THE SEWING BOOK

THE SEWING BOOK

A COMPLETE **P**RACTICAL **G**UIDE

ANN LADBURY

LONGMEADOW
PRESS

This key explains the use of colour, tone and texture that has been applied to the design of the step-by-step drawings in *The Sewing Book*.

Key

Main fabric, right side (RS)

Main fabric, wrong side (WS)

Lining or facing, right side (RS)

Lining or facing, wrong side (WS)

Interfacing

Tailoring canvas

Bias binding (except on pp.54–57)

Adhesive tape

The Imperial and metric measurements given throughout the book are working equivalents rather than exact conversions.

The Sewing Book was written by Ann Ladbury. The following specialists contributed to the home and decorative sewing sections: Jeanne Argent, *Sewing for the Home*; Eirian Short, *Quilting*; June Thorpe, *Appliqué*; Marian Bryan, *Patchwork*.

Consultant Editor
Linda Seward

Editors
Margaret Ramsay
Gilly Abrahams

Art Editor
Jill Raphaeline

Production
Philip Collyer

Artists
The Basics of Sewing, Perfect Dressmaking and *Traditional Tailoring*: Jil Shipley. Technical Arts Services 10–15; Pamela Hardman 22–7; Studio Collins International 9; Ann Winterbotham 9, 140–52; Lyn Gray 141–2
Sewing for the Home: Janet Sparrow;
Jil Shipley 190
Decorative Sewing: Janet Sparrow;
Jil Shipley 206–8
Pfaff, Germany (technical drawings of sewing machine parts) 13–17, 59, 60–4, 68, 89, 205

Photography
Nigel Heed 29–30
Angelo Hornak 77

Consultants
David Bowers, Bedding Federation; Malcolm Hedges; John O'Gorman, British Man-made Fibres Federation; Christopher Thompson

Acknowledgments
The Publishers would like to acknowledge the kind cooperation of the following: Anything Lefthanded; J. and P. Coats Ltd; Danasco Fabrics Ltd; Dickins & Jones (Harrods) Ltd; Mrs Millicent Nicoll, Butterick Archives; Mary Peacock; Pellon Corporation, New York; Pfaff (Britain) Ltd; Pfaff, Germany; The Vilene Organisation

The Sewing Book
© 1985 Mitchell Beazley Publishers
Reprinted 1987, 1988
Paperback edition 1990
Reprinted 1991
This book is adapted from
The Joy of Living Library – Sewing
© Mitchell Beazley Publishers 1978
Edited and designed by Mitchell Beazley Publishers, part of Reed International Ltd, Michelin House, 81 Fulham Road, London, SW3 6RB

This 1992 edition published by Longmeadow Press, 201 High Ridge Road, Stamford, CT 06904

ISBN 0-681-41640-8

Filmset by Servis Filmsetting Limited
Reproduction by Chelmer Litho Reproductions, Maldon, Essex
Printed and bound in Spain by Grafos S.A. Arte sobre papel

CONTENTS

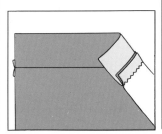
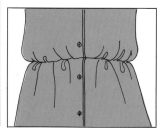

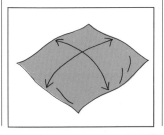
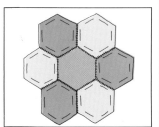

|

THE BASICS OF SEWING

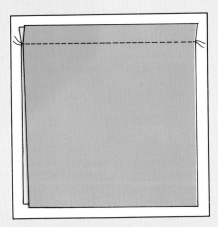

Everything a beginner needs to know: choosing and using a sewing machine; hand and machine stitches; textiles and their applications; the importance of pressing; making seams, hems and bindings; inserting zippers and other fasteners; and hints on sewing with suede, leather and fur

SEWING MACHINES

Mob violence and lengthy acrimonious litigation are but two of the problems that have beset the evolution of one of the most useful of all domestic and industrial appliances, the sewing machine.

Although the first patent was taken out by an English cabinetmaker, Thomas Saint, in 1790, the first person to make his model truly productive was a French tailor, Barthélemy Thimonnier. His heyday was, however, short. In 1830 he had 80 machines in a Paris workshop making French army uniforms; the next year the machines were destroyed by rival tailors fearful for the future of hand sewing that was their livelihood.

Thimonnier's machine worked a chain stitch in imitation of a form of embroidery. The first to design a machine that broke away from the principles of hand sewing was the American Walter Hunt. Hunt's needle had an eye at the point, thus eliminating the need for the needle to go right through the fabric as in hand sewing. The stitch formed was known as lock stitch and was more secure than the earlier chain stitch. Hunt never patented his machine, however, and it was his compatriot, Elias Howe, who developed and in 1846 patented a very similar machine, which heralded the start of the sewing machine industry.

Litigation ensued when Howe discovered that other inventors, among them Isaac M. Singer, were beginning to produce imitation models. Like Howe's, Singer's machine had a shuttle that created a considerable noise. Relief for the noise-afflicted ears of seamstresses and tailors came with the invention, in 1852, of a machine that, instead of a shuttle, had a crude version of the bobbin used today. Two years later its American inventor, Allen B. Wilson, added the further refinement of a four-motion feed so that fabric was automatically moved on between stitches. Here at last was the prototype of the modern domestic machine.

Eventually, to avoid further litigation, four companies agreed, in 1856, to pool their patent interests, thereby setting up the first large-scale patent pool. The manufacturers were Howe, Singer, Wheeler & Wilson and Grover & Baker.

Although few machines were manufactured before 1850, in 1860 more than 111,000 were produced by 74 US companies, and the production figures had risen to 700,000 by the beginning of the 1870s. By 1900 patents had been issued worldwide for machines that could hem stitch (the inventor's name, Gegauf, became synonymous with the process in Germany), zigzag, stitch buttonholes and sew two parallel seams simultaneously.

Buying a new machine

Apply the same rules to buying a sewing machine and to deciding on the make and model as you would to buying a car. Take a good look around at the variety of makes on the market and study brochures of models that are in your price range. Discuss the choice of machine with friends and try out their machines. Find out from dressmaking students which makes are used in their schools and colleges.

Choice

Sewing machines are divided into categories according to what they will do. An explanation of their capabilities may help you to decide which category to look at, even if it does not tell you which model to buy.

Basic zigzag These will do a zigzag stitch up to about 5 mm/¼ in which can be closed up for buttonholes and satin stitch. Straight stitching can usually be done with the needle at right, centre or left, a fact which helps if stitches miss on fine synthetics.

Semi-automatic On these machines the zigzag width can be varied while sewing which means that stitches such as blind hem and embroidery stitches can be made. The number of these stitches is usually limited to those most often used in sewing.

Automatic On these machines the material can be moved back and forth while it is being stitched, enabling such stitches as knit and pullover stitches, overlocking and automatic buttonholes and many elaborate decorative stitches to be made.

Electronic computerized On these, the most advanced machines, stitches are selected by touching a button; the variety of stitches is enormous. They have a visual display panel which shows details of the stitch being used and they offer a number of very sophisticated operations.

Once you have narrowed down the choice, look at the machines you are interested in. Be wary if the dealer tries to persuade you to take a particular one as he may be receiving additional commission for disposing of an obsolescent model. Beware, too, of enormous price reductions as these may indicate that the model is about to be withdrawn. Be suspicious of a manufacturer with many different machines on the market who is constantly offering them at giveaway prices.

Do not be impressed by the ease with which the demonstrator uses the machine; try it out yourself. Lift it up and make sure you can carry it. Even if you have a sewing room you will have to move the machine sometimes.

Take with you to the showroom a selection of fabrics of different thicknesses, including a thin silk and a synthetic knit, and try them, folded double, in the machine. Do this yourself after being shown how to operate the machine and after carefully reading the instruction manual.

Always try out the threading procedure. Unthread the machine and rethread. Was it easy, and in sequence? Were they easy loop-over actions or did you have to keep licking the thread and peering through a hole? Do not worry unduly about bobbin threading as this is always the most difficult part of the process and comes with practice.

Check that the light is over the needle. Look at the construction of the machine for easily breakable plastic. Look at the plugs on the cord connecting the machine to the foot; they should be moulded to prevent them coming loose.

During the test, find out if the machine is versatile but still simple to use. Basic operations, such as winding the bobbin and threading, are the same on all machines. Do not select a model if there is anything irritating or awkward about any of these operations.

Check the following points when trying out the stitching. Do the two unbasted layers of fabric travel evenly under the foot or are you left with a surplus on the top? (This indicates teeth that are too high or an uneven feed.) Does the machine stop quickly when you lift your foot, or, if you prefer a knee control, your knee, or does it run on? An electronic control stops at once, a good electric one stops within three stitches.

After you have taken all these points into account, consider what else you want the machine to do. Check which machine feet are included in the purchase price.

Consider, too, whether you require a free-arm model or a flatbed. The flatbed, the original type, has a solid base and is useful for big articles such as curtains and sheets. On the free-arm, the plate, or bed, and the bobbin case are fitted into an arm that stands free of the base, so that fabric can easily be moved across and around underneath when sewing. This is useful for such purposes as setting in sleeves and cuffs and children's clothes. Some models simply convert to free-arm by unclipping the accessory box.

Ask the dealer about servicing, repairs and speed of repair. If in doubt, check these points with the wholesaler.

Read the guarantee carefully.

Buying second-hand

Test a second-hand machine thoroughly, preferably in two separate sessions, and do not buy it until you have checked that the make is not obsolete, that the machine works and that you can get it repaired. Be suspicious if it is a new model; it may be for sale because it is defective.

Since they were invented, sewing machines have been heirlooms, handed down, still functioning perfectly, for generations. Buy a good-quality machine, pay as much as you can afford, and you might well have something to hand on in your family.

Maintaining your machine
Use the machine as much as possible and occasionally check that the cord casing is not badly worn and exposing wires. Store the machine in a warm place and keep it dust free. If you leave it out between sewing sessions, make a loose protective cover for it. Brush out all fluff repeatedly—several times when making a garment. New models can be stiff and are easier to use when broken in.

Cleaning
Clean your machine regularly, preferably at the end of each garment. If it is being put away for any length of time, clean and oil it beforehand.

To clean the machine, remove the needle and throw it away. Open all doors, remove all plates, take out the bobbin case and remove the bobbin. Clear out any pins from the bottom of the machine. Brush out all fluff and bits of thread, especially on and under the teeth, with the machine brush. Blow hard to remove the last traces. Wipe all parts with a clean cloth.

Oiling
Oiling points may be marked on the machine; they will certainly be indicated in the handbook. Put two drops of oil in those positions only. Many modern machines are self-lubricating and it is harmful to oil them, although you may find the bobbin socket requires oil. To do this unclip the ring holding the sewing hook in position, remove the bobbin case, clean the socket and apply a drop of oil. Clean the bobbin case, wipe it with an oiled

cloth, replace the case and ring. Run the machine unthreaded to distribute the oil. Before using the machine again wipe the needle and needle plate then stitch on a scrap of fabric to remove surplus oil. Do not over-oil. Always use oil purchased from a sewing machine dealer.

Position
The machine should be about 10 cm/4 in away from the front edge of the supporting surface, and your eyes should be between 15 and 24 cm/6 and 9 in diagonally above and directly in front of the needle. Try a chair or, preferably, an adjustable stool for comfort—when sewing you should be able to lean forward with both hands on the machine bed. Make sure your foot rests easily on the foot control. Have the maximum table space to the left to take the weight of the fabric. When making large items, place a chair near the machine with its back to the table and push the fabric onto it as you sew.

EQUIPMENT
Keep nearby a supply of machine needles, a small pair of scissors, a dish or magnet for pins, a brush and a screwdriver (supplied with the machine), machine oil, a clean duster, bobbins, a wastepaper basket and additional machine feet.

Thread
Buy enough thread—core-spun, polyester or mercerized cotton, unless otherwise directed under the individual stitches—to complete the garment. If seams are to be finished, you will generally need two spools; a long dress or other garment with long edges to be finished will usually require three spools.

Needles
For normal sewing, needles range in size from small, 70 (9), to medium, 90 (14), and large, 110 (18). Choose the one most suitable for the fabric. In general, the finer the fabric the smaller the needle so that it does not make ugly holes. A medium size is suitable for most medium-thickness fabrics, but sometimes a very close weave or knit is better stitched with a finer needle. Change to a new needle frequently, particularly when working on synthetic fabrics.

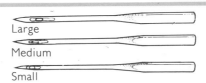

Large
Medium
Small

The various needle points available for different types of fabrics are: basic *sharp point* with short cut-out or scarf, for most basic fabrics; sharp point with long scarf, for fine synthetics, often the solution when missed stitches occur; *ball-point*, for knits and jerseys—the rounded point forces its way between the yarns instead of trying to pierce them; *jean-point*, specially elongated and sharper to penetrate the hard texture of denim, canvas etc; *wedge-point* or leather needle, with three-sided sharp tips for easy cutting of leather and suede—never use it on any other types of material; *twin*, with two or three blades, for pin tucks and double or triple stitching—the sizes vary and so do the spaces between the needles; *wing* with a wide shaped blade which makes larger decorative holes in the fabric.

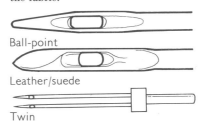

Ball-point
Leather/suede
Twin

In addition to size make sure you always use the correct needle *system* for your machine. The system number will be given in the sewing machine handbook and it is also shown on the needle pack: 705H, 130H, 705B or 130R, or for some old machines 15 × 1 or 206 × 13. The system relates to the machine mechanism.

Bobbins
There is little variation in size and shape. Some bobbins have holes all around which make it easy to see how much thread is left. At the start of winding the bobbin, the end of the thread can be passed through either of the two smaller holes, whichever is uppermost, but this is not essential. Others have a groove at the top and bottom to fit onto certain types of bobbin winder. Metal bobbins are more durable than plastic ones.

Inserting threaded bobbin in case Place in socket of bobbin case and pull thread around under spring until it emerges from hole in socket.

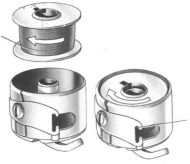

Inserting bobbin Open bobbin cover on front of machine, pull out central latch on bobbin case, push bobbin into socket on central bar until it clicks into place. Release latch. Close the front cover.

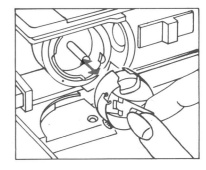

Raising bobbin thread Insert threaded bobbin into machine. Hold end of upper thread. Turn hand wheel toward you until needle has moved down and up again or, on some machines, you can tap the foot control once to activate one stitch and this will raise the bottom thread. Pull the upper thread to bring bottom thread right out.

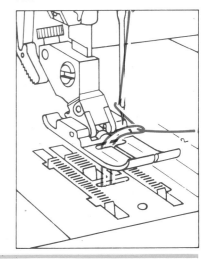

SEWING MACHINE FEATURES

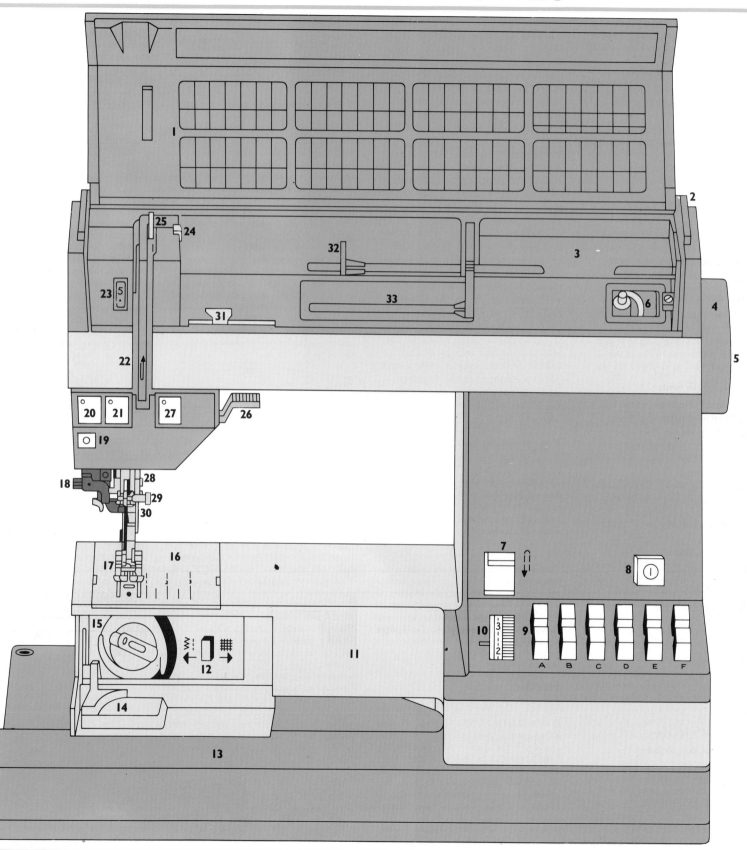

The illustration opposite is an example of a basic, middle price range sewing machine with push-button stitch selection.

Many of the features shown in the illustration are standard on all sewing machines, but some such as nos. 18, 19, 20, 21, 28 and 33 are exclusive to this model.

Refer to the manufacturer's manual for precise details of what each model is capable of doing.

Key

1 Stitch programme chart—illustrates the range of stitches
2 Carrying handle—lifts when lid is closed
3 Compartment for stitch cards
4 Hand wheel
5 Stop motion knob
6 Bobbin winder
7 Reverse-feed control
8 Master switch
9 Fingertip stitch buttons
10 Stitch length control
11 Free-arm—converts to flatbed by attaching accessory box
12 Drop feed control
13 Base plate
14 Free-arm cover
15 Sewing hook
16 Needle plate
17 Sewing foot holder with sewing foot
18 Needle threader
19 Bobbin thread indicator light
20 'Needle down' button
21 Slow sewing button
22 Threading slots
23 Needle thread tension control
24 Bobbin winder thread guide
25 Take-up lever
26 Presser bar lifter
27 Basting stitch button
28 Dual feed with thread cutter
29 Needle holder with tightening screw
30 Presser bar
31 Bobbin winder thread guide—swings out
32 Spool holder with disc
33 Second spool holder—swings up

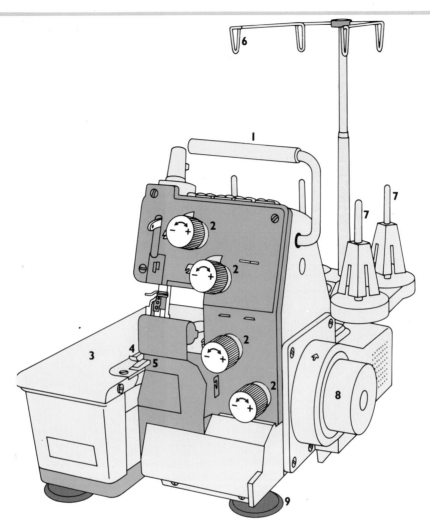

Overlock or serging machine
An overlocking machine is expensive and uses a lot of thread but is a great time saver, not only because it stitches very fast, but because it stitches, finishes and trims a seam in one operation. It reproduces the seam finish found on ready-to-wear clothes; ideal for sewing knits, stretch fabrics and hand knitting. Stitch length and width can be adjusted to hem fine fabrics, to overlock and blind hem in one operation, and to stitch hems decoratively. Remember that all fitting of garments must be complete before stitching and that overlocking is very difficult to undo. Apply the same rules to choosing and buying as for a sewing machine. Try out various types: some need two spools of thread to operate, others need three or four. For most people a three-thread model is probably the most useful.

Key

1 Carrying handle
2 Tension controls
3 Machine bed
4 Sewing foot
5 Cutter
6 Thread guide
7 Thread holders
8 Hand wheel
9 Rubber suction cups

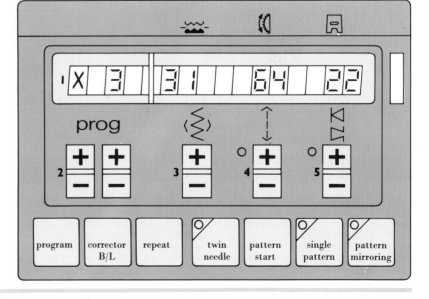

Selector panel on a typical computerized sewing machine
Many computerized machines are now available. The manufacturer's handbook will explain how to programme them. Here is an example of a computer panel (right).

Key

1 Display panel
2 Programme selector keys
3 Stitch width key
4 Stitch length key
5 Balancing key

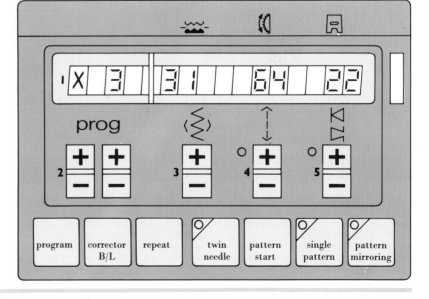

SEWING MACHINE FEATURES

ATTACHMENTS

All machines have attachments for special kinds of stitching. Some make sewing easier on certain fabrics, some save time and some are essential, sometimes in conjunction with a particular needle, for forming various stitches.

The machine manual will explain how to attach and use the feet. Those illustrated here are the most useful ones; some may have to be purchased as extras, but they are worth the investment for a more professional result. Keep the additional feet near the machine so that you will be more inclined to use them.

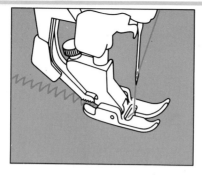

General purpose foot The general all-purpose foot for all straight and zigzag stitching.

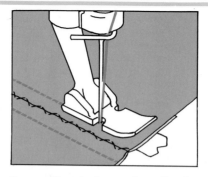

Conventional zipper foot Simple zipper/piping foot found with most basic machines for stitching close to zipper teeth or filled edge of piping. The needle is adjusted to enter the appropriate hole.

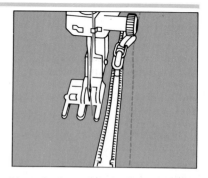

New-design zipper foot Modern zipper feet vary in shape. This one features three toes; the side toe rests on the fabric to prevent puckering while the needle falls beside it. The foot is adjusted from side to side, the needle remains in the same position.

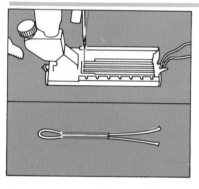

Buttonhole foot This has a metal runner with marks on it indicating buttonhole size. A gimp or filler thread can be looped around the central toe. After stitching, pull up gimp and trim.

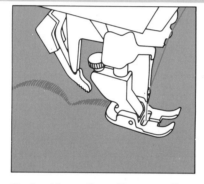

Embroidery foot Perspex allows greater visibility and accuracy; you can see through the foot and watch the stitches form. Use for all satin stitch and decorative stitching. The underside of the foot is cut out to allow the thickness of the stitching to pass through.

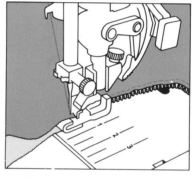

Gathering foot Gathers a length of fabric in fixed amounts as you stitch. If the piece to which it is to be seamed is placed flat on top, it will gather the underneath fabric and stitch it to the upper fabric in one operation.

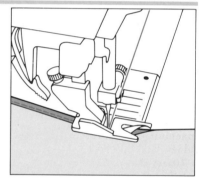

Hemming foot Most suitable for fine fabrics. Has a long toe and a central curl that turns under the raw edge to form a narrow hem, which is fed under the needle.

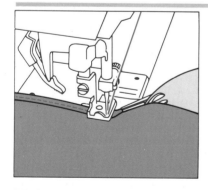

Binding foot The fabric is fed through the central groove inside the raised cone. The edge is encased in the binding which is fed into the cone. Use prefolded binding, bought or made with a tape maker; use straight or zigzag stitch.

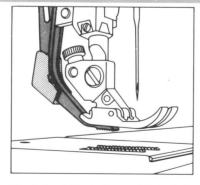

Dual feed foot Foot with built-in dual feed which means the top layer is fed under the needle as well as the bottom layer. It eliminates puckering and uneven movement of fabric. Particularly useful for velvet and pile fabrics and for matching checks and patterns.

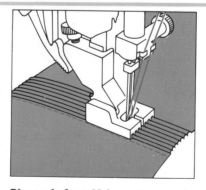

Pin tuck foot Makes narrow tucks that fit into the grooves under the front of the foot. Use with twin needle. Tucks can be filled with cord, which is fed up through the hole in the needle plate.

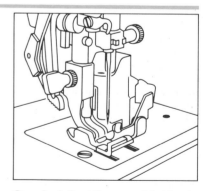

Overlock foot Seams and finishes in one operation. An attachment worth having if making lots of clothes and you like this form of seam finish.

12

MACHINE **S**TITCHING

Learn to control a new machine by practising first on paper and then on spare fabric. Do not thread the machine up but put a sheet of lined or squared paper under the foot, lower the foot and stitch on the lines. Practise lines, curves and corners, practise reversing and stopping and starting at marked points and try going very slowly.

When you are thoroughly familiar with the feel and speed of the machine, thread it and do the same things on a double piece of check fabric. Then fold a piece of fabric and practise edge stitching. Finally, start on a garment, but confine yourself to straight and zigzag stitching for a while before embarking on more ambitious features such as buttonholes and automatic patterns. Work slowly at first, stitch by stitch, for good, professional-looking results.

Rules for good machining
1 Make sure that the fabric is flat and smooth before machining. Press it if it has been folded.
2 Insert the correct new needle for the fabric.
3 Check that all dials on the machine are on 0 or set for straight stitch.
4 Set the stitch length to approximately what you think will be correct—between 2 and $3\frac{1}{2}$ for most fabrics—and try out the stitching on a folded piece of spare fabric. Press and then examine both sides of the fabric to see if the length needs adjusting. If necessary, change the stitch length and test again.
5 Pull stretch knit fabric to make sure that the amount of zigzag is correct for the fabric.
6 Use the same colour and type of thread top and bottom, unless decorating.
7 After machining, press the line of stitching on the upper side to smooth it out and to help embed the thread in the fabric.
8 Trim off any fraying edges of fabric after pressing.

Threading the needle
The illustration above right shows an automatic needle

threader in action. An alternative is the simple wire threader. To thread the needle manually, cut the thread at an angle, moisten the end and thread through the eye from front to back.

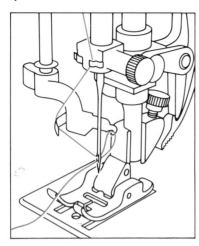

Threading
Many thread spools now have a continuous groove right around one end which grips the thread end and stops it unwinding, but if you use the older type of spool that has a notch cut in one end, take care to place the reel on the machine with the notch at the end opposite to the direction the thread takes.

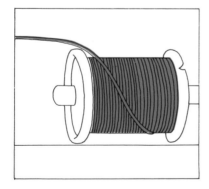

Ends of threads to be fastened off can be avoided if you have a machine that can wind the bobbin with the thread through the needle. This is suitable for short lengths of stitching only, e.g. darts. Wind a small amount of thread onto the bobbin and insert it without breaking the thread. Begin stitching exactly at the fold of the fabric or the point where you wish to begin.

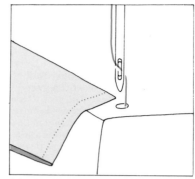

How to start
Switch on machine. On basic machines turn the hand wheel toward you until the thread take-up lever *and* the needle are at their highest point. On modern machines with an automatic needle-up facility they will be in position. Check that the ends of both threads are long enough—approximately $6 \text{ cm}/2\frac{1}{4}$ in. Pass both of the threads through slot in foot and take the ends to the side.

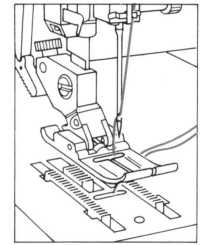

Place a test piece of fabric, doubled, right under the foot, not part-way, with the bulk of it to the left and the width of a seam allowance only to the right. As you do this the thread ends will move toward the back; take hold of them, draw them out behind the foot and place your fingers lightly on them to prevent them being drawn into the needle hole with the first stitch. On a basic machine lower the needle into the fabric by turning the hand wheel toward you. Lower the foot and press the foot control.

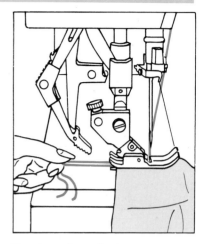

Testing the stitch
Try out straight and zigzag stitches on a folded piece of fabric and adjust size until satisfactory. Also check any other stitches you intend using; some may not look right on the fabric and you may thus have to consider an alternative one. If the stitch proves to be unsatisfactory, rather than immediately twiddling knobs, quickly unthread machine, check that needle is in correctly, reinsert bobbin, rethread top, bring bottom thread out onto plate and test again. If the stitch is still unsatisfactory, consult the list of machine faults on p. 19.

Tension
The thread on the top of the machine, coming from the spindle, passes through three or four points of control before going through the needle. The underneath thread, wound evenly onto the bobbin, is controlled only by a spring. The two threads loop together to form each stitch, the carefully controlled top thread catching as much or as little of the underneath one as is needed to form the stitch. It is, therefore, usually only the top thread that needs to be adjusted if the stitch is not properly formed.

Many modern machines have a self-adjusting tension mechanism and sew perfectly on all fabrics; in fact, any machine, even an old one, should stitch correctly if it has been cared for and the springs have not been strained. Never make any large adjustment to a tension control; a very small one should be enough to correct the feed of the thread. If it is not, have a new disc or spring fitted.

To check tension, work a row of straight stitching through double fabric. Examine both sides of fabric and run a finger along stitching. It should feel smooth. If it feels lumpy on either side, the tension needs some adjustment.

MACHINE STITCHING

Top tension too loose

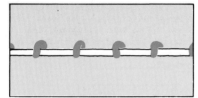

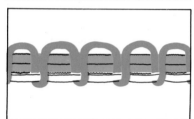

Top thread forms loops on surface of fabric because too much thread is being allowed through controls. The underneath stitching feels lumpy where loose top thread has passed right through fabric and the two threads interlock. Correct by tightening top tension control wheel; on most machines there is a central line with numbers each side.

Top tension too tight

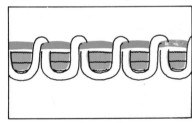

Top thread pulls on bottom one, drawing it up through fabric to RS. The stitching on top feels lumpy where underneath thread has come through. Correct by loosening top tension control to a lower number.

Correct tension

The two threads loop together evenly, almost between the two layers of fabric. The stitching on both sides feels smooth and looks alike.

If adjusting top tension does not correct stitch, slightly loosen or tighten tiny screw on side of bobbin case or socket. This remedy should only rarely be necessary, possibly on very thick fabrics or when using shirring elastic or topstitching thread, and should not be regarded as a regular remedy for a poor stitch. When adjusting for a particular thread or stitch remember to readjust after use.

Direction of stitching

Always have a guide on, or beside, which to stitch, such as tailor's tacks, basting, a chalk line or an edge. Do not machine on a row of basting but beside it, on raw edge side, so that it can be removed easily afterward. Always work from the wide to the narrow end of a piece of fabric.

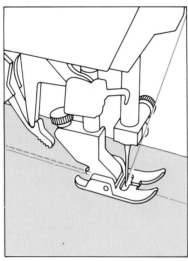

On edges that are not exactly on lengthwise or cross grain the finished result is improved if you stitch, both by machine and by hand, in direction of grain. Take a piece of plain-weave cloth, cut it at an angle and slightly fray it. The yarns will come off at a

sharp outward angle in one direction, but will lie flat against the fabric in the other.

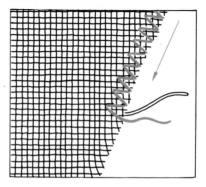

These directions particularly apply when zigzagging seam allowances, in order to keep angled fibres lying as close to raw edge as possible.

Feeding in

Except for certain special effects, such as fluting an edge or working embroidery with a hoop, your hands should only guide the fabric; you should not need to push at the front or pull at the back.

Keeping straight

Run edge of fabric level with one side of machine foot, or watch needle closely for accuracy on fabric motifs such as stripes. Some machines have marked measured lines on needle plate for guiding edge.

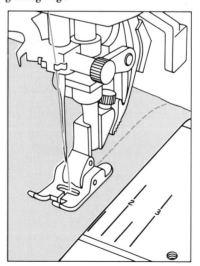

Needle position

If you find it difficult to keep stitching straight on soft fabrics or knits or if the stitching puckers unduly on fine fabrics, move the needle to the left position. This closes the gap between needle and foot and allows less movement of fabric.

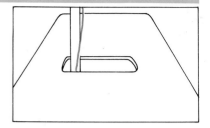

Turning corners

On machines with automatic needle stop facility set it to 'needle down'; on basic machines stop sewing, turn hand wheel until needle is lowered into fabric. Raise the foot, swivel the fabric clockwise to new position, lower the foot and continue stitching.

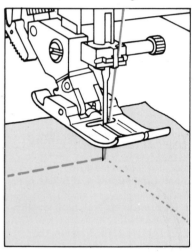

On fine fabrics and those that fray easily adjust the stitch to a smaller size just before turning the corner. On completing the corner return the stitch to the correct size.

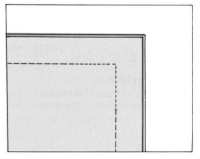

Turning corners to be trimmed

Stop one stitch away from corner with needle down. Raise foot, swivel fabric and lower foot. Using hand wheel, work one stitch across corner. With needle still in fabric, raise foot again, swivel fabric so that you can stitch along seamline, lower foot and continue stitching.

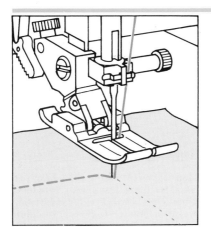

Working curves

On a gentle curve, stitch very slowly, holding fabric in both hands and easing it around gradually. For tight curves, stop at beginning of curve, and, with needle still in fabric, lift foot and turn fabric slightly into curve. Lower foot and work two stitches, using hand wheel for greater control. Repeat this sequence until end of curve, making sure that the stitching remains at the same distance from the edge of the fabric all the way around.

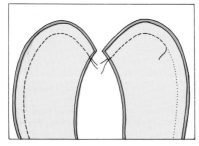

To ensure that matching curves are identical cut a template to size excluding seam allowances, place on the fabric and mark the stitching line with dots using a fabric pen. Stitch in the usual way, stopping frequently and easing the fabric around.

Missed stitches

With knits, stretch and pliable or fine fabrics, particularly synthetics that

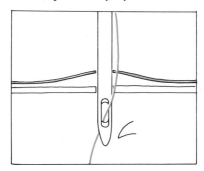

tend to build up static, stitches may fail to form. The fabric clings to the needle and either lifts above the needle plate or is pushed down below it. The thread is also gripped by the fabric and so the hook below fails to catch the thread. Burrs or snags on the needle, or a blunt needle, will cause this to happen; so will one of the wrong type or size. It can be cured by placing paper below or on top of the fabric.

How to stop

As you approach the point where you want to stop, slow down, put your hand on the hand wheel to act as a brake and ease off on the foot control. All machines will stop within one or two stitches but to stop accurately use the wheel to make the final stitch. Do not stitch beyond end of fabric.

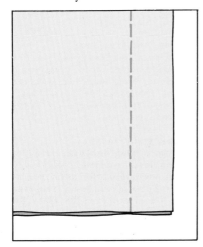

With needle at highest point, raise foot, draw fabric to the back until 12 cm/4½ in or so of thread appears, then cut the threads mid-way or very close to the fabric, using the cutter on the back of the presser bar.

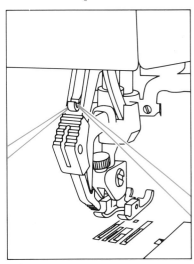

Fastening off ends

It is important to fasten off stitching securely, neatly and as unobtrusively as possible.

Reversing is the quickest way of finishing, although it adds a little stiffness and should be avoided on luxury or examination articles. Start machining a little way in from the edge—1 cm/⅜ in is enough—and reverse to the edge before going forward. On reaching the end of a line of stitching, reverse as at beginning of stitching to fasten off.

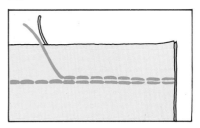

Alternatively, fasten off both RS and WS ends of thread in turn by backstitching a little way along machine stitching on WS or by running the threads, again in turn, in and out of stitches on WS.

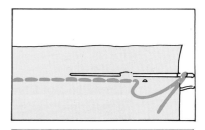

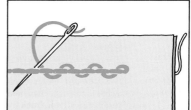

A knot is awkward to tie and not very durable in washing. To fasten off ends of thread when stitching on RS of fabric, pull ends of WS thread gently until a loop of RS thread forms.

Pull the loop up with a pin or with your fingers to bring the thread through from RS.

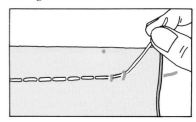

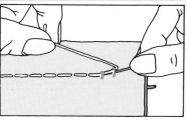

Fasten off both ends by above methods. Cut off thread, close to fabric. This keeps the work neat, prevents the ends from being caught in the machine and avoids marks when the stitching is pressed.

Removing stitches

To remove machine stitching quickly on all fabrics except very fine ones, slip end of pin or unpicker/seam ripper under a stitch on upper side of work and lift and cut thread with small scissors or on curve of unpicker/seam

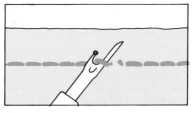

ripper. Continue to undo stitches by lifting, but not cutting, until you have enough thread to grip firmly between thumb and forefinger (wet fingers for a firmer grip). Tug very hard on thread against line of stitching—toward part still stitched. The thread will snap six or seven stitches farther on.

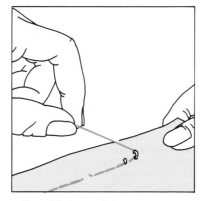

Turn fabric over, lift end of thread on WS and pull hard to snap it. Turn to RS again, lift thread and snap, and so on. This will not harm the fabric and is soon mastered with practice. On very fine fabrics such as chiffon, lift and cut each stitch in turn.

Place fabric on sleeve board and press with steam iron or with dry iron and damp cloth to smooth out fabric and close up holes.

MACHINE STITCHES

STRAIGHT STITCHES
Straight stitching

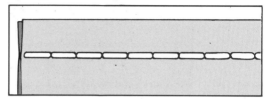

The most widely used stitch for joining two pieces of fabric. Suitable for all except stretch fabrics. Following tailor's tacks, chalk marks or basting, machine slowly to keep straight and to avoid top layer of fabric moving. If working parallel with an edge, use edge of foot as guide.

Edge stitching

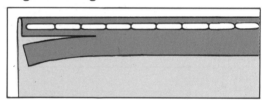

This can be done with a straight or zigzag stitch, with the needle penetrating the fold of the fabric. Fold the edge under and press it, basting first if necessary. Put the fabric under the machine foot with the narrow edge underneath so that it is held flat. Turn the wheel to lower the needle into the fold, lower the foot and stitch slowly, watching the needle.

Basting

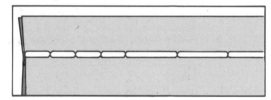

Some modern machines can be set to baste, generally using a special foot and needle. Although a fast method of basting, this must be carefully controlled to keep it straight. Useful for preparing several garments with long seams for fitting.

Topstitching

Decorative stitching, straight, zigzag or embroidery stitch, helps to keep edges flat on bulky fabrics such as quilting and breaks up the surface of plain fabrics, particularly cottons and denim. With all kinds of topstitching adjust size for the best effect. Always work from RS and leave long ends of thread that can be neatly sewn in on WS. There are several methods of top stitching:

With ordinary, matching sewing thread top and bottom of machine. On many fabrics the stitch does not show on RS but an attractive ridge results on both sides.

With two spools of ordinary sewing thread on top of machine, to match or contrast with fabric, threaded and put through needle together. Thread bobbin with ordinary thread to match fabric. This produces a slightly heavier, more obvious stitch.

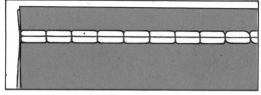

With a twin needle and two spools of ordinary sewing thread on top and bobbin threaded in usual way with thread to match fabric. The two top spools can match the fabric or be a contrast. This produces two parallel lines of stitching.

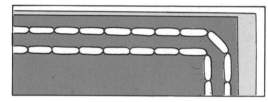

With a large needle, no. 110 (or 18), and heavy topstitching thread on top and ordinary sewing thread on bobbin. This produces a very bold single line of stitching on RS only. If the effect of the heavy thread is required on both sides, wind bobbin with topstitching thread. Both threads should be the same colour and either match the fabric or contrast with it. Test stitch; you may have to loosen top tension slightly to prevent bobbin thread coming through to RS or loosen tension on bobbin case slightly to obtain a good stitch. If so, remember to readjust tension screw. Stitch very slowly. Bold or topstitching thread may strain the bobbin case if used a lot. To prevent this, buy a spare case, adjust it and keep it only for topstitching.

Triple straight stitching

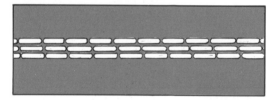

A stitch for plain open seams on knits, jersey and stretch fabrics, especially where there could be strain in wear, for example crotch seams. The machine takes two stitches forward and one back. It makes the seam stronger but allows it to stretch without splitting.

ZIGZAG STITCHES
Zigzag

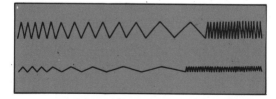

Used for finishing edges and for decoration. If using the stitch for decoration, experiment with the length and width to achieve the desired effect, which can range from close-up stitches, barely discernible as zigzags, to more widely spaced, more obvious zigzags.

For zigzagging along an edge, the length and width of the stitch must be carefully set for each fabric to ensure that the zigzag prevents fraying. Try out various sizes of stitch until you find a satisfactory one. The stitch should be as small and narrow as possible

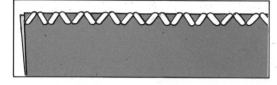

for the fabric, as with a wide zigzag the fabric frays between stitches. If the fabric frays badly or tends to curl up when stitched, set to widest stitch but run raw edge of fabric under needle. Half the zigzag is, therefore, lost and curling eliminated.

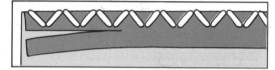

On fine fabrics turn under raw edge, baste it down, press and work a very small zigzag over fold. Trim away surplus fabric on WS.

If any version of a zigzag stitch makes edge of fabric flute or stretch, lay an extra length of thread on fabric and zigzag over it. Use this thread to pull fabric flat after completing stitching.

Slight zigzag

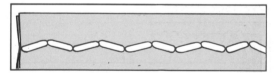

Useful for seams on fabrics that have give, such as knits, as the stitch also has give and thus prevents seams splitting in wear. It can be used as an alternative to stretch stitch and gives a neater seam finish. Always use polyester thread. Set zigzag control to slightly off 0. Test stitch and pull to make sure there is enough give. The zigzag should be so slight that it is barely distinguishable from a straight stitch. If it is too wide, it prevents the seam from being pressed open correctly.

Stretch stitch

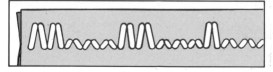

Some modern machines have stretch stitches that should be used on fabrics with give, such as knits, velours and stretch towelling. These stitches are usually made up of combinations of wide and narrow zigzag. Do not use on crisp fabrics where a neatly pressed open seam is required.

Multi-zigzag

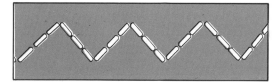

May also be called running zigzag or serpentine stitch. A stitch with maximum stretch but the minimum amount of thread, so it is fine and soft. Used for attaching elastic but it also makes an attractive decorative stitch. Useful too for preventing edges of knit fabrics such as stretch towelling from curling up.

Blind hem stitch

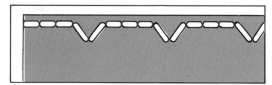

Used for holding up the hem on firm, fairly heavy fabrics and as a seam-finishing stitch on non-fraying knit fabrics, where it helps to prevent the edge from curling up. It should not be used on hems of lighter weight fabrics as it may show. The stitch is made up of several straight stitches followed by a zigzag to the left of the needle and away from the edge. On a hem, work the stitch so that the zigzag catches down the top edge of the hem onto WS of garment; use hemming foot and make sure fabric is folded and fed into machine accurately.

Overlock stitch

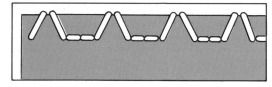

Many modern machines have an overlock stitch for finishing edges that is similar to a commercial over-locking stitch. It consists of a zigzag to one side followed by two straight stitches and prevents fraying better than a normal zigzag. Work zigzag part right over raw edge and not within it.

Closed overlock

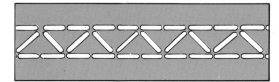

Used for joining seams on loosely knitted fabric and pieces of hand knitting. If the stitching stretches the fabric, place a length of wool on the edge, pulling it as you stitch over it.

Combination overlock

In addition to the basic overlock stitch most machines offer several stitches that combine seam stitching with an overlock stitch for the edge. Trim the seam edges to the correct width after setting the stitch size. This type of stitch makes an attractive hem finish and it has the advantage of preventing wavy fabric.

Satin stitch

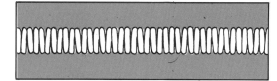

Used mainly for machine-made buttonholes and machine appliqué; also for embroidery and for bar tacks through several layers if hand bar tacks would look wrong or inexpert. Use ordinary sewing thread or, for embroidery or appliqué, machine embroidery thread and satin stitch foot, which allows you to see the fabric more easily than the ordinary foot and helps to make the stitching more accurate. Watch hole in centre of foot while stitching. The stitches, tightly worked zigzags, should be very short and appear as closely packed parallel lines.

Machine shell edge

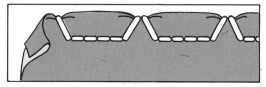

Successful only on fine fabrics, it can be worked using the hemming foot and a small zigzag.

Alternatively, on non-fraying fabric, turn under raw edge and feed under needle with stitch on no. 4 zigzag. Allow needle to go off edge of fold on righthand side which will draw fabric into shells. If fabric frays, turn and baste a narrow hem before machining. The machine can also be set to a blind hem stitch, which is worked so that, when the needle jumps to the side, it goes right over the edge. Use a long stitch and no. 4 stitch width.

Honeycomb stitch

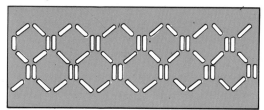

Can be used for attaching elastic but is mostly used for stitching hems on fine knits.

DECORATIVE STITCHES

There seems to be no limit to the variety of decorative stitching that is possible with modern machines. An electronic machine containing a computer not only offers a very wide range of stitches, alphabets and numbers but also free programming which is the facility to create individual designs and store them in the computer. It is possible to recreate handwriting and design motifs as well as adjust the length of a design, mirror a design and balance the stitching.

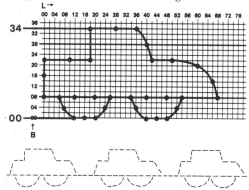

Top: design outlined on chart ready for plotting and input. Bottom: the finished motif

Freely programmed writing combined with a stitch from the computer memory

At the opposite end of the scale creativity is limited but possible even on the most basic machines. Decorative stitching can be done just by using two threads of different colours on the top of the machine. Between these two extremes make use of whatever facilities are offered on the model you have.

Stitch on the RS whenever possible. Except with open stitching stitch on two or more layers of fabric. If this is not feasible put a non-woven embroidery backing such as Stitch-n-Tear under the fabric, or use typing paper. If it is not to be torn away afterward, iron-on interfacing may be used to support the fabric.

Mark the design or selected position for starting or centralizing a design, using basting stitches, or a fabric marking pen of the type that fades automatically. Another method is to draw the design on wax paper using an embroidery transfer pencil, place face down on the fabric and press to transfer the design.

Use a thread of suitable thickness, e.g. machine embroidery 30 or 50. Adjust the tension if necessary, especially for satin stitch,

MACHINE STITCHES

to give a rounded appearance to the stitches on the RS. Always test the stitching on spare fabric.

Free-style embroidery requires a hoop to hold the fabric taut. Put the fabric RS up

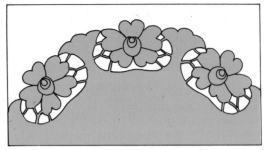

across the base of the hoop. Remove the sewing foot, lower the teeth; remember to raise and lower the presser bar as usual as it controls tension discs.

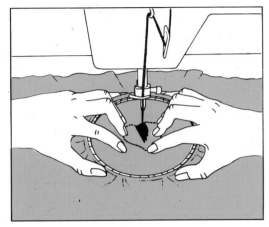

Couching

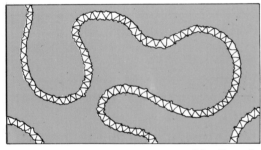

Decorative threads, knitting yarns and braid can be couched in place using a zigzag or more decorative stitch set to a wide width to cover the couched yarn or braid.

Cross stitch

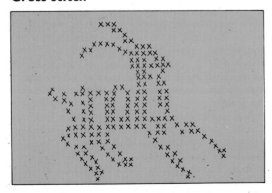

With an automatic cross stitch facility lines can be stitched to form borders; separate motifs and designs can be made and solid areas filled. It takes time to learn how to turn corners.

Cut work

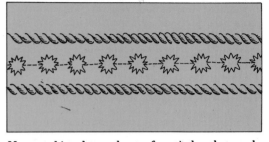

This heavy form of embroidery can be worked using satin stitch. Make sure the fabric is well supported; cut away the edges and intervening areas carefully after stitching.

Eyelets

These are an automatic feature on some electronic machines but they can be made with care on other machines, using satin stitch. After sewing reshape the eyelet with a bodkin.

Hemstitch

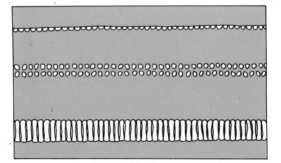

An attractive punched decoration for fine fabrics made with various zigzag and triple stitches, or the machine may have programmed stitches. Use as borders between tucks etc., through double fabric as a hemstitch, or the edge can be trimmed after stitching to produce picot edging.

Monograms

Use plain satin stitch or ornamental satin stitch, reducing stitch width on some parts of the letters for

good effect. On pile fabrics draw outline on paper or Stitch-n-Tear, pin to RS fabric and stitch monogram through paper, tearing it away afterward. All fabrics must be well supported for monogramming.

Ornamental borders

Most machines have a least a few stitches that can be used for border designs but with imagination interesting effects can be achieved, making the border look like braid and not like a stitch sampler. With computerized machines there is no limit to the variety of creative designs that are possible.

Scallops

Even machines offering as few as five ornamental patterns include a satin stitch scallop. It can be used effectively on edges of collars, cuffs, necklines, frills etc., and also on household items. Baste two pieces of fabric WS together with iron-on interfacing pressed to one piece. One layer of fabric may be omitted from some household items. Mark outer edge to be stitched and work the scallops, adjusting length slightly if necessary to make neat corners. Trim off surplus fabric.

Twin-needle

A simple method of stitching that can be worked with a straight or zigzag stitch using matching or contrasting colour threads. Some elaborate patterns can result from combining various ornamental stitches.

MACHINE FAULTS

The main faults are given below with, where appropriate, a general remedy. If this remedy does not overcome the problem, check each point listed until the fault is diagnosed.
All remedies are listed in italics.

Neither motor nor light work
1 Machine plug or foot control plug may not have been pushed right in. Alternatively, wall socket switch or master switch on machine may not have been switched on.
2 Faulty fuse or wiring in plugs.
3 Main house fuse has blown.
4 Area power failure.
If power is still not reaching the machine, consult a dealer.

Motor does not run but light functions
Power is reaching the machine if the light comes on so the problem is caused by motor failure, which must be dealt with by a dealer.

Excessive noise in sewing
Insert a new or smaller needle or different point.
1 Poor-quality oil may have solidified.
Clean and oil thoroughly; if noise continues, have poor oil flushed out by a dealer.

Machine works too slowly
Open up machine and oil it.
1 On two-speed machines, speed indication may be on minimum.
Check and regulate if necessary.
2 Machine out of use for some time, or cold.
Keep running until it warms up.
3 Something may have rolled under foot control, preventing you pushing it right down.
4 Tension belt too tight.
Must be corrected by dealer.
5 Motor not running properly.
Consult a dealer.

Needle does not move
Tighten wheel, which may have been loosened for bobbin winding.
1 An end of thread or dust may be caught in bobbin case.
Remove dust or thread and check bobbin is correctly inserted.

Machine jams after making one or two stitches
1 Ends of thread or fluff trampled in and tangled under needle plate.
Clean out plate area thoroughly.
2 Thread caught in bobbin case.
Remove plate and bobbin unit and gently rock hand wheel back and forth until you can see the thread. Pull it out.
3 Machine incorrectly threaded.
Check handbook and rethread.
4 Fabric not completely under presser foot.
Adjust so fabric edges farther under foot.

Machine runs but no stitches form
1 Needle has come unthreaded.
Make sure take-up lever is at high position to start and rethread.
2 Needle inserted wrongly.
Unscrew and adjust.
3 Bobbin has run out.
Remove and fill.

Fabric does not feed through
1 Incorrect foot inserted for stitch (satin stitches get caught up if wrong foot is used).
Change to correct foot.
2 Teeth may accidentally have been lowered.
Raise to usual sewing position.
3 Machine bed damp, causing fabric to stick.
Polish bed and sprinkle talcum powder on it.

Wrinkled stitching
Place tissue paper or thin typing paper over teeth and over top of fabric.
1 Needle bent, too large for fabric, of poor quality and roughly finished, or ball-point needle being used on woven fabrics.
Replace with new, correct needle.
2 Thread too coarse for fabric.
Replace with suitable thread.
3 Incorrect foot inserted for stitch.
Replace with correct foot.
4 Stitch too wide or too long for fabric.
Adjust stitch size until it suits fabric.
5 Top tension too tight.
Adjust tension screw if the machine has one, or check handbook for method of adjusting.
6 Pressure too great for thickness of fabric.
If machine has a pressure screw, loosen slightly. If there is no screw, the machine should be self-adjusting; consult a dealer.
7 Teeth set too high.
As a temporary measure, lower teeth slightly by turning knob toward darning position; have the setting adjusted properly by a dealer.

Occasional missed stitches
If sewing on fine fabric, e.g. silky jersey, use a ball-point or long scarf needle; try a different stitch and foot; if possible stitch with needle at right or left position instead of centre; change to a different type of thread; or put tissue paper or typing paper under fabric.
1 Needle blunt, bent or too fine for fabric.
Replace with new, correct needle.
2 Needle incorrectly inserted.
Check handbook and reinsert.
3 Top tension too tight.
Adjust tension screw if the machine has one, or check handbook for method of adjusting.
4 Pressure too high for fabric.
If machine has a pressure screw, loosen slightly. If there is no screw, the machine should be self-adjusting; consult a dealer.
5 Starting off too violently.
Use hand wheel.

Needle breaks
1 Needle bent or too fine for fabric.
Replace with new, correct needle.
2 Needle loose.
Unscrew and insert firmly.
3 Knot in thread.
Cut off knotted section and rethread machine.
4 Bobbin case incorrectly inserted.
Check handbook and reinsert.
5 Presser foot loose.
Tighten screw attaching it to machine.
6 Zigzag stitch worked with unsuitable straight stitch foot, e.g. zipper foot.
Use zigzag foot or general straight stitch foot.
7 Pulling out fabric without raising needle.
Always raise both needle and presser foot.
8 Pins left in fabric.
Sew over them slowly if they are at right angles to stitching line or remove completely.
9 Approaching thick area too fast.
Slow down and, if area is very thick, use hand wheel to bring needle into layers of material.
10 Pulling material and bending needle.
Do not pull fabric faster than machine sews.

Top thread breaks
1 Needle blunt, rough, too fine or incorrect for fabric.
Insert new, correct needle.
2 Needle inserted wrongly.
Unscrew and adjust position.
3 Knot in thread.
Cut off knotted section and rethread machine.
4 Thread caught twice around take-up lever or other part.
Rethread.
5 Thread dried out or wrong for fabric.
Replace with new thread.
6 Hole in needle plate rough.
Ask dealer to smooth it or supply new plate.
7 Top tension too tight.
Adjust tension screw if the machine has one, or check handbook for method of adjusting.

Bottom thread breaks
1 Bottom thread caught up.
If the bobbin is the two-piece type, check that the pieces are properly aligned and joined. Otherwise remove bobbin and reinsert.
2 Knot in thread.
Cut off knotted section and rethread.
3 Top or bottom incorrectly threaded.
Check handbook and rethread.
4 Bobbin overfilled.
Cut off surplus thread.
5 Tension on bobbin case too tight.
Adjust screw on bobbin case.
6 Bobbin wound unevenly.
Rewind.
7 Fluff in bobbin case.
Remove and brush out case and bobbin area.
8 Rough edges on bobbin case.
Buy a new one.

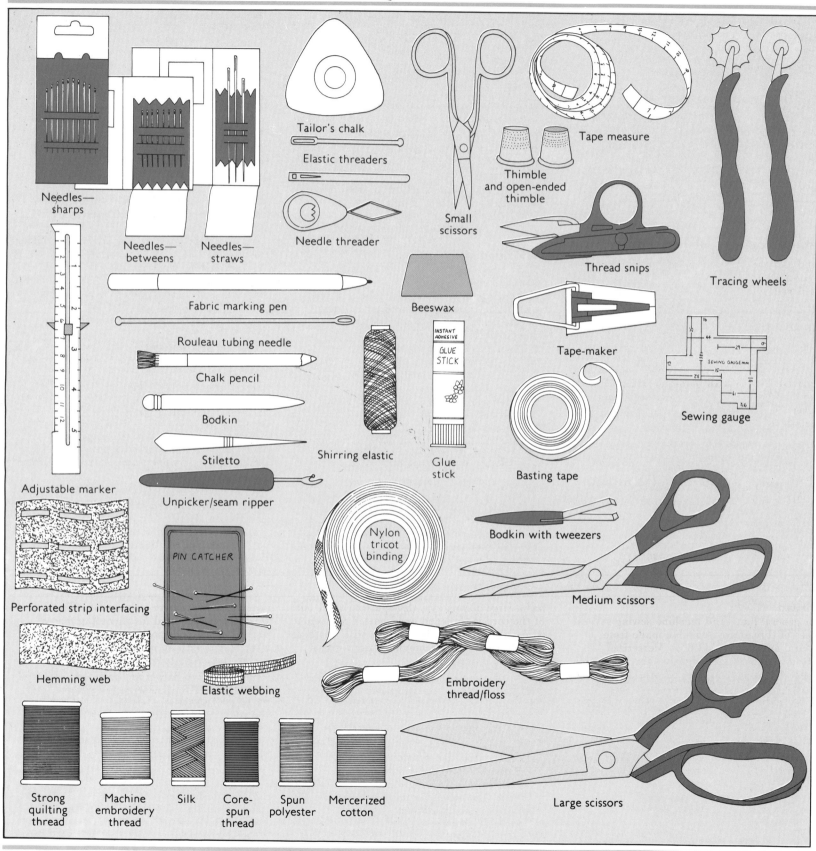

Needles—sharps

Needles—betweens

Needles—straws

Tailor's chalk

Elastic threaders

Needle threader

Small scissors

Tape measure

Thimble and open-ended thimble

Thread snips

Tracing wheels

Fabric marking pen

Beeswax

Rouleau tubing needle

Tape-maker

Sewing gauge

Chalk pencil

Bodkin

Shirring elastic

Glue stick

Basting tape

Stiletto

Adjustable marker

Unpicker/seam ripper

Bodkin with tweezers

PIN CATCHER

Nylon tricot binding

Perforated strip interfacing

Medium scissors

Hemming web

Elastic webbing

Embroidery thread/floss

Strong quilting thread

Machine embroidery thread

Silk

Core-spun thread

Spun polyester

Mercerized cotton

Large scissors

Good sewing equipment is essential for professional results. The range of gadgets and aids is continually increasing, but the basic items required are few.

Scissors

Good-quality scissors are a sound investment; have several pairs in different sizes making sure they are all comfortable to hold. Choose between drop-forged scissors with strong blades which can be sharpened, and lightweight stainless steel blades with plastic handles. A sharpener is available for these.

Thread snips are useful but a small pair of scissors with large finger holes is also needed for cutting thread, clipping fabric edges and cutting buttonholes. Larger scissors must be side-bent—shaped so that the handles fit the hand and the blade rests flat on the table to give an accurate cutting line. Have a medium-sized pair with blades 10–12 cm/4–5 in long for trimming seams and cutting small pieces of fabric. A bigger pair with 28 cm/11 in blades will be required for cutting out and good drop-forged scissors are easier for this, especially in tailoring. For left-handed people shears are available with handles and blades reversed. People with manipulative problems may find battery-operated scissors helpful. Never use dressmaking scissors for any other purpose or they will become blunt.

Needles

Betweens are short needles, ideal for hand sewing as it is easier to make small, correctly formed stitches with a short needle. Keep a variety of sizes and select needles according to the weight of the fabric. Sharps, long needles, are used for fly-running or for gathering when a lot of stitches are collected on the needle. Very long needles known as straws are used for working through many layers. Needles soon become blunt so replace them often.

Thread

For general hand and machine sewing several types of thread are available made from natural and synthetic fibres. Mercerized cotton is smooth and slightly shiny, available in size 40 for general use and sizes 50 and 60 for fine fabrics and hand stitching. Use on natural fabrics. Spun polyester thread is fine and very strong and has elasticity. It is suitable for all fabrics; always use on jersey and stretch fabrics. Core-spun thread is fine polyester covered with cotton, which makes a strong thread that is slightly thicker than polyester. Use on all except fine fabrics. Use instead of polyester for machine stitching if problems of static—missed stitches—are encountered.

Silk thread is soft and lustrous, good for hand sewing and can be used on silk and wool. A thicker silk thread, buttonhole twist, is used for tailor's buttonholes and also as a filler thread for machine-made buttonholes. Gimp is a thick cotton covered with silk or cotton, used as filling in tailor's buttonholes.

Bold polyester thread is for heavy-duty stitching, for example on furnishings. This or linen button thread is used for sewing buttons on tailored clothes. Machine embroidery cotton thread, sizes 30 and 60, can be used for basting very delicate fabrics, for machine and hand embroidery and for machine-made buttonholes. Extra-strong fine polyester thread is for hand quilting and other strong hand stitching on fine fabrics.

Various metallic and fibre yarns create interesting effects. Basting thread breaks easily so it can be removed without harm to the fabric. Use for all temporary stitching. Long pieces can be reused.

Thimble

A thimble is worn on the middle finger of the hand holding the needle and makes hand sewing more comfortable and efficient. An open-ended thimble is pleasant to use as air can reach the finger.

Beeswax

It is essential to strengthen thread for sewing on buttons by coating it with beeswax, and it is helpful to wax double thread to prevent the two strands from parting. A covering of wax on synthetic thread stops it twisting.

Bodkin

Bodkins are used for removing basting stitches, easing out corners and points, turning belts, shaping eyelets and buttonholes, and threading elastic or cord through a casing. The elastic is tied around the grooves at the end of the bodkin and then inserted. An elastic threader can be used instead of a bodkin. A flat metal needle, it has a large oblong eye, through which one end of the cord is threaded and knotted to anchor it. A wooden bodkin is available with tweezers set into the end for removing stray threads and tailor's tacks.

Tailor's chalk

Stitching lines, darts and alterations can all be marked with tailor's chalk. Always use white chalk as colours may not brush out easily—even on white fabric it is visible as a dull mark. Keep the chalk sharp by shaving the edge carefully with the medium scissors.

Chalk pencils are easier to sharpen and are available with a brush fitted to the end. Another way of marking points on single layers of fabric is to use a fabric marking pen—some of these wash out and others disappear automatically.

Measures

A fibreglass tape measure, marked with metric and Imperial measurements, is the best buy. Linen and other fabric tape measures eventually stretch. An adjustable marker, a short metal rule with a movable arrow, is useful when the same measurement has to be used repeatedly as, for example, when making tucks or buttonholes. Use a metre rule or yardstick for long straight measurements and for checking grain lines and hems.

Pins

Buy good steel pins in a container. Always keep the dark absorbent paper with the pins as it prevents rust. Cheap pins can damage or mark fabric. Long pins with coloured plastic heads are useful for fitting or for open or hairy fabrics where they are easily visible. Pincushions are a handy way of storing pins. A magnetic pin catcher should be kept by the sewing machine or stuck to it.

Notions

Various iron-on strips and tapes are available: narrow webbing for holding down hems and facings; webbing in sheet form with paper backing for use in buttonholes and pockets and for appliqué; perforated strip interfacings in various widths and weights to make construction of cuffs and waistbands easier.

Basting tape is very narrow tape with many applications such as temporarily holding facings in place and, with the backing removed, inserting zippers and applying braid. Provided it is covered by fabric it need not be removed. A glue stick is also useful for sticking patterns together.

A tape-maker, a tool for making accurately folded bias strips from your fabric, is a great time saver. Raw edges can be enclosed and edges can be faced, using either stretch lace or nylon tricot bias strip.

A needle threader is helpful but most will only work with larger size needles. The wire type can also be used for threading machine needles. Take out stitching and slit buttonholes with an unpicker/seam ripper (see p. 16). A rouleau tubing needle, a long needle with a ball end, makes the business of turning narrow tubing very easy; it can also be used for threading elastic and cord. A stiletto is a sharply pointed tool used to make holes in fabric and leather.

Markings can be transferred from pattern to fabric using dressmakers' carbon paper (keep to pale colours) and a tracing wheel—the plain wheel is more efficient than the toothed wheel as it makes a solid line.

An embroidery transfer pencil can also be used for marking designs on fabric. Draw the design on greaseproof or wax paper then press onto it to transfer design to fabric.

HAND SEWING

To achieve the best results in hand sewing, try not to hurry your work and allow enough time at each session to complete a particular feature, such as a hem or set of buttonholes. It is also important not only to have the right equipment but to know how to use it properly. Left-handed people should reverse the instructions given below.

Threading a needle
Pull the thread from the spool, cut and smooth the end. Holding the needle with the left hand, rest both hands lightly against each other to steady them while pushing the thread through the needle. Pull the thread through the eye with the right thumb and forefinger. The thread pulled through should be about one-quarter of the total length. It is often necessary to cut the end again cleanly at an angle if it does not thread the first time.

Making a knot
After threading the needle, keep hold of the thread between the left thumb and forefinger and wind it once around the forefinger, about halfway along the pad (1)—not less or it will be impossible to form the knot. With the thumb pad roll the thread to the end of the forefinger to make a loop (2). Turn that into a knot by running both thumb and second finger nail down the thread to the end (3). The dampness of the thread end helps to form the knot. Do not make big knots and keep practising if "tails"—spare lengths of thread beyond the knot—persist in forming.

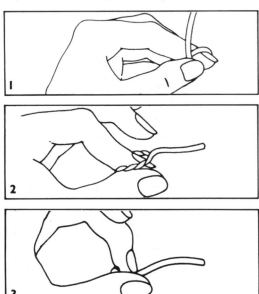

Holding the needle
Hold the needle fairly near the point with the right thumb and forefinger. The other fingers should be bent, almost clenched. The thimble,

on the middle finger, should have its side resting on the eye of the needle.

Insert the needle through the fabric, pushing the blunt end with the thimble. With the thimble still against the needle, move thumb and forefinger to grasp the needle point and pull the needle through the fabric. Stitches should generally be made in a smooth, continuous movement, not in a series of jabs and pushes. The fingers should control the needle all the time and hardly ever let go while working a row of stitches.

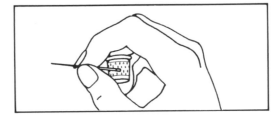

Starting off
Most permanent stitches and also basting are best started with a knot, as it is strong. Hide the knot on the wrong side under a fold or an edge of the fabric for permanent stitching. Knots in thick thread are later cut off, as, for example, in sewing on buttons. Sometimes, knots are hidden well away from the stitching, as in buttonholes.

If the fabric is transparent or the work delicate, start with two small backstitches on top of each other. The easiest way to do this is to use a knot, make the stitches and then cut off the knot. Work them under a fold or an edge of the fabric.

Finishing off
Fasten off with at least two backstitches worked on top of each other, hiding them under a fold or an edge. Cut off the thread close to the surface of the fabric. See individual stitches for exceptions to this rule.

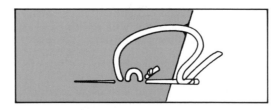

Working temporary stitches
The main temporary stitches are tailor's tacks and basting. They are quicker and easier to work and the results more accurate if the fabric is flat on the table. It is also better and generally quicker to work temporary stitches standing up, so that your eyes are directly above the stitches and your body weight is forward. Not only is this more comfortable than working with outstretched arms, but, as

such stitches are generally worked over a large area, it is easier to gain an overall picture and to watch for wrinkles.

Use a long piece of basting thread, stretching from shoulder to wrist when threaded, and a large between needle—4 to 6, depending on the thickness of the fabric. Arrange the work on the table and stitch, using the other hand to ease and push the fabric on to the needle. The table surface is used almost to bounce the needle point off again and up into the fabric, and so wood, which is soft, is the best surface on which to sew.

Working permanent stitches
Sit on a comfortable chair, near a window or directional lamp, as good light is essential. It can even be an armchair if you sit sideways and on the edge (the padded arm is handy for needles and pins).

Bend well over the work and relax. Even if sitting at a table, always hold the work, as it is important to retain the shape already inserted. Tailors sit cross-legged, or with one leg crossed over the other while sitting on the edge of a table or work board, so that they can build shape into the garment over their knees.

Unless otherwise indicated under the individual stitch, use a small between needle—6 to 9, depending on the thickness of the fabric—and a short piece of thread, no longer than from elbow to wrist when threaded, so that when you stitch, only the forearm should move. Working with a short thread makes the tension easier to control and also leads to neat identical stitches.

Have small scissors, thread and wax handy, and a bodkin for pulling out basting. Use the wax for smoothing out synthetic thread if necessary. Always press the stitching when finished, after removing basting stitches.

Tension
Correct tension in hand sewing is just as important as in machining. The tension must be correct for the fabric, neither too tight nor too slack, and the tension of all the stitches must be even. This is one reason for trying to complete a particular feature in one sitting.

Pull the thread through to finish each stitch with the same amount of tug. This takes concentration and practice because the thread becomes shorter and so the pull has to be adjusted fractionally for each stitch. Some hand stitches are pulled taut to embed the thread in the fabric. If several stitches are being made at one point, some are left taut on the surface, either for effect or to prevent wrinkling of the fabric, and others are left fairly slack to make sure a line does not show on the right side of the fabric.

A-Z OF HAND STITCHES

BACKSTITCHES

Backstitch

Strong stitch used for fastening off almost all hand stitches, for repairing seams and for small areas where machining might be awkward. The stitches should form a continuous row.

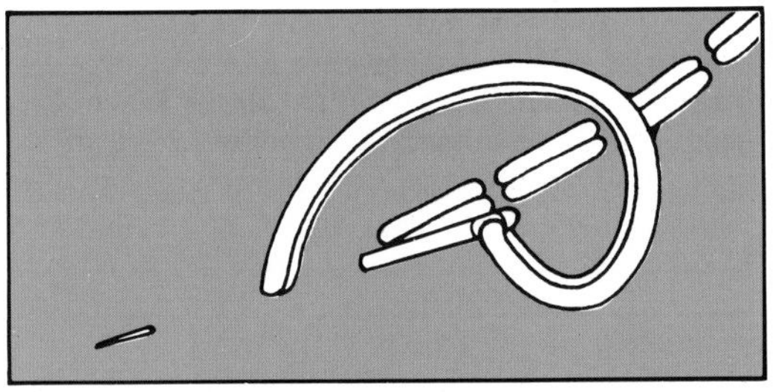

Used waxed double thread for strength. Work from right to left keeping stitches as small as possible, no more than 4 mm/$\frac{1}{8}$ in on top of work. Stitches on WS are twice the length of those on top and look rather untidy. Start with a knot. If knot is on RS, bring needle up to RS 4 mm/$\frac{1}{8}$ in farther on. Insert needle back by knot and bring out 4 mm//$\frac{1}{8}$ in in front of this first stitch. Take needle below by end of first stitch bringing it up another 4 mm/$\frac{1}{8}$ in in front of where it last emerged. If starting with knot on WS, bring needle straight through to RS and insert 4 mm/$\frac{1}{8}$ in behind knot. Bring out 4 mm/$\frac{1}{8}$ in in front of this first stitch and take further stitches as described above.

Half backstitch

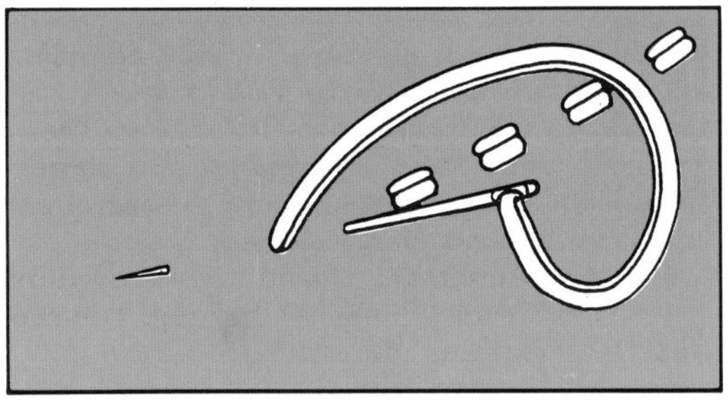

Neater, more attractive and stronger than an ordinary backstitch, although still untidy on WS so use only where this does not matter. The stitches do not form a continuous row; the space between them equals the length of the stitches—2 mm/$\frac{1}{16}$in. Suitable for setting in sleeves by hand and for other places where a full backstitch would produce too large a stitch, causing the fabric to part.

Work as for backstitch, using double waxed thread, but take needle back and through WS only 2 mm/$\frac{1}{16}$in behind emerging thread. Bring up to RS 4 mm/$\frac{1}{8}$ in in front of stitch as in backstitch. Pull thread tight with each stitch if working on a seam to ensure that the seam does not open up in any part and show threads.

Prick stitch

A type of backstitch which, although untidy on WS, can be almost invisible on RS if worked with single thread. Use where hand stitching will enhance the finished appearance or where the pressure of machining would cause a ridge on layers of fabric, e.g. holding a binding over a hem or pocket, stitching through a seam join from RS, as at the back of a collar. On fine fabrics such as chiffon and georgette insert zippers with prick stitch rather than by machine.

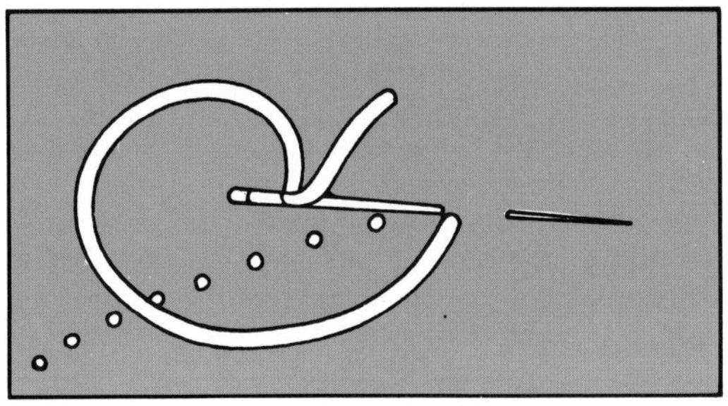

Use single thread and work from right to left. Begin with a knot or backstitch and bring needle through to RS. Make stitch by inserting needle again slightly behind point where it emerged, but almost in same hole. Take needle underneath for shortest distance fabric allows, and bring up to RS. Do not pull thread too tight.

Bar tack

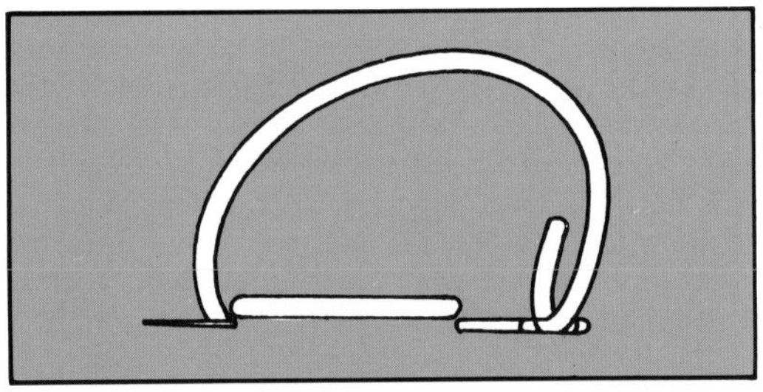

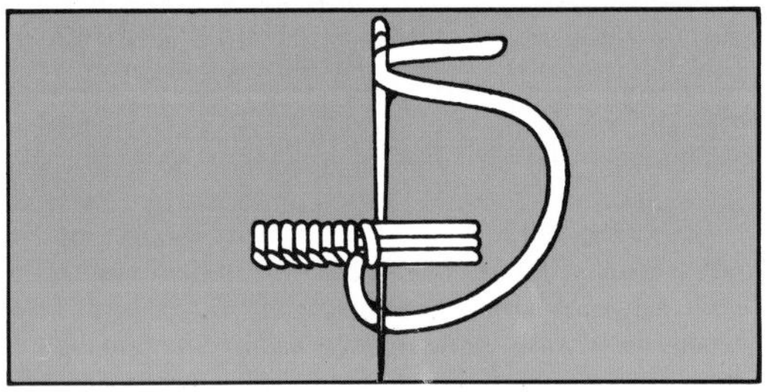

Strengthening bar used across ends of sleeve opening and base of zipper opening to prevent fabric tearing. Use ordinary sewing thread.

Start with a knot on WS. With RS of work toward you, bring needle through to RS and take three or four satin stitches on top of each other through fabric at point of strain. If there are several layers of fabric to be held, make stitches with stabbing motion. The length of the stitches will be the length of the bar tack. Cover these threads with closely spaced loop stitch, taking needle under strands. Pass needle to WS and fasten off firmly with a backstitch.

BASTING STITCHES

Diagonal basting

A big stitch used to cover large areas quickly. Keeps fabric flat, whereas ordinary straight basting would cause ridges. Particularly suitable for inserting interfacings, holding linings and holding roll line of collars. Unless working to a moulded curve, keep material flat on table and stand up to sew.

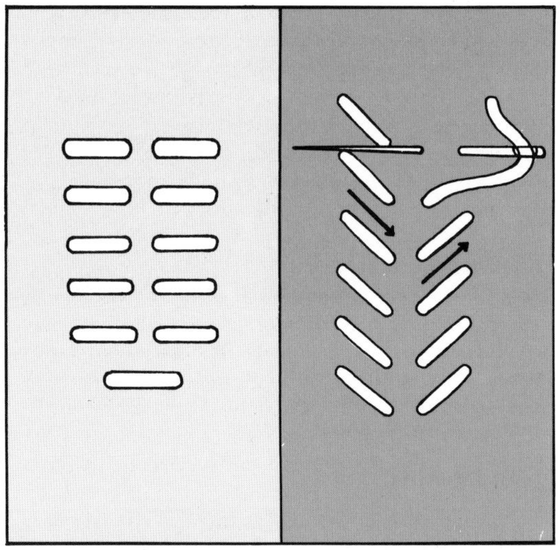

Work on RS, starting with a knot. Take a small horizontal stitch from right to left through fabric. Working toward you, take another stitch the same size as, and parallel to, the first, so that a diagonal stretch of thread on RS links end of first stitch with beginning of second. The parallel horizontal stitches show only on WS. Do not pull thread tight or ridges will form. The length of the parallel stitches and the distance between them varies according to the amount of control required. Take short stitches close together for greater control, longer ones more widely spaced if less control is needed. Several rows can be worked, about 3 cm/$1\frac{1}{4}$ in apart. Finish each with one loose backstitch for ease of removal.

Even basting

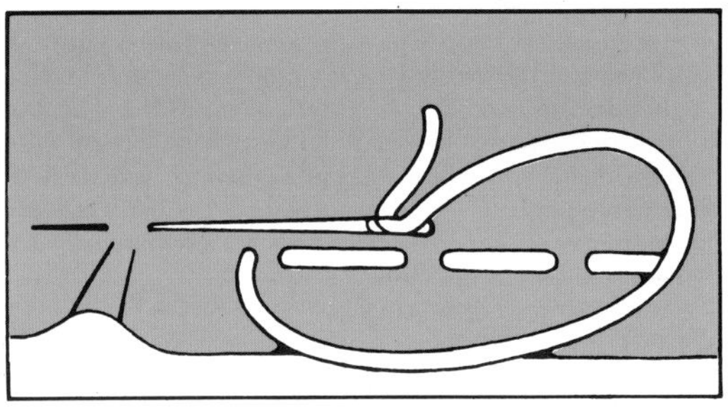

Used to hold two or more layers of fabric together or for marking single layers.

Start with a knot on RS and work from right to left. Stand up when stitching long straight lines and work on a flat surface. Push needle through fabric in one continuous in-and-out movement, making stitches about 2 cm/$\frac{3}{4}$ in long, shorter around curves or difficult areas. Pick up on needle as little fabric as possible between stitches—about 3 mm/$\frac{1}{8}$ in. If too much fabric is picked up, the layers of fabric part and seams open when the garment is being fitted, or the fabric moves when it is machined. Finish with one backstitch, or two if preparing for fitting. To remove, pull starting knot gently.

Flash basting

Limited almost entirely to attaching seam allowances of loose linings to seam allowances of garments, e.g. at shoulders and side seams.

A-Z OF HAND STITCHES

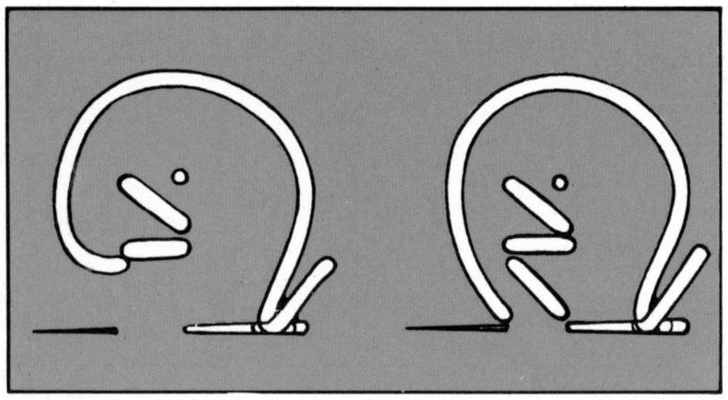

Work as a single row as for diagonal basting, strengthening the bottom of each diagonal with a backstitch instead of the ordinary horizontal stitch. Finish as for diagonal basting.

Slip basting

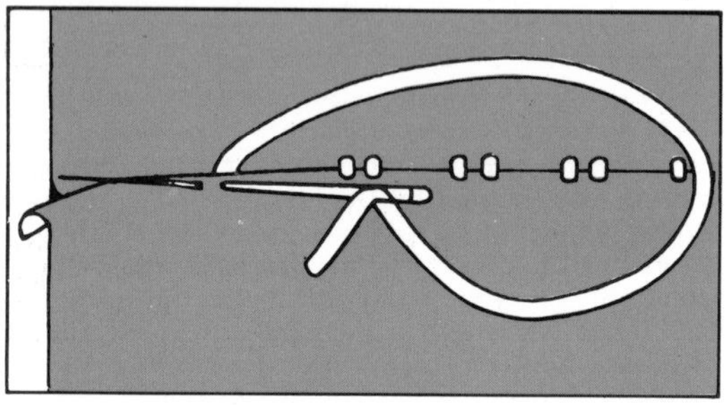

Worked from RS to hold together pieces of fabric on which the design has to be matched or where a folded edge has to be caught down accurately before being pressed or stitched permanently.

Fold top layer of fabric under at seamline and pin at intervals to hold. Start with a knot on RS. Working right to left, slip needle into fold and bring out about 5 mm/$\frac{1}{4}$in farther on. In single layer of fabric, directly opposite point at which needle emerges from fold, take a horizontal stitch of about 3 mm/$\frac{1}{8}$in. Directly opposite the end of this stitch, insert needle in fold and take another 5 mm/$\frac{1}{4}$in stitch, and so on. Finish with one backstitch. If the two joined pieces form a seam, the top layer is flapped over to reveal a row of ordinary straight basting stitches.

Strong basting

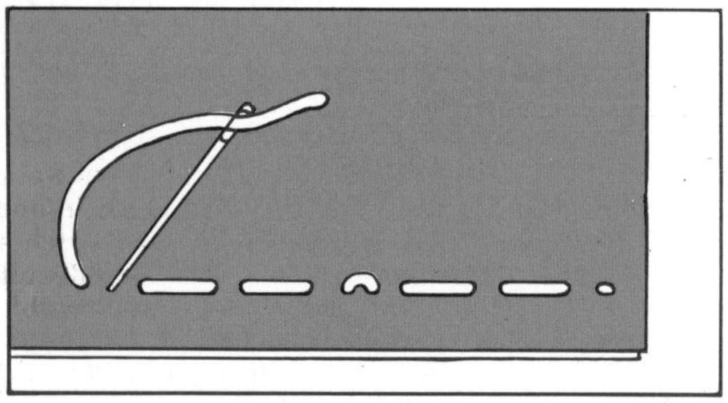

Used particularly in tailoring and where fabrics of very different weights are inclined to slip and part. Use on main seams to provide strength for fitting. Strong basting is often left in place inside tailored clothes and later covered by lining, for example around armholes. Work as for even basting but make a small backstitch every alternate stitch or every two stitches.

Uneven basting

Used for the same purpose as even basting and also on fine or slippery fabrics for a better grip.

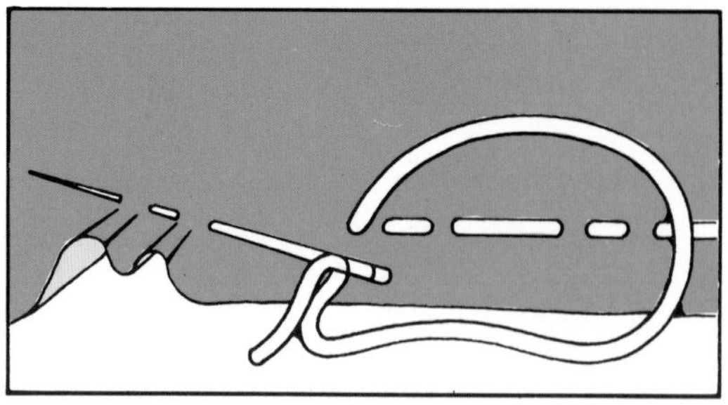

Work as for even basting, with same needle movement, but take a small stitch, e.g. 5 mm/$\frac{1}{4}$in, alternately with a long one, keeping space between stitches equal. Finish and remove as for backstitch.

Blanket stitch see Loop stitch

Buttonhole stitch

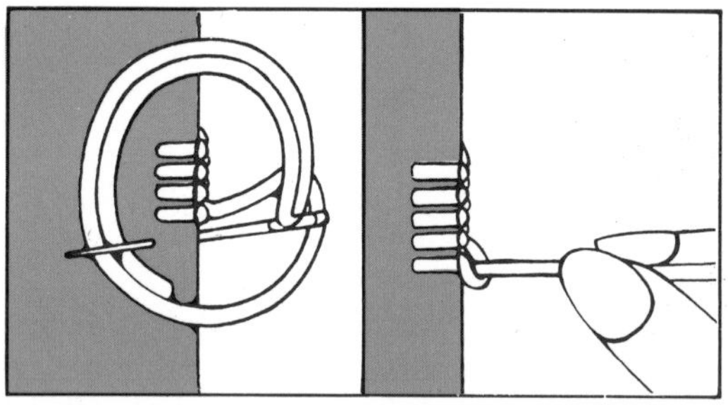

Used for hand-worked buttonholes, and also for finishing a short length of raw edge to prevent fraying. Difficult to work neatly because a knot is formed with each stitch and an even tension must be kept on all knots. For hand-worked buttonhole method see p. 66.

Begin with a knot on WS and work toward you with cut edge to right (to left, if left-handed). Take thread over edge and insert needle from WS beside knot. Bring needle point through to left of edge on RS. To form a knot rather than a loop, wind double section of thread by eye of needle around needle point toward you. Although the fingers should leave the needle at this stage, keep thimble in place at eye of needle to steady it while knot is formed. Let go of thread and finish pulling needle through fabric. To settle knot on edge of fabric, grasp thread near knot and tug it gently into position. Work next stitch beside it, nearer to you. The depth of stitch depends on how much the fabric frays; the more it frays the deeper the stitch (a fabric adhesive strip on WS helps to lessen fraying). The closeness of the stitches depends upon the thickness of the thread but keep spacing even and make sure that the knots touch.

Catch stitch

Used almost entirely to hold up hems in medium and heavy fabrics, and sometimes over a raw edge in short lengths. Although weak, it is invisible on RS. It serves the same purpose as herringbone, but is neater.

To avoid a ridge on hems, work stitch just under hem edge, 3 to 5 mm/$\frac{1}{8}$ to $\frac{1}{4}$in down, depending on thickness of fabric. If it is worked lower, the weight of the edge eventually pulls and makes a line; you may also catch your heel in it. Work from right to left. Lift up hem edge and fasten thread inside with a knot or backstitch. Take a very small stitch in hem fabric and 3 to 5 mm/$\frac{1}{8}$ to $\frac{1}{4}$in to left, depending on thickness of

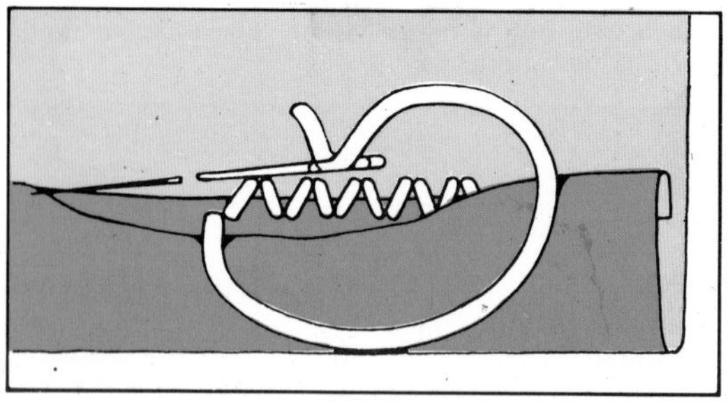

fabric, a small stitch in garment. If possible, pick up one thread or less in garment, a little more in hem edge, keeping thread loose. If working over an edge, make stitches same size.

Chain stitch

Although mainly an embroidery stitch, it has its uses in dressmaking and can be worked, with a single or double thread or buttonhole twist, to make a chain to form a belt loop or French tack.

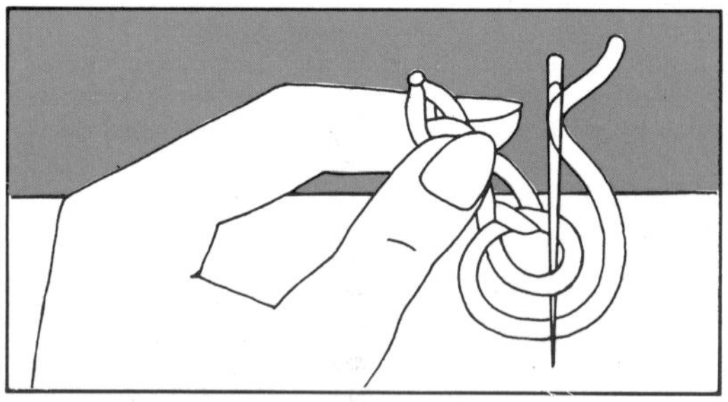

Start with a knot on WS and bring thread through to RS. Make a small loop and insert needle at point where it emerged, holding loop out to a length of 2 mm/$\frac{1}{16}$in. Bring needle out just inside end of this first loop and continue to form chains until desired length is reached, holding line of chains away from fabric. Fasten off by taking needle through last loop and working several backstitches on WS.

Cross stitch

Like chain stitch, it is mainly an embroidery stitch, but is useful in dressmaking for finishing off a raw edge and, in groups of a few stitches, for strengthening weak areas such as pocket ends. The needle must be stabbed through the work with each movement. This makes the other side untidy so use only inside a garment, e.g. for linings and seam allowances. Work on RS for decoration only.

Working from left to right, start with a backstitch and bring needle through to RS. To form first diagonal of cross, take needle below the point at which it emerged and insert same distance to right, bringing it up again at left exactly below start of diagonal. The distance the needle is taken down and across is 3 to 5 mm/$\frac{1}{8}$ to $\frac{1}{4}$in, depending on thickness of fabric. To form second diagonal, insert needle at top righthand corner of cross and bring out at start of first diagonal. If room, work another two or three stitches beside initial stitch, but if space is limited and more strength needed, work second cross stitch over first.

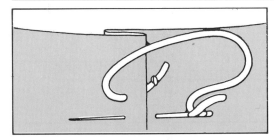

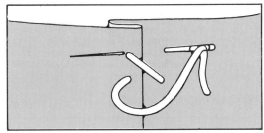

To finish off a raw edge with cross stitch, work first diagonal of each stitch, from top left to bottom right, in a row toward you. When row is finished, work back in opposite direction, forming diagonals from bottom left to top right to complete each cross.

Diagonal basting see BASTING

Draw stitch

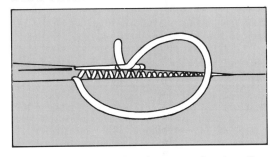

Used in dressmaking, but far more often in tailoring, to join two folded edges invisibly from RS, e.g. collar and lapel. The join is often shaped or has more fullness in one edge than the other, so it is important to draw up thread on each stitch.

Begin with a knot well tucked away. Working from right to left, take a tiny stitch of 1 mm/$\frac{1}{16}$in through one fold and insert needle in opposite fold slightly behind this first stitch. Pull thread through and draw folds together. Move forward 1 mm/$\frac{1}{16}$in and repeat stitches. Do not pull thread too tight or fabric will wrinkle. Keep an even tension on all stitches. If join is curved, take a slightly longer stitch in concave curve to keep edges even. Slide needle to WS and fasten off well away from join.

Even basting see BASTING

Feather stitch

When used in dressmaking, this embroidery stitch can be both decorative and functional; particularly suitable for faggoted seams and sewing on braid.

Use ordinary sewing thread or embroidery thread and work with RS toward you. Start with a knot or, on fine fabrics, a backstitch. Bring needle through to RS

of fabric and take a small stitch toward you, holding thread down against fabric to form loop and bringing needle out just above loop to form stitch. The amount of fabric picked up should be between 2 and 5 mm/$\frac{1}{16}$ and $\frac{1}{4}$ in depending on thickness of fabric. Begin second

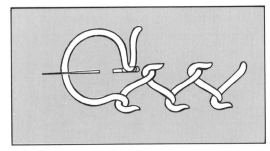

stitch slightly below loop to left, the distance below depending on thickness of fabric and size of stitch, and work third stitch slightly below second loop to right, and so on.

Fell stitch

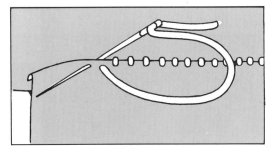

Sometimes called felling. A tailoring stitch used for attaching loose linings to the neck, front edges and seams of coats and jackets.

Baste lining in position with raw edge folded under. Hold work with fold of lining away from you. Start with a knot hidden under fold and, working from right to left, take a tiny deep stitch into fabric of garment, bringing needle out in edge of lining, no more than 2 mm/$\frac{1}{16}$in away. Insert needle again in garment fabric slightly behind where thread emerged for an almost invisible stitch. Pull thread just far enough for the stitch to disappear; if it is pulled too tight the lining will wrinkle. Fasten off with two backstitches under the fold but in the garment. Although the stitch must be so small that it is virtually invisible, it is extremely strong. For a more professional result and a stronger finish, it can also be used as an alternative to hemming stitch to hold down a fold of fabric.

Flash basting see BASTING

Fly-running see RUNNING STITCHES

Half backstitch see BACKSTITCHES

HEMMING STITCHES

Hemming stitch

Moderately strong and worked on WS to hold down a fold of fabric. It shows on RS and is, therefore, unsuitable for skirt and dress hems. It should also be avoided on jacket and trouser hems.

Work toward you. Begin with a knot, on WS of edge

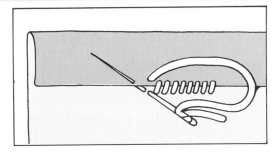

if possible, but if working on sheer fabric start with a small backstitch on WS. Take a slanting stitch 1 mm/$\frac{1}{16}$in long, picking up part of single fabric and fold in one movement. Take another slanting stitch 1 mm/$\frac{1}{16}$in farther forward. The length of the stitches and the distance between them can be a little more on thicker fabrics.

Hemming into machining

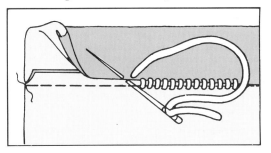

Stronger and more versatile than hemming. Use anywhere where a row of machining has been worked, e.g. on WS of waistbands or on cuffs.

Work toward you. Instead of picking up fabric, pick up thread of machine stitch and then run needle into fold at a slight slant. Pull thread fairly tight. Work a hemming stitch into every machine stitch for maximum strength and neatness.

Shell stitch

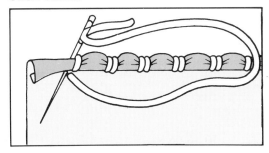

A decorative stitch, equally visible on both sides, and used on fine fabrics only to hold a narrow hem or for making tucks.

Work from right to left over a folded edge, usually 5 mm/$\frac{1}{4}$ in deep. Begin with a small backstitch—on WS if working a hem, on one of the two RS if working a tuck. Take needle over and behind folded edge, insert below it and bring through at same level toward you. Pull thread sufficiently to wrinkle fold attractively. Hold thread with thumb of other hand, take another stitch over fold in same place as first and pull thread tight to hold stitch firmly. If working tucks, make three tiny running stitches between shells. If holding down an edge, run needle through fold for 5 mm/$\frac{1}{4}$ in or, if fabric is springy, work three hemming stitches along fold. Take needle over fold twice to make second shell, and so on. Press carefully to avoid squashing shells, pushing tip of iron into each shell.

Slip hemming

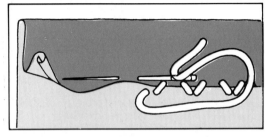

Used for holding down a folded edge, e.g. skirt hem, on light fabrics. Stitched with care, it can be almost invisible on both sides.

Work from right to left, beginning with a knot or a backstitch in fold. In one continuous movement take up one thread of single fabric on needle and, slightly in front of this, pass point into fold. Slip needle through fold for 2 to 5 mm/$\frac{1}{16}$ in to $\frac{1}{4}$ in and bring out. Below the point at which the thread emerges and 1 mm/$\frac{1}{16}$ in farther on, take up another thread of fabric and insert needle in fold. Keep thread fairly loose as the hem shows if it is taut.

Slip stitch

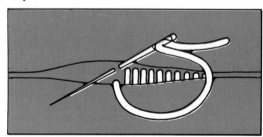

Used for joining two folded edges. It can be invisible if carefully worked, so is useful for anything that has to be sewn from RS, such as a split in a seam, the gap in a belt, the ends of a tie, cuffs and collars.

Start with a knot hidden inside one of the folds. Working from right to left, take a tiny stitch along this fold and then take another in opposite fold about 1 mm/$\frac{1}{16}$ in farther on. Pull thread tight enough to join folds but not to wrinkle them. Fasten off slightly away from join.

Herringbone stitch

Similar to cross stitch, but not an even cross and quicker to sew. Worked over a raw edge to hold it down, e.g. on facings, and, worked in embroidery thread, to attach rickrack or zigzag braid. Used frequently on medium and heavy fabrics, less on lightweight materials as the edge tends to curl up. Can be used to finish the hem of a thicker fabric, but inclined to be visible as a ridge after some wear.

To work over a raw edge, sew from left to right and begin with a knot or backstitch slightly below edge. In garment fabric above edge, diagonally to right of starting point, take a small stitch, 2 to 4 mm/$\frac{1}{16}$ in to $\frac{1}{8}$ in

long, depending on thickness of fabric, from right to left. Diagonally to right below first stitch and below raw edge, take another small horizontal stitch in same direction. Take a third stitch to right above second stitch on same level as first, and so on. Do not pull thread tight. Rows of horizontal stitches should be between 4 and 8 mm/$\frac{1}{8}$ and $\frac{3}{8}$ in apart.

Herringbone can be worked in various ways to

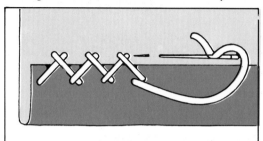

attach braid, depending on the width and style of the braid. It is worked across thin braid, down the middle of a wider strip and, with rickrack braid, the horizontal stitches are taken in opposite curves.

Loop stitch

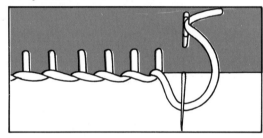

Also called blanket stitch. Sometimes confused with buttonhole stitch but less lumpy and a loop is made rather than a knot. The stitches can be close together or spaced out, depending on where they are used. Close loop stitch, with no space between stitches, is used over bar tacks, at the back of buttons and for eyelet holes (where there would be no room for the knots of buttonhole stitches); open loop stitch is used as an alternative to herringbone for finishing raw edges or holding them down.

Work from left to right with edge toward you and start with a backstitch on WS. Bring needle and thread around to RS and insert needle above edge on RS, holding thread below edge. Bring needle out below edge over held thread. Pull thread and settle so that it lies along edge. The distance from the edge at which the needle is inserted varies according to the fabric—on non-fraying fabrics from 3 to 5 mm/$\frac{1}{8}$ to $\frac{1}{4}$ in, depending on thickness of fabric, on fraying from 4 to 8 mm/$\frac{1}{8}$ to $\frac{3}{8}$ in. Hold thread below edge and take another stitch a little to right for open loop stitch, immediately to right for close.

Overcasting

Used for finishing raw edges. If the material frays badly, work a row of machining first and trim away very close to it before overcasting over it.

Work from left to right and start with a knot on WS if possible. Take needle over raw edge and insert in back of edge at right angles to fabric, bringing it through to the front at same level. Pull thread through

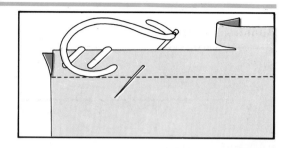

quickly to form sloping stitch, but not too tightly as edges will curl. If worked slowly, the stitches become upright and unattractive. Use thumb of other hand to hold edge flat while working. The depth of stitch and the distance between stitches depend on the thickness of the fabric, but make the depth as shallow as possible without pulling the fabric away.

Oversewing

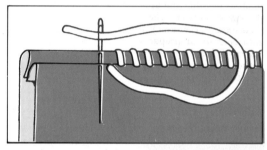

Used for joining two folded edges where greater strength is needed than slip stitching can provide.

With the two folded edges together, work from right to left, starting with a hidden knot in back fold. Pass needle at right angles to body through top of both folds, picking up one fabric thread from each. Pull sewing thread through fairly tightly. Repeat to produce a row of tiny, neat, slanting stitches on RS. The distance between the stitches varies from 1 to 3 mm/$\frac{1}{16}$ to $\frac{1}{8}$ in, depending on thickness of fabric.

Prick stitch see BACKSTITCHES

RUNNING STITCHES

Fly-running

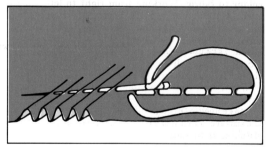

Quicker to work than running stitch and used where several long rows of running stitches are to be inserted, as, for example, in preparation for smocking.

Use a sharps needle and work from right to left in a straight line. Start with a small backstitch. Hold needle near point and, instead of taking single stitches, wiggle point in and out of fabric quickly.

26

Running stitch

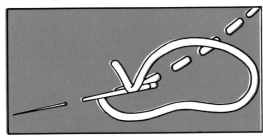

Weak stitch used for inserting gathering threads, for preparing for smocking or for working French seams by hand on lingerie or baby wear—for seams practise the stitch first to ensure a good finish.

Start with a small backstitch and, working from right to left in a straight line, pass needle in and out of material at regular intervals. The stitches should be as small as possible and approximately the same size as the spaces between them (it is impossible to make them exactly the same). If working running stitch for gathering or in preparation for smocking, do not fasten off but leave an end of thread for pulling up gathers when all rows are in place. On a French seam, insert an occasional half or full backstitch for extra strength.

Saddle stitch

Decorative topstitching worked from RS only.

With chalk or basting, mark out a line to follow, as stitch is invariably parallel with a finished edge and any deviation from its line is immediately noticeable. Using thick topstitching thread and a needle large enough to take the thread, e.g. 4, begin with a well-hidden backstitch, especially if thread is a contrasting colour to fabric. Working from right to left, take a stitch 6 to 13 mm/$\frac{1}{4}$ to $\frac{1}{2}$ in long. Take needle back almost to where it was first inserted and take it below, bringing it out 6 to 13 mm/$\frac{1}{4}$ to $\frac{1}{2}$ in in front of first stitch. Take needle back almost to end of first stitch on RS, pass through to WS, and so on. The stitches should be longer than the gaps in between.

When working on a completed edge, or if stitching is to show on both sides, e.g. where a lapel turns over, do not take needle through all thicknesses, but just stitch the surface. Turn work over and repeat on other side if stitching is to show.

Satin stitch

Primarily an embroidery stitch, but useful for strengthening where a bar tack would be too lumpy, e.g. at ends of pockets and of hand-worked buttonholes.

Work in ordinary sewing thread, or, for buttonholes, buttonhole thread. Begin with a knot on WS and on RS make parallel small stitches on top of each

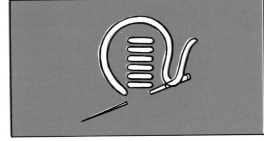

other or very close together. With thick fabrics, stab needle back and forth from RS to WS. Pull thread tight.

Shell stitch see HEMMING STITCHES

Slip basting see BASTING

Slip hemming see HEMMING STITCHES

Stab stitch

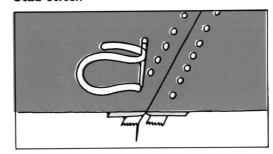

Strong stitch worked in a short length through several layers of fabric, e.g. at the base of a zipper. The effect should be like prick stitch—an almost invisible dent rather than a stitch—but stronger.

On WS a row of small stitches will show, so work stitch from whichever side is the more important to the appearance of the garment. Work as for prick stitch, but instead of running the needle through the fabric, stab it backward and forward through all layers.

Tailor tacking

Also called tailor's tacks. The best and most accurate way of making marks through two layers of fabric. Used for marking seam allowances, balance marks, pleat lines, etc., after cutting out but before removing the pattern; also for marking two sides of a garment accurately, e.g. after making a fitting adjustment, or for marking position of pockets after the garment has been fitted.

Follow the rules for temporary stitches on p. 22, using double basting thread. Work from right to left. Do not use a knot, but take a small stitch in double fabric about 2 to 4 mm/$\frac{1}{16}$ to $\frac{1}{8}$ in long depending on thickness of fabric. Move forward about 2.5 cm/1 in, less if working a curve, and take another small stitch. On a long straight line, the stitches on the surface can be longer, but never pick up more on needle than 4 mm/$\frac{1}{8}$ in. Do not fasten off end of thread but leave on surface and carefully clip in half all stitches on surface. Open the two layers of fabric until thread is revealed and clip across each pair of threads, leaving equal tufts on either side. This produces an accurate marking on two layers of fabric. Good tailor's tack tufts are so

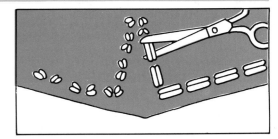

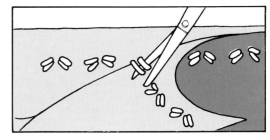

short they can be hard to remove (use your teeth or a pair of tweezers). To save thread on long runs, pull the thread through at the end of each stitch until it leaves a small tuft and clip before making the next tailor's tack.

If tailor's tacks worked this way fall out prematurely, it is for one of the following reasons: you are not using proper basting thread, which is hairy and grips the fabric; you are not using double thread, which jams the tuft in the material; you are using too big a needle, making a hole in the fabric that allows the threads to escape; you are leaving long ends of thread that trail across the fabric, get caught in your fingers and so come out.

Uneven basting see BASTING

Whipping

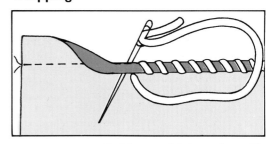

Used to finish a rolled hem on fabrics such as silk, chiffon and georgette.

Work from right to left with a fine needle, 8 or 9 between. Anchor thread in raw edge with backstitch and roll raw edge under toward you between left thumb and forefinger. Pass needle over rolled edge to RS, insert at back of edge at an angle and bring through to garment fabric below roll. Re-roll next short section and hold with other hand while taking second stitch, and so on. The distance between the stitches varies according to the type of fabric—fairly close together on fine fabrics and more widely spaced on thicker ones. On fabrics such as polyester chiffon, polyester georgette, nylon chiffon and polyester lawn, work a row of machining first about 4 mm/$\frac{1}{8}$ in from raw edge and trim edge close to machining. Roll edge over toward you and whip stitch as above.

TEXTILES

At one time it was fairly easy to identify the fibre used to make a fabric. Not only were the natural fibres such as cotton and wool recognizable, but so were nylon and polyester. Consequently, it was possible to make a reasonable guess at how the fabric would behave in wear and how it would have to be treated during sewing. The fabrics, too, were fairly standard, but due to great technological advances in mixtures of fibres it is now rarely possible to distinguish the fibre content instantly.

Fortunately, rolls of fabric now have to have their fibre content labelled. The fibres are listed in order of predominance; those present in quantities of 5 per cent or less do not need to be named unless they significantly affect the behaviour of the main fibre. It is, therefore, important to be familiar with all the main fibres, both natural and synthetic, and with their properties in order to know what to expect from the fabric. All fibre names have been standardized; if the trade name is used on the label, the generic name is also shown.

Fibres are produced either in staple form, as short tufts, or in filament form, as long continuous strands. The spun fibre is known as yarn. All synthetics are produced as filaments, but most can also be processed to form staple yarn. Silk is produced in filament form only, whereas wool and cotton come only in staple form.

Natural and synthetic fibres may be blended with other fibres before spinning, or spun first and then combined with other fibres before being made into cloth.

Natural fibres
Prehistoric people made clothing out of natural fibres, either from animal hair or from parts of plants or vegetables. The fibres were spun to form yarn. The oldest evidence of fibre use is probably the specimens of flax and wool fabrics found in primitive lake dwellings in Switzerland, which date back to the 6th and 7th centuries BC. Mummies wrapped in linen

bandages and wall paintings depicting the process of preparing the fibre indicate that linen was known to the Egyptians more than 5000 years ago. The first cotton cloth is believed to have been woven in India in 3000 BC, and the production of silk was an industry in China in 2640 BC.

These four principal natural fibres—cotton, linen, silk and wool—continued to monopolize the textile market until the late 19th and early 20th centuries, when the first manmade fibre—rayon—and later the first synthetic fibre—nylon—were introduced. Even today, despite the rapid increase in the range of synthetic fibres, natural fibres maintain their lead in the world's fibre production.

Among the other natural fibres are ramie, which resembles linen and is taken from the stalk of a species of nettle, and the luxurious hair fibres, rabbit, angora, mohair, cashmere and vicuna.

Ramie, a lustrous pure white fibre, is sturdy and coarse and can be blended in small amounts with wool, cotton, nylon and viscose/rayon to increase their durability. As it withstands wear and heat, treat the resulting fabric according to its main fibre.

Of the hair fibres, rabbit has been used in Europe as a fibre for clothing for more than a century and is warm, soft and lightweight. As the hairs are short they are unsuitable for spinning on their own and so are usually mixed with wool. Many woven and knitted fabrics have rabbit hair included, for extra beauty and warmth. Angora rabbit hair is occasionally used alone for knitwear and expensive dress fabrics.

Mohair, a very fine, thin, smooth fibre, is derived from the hair of the Angora goat. The most valued mohair comes from Turkey. Mohair is commonly combined with wool to make top-grade, lightweight, fine suitings for men. It is also used for scarves, sweaters and stoles as well as dress materials, linings, velvets and imitation furs.

Cashmere was originally

produced in Kashmir from the hair of the indigenous goat, but now comes also from Mongolia, Tibet, Iran and Iraq. Smooth and soft, cashmere is used mainly for sweaters and some woven fabrics.

The finest and costliest of all hair fibres is vicuna, from the animal of the same name, a member of the llama family.

Follow the care instructions on the fabric label closely for all luxury hair fibres. In general, if the fibres are washable, treat them the same way as wool.

Synthetic fibres
When future historians and archaeologists name and categorize the present era, the Stone Age, Iron Age and Bronze Age may well be joined by the Age of Synthetic Fibres. Although the history of these fibres begins in the last century, it is during the 20th century, particulary in the 1930s and 1940s, that the most rapid changes have taken place.

Synthetic fibres owe much to the producer of a natural fibre, the silkworm. Although silk was first produced commercially in China in 2640 BC, it was not until 1664 that an English chemist and mathematician, Robert Hooke, suggested that the silkworm's work could be emulated by man.

The first to put this idea into practice was Count Hilaire de Chardonnet. In 1885 he was granted the first artificial fibre patent and in 1891 his first artifical silk factory went into production in France. The fibre was based on cellulose. In this de Chardonnet was indebted to the discovery of his compatriot A. Payen, who, in 1839, had extracted cellulose from wood, so providing the basis for all the early synthetic fibres.

A new impetus to the industry came with the manufacture of rayon, also known as viscose. (The name comes from the Latin *viscosus*, sticky.) A cellulose-based fibre, it was invented in 1892 by three British scientists, Cross, Bevan and Beadle, and proved to be a more economic means of producing artificial silk

than any previous methods—as such it was responsible for the birth of the modern stocking.

Acetate, the nearest to silk of all artificial fibres, finally went into production at the end of World War I. Like rayon, acetate revolutionized women's clothing and was widely used for underwear and for nightwear.

The ultimate breakthrough in the production of artificial fibres came in 1931 with the so-called Pe-Ce fibres, the first completely synthetic textile fibres manufactured from the chemical polyvinyl chloride by the German company IG-Farben. The artificial fibres industry no longer had to rely on natural substances or regenerated extracts from them, such as cellulose, for making fabrics, but could instead turn to the increasingly wide range of petroleum or coal-tar chemicals for the production of fully synthetic fibres.

The pin-up era
The greatest textile revolution was the development of nylon in 1938. Not only did it inaugurate, in 1939, the era of the nylon stocking and the pin-up, but, because nylon was thermoplastic, for the first time fabrics and garments could be set by heat so they kept their size and shape in wear and wash. Within months of each other, Du Pont in the United States and IG-Farben in Germany patented the fibres which, although made quite differently, were almost identical in their characteristics. It was Du Pont who called theirs nylon. Originally made from coal-tar products, nylon is now mainly made from petroleum chemicals.

The 1940s saw the discovery of acrylic and polyester, both synthetic fibres. Polyester was developed by two British researchers, Whinfield and Dickson, in 1941 and manufactured by Imperial Chemical Industries (ICI)—the biggest of the European chemical concerns—and Du Pont. Acrylic was patented by a German fibre chemist, Herbert Rein, in 1942 and two months later by Du Pont.

Since the 1940s other cellulosic and synthetic fibres including triacetate and modacrylics have been invented. In 1962 the production of synthetic fibres exceeded the million tons mark. By 1975 the figure had risen to above seven million tons. For many years the cellulose-based fibres dominated the manmade market, but in 1968 synthetics overtook them.

At their best synthetic fibres produce textiles that are tough, washable, crease-resisting, hard-wearing and less likely than their natural counterparts to shrink, fade or become matted. They have also had considerable effect on how textiles are made up. More suitable than natural fibres for other methods of fabric production besides weaving, synthetic fibres are continually increasing the range of fabrics available.

FABRICS

Woven fabrics
Yarns of different colours, strengths and thicknesses can be combined to produce a wide range of woven fabrics. The thickness of a yarn is defined by its denier, the weight per standard length of fibre (9,000 metres/9,846 yards); the lower the denier the finer the yarn and the lighter the resulting cloth. In some fibres singlespun yarns are weak, so they are often twisted together in sets of two, three or four to strengthen them and sometimes also to produce a combination of colours within a yarn. The resulting yarns are referred to as two ply, three ply and four ply.

Two ply

Three ply

When fabric is woven, the vertical threads, or warp yarns, which run the length of the finished fabric, are held on the loom and the horizontal, or weft, yarns inserted through them. The warp yarns are sometimes known as selvage threads because they run parallel with the strengthened edge, or selvage, of the fabric.

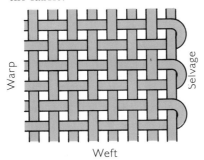
Warp
Weft
Selvage

The most common pattern of weaving the weft through the warp is alternately over and under the warp threads. This produces a plain-weave fabric. If

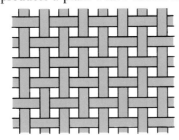
Plain weave

both weft and warp yarns of the plain weave are of identical weight, the finished fabric is known as even-weave. When yarns of different strengths are used, the warp threads are stronger, so it is wise to cut out with the warp running in the direction of most strain. Other patterns in the weave are produced by varying the order in which weft threads pass over and under the warp. Hopsack and twill are examples of two-over-two-under weaves. Patterns, as in

Hopsack

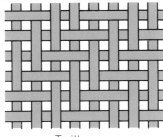
Twill

brocade, can be woven into a fabric by passing the weft over many warp threads. This process is known as Jacquard weaving after the special apparatus and loom and their French inventor Joseph Marie Jacquard.

Brocade

Jacquard weave, RS and WS

Knitted fabrics
Knit or jersey fabrics are produced from a continuous length of yarn, and most yarns can be used to make them. There are two basic knit structures—weft and warp. Weft knit is

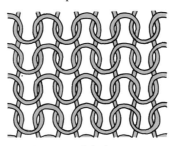
Loose weft knit

modelled on hand knitting with one yarn knitted in the horizontal, weft, direction. For a warp knit several yarns are knitted at once in the lengthwise, warp, direction. Warp knits generally have less stretch than weft because each yarn interlocks with the one beside it.

Knits can be close and firm, loose and ribbed like hand knitting, or lacy. A surface pattern may be created by introducing another yarn, but the back of the fabric will show that it is knitted. Knits can also be identified by their cut edges, which do not fray. All knits stretch across the width, sometimes by an enormous amount. There may be no selvage, but if there is, it may be rough and uneven or curled.

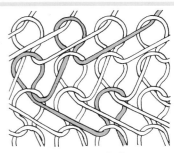
Single-warp knit

Weft knit with selvage

Bonded fabrics
Bonds, or laminates, are woven or knitted fabrics specially produced for sticking to a backing, which is often thin acrylic or nylon knit or aluminium-backed cotton/Mylar. A very thin sheet of polyurethane foam may be placed between the fabric and the backing. This adds warmth to the fabric and reduces creasing. The main uses of bonded fabrics are for furnishing and upholstery.

Stretch fabrics

Elastane yarns have long been woven into fabrics used for making garments such as swimsuits, but today stretch versions of woven fabrics, including gabardine, denim, lace, twill, towelling and many others, can be produced. The stretch usually runs lengthwise with the warp, but can be incorporated into both warp and weft.

FABRIC FINISHES

Demand for easy-care, resilient and hard-wearing fabrics has led to rapid development in fabric finishing. The handle and performance of a fabric is greatly improved by finishing, but unless the treated fabric is particularly smooth, rough, dull or shiny the finish may be invisible. Because finishes may be destroyed by incorrect treatment and often are not labelled, it is best to inquire before buying.

Colourfast

Most fabrics, such as cotton and silk, that are liable to fade in sunlight are treated to resist fading unless, as in denim, fading is deliberately required.

Shrink resistant

Absorbent fibres such as cotton often shrink when penetrated by water. Many fabrics (voile and loosely woven cotton are two of the most notable exceptions) can be pre-shrunk, but the process is sometimes known as "shrinkage control" because it is virtually impossible for manufacturers to guarantee no further shrinkage, although good quality cloth will not shrink.

Crease resistant

Fabrics made from fibres such as cotton, silk, linen and viscose/rayon tend to crease badly and thus benefit from the application of a crease resistant finish. Because all fabrics crease, if only for a moment, when placed under pressure, manufacturers often call this a "crease recovery" finish. Crease resistance is achieved by various processes and fibres react differently, so guarantees vary accordingly. For example, some fabrics are guaranteed to shed creases within a quoted period out of wear, whereas for others the period is not quoted.

Non-iron

Many manufacturers name their non-iron finishing process "minimum iron" or "drip dry" because the results after washing may not satisfy everyone and most fabrics do not dry entirely flat. Repeated washing eventually destroys the finish.

Water repellant

Various chemical methods are used to treat fibres to reduce water absorption. The finish, applied to gabardine, poplin and nylon, is not completely waterproof and is often described as "showerproof". Spray-on finish to reduce water absorption can be bought to treat fabric at home.

Stain and alcohol repellant

A few fabrics such as dress velvet are treated to resist staining and repel alcohol. Always check fabric care instructions.

Flame resistant

Fabrics cannot be made fireproof, but those that flare up readily, such as cotton and viscose/rayon, can be treated to make them slow to catch fire. When choosing fabric for children's nightwear, clothes for the elderly, or when buying dress net check whether it is flame resistant. The finish is usually destroyed by boiling or bleaching the fabric.

Mothproof

Fabrics such as wool and silk that form the food of clothes-moth larvae can be treated to prevent them from being eaten in this way. A spray can be used for home treatment of fabric.

Anti-bacterial

Fabrics liable to rot when attacked by mildew or the bacteria that break down human perspiration can be treated by a process undetectable on the fabric. The treatment is usually applied only to more expensive materials.

Brushed

Cotton, viscose/rayon acrylics and nylon can be finished so that they have a soft, slightly furry surface. Brushed fabrics are warmer than unbrushed ones because additional air pockets are formed on their surface, but the brushing process weakens the fibres and increases their flammability.

Glazed

A polished effect, which reduces soiling, is produced on the fabric surface. Furnishing fabrics made from absorbent fibres and some dress fabrics, particularly cottons, may be glazed.

Mercerized

Caustic soda is applied to cotton and other natural fibres to create a slight shine and increase fibre strength. This important finish is applied to cotton sewing yarn as well as to cotton fabric.

Embossed

Most fabrics can be embossed with a raised design by passing them between engraved rollers. The finish is not always permanent, so follow washing instructions carefully.

Moiré

A moiré, or watermark, effect is created by spraying silk, viscose/rayon, and sometimes cotton fabrics with water and then heating them. Do not damp press these fabrics or the effect is destroyed. A more permanent watermark is produced by making small engravings on the right side of the fabric. The life of the finish depends on both the fibre and the way it is treated, so follow care instructions meticulously.

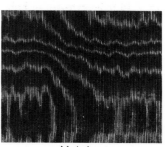
Moiré

SELECTING AND BUYING FABRICS

Successful sewing depends very much on a careful choice of fabric. It is wise not to buy entirely on impulse, nor to have a totally preconceived idea, although the type of garment to be made narrows the choice. A tailored garment, for example, needs crisp fabric. To make a good choice, follow these guidelines:

1 Stand in front of a mirror and hold the fabric over you to see if the colour is suitable. Check by comparing it with a colour you know to be unflattering.

2 Hold the fabric against you flat, pleated, gathered or draped, depending on the garment style, to check that it reacts correctly.

3 To see how the fabric looks against your legs, hold it so one end reaches your hemline. If choosing fabric for trousers or a long dress, lower its edge to the floor. Examine the effect of the fabric over the whole area of the planned garment, particularly if the fabric is checked, striped or has a very large or small pattern.

4 Crush a corner of the fabric to see if it creases badly or springs up. Note that springy fabric is hard-wearing, but can be difficult to sew.

5 Examine the raw edge to see if the fabric frays. If the fabric has no other disadvantages, fraying can be coped with by cutting out with seam allowances 5 mm/$\frac{1}{4}$ in wider than usual.

6 Hold the fabric up to the light to examine the weave or knit. Use close weaves and knits for garments that will have heavy wear.

7 Pull knit fabric lengthwise and widthwise to check its give. Make sure that the fabric springs back after stretching.

8 Look at the design or weave to see if the fabric has nap or is "one way" (see Nap).

9 Check the straightness of the grain (see Grain).

10 For checked or striped fabric fold over one corner to make sure the lines match. If they do not match, the fabric cannot be used on the bias because the pattern is uneven.

11 Unroll the fabric and look for any flaws (see Flaws).
12 Check the washability of the fabric and the finishes, such as crease and flame resistance.
13 Select the fabric you like best, that will be most suitable for the garment and will mix well with existing clothes and accesories.

Flaws

Flaws in fabric include knots or uneven patches in the weave, knit or print, dirty marks and, particularly in synthetics, dirt along the folded edge of the fabric. On good-quality fabric flaws are marked at the selvage with coloured thread. Fabric with a flaw on the wrong side may be acceptable. If a flaw is on the right side, decide whether you have sufficient length to accommodate the pattern pieces before the flaw appears or estimate whether main pattern pieces can be placed on either side of the flaw to avoid it. By asking for extra fabric you should be able to avoid one flaw, but do not buy a length with several imperfections.

Remnants

If bought wisely, remnants can be bargains, but remember that if the length was saleable for its purpose, as with trouser fabric, it would not be offered as a remnant. Small remnants are always usable. Cotton, for example, can be used for patchwork, repairs and contrasting yokes and cuffs, and fabrics of all kinds are ideal for toys. Larger remnants can be made into scarves, aprons and children's clothes, while whole lengths make blouses.

Grain

The grain is the straight thread of a woven fabric. The warp threads are usually known as the lengthwise grain, the weft threads as the cross grain. Knitted fabrics do not in fact have a grain, although the term is used to refer to the lines of knitting.

If fabric is "off grain", the selvages will not meet when the fabric is folded in half along the cross grain—the simplest check.

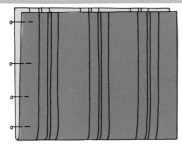

Forcing the selvages to meet causes wrinkling and the fabric will not lie flat with both the straight grain of the fabric and the straight grain lines of the pattern pieces matching. (The

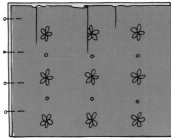

straight grain is generally the warp, but small pieces of fabric are often cut on the weft.)

Woven fabric in a natural fibre can be straightened by pulling it from the two opposite "short" corners, although synthetics may not respond to this treatment.

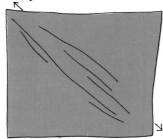

If the fabric has a finish that prevents this method of straightening, dampen the whole length, pull it to correct the grain, fold it lengthwise in half and baste it together around all edges before drying and pressing it. The basting can then be removed. Knitted fabrics can be straightened in a similar way. It is impossible, however, to straighten synthetic knit.

Fabric such as brocade that has the pattern woven into it can also be straightened, unless it is synthetic, but fabric that has

been printed off grain cannot be corrected and the pattern pieces must be cut according to the print, ignoring the straight grain. If a piece of off-grain fabric must be used, choose a pattern with many small pieces and cut each out on single fabric one at a time.

Nap

A true nap is a pile or finish on the fabric surface that lies in one direction only. Napping or brushing one side of fabric increases warmth. If two pieces of fabric are joined with the nap facing in different directions, the piece with the nap lying the wrong way will appear lighter

than the other one. Brush your hand across the fabric in both directions to see which way the pile lies smoothly. Examples of fabrics with a true nap are faced cloth, velours and velvet. A large number of other fabrics are "one way" for different reasons. Many fabrics have prints, checks or uneven stripes that lie in one direction. Satins, gabardines, knits and fabrics containing metal loops should be treated as one way because of the direction of the weave or the effect of light on them.

If you are in any doubt about a fabric, always buy extra to allow for nap. Check the pattern envelope for the amount to buy. Cut all pattern pieces with the nap lying in the same direction.

Matching patterned fabrics

Before selecting a checked or striped fabric, make sure that the pattern envelope does not advise against it. If matching is necessary, avoid a pattern with many joins and remember that gathers, pleats and folds are easier to manage. Buy enough

extra fabric so that there is room to move each main pattern piece one whole pattern repeat on the fabric to make it match. When cutting out, add an extra 1 cm/ $\frac{3}{8}$ in seam allowance for a small pattern, more for a larger one, so the seams can be moved at fitting to improve matching. If in any doubt, choose plain fabric for part of the garment, or turn some pieces such as yokes onto the cross.

Wherever possible, matching should be perfect at garment seams. It is not always possible

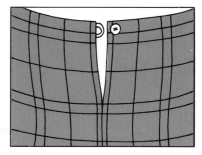

to do this completely if, for example, the two matching edges are cut at different angles or one edge of a seam has a dart. A

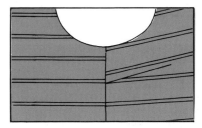

stripe or check may be perfectly matched around the body, including shoulder seams, but it

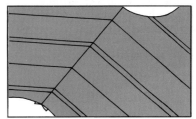

may be impossible to chevron vertical lines at the side seams. Always try to match patterns perfectly at the centre front and centre back and, on a skirt, at the side seams. If a shoulder dart prevents matching, leave it out and adjust the fit.

Both natural and synthetic fibres can be made up into such a wide variety of cloths that it is impossible to give detailed sewing instructions for each fibre. Refer to the individual fabrics in the following list of popular, widely used materials. If in doubt about how to handle a particular fabric, stitch and launder it in the same way as a fabric of a similar weight and thickness. Machine needle size, hand needle size, the type of thread and stitch length are given at the end of the entry for each fabric. Washing and pressing instructions are given at the end of the entry for each fibre. *Fibres are set in italics.*

Abercrombie Blue, black and green Scottish tartan; wool or wool with polyester or acrylic. Used for pleated skirts, jackets, dresses, children's clothes. 90 (14); 7; polyester or mercerized; large.

Acetate
One of the cellulosic group of synthetic fibres. Not available in fibre form until 1918. Made by dissolving cotton linters—short cotton fibres—or nowadays generally wood in chemicals. The result is extruded to form an acetate yarn, which can be a filament or staple yarn. The first acetate was referred to as "artificial silk".

Has low rate of absorbency and does not conduct heat readily—acetate garments are cool in summer and warm in winter. Dyes readily and can be embossed with patterns easily. Soft and pliable: drapes well. Weaker when wet and not hard-wearing; tends to tear at seams.

Made into woven dress fabrics such as satins, taffetas and brocades and knitted fabrics for blouses, dresses, underwear, men's ties, shirts, socks and suits.

Wash often in warm water; do not wring as creases can be permanent if the fibre cracks. Iron on WS with a medium iron and damp cloth.

Acrylic
A synthetic fibre widely available since 1950. Contains at least 85 per cent acrylonitrile, a liquid derivative of oil refining and coal carbonization.

Can be filament but mostly produced in staple form, which tends to be warmer and woollier than the other synthetics, polyester and polyamide. Fairly strong and hard-wearing. Feels warm and soft and is thermoplastic, so can be permanently pleated by heat. Has a fairly low rate of absorbency and is moderately flammable.

The discovery of acrylic made it possible to produce less expensive wool-like fabrics because it can be bulked successfully. Used in all kinds of clothing, knitwear, blankets and carpets. Blends well with other fibres.

Washes well in warm water. Avoid wringing. If necessary, use a cool iron. Take care to avoid stretching when pressing.

Alpaca The soft, fine hair of the South American alpaca makes a thin fabric that is both lustrous and crisp and also warm and durable. Used mainly for men's wear. Alpaca also denotes fabric made from other fibres and blends, such as viscose/rayon and acetate, with a similar finish. 70–90 (9–14); 7–9; silk or polyester; medium.

Angora Formerly described any long, white rabbit hair included in fabric; now refers only to the hair of the angora rabbit. Expensive; generally mixed with other fibres. 70–90 (9–14); 7–9; silk; medium.

Antung Cheap, crisp plain-weave silk often with a woven pattern. Can be used as a base for chiffon, as a lining, and for petticoats for evening and wedding outfits. 80 (11); 7; polyester; medium.

Astrakhan Very expensive curly fleece of the astrakhan lamb. Astrakhan fur fabric, usually made from acrylic fibres, is a good imitation. Do not press. Used for hats and as coat trim. 100–110 (16–18); 6; polyester; large.

Barathea Very closely woven, smooth, fine fabric usually of wool. Used for coats, skirts and suits. Marks easily in pressing. 90 (14); 6; polyester or mercerized; medium to large.

Batiste Soft, fine fabric, usually in plain colours. Can be of cotton or polyester yarn. Easy to sew. Washable. Used for dresses, lingerie, blouses, children's wear. 70–90 (9–14); 7; polyester or mercerized; small.

Bedford cord Long-wearing corded fabric, first made in New Bedford, Massachusetts. Made from wool, cotton or polyester. Can be attractively topstitched. Used for coats, jackets, riding habits and trousers. 100 (16); 6; polyester; medium to large.

Blazer cloth Once a traditional napped, striped, woollen flannel but can now be plain colours and may contain polyester. Used for unlined tailored jackets. 90 (14); 6; polyester or mercerized; large.

Bolivia Soft, luxurious woollen ribbed-pile fabric, often with some mohair or alpaca. An excellent fabric for tailoring. 90 (14); 7; mercerized; large.

Bonded fabrics Layers of fabric of any fibre, but usually acrylic, joined to a knit backing, generally of nylon. The layers are held by adhesive, but sometimes a thin layer of polyurethane foam is also added. Non-fraying, easy to handle but springy. Topstitch seams. Used for loose coats and jackets. 90 (14); 6–7; polyester; large.

Bouclé Woven or knitted fabric in various weights, characterized by surface loops. May be wool, mohair or acrylic, or a mixture of several fibres. Used for women's coats, jackets, dresses. 90 (14); 6–7; polyester; medium to large.

Bouclé knit Synthetic knit fabric with bouclé effect. Often a mixture of fibres. Used for women's suits, sweaters and dresses. Stretchy fabrics, so tape horizontal seams and use suitable machine stitches. 90 (14); 6; polyester; medium.

Brocade Fancy-patterned fabric produced by mixing dull and shiny yarns in matching or contrasting colours and sometimes including metallic yarns. Additional threads are often introduced which run along WS and come to the surface only occasionally. Can be made from any yarn but now usually acetate. Frays, particularly if there are additional threads on WS. Dry press. Avoid too close a fit. Used for wedding and evening dresses; thicker types for furnishings. 70–90 (9–14); 8–9; polyester; medium.

Broderie anglaise or eyelet lace Plain white or pale coloured cotton or polyester cotton, with crisp, fresh, embroidered eyelet patterns. Used for dresses, blouses, children's clothes. 70 (9); 6; mercerized or polyester; medium.

Brushed acrylic Lightweight woven fabric, often printed, with a brushed surface. Inexpensive and easy to sew. Used for dresses, shirts, children's clothes. 70 (9); 6; polyester; medium.

Brushed cotton Plain-weave cotton with brushed surface. Easy to sew. Washes well. Used for dresses, shirts, children's clothes. 90 (14); 6; polyester or mercerized; medium.

Buckram Plain-weave, specially stiffened, coarse cotton fabric. Used for hats, belts and upholstery. Not usually washable. 90–100 (14–16); 5–6; polyester; large.

Calico Sometimes known as muslin in the United States. A firm, plain-weave cotton fabric, generally cream coloured but also available in a variety of colours and patterns. Strong and hard-wearing. Used for dresses, shirts, blouses and children's clothes. 90 (14); 6–7; core-spun or mercerized: medium.

Cambric A fine, closely woven cotton fabric with a slight shine on the RS. Easy to sew. Washes well. Used for children's clothes, blouses, nightwear. 70 (9); 7; mercerized; medium.

Camel cloth Woollens or blends the colour of camel hair. Usually coat weight with a slightly brushed surface. "Camel hair" denotes very expensive cloth containing real camel's hair; sheep's wool is often added to reduce the price. 100 (16); 6–9; polyester, mercerized or silk; large.

Canvas Various types and weights of plain-weave cotton and linen yarns made for use as interfacing in tailored clothes. Also, in open weave, used for embroidery. Choose needle size and thread according to weight of canvas.

Cashmere Expensive, fine, soft, lightweight fibre from hair of Kashmir goat. Often mixed with wool, it is made into knitwear and top-quality coatings. 70–90 (9–14); 6–9; silk or mercerized; medium to large.

Cavalry twill A strong, smooth worsted cloth used for tailored sporting jackets and trousers. Very hard-wearing. 90 (14); 6; mercerized; medium.

Challis A fine, lightweight fabric previously made from wool but now from any fibre or blend. Often printed with a floral or paisley pattern. Used for blouses, dresses and children's wear. 70 (9); 7–8; polyester or mercerized; medium.

Chambray Cotton fabric made by using white weft yarns and coloured warp, forming a variety of stripes and patterns. Hard-wearing and easy to wash. Used for dresses, shirts, trousers and children's clothes. 70–90 (9–14); 6–8; polyester or mercerized; medium.

Charmeuse A crêpe-type lightweight fabric made from polyester or silk. It is fairly firm with a dull, smooth surface. Used for soft dresses, blouses, evening clothes. 70 (9); 8; polyester or silk; medium.

Cheesecloth Originally used for wrapping cheese. A rough-surfaced fabric, usually Grade 4 pure cotton, with an unfinished look, but soft and comfortable in wear. In natural ecru or coloured. Washes well; need not be ironed. Used for blouses, skirts, shirts and dresses. 70 (9); 7–8; mercerized or polyester; medium.

Chenille Thick, tufted, fabric made from cotton, sometimes mixed with synthetic fibres such as viscose/rayon; also made occasionally from silk or wool. Dry cleaning advisable. Do not press. Once confined to furnishings but now produced for coats, bathrobes and jackets. 100 (16); 5–6; polyester; large.

Cheviot A wool suiting with a tweedy appearance originally from the sheep of the Cheviot Hills in Britain. The yarn is rough and uneven which makes it very hard-wearing cloth. A good tailoring fabric. 100 (16); 5–6; mercerized; large.

Chiffon Sheer, soft fabric, sometimes made from silk, more often from nylon or polyester. Difficult to handle, especially the synthetic chiffons, which fray readily. Dry press. Used for scarves, blouses, dresses and evening wear. 70 (9); 8–9; polyester or silk; small.

Chintz Closely woven cotton fabric with glazed or permanent finish. Usually printed with flowers or birds. Wears well. Used for furnishings. 90 (14); 5–6; mercerized or core-spun; large.

Ciré Fine, silky fabric with a shiny wet look. Made from silk or, more usually, nylon or polyester and sometimes acetate. Used for bathing suits, blouses, dresses and rainwear. 70 (9); 7; polyester; small to medium.

Cloqué Fabric with a raised surface resembling irregular blistering. Made from polyester or acetate. Used for dresses, blouses, evening and bridal wear. 80 (11); 7; polyester; medium.

Corduroy Cord du roi—cloth of the king—is a ribbed fabric usually of cotton but it can contain some polyester or be entirely synthetic on a knitted backing. The pile, running the length of the fabric, is made by weaving additional threads into a plain- or twill-weave fabric and looping them over the surface. The loops are cut after weaving is complete. As the pile shades, cut out with it running upward on the body. Press lightly on WS only. Used for jackets, trousers, suits, skirts, dresses and furnishings. 90 (14); 6; polyester or mercerized; medium to large.

Cotton

A natural fibre extracted from the boll, or seed pod, of the cotton plant. Cotton is the most widely used textile fibre.

Various types of cotton yarn are produced depending on such factors as climate and soil. Length of staple fibre varies between 2 cm/¾ in and 5 cm/2 in. Egyptian and Sea Island fibres are generally long; North American and Indian fibres are short. All cotton fibres are thin, fairly smooth, soft to wear, absorbent and very strong. Can be dyed, glazed and mothproofed, as well as given many other finishes. Flammable and creases easily unless specially treated.

Numerous uses including underwear, towels, shirts, dresses, sheets, children's clothes.

Hard-wearing so can be washed frequently. Iron slightly damp with hot iron; do not leave cotton damp as it is subject to mildew.

Cotton broadcloth Soft woven mercerized cotton fabric, medium weight. Used for casual clothes. 70 (9); 7; mercerized; medium.

Cotton jersey Knitted cotton fabric used for T-shirts and track suits. Easy to sew, but use stretch techniques. 80 (11); ball-point; 7; mercerized; medium.

Cotton velvet Pile fabric composed of cotton pile and backing. Usually washable, not difficult to sew. Used for children's clothes, dresses, furnishings. Cut with pile running upward and stitch in the same direction. Press pile down on a piece of the same fabric. 80 (11); 6; mercerized; medium.

Covert A closely woven twill-weave wool usually in brown or beige. Used for tailoring. 100 (16); 6; mercerized; large.

Crêpe Fabric with crinkled appearance produced by chemically twisting the yarn before weaving. Made in wool, acetate, cotton, silk, polyester and acrylic yarns. Liable to shrink. Drapes well; used for dresses and blouses. 70–90 (9–14); 6–7; polyester or mercerized; medium.

Crêpe de Chine From the French name "Chinese crêpe". Originally made from silk but now often polyester. Slippery to handle. Characteristic matt surface. Used for soft dresses, blouses. 70 (9); 8; polyester; medium.

Crepon Cotton fabric made from pre-crimped yarns. A soft fabric for blouses, lingerie, full skirts. 70 (9); 7; mercerized; medium.

Crinkle crêpe Puckered cotton fabric, design is usually random. A crisp fabric for dresses, shorts and children's clothes. 90 (14); 6; mercerized; medium.

Cupro

One of the original rayon fibres, first produced commercially in 1919. The raw material, wood or cotton, is dissolved in copper sulphate, soda and ammonia.

Produced in filament form only. Fine, soft and lustrous and so closely resembles silk that the best hosiery and underwear were made from it until nylon came into general use. Absorbent, drapes and wears well, but burns readily.

Sometimes blended with acetate or cotton and usually made into fine, soft, woven fabrics for sportswear, curtains, lining material and upholstery fabrics. Also found in soft, expensive, luxury dress fabrics such as chiffons, satins, ninons and nets. Washes easily. Short spin only.

A-Z OF TEXTILES

Damask Jacquard-weave fabric, mixing shiny and dull yarns. Pattern textures or colours on WS are reversed on RS. Made from cotton or linen for table linen and soft furnishings; from acetate, viscose/rayon and other synthetics for dresses. 90 (14); 6–7; mercerized or polyester; medium.

Denim Name derives from French town of Nîmes ("de Nîmes"). Hard-wearing twill-weave cloth of white yarns mixed with blue or another colour. Usually cotton but sometimes mixed with polyester. Washes well. Cotton varieties fade. Used for work clothes and informal wear, particularly jeans. 90 (14); 6; polyester or core-spun; medium to large.

Doeskin Close-weave plain or twill cloth, usually fine wool, with a soft nap on RS producing a silky sheen. Press on WS only, using a damp muslin cloth. Used for coats, skirts and dresses. 90 (14); 6–8; silk, mercerized or polyester; medium to large.

Donegal Rough tweed of wool or mixtures including cotton, polyester, viscose/rayon, acrylic, characterized by a white nubbly effect. Used for coats, jackets, trousers and skirts. 90–100 (14–16); 5–7; polyester or mercerized; medium to large.

Downproof cambric Plain-weave waxed cotton fabric for pillowcases and quilt covers. Usually white or cream. 90 (14); 7; core-spun; medium.

Drill Very strong, twill-weave cotton. Launders well. Used in white and khaki for uniforms and can also be striped. 110 (18); 6–7; core-spun or mercerized; large.

Duchesse satin A firm, heavy satin with a high gloss. Usually viscose/rayon or acetate fibre. Used for evening and bridal clothes and furnishings. 90 (14); 6; polyester; medium to large.

Duck Very strong, closely woven heavy cloth, usually of cotton.

Plain-weave canvas effect. Used for furnishings, protective clothing and trousers. 100 (16); 6; core-spun; large.

Dupion Comparatively inexpensive silk fabric, made from a thick, uneven yarn reeled from double cocoons. The effect can be imitated in acetate and synthetic yarns. Creases easily. Press dry if silk. Used for dresses and coats. 70 (9); 8–9; silk or polyester; medium.

Duvetyn (also Duvetyne) Fabric with a smooth, brushed RS resembling suede finish. Often wool but can also be cotton or synthetic fibre. Cut pattern pieces with nap in one direction. Used for lightweight jackets, coats and dresses. 90 (14); 6–8; polyester or mercerized; medium.

Face finished or faced cloth Any fabric that has a raised or brushed surface on RS, or face side. Unlike pile fabrics such as velour, these are not one-way fabrics. Usually wool but may also contain synthetic fibres such as acrylic or polyester. Medium and heavyweight fabrics used for dresses, suits, coats and blazers. 90 (14); 7–8; polyester or mercerized; medium to large.

Façonné Soft shiny fabric, usually viscose/rayon or polyester, with small self-colour designs. Used for blouses, dresses, evening and bridal clothes. 70 (9); 7; polyester; medium.

Faille Cross-ribbed fabric with close weave. Sometimes silk but generally acetate or polyester. Used for dresses and coats. 70 (9); 7; polyester; medium.

Felt Non-woven fabric with no grain made by pressing short lengths of wool fibre, cotton or synthetics and bonding them with heat and moisture. Weak, not washable. Used primarily for soft toys, decoration and hats. 90 (14); 6; core-spun; large.

Felt cloth Woven fabric made of wool or blends with surface brushed or felted to obscure

weave. Treat as ordinary plain-weave fabric. Used for coats and jackets. Sew as for felt.

Flannel Soft, warm, all-wool fabric with a slightly napped surface on RS. Often made into sportswear, blazers and skirts. 90 (14); 6–7; silk, mercerized or polyester; medium to large.

Flannelette Soft plain-weave cotton fabric with brushed surface. Warm and washable. Used for baby clothes, nappies/diapers and sheets. Also suitable for nightwear if flameproofed. 70 (9); 7–8; mercerized or polyester; medium.

Flouncing Cotton or nylon lace fabric with finished scallops along one or both edges. Used for lingerie, evening and bridal clothes. 70 (9); 7; mercerized or polyester; small.

Foulard Soft twill-weave fabric in acetate, viscose/rayon or polyester but also can be silk. Slippery to handle, frays easily. Usually printed with small-spaced print. Used for blouses, bathrobes, scarves. 70 (9); 8; polyester; small.

Fur fabric Smooth or curly fur pile on woven or knit backing. Pile usually acrylic but can be nylon or another synthetic. Backing generally synthetic. Cut all pieces with nap, i.e. in same direction. Do not press. Used for jackets, coats and trimming. 100–110 (16–18); 5 or 6; polyester or core-spun; large.

Gabardine Closely woven twill-weave cloth in wool, cotton or polyester. The diagonal twill weave discourages water absorption, making gabardine ideal for raincoats. 100–110 (16–18); 6–7; polyester; large.

Gauze Soft open fabric, usually cotton but may be polyester. Used for full, gathered items such as curtains and drapes. 70 (9); 7; core-spun; medium.

Georgette Fine sheer fabric with crêpe appearance, made from

twisted yarns of silk, nylon or polyester. The synthetic fabrics tend to slip and fray. Dry press. Used for blouses and evening dresses. 70 (9); 8–10; polyester or silk; small.

Gingham Hard-wearing cotton fabric in which white and dyed yarns form checks and, less commonly, narrow stripes. Used for casual clothes, children's wear, tablecloths, curtains. 70 (9); 7–8; mercerized, core-spun or polyester; medium.

Gold tissue Luxurious and expensive fabric made from silk or polyester with metal thread. Frays easily. Used for evening wear. 70 (9); 7; polyester; small.

Grosgrain One-way horizontal-ribbed fabric, often narrow. Made from acetate, polyester or even silk. Used for ribbons and evening wear. 70 (9); 7–8; polyester; medium.

Habutai Very light, soft, silk fabric in plain or twill weave, at one time produced exclusively in Japan. Creases easily; needs mounting to add body. Used for dresses and linings. 70 (9); 8; silk or polyester; medium.

Harris tweed Durable plain or herringbone woollen cloth made from coarse wool showing slightly white hairs. Officially the term refers to cloth from the Outer Hebrides only but it is often used to describe a Harris-type tweed. Used for coats and jackets. 100 (16); 6; silk or mercerized; large.

Holland Fine linen cloth used in furnishings and upholstery under the main fabric and also in tailoring for reinforcing pockets. 90–100 (14–16); 5–6; polyester, mercerized or core-spun; large.

Houndstooth Distinctive small or medium-sized check woollen fabric with a star-shaped design. A tailoring fabric for men's clothes, women's suits and coats. 90 (14); 5–6; mercerized; large.

Indian silk Crisp, slightly rough-surfaced fabric suitable for evening and bridal clothes and furnishings. Used for loose styles as it pulls and creases easily. 70 (9); 7–8; polyester; medium.

Jersey First made on the island of that name. Any knitted fabric may be so called, although the word is usually reserved for plain or stocking-stitch knits. Jersey fabric was always made of wool, but it can now be of any fibre and can be plain, printed or jacquard. 70 (9), ball-point if necessary; 7–8; polyester; medium, slight zigzag.

Knit Normally used to describe knitted fabrics with a lot of give; they may be thick, ribbed, lacy or open. Knits are made in all fibres and blends, but some lose their shape and should be avoided for trousers. 90 (14); 6–7; polyester; large, slight zigzag.

Lace Fine openwork fabric made in various ways from a range of fibres such as cotton, nylon, polyester and blends. Some lace includes acetate. Wash carefully or dry clean. Piece lace is used for dresses and bridal gowns, lace edging for decoration. 70–90 (9–14); 6–9; polyester or mercerized; medium.

Lamé Fabric made from any of various fibres into which metallic threads have been woven. Used for evening wear. 70 (9); 7; polyester; medium.

Lawn Name derives from Loan, France, the place where it was initially made. Fine plain-weave fabric of cotton, polyester or linen. Crisp finish. Used for blouses, dresses, nightwear, for mounting other fabrics and for lining yokes and small areas. 70 (9); 7–9; mercerized or polyester; small.

Linen
An ancient natural fibre taken from the stem of the flax plant. Grown principally in the Soviet Union, Ireland, Belgium and Holland.

Length of staple fibre varies from 15 cm/5½ in to 1 metre/1 yard, depending on length of flax plant

stem. Slightly uneven texture and dull in appearance. Expensive, but is very strong and highly absorbent. A good conductor of heat, it feels cool to the touch. Fabrics crease easily, so dress linens should be treated to make them crease resistant. Burns easily.

Used for tea towels, table linen, best-quality bed linen, shirts, dresses, suits.

Wash often, bleaching white linens. Iron fabric while evenly damp with a hot iron.

Madras Cheap cotton fabric, often unfinished, so may shrink. Hand-woven in Far East in bright-coloured stripes or checks. Used for dresses and shirts. 70 (9); 6–7; mercerized, core-spun or polyester; medium.

Matelassé Fabric with a raised pattern producing a quilted effect. An extra weft thread is added, making it look almost like double fabric. Dress fabrics are often acetate or nylon, furnishing fabrics usually viscose/rayon or cotton. 90 (14); 6–7; polyester; large.

Modacrylic
A modified acrylic yarn containing less than 85 per cent acrylonitrile (see acrylic); other synthetic ingredients, their percentage varying according to the manufacturer, make up the balance. Very similar to acrylic but almost completely flame resistant.

Because of its flame resistance particularly suitable for children's nightwear and fabrics with excessive pockets of air in the surface such as fake fur.

Wash and iron as for acrylic.

Modal
A cellulosic fibre. It is polynosic, a term used to describe a higher strength viscose/rayon that is stronger when it is wet.

Produced only in staple form, the fibre is soft and fuzzy, not shiny. Very strong and similar to cotton but more absorbent. Cool and soft, so pleasant to wear in the heat. Like cotton, it burns readily.

Mainly blended with cotton or polyester to produce a softer, less expensive fabric, suitable for

blouses, shirts, nightwear, bed linen, dresses, children's clothes and some furnishing fabrics.

Wash in hot water and iron with a hot iron.

Mohair/wool Fine, light suiting with slight sheen. Excellent for tailoring. 90 (14); 6; mercerized; large.

Moiré Ribbed or corded fabrics subjected to heat and heavy pressure after weaving to give a rippled appearance. Made from acetates and triacetates and, occasionally, silk and cotton. Used for evening wear. 70 (9); 7–8; polyester; medium.

Moleskin Closely woven twill cotton fabric, with a slightly velvety finish on RS. Used for jackets, shirts and trousers. 90 (14); 6; mercerized, polyester or core-spun; large.

Mousseline Shiny, soft, satin-weave fabric of silk, acetate or polyester. Used for evening blouses. 70 (9); 8; polyester; medium.

Mungo Cheap woollen cloth made from short, waste-wool fibres. Often blended with cotton or other wool. Used for duffle coats, casual trousers and unlined wear. Does not wear well. 90 (14); 6; polyester; medium.

Muslin Cheap, open-weave cotton fabric with a tendency to crease and shrink. Often used for lining lightweight materials. Plain white household muslin is excellent as a pressing cloth; bleached and dyed muslin are used for dresses and blouses. 70 (9); 7–8; mercerized or polyester; small.

Needlecord Lightweight cotton or synthetic fabric with short, fine-ribbed pile. Often printed. Washable. Used for blouses, shirts, skirts, dresses and children's clothes. 70 (9); 6–7; polyester, core-spun or mercerized; medium.

Ninon Sheer, plain-weave fabric made from cotton or synthetics such as polyester or nylon. Used

for sheer curtains. 70 (9); 9; polyester; medium.

Nylon See Polyamide.

Ombré From French word meaning "shaded". Refers to many knitted or woven fabrics with a design in which the colour graduates from light to dark. 70 (9), ball-point if necessary; 7–8; polyester; medium to large.

Organdy Fine, plain-weave, transparent, permanently stiffened cotton. Creases readily. Used for accessories, blouses, dresses, curtains, bedspreads and in book binding. 70 (9); 7; mercerized or polyester; small.

Organza Slightly lustrous, transparent, plain-weave fabric in silk or synthetic yarn. Used for evening wear, bridal veils and linings. 70 (9); 9; polyester or silk; small.

Panama A fine plain-weave suiting made from cotton and worsted yarns with perhaps some polyester. Usually plain colours. Can be used for women's shirtwaister dresses and suits but mainly for lightweight clothes for men. 90 (14); 6; mercerized or polyester; medium.

Panné Pile fabric, usually velvet, with pile pressed flat in one direction to give a lustrous surface. Made from any fibre. Jersey-backed panné velvet is very easy to sew. Cut with pile running upwards. Press lightly on WS. Used for dresses, trousers. 70 (9); 7–9; polyester; medium.

Percale Plain close-weave fabric, generally cotton but may also contain some polyester. Sometimes has a slight sheen. Used for nightwear, children's clothes and blouses. 70 (9); 7–8; mercerized or polyester; medium.

Petersham Usually refers to the narrow-width ribbed belting material for skirts and trousers. Can be viscose/rayon, polyester or cotton. Sew by hand with small needle and use the same thread as for garment.

A-Z OF TEXTILES

Plissé Cotton fabric with part of the design, usually stripes, puckered. Washable but do not iron. Used for children's clothes and also for blouses and underwear. 70 (9); 7; mercerized or polyester; medium.

Point d'esprit Usually describes a net or voile fabric that has woven spots on it. Used for blouses, dresses, evening and bridal clothes. Handle as for voile.

Polyamide
A synthetic fibre more commonly known as nylon, the name it was given after its discovery in 1938. Polymer chips, produced from a nylon salt composed of benzine, oxygen, hydrogen and nitrogen, are melted then extruded into yarn.

Initially mainly a filament yarn used for stockings and subsequently for parachutes and overalls. Now also produced in staple form. Very strong and highly elastic. Not very absorbent and so accumulates static electricity. Polyamide melts but does not burn.

Makes up well into fine materials such as chiffon, organza, surah and brushed and knitted nylon, for light garments, scarves, hosiery and underwear. Mixes well with other fibres and used in a wide range of fabrics from taffeta to laminates for protective clothing such as anoraks.

Wash often, as nylon attracts dirt particles. White and light-coloured nylon may pick up tints from other fabrics, so wash separately. If necessary, use a cool iron.

Polyester
A synthetic fibre. Experiments for making polyester yarn from petroleum and other chemicals were being made as long ago as 1938, but polyester was not in general production as a fabric until 1946.

Can be made in continuous filament form which produces a smooth fabric, or in short staple lengths, producing a fuzzier, often thicker fabric. Very strong, resilient and hard-wearing. Has low moisture absorbency and so dries fast. Melts when heated, but does not burn.

Mixes well with, and often improves the performance of, other fibres. Can be knitted or woven into a wide variety of weights of cloth from voile, georgette, dress and knitted fabrics to suitings, furnishing fabrics and padding for quilting. Also used to make thread.

Attracts dirt particles, so wash often. Do not boil. If necessary, press with a warm iron. Can build up static electricity, especially in dry weather; rinse in fabric softener to reduce this tendency.

Polyester cotton A small percentage of polyester fibre added to cotton produces a soft hard-wearing fabric with less tendency to crease than pure cotton. Easy to sew. Used for all types of garments. 70–90 (9–14); 6–9; mercerized, core-spun or polyester; medium to large.

Polyester jersey knit The term is commonly used to describe the smooth silky fabrics, often printed, that are shiny in appearance and slippery to handle. Polyester jersey can also be matt and dull and any thickness. The lightweight fabrics can be difficult to stitch by machine. Used for long or short dresses in fluid or full styles. 70 (9), ball-point or scarf with tissue paper under the fabric; 7; polyester; medium.

Poplin Closely woven fabric made of cotton fibre that is mercerized before weaving. Thick weft thread gives fabric its distinctive appearance—a smooth tight weave with a slight shine. Difficult to sew and press. Seams liable to wrinkle. Pins may leave holes. Used for shirts and dresses. 70 (9); 7–9; polyester or core-spun; medium.

Quilting Any fabric stitched in a pattern to a padded backing, sometimes with another fabric under the backing. Easy to sew. Used for casual clothes, nightwear, children's clothes. 70 (9); 6; core-spun; large.

Raschel knit A coarse fabric with limited give that is very easy to sew. Used for all types of clothes; some furnishing fabrics are also available. 70 (9); ball-point; 6; polyester; medium.

Rayon See Viscose.

Reversible cloth Double-sided fabric made by joining together two layers with adhesive or thread. Usually wool but can be acrylic. Used for coats, capes, jackets. 100–110 (16–18); 6–7; polyester or mercerized; large.

Sailcloth Thick, strong fabric usually made from cotton but can include some polyester. Creases, so normally treated for crease resistance. Used for crisp outfits, dresses, suits, trousers and jackets. 90 (14); 6–7; polyester or core-spun; medium to large.

Sateen Satin-weave cotton fabric, shiny on RS. Used for curtain linings, bedspreads and some garments. Not hardwearing under strain. 90 (14); 6; mercerized or polyester; medium.

Satin Slippery fabric, shiny on one side. Fabrics for evening wear, lingerie and blouses made from silk, acetate or polyester. Cotton and crêpe-backed satin look similar and are used for dresses and blouses. Dry press on WS only. 70–90 (9–14); 7–9; polyester or mercerized; small to medium.

Seersucker One of the first non-iron dress fabrics. Usually made of cotton with rows of warp threads pulled tightly to create wrinkled effect. Generally produced in coloured stripes. Washes well. Ironing flattens but does not eliminate wrinkles. Used for summer suits, dresses, sportswear and table linen. 70 (9); 6–7; mercerized or polyester; medium.

Shantung Originally a natural-coloured Chinese silk used for blouses, suits and dresses. The term now denotes a plain-weave cloth with an uneven surface; made of any fibre, from yarns of irregular thickness. 70–90 (9–14); 6–7; polyester; medium.

Silk
An ancient and expensive natural fibre, produced by the silkworm. Although the cultivated silkworm can spin almost one mile of continuous filament on one cocoon, the filament has to be carefully unwound and spun into yarn. Primarily produced in Japan, China, the Soviet Union, India and Italy.

Removal of sericin, a gummy substance in the raw filament, gives silk its expensive lustrous appearance and may reduce its weight by as much as one-third. Weight loss is compensated for by addition of metallic salts. Some silk, such as taffeta, is heavily weighted, some, such as crêpe de Chine, less so; the amount of weighting gives the fabric its firmness. Spun silk is made from shorter, waste lengths of filament and is less expensive. Wild silk is reeled from the tusser moth and produces a rough, irregular filament. All silk is very strong, soft, smooth and comfortable next to the skin. It is extremely elastic and does not tear easily.

Numerous uses including scarves, dresses, suits, shirts. Fabrics made from silk fibre include crêpe de Chine, georgette, chiffon, twill and jersey.

Wash gently in warm water and pure soap flakes or dry clean before it is very soiled. Creases easily so do not squeeze or wring out. Iron cultivated silk when damp with a warm iron; iron wild silk when completely dry.

Spun silk A medium-weight matt silk, inexpensive and suitable for crisp styles in shirts, blouses and dresses. Creases easily. Wash carefully. 70 (9); 8; silk or polyester; small to medium.

Stretch towelling Very stretchy knit with a loop pile on one side. Not difficult to sew but stretch stitches are needed. Used for sportswear, nightwear, casual clothes and children's clothes. 70 (9); ball-point; 7; polyester or core-spun; medium.

Suede cloth Any fibre, knitted, woven or non-woven, and often brushed on RS, which resembles real suede. Cut woven or bonded suede cloth with nap in one direction. Sew knit suede cloth as for heavy synthetic knit. 90 (14); 6; polyester or core-spun; medium, slight zigzag.

Surah Fine twill-weave fabric made from polyester, acetate, triacetate or occasionally silk. Often printed. Used for blouses, dresses and men's ties. 70 (9); 8–9; polyester; medium.

Taffeta Plain-weave, smooth, crisp fabric made from acetate, polyester or triacetate and occasionally silk. Creases easily. Dry press. Used for evening wear, trimmings. 70 (9); 9; polyester or mercerized; medium to large.

Ticking Firm cotton fabric, usually twill weave, often striped. Washes well. Very hard-wearing. Used for mattress and pillow covers when down-proofed, but also for dresses, shirts and trousers. 100 (16); cotton, core-spun or polyester; large.

Towelling Sometimes called terry weave or terry cloth. Additional cotton threads are inserted to form loops on one or both sides. Varieties with loops on both sides are thick and bulky to handle. The loops fall off when cut, so the edges must be finished. Soft and highly absorbent. Used for beachwear, towels, curtains and robes. 90 (14); 5–6; mercerized or polyester; large.

Triacetate
Fabrics were first produced from triacetate in 1954. It is hard to distinguish triacetate from acetate although it is more lustrous. The initial processing of wood pulp or cotton is the same for both, but the final processing differs.

Can be a filament or staple yarn. Moderately strong but gives way at the seams. Drapes well; feels crisp and firm. Not absorbent and dries quickly. Thermoplastic so can be permanently pleated by heat. Melts and burns readily.

Woven and knitted into various fabrics of different thicknesses. Can be mixed with nylon, especially in knit fabrics, cotton, viscose/rayon
or wool. Used for underwear and lingerie, and in weaves and knits that do not shrink. Also found in some pile and furnishing fabrics.

Wash often in warm water, but do not wring or squeeze, as the fibres can crack. Almost drips dry. Press while damp with warm iron on WS.

Tussah Sometimes called tussore. Heavy silk fabric with attractive uneven appearance. Fabric frays and creases easily. Used for suits, dresses. 90 (14); 6; silk or polyester; medium to large.

Tweed Any thick, rough, heavy-weight woollen fabric with white hairs in surface. Can be in plain herringbone or twill weave. Used for coats, jackets and suits. 100 (16); 5–6; polyester or mercerized; large.

Uncut velvet Made from any fibre. Some of the pile is left uncut, so forming loops. Often used for furnishings. Cut with nap in one direction. Press and sew as for velvet.

Velour Knit or woven fabrics with short pile. Can be made from variety of fibres including cotton, polyester and modal. Used for casual as well as elegant clothes. 70 (9); ball-point; 7; polyester; medium.

Velour frappé Velvet with a raised pattern. Uses as for velvet and also suits and coats. Treat as velvet.

Velvet Rich-looking pile fabric made from cotton, silk, polyester, nylon or other synthetics. Additional warp threads used to form the pile, which is even but shades. Cut out with pile running upward. Various types of velvet dress and furnishing fabrics are available. Press lightly on WS, with another piece of velvet RS up on pressing board. When stitching insert tissue between layers to prevent wrinkled seams. 70 (9); 8–9; polyester or mercerized; medium to large.

Velveteen Has rich appearance of velvet but made of cotton. The
pile is added by inserting additional weft threads. These are looped in the weaving and cut afterward. Usually frays readily. Cut out with pile running upward. Press lightly on WS only, with a piece of velveteen RS up on the pressing surface. Used for dresses, trousers and suits. 90 (14); 7–8; polyester or mercerized; medium to large.

Vinyl-coated fabric or PVC Knitted or woven fabric, often cotton, which is coated to add a dull or shiny waterproof finish. May be quiet and soft if vinyl in coating is porous, or noisy if vinyl is non-porous. Do not press. Sponge to clean. Avoid bringing the fabric into contact with sharp edges as its splits easily. Used for children's clothes, aprons, rainwear and furnishings. Apply a drop of oil to machine needle before stitching. 90 (14) and roller foot; 6–7; polyester or core-spun; large.

Viscose/rayon
Viscose is known as rayon in the United States. A cellulosic fibre, it is produced by making sheets of cellulose from wood or cotton and soaking them in caustic soda to form crumbs of cellulose. Widely available from 1910 onward and the first artificial fibre to be produced on a large scale. Combines well with other fibres.

Can be a staple or filament yarn. Fairly strong but loses as much as half its strength when wet. Feels soft, cool and limp against the skin. Burns very easily and is not hard-wearing. Viscose/rayon fabrics are often dull in texture.

Woven viscose/rayon fabrics are available in dress and blouse weights. Can be brushed for children's clothes, nightwear, housecoats and long casual wear.

Warm wash. Use a medium-hot iron when slightly damp.

Viyella Trade name for a well-known lightweight plain or printed fabric made from wool and cotton. Easy to sew. Can be used for many clothes including shirts, blouses, dresses, nightwear and children's clothes. 70 (9); 7; mercerized or polyester; medium.
Voile From French word meaning "veil". Sheer, plain-weave fabric, made from cotton or polyester; cotton voile is softer and more comfortable. Used for full sleeves, gathers, frills and curtains. 70 (9); 9; polyester or mercerized; small to medium.

West of England A traditional English woollen cloth which can be beautifully tailored. Used for men's and women's suits. 80 (11); 6; mercerized; large.

Wool
The wool from the fleece of sheep has been used for clothing since earliest times. The best wool comes from the shoulders of the sheep.

Cylindrical but scaly, with a natural crimp: still air is trapped under the scales insulating the body against heat loss and making the fibre feel warm to the touch. Fibre length varies from 4 cm/2 in to 40 cm/15 in; it is fine or coarse depending on the type of sheep. Extremely resilient and absorbent.

There are two kinds of yarn: woollen and worsted. Woollen yarns, made mainly from the shorter fibres, are thick and fluffy with a hairy surface. Worsted yarns, made only from the longer fibres, produce a smoother, clearer pattern when woven and can be printed. Both can be woven in any pattern, and mix and blend well with all other fibres. The label "pure new wool" indicates that the yarn has not been reprocessed, either by combing and carding old woollen cloth, or by using the combings and scraps left over from the processing of the fleece.

Woollen yarn is made into dress-, skirt- and coat-weight fabrics, and into blankets and furnishing fabrics. It is excellent for overcoats and raincoats and is rewarding to tailor. Worsted yarn is made into men's suiting.

The scales on the fibre become entangled during frequent and incorrect washing. Woollen cloth varies in its finish: much of it is now processed so that it is machine washable. Follow label instructions carefully. To wash by hand, wash, rinse and squeeze gently in warm water. Do not soak or bleach. Dry without stretching the garment.

PRESSING

One of the most important processes in sewing, pressing contributes more than anything else to a professional result. It is essential at each stage in the construction of a garment to build in shape and set the seams; it can also, if properly done, greatly improve the look of slightly unsatisfactory sewing.

Pressing surface
The ideal surface is a firm, custom-built bench padded with one or two layers of blanket and a layer of sheeting or other cotton material. Alternatively, use a work surface padded with a blanket and sheeting. Have a piece of heatproof plastic or asbestos on which to stand the iron. The ironing board can be used for pressing, although it may wobble under the pressure.

Irons
A good steam iron (**A**) is best for dressmaking and household sewing, used on its own for lightweight fabrics or with a damp cloth for heavier ones and for fusing interfacing. Pressing heavier fabrics such as those used in tailoring will be more effective, quicker and much easier if a heavy dry iron is used, in conjunction with a damp cloth. A domestic press is excellent for all flat construction pressing, especially in tailoring.

When pressing, stand steam irons on their specially constructed heel to prevent water leaking onto the ironing surface. Lay dry irons flat on the ironing board well or heatproof mat. Always unplug irons after use and empty steam irons. Clean the sole plates by wiping with liquid household cleanser on a damp cloth or according to manufacturer's instructions.

Pressing cloths
A fine, open-weave cotton such as muslin makes a good general pressing cloth. Thicker cotton cloths hold more water and are used for the heavier fabrics of tailored clothes. Alternatively, fold the muslin cloth so that it holds more moisture.

Water
Ideally, there should be a sink in the work room but if not, have a bowl of water handy. A spray bottle (**B**) is also useful.

Sleeve board
An essential piece of equipment, the sleeve board (**C**) is padded on one or both sides and has a selection of different-sized ends for different areas of a garment. Wooden sleeve boards are stable and easy to use; the metal ones supplied with some ironing boards are rather springy. When pressing, stand the sleeve board on a table covered with a blanket and sheeting, or on the ironing board.

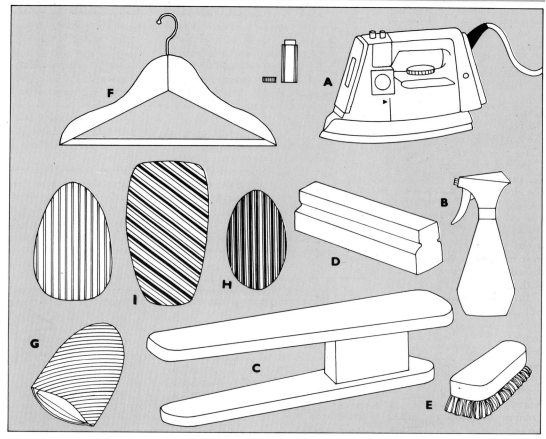

Pressing block
This is a smooth block of wood (**D**) for banging steam into heavy fabrics immediately after the iron has been applied and for making strong creases such as trouser creases. If you cannot obtain a block, use a book or the back of a large clothes brush.

Clothes brush
Keep a brush (**E**) handy for bringing up the nap on fluffy fabrics when they are still warm from pressing. Use it also to remove tailor's chalk marks from fabric, preferably before pressing so that they do not "set".

Coat hangers
Have a few shaped wooden hangers (**F**), some with bars, for hanging each piece of pressing while the fabric cools.

Pads, hams and rolls
A pressing mitt (**G**) or small oval pad (**H**) is useful in dressmaking. Hold it in your hand while pressing shoulders, sleeve heads and any shaped area such as below the waist of a skirt. Bigger, harder pressing pads and hams (**I**) are used in tailoring and also a soft flat sleeve-shaped pad. A padded seam roll is also useful. A substitute can be made by wrapping a rolled up magazine in a towel.

Essentials of pressing
Pressing, as the word suggests, is the application of pressure—and also heat and usually moisture—to the fabric for as long as is necessary to achieve the desired shaping. Experience teaches you how to achieve the right result on every fabric, but there are a few basic principles, which, if followed, will produce good results. Before pressing, take into consideration the fibre content, weave, thickness and texture of the fabric.

Most irons are thermostatically controlled to keep them at the chosen temperature setting. Some irons have fibre names instead of temperatures on the indicator, others have both.

Before pressing the garment, allow the iron to heat up fully and test the temperature by pressing a crease into a spare piece of fabric. Adjust the temperature if necessary. If you are pressing with a damp cloth, select a higher temperature as the cloth prevents the heat fully penetrating the fabric.

One method of providing moisture for pressing is by using a steam iron. Water drips onto a hot plate inside the iron and the resulting steam escapes through holes in the sole plate. Some irons also have spraying equipment, but be careful when using this on the right side of the fabric, or on unfamiliar materials, as water can leave a mark.

An alternative method of providing moisture is to use a damp muslin pressing cloth, which enables you to control the amount of steam going into the fabric. Wring out the cloth thoroughly for pressing lightweight fabrics, but leave water in it for fabrics requiring more steam. The cloth cools the base of the iron so the damper the cloth the hotter the iron must be to ensure that the water is converted to steam immediately.

Do not cover the whole of the work with the pressing cloth—use only a small area of the cloth at a time to cover the section to be pressed. Lift the cloth off the fabric as soon as you raise the iron to stop water soaking into the garment. Keep the cloth damp, wringing it out with care, so that the amount of water in it remains constant. When pressing small, difficult areas, cover only the tip of the iron with the cloth.

Pressure is applied by the weight of the iron and by leaning on it. The iron is never actually allowed to rest on the fabric, but its weight is controlled according to the fabric being handled. Only light pressure is needed on soft fabrics and on fabrics with a pile or surface that you do not want to flatten. Much more weight and pressure are needed on heavy, closely woven and springy fabrics. Lean on the iron to apply extra pressure when pressing features such as pleats or trouser creases. Apply pressure in short, sharp, almost banging movements, not sliding ones. Press for a couple of seconds only, less on some fabrics.

The pressing sequence

After testing the temperature on a piece of fabric, arrange and smooth out a section of the part to be pressed on the pressing surface. Wring out the pressing cloth. Arrange a part of it on the work and immediately apply the iron. Lift the iron and cloth and examine the fabric. It is unlikely to be completely pressed so arrange another damp part of the cloth on the fabric and press again. Continue until satisfied that the fabric is permanently shaped into its new position. Quickly re-press any wrinkles while the fabric is warm and easy to handle. The muslin is sufficiently transparent to enable you to see whether the iron is being applied correctly. If using a steam iron, follow the same procedure without the cloth. With both dry and steam irons use only as much of the iron as is necessary—the whole plate can leave an iron imprint on the fabric.

After pressing a section leave it to cool for a moment before moving on to the next section or the fabric may crease; some fabrics may also stretch. If the work has been pressed on the wrong side, check the right side, as most fabrics need pressing on both sides.

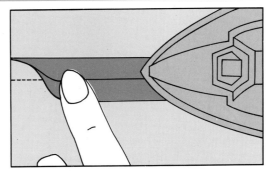

1 Seams Place seam WS up on sleeve board. Open it out with fingers and closely follow fingers down seam with tip of iron. Press same section again more firmly until seam stays open. Continue to end of seam.

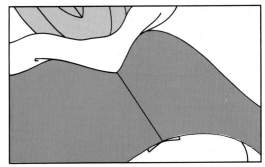

2 Turn work RS up and press again lightly, protecting the fabric with a cloth if necessary and correcting any wrinkles.

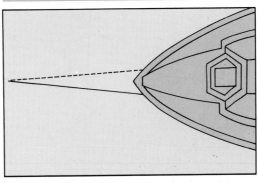

1 Darts Place fabric WS up with point of dart at the end of a sleeve board or pressing pad. Fold dart toward the centre of the garment or upward, depending on its position, and press lightly. Press again more heavily to flatten. Turn fabric RS up and press lightly, keeping the point of the dart at the end of the board. On thick fabrics cut darts open before pressing.

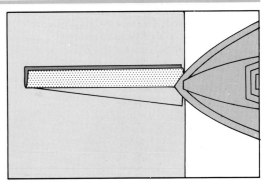

2 On small darts with a piece of tape or lining stitched into them, press the dart one way and the tape the other, following the previous method.

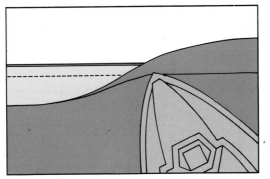

Bindings With binding stitched to RS, place fabric on pressing surface RS up; if stitched to WS place fabric WS up. Run tip of iron along join, lifting strip to make a good line. Do not run iron right over strip or seam allowance will make a ridge.

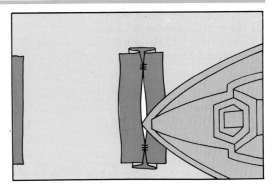

Buttonholes Place work RS down on a folded towel. Press back of buttonholes with tip of iron; work tip into each opening to flatten and straighten it.

PRESSING

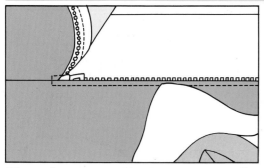

Zipper Open zipper and lay flat on sleeve board, RS up. Wrap damp pressing cloth around toe of iron and run toe along stitching, not over zipper teeth.

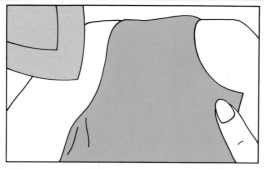

Sleeve heads With garment and sleeve RS out and sleeve hanging loose, arrange a pressing pad or folded towel in armhole of garment. Hold pad in one hand to avoid creasing. Place a small section of damp cloth over the sleeve head seam and press around seam with tip of iron.

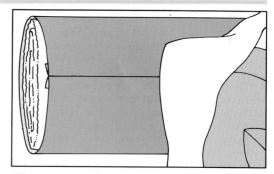

Sleeves Roll up a towel long enough to fill the entire length of the sleeve and push it into the sleeve, RS out. For extra firmness roll a magazine inside the towel. Place damp cloth over sleeve and press lightly, revolving sleeve and towel together after each section is pressed.

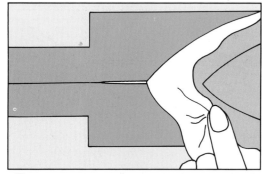

1 Pleats Lay finished pleat, basted into position, WS up on sleeve board and press well with a damp cloth, pressing inverted and box pleats open and knife pleats to one side.

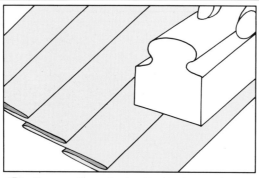

2 Remove iron and cloth and bang in the steam with a block. Allow to cool slightly before pressing next pleat. When all pleats have been pressed on WS, turn work to RS and press again lightly, removing any unevenness in the pleat line.

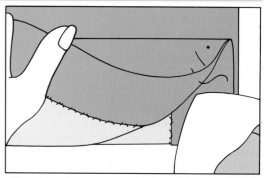

3 To press the hem of finished pleats, turn up hem and, one by one, place pleats, basted into position, RS up on sleeve board. Lift top section of pleat and re-press fold of pleat underneath.

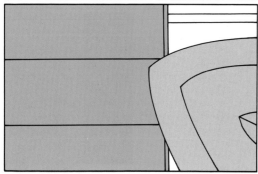

4 Rearrange pleat with top section in place and RS up. To avoid an imprint on fabric under pleat fold, place a folded towel under garment and press pleat on RS.

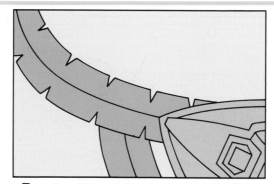

1 Collars When making a collar, arrange neck join of under-collar to neckline WS up on the end of a sleeve board or pressing pad and press as an open seam using toe of iron. Move neck join around as each section is pressed. Finish by turning work over to RS and pressing again lightly as for an open seam.

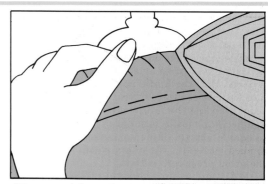

2 On a finished collar with a fold or roll, baste roll diagonally and arrange collar RS out on a dummy or stand, or on a pressing ham, or around a rolled-up towel, all of which act as a neck. Press along the roll, using the other hand to shape the collar by easing it around the neck as you press.

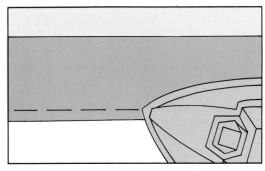

1 Hems Arrange basted hem WS up on sleeve board, with weight of garment resting on surface beneath to prevent stretching. Use side of iron and press basted fold in sections. Do not press over top, raw edge of hem. Allow to cool before pressing next section.

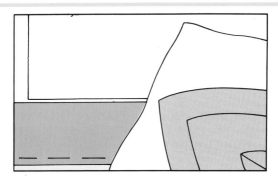

2 For a finished hem, place garment WS up on sleeve board and arrange a piece of fabric of equal thickness to hem, or a piece folded to equal its thickness, against bottom edge of hem. Press lightly over edge using a damp cloth to avoid a ridge.

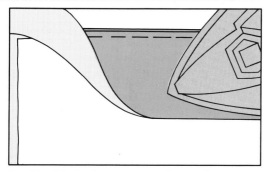

Double fabric On a garment that is almost completed, the iron is likely to press the outline of double areas such as facing joins, tucks, cuffs or collars through onto the garment. Avoid this by slipping part of a dry pressing cloth between the garment and the section to be pressed.

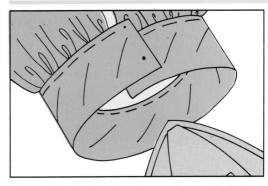

1 Finished edges On edges such as cuffs, facings and certain kinds of collar such as a straight stand, the join is often rolled slightly to the inside of the garment. To stop the join making a ridge on RS, press on the inside with tip of iron only.

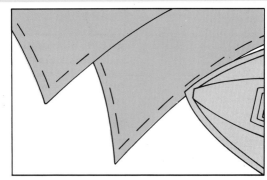

2 On a collar that turns over, such as the shirt collar, the join is generally rolled slightly to the underside; press from this side using tip of iron.

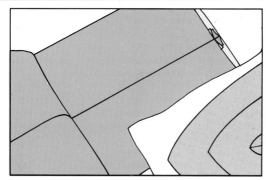

1 Trousers Hold one trouser leg up, RS out, by the hem; arrange with inside leg uppermost and inside seam 1 to 2 cm/⅜ to ¾ in toward front. This places the front crease centrally over the knee and gives a better hang than when seams are together. Front fold should run from hem up to a point at waist about 7.5 cm/3 in from centre front seam. Using a damp cloth, press up front crease a little way.

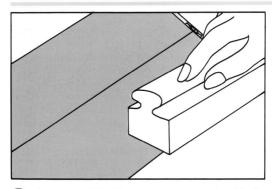

2 Remove iron and bang steam in with a block.

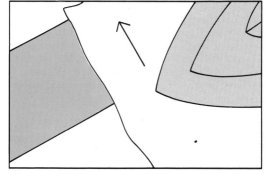

3 Press across leg to establish back crease. Complete front crease up to waist but do not force it to meet a dart point on women's trousers or the crease may not be straight. On some styles of men's trousers the crease runs into the front pleat. Press back crease so it meets centre back seam at waist. Allow the first leg to cool and then repeat the procedure for the other leg.

Pressing tips
1 Press at a comfortable height—the sleeve board placed on the table or ironing board will raise height.
2 Wait for soft fabrics to cool before moving on to the next area.
3 After careful pressing, give a final all-over press, then hang garments up immediately; tailored clothes should be hung on a dummy, trousers over the bar of a hanger.
4 Water is essential; keep some nearby, with the water bottle for the steam iron.
5 Use a damp cloth for all trouser pressing, to avoid shiny patches.
6 Make your own pressing pads, hams and rolls with cotton covers and a filling of cut-up tights or stockings.
7 Complete the stitching on several garment pieces, accumulating enough for a lengthy pressing session.

41

SEAMS

There are two basic types of seam—the functional, which holds the pieces of a garment together, and the decorative. Most functional seams have some shaping, which provides style, or allows for the slopes and bulges of the body, or both. The edges of the fabric pieces can be either angled or curved so that when joined they form a shaped area. Sometimes, however, a functional seam is perfectly straight, as, for example, when joining narrow widths of fabric together to form one piece of a garment.

The fabric, the type of garment, possible strain of constant wear and washing and the effect wanted on the right side should all be taken into consideration when deciding on the type of seam to use.

Handling seams

The same preparatory stages apply to all seams, but certain things, including the seam allowance, vary according to the type of seam. For accuracy, mark all seamlines before beginning to sew. Where possible—this depends on the type of seam—place the pieces of fabric flat on the table. Whether they are right or wrong sides together is again governed by the kind of seam.

With raw edges toward you, lift and flap (rather than drag or pull) the fabric until the seamlines are level. Pin only if there is ease to control or if it is imperative to match the pattern of the fabric on both sides of the seam. Insert pins across the seam, not along it.

Baste the seam on the seamline, keeping the fabric flat, but helping it onto the needle with each stitch. Machine close to raw edge side of basting rather than on top of it. This enables you to remove the basting easily.

Unless, for example, you are working with material cut on the bias, always baste and stitch with the grain: from the wide part to the narrow, skirt hem to waist, neck to shoulder point, underarm to wrist, and so on. Press seam with the grain to prevent stretching. Press curved areas over a sleeve board.

FUNCTIONAL SEAMS

Open seam

Straight stitched Often called plain seam. The most widely used functional seam because it is flat and neat, produces the most tailored look of all seams, and is one of the most inconspicuous.

Can be used anywhere except where there is gathering and on any material except transparent or fine fraying ones. As there is only one row of stitching, a split shows up immediately, so the seam may not be suitable for children's clothes or other garments intended for hard wear, such as jeans, dungarees and protective clothing.

Zigzag Seams on knits and other fabrics with give, such as crêpe, are best stitched with a slight zigzag for additional stretch.

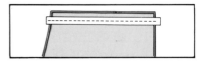

Pressed open, this looks like an open seam, but will not split in wear.

Finishing open seams To prevent fraying and to help keep seam allowances flat, always finish the raw edges of open seams. Finished allowances should be 1 to 1.5 cm/$\frac{3}{8}$ to $\frac{5}{8}$ in wide to support the seam. Choose a method that will be effective on the fabric without adding bulk. Finish raw edges for the whole length of the seam, even if you intend to insert a zipper later on.

French seam

A narrow seam that looks identical to an open seam on RS but forms a ridge on WS, so restrict to fine fabrics. Useful if

fabric frays as edges are enclosed, and excellent for blouses, nightwear and children's clothes. Can be worked by hand on fine garments. It is started on the right side, which makes fitting awkward.

Narrow finish seam

Use only on lightweight or transparent fabrics as seam allowances lie to one side.

Taped seam

A method of reinforcing or stabilizing seams on fabrics tending to stretch or in areas such as the shoulder or the crotch.

Machine flat fell seam

Strong and flat and suitable for all medium-weight fabrics, but not for very fine or bulky fabrics.

Two rows of stitching show on one side of the fabric; they can be worked in a contrasting thread. If you have difficulty in working neat edge stitching, work the seam so that stitching is visible on wrong side only. If the seam is worked so that the edge stitching appears on the right side, you will have to undo the seam basting and rebaste when fitting the garment.

Angled seam

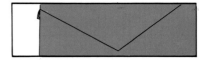

The angle formed by the seam is part of the design, but there is usually some additional shaping, which may prevent the two edges from fitting together easily.

Curved seam

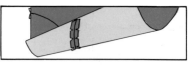

Often provides shaping for the bust and, therefore, the two edges of fabric to be joined differ in shape, one generally being more curved than the other.

Self-finished seam

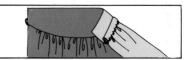

Useful for fraying fabrics as raw edges are enclosed, but forms a bulky ridge so confine to thin materials. Very useful on curves such as armholes and where one edge is gathered, as on yokes and waistlines.

Double-faced seam

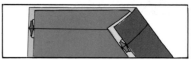

Use for reversible garments, and where a facing rolls back to show a join. Suitable only if the two layers of fabric are joined by threads, not adhesive.

Welt seam

A strong seam suitable for most fabrics, except very fine fraying ones. As a row of stitching shows on RS, the welt seam is an effective way to add interest to plain fabrics and to add style to casual coats, safari suits, shirtwaister dresses and trousers.

Rolled seam

Used on fine fabrics. There is only one row of stitching so confine to loose-fitting items as otherwise the seam may split.

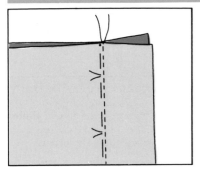

1 **Open seam** With fabric RS together, baste along seamline and machine with straight stitch or, on stretch fabrics, zigzag. Remove basting and tacks. If zigzagging, use synthetic thread and set stitch width dial to slightly off 0. The stitch is slightly wobbly, not a defined zigzag.

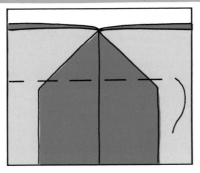

2 Where open seams meet, cut away seam allowances at an angle before stitching to reduce bulk.

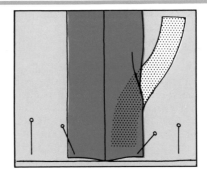

3 Open seams in fine knits wrinkle for the last 20 cm/8 in to the hem because no weight pulls them down. Stretch out this section and pin it to a sleeve board. Slip narrow strips of fabric adhesive web under seam allowances and press. Leave to cool before removing pins.

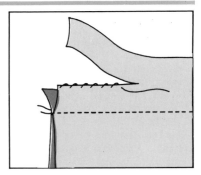

1 **Finishing open seam** To finish by hand on any type of fabric, overcast, trimming away surplus fabric as you sew.

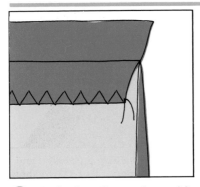

2 To finish medium or heavy fabrics by machine, place fabric with raw edge under machine and zigzag over raw edge.

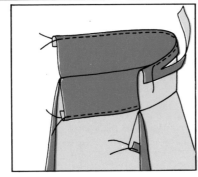

3 To finish thin fabrics by machine, turn edge under 5 mm/$\frac{1}{4}$ in and zigzag or straight stitch close to fold. Press and trim away surplus on WS almost down to stitching.

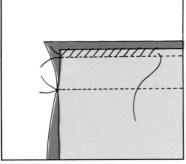

4 On fraying medium to heavy fabrics, trim 5 mm/$\frac{1}{4}$ in off seam allowances and machine each one separately a little way in from the trimmed edge—not too close as this encourages fraying. Overcast, taking stitch down over the machining.

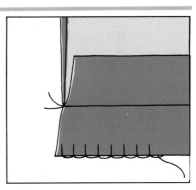

5 On firm fabrics such as polyester that fray only a little, loop stitch raw edges of seam.

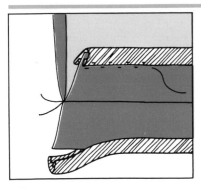

6 Badly fraying lightweight fabrics, e.g. brocade, can be bound with bias binding or net.

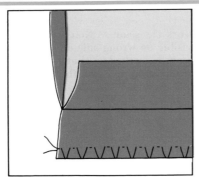

7 Prevent raw edge of fine knit from rolling up by working blind hem stitch or any wide decorative machine stitch along it.

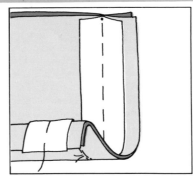

1 **Taped seam** Place fabric RS together and baste on seamline. Baste a length of seam binding or tape (pre-shrunk) with centre over seamline. Ease it around a curve. The tape can be applied to either piece of fabric.

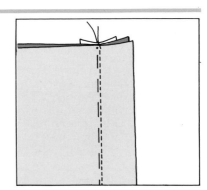

2 Turn work over with taped side down and machine beside basting. Remove basting and tacks. Press stitching, press seam open and finish seam allowances as for open seam.

SEAMS

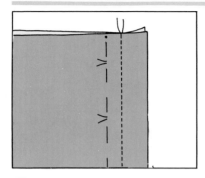 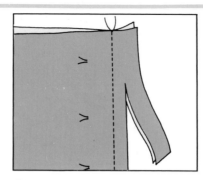 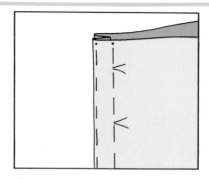 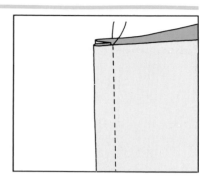

1 **French seam** Place fabric WS together and baste along seamline. Work first row of stitching about 5 mm/¼ in from seamline (a little more on firm fabrics such as cotton). Remove basting and press stitching flat. Press seam allowances open onto RS, turn work over and press.

2 On RS press seam allowances together lightly. Trim both seam allowances down to within 3 mm/⅛ in of stitching.

3 Open out fabric, fold so that RS are together, roll seam so that join appears right on edge and baste fabric together near edge. Hold seam to light to find edge of turnings on inside and baste slightly beyond edge. Press.

4 Machine beside second row of basting. Remove basting and tacks and press stitching. Open out fabric and press seam toward back of garment. Press again on RS. Where two French seams cross, press each one in a different direction to eliminate excess bulk.

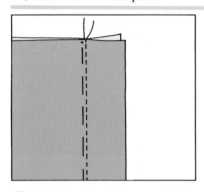 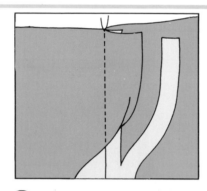 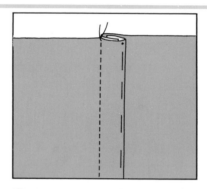 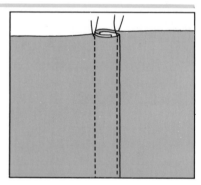

1 **Machine flat fell seam** Place fabric RS together if second row of stitching is to show on WS, WS together if to show on RS. Baste on seamline and machine. Remove basting and tacks and press stitching. Press seam allowances open on WS and RS to remove wrinkles.

2 Press both seam allowances to one side—toward either the back or the front, but be consistent throughout the garment. Lift top seam allowance and trim underneath one to 5 mm/¼ in. Press both seam allowances again to one side to flatten them.

3 Turn under raw edge of upper seam allowance and tuck it as far as it will go under trimmed edge. If seam appears clumsy, trim a little off wide seam allowance before turning it under. Baste to garment keeping folded edge an even distance from machining. Press on RS.

4 Machine on fold, with exactly the same size stitch as the initial row of machining. Press on RS.

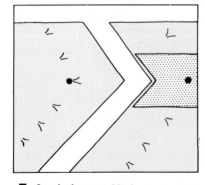 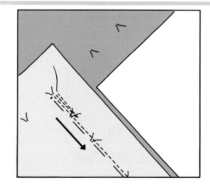 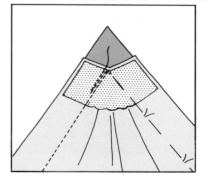 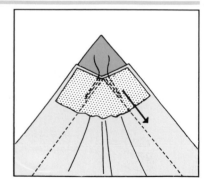

1 **Angled seam** Mark exact point of inner corner on both pieces of fabric at A and B and press a small piece of lightweight iron-on interfacing over B on WS. Cut interfacing down to fit shape of angle.

2 With RS together and corner marks matching, baste on seamline parallel with two aligned edges from corner right to end of seam. Lower machine needle into corner, lower foot, stitch forward a little, reverse to corner and sew forward to end of seam.

3 Press and finish as a normal open seam. Turn work over and clip reinforced corner to within a thread of start of machine stitching. Swing fabric around with RS still together until the two unstitched edges align. With this side of work toward you, baste from corner to end of seam.

4 Lower machine needle into corner exactly where previous stitching ends. Stitch as before, reversing to fasten ends. Remove basting and tailor's tacks, press seam open and finish. If you are unsure of reversing accurately at corner, leave long ends of thread to sew in by hand.

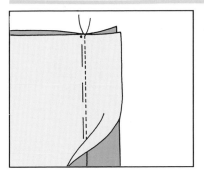

1 **Narrow finish seam** With RS together, baste along seamline and machine. Remove basting and press seam open.

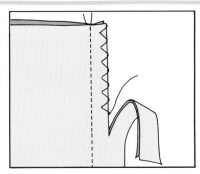

2 Press both seam allowances to one side. To finish by machine, trim raw edges down to 5 mm/¼ in from machine stitching and zigzag over both together. Press on RS.

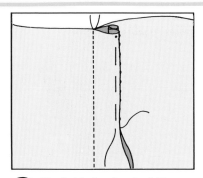

3 To finish by hand, fold seam allowances in to meet each other, baste, press and slip stitch together. Press on RS.

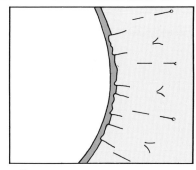

1 **Curved seam** With the more curved piece on top, match balance marks and notches and pin fabric RS together, exactly on seamline, taking care to pick up only a little fabric. Ease shaped piece into position and hold seam over your hand to pin so that it remains in a curve.

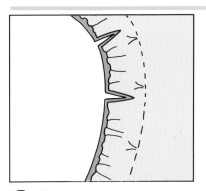

2 Baste on seamline with small stitches along curve. If the fabric is stiff or unyielding, as you baste clip seam allowances at intervals almost down to basting. Remove pins.

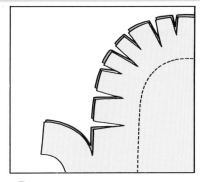

3 Still working from shaped side, machine slowly beside basting, following curve. Remove basting and tacks and press stitching. Trim seam allowances and clip at frequent intervals. Press seam either open or to one side and finish seam allowances separately or together.

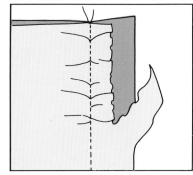

1 **Self-finished seam** With RS together, baste along seamline and machine. Remove basting and tailor's tacks and press seam allowances to one side. Trim upper seam allowance—always the gathered edge if there is one—to 5 mm/¼ in.

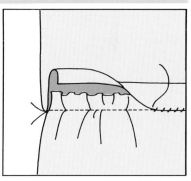

2 Fold wider edge down twice by rolling and bring it over to meet machining. Baste and press. Hem into machine stitches to finish or, for speed but a harder ridge, machine near bottom fold on WS. Remove basting and press seam.

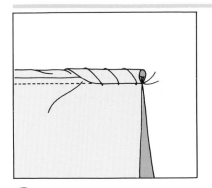

3 On very fine, flimsy fabrics, particularly at waists and armholes, make seam narrower so that it shows less. Trim down wider seam allowance to 6 mm/¼ in, fold down as in (**2**) and whipstitch over edge, bringing needle through just above machining.

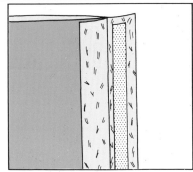

1 **Double-faced seam** Open layers of fabric and clip threads in from edge to a depth of about 4 cm/1½ in along seam edges to be joined. Counteract stretching by sewing or ironing narrow strips of interfacing beside opened raw edges on WS of two outer layers.

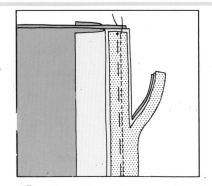

2 Place edges of two reinforced pieces RS together and baste, making usual seam allowance. Machine beside basting, trim raw edges, remove basting and press seam open.

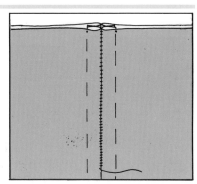

3 Turn in the two remaining raw edges so that they meet over centre of seam, baste and press. Slip stitch edges together. Remove basting and press both sides of fabric.

SEAMS

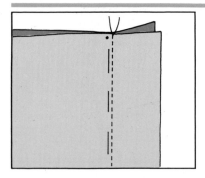

1 Welt seam With fabric RS together, baste on seamline and machine. Remove basting and tailor's tacks, press seam open and press seam allowances to one side—toward the back or front of the garment, depending on where you want the additional stitching to show.

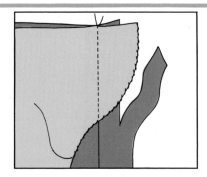

2 Lift seam allowances and trim down the underneath one to a little less than 1 cm/⅜ in. Finish raw edge of wider seam allowance unless fabric is non-fraying or garment is to be lined.

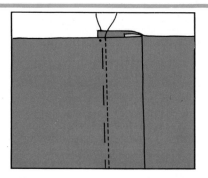

3 On RS baste parallel to seamline, stitching through wider seam allowance and encasing the narrower one. Press lightly. Machine stitch or prick stitch parallel with seam, making sure that you stitch through the wider seam allowance underneath. Remove basting and press seam on RS.

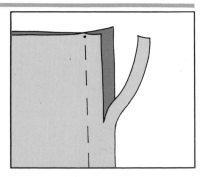

Rolled seam With RS together, baste fabric on seamline. Trim down one layer to within 3 mm/⅛ in of the basting.

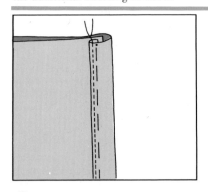

2 Bring wider seam allowance over trimmed layer, fold down twice and baste down on seamline. On very fine fabric trim wider seam allowance a little before folding over. Machine along edge of fold. Remove basting and on WS press seam to one side.

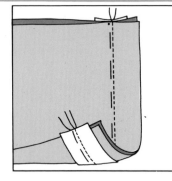

Seams on transparent fabrics To stop wrinkling and to ensure the machine stitches properly and the teeth do not mark the fabric, place strips of tissue or thin typing paper under the fabric as you baste the seam. Machine through paper, and tear it away when removing basting.

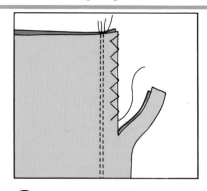

2 Use narrow finish, French or rolled seams on these fabrics. On the narrow finish, work a second row of machining to stabilize edges, trim edges down to within 3 mm/⅛ in of this machining and zigzag or overcast together.

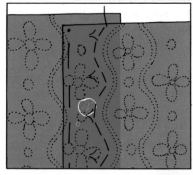

Seams in lace Cut out with slightly wider seam allowances than usual and mark seamlines. Matching seamlines, with both pieces RS up, lap one piece over the other and baste together. Near seamline on top piece use basting to mark out a stitching line around each lace motif.

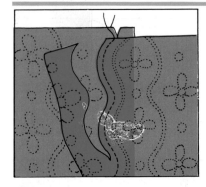

2 Using perfectly matching thread, work over basted line with satin stitch or a close machine zigzag. Remove basting and tailor's tacks. Close to stitching clip away surplus lace on both top and bottom pieces. Press RS down on a folded towel.

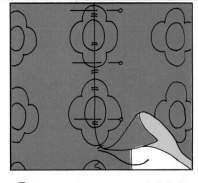

Seams in patterned fabrics Make sure pattern matches exactly at seams by working first from RS. Fold under one edge of fabric on seamline and place it on RS of second piece, matching seamlines and pattern of fabric. Place a few pins across seam. Slip baste fabric together.

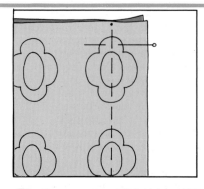

2 Remove pins. With fabric RS together, replace pins across seam at start of each motif. Check the underneath to make sure pattern is level. The pins should be inserted so that the heads project well beyond the raw edge or they may get caught under the machine foot.

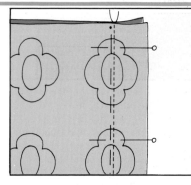

3 Machine seam, stitching over pins, but slow down as you approach them so that the needle slides in easily to one side of them. Alternatively, stop at each pin and work machine by hand wheel. Remove pins and basting and press. Finish as for an open seam.

DECORATIVE SEAMS

Decorative seams add style to an outfit and provide a focal point. It is important, however, not to overdo the decoration. Consider the type and design of the fabric, the outfit itself and the finished effect before working a decorative seam.

Do not attempt any of the following until you have mastered the decorative stitches involved and have tried out the techniques on spare fabric.

Piped seam

Matching or contrasting piping can be inserted into a seam to provide a focal point on clothes and soft furnishings. As it tends to make the seam more rigid, it is unsuitable for most softly draped styles. It can be soft, or unfilled, or filled with a length of cord that has been pre-shrunk.

Lapped seam

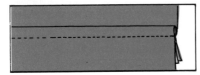

One side of the seam laps over the other. Suitable for any fabric.

Topstitched seam

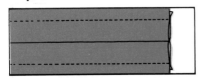

Any open seam can be decorated with additional stitching, worked in matching or contrasting bold or double thread, or using a twin needle to produce double stitching. The stitching can be on one side of the seam or both; try it out on correct number of thicknesses first. If you wish to stitch farther from the seam than the standard width of the trimmed seam allowance, add extra fabric at seams when cutting out the garment pieces.

Faggoted seam

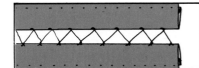

The seam is joined with faggoting, or feather stitch, to leave a gap between the seam edges. This can be a weak area, so avoid on clothing that will be subjected to a lot of wear. If the pattern does not include the seam, work it on fabric larger than you will need and cut the fabric around the pattern piece later.

Insertion seam

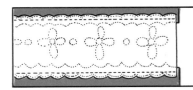

Lace is the usual insertion on fine fabrics for blouses, lingerie, etc., but any suitable open-weave braid or trimming can be used, and on almost any garment. The insertion can be added after the pattern pieces have been cut out; no extra allowance is needed.

Slot or channel seam

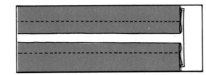

Use on any fabric, but most effective on plain, firm materials. Backing, cut from a contrasting coloured or patterned fabric, shows between the seam edges. It should be similar in weight to the garment fabric; if it is lighter, mount it on iron-on interfacing. The width of the backing depends on the weight and bulk of the fabric and on how visible the backing is to be. Generally, the maximum that should show is 5 mm/¼ in, but on some styles the gap can be larger.

If the pattern does not include the seam, cut through a large enough piece of fabric, work the seam and cut out the fabric around the pattern piece later.

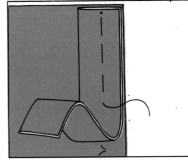

1 Piped seam—soft Cut and join enough crosswise strips of fabric, 3 cm/1¼ in wide, to make the required length. Fold joined strips in half, WS together, and press. Baste strip to RS of one of seam edges along seamline, allowing fold of piping to extend beyond seamline.

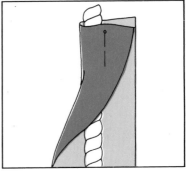

1 Piped seam—corded Cut a small piece of fabric on the true cross or on the bias, wrap it around the piping cord, pin and trim, leaving two 3.5 cm/1¼ in seam allowances. Unpin and measure width of strip. Prepare strip this width and required length.

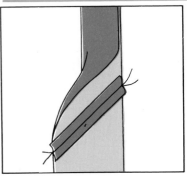

1 Piping a circular edge If the fabric has been joined so that it is no longer flat, make piping about 12 cm/4½ in longer than seam and join before applying it. Insert cord and stitch, leaving area unstitched where cord ends are to be joined.

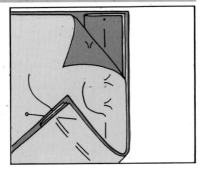

2 Place second garment piece over strip RS down. Baste, piercing top and bottom layers of fabric with pins, turning fabric back to check that seamlines coincide. Machine beside basting. Remove basting and tailor's tacks and press seam. Trim off excess piping.

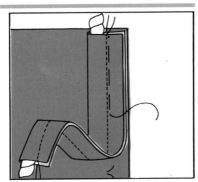

2 Wrap strip RS out around cord and machine with zipper foot as close as possible to cord. Do not baste first as the stitches pull open. Baste piping down onto seamline, machine and finish as for soft piping.

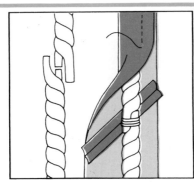

2 To join the cords of filled piping, trim ends of cord so they overlap slightly, unravel them a little and cut half the strands. Wrap overlapping strands around shorter ones and work a stitch over and over across join. Wrap fabric strip over cord.

SEAMS

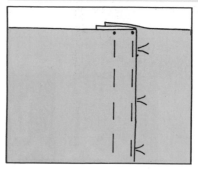

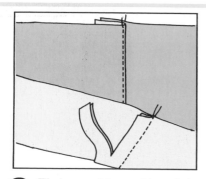

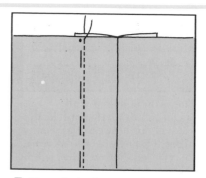

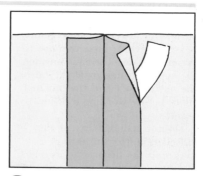

1 Lapped seam Decide which way seam is to lap. Turn under top layer of fabric on seamline, baste fold and press. Place this WS down onto RS of underneath piece, matching notches and seamlines and baste two pieces of fabric together slightly away from fold.

2 Work a straight machine stitch along fold or use a hand or machine embroidery stitch. Remove basting and tacks and press. On WS trim and finish the two raw edges together.

1 Topstitched seam Press and finish open seam. At desired distance from seam, baste through garment and seam allowance. Machine beside basting on RS, using machine foot as a guide, or embroider by hand or machine. If stitching both sides of seam, sew in same direction.

2 For a more raised effect, cut bias strips of lining or other thin material such as cotton lawn and slip these under the seam allowance on WS before basting. Baste and stitch as before.

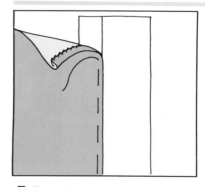

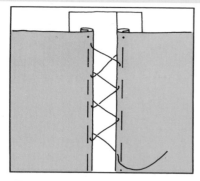

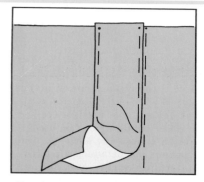

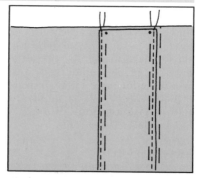

1 Faggoted seam Baste a line on RS of fabric to mark position of faggoting. Cut on line and turn in about 3 mm/⅛ in on each edge and stitch. Press. On fine typing paper or tissue, pencil a straight line and baste one hemmed edge WS down to paper.

2 Place other hemmed edge about 3 mm/⅛ in away and baste. On wool or thicker fabrics the hems can be a little wider and the gap on the paper 1 cm/⅜ in. Join edges with feather stitch, worked in a thread of suitable thickness. Remove paper and basting.

1 Insertion seam The insertion can be as wide or as narrow as desired. Mark position of one edge of insertion with basting or tailor's tacks on RS of main fabric. Place one edge of insertion along basting and baste to garment. Holding insertion flat, baste second edge to garment.

2 Attach insertion to RS by machine with a straight, zigzag or embroidery stitch, or by hand with hemming or an embroidery stitch. Match the thread to the insertion for less conspicuous stitching. Remove basting. Press stitching and insertion with RS down on a folded towel.

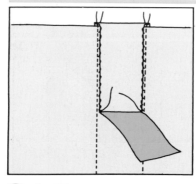

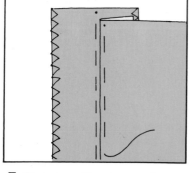

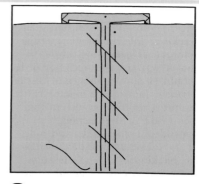

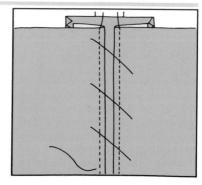

3 On WS cut fabric carefully between rows of stitching, about 4 mm/⅛ in away from each row. Trim edges and finish—hand overcasting is easier than machine zigzag. To prevent fabric edges showing through transparent insertion, roll them back beside insertion and hem.

1 Slot seam Turn in raw edges on seamline, baste and press. Finish edges. Cut bias backing strips at least 3 cm/1¼ in wide. Baste along centre of strip, finish edges and press. Baste one folded edge of fabric, RS up, to strip 2 mm/1/16 in from centre, with top edge below backing edge.

2 Baste other fabric edge to strip the same distance away from the centre. Work a row of diagonal basting across folds and backing strip. Fit garment carefully, adjusting seam if necessary.

3 On RS machine along seam edges, 3 mm/⅛ in away from each fold, using machine foot as a guide. Remove all basting. Press seam RS down on a folded towel.

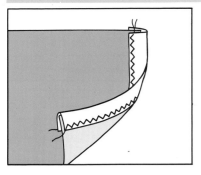

Nylon tricot binding Fold nylon tricot seam bias to enclose seam edges of fraying fabrics or unlined clothes. Using a decorative zigzag stitch, sew through binding edges and seam edge together.

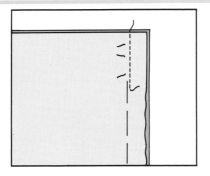

Velvet seam For pile fabrics. With fabric RS together baste seam in the direction of the pile—usually from hem upward. Do not fasten off the basting. Stitch seam in the same direction, cutting basting stitches when neccessary to allow top layer of fabric to move. Trim fabric edges.

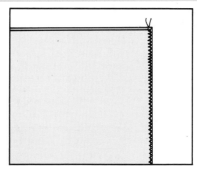

Hairline seam For fine fabrics and full styles, also for bias seams. With fabric RS together stitch seam with a very small, close zigzag stitch on the seamline. Trim away surplus close to stitching. Press seam to one side.

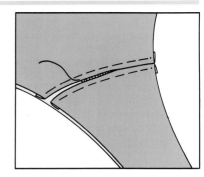

Draw seam A hand-sewn open seam used in tailoring where there are two layers of garment. With RS up trim and fold under each edge in turn and baste to the layer beneath with the folds meeting. Press, then slip stitch together from RS with very small, tight stitches.

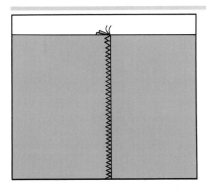

Zigzag seam Strong seam suitable for denim, canvas, etc. Stitch seam with fabric RS together. Press both seam allowances to one side. On RS of seam stitch with medium-size zigzag stitch in contrast colour, stitching close to seamline.

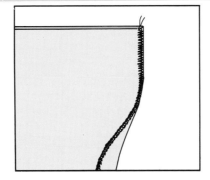

Ridge seam For medium-weight non-fraying fabrics such as jersey, felt, suede fabric and non-fraying cotton. Trim seam allowances to $3\,\text{mm}/\frac{1}{8}$ in or less. Set the machine to satin stitch of a similar width and stitch seams with fabric WS together.

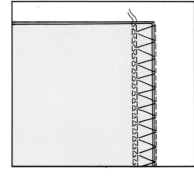

Pullover seam A firm seam for open knits, stretch towelling and velour. Pin fabric RS together. Trim seam allowances to $2\,\text{mm}/\frac{1}{16}$ in. Set machine to a wide stretch stitch and stitch seam, making sure the needle clears the edge when it moves to the right. Remove pins as you come to them.

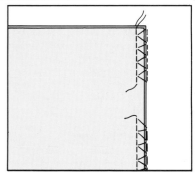

Closed overlock seam Use on close, fine jersey knits such as T-shirt fabric. Select a wide overlock stitch that has a stitch to run beside the raw edges. Pin fabric RS together, trim seams to $2\,\text{mm}/\frac{1}{16}$ in and stitch, making sure needle clears the edges to the right. Keep fabric taut while stitching.

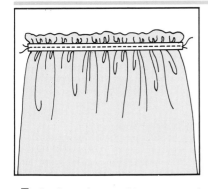

1 Gathered seam If two pieces of fabric are to be gathered and joined, cut a piece of tape the length of the finished seam, gather up one piece to fit and stitch the tape to the WS.

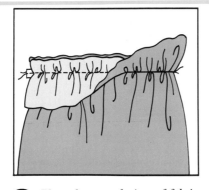

2 Place the second piece of fabric on the first, RS together, pin and pull up gathers to fit. Turn the seam over and stitch along the tape close beside the first row of stitching.

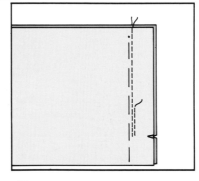

1 Reversing a seam Do this where facing hems or cuffs are to be finished on the RS. Baste the seam. Mark the exact position of the hemline by clipping the seam allowances. Stitch the seam as far as the clip and fasten off.

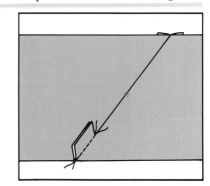

2 Clip again as far as the stitching. Press seam open and finish the raw edges. Fold the unstitched sections of seam to the RS of the garment and stitch from clip to raw edge. Press open and trim edges. Finish hem, facing, etc. as necessary.

By the time you turn up a hem you should be sufficiently familiar with the fabric, through handling and pressing it, to be able to decide on the type of hem finish. However, if the decision seems difficult, consider whether a plain invisible hemline is best or whether the fabric lends itself to a machined or decorative finish. Consider, too, the weight of the material and remember that narrow hems work well on fine fabrics such as voile, cotton, polyester cotton, but that a deeper hem is needed for heavier materials.

Wherever it is essential that the hem is absolutely level—at the bottom edge of dresses, skirts and trousers—leave it until all other processes have been completed, as these may affect the hang of the garment. At the fitting stage, however, it is sometimes easier to assess the finished effect if the hem is turned up and basted.

Hems on nightwear, blouses and other tops can be turned up and finished fairly early in the construction. It is also simpler to hem certain kinds of sleeves before inserting them in the garment—those with cuffed and elasticated finishes and short sleeves. If, however, the sleeves are loose at the wrist and full length, they must be set in before being hemmed, as the extra fullness makes them appear longer.

Measuring the hem

Pins, tailor's chalk, a full-length vertical mirror, a hand mirror—to see the sides and back—and a hem marker are needed for measuring and marking the hemline. There are various kinds of hem markers: some merely gauge the hem level, which is then marked with pins; others also mark it by puffing chalk onto the fabric or by firing pins. Alternatively, screw a long ruler or a straight length of wood onto a block of wood.

Deciding on the length

Put the garment on and fasten it. Wear a belt or anything, such as a jacket, that may affect length. When deciding on the length of a skirt or dress, remember to make it 1 cm/⅜ in shorter than the coat with which it will be worn. Wear shoes that correspond in height of heel to those you will wear with the outfit.

When turning up the hem on a sleeve before setting it into a garment, measure underarm seam of a sleeve on an existing garment as a guide to correct sleeve length.

Turn up and pin front of hem to approximately the required length. Look in mirror and adjust until correct. Consider overall height and any proportional problems: for example, avoid hemlines low across the calf if your legs are short from knee to ankle. Put one pin on turned-up fold of fabric to mark length at front; remove all other pins.

Marking the length

If possible enlist help in marking the length. Adjust hem marker to level of pin. If using a length of wood or ruler, make a pencil mark on it at level of pin. Stand still while your helper moves around inserting pins horizontally at this level at intervals of about 6 cm/2¼ in. If the marker has a container of powdered chalk, pins need not be used (1). The marker must be kept close to the skirt so that the fabric is not pulled out at an angle.

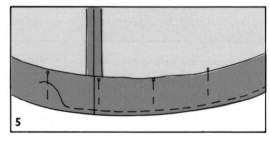

If the skirt is full and hanging in folds, mark outer folds and re-arrange skirt so that remainder can be marked. Before marking a level hem on a skirt that is flared, circular or cut on the bias at any point, hang the garment on a hanger or dressmaker's dummy for a few days to allow the bias areas to drop. Avoid a dragged or lopsided finish on a slightly shaped wide skirt hem by turning up and pinning first across centre front area, then centre back, then sides.

Trousers cannot be measured from the floor, but should be turned up and pinned to rest on shoes at front and slope down about 1 cm/⅜ in at back (2). They should be fractionally shorter at inside leg than outside. Pin up both trouser legs, inserting pins vertically and checking that the two hems are equal in length by placing leg seams together and adjusting hems if necessary. If you still have difficulty in deciding on correct length, use inside leg seam of an existing pair as a guide.

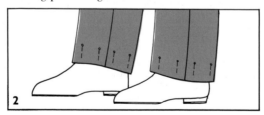

Take off garment; spread hemline out on table RS up. Using tailor's chalk, make chalk dashes between pins (3). Do not attempt a continuous line as it will invariably be uneven. Remove pins, one by one, and insert more chalk marks where pins were. If a chalk puffer was used, mark line again with chalk dashes as powdered chalk rubs off easily. If tailor's chalk is not visible on fabric, baste around hem at level of pins, picking up fabric between them and removing them afterward. Correct any pins or chalk marks that are out of line. The hem should appear as a curve—the more flared the hem, the more curved the line.

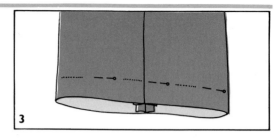

With fabric RS out, fold back upper layer of garment to leave under layer clear to work on. Turn up the section of hem in front of you so chalk or basting is exactly on fold. Holding a short section with one hand, baste with stitches no longer than 1.5 cm/¾ in just inside fold (4). The exact position of this row of basting varies with the fabric: with thin fabrics it should be about 2 mm/1/16 in from the fold; with thick or springy ones about 4 mm/⅛ in.

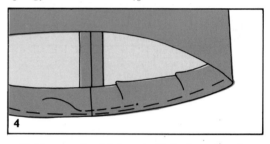

Hold up surplus fabric on inside by inserting pins at intervals, ignoring any fullness (5).

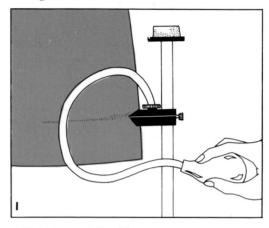

Try on garment and check that hem is level and required length. Remove garment and all pins. If your posture is upright and your hips are level, measure length of side seams and any pairs of seams in front or back sections. Adjust hem if necessary. Do not compare the length of the centre front seam with that of the centre back seam as these are rarely equal.

On check fabric make sure curve of hem runs evenly on checks on either side of centre front and centre back, even if you have lopsided hips.

Marking length unaided

If you have no one to help, pin the hem up and check that it is level in a mirror. Check that corresponding seams are equal in length (except centre front and centre back), allowing for any hip peculiarities. Mark hemline in a curve with chalk or pins, paying great attention to grain to see that angles of threads in weave are the same on either side of centre front and centre back. Turn up and baste as above but try on and check carefully from front, back and sides before proceeding. Alternatively, if you have a dressmaker's dummy that has exactly the same posture as you, put the garment on it to mark the hemline.

Pressing the bottom fold

Use sharp, heavy movements, never leaving the iron in position for more than an instant. It is preferable to bang the iron down in sharp bursts rather than to apply prolonged pressure. Work slowly in short stretches and press only the bottom fold, not along edge of surplus fabric or a mark will be visible on RS.

Depth of hem

The depth of hem depends partly on the style and general finish of the outfit, but mainly on the fabric and the shape of the hem. Use narrow hems—2 mm to 1.5 cm/$\frac{1}{16}$ to $\frac{5}{8}$ in—on long skirts and dresses, sleeves, frills, blouses, nightwear and shirts and on circular or flared edges. Straight or nearly straight hems can be wide—4 to 7 cm/1$\frac{1}{2}$ to 2$\frac{3}{4}$ in—in all fabrics. Short skirts and coats need a deep hem to provide weight and, therefore, a better hang. Trouser hems should be between 2.5 and 4 cm/1 and 1$\frac{1}{2}$ in. The hem on all these garments can be single or double, depending on the fabric and style.

Mark depth of hem by using a ruler or adjustable marker and tailor's chalk and measure evenly from pressed edge, marking all around hem. If chalk does not show, insert pins horizontally through hem only (**6**). If you want to use strips of adhesive to hold hem

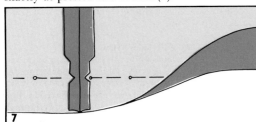

down, make hem the depth of the adhesive, allowing an extra 3 mm/$\frac{1}{8}$ in for basting at fold and the same for finishing. If the hem edge is to be turned under to form a double hem, allow slightly more fabric than the depth of the hem.

If the fabric is transparent and a neater finish is required, make hem deep enough to allow raw edge to be turned down as far as bottom fold.

Seams within hem depth

After marking depth of hem, remove basting at seams, open out fabric and cut down seam allowances of open seams within hem depth to 3 to 5 mm/$\frac{1}{8}$ to $\frac{1}{4}$ in to reduce bulk. On curves, clip these trimmed seam allowances exactly at pressed fold of hem (**7**).

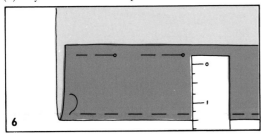

Finishing the raw edge

There are various methods of finishing raw edges, but the neatest and least visible methods—and the most widely used—are overcasting, machining and overcasting, and zigzagging.

To overcast, trim hem down to chalk line or pins and sew along edge (**8**). Work in small sections to minimize fraying. Pull thread fairly tight to bring edge up slightly and so counteract stretching.

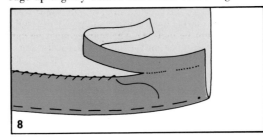

If the fabric frays badly or is a loose weave, work a row of straight machine stitching along chalk line marking raw edge. Trim close to machining, a little at a time, and overcast, taking needle just below machining and pulling thread fairly tight (**9**).

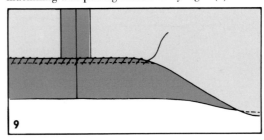

To zigzag, stitch along edge. This will probably cause stretching, so do not use on stretch fabrics.

A hem edge can be finished with herringbone stitch or binding, but do not cover a wide hem edge with straight seam binding, tape or even with herringbone stitch, because the hemline will eventually show on RS.

Holding the hem down

Hems can be held down in a variety of ways, depending on the type and weight of fabric and on whether the stitching is to show on RS.

On medium and thick fabrics catch stitch (**10**) is used for an invisible deep hem on coats, dresses, trousers and skirts. Baste finished edge, just below finishing, to WS of garment. Pull back edge toward you and start thread under it. Keeping edge away from garment, work catch stitch between hem and garment, stitching slightly below finished edge. Do not pull thread tight or hemline will show on RS. Finish off in hem edge, remove basting and press up to, but not over, edge.

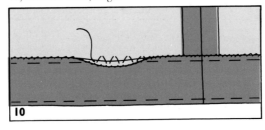

On fine or thin fabrics the raw edge can be turned under and held down by slip hemming (**11**). Turn edge under about 1 cm/$\frac{3}{8}$ in and baste. Open out hem, press turned-under edge and baste it down to WS. With

edge toward you, slip hem along it. Do not pull thread tight. Remove basting on WS and press up to, but not over, turned-under edge.

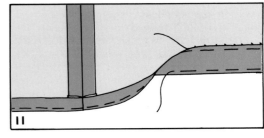

If the hem is likely to be let down later, edge stitch top of hem allowance by machine after basting.

Hold the hem down by machining (**12**) only if you want a decorative effect or if the stitching is to show, e.g. on narrow hems and jersey. Turn raw edge under and baste. Open out hem, press turned-under edge and baste it down to WS. Place under the machine with WS of garment uppermost. Lower needle into turned-under edge, lower foot and complete hem with edge stitching. Remove basting and press. The appearance of a machine-finished hem is often improved by working another row of stitching on lower fold. Press stitching with tip of iron to remove wrinkles.

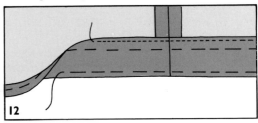

All widths of hem can be held down with an adhesive strip (**13**), but try this method out on a small piece of fabric as it is not always successful on fine materials. It is ideal for trousers, giving a lasting crisp finish. Turn up, baste and press lower fold as usual and trim and finish raw edge. Place hem on sleeve board and slip adhesive strip under hem edge so that it is covered. Insert only about 20 cm/8 in at a time. As the strip tends to break, it may not be possible to use one continuous piece. Butt edges of strips or overlap. Take hold of fabric, not adhesive, and pull gently outward to counteract any slight drawing up. Press hem well until adhesive is melted, using a medium hot iron over a damp cloth and placing it three or four times on each spot. Remove basting and press again lightly.

On denim and canvas use blue hemming web which is extra strong for heavier fabric. Hemming web can also be used to add crispness and to make a firm base that can then be topstitched, a technique that is successful on suede fabric, linen, etc.

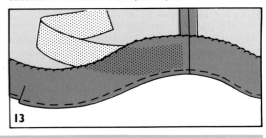

HEMS

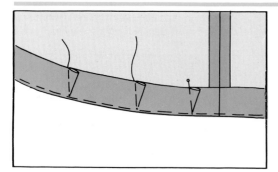

1 **Dealing with fullness** Excess fullness in lightweight or thin fabrics can be made into very small darts. Before trimming and finishing edge, pin darts, all in same direction, exactly where flutes occur, which is often near seams, and baste in place. Do not force them in for the sake of symmetry. Remove basting before final press.

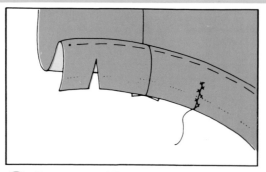

2 To counteract fullness in thick or heavy fabrics, lay hem on table and, where fluting occurs, cut fabric down through hem edge to within 3 mm/$\frac{1}{8}$ in of basting at fold. Clip out a "V" of fabric at this point so that hem lies flat with raw edges close together. Take care not to cut too much. Re-join raw edges with a wide zigzag or herringbone. Trim hem edge on chalk marks and finish.

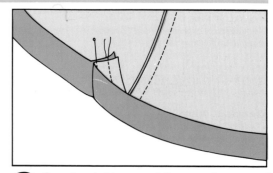

3 On a flared skirt some fullness can be removed at the sides by restitching the seams. Mark the hemline fold, turn up the hem and baste near the fold. Pin the seam so that the hem depth lies flat. Restitch the seam from hem fold to lower edge. Trim off surplus fabric. Clip seam allowances toward stitching level with hem fold. Press seam open. Fold up hem and complete.

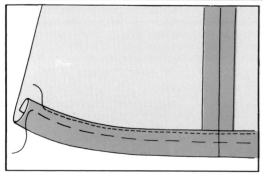

Curved hem If the hemline is very curved, make the hem narrow to minimize fullness. On medium fabrics allow 5 mm/$\frac{1}{4}$ in beyond marked hemline, cut off surplus, finish edge and catch stitch to garment. On fine fabrics cut away surplus 1 cm/$\frac{3}{8}$ in beyond mark, fold hem twice, baste and press. To finish slip hem or machine on WS, using a straight stitch close to top of hem or a zigzag over it.

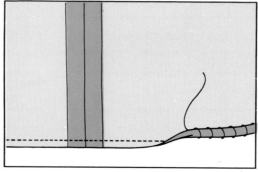

Circular hem As little of a circular hem is on the straight grain it easily stretches and flutes, and should be as narrow as possible. Mark hemline and machine with a straight stitch 5 mm/$\frac{1}{4}$ in below line. Trim surplus, a little at a time, very close to stitching. Lick thumb and forefinger and roll a section of raw edge toward you. Tack down with whipping or slip hemming and proceed to next section.

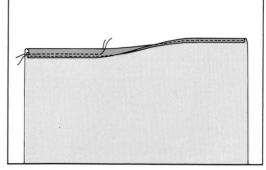

Rolled hem Trim hem allowance to 1.5 cm/$\frac{5}{8}$ in. Fold under 1 cm/$\frac{3}{8}$ in and edge stitch with straight stitch. Trim off surplus close to stitching. Fold hem up again and stitch with straight or small zigzag stitch, pulling fabric slightly to avoid movement on the edge.

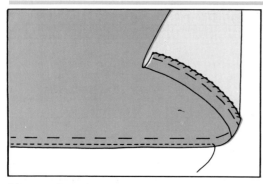

Narrow hem Use where weight is not needed. The trimmed hem depth should be 2 mm to 1.5 cm/$\frac{1}{16}$ to $\frac{5}{8}$ in. On medium or thick fabrics finish raw edge, baste to garment and hold down by catch stitching on WS or by machining along fold on RS, using machine foot as a guide. On fine fabrics turn raw edge under 1 cm/$\frac{3}{8}$ in, baste and press. Slip hem or machine, on WS, along bottom of turned-under edge.

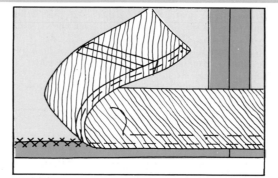

1 **Faced hem** Useful if not enough material to turn up a suitable hem. Trim to within 1 cm/$\frac{3}{8}$ in of marked hemline. Turn up hem, baste and press. Catch stitch or, on medium or thick fabrics, herringbone raw edge down. Remove basting and press up to edge. Cut crosswise strips of lightweight fabric 5 cm/2 in wide. Fold in 5 mm/$\frac{1}{4}$ in, baste and press. Place fold 2 mm/$\frac{1}{16}$ in over hem edge; baste.

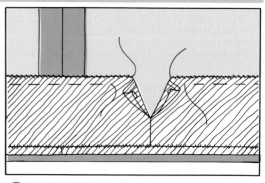

2 Attach centre of strip to garment with diagonal basting. Turn in other raw edge 5 mm/$\frac{1}{4}$ in and baste to garment. Press edges of strip lightly. Slip hem upper edge to garment, turn fabric around and hem lower edge down. Turn in ends and slip stitch together. Remove all basting.

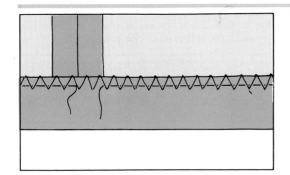

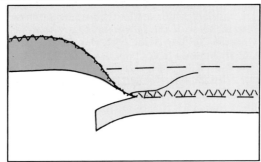

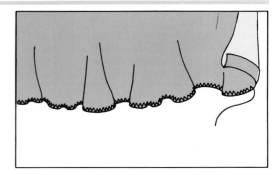

1 Jersey knit hems To make a wide hem, finish raw edge of hem by zigzagging or overcasting over a length of synthetic thread laid near raw edge. Leave ends of thread long enough to grasp. Baste hem to WS of garment, pulling up loose ends of thread to draw edge up and so correct any stretching. Catch stitch edge to garment; cut off loose ends or pull the whole length of thread out.

2 To make a narrow hem, zigzag along chalk line marking depth of hem on RS and trim away surplus close to stitching. Baste hem edge to WS of garment and catch stitch or machine close to edge on RS. Remove basting and press.

3 To achieve a fluted edge on fine knits, trim fabric to leave 5 mm/$\frac{1}{4}$ in beyond hemline mark. Place garment RS up under machine and turn under the 5 mm/$\frac{1}{4}$ in. Set machine to a medium-width stitch—$2\frac{1}{2}$—and medium length. Zigzag over fold, but pull fabric to stretch it as it goes under foot to give a close satin stitch. On WS trim fabric close to stitching. Do not press.

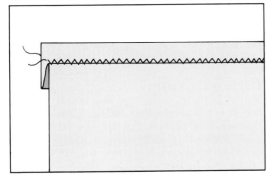

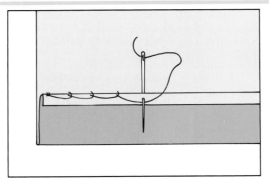

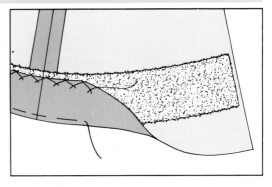

4 On soft or heavy knits turn up, baste and press the hem fold, mark hemline depth and stitch along edge to prevent stretching. Fold hem halfway into position, baste and catch stitch. Complete hem by folding remainder of hem depth into place and stitching.

Extra strong hem Use loopstitch on slippery or fine fabrics where little fabric can be picked up on the needle.

Interfaced hems Add weight or crispness to evening and bridal clothes by inserting medium or heavy interfacing. Cut interfacing 2 cm/$\frac{3}{4}$ in deeper than hem and shaped to fit the hem curve. Insert under hem, press in place if iron-on or attach with catch stitch. Complete hem by attaching it to interfacing.

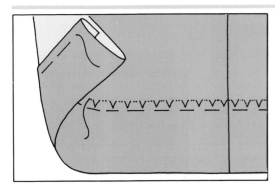

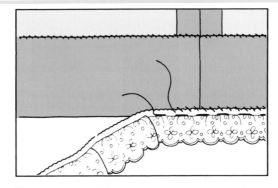

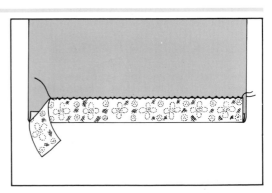

Decorative finish—blind hem stitch Hems on lightweight fabrics for loose linings and lingerie can be finished decoratively by machine. Turn under raw edge of hem, baste and press. Set machine to blind hem stitch, or to an embroidery stitch, place work under machine with RS of garment uppermost and stitch close to turned-under edge with matching or contrasting thread.

Decorative finish—lace Press turned-up hem. Attach narrow lace (stretch lace eliminates wrinkling) or other trimming to WS of hem either by basting and oversewing top edge to fold of hem (thus making the garment a little longer) or position trimming on RS of hem so that bottom edges align. Attach top edge to RS with hemming, feather, herringbone, zigzag or machine embroidery stitch.

Lace hem On light fabrics for lingerie and linings the hem depth can be provided by using stretch lace. Stitch the lace to WS of garment with one edge on the marked hemline, using a small zigzag. Fold lace to RS and baste with lace edge on hemline. Stitch remaining edge of lace to garment.

BINDINGS

Binding is a method of finishing an edge by enclosing it in a strip of fabric. It is easier to work neatly with strips of fabric cut on the bias, as fabric cut like this stretches, making it possible to bind shaped edges.

Binding can be single or double except on bulky fabrics, where single binding should be used. It can be in the same fabric as the edge to which it is to be joined but a different colour, or it can be a contrasting print or texture. A lighter weight fabric can be used to bind a heavier one, but the reverse is more difficult and may entail doing all the sewing by hand to avoid puckering. Often binding can be cut from leftover scraps. If a lot of strips are needed, buy additional fabric.

Single binding can also be bought in several widths, pressed and folded ready to apply, available in plain and printed cotton, mercerized cotton, polyester cotton and viscose/rayon satin.

True cross and bias

As a general term, bias binding denotes all binding cut diagonally to the grain of the fabric. More specifically, it refers to binding cut at an angle of less than 45° to the selvage, as opposed to true cross, which is cut at an angle of 45°. True cross, or crosswise, strips have maximum stretch, the amount varying according to the fabric. If a patterned fabric such as stripe or check or a plain fabric with a distinctive weave is used for binding, the strips must be cut in this way or the pattern will not look right. True cross strips must also be used on very concave edges such as scallops.

Some stretch fabrics, notably knits, should be cut on the bias rather than the true cross as otherwise they have too much stretch and become unmanageable. The resulting edge finish can also be bubbly.

The amount of material available also determines the way in which the binding is cut; if you have plenty, cut non-stretch fabrics on the true cross; if not, cut on the bias.

Both crosswise and bias strips have numerous other uses besides finishing edges. They can be worked into rouleau tubing to form ties and skirt or coat tabs; they can be used to lengthen garments; and they can also be applied decoratively, in strips or as piping.

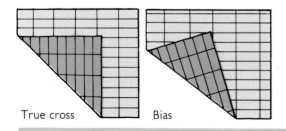

True cross   Bias

Calculating the width

The finished width of the binding depends on the thickness of the fabric. It is easy to apply a narrow binding made with thin fabric, but a narrow binding looks bulky in thick fabric. Aim for a finish of between 3 and 6 mm/$\frac{1}{8}$ and $\frac{1}{4}$ in. To calculate the width, cut a short piece of fabric, pin it to an edge and fold it over to see if the width is correct. Adjust and then measure width needed.

For single binding cut strips twice the finished width, plus a seam allowance on both sides of about 5 mm/$\frac{1}{4}$ in. The strips can be trimmed later if they are too wide, although it is difficult to keep the edges straight.

Single

Double binding should be four times finished width, plus two seam allowances of 5 mm/$\frac{1}{4}$ in. The width cannot be reduced without removing stitches.

Double

Joining cross and bias strips

Join strips of equal width end to end to form a strip about 7.5 to 10 cm/3 to 4 in longer than needed. The ends of the strips and the joins must be on the straight grain of the fabric as otherwise the joins bubble. When cutting bias from odd-shaped scraps that are not on the straight grain, lay all the strips end to end WS up and trim each one on the straight grain (1), pulling out a thread as a guide. Cut off ends with selvages.

1

Press a small seam allowance to WS at end of each strip. Lay strips out end to end and WS up (2). Lift each pair of adjacent pressed seam allowances and place creases together, so the long edges are still running level. Little triangles of fabric will jut out at each side.

2

Joining the strips accurately is difficult and the easiest and most satisfactory method is to backstitch or half backstitch them together by hand, while they lie flat on the table (3). Joins can be machined, but they often end up

slightly off the grain or with the long edges out of line. Also, fastening off by machine can produce hard lumps in the joins.

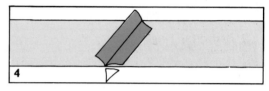

3

Press joins; cut off extending triangles (4).

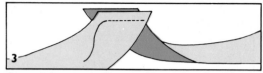

4

Pressing the strips

If the strips are in a very stretchy fabric, remove any excess stretch that might cause bubbling. Pin end of strip WS up onto ironing surface. Pull gently from other end; press pinned end. Move pin along and continue pressing whole length, shaping strip into a curve if it is for a scalloped or curved edge.

Cutting the strips

To cut both crosswise and bias strips, insert a few pins to hold folded fabric in place, leaving the fold free. Flatten the fold against the table and cut carefully along the crease (5) or, to ensure that you keep straight, run the tip of the iron lightly along the fold, unpin, open out and cut, but place the cut edges together again afterward.

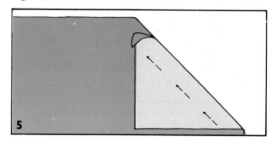

5

Using an adjustable marker, mark and cut a straight line parallel with edges to give a pair of strips. Continue cutting strips of even width, pinning near the cut edges before measuring the next strip (6).

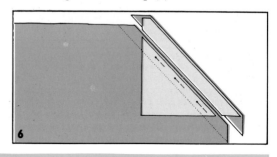

6

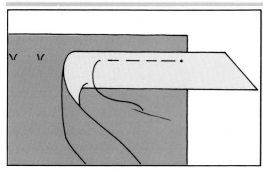

1 **Attaching single binding** Place one edge of binding RS down against RS of edge to be bound, taking 5 mm/¼ in seam allowance on the strip but normal one on the garment. Leave about 2 cm/¾ in of strip extending at the start. Anchor difficult sections by pinning across the strip, but do not pin the entire length as the binding stretches. Baste about 2 cm/¾ in of the fabric at a time, taking small stitches.

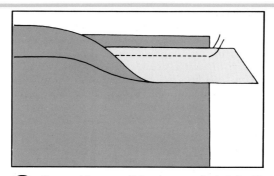

2 Set machine to a slight zigzag and stitch beside basting, strip uppermost. Remove basting and press stitching. On RS push tip of iron up under strip toward stitching and edges and run it along join, lifting strip slightly. Trim raw edges to fractionally less than finished binding width. On a very curved edge, clip seam allowances in toward the machining every 5 mm/¼ in.

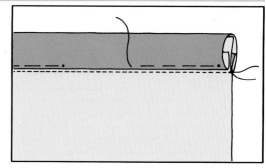

3 With WS of garment toward you, fold over raw edge of binding 5 mm/¼ in and bring fold onto machining. Baste into position in sections of about 6 cm/2¼ in, starting in the centre, followed by the ends, then the sections between. If you baste along from one end, the binding may not lie flat. Run tip of iron lightly along fold by machining.

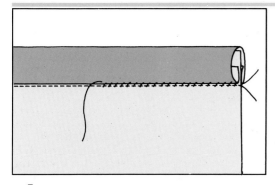

4 Hem into machining, picking up every stitch. Remove basting. Press WS lightly with edge on a towel to avoid compressing the binding. Alternatively, apply binding to WS of garment and fold over to RS so folded edge covers machining. Finish with hand or machine embroidery along fold. If fabric is bulky, bind it with dress net cut on straight grain. Trim edge so that fabric fills net.

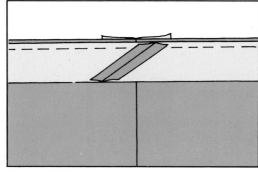

1 **Joins—single binding** On a continuous edge put final join of binding strip in an inconspicuous place, e.g. underarm, back of neck or side seam on hem. Baste strip to garment, leaving 2.5 cm/1 in surplus unstitched at start and 1.25 cm/½ in at end. Fold back the ends on WS on straight grain so folds meet and press. Backstitch along fold, press open and trim ends. Machine binding to garment.

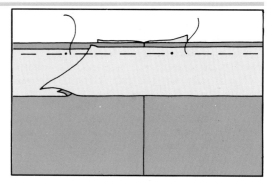

2 An easier method of joining the ends is to fold back the 1.25 cm/½ in on one end of the strip and lay the other end, unfolded, on top, overlapping at least 1 cm/⅜ in. Baste ends to garment along seamline. With binding uppermost, machine beside basting. Remove basting.

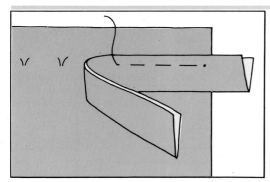

1 **Attaching double binding** Quicker and easier than applying single binding, but the strip must be very carefully cut. Fold strip in half WS together. Press lightly. Baste raw edges of double strip to RS of garment edge, taking normal seam allowance on garment and 5 mm/¼ in on edge of strip and leaving 2.5 cm/1 in surplus unstitched at the start and about 1.25 cm/½ in unstitched at the end.

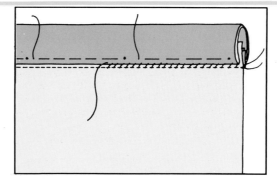

2 Machine beside basting, using a slight zigzag. Remove basting and press as for single binding (**2**). Trim all seam allowances, but not too narrow. Turn work over and, with WS facing you, roll fold of binding over to meet machining. Baste, starting at the centre, then two sections at either end, followed by areas between. Press lightly. Hold down by hemming into machining. Remove basting.

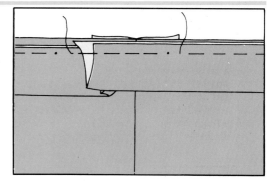

Joins—double binding Can be made on the straight grain as for single binding. This is, however, difficult to do neatly after the strip has been basted in position as the strip has to be completely opened out before joining. It is generally easier to use the overlapping method described in single binding.

BINDINGS

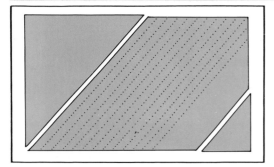

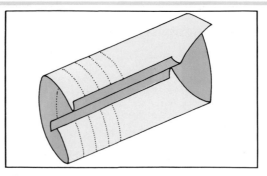

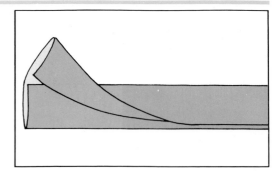

1 Cutting continuous binding A continuous bias strip can be cut from a large rectangle of fabric. Cut off two opposite corners; draw lines 2 cm/¾ in apart on WS between the diagonal edges across the whole piece.

2 Fold fabric with two short crosswise edges RS together, but with one edge extending on the long bias side, so that the other edge lines up with the first chalk line. Baste and stitch along marked seamline to form a tube. Remove basting. Press seam open and trim seam allowances. Start cutting the continuous strip at the extension and cut around, following the marked lines exactly.

1 Applying by machine Cut a strip of binding wide enough for equal seam allowances to be folded in along each side so that edges almost touch. Fold strip again slightly off centre and press. The narrower section is finished binding width. Alternatively, use purchased bias binding. If you intend to use a binding foot, make sure that the width of binding fits the foot.

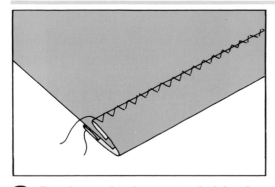

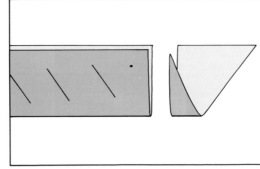

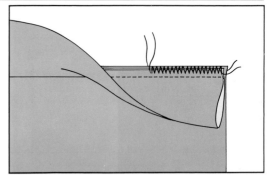

2 Trim the raw edge of garment to a little less than the finished width of the binding. Place binding over the trimmed edge so that the edge is sandwiched between the turned-in edges of the binding. On RS baste through all layers and edge stitch, using a wide stitch such as zigzag or blind hem to ensure that the underneath fold is caught in place on WS. Remove basting. Press binding on WS and RS.

1 Double edge finish A quick and simple way of using binding, especially effective if fabric is knit or is a contrast to main fabric. Can have a finished width of up to 4 cm/1½ in. Cut bias strip twice finished width plus 1 cm/⅜ in, fold with WS together, press to shape and baste down the middle. Cut ends straight.

2 Trim garment seam allowance to 5 mm/¼ in. Place folded binding on RS, matching raw edges. Stitch in place. Zigzag over raw edges. Press binding to extend beyond garment edge. Join garment seam.

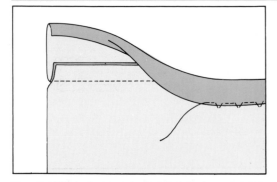

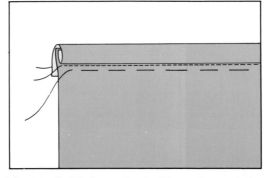

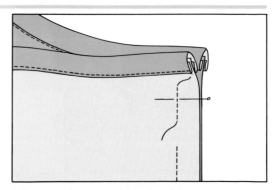

Flat finish Binding can be finished flat on either RS or WS of edge. Stitch strip to fabric, press strip to extend then roll it over the edge. Baste and press close to edge. Baste remaining edge flat and stitch with straight or decorative stitch. Trimming can be inserted under edge before stitching.

Narrow finish A neat finish when applying a light fabric to a medium one. Stitch binding to RS, trim both seam allowances to 2 mm/1/16 in. Roll binding over to WS and baste below the join. Stitch again either on the edge of the binding or in the seamline—the zipper foot may help.

Joining seams Whenever possible leave one seam or part of a seam open. After completing the binding, flat finish or double edge finish, place seam RS together matching bindings. Pin across the binding and make a few machine stitches to hold. Complete the seam from hem upward.

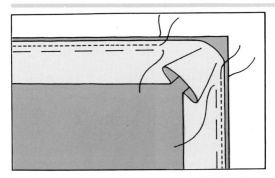

1 Angled corners These are difficult to keep neat. To attach single or double binding to a garment edge with an angled corner, baste a strip of binding to garment, stitching up to within 2 cm/¾ in of corner on either side. Machine to end of basting on each side. Remove basting.

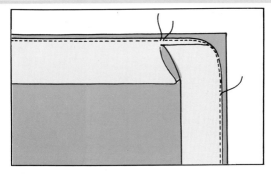

2 Tuck surplus binding in at the corner and press flat. Complete stitching at corner—this is easier by hand than by machine.

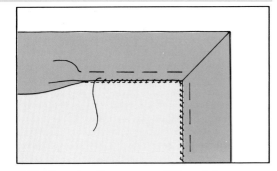

3 Turn binding over to WS and baste up to corner along both sides. Tuck surplus fabric under at corner and press flat. Hem binding into machining. At corners on WS and RS, slip stitch folds of surplus binding together. Remove basting.

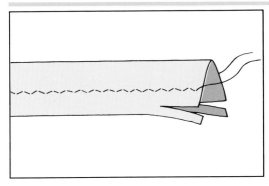

1 Rouleau tubing Bias strips stitched and turned RS out can be used as belt loops, ties, frogs, ball buttons and decoration. Cut and press strips of fabric on the true cross or bias. Fold strip WS out, press lightly if fabric is springy. Stitch along the strip 5–10 mm/¼–⅜ in from fold. The exact distance depends on fabric thickness—practise first. Pull fabric slightly while stitching.

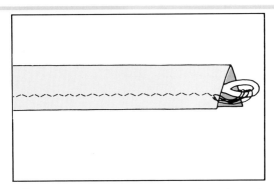

2 Slip a rouleau needle into the tube and sew the eye of the needle to the seam allowances at the end using the thread ends.

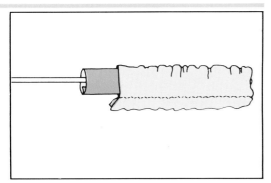

3 Ease the fabric back over the eye of the needle. Work it along section by section, grasp the ball end of the needle and pull it out so that the tubing turns RS out.

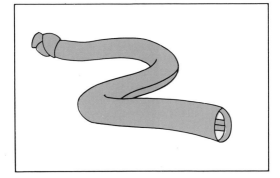

4 Cut the threads at the end and remove the needle. Finish the ends by tying a knot or push in the raw edges with a bodkin. Push far enough to stop ends coming out. The tube can be left open and unstitched or it can be drawn together and a bead attached.

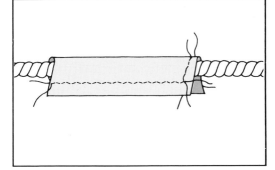

1 Filled tubing Use thin piping cord to fill tubing to make it firmer and more obvious. It requires twice the amount of cord as tubing. Cut and join bias strips. Find the centre of the cord and start wrapping the strip around it WS out. Stitch across end of the bias through the cord, turn and stitch along beside the cord. The zipper or piping foot will help.

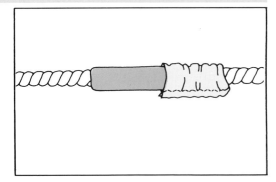

2 Gently pull the cord protruding from the un-stitched end and wrinkle the tubing back over the other half of the cord until the tube is RS out. Trim off surplus cord.

ZIPPERS

It is often advisable to leave buying a zipper until you are ready to insert it in the garment. You will find it easier to decide on the kind of zipper and on its length and position after handling the fabric and fitting the garment. A small or short person may, for example, be able to insert a shorter zipper more in proportion to the total length of the garment than that specified by the pattern; a larger figure may need a longer zipper. You may decide to insert the zipper in a different position from that on the pattern or even dispense with it altogether.

Never insert a zipper at the centre back of trousers or a skirt if it can be placed elsewhere. The back of the figure is hollow, so a zipper always appears to bulge outward. And, on trousers, a zipper prevents the back seam from giving as you move.

Types of zippers
There are three main types of zipper—metal, nylon and concealed.

Metal zippers have nickel alloy teeth attached to a strong, coloured, twill tape. The teeth can be coloured to match the tape or uncoloured.

Nylon zippers consist of two continuous coiled filaments of nylon, which are attached to a coloured, usually lightweight tape. When the zipper is closed, the coils interlock. Do not use this zipper on tight-fitting clothes. Soft and smooth-edged, it can be used on all fine fabrics and knits.

The concealed zipper looks like a seam on the right side. Use on fabrics such as velvet and satin but not on tight-fitting garments.

Choosing the type of zipper
Choose the nearest available colour to the fabric or one a shade darker. With multicoloured materials match the zipper to your thread colour. If a closely toning colour is not available, or if your fabric is ombré, border patterned, striped or checked, insert the zipper by an uneven hems method or use a concealed zipper.

PREPARING AND STITCHING
From preparing the opening before starting to insert a zipper to basting it in and stitching it by hand or machine and finishing off, the same basic processes are common to all types of zippers and apply to all the methods of inserting them given on the following pages.

Permanent stitching
All zippers can be inserted by hand or machine, depending on how confident you are (it is easier by hand); on the position of the zipper; on whether you want to make a feature of the zipper with decorative machining; and on the strength required. Machining is stronger than hand sewing, but no quicker—by the time you have prepared the machine and adjusted the foot you can be halfway down one side by hand.

Direction of stitching
Baste and machine or hand stitch both sides of the zipper in the same direction where possible. Always work toward a raw edge if you have one and away from a finished edge. Stitching from the bottom upward prevents a bulge at the bottom. If it is not possible to work in this direction, avoid the bulge by hand stitching rather than machining.

Tips
1 Make sure the zipper opening is long enough for you to put the garment on easily.
2 If the zipper has been folded, press the tape flat.
3 Always have at least 1.5 cm/$\frac{5}{8}$ in seam allowance on both sides of the zipper opening. If fitting has reduced this, stitch on fabric or tape to make up the width.
4 Make the length of the opening 3 mm/$\frac{1}{8}$ in shorter than the zipper to prevent the end stop showing.
5 With the zipper basted in position, try the garment on to check the fit. Adjust seamline if necessary.
6 Keep all zippers, except concealed, closed while inserting.
7 If the zipper is stiff, run a special wax pencil, beeswax or lead pencil along the teeth.

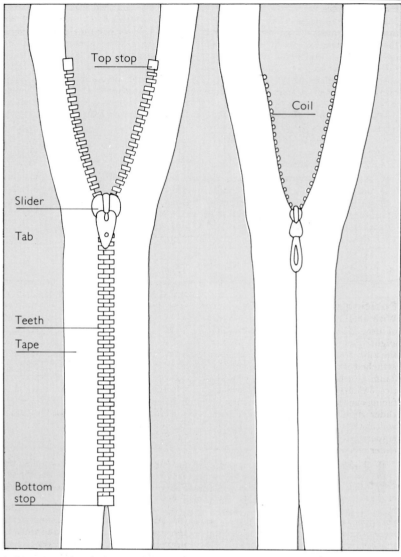

Left, conventional zipper; right, concealed zipper

Basting tape
This narrow adhesive double-sided tape is invaluable as it eliminates basting and keeps the zipper and fabric flat while being stitched. Fix a length of tape to RS of each zipper tape, remove peel-off backing. Place zipper in position on prepared fabric and press in place. Zipper is ready to be stitched. Basting tape is left in position and will not harm fabric.

When to insert
A long zipper is easiest to insert while the fabric is flat, before it is joined into a tube shape, but insert it at this stage only if you are sure that this area of the garment will not require any fitting alterations. Short zippers are easier to insert and often, as in trousers and at wrists, they are left until the main parts of the garment are joined.

Choosing the method of insertion
The method depends on the position of the zipper in the garment, the effect desired and the fabric. Take into consideration the type of edge at the top of a zipper opening and whether the zipper is a good colour match. If you are a beginner, bear these factors in mind, but, even more importantly, choose one of the easier methods.

Preparation

Stitch the seam right up to the zipper opening and press. Finish raw edges for the whole length of the seam and opening. Turn under, baste and carefully press the edges of the opening—the way in which you do this depends on the method of inserting the zipper. Avoid stretching the opening when pressing by pinning the folds of the opening edges to a sleeve board, so that both edges are level (**1**) before you start to press.

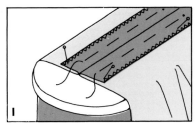

Position of slider

With all zippers and with all methods of inserting them the slider must be set slightly below the seamline at the top of the zipper opening. If a facing is to be attached at the top, the slider should be $2\,mm/\frac{1}{16}$ in below the line on fine fabrics, $5\,mm/\frac{1}{4}$ in on bulky materials. The facing can then roll to WS, bringing the slider right to the top. If a collar or waistband is to be added after the zipper has been inserted, place the slider $2\,mm/\frac{1}{16}$ in below the seamline when positioning the zipper.

Basting

Hold the zipper in position at the slider end and baste it down to the edges of the opening. Do not use pins; they cause the zipper to snake and become uneven, which makes it impossible to insert the needle at the correct angle and quickly enough to ensure that the zipper is fitted into the opening properly.

If you need to anchor the zipper while you check the position of the slider or the length of the opening, place one pin from RS across and under teeth close to where you intend to start basting. With RS up, hold $2\,cm/\frac{3}{4}$ in at a time in position with one hand and, with a small needle, take two basting stitches (**2**).

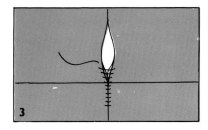

Remove pin and continue basting. Always baste right to both ends of the tape to help anchor the zipper and keep it straight. The tape ends may be trimmed later.

If inserting a zipper where two seams meet, e.g. at a waistline join, oversew the join together firmly from RS before basting in zipper from the bottom of the opening upward (**3**).

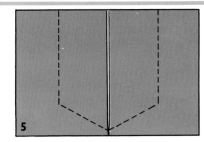

Where to stitch

Do not stitch too close to the teeth; it makes the zipper look bulky and shortens its life. The optimum distance away varies according to the type of zipper and the method of insertion.

Stitching must be parallel with the fabric edge or zipper teeth, particularly if it will show down both sides. A stitching line can be marked with sharp chalk, but learn to judge the distance from the fabric edge. With practice this is the more accurate method as sometimes you can follow the grain of the fabric. With visible zippers work the final row of stitching from RS.

Some zippers have a stitching line woven in the tape, but, as this is on WS of garment, use it only if in difficulty as a guide for basting.

If inserting a zipper with a big slider (**4**), stitch at the usual distance from the teeth nearly to the top and then, to prevent a bulge, stitch outward at an angle, still keeping the line straight, for the final $1\,cm/\frac{3}{8}$ in. Make sure that the angle is the same on both sides of the tape to give a Y-shape at the top.

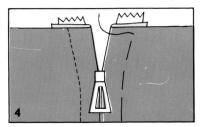

Stitching across the bottom of a zipper causes a bulge, so avoid except for decoration or unless, as with a fly opening, the stitching is far enough away not to cause a bulge. If stitching for decoration, make a "V" (**5**), which will not bulge as much as a horizontal line straight across the bottom; it will also look much better.

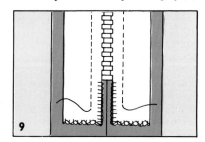

Stitching by hand

This is much easier than machining, as you have more control and it is easier to keep the stitching straight.

Always stitch a bulky fabric by hand. Using a small needle, begin with a knot and backstitch on WS, stitching through tape and seam allowance only

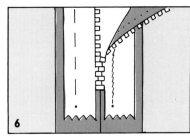

(**6**). Turn work over and bring needle up to RS and work prick stitch, making the stitches as short as possible. Do not pull thread tight. Fasten off firmly on WS.

If the stitching will not show, use a half backstitch instead of prick stitch, but make quite sure that you keep the same tension on both sides of the zipper.

Stitching by machine

Set the machine to a straight stitch slightly larger than that for the rest of the sewing; a small stitch causes puckering. Attach the zipper foot and adjust to correct position. Check that the needle does not hit the foot. Place the work under the foot, RS up, lower the needle and then the foot, and machine very slowly (**7**). If stitching at

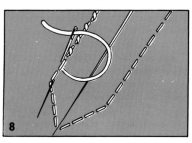

an open end, e.g. at a neckline, do not finish off by reversing but stitch to the end of the tape. At the bottom of the zipper leave long ends of thread to sew in by hand on WS.

Stitching by hand and machine

If hand stitching alone will not be strong enough, add a row of machining on WS along edge of tape through tape and seam allowance only. This will not prevent the hand stitching breaking, but it will avoid a gap if it gives way. To achieve the decorative effect of machine stitching when inserting the zipper by hand, first machine along the prepared edges of the fabric where you intend to stitch in the zipper. Then set the zipper in by hand, working prick stitch but taking the needle over the machine stitches (**8**).

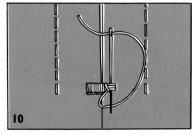

Finishing off

On WS trim tape ends if desired and neatly loop stitch excess tape at the base of the zipper to the seam allowances to prevent the tape rolling up (**9**).

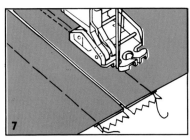

Finish the base of the zipper opening by working a very small bar tack by hand (**10**). If this will be too obvious, for example on a plain pale fabric, work it on WS.

For additional strength on trousers, jeans and other articles of clothing or home furnishings, such as cushions, that will be subjected to hard wear, work a second row of machining on WS through tape and seam allowance only 2 to $3\,mm/\frac{1}{16}$ to $\frac{1}{8}$ in from edge of tape.

ZIPPERS

METHODS OF INSERTION

None of the following methods is difficult if each stage is followed carefully. Stitching by hand is often easier for beginners. Avoid stretching the fabric at all stages. Lightweight or loosely woven fabrics will be easier to handle if a strip of light iron-on interfacing 2.5 cm/1 in wide is first pressed to the WS of each edge. Place one edge of interfacing on the seamline of the garment. The interfacing will also prevent wrinkled stitching. On very fine fabric such as chiffon use a strip of the fabric instead.

To help keep the seam flat make sure that the seam allowance is marked on the garment. Mark with chalk or stitch right across both edges of fabric after the seam is made. Mark the zipper tape in the same way, 5 mm/¼ in above the top stop. Threads are clipped leaving a marker on each side of the zipper and the garment; match up these markers when inserting the zipper.

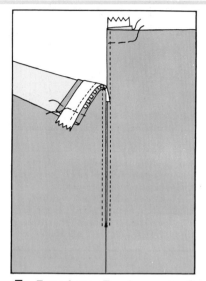

1 Even hems Equal amounts of fabric are left between the stitching and the zipper on either side and the fabric edges meet down the centre of the zipper teeth. There are two easy methods of doing this, but neither is suitable for bulky fabrics. Both methods can be used at side openings, wrists, centre front, underarm, short neck openings and centre back.

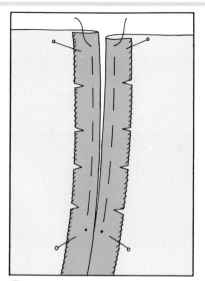

2 For the first method, if the seam is curved, clip the fabric every 5 cm/2 in on finished edges where zipper is to be inserted. Turn in both edges along marked seamlines. Baste and press without stretching seam allowances.

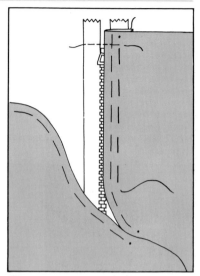

3 With zipper and fabric RS up, place one of pressed folds along centre of closed teeth. Hold zipper in correct position with one hand, so slider is just below seamline at top of opening, and use other hand to baste in centre of zipper tape, about 5 mm/¼ in from fold. Take care not to stretch the fabric—ease it onto the zipper. Baste second side from same end with folds of opening meeting.

4 To prevent fabric being pulled off teeth when stitching, hold folded edges together with big oversewing stitches or catch stitch, both worked in basting thread through edges only. Stitch zipper from RS by hand or by machine. Remove basting. Work a bar tack at base of zipper. Remove oversewing. Press on RS along stitching and on WS with zipper RS down on a towel.

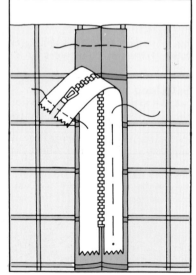

1 Alternative even hems Use where pattern has to be matched or where seam is curved. Stitch seam to base of zipper position. Close up seam where zipper is to go with a large machine stitch or hand basting. Press seam open. With fabric WS up put zipper face down over seam. Centre teeth over seam, position slider correctly. Baste each side of teeth or secure with basting tape.

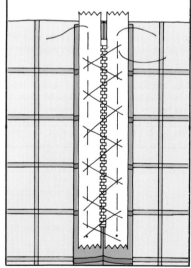

2 To keep zipper in position if inserting by machine, anchor it further by working a row of close herringbone stitch on WS right across zipper; use basting thread.

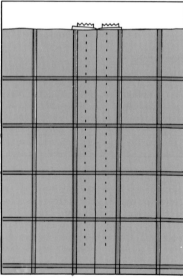

3 Sew zipper in by hand or machine; do not stitch across the bottom. The thicker the fabric the further from the seamline the stitching should be to ensure the teeth remain covered. A large machine stitch looks good on fabrics such as denim, canvas and linen; the bigger the stitch the less of a ridge will be formed. Remove basting (not basting tape). Press stitching with tip of iron.

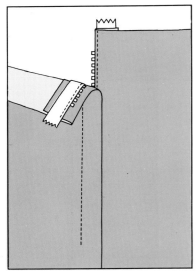

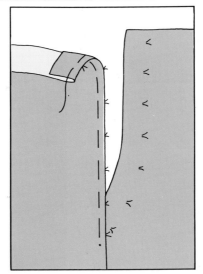

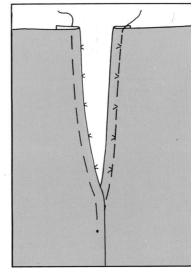

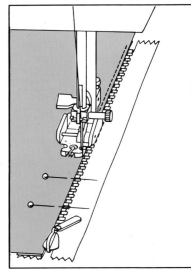

I **Uneven hems** There are two uneven hems methods of inserting a zipper. In both, one edge of the opening is wider than the other and the zipper teeth are completely covered by a fold of fabric, so they are ideal methods if the zipper is not a good colour match. Select uneven hems methods for skirts, front or side trouser openings and long back openings.

2 Cut out fabric, leaving slightly more than $1.5\,\text{cm}/\frac{5}{8}\,\text{in}$ seam allowance on both edges of zipper opening. Decide which side of the opening will be the wider edge. At the front, the wide edge is to the right; at the left side to the front; at the back it is on the right side of the body (or left if left-handed), to make it easier to fasten the neck. Fold under wider seam allowance on seamline; baste; press.

3 On second, or under, side turn under finished edge $3\,\text{mm}/\frac{1}{8}\,\text{in}$ from seamline to make a narrower seam allowance. This ensures that the zipper is well under the top edge and stops it being seen. The narrower seam allowance should extend as far as the bottom of the zipper tape. Baste on seamline and press without stretching. If the seam is curved, clip seam allowances.

4 Starting at the top, with both zipper and garment RS up, place fold of underside against teeth of closed zipper and baste to zipper tape. Stitch by hand or machine close to fold of fabric right to end of tape. Remove basting but not tailor's tacks. Press up to zipper teeth.

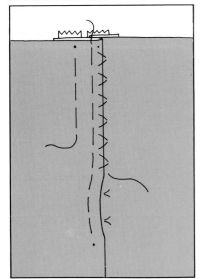

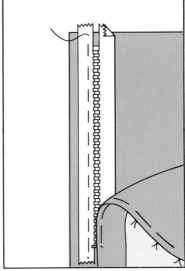

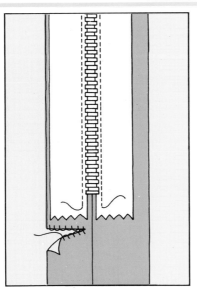

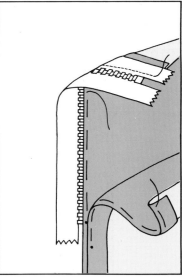

5 Bring wider fold over teeth until it meets original seamline of underside. This ensures that garment fits correctly and that zipper is covered. Starting at the top, catch stitch fold down to underside with basting thread. Baste fold to free side of tape beside teeth and stitch close to basting. Remove basting but not catch stitching. Press stitching on RS; remove catch stitching and tailor's tacks.

6 At base of zipper, clip narrower seam allowance in toward the zipper so that it lies flat. Loop stitch clipped raw edges of turning to finish. Press well on WS.

I **Alternative uneven hems** Use this method for extra strength; it has same top fold as in the first method, but as no stitching shows on the fold underneath, the zipper can be attached to the under fold by machine. Prepare and press wider fold as before. Place closed zipper RS down on RS of second, or under, side, centring teeth on seamline, and baste along one side of tape beside zipper teeth.

2 Machine or backstitch $2\,\text{mm}/\frac{1}{16}\,\text{in}$ from zipper teeth. Remove basting and press stitching. Roll both zipper and seam edge over so zipper is RS up. Baste along narrower seam allowance side of zipper through all layers—garment, seam allowance and zipper tape. Press up to teeth. Complete wide fold as before, clipping and finishing narrower seam allowance on WS so it lies flat.

ZIPPERS

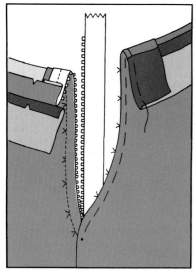

1 **Uneven hems—faced edge**
Baste and stitch narrow seam
allowance to zipper tape as far as
seamline, leaving top of tape free to be
trimmed. Remove basting and press.
Attach facing to neck in the usual way.
Clip seam allowances and trim, with
tape, so that one allowance is smaller
than the other. Fold under wider edge
of both zipper opening and facing on
marked seamline. Baste and press.

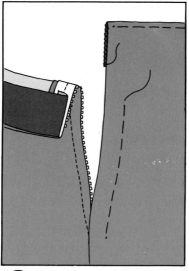

2 Roll facing to WS, baste along
neck edge and press. Slip stitch
edges by zipper together. Lay
wider seam allowance over zipper,
baste and complete. Hold neck edges
together neatly at top with a very small
hook and a worked thread bar.

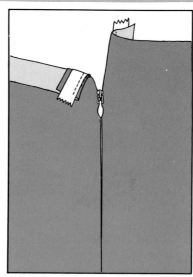

1 **Concealed zipper** The easiest
and quickest of all zippers to
insert. Invisible from RS. Use
when a good colour match is not
available or when any other type of
zipper and method of insertion would
break up the pattern on the fabric. It is
ideal, too, for fabrics that are difficult
to sew.

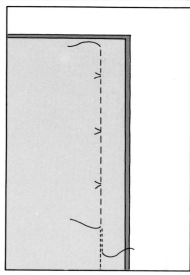

2 Close up zipper section of seam
with a large machine stitch (this
section should be 1 cm/$\frac{3}{8}$ in shorter than the zipper as the bottom part is
difficult to reach). Carefully press open
entire seam length as it will be impossible to press the zipper section
again.

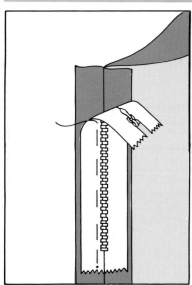

3 Place closed zipper on WS of
seam, centring teeth over join.
Baste both sides through tape
and seam allowance only, not right
through to garment. To do this, slip
your fingers underneath the seam
allowance as you baste.

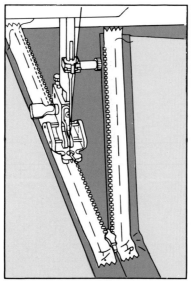

4 Undo original line of large
machine stitches and open zipper
right to its base. Roll teeth over
so they are flat. Open out fabric and
machine or backstitch down each side
of zipper beside teeth, stitching
through tape and seam allowance only
and working from WS. Sew down as far
as the slider, leaving ends of thread
long enough to sew in by hand if
stitching is done by machine.

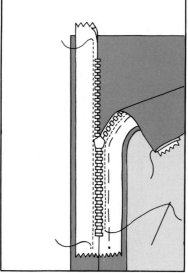

5 Move the slider up a little and
backstitch from previous stitching down to end of tape. Remove
basting. Run slider up and down gently
a couple of times to roll teeth into
position again. If zipper needs pressing,
place it on a folded towel WS down and
press lightly on RS.

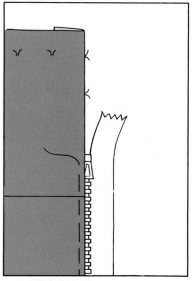

Finishing with a roll collar.
Machine roll collar to neckline, but do
not finish. Turn in edges of zipper
opening and collar and press. Insert
zipper by an even hems method,
placing top of zipper so that it extends
into the collar by less than a quarter the
depth—2 to 3 cm/$\frac{3}{4}$ to 1$\frac{1}{4}$ in. This conceals the slider and holds the collar
upright. Complete collar in the usual
way.

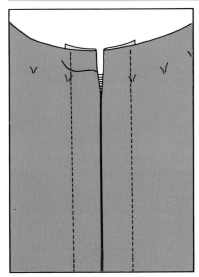

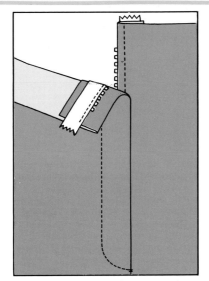

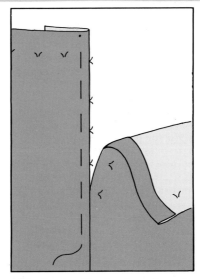

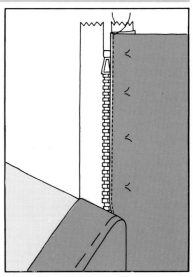

Side seam zipper A short, back neck zipper and an underarm zipper are easier to reach than a long back zipper and avoid a long row of stitching. Before setting in sleeves, insert back neck zipper and underarm zipper, keeping tape 5 mm/$\frac{1}{4}$ in below seamline of armhole. Continue the stitching right up to the armhole edge. Slip stitch folded edges together above zipper to underarm edge.

| **Fly insertion** Use at centre front of trousers, jackets or wherever a concealed but flat zipper insertion is needed, or where a wide edge is part of the design. Extra seam allowances of a total of 3 cm/1$\frac{1}{4}$ in are needed for trousers, but allow a little more for a jacket. Add this on when cutting out or join an extra piece of fabric to wider edge.

2 On the side that is to form the wide covering flap, fold under seam allowances on seamline, baste near fold and press. On second, or under, side turn under finished edge 5 mm/$\frac{1}{4}$ in from seamline to make a narrower seam allowance. Baste into position and press. Clip narrower seam allowance at the base to ensure that the zipper lies flat.

3 With garment and zipper RS up, place narrower fold against zipper teeth and baste to tape. Stitch to end of tape by hand or machine. Remove basting and press stitching. With zipper still closed, bring wider fold over until it meets seamline on fabric on underside of opening. This ensures that the garment fits correctly and that the zipper is completely covered.

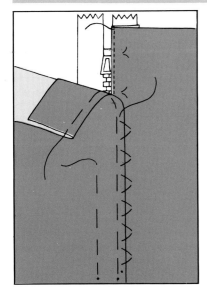

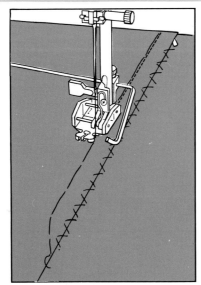

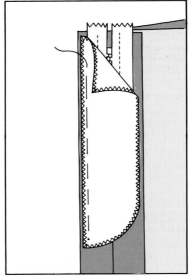

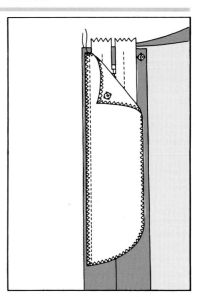

4 Hold down wider fold on seamline of narrower one with large catch stitch in basting thread. Baste fold to zipper close to teeth. To ensure that the distance between stitching and edge is even, use an adjustable marker to mark out, close to basting, an accurate stitching line with sharp chalk, or work another more accurate row of small basting stitches in coloured thread.

5 A further alternative is to attach the edge guide to the back of the foot holder. Stitch the zipper. At the base of the zipper the stitching is usually curved around to meet the seam; make sure the point at which the stitching and seam meet comes below the end of the zipper. Remove basting and press. Work a bar tack at base of zipper. Remove catch stitch.

| **Guards** Add a guard to the back of a zipper to protect sensitive skin or fine underwear. Cut a piece of lightweight fabric to the length of the opening, curved at one side of the base to keep it flat, and finish it all around. Petersham ribbon is less bulky than fabric. On WS, baste one edge of guard level with edge of one seam allowance.

2 Machine near edge through guard and seam allowance. Remove basting. If adding a guard to the back zipper of a dress, finish by sewing a very small snap to the unattached top corner and opposite garment edge. This helps to keep the zipper closed during wear.

Fasteners fall into three main groups: decorative fasteners such as frogs and loops; hooks, snaps and Velcro, which are concealed; and visible functional fasteners such as buttons and buttonholes. However, many fasteners are decorative as well as functional. For example, the positioning of buttonholes and buttons can produce a decorative effect, and special snaps are available which include a button cap to be covered with fabric.

Before choosing the fasteners, consider the requirements and features of the garment. If there is likely to be strain at the fastening point, choose strong fasteners such as hooks or buttons. Snaps are not strong by themselves, but can be used with other fastenings or a single one can be placed at, for example, the neckline of a garment that has buttons as the main fastening. Use frogs on loose garments only as they are not strong and come undone easily.

Positioning

Consider the position of every fastening. Lumpy fastenings at the back of a garment can be uncomfortable, while hooks at the back tend to be rather unmanageable. Use a fastening the wearer can manage, and place it in an accessible position. For example, back fastenings are unsuitable for young children who dress themselves.

In general, on everyday garments choose fasteners that are easy to use. Complicated ones such as loops should be confined to special garments that are not often worn. Many fastened openings must have an overlap, so bear this in mind as some fasteners, such as hooks and eyes, cannot be used in this way.

Buttons and buttonholes are suitable for any fabric provided that the right type of buttonhole is made. Other fastenings should be chosen carefully to suit the fabric and garment. Do not spoil the appearance of the garment by choosing unsuitable fastenings, and avoid mixing different kinds of decorative fasteners on one garment.

BUTTONHOLES

There are four methods of making buttonholes. Always calculate the exact size of buttonhole needed, rather than abiding by the pattern markings. Work buttonholes before attaching buttons.

To calculate the size, measure the diameter of the button and allow for its thickness and for ease—the amount of ease required varies with the thickness of the fabric and the type of buttonhole. After calculating the size, make a trial buttonhole. To ensure a uniform set of buttonholes, use an adjustable marker set to the measurement required.

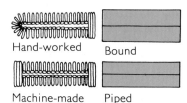

Hand-worked   Bound

Machine-made   Piped

Machine-made buttonholes

Suitable for all fabrics and easy to make. They can fray a little so do not use on special garments or expensive fabrics. Allow 3 mm/$\frac{1}{8}$ in ease on fine fabrics, 5 mm/$\frac{1}{4}$ in on thicker ones. Work them when the rest of the garment is complete.

Piped buttonholes

The easiest method and suitable for all other than fine fabrics. Allow 2 mm/$\frac{1}{16}$ in ease on medium fabrics and 4 mm/$\frac{1}{8}$ in on thicker fabrics. Work first eight stages early on in the garment.

Bound buttonholes

Difficult to work neatly and best restricted to lightweight fabrics. Allow 2 mm/$\frac{1}{16}$ in ease. Work early on, but finish off the backs when the garment is complete.

Hand-worked buttonholes

Should be attempted only by the very experienced who enjoy hand sewing. With correct thread, they are suitable for all fabrics. Allow 2 mm/$\frac{1}{8}$ in ease on fine fabrics, 4 mm/$\frac{1}{8}$ in on heavier ones. Work buttonholes when garment is complete.

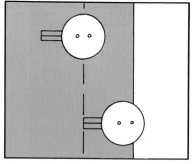

Horizontal buttonholes Place buttonholes horizontally at points of strain such as cuffs and waistbands. The amount of fabric extending beyond button placement line limits the size of button and buttonhole. A button must never be so large that it hangs over garment edge.

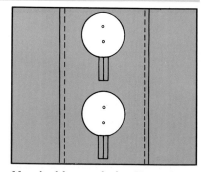

Vertical buttonholes Use on loose-fitting clothes or for decorative purposes, such as on pocket flaps, as the button tends to come undone easily if strained. Suitable also where the style limits buttonhole width, as on a narrow fly opening.

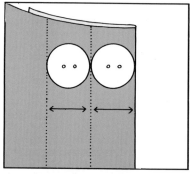

1 **Marking positions** Place button against garment edge and mark position of other side to establish outer end of a horizontal buttonhole, or placement line for a vertical one. Chalk a parallel line the button diameter away to mark inner end.

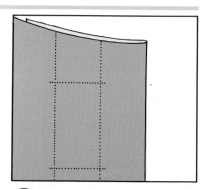

2 Lay the buttons out to decide how many are needed to be effective. Do not place them too near top or bottom where it might be difficult to make buttonholes. Calculate buttonhole length and, using an adjustable marker, mark positions with chalk lines.

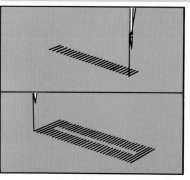

1 **Machine-made buttonholes** Mark position of buttonholes. Attach buttonhole foot and set machine as shown in handbook. Press hemming web between garment and facing to minimize fraying. Work buttonholes as shown in handbook, beginning at inside end.

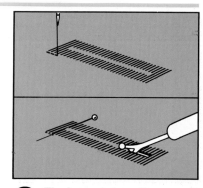

2 The buttonholer will automatically fasten the threads by finishing with three straight stitches. With small sharp scissors or unpicker/seam ripper, slit the buttonhole, but place a pin at end of buttonhole to prevent it cutting too far.

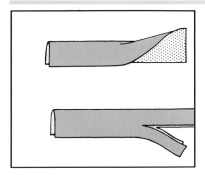

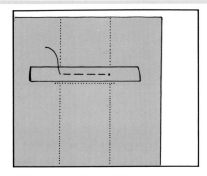

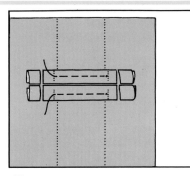

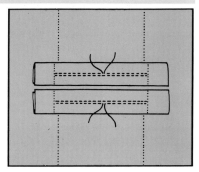

1 **Piped buttonholes** Cut a long strip of fabric 2.5 cm/1 in wide on straight grain, unless a special effect is required. Press paper-backed hemming web to WS of strip. Fold strip WS together and press. Trim width to 4 mm/⅛ in for fine fabrics, 6 mm/¼ in for thick.

2 Cut a strip of piping the required length and place with cut edges against the buttonhole mark on RS of garment, leaving at least 1 cm/⅜ in extending on each side. Baste along centre of piping, stitching through garment and interfacing only, not through facing.

3 Cut a second piece of piping. Place on other side of buttonhole mark with cut edges close to first strip. Baste in position as in (2). Trim piping to 1 cm/⅜ in from buttonhole ends. Re-mark the exact length of the buttonholes by chalking firmly across the piping.

4 Starting in the middle of one piece of piping, machine with a small stitch to chalk mark. Turn and, counting the stitches, machine to other chalk mark. Turn and stitch back to centre. Stitch second piece, counting stitches to ensure equal length. Remove basting and cut off threads.

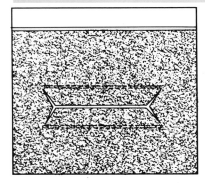

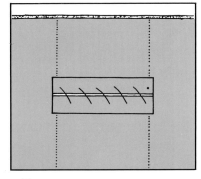

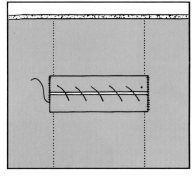

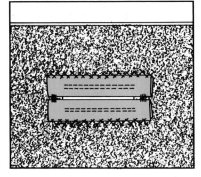

5 On WS of work, clip with small scissors between the parallel rows of stitching. Cut diagonally out to ends of machine stitching through garment and interfacing only. To make sure you do not cut the piping, insert a finger between the piping strips.

6 From RS push piping through slit to WS and also the triangles of garment fabric at ends of buttonhole. Work piping flat with fingertips. Diagonally baste folded edges of piping together. Place work on folded towel and press WS with tip of iron.

7 To finish ends of buttonhole on RS, work stab stitch across each end, taking needle down through fold at ends of buttonhole and up through piping. Press stitching lightly on RS using a cloth.

8 On thick or springy fabrics it may be necessary to hold raw edges of piping down on WS by herringboning them to interfacing. On all fabrics oversew ends of piping beyond the buttonhole opening to hold them together securely.

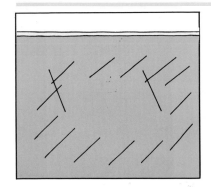

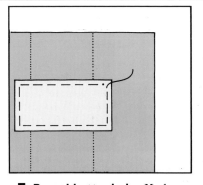

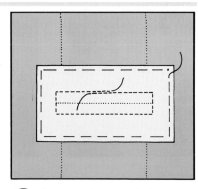

9 When garment is complete a facing will cover the back of the buttonholes. If fabric frays badly, press paper-backed hemming web to WS of facing. Baste around buttonholes on RS of garment and through facing. At each end of buttonhole stab a pin through to facing layer.

10 On WS of garment clip facing between pins. Remove pins and clip into holes left by them. Turn raw edge under with point of needle and hem around making an oval shape. Press buttonhole again on RS and WS and remove basting.

1 **Bound buttonholes** Mark position of buttonholes. Cut rectangles of fabric on the straight grain which are 3 cm/1¼ in wide and at least 3 cm/1¼ in longer than the buttonhole. Place rectangle RS down on RS of garment over position mark. Baste.

2 Re-mark buttonhole length on rectangle. Starting in centre, work a rectangle of stitching around position mark exactly the length of the buttonhole and three or four machine stitches wide. Work the final stitches over the first ones and cut off thread ends. Remove basting; press.

FASTENERS

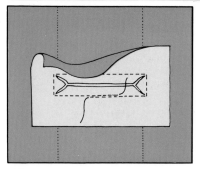

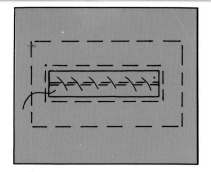

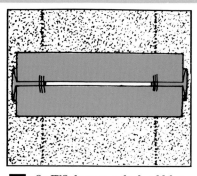

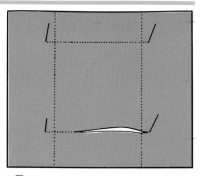

3 Clip centre of buttonhole with small scissors. Cut out to corners of rectangle, clipping right up to the machining. Press sides of rectangle toward centre by running tip of iron around seam on RS between garment and rectangle.

4 Push rectangle through slit. Press join from RS. Roll fabric until two folds of equal width fill the buttonhole opening. Hold the narrow seam edges on each side away from buttonhole and baste rectangle to garment. Press. Baste folds diagonally together at buttonhole centre.

5 On WS the rectangle should form inverted pleats at each end. Hold pleats with bar tacks. Attach sides of rectangle to garment with small pieces of paper-backed hemming web. Press. Complete garment. Finish back of buttonholes as for piped method (**9**) and (**10**).

| **Hand-worked buttonholes** On fraying fabrics it may help to press a strip of paper-backed adhesive or hemming web to underside of work, but this makes the edge stiffer to sew. Insert a pin at each end of mark and cut between pins. Start with an inconspicuously placed buttonhole.

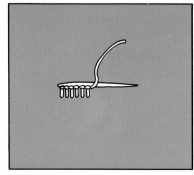

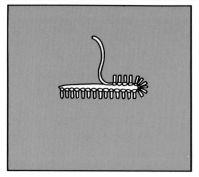

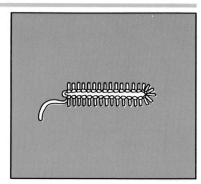

2 Work on RS with a small needle and single thread with knotted end—thick on heavy fabrics, otherwise normal sewing thread. Start between garment and facing, hiding knot slightly away from buttonhole. For vertical buttonholes start either end; for horizontal ones start at inside.

3 Work close buttonhole stitch through garment and facing toward you down first side. Pull thread to settle each knot on raw edges; the knots should touch.

4 At outer end of horizontal buttonhole, nearest garment edge, work five stitches in a semicircle. The five stitches must be shorter than the side stitches and the knots should lie on top of the fabric. This end accommodates the shank of the button.

5 Work down second side in same way as first, as far as inner end. Pass needle through knot of first stitch worked on first side and draw sides together.

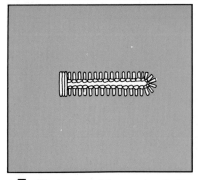

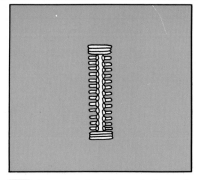

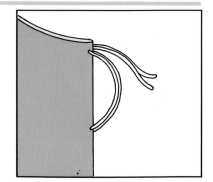

6 Work a bar of short satin stitches across end of buttonhole to depth of both rows of stitching. Pull thread fairly tight. Pass needle to WS and loop stitch over bar to finish. (Do not stitch over bars on RS or you will have a clumsy end just where the buttonhole is always visible.)

7 On a vertical buttonhole work another satin stitch bar at the other end of the buttonhole. On RS oversew both horizontal and vertical buttonholes with basting thread to draw sides together. Press lightly on RS and WS. Remove basting thread.

BUTTONS AND LOOPS

Thread or rouleau tubing loops may be substituted for buttonholes if appropriate for the garment style. Both suit an edge-to-edge opening and tubing can also be used for an overlap.

For a single small fastening, use a thread loop with a button. This can be made on a folded edge, but a seamed edge is desirable for tubing, so that the loops can be sewn into the seam. Tubing is preferable if more than one fastening is needed.

Tubing can also be formed into decorative ball buttons, which are fastened with tubing loops or frogs—intricate loops made with rouleau tubing or cord.

| **Thread loop** Using double thread, work a backstitch on WS and bring needle up in loop position. Allowing for button diameter, insert needle into edge a little below, leaving enough thread extending to pass over button. Work three more equal stitches in the same place.

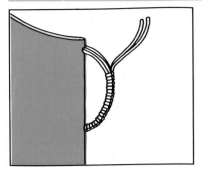

2 Work loop stitches closely over the extending stitches. Fasten off with a backstitch on WS of fabric.

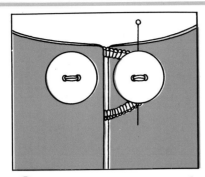

3 Close the opening by pinning the loop in fastened position. Stitch button (see over) to garment at farthest end of loop. If the button and loop are at the centre front, improve the appearance by sewing a second button beside the loop to balance the first one.

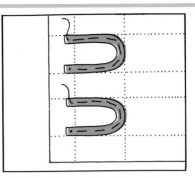

| Rouleau tubing loops For separate loops make a paper diagram as a position guide. Cut paper to length of opening. Mark seamline and loop positions. Cut pieces of tubing to correct length for buttons. Baste loops to paper with ends extending past seamline toward garment edge.

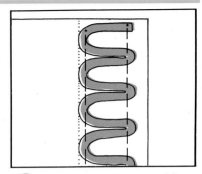

2 For a continuous row of loops, cut paper and mark seamline as before. Mark extent of loops according to button size. Baste tubing to paper in snake-like curves, keeping loops close together. Allow outer edges to project over seamline and clip to ease strain.

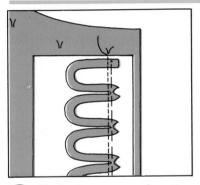

3 For both separate and continuous loops, place paper on RS of garment with seamline on garment seamline and loops extending back into garment. Baste. Machine through loops, paper and garment on seamline. Remove paper and basting.

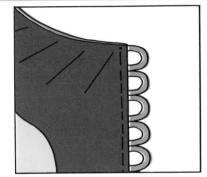

4 Place facing over loops RS down and baste on seamline. Stitch through facing loop ends and garment; work from garment side and follow first machine stitching. Remove basting. Turn facing to WS and baste diagonally in position. The loops now extend from the edge. Press facing.

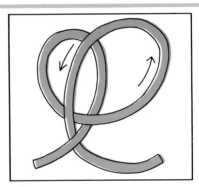

| Ball buttons To form a button, take a piece of tubing and, with one end at the lower left, make a loop and hold it. Make another loop to the right of the first. Pass the long end of second loop over and back under the starting point from left to right.

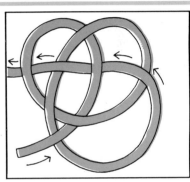

2 Weave the long end over and under across the four strands of the two loops. Pull the long end gently to ease the tubing loops into a ball.

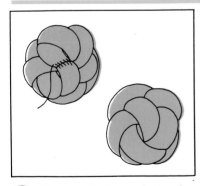

3 Oversew the two ends together. This join now becomes the underside of the button. Use the buttons with loops or frogs.

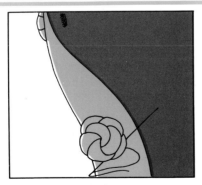

4 To attach ball buttons on fine fabrics, position button on RS of fabric. Working from WS, backstitch over and over through fabric and base of button. Loop stitch over bar of stitches on WS. On thicker fabrics, sew button on from RS, working stab stitch through base of button.

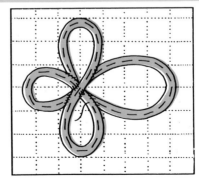

| Frogs On squared paper draw size and shape, making one horizontal loop the correct size for the button. Following the design, baste tubing or cord to paper. Secure frog by oversewing ends and hemming loops to each other at centre.

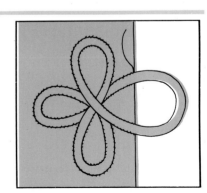

2 Remove frog from paper. Tucking ends out of sight at the back, position frog on RS of garment with button loop extending from edge. Slip stitch in place up to edge of garment. Alternatively, backstitch it to garment from WS, working through fabric into back of frog.

FASTENERS

BUTTONS

Choose buttons to suit the garment. For functional fastenings on casual or work clothes, use plain buttons that blend with the fabric. Decorative buttons will be noticeable, so make sure they harmonize with the garment. They will also draw attention to buttonholes. If your chosen type of button is not available, use buttons covered in the garment fabric.

Spacing is important: use plenty of small buttons close together, but spread large ones out. Before buying buttons check the size recommended on the pattern as the fastening overlap is calculated for that size.

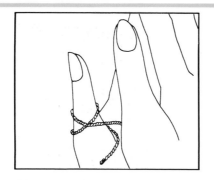

1 **Sewing on buttons** Thread a slightly larger needle than for most hand sewing. Pull thread through until double and knot ends. Run beeswax along thread. Twist a section by rubbing it between your palms. Wind twisted part around thumb and twist next section.

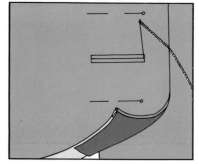

2 To position button in horizontal buttonhole, pin buttonhole over-lap onto button side in position it will be during wear. Insert needle into buttonhole at end nearest garment edge, where button shank will rest, and into fabric below. Remove pins and turn back overlap.

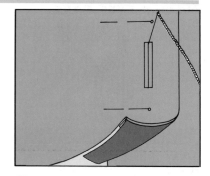

3 The button sits at the top of a vertical buttonhole. To position, pin overlap in place as in (**2**). Insert needle at top of buttonhole opening and pass through to fabric beneath. Remove pins and turn back overlap.

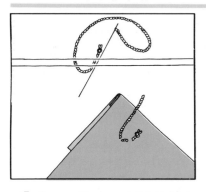

4 Pass needle through fabric, leaving knot on RS. Bring needle up 2 mm/$\frac{1}{16}$ in to left of knot—for vertical buttonhole, turn work sideways. Insert needle again by knot and bring up to the left to make another stitch. Cut off knot. The next stages vary according to type of button.

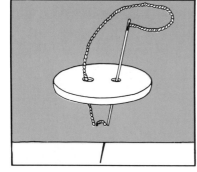

1 **Purely decorative buttons** Slip button onto needle. Pass needle through opposite hole and through to WS. Bring up through first hole and stitch twice more with button flat on fabric. For a four-hole button make two stitches through each pair of holes—more make the centre lumpy.

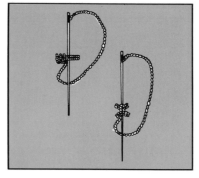

2 Turn work to WS and, for a two-hole button, work loop stitch over the bar of stitches. Fasten off with two stitches through fabric under bar. Cut off thread. For a four-hole button, draw the threads together on WS and work a few loop stitches over them.

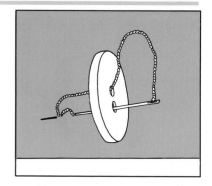

1 **Functional buttons** must be lifted off the fabric by a shank of 2 to 5 mm/$\frac{1}{16}$ to $\frac{1}{4}$ in, depending on thickness of fabric. Slip button onto needle and hold slightly above fabric. Pass needle through to WS and up through second hole of button, making a stitch over starting stitch.

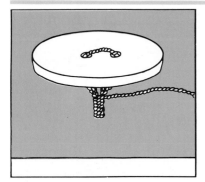

2 Continue stitching until shank is strong enough for fabric and button. Finish shank so needle is between button and fabric. Wind thread around shank from base to button. Pull to tighten and wind back to base of shank. Pull sharply again. Pass needle to WS and work bar tack.

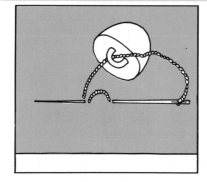

Dome buttons have a metal loop at the back that acts as a shank. Start as in (**4**) and attach by taking a stitch through fabric, then passing needle through loop and so on. Make plenty of stitches until firm. Finish with a bar tack on WS.

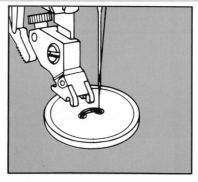

Machine sewing Attach button-sewing foot or remove base of foot. Set stitch length to 0 and zigzag width to fit holes in button or press button-sewing knob. Drop feed teeth. Insert needle in hole, lower foot, and stitch. To make shank, stitch over a matchstick, or attach sewing foot.

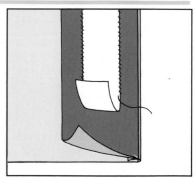

Reinforcing Always sew on buttons through two layers of fabric with inter-facing or other reinforcement between them. If there is no interfacing in the garment, hem a length of tape or straight seam binding to WS of opening before sewing on buttons.

HOOKS, EYES, BARS, SNAPS AND PRESS STUDS

Usually available in black and silver metal, these fasteners come in a range of sizes to suit different types of fabric and garment. The largest sizes are used mainly in soft furnishings. Snaps or press studs are also available in a few colours but the size range for these is limited. Although they are not very strong, and are unsuitable for clothes that will undergo heavy wear, transparent plastic snaps are useful on some garments as they are virtually invisible.

Attach fasteners to double fabric or to one layer of fabric and one of interfacing. Work with single synthetic thread that matches the fabric or with black thread to coordinate with black hooks and snaps.

Hooks and bars are strong and give a firm fastening for openings such as waistbands. In some openings, where the bar would be too noticeable, the hook can be used with a hand-worked thread bar. Hooks and eyes provide a slightly movable fastening but they are easier to use.

On overlapping openings, use hooks and bars—an eye would be visible. The hook is placed slightly back from the edge of the garment on the wrong side of the upper part of the overlap. The bar is positioned on the right side of the other edge, or underside, so that it is just under the edge of the upper layer when fastened.

Hooks and eyes are best where they will be invisible as, for example, on the inside of the garment or where there is a flap to cover them. Edges which are to meet, as at the back of a collar, can be brought loosely together with a hook and eye.

Snaps or press studs are generally suited to overlapping openings. On an opening where the two edges meet, snaps can be attached if the second half, the well section, is sewn to the edge through one hole only and thus extends from the edge. Tape with snaps already attached is available. It is stitched into position by machine and can save time if several snaps are needed.

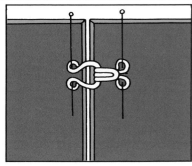

1 **Hooks and eyes** Fasten hook into eye and position on WS of garment. The hook is set back from one edge and the eye should project from the other edge. Insert a pin through loops of hook and one through loops of eye. Unfasten hook.

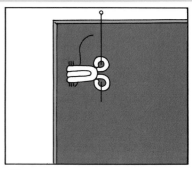

2 Work a backstitch beside end of hook. Pass thread under head of hook and take a stitch through the fabric, passing needle under hook. Work at least six stitches across the hook in this way to hold it down. Be careful not to go through to RS of garment.

3 Pass needle through fabric, again taking care not to go through to RS, and bring through beside one loop of the hook. Remove pin. Work close buttonhole stitch toward you around the first loop. Continue around the second loop. Fasten off with a backstitch beside hook.

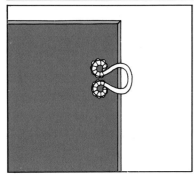

4 Fasten hook into eye and check position of eye on garment. Adjust until correct. Unfasten hook. Start with a backstitch and bring needle up beside one loop. Work close buttonhole stitch around each loop, removing pin after starting stitching. Fasten off with a backstitch.

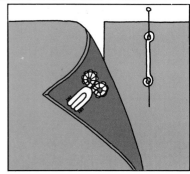

1 **Bars** If garment edges overlap, use bars rather than eyes. Attach hook, as before, slightly back from edge on WS of overlap. Pin opening together. Pin bar in position on RS of underside of opening. Fasten hook and bar to check opening closes properly. Unfasten hook.

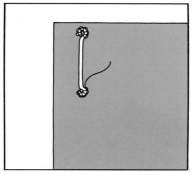

2 Work a backstitch on WS of garment beneath bar. Bring up thread beside bar. Remove pin and work close buttonhole stitch around first loop of bar. Take needle underneath fabric, bring up at second loop and stitch as first. Fasten off with a backstitch.

3 Make a thread bar if the metal bar is liable to be conspicuous. Close and pin opening after attaching hook. Insert needle in bar position and work a bar of four stitches the length of the hook head. Work close loop stitch over threads. Fasten off thread on WS with a backstitch.

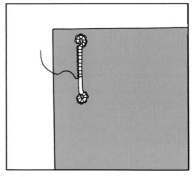

4 If a metal bar is required to give strength but is too obvious on the fabric, work loop stitch across central part of bar when it is attached. Use thread that matches the fabric, thus camouflaging the bar.

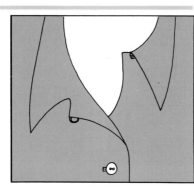

5 For a neck fastening that can be adapted to form a lapel, use a hook and thread bar. Sew a tiny hook under the collar and make a thread loop on top corner of other side of opening. Attach a top button to upper layer of opening to give an even appearance when neck is fastened.

FASTENERS

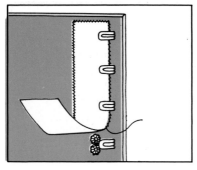

6 If using a row of hooks that may appear unsightly, cover ends of hooks with a piece of coloured seam tape to match fabric. Hem all around tape.

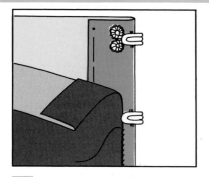

7 On a faced edge hooks can be inserted into a seam. Turn in garment edge and baste. Sew hooks, with heads extending, to WS of edge. Turn in edge of facing and attach by hemming to WS of garment over hooks.

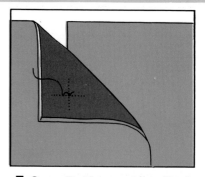

I **Snaps** Decide on position of knob section on WS of top layer of opening overlap and mark position with chalk. Knot end of thread and take a stitch at the snap position. Be careful not to take needle through to RS.

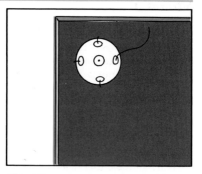

2 Place snap over knot and anchor with one oversewing stitch worked through each hole.

3 Work close buttonhole stitch in each hole of snap, settling knots on fabric at edge of snap. Take three to five stitches in each hole, depending on size of snap. Pin up garment opening.

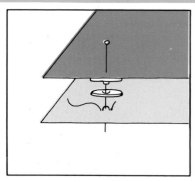

4 Insert a pin from RS of garment through centre hole of snap. Slip the under, or well, section onto pin and insert pin into under layer of opening, to position the well. Start with a backstitch and work an oversewing stitch through each hole of well. Proceed as in (**3**).

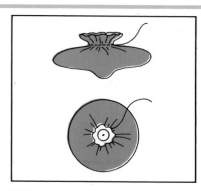

5 Snaps can be covered with lining fabric to match the garment. Cut two circles of woven lining to size. Work a row of gathering around edges. Place circles over both halves of snap, draw up gathering at back and fasten off. Trim surplus. Attach as for ordinary snaps.

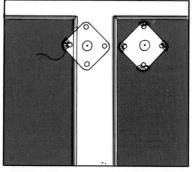

6 Snaps can be used to fasten edges that meet rather than overlap. Attach first half of snap in usual way. Sew well, or second half, to other edge attaching it by only one hole. Leave remainder of snap extending from garment edge.

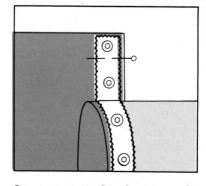

Snaps on tape Cut the tape to the length required and anchor in place with a few pins or basting tape. Turn under each end and attach with hemming or a small zigzag stitch or a straight stitch using the piping or zipper foot.

DECORATIVE SNAPS AND STUDS

Various kinds of decorative snaps are available. Button-snaps, in several sizes, consist of button caps that you cover with fabric, a backing plate to cover the raw edges of the fabric and a standard press fastener that fits the socket in the backing plate.

Popper snaps with fancy metal tops or coloured pearl tops can be used on shirts, jackets, bags, and for detachable items such as hoods. A simple tool for fixing is included in the pack.

Buttons and studs for jeans can be bought. The studs are decorative but can be used at pocket corners for strength.

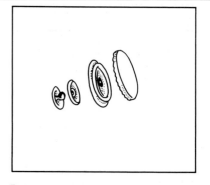

Button-snaps Attach upper snap (knob) to underside of outer layer of opening with one or two straight stitches across the four holes. Fit backing plate over it on outside of garment. Align slots in plate with those in snap. Stab needle back and forth until both are attached. Snap button onto plate.

Jeans buttons Pierce a hole in the fabric using a stiletto or awl. Oversew or loopstitch around the hole. If this is a replacement button strengthen the fabric with interfacing first. Pass shank of button through the hole and fit cap on the end.

VELCRO

Velcro is a very versatile fastener that can be used in many places to augment or replace other fastenings. It also provides instant adjustment to size which makes it useful for children's wear and maternity clothes, in positions such as waists. It is invaluable as a fastener for the disabled and those with manipulative problems.

Velcro consists of a nylon tape in two parts, one covered with tiny hooks, the other with soft loops. When the two parts are pressed together, the hooks engage in the loops; they can be undone by lifting and peeling one part from the other. Various widths are available in strip form: 20 mm/$\frac{3}{4}$ in, for most dressmaking applications, in many colours; 15 mm/$\frac{5}{8}$ in, for use where there is little strain and for furnishing items, in several colours; and 30 mm/$1\frac{1}{4}$ in, for heavy duty use on bags and some waistbands. Another form has adhesive on the back of the hook side for attaching to pelmet/valance boards, furniture etc. The loop side is sewn as usual to fabric. Velcro is also available as 20 mm/$\frac{3}{4}$ in discs. These have a small amount of adhesive on the back which bastes them to the fabric while being stitched.

Keep Velcro fastened when not in use and while articles are being laundered so the hook section does not catch on other things. When attaching it to clothes, place the hook part so that it is not in contact with the skin during wear, to avoid irritation. It can be used to fasten waistbands, cuffs, necklines, straps, bags, belts, and for detachable items like hoods, bibs, collars and appliqué motifs.

Mushroom fastener

This is similar to Velcro in appearance, with one tape covered in soft loops, but the other tape has nylon mushroom-like shapes instead of hooks. The mushrooms engage in the loops to fasten. It can be used on furnishing items but will not stand up to constant use on clothes.

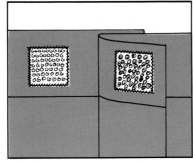

Hook and loop fastener The hooks of the upper layer catch in the closely packed loops of fibre to form a firm bond. Lift one corner or edge to peel them apart; the hooks will open to disengage and then spring back to shape. Stitch by machine to under layer but by hand to outer layer.

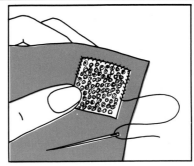

Attaching by hand Hold each piece in place—it is difficult to pin—and hem around outer edge. Begin and end away from corners which is where the strain of opening occurs. Use a small needle and polyester thread; tuck the knot under the edge. Use small close stitches and fasten off firmly.

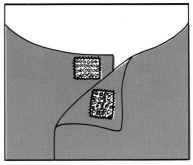

Attaching by machine Put Velcro in position, lower the machine needle into the edge, adjust position of Velcro, lower the foot and stitch. Use a small zigzag or blind hem stitch worked over the edge to hold it flat.

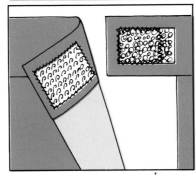

Overlap opening Cut the strip to the length required; allow at least 4 cm/$1\frac{1}{2}$ in on a waistband, 1.5 cm/$\frac{5}{8}$ in on a cuff. Separate the two parts and trim 2 mm/$\frac{1}{16}$ in from the hook section to make sure it will be covered by loop section when fastened to avoid catching. Attach each part.

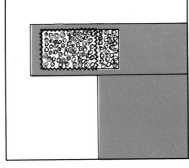

Long overlap If the opening overlaps by more than 5 cm/2 in, stitch the loop side of the fastener to the outer part of the overlap but cut the hook part into small pieces about 2.5 cm/1 in long. Space out the pieces on the under layer and stitch in position.

Waist openings To avoid Velcro creaking at waist fastenings, stitch across the under section 5 mm/$\frac{1}{4}$ in from the end.

Edge-to-edge opening Cut strip to required length, separate the two parts and trim hook section so no hooks are exposed when fastened. On WS place one part level with one edge and hem or work small zigzag all around. Sew second part to WS of other edge so it extends beyond the edge.

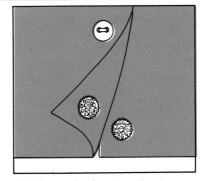

Circles under buttons Sew buttons on the outside of the garment. Sew Velcro circles between the garment layers. Stitch the loop side to the outer layer, hemming around the edge, and the hook side on the under layer. Use on all types of openings including cuffs, and at neckline in place of a snap.

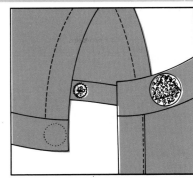

Detachable items Use as many Velcro circles as are necessary to keep the detachable part in place: one is sufficient on a bow; five are needed to fix a hood to a collar. Stitch the hook side to the detachable part. Hook side can be attached by machine, stitching in a triangle across the circle.

SUEDE, LEATHER AND FUR

Real suede, leather and fur comes in odd shapes that may have to be adapted to meet your requirements; the synthetic versions are manufactured in standard widths, usually between 145 and 160 cm/58 and 64 in, and have straight edges.

Marking and cutting
Spread pattern out on WS of real or synthetic suede, leather or fur, placing all pieces in one direction so the pile is facing the same way. Anchor the pattern and mark around each piece using tailor's chalk, wax chalk, fabric marking pen or even a sliver of white soap. Avoid pins. Remove the pattern. Cut each piece singly, reversing the pattern to cut the second piece. Use cutting-out shears for soft suede, suede fabric, thin leather and fake fur. Allow wider seam allowances for thick fake fur. Cut real fur with knife or cutting tool. No seam allowances are needed for real fur but pattern must be pre-fitted. On suede and leather, mark seam allowances, balance marks etc. by clipping the edge of the skin.

Patterns
For suede fabric and fake fur use pattern layout, but real skins are small and uneven so select patterns composed of small pieces. Edges of skins are often thin so avoid them.

Adhesive
Hems in leather and suede may be held in place with pliable adhesive. Use sparingly, and try out on scrap piece to make sure it does not show on RS. If hem does not lie flat, hammer it before it sets. Use basting tape to hold down hems, seams and facings in leather, suede and suede fabric to be topstitched.

Needles
Use leather needles for machine stitching real suede and fur. Spear-pointed hand sewing needles should be used for sewing on buttons and for stitching two layers of real suede. Use a ball-

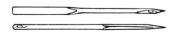

point machine needle for stitching fake fur and suede fabric which is jersey backed. Use a large machine stitch on all fabrics.

Thread
Use a thick, strong polyester or core-spun thread for machining, and beeswaxed thread for all hand sewing.

Interfacing
Use soft or medium iron-on non-woven interfacing on suede, suede fabric and fur fabric, testing it first on lightweight fabrics. Use heavy sew-in interfacing or canvas on real fur. Reinforce edges for zippers and buttons with linen tape or perforated interfacing band. Real fur can be backed with muslin, cheesecloth or domette.

Seams and hems
Use open seams on real and fake fur. Use taped open seams, piped, or welt seams on suede, leather and suede fabric; overlapped and right-side seams also look good. Use adhesive or topstitched hems on suede fabric. Hand sew fake fur hems and face hems of real fur. Stitch suede and suede fabric as for pile fabrics using dual feed or roller foot if possible.

Fastenings
Choose fastenings to suit weight and style, for example large wire hooks and eyes on real and fake fur. Suede, leather and suede fabric can be fastened with snaps, frogs, buttons and elastic or braid loops, Velcro, buttons and buttonholes. Make piped buttonholes; use ordinary fabric or suede to make them on real and fake fur. Use buttons with a metal shank if possible, backed with a small button. Zippers should be heavyweight with topstitching beside the teeth, or use concealed zippers.

Pressing
Press suede and leather on WS only with a warm dry iron over brown paper. Press suede fabric and fur fabric on WS with steam iron or dry iron and damp muslin. Do not press real fur.

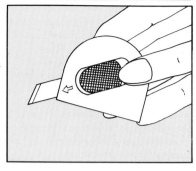

Trimming (Stanley) knife or razor blade Use to cut real fur. Place fur WS up and slice carefully through the skin only.

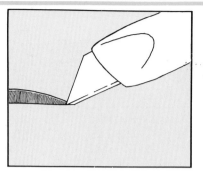

Small pointed blade in holder Push blade forward and hold while cutting. When released it springs back into the holder for safety. Use to cut leather and suede, the skin side of real fur and the backing of fake fur.

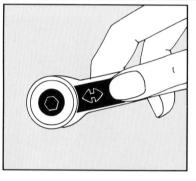

Fine, smooth, circular blade attached to a handle Safety lock prevents misuse. Easy to cut around curves with this blade. Cut suede and leather, placing it on a board or bench and pressing hard with wheel.

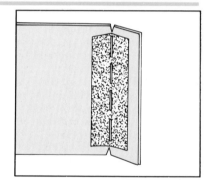

Reinforce fastening edges and hems of suede and suede fabric with iron-on interfacing band. Align the perforations with the fold line or seamline. Alternatively use linen tape, placing one edge on the fold line and attaching it with fabric adhesive.

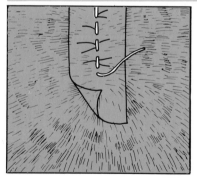

Cellophane If machining is necessary on RS of fur or fur fabric, place cellophane between fur and machine foot to prevent the pile being caught up.

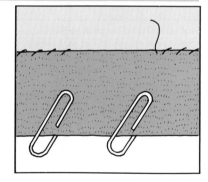

Transparent adhesive tape, clothes pegs/pins and paper clips Use these aids instead of pins and basting on real and synthetic suede and leather and on real fur to avoid making holes that will show in the skins.

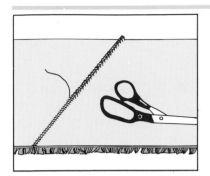

Fur seam Hold edges together, over-sew on WS using waxed thread and spear point needle. Pull thread tight and work back over stitches a second time for extra strength and to fasten off. On WS beat seam with scissor handles to flatten the oversewing. On RS tease out fur with a pin.

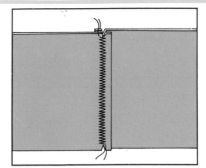

Overlap seam Have a seam allowance of 5 mm/¼ in only where this seam is to be used. Clip edges of suede to mark seam allowance. With RS up, lap one piece over the other, match up the clips and stitch. A single line or two lines of straight stitching can be used or a row of decorative stitching.

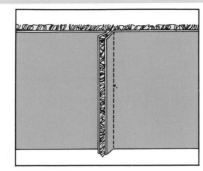

Right-side seam Decorative ridged seam for sheepskin, fur-backed suede and fur-backed fabric. After stitching trim seam allowances carefully and evenly.

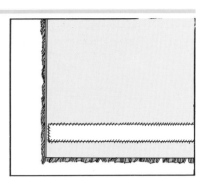

Fur or fake fur hem Allow 1 cm/⅜ in hem, more if fabric is bulky. On real fur, hem linen or twill tape to WS with lower edge on hemline.

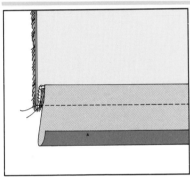

2 Cut bias strips of lining or cotton fabric 5 cm/2 in or more wide. Fold in and press one long edge. Place right side down on fur and stitch on hemline or beside edge of tape.

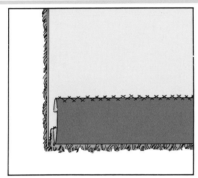

3 Fold all seam allowances up into garment and secure with herring-bone stitch. Fold bias strip to WS of garment, baste in position and stitch remaining edge to garment.

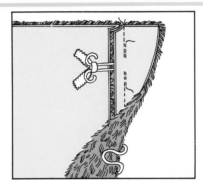

Fur hook Leave a small gap in the seam stitching at the edge of the garment. From WS push hook through gap and knot a short piece of stay tape over the loops. Secure by hemming the ends of tape to the back of the garment.

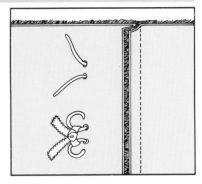

Eye Straighten the ends of the eye by forcing closed scissor points into them. Make holes in the fur backing using a stiletto or awl, push ends of eye through from RS. Re-shape the ends. Tie a piece of stay tape through the loops and hem in place.

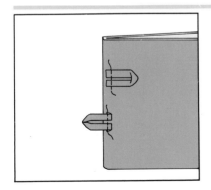

Braid loops Use with toggle buttons on fur, fake fur, suede and leather. Fold pieces of twill tape or firm braid and place face down on the finished edge of the garment on RS. Stitch across loop ends. Fold loops to extend beyond garment edge and stitch again.

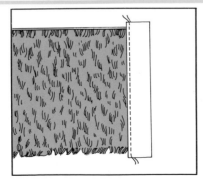

Open-ended zipper in real and fake fur Cut lengths of 2 cm/¾ in grosgrain ribbon 3 cm/1¼ in longer than fur edges. Place ribbon on RS with the edge on the seamline and stitch close to the edge with straight or zigzag stitch. Trim off surplus fur underneath.

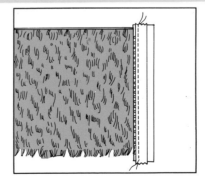

2 Separate the zipper and place each half face down on the ribbon. Align the edge of the teeth with stitched edge of ribbon. Stitch beside teeth through zipper tape and ribbon.

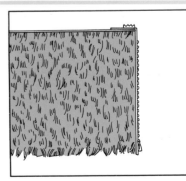

3 Fold ribbon and zipper to WS. Allow zipper teeth to extend beyond edge. Hold in place by hemming along remaining edge of ribbon.

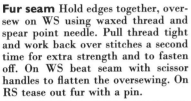

73

2

PERFECT
DRESSMAKING

How to make clothes to *haute couture* standard: how to adjust patterns, use interfacing, apply functional and decorative shaping, add facings, make many types of waists, sleeve openings, yokes, pleats, collars, pockets and belts; and how to set in sleeves, line clothes, and make alterations

PATTERNS

Each pattern company designs from its own set of basic pattern shapes, or blocks, so you may well find that certain makes are better suited to your figure than others.

Some patterns contain several sizes and are referred to as multi-size. This is an advantage as sizes can be mixed to accommodate individual figure needs.

Ease for movement in the garment is allowed for when the pattern is produced but the amount allowed varies with different makes of pattern. Some garments require more ease than others; a blouse, for example, has more ease allowed than a fitted dress, and a coat more than a jacket. Some patterns have the instruction "use knit fabrics only", which indicates that very little ease has been added as the fabric itself should stretch to allow room for movement and shaping. More ease is allowed on large-size patterns.

Seam allowances of 1.5 cm/⅝ in are usually included but some patterns are the exact garment size so allowances must be added.

When choosing a pattern select the size which most closely resembles the measurements of the wearer of the garment although it is unlikely to be a perfect fit. As a general rule, choose patterns for tops and full-length clothes by the bust or chest size, and for skirts and trousers by the hip size.

However, there may be exceptions to this. A short, small-boned person with a large bust will have fewer alterations to make if a small pattern to suit the rest of the figure is used and the bust shaping enlarged. A tall person with a large bony frame may use a large pattern, reducing it at small features such as bust or hips. Buy the size that fits in the most places.

If dealing with a particular figure problem other than length, choose a pattern with a seam, dart or gathers at that point so that it can be adjusted easily. Inexperienced dressmakers will have more success with loose styles which do not need detailed fitting.

MEASURING

Before buying a pattern, take a few important body measurements to use as a guide when choosing pattern size. A chart of the measurements for each size is usually found at the back of pattern catalogues and on the pattern envelope.

Measure the bust or, on men and children, the chest firmly around the fullest part of the figure, taking the tape measure under the arms, and measure the waist firmly around the natural waistline. Take the hip measurement around the pelvic bone.

A back neck-to-waist measurement is often indicated on the chart but as this is easy to adjust it need not be considered when buying the pattern unless you are very short-waisted and there is a special pattern.

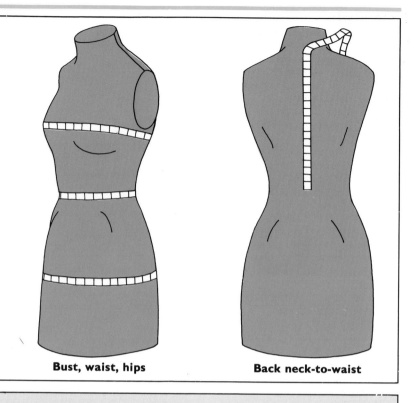

Bust, waist, hips   **Back neck-to-waist**

UNDERSTANDING PATTERN MARKINGS

Pattern markings enable the manufacturer to convey information about the construction of a garment to the dressmaker. Some vary from manufacturer to manufacturer. Most markings should be transferred to the fabric before the pattern is removed and used as a guide when making up the garment.

A Lengthening/shortening line
B Grain line—also indicates nap or one-way fabric
C Fold line
D Centre front line
E Waistline
F Stitching line
G Seam allowances—not included in all patterns
H Sleeve inset point
I Button and buttonhole positions
J Topstitching line
K Centre front fold
L Balance marks or notches—useful on curved seams
M Zipper position
N Cutting lines on two-size pattern
O Alternative cutting line for shorter version

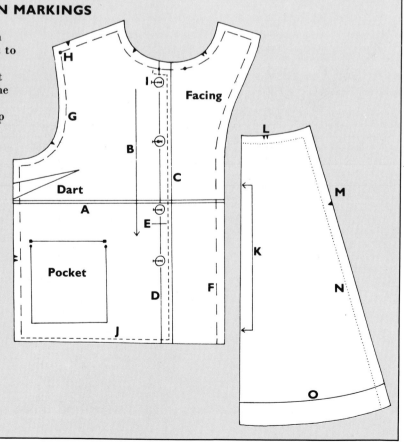

CHECKING

Before cutting out, check all the measurements on the pattern even if the basic measurements of bust or chest, waist and hip suggest it will fit. As the pattern is chosen by its width measurements these should be virtually correct. It is difficult to measure widths on the pattern because no indication is given of the amount of ease allowed. If, however, the pattern is not wide enough at any point, add extra fabric when cutting out.

The important feature to check on the pattern before cutting out in fabric is the length of each pattern piece, as this makes a great difference to the fit of the garment. Compare the length of each body area with the length of the pattern and adjust accordingly to ensure that the balance of each piece is correct. You can solve any remaining problems when the garment is being fitted.

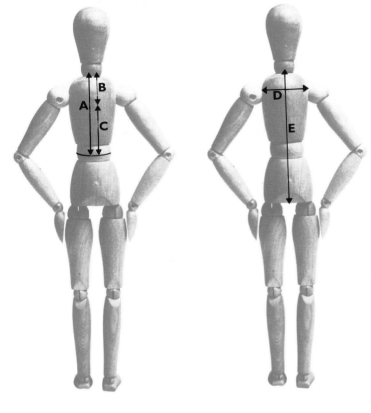

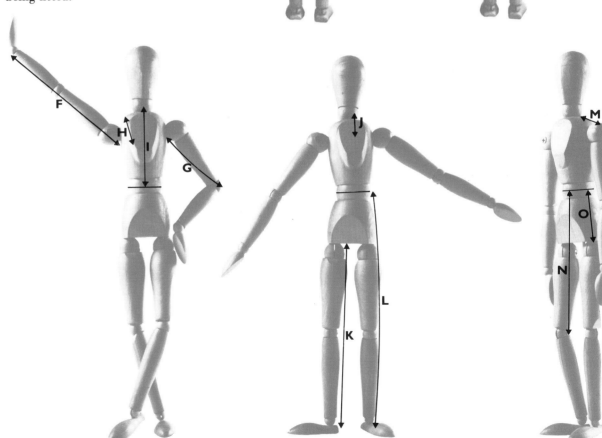

A Back neck to waist Establish waist level by tying a tape around waist or wearing a narrow belt. Measure from top spinal bone to natural waist. Add 5 mm/$\frac{1}{4}$ in for ease of movement.

B Back neck to underarm Measure from top spinal bone down centre of back to underarm level.

C Underarm to waist An exact measurement can be taken from an existing garment. Alternatively, measure at centre back from underarm level to waist.

D Shoulder width Measure across shoulder blades halfway down armhole. Add 1.25 cm/$\frac{1}{2}$ in for ease.

E Jacket length Measure from centre of base of neck at back to base of seat.

F Sleeve seam Measure from underarm to wrist and add on 2.5 cm/1 in for ease. Alternatively, take the measurement from an existing garment.

G Underarm to elbow Measure with arm bent or take from existing garment.

H Shoulder to bust point Measure from centre of shoulder down to point of bust. The bust dart position is established from this measurement.

I Front neck to waist Measure from hollow of neck straight down to waist level. Add 5 mm/$\frac{1}{4}$ in for ease.

J Neck to chest Measure from hollow of neck to chest level—about halfway down armhole level but just before bust rises. Make a note of how far down the bust rises.

K Inside leg Measure from crotch point to just below top of appropriate shoe for trousers. This measurement is more accurate if taken from an existing pair of well-fitting trousers.

L Outside leg Measure at side from waist down to just below top of appropriate shoe for trousers. To measure yourself, hold the tape so the end is level with the ankle and read off the measurement at the waist.

M Shoulder length Measure, over a well-fitting jacket, from edge of undercollar to armhole seam. Add 5 mm/$\frac{1}{4}$ in for ease.

N Waist to hem Measure at centre front from waist to hemline. This gives a rough guide and the exact length is established when fitting the garment. To measure yourself, hold the tape so the end is level with your hem and read off the measurement at the waist.

O Waist to hip level Measure at side from waist down to level of pelvic bone. This ensures skirt balance is correct as pattern hip level is often too low. Make a note of how far down this measurement is taken.

PATTERNS

ALTERING PATTERN PIECES

Assemble the necessary equipment: a ruler, tape measure, pencil or felt pen, transparent adhesive tape, pins and extra paper. Using old scissors (dressmaking scissors will lose their sharp edges if used on paper of any kind), cut out the pattern pieces from the sheet of tissue on which they are printed; cut exactly on the printed outline or, on a multi-size pattern, on the line for your size.

Press pattern pieces flat with a cool iron. Draw a line in pencil or felt pen to mark the chest and bust level on the front bodice, measuring from the front neck to the depth previously noted (see p. 77). If the pattern has a yoke, use the yoke edge as the chest line. Draw in the hip level on the skirt in the same way. Draw a line across the back bodice at underarm level. Draw the crotch level on trousers and the elbow level on a sleeve.

Spread out each piece in turn and check against all the figure measurements taken. If the pattern has seam allowances included, measure within them; otherwise measure from the edge. Measure and mark at each point. If the pattern differs from the figure by more than 1 cm/⅜ in at any measuring point, it must be altered. Less than 1 cm/⅜ in can be adjusted when fitting or may even be taken up in ease.

Make the alteration at the measuring point. If an adjustment of, say, more than 2.5 cm/1 in is needed, make two smaller parallel alterations, about 2.5 cm/1 in apart, as too big an adjustment at one point may disturb the balance of the pattern too much. Larger pattern pieces such as trousers, a one-piece dress or a long skirt, should be adjusted by a small amount at two or even three places in order to preserve the balance of the design. Some patterns have a printed line as a position guide for lengthening or shortening the pattern piece. Use this only if it is close to your marked adjustment point. The length of a skirt or trousers or the length of a bodice below the armhole can generally be adjusted on this line.

Make sure the paper is still flat after the alteration has been made.

Checking edges

Adjusting the pattern may throw out edges slightly, so check the following points:

1 Straighten or gently curve any seam edges that are uneven.
2 If darts are affected by alterations, redraw the dart, making sure it is the correct width at the pattern edge. To reshape the edge of the paper fold the dart and pin it, then cut along the pattern edge. Open it out and the edge will be the correct shape.
3 Make sure the straight grain line is still straight. If not, draw a new grain line parallel with main edge or, on a sleeve for example, exactly down the centre of the piece.
4 If the depth of the armhole is shortened, either take a small pleat across the sleeve head at the same point so that the sleeve fits, or, for a square-shouldered figure, lower the bodice armhole slightly.
5 Check the length of all seam edges to make sure they match corresponding edges. For example, measure side seam edges of front and back bodices if an alteration has been made to one of them.

Mounting patterns

If you intend to use a particular pattern fairly often, make it more durable by pressing the pieces onto lightweight iron-on interfacing. An adjusted pattern can be a useful reference for altering other patterns. However, before using it, make sure that your measurements (or those of the person who is going to wear the garment) have remained the same. Bear in mind that as you get older your shape is quite likely to change, even though your weight may remain the same. Remember also that hemlines fluctuate from season to season.

BASIC ALTERATIONS

The difference between the vertical measurements taken on the body at various positions and the length of the pattern piece at the same point, will indicate the amount to be inserted or removed at each level. Remember that ease has been allowed in the pattern length so do not remove that. Lengthen or shorten the pattern to no less than 5 mm/¼ in longer than the body measurement. Remember too that seam allowances of, usually, 1.5 cm/⅝ in have been included, more at hems. Subtract these when measuring patterns.

Cut and open pattern or fold away on dotted lines shown. Some alterations will have to be made all around the body, i.e. evenly across the back and front pattern. Some require different amounts back and front—your measuring will reveal this. Uneven or wedge-shaped pieces have therefore to be inserted or removed but matching pattern edges must finish up equal in length. On a yoked style make the alterations at the edge of the lower piece. Also remember that other adjoining pieces must be altered to correspond, such as armhole depth on sleeve, length of facing, fly piece etc.

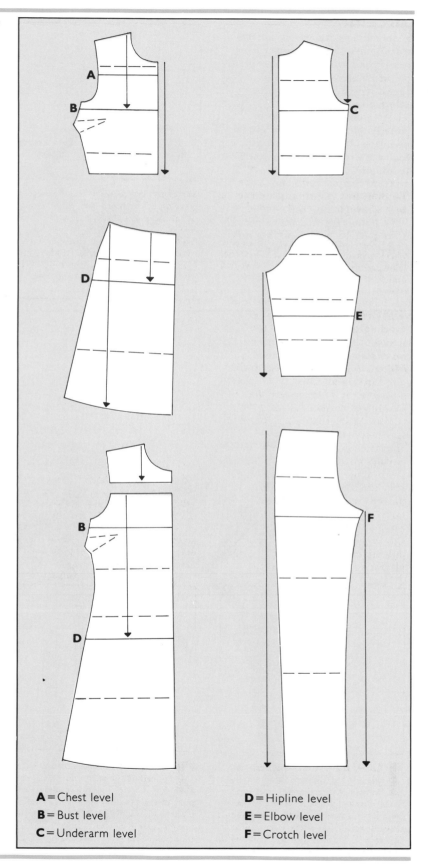

A = Chest level
B = Bust level
C = Underarm level
D = Hipline level
E = Elbow level
F = Crotch level

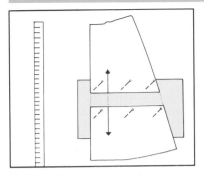

To lengthen a pattern place it on a piece of paper. Cut pattern on adjustment line. Separate pieces until distance between them is equal to length to be inserted. Pin pattern to paper. Check measurement. Replace pins with transparent tape. Trim away surplus paper.

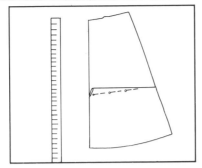

To shorten a pattern fold pattern piece on adjustment line. Make a pleat equal in total to the length to be removed, remembering that fold is double. Pin the pleat and check that pattern is correct length. Replace pins with transparent adhesive tape. Trim pattern edges to make them even.

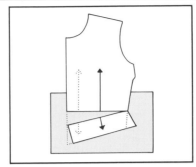

To lengthen unevenly, cut pattern from edge to be lengthened almost to other edge. Swing lower half of pattern down to insert extra length. Pin; check measurement. Replace pins with tape. Trim side seam, straighten lengthened edge and redraw straight grain line parallel with edge.

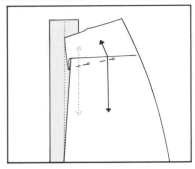

To shorten unevenly, make a tapering fold across the pattern and pin. Smooth out from fold to opposite edge so nothing is taken up at that edge. Check measurement. To straighten shortened edge, add an extra strip of paper or correct when cutting out fabric. Redraw straight grain line.

SPECIAL ALTERATIONS

After sewing a few garments you will probably become more familiar with the problems of fitting. If you have to make the same fitting alterations on each garment the patterns are not absolutely correct for the figure. Once you are sure where these differences lie, make the alterations on each pattern before cutting out.

The following adjustments may affect the shape within the pattern piece but the basic method and equipment are the same as for lengthening and shortening. Remember to correct any edges affected by the alterations.

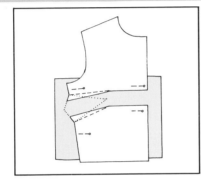

1 Prominent bust To enlarge the shaping area, pin pattern on a piece of paper and cut along centre of dart to point. Cut across to centre front edge. Separate pieces by the amount to be added and redraw edge of dart. Stitch dart from original base to new point by usual method.

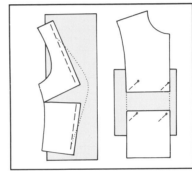

2 On a panel style cut across both pieces at bust level. Open side panel at bust point keeping edges closed at underarm seam. Pin to paper, redraw bust seam edge adding more shape. Open centre panel evenly across inserting the same amount as for side panel.

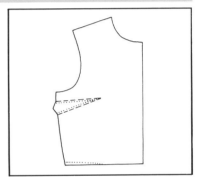

Small bust Reduce width at base of dart and redraw stitching lines. This makes the front side seam longer than the back, so match patterns at underarm and trim surplus at waist. Alternatively, take a fold in across pattern from side edge if pattern has no waist seam.

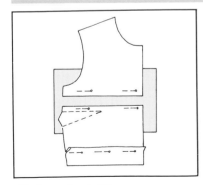

1 Low bust Place pattern on a piece of paper and cut across it between side seam and centre front above bust dart level. Separate the pieces, inserting amount needed to bring dart down to correct level and pin to paper. Fold and pin pattern below dart to take up any extra length.

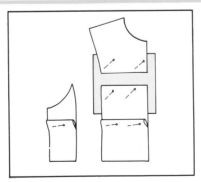

2 On a panel style cut across centre panel at chest level. Insert sufficient paper to lower the curved part of the seam to bust level. Make a pleat above waist to remove an equal amount; slightly less if bust is big. On side panel fold out a pleat of equal size.

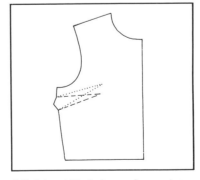

High bust Mark the new bust point on the pattern. Redraw dart to this higher point from the original base. To raise or lower bust line on a princess style, lengthen or shorten pattern pieces above and below bust point to bring shaping to correct level for figure.

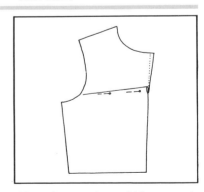

Flat chest Take a fold across the pattern from the centre front edge above armhole level, tapering it away at armhole edge. To straighten the centre front line, it is usually helpful to take a little off the neckline.

PATTERNS

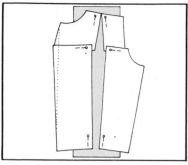

Broad back Cut across pattern nearly to edges, above or below armhole, depending on where width is needed. Cut down centre from shoulder to waist. Pin to paper and open out at vertical cut. Keeping shoulder edges together, overlap horizontal cut edges and pin. Straighten centre back.

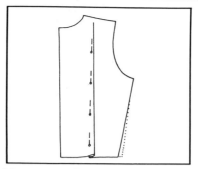

Narrow or flat back Take a fold down centre of back pattern piece from shoulder to waist. If shoulder is the correct width, take fold upward from waist, tapering it away at shoulder edge. If the waist width is reduced too much, add a little at side seam to compensate when cutting out.

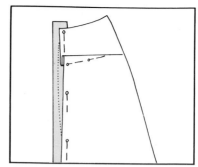

1 **Hollow back** To alter either a skirt or trousers, take a small fold across pattern from centre back edge about 5 cm/2 in below waist. Taper fold away at side seam. Redraw centre back edge, curving it slightly at alteration point. Try to choose a pattern with a centre back seam.

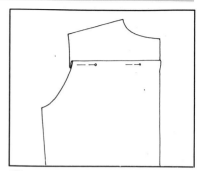

2 On a one-piece dress a hollow back produces excess material at waist. Take out a pleat across back, level with the middle of the armhole. Adjust the slight reduction in armhole size when constructing the dress and inserting the sleeve.

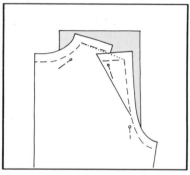

Narrow shoulders Cut pattern at an angle from middle of shoulder to halfway down armhole but not through edge. Overlap pieces at shoulder and pin onto a piece of paper. Redraw shoulder seamline across overlap from original neck point to original shoulder point. Alter back and front.

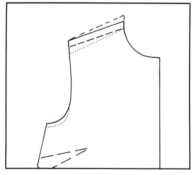

Sloping or hollow shoulders Draw a new shoulder line from original neck point to armhole edge. Do this on front or back, or both, as required. Lower armhole to correspond.

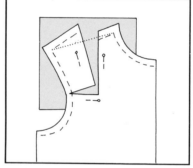

1 **Broad shoulders** Cut pattern down from mid-shoulder to a point level with middle of armhole. Cut across nearly to armhole. Swing cut piece back. Pin to paper; redraw shoulder seam from original points. Alter back and front. Adjust shoulder line when fitting.

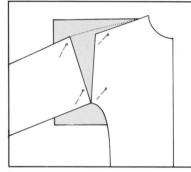

2 On a kimono style cut the pattern from underarm curve up to shoulder edge. Extend shoulder length by swinging out and opening the upper edge, keeping underarm edges together. Pin to new paper; redraw shoulder seam.

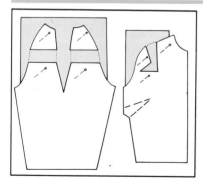

3 On a raglan style cut across sleeve pattern half way down armhole and raise each piece. On front cut pattern horizontally at same level as sleeve then cut vertically to mid-shoulder. Open out at shoulder only by same amount as sleeve. Redraw seam edges.

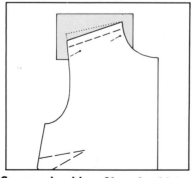

Square shoulders If surplus fabric appears at neck edge, draw a new shoulder line from neck, tapering to original level at outer edge. If neck fits but armhole is tight, add extra at armhole edge and redraw seam.

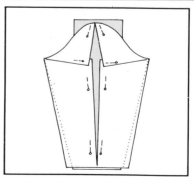

1 **Plump arms** Cut pattern through centre from sleeve head to wrist and cut across it just below underarm but not through edges. Open pattern at vertical cut to extra width needed, overlapping horizontal cut edges to keep pattern flat.

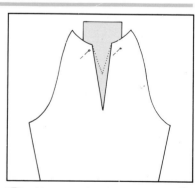

2 Alter a raglan sleeve pattern by shortening the dart that runs from neck edge along shoulder, or, if the sleeve is in two pieces, add extra to each edge. If more room is needed cut pattern from dart to wrist and cut fabric adding extra to cut edges and making a seam in the sleeve.

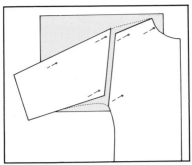

3 Tightness across the top of a kimono sleeve may be relieved at fitting. If always a problem an extra 1 cm/⅜ in can be allowed when cutting fabric. If this is insufficient cut the pattern from shoulder to underarm, raise the sleeve section and redraw shoulder and underarm seam edges.

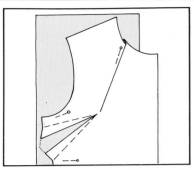

Gaping neckline This can be caused by a prominent bust or a hollow chest. If it is the former, cut pattern through centre of bust dart and place on paper. Fold and pin surplus at neckline, open dart wider and redraw neckline. Redraw outer edge of dart. Stitch along original lines.

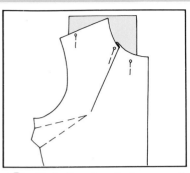

2 If a hollow chest is the cause of a gaping neckline, pin pattern to paper and take a tapering fold from neckline only toward point of bust dart. Redraw neckline.

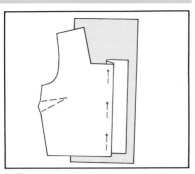

3 If a square neckline gapes, pin pattern to paper and take tapering fold from neck edge to waist. Redraw neckline.

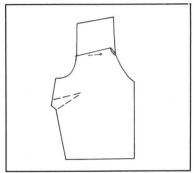

4 If a V or wrapover neck gapes, shorten the neckline by taking out a pleat across the chest. Taper it to nothing at armhole unless the armhole also gapes, in which case take an equal amount right across.

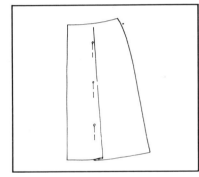

Flat bottom One remedy is to omit the waist dart and take in the resulting surplus at waist in side seams. If this is insufficient, take a fold in centre of back at the hemline and taper it away at the waistline.

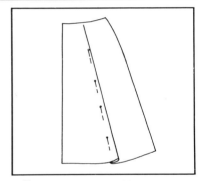

Thin thighs and legs To adjust a skirt, take a fold up the centre of the pattern piece, tapering it away toward waist. Add fabric at side seam when cutting out if hip width has been reduced too much. Alter back and front.

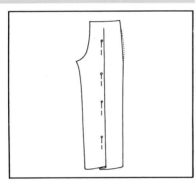

2 To adjust trousers for thin thighs and legs, take a fold up the centre of each leg, tapering it away toward waist. Add fabric at side seam when cutting out if hip width has been reduced too much. It is not always necessary to alter back and front.

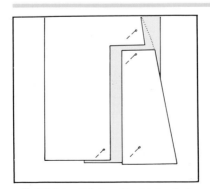

Thick thighs If thighs bulge below hip line, skirt and trouser patterns should be altered by cutting horizontally for 10 cm/4 in just above thigh bulge. Cut vertically to hem edge. Move cut section outward to add the amount necessary. Redraw side seam edge smoothly.

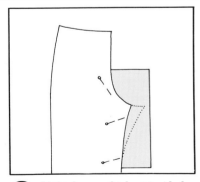

2 If thighs are thick at inside leg, extend crotch point of a trouser pattern. Extend inside leg seamline from about 12 cm/5 in below the crotch upward. Extend centre back seamline, in a curve, by a maximum of 5 cm/2 in to meet inside leg seam.

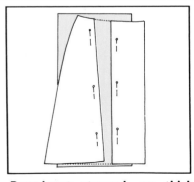

Prominent stomach or thick waist If omitting darts is insufficient to accommodate figure, cut down centre of pattern from waist to hem. Pin to paper, separating pieces to allow extra width at waist and stomach area. Redraw hemline and waistline.

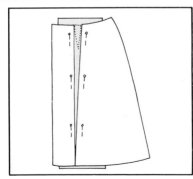

Large buttocks If the size of the waist allows, increase width of waist dart or add a dart to provide extra buttock shaping. Alternatively, cut down centre of pattern from waist to hem. Open out pieces at waist, pin to paper, inserting enough width at waist level to make new dart. Draw in dart.

PATTERNS

USING THE PATTERNS

Once the pattern is adjusted satisfactorily, check the fabric carefully before cutting out the garment. Examine the whole length and mark any flaws, marks or faded patches to be avoided with chalk.

Press out creases, such as the centre fold crease, with a damp cloth. It is particularly important to do this on synthetic knits although sometimes the crease cannot be removed and has to be avoided when cutting out. Synthetics tend to attract dirt particles on the fold, which, if folded on the right side, will show up as a dirty mark when pressed. Wash the fabric, or have it dry cleaned if necessary, to remove this mark.

Knit fabrics often have an untidy selvage which should be cut off. On all fabrics straighten one end of the length. If the grain is not perfectly straight, the fabric should be stretched from opposite corners—you will need help with this.

If the fabric contains natural fibres, test it for shrinkage. Using a ruler and a chalk pencil, measure and mark out a square of about 16 cm/6¼ in at the centre of the fabric. Press the square with a damp cloth and allow the fabric to cool. Measure the square again and note any difference in its dimensions. Any slight shrinkage on that small square is multiplied if it occurs on the whole length so before use the fabric must be shrunk. Washable fabrics may be squeezed in warm water, or put in a washing machine without soap, then dried and pressed. Alternatively, press the single thickness of fabric all over with a damp cloth. Take care to press evenly and keep the cloth damp. Another method is to fold the fabric lengthwise, place it on a damp sheet, roll it up and leave overnight. The next day press the fabric until it is completely dry.

Fold fabric right side out so that marks, flaws and pattern designs are visible. Pin straightened ends together and pin selvages together at wide intervals. If short of space on the cutting-out surface, roll up the surplus length of fabric to prevent it from hanging off the table and stretching.

Facings, pockets and other small pattern pieces can be cut from any fabric that is left over after the main pieces have been cut out, but make sure that you leave enough room for them when cutting out the main pattern pieces.

Folding the fabric

Each pattern is usually only half the garment area and is cut out on double fabric, sometimes on the fold. The material, therefore, must be folded in such a way as to accommodate all the pattern pieces on the correct grain.

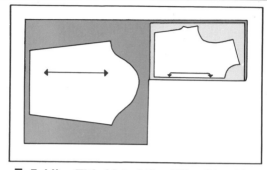

1 Folding Wide fabric, 140 to 175 cm/54 to 70 in, can usually be folded down the centre for cutting out the pattern. If one pattern piece is very wide and will not fit on folded fabric, open the fabric out and cut the piece on single fabric. Fold all narrower fabrics down the centre, provided pattern pieces are not too large.

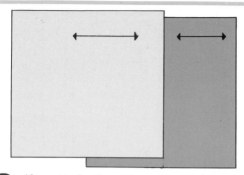

2 Alternatively, if some large pattern pieces have to be cut, measure and cut off the length needed and fold and cut the fabric across the width. Turn the top piece of fabric around so that any nap or pattern is facing in the same direction on both pieces of fabric.

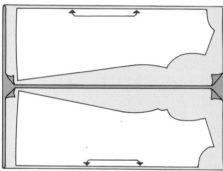

3 Where there is a pattern instruction "place to fold", the fold must be made on the straight grain of the weave or on the straight line of knitting on a knit fabric. If most, or all, of the main pattern pieces have to be placed against the fold, fold the fabric sides to middle with selvages meeting at centre. Make sure the grain is straight on both the folded edges.

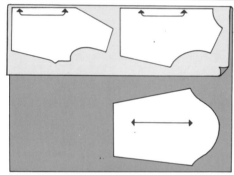

4 If short of fabric, fold in one side of fabric to a width just sufficient to take pattern pieces which have to be cut on the fold. This leaves a wide strip along the other side where smaller pieces, such as the sleeve, can be cut on single fabric. Turn the pattern piece over to cut the second piece where necessary.

PLACING THE PATTERN

Place each pattern piece in position on the fabric, checking that the grain line is straight by measuring an even distance from the fold or selvage at each end of the grain line. Anchor the grain line to fabric with two pins. Position all the main pattern pieces to check that everything fits. Position smaller pieces but do not pin finally or cut until after fitting. Observe all instructions such as "place to fold" or "cut twice". Leave room between the pieces for seam allowances if the pattern does not include them, and for any extra width or length to be added for fit.

On particularly bulky fabric, pinning the pattern to the fabric can tear the pattern and cause the fabric to lie unevenly. Anchor the pattern pieces on the fabric with a few heavy objects and chalk around the pattern. Remove the pattern and cut out.

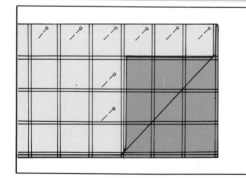

Checked fabric Fold fabric along a stripe suitable to fall at the centre of any pattern piece. Pin along fold. Beginning in centre of length of fabric, insert pins across width, ensuring that checks match exactly on both layers lengthwise and crosswise. Continue inserting pins across width and matching checks at intervals of 8 to 10 cm/3 to 4 in. Do not remove pins when cutting out fabric.

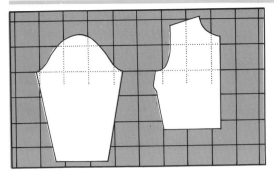

Placing checks on pattern Decide how checks are best placed on body, taking into account any figure problems. Dealing with problem pattern piece or front pattern first, draw guidelines on pattern, tracing checks of fabric. Mark other pattern pieces to match. When all pattern pieces are marked, place on fabric and cut out, matching checks and guidelines.

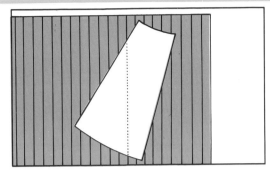

Striped fabric Prepare as for checked fabric to match the stripes. Turn each pattern over to cut it the second time if necessary.

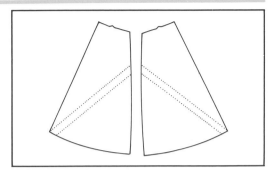

Chevron stripes Decide on angle of stripes. Draw a stripe on front pattern piece at that angle. Place back pattern beside front and draw a stripe at same angle, but in other direction, to match first one. Arrange pattern on fabric so that drawn stripe aligns with fabric stripe. Use the same method if cutting a pattern piece such as a skirt or sleeve on the bias instead of on the straight grain.

Geometric or floral fabric Large bold designs must be carefully positioned on a garment. To help balance the design when cutting out, cut an additional paper pattern for a sleeve or cut a whole pattern piece for a back skirt or bodice front instead of placing a pattern piece on folded fabric. Each piece can then be cut out in single fabric and the design attractively placed.

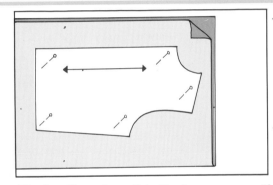

Pinning Place pins well inside the paper to avoid disturbing pattern edge, and pin at each corner of the pattern and between corners on a long edge. Insert pins diagonally, as the fabric gives and lies flatter than if pins lie with straight grain. Use only a few pins—too many make the fabric uneven and inaccurate when cut out.

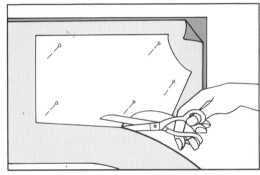

Cutting Keep the fabric flat on the table. Cut with the bulk of the pattern to the right of the scissors; reverse if left-handed. Use the whole blade and close the scissors right to the tips; do not make short chopping movements. Make sure the open blade fits snugly into the cut each time to avoid a chopped edge. Move around to reach all parts rather than moving fabric.

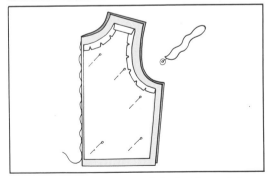

Marking Tailor's tacks mark both sides and do not harm fabric. If pattern has a seam allowance, fold it back and clip curves. Work tailor's tacks on fabric close to paper. Tailor's chalk can also be used.

If the pattern has no seam allowance, work tailor's tacks around edge. Work single tacks at right angles to seam to mark balance marks. Mark a fold with a row of basting before removing pattern.

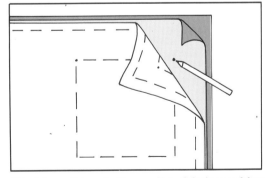

Marking with a chalk pencil or fabric marking pen Both are suitable for making occasional marks, such as a pocket position, but not for marking seam allowances all around a piece. Cut fabric out RS together, fold pattern back and make marks on WS of both layers of fabric. One type of pen makes marks that disappear in a day or so; others need removing with water.

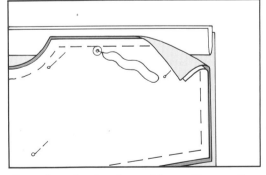

A tracing wheel can be used for marking seamlines. The type with a smooth edge is best as it makes a continuous line. Cut dressmaker's carbon paper into strips about 5 cm/2 in wide. Fold strips carbon side out. Slide carbon between two layers of fabric so carbon is against WS. Pressing hard, run wheel along seamlines on pattern; check that marks are transferred before removing pattern.

INTERFACING

Interfacing is an additional layer of specially manufactured material that is put on the inside of selected areas of a garment. This extra layer helps edges such as necklines and style features such as yokes to keep their shape, reduces wear at points that are frequently handled, such as fastenings and pockets, and at any point that fits the body closely, such as waistband and cuffs. It also gives collars, cuffs and pocket flaps a crisp appearance. The interfacing material is placed on the wrong side of the fabric so that it supports the garment.

Interfacing materials are either woven or non-woven, iron-on or sew-in. Those with heat-sensitive granules on one side stick to the fabric when pressed in place. Sometimes ordinary fabric is used as interfacing. It is important to use the correct weight for the fabric in order to retain its draping qualities. Select a suitable weight by feeling the fabric with a piece of interfacing underneath it. If interfacing is visible in any way—ridges, lines or an unacceptable stiffness to the fabric— then the wrong weight or type has been used. Similarly if collars, cuffs or edges are limp, the interfacing is wrong.

Interfacings are available in rolls of various widths, from 60 cm/24 in to 130 cm/50 in, and interfacing bands and tapes can be purchased pre-packed, on reels, or by the length.

With a collar that rolls or folds it is the under-collar, which is the extended edge of the garment, that should be interfaced. A collar without a seam at the outer edge may have interfacing across its full width, but it then becomes a double layer when the collar is made so a less crisp interfacing should be used. It is not correct to attach interfacing to a facing—it is pointless to stiffen a piece of fabric that simply lies inside the garment— and this should be done, with soft interfacing, only if it is impossible to interface the garment. Where it is applied to an edge it may be covered by a facing or a lining; often it is sandwiched between two pieces and completely hidden, for example in collars. One layer of interfacing is usually sufficient, except in traditional tailoring where much of the skill lies in shaping the fabric over layers of various types of interfacing.

Tips

1 Be guided by the suggestions made in the pattern instructions as to which parts should be interfaced, but add others if necessary.
2 A pattern piece may be provided for cutting interfacing but if not, work out the shape by drawing a line on the pattern to indicate the extent you want to interface and cut from that.
3 Check washing and dry cleaning instructions and whether pre-shrunk.

	Type, weight and colour	Application
IRON-ON Non-woven	**Ultra soft** Fine: white	Roll collars, edges, yokes: *very soft fabrics*
	Light Soft: white, charcoal	Flat collars, edges, pockets, hems, cuffs: *lightweight fabrics*
	Medium Springy: white	Stand collars, edges, pocket tops, tabs, cuffs: *medium fabrics*
	Heavy Firm opaque: white	Belts, bags, long dress hems: *all fabrics*
Woven	**Light** Soft cotton: white	Collars, cuffs, yokes: *light and medium fabrics*
	Medium Stiff cotton: white, black	Collars, cuffs, jacket-fronts, bows: *medium fabrics*
Tapes	**Perforated band** Light: white	Cuffs, bands, pocket tops, pleats, straps, belts, edges, welts: *all fabrics*
	Firm: white	Waistbands: *all fabrics*
	Adhesive web: white, blue	Hems, facings, frills, flounces: *all except fine fabrics*
	Paper-backed adhesive: white	Appliqué, pipings, openings: *all except fine fabrics*
SEW-IN Non-woven	**Soft** Light: white, charcoal	Collars, edges, yokes, pockets: *soft, delicate fabrics*
	Medium Springy: white	Collars, lapels, pockets: *medium fabrics*
	Heavy Stiff: white, opaque	Belts, waistbands, pelmets/valances: *all fabrics*
Woven	**Haircloth/hair canvas/laptair** Springy, wiry, cotton or wool and horsehair: grey. *Shrink before use*	Chest area: *all suit and coat fabrics*
	Soft canvas/flax canvas Soft, closely woven linen or cotton, various weights: beige. *Shrink before use, press using damp cloth*	Lapels, chest, front, back, shoulders, pocket flaps: *all suitings and coatings*
	Domette Soft, fuzzy open cotton: white, black	Chest area, coats and jackets, to prevent horsehair from scratching: *all suitings and coatings*
	Wigan Loosely woven cloth: black, white, drab colours. *Shrink before use, press using damp cloth*	Hems and sleeve hems, coats and jackets, backs of pockets and stays: *all suitings and coatings*
	Holland Loosely woven linen	Same purpose as wigan
	Silesia/pocketing Closely woven strong fine cotton: black, white, drab colours	Pocket bags, fly facings, waist facings, reinforcements: *all tailoring fabrics*
	Collar canvas Stiff cotton or linen: dark beige. *Shrink before use, sprinkle with water and hot press*	Collars: *all tailoring fabrics*
	Melton Felt-like non-fraying wool: all basic colours	Under-collar on coats and jackets: *all tailoring fabrics*
	Cotton Permastiff Medium: white	Collars, cuffs: *medium fabrics*
	Cotton Victoria Crisp: white	Collars, cuffs, edges, yokes: *medium fabrics*
	Mull muslin Soft, light: white	Collars, edges: *medium fabrics*
	Lawn Soft: many colours	Collars, edges, soft features: *very soft fabrics*
	Organdy Crisp, springy. *Will not show*	Collars, bows, cuffs: *soft fabrics*
	Marquisette and net Crisp, springy. *Does not add bulk*	Collars, necklines: *sheers*
	Self fabric. *Will not show*	Collars, necklines, edges: *sheers*
Tapes	**Stay tape** Strong linen twill tape. *Shrink before use*	Edges of coats and jackets: *all tailoring fabrics*
	Linen tape Woven linen strip without selvage	Edges, hems, pockets: *all tailoring fabrics*

IRON-ON INTERFACING

Buy an interfacing that feels softer than the effect you want, because it will become crisper after being pressed. If you find you have used one that is too heavy, gently peel it off. Always test interfacing on a scrap of fabric because occasionally fabric will bubble. Follow manufacturer's instructions for fusing in place; most have to be applied with a warm iron and damp cloth. If your fabric may be marked by this treatment, change to sew-in interfacing. Because iron-on interfacings extend to the edge of the garment piece, the adhesive helps to control fraying. Woven iron-on interfacings should be cut with the grain arrow of the pattern pieces on the straight grain of the interfacing. Some non-woven interfacings can be cut with pieces lying in any direction but many have a sort of grain, which should be followed.

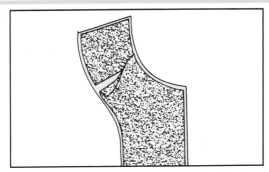

Joining Pieces can be joined simply by overlapping. Cut allowing 1 cm/⅜ in or so at the edge to be joined, press one piece to the fabric and then the other. The join will be stiffer than the remainder so try not to have it where the garment should be soft.

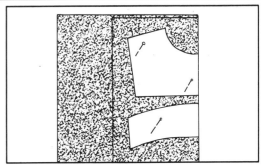

Cutting Fold interfacing RS out, pin pattern pieces in position, cut out around pattern edge. If interfacing is particularly heavy, mark around pattern with fabric pen instead of pinning. With pieces to be interfaced right to the edges, such as collars, pockets and yokes, reserve the piece of fabric for them but do not cut them out; cut the interfacing first.

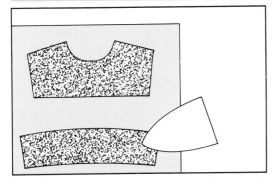

Attaching and marking Place interfacing in position on WS fabric; anchor with one pin. If fabric has not been cut out, place interfacing with straight grain correctly positioned. Attach interfacing using a warm iron and, usually, a damp cloth, placing the iron down firmly. Hold for a couple of seconds and lift. Remove pin; press entire area. Cut out fabric, turn RS up and press again.

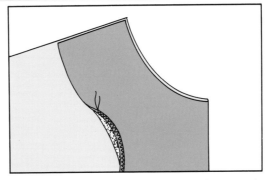

Edges The method described for attaching avoids any possibility of getting adhesive on the iron or the pressing board. Outer edges of facings and any edges that will not be enclosed in a seam should be zigzagged to the fabric to make sure the interfacing will not become detached. On very fine fabrics fold edge under and stitch.

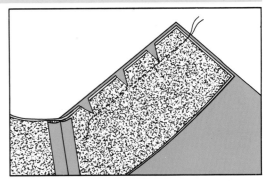

Curves Iron-on interfacing makes edges unyielding, which has the advantage that they will not stretch. To counteract this when handling curved edges and joining them to straight or curved pieces, clip the edge at intervals to a depth of 1 cm/⅜ in.

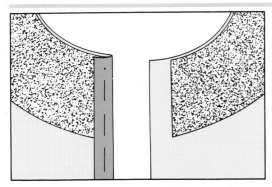

Reducing bulk Bulk in seam allowances will normally be reduced by the usual trimming after stitching but it should be reduced *before* stitching where additional thickness is to be added, such as a zipper. Apply the interfacing to the garment edge, but before pressing the zipper edges, trim 1.5 cm/⅝ in from the interfacing.

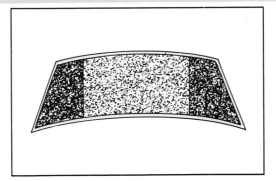

Extra stiffness One of the advantages of iron-on interfacing is that additional crispness can be quickly added to selected areas. On collar points, decorative features, waistbands, ends of shaped cuffs, an extra piece of interfacing can be pressed on top of the first. This is a useful technique, especially on shirts.

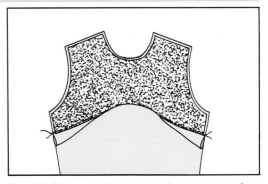

Combining areas Iron-on interfacing may produce a line along the free edge which is visible on the RS of fabric. If this happens to your test piece, see whether you can extend the interfacing into another seam, possibly combining two areas and using one piece of interfacing. A longer curved edge will show much less. Avoid darts or trim interfacing and stitch it on one side of the dart.

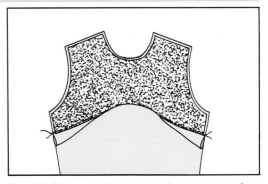

INTERFACING

SEW-IN INTERFACING

Sew-in interfacings, even non-wovens, are more flexible than the iron-on type, so use them for preference for draped or softly folded features. Most woven interfacings need shrinking before cutting, and should be cut with the grain corresponding to the straight grain arrow on the pattern. The exceptions are pieces that are cut on the bias in tailoring, and when you are interfacing stretch fabric. At least two edges of the interfacing must be either stitched into a seam or sewn down at the seamline, otherwise it will wrinkle in wear and washing.

Interfaced edges provide a good base for neat topstitching; and strips of light sew-in interfacing can be put in yoke, zipper and sleeve edges to eliminate puckered stitching. Cut interfacing to avoid darts or at least cut it away from the points of darts.

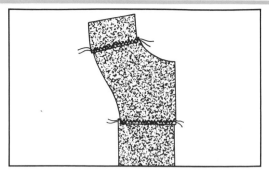

Joining Joins in interfacing should normally fall at garment seams. If it is necessary to join pieces because there is not enough interfacing to cut a pattern piece, cut sections of interfacing a little longer than required and overlap at join. Work zigzag stitch along join.

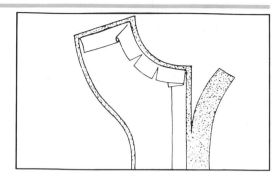

Marking and cutting With medium and light-weight interfacing pin pattern on folded interfacing and cut around outer edge. Mark essential points and seam allowances with fabric pen or tracing wheel and carbon paper. To cut heavy interfacing without seam allowances trim off or fold back 1.5 cm/⅝ in along edges that extend to a seam. Cut around outer edge.

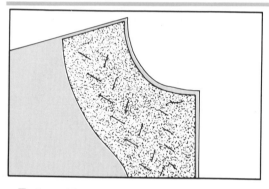

1 Attaching Cut out interfacing. Light and medium weights should be cut with the edge level with the garment, heavy interfacing should be cut without the seam allowance. Place fabric on table WS up, place interfacing on top matching edges or having interfacing edge 1.5 cm/⅝ in inside edge. Begin in the middle and baste together in rows, stopping 1.5 cm/⅝ in from outer edge.

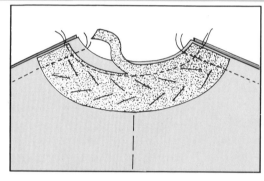

2 Make up the garment, stitching through interfacing and garment fabric. After stitching, trim interfacing away close to seamline to avoid bulk.

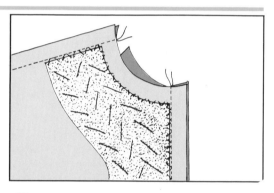

3 Trim away interfacing so that it lies inside any corners. Work catch stitch around the edges of the interfacing that lie against garment seam allowances. Baste and machine garment sections. The stitching should fall just beyond the edge of the interfacing to prevent bulky seams. In tailoring the edges are also taped.

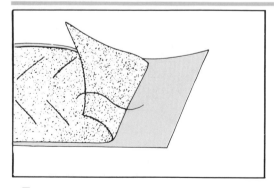

1 Interfacing collar Use a soft interfacing for collars that fold or roll, a crisp one for flat or stand collars. Baste interfacing to WS under-collar. Heavy interfacing should be cut without seam allowances and attached to fabric around outer edge. A tailored collar is covered with padding stitch and shaped as it is being stitched.

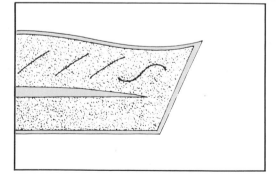

2 Firm non-woven interfacing may be bulky at the fold of a collar. To achieve a good roll line, press collar along fold and then cut away an oval slit in the interfacing on the fold line. At its widest point the slit should be about 3 mm/⅛ in wide, and it should extend to within 1 cm/⅜ in of the edges.

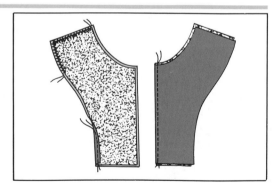

Attaching interfacing to facing If this is necessary, place interfacing on WS facing with edges level and baste. At outer edge either zigzag over both edges or trim a little off the interfacing, fold fabric over edge and stitch. Alternatively the interfacing can be stitched flat onto the RS of the outer edge of facing then folded into position inside. Use straight stitch or bind hem.

BANDS, STRIPS AND TAPES

These are used where a narrow piece of interfacing is required to stiffen and define an edge or to provide a stitching or fold line. Lightweight perforated iron-on banding is manufactured to an accurate width of 3 cm/$1\frac{1}{4}$ in each side of the perforations and it is worth adapting the width of hems and features in order to make use of it. Add seam allowances when cutting out fabric.

Adhesive hemming web is in strip form. Use small pieces to hold facings in place on WS, use it to stiffen hems, put a strip between facing and garment to prevent machine-made buttonholes fraying and push little pieces into collar corners to stiffen and prevent fraying. Paper-backed webbing is similar but in sheet form. Sew-in tapes are used mainly in tailoring to soften edges and to prevent stretching.

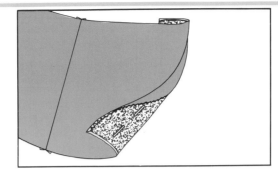

Wrap-over edge Stiffen the outer flap of a wrap-over skirt by pressing perforated banding to WS of fabric. Mark fold line by pressing or with chalk, locate the perforations along the line and press, adhesive side down. Fold outer edge of fabric over banding and edge stitch or trim fabric and zigzag the two together. Fold facing to WS, press.

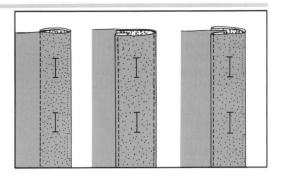

Foldline Where interfacing has been used over a wide area define the fastening edge of the garment and make an easy foldline by pressing banding on top of the interfacing on WS. The perforations must match up with the foldline of the garment. The buttonholes must fall on the banding; if horizontal, use small buttons.

Shirt strap If button strap is cut in one with shirt front press perforated banding to WS with perforations along fold line of garment. Fold strap to WS, tuck edge of fabric under banding and stitch. For separate button strap, press banding to centre on WS, attach strap to RS and finish on WS, or reverse this, finishing strap on RS.

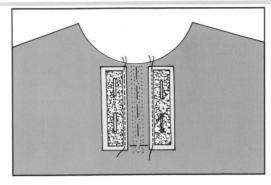

Strap opening When making a strap opening, begin by pressing a narrow strip of paper-backed adhesive over the marked opening. Make straps by pressing perforated banding to fabric and cutting out. Attach straps to RS each side of marked opening, cut opening, press strips to extend them, then fold along perforations and finish on inside of garment.

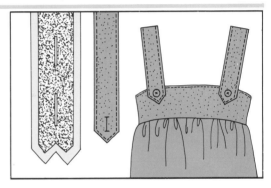

Tabs Reinforce tabs, shoulder straps, added hem bands, bag handles, by pressing perforated banding to WS fabric. Add seam allowance and cut out. Ends of banding should be cut to desired shape before pressing to fabric.

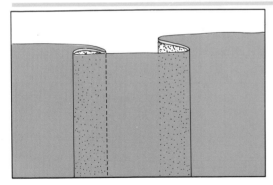

Tucks Flat tucks in all except light fabrics will be improved by being interfaced with perforated banding. Decide on position of tucks and allow sufficient width for each. Mark centre line of each tuck. On WS fabric press banding with perforations on tuck markings. Fold fabric WS together and press. Attach edge guide to machine foot, adjust to 3 cm/$1\frac{1}{4}$ in and stitch tucks. Press.

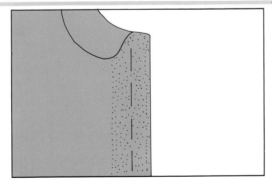

Buttonholes Insert a strip of hemming web between facing and garment just before making machine-made or hand-worked buttonholes. Fraying in use will be eliminated and the edge will be crisper. Make vertical buttonholes to fall within the webbing.

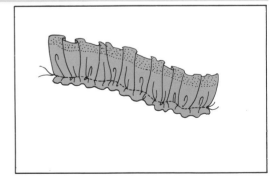

Crisp hems Hemming web is used to hold up hemlines without stitching, but it can also be used as an interfacing. Inserted in the edge of frills and ruffles it will make them stand up crisply in wear. It is particularly useful on furnishing items.

SHAPING

Pattern pieces are shaped so that, when they are joined, the garment fits the curves of the figure. Additional shaping is often needed within the pattern pieces, either as a style feature or in order to accommodate parts of the body. Fullness is controlled by various methods—darts, tucks, gathering, shirring, gauging or waffling.

Use synthetic thread for all processes where threads are to be pulled or where there will be strain, as in shirring.

Frills and ruffles can also provide fullness, but usually only as an attractive style feature.

DARTS

Suitable for any fabric, correctly adjusted darts give a smooth fit.

The size of the pocket of fullness at the point of a dart depends on the width of the fold of fabric at the base. Small, or narrow, darts are used where only a little shape is needed, as at shoulders or elbows, while wider darts create fullness at the bust or bottom.

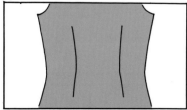

Above left, bust and front waist darts; above right, shoulder darts.

On garments without a waist seam the fullness can be controlled by a dart that is wide at the middle but runs to points at each end. If fullness has to be taken out as a curve, fit and cut dart before stitching.

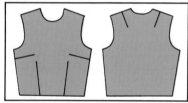

Double-ended darts

Very small darts, which may make a ridge if pressed to one side, may be balanced by sewing a piece of fabric into the dart.

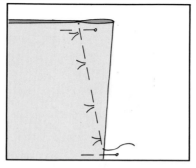

1 Standard dart Mark the stitching lines of the dart with tailor's tacks and fold fabric RS together with marked lines meeting. Insert two pins to hold the dart—one just beyond the point. Baste on stitching line from base to slightly beyond the point and remove pin at base.

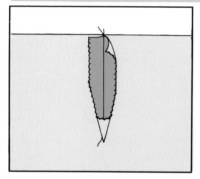

4 If the fabric is bulky, cut along the fold of the dart, almost to the point, after stitching. Trim and finish the raw edges by hand. It is hardly worth using the machine for sewing such a short distance.

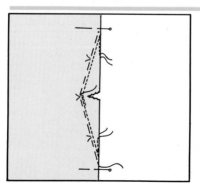

2 Overlapping the first stitching, stitch from the centre to the other point, reversing along fold. Remove tailor's tacks, pins and basting. Press dart, WS up, as two separate darts. Clip the fold at the centre of the dart and finish the cut edges. Press finished dart firmly.

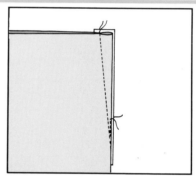

2 Place the wide base of the dart under the machine with the point directly in front of the foot. Stitch slowly from base to point, ending exactly on the fold. Reverse along fold to fasten ends or leave ends to sew in later. Remove basting, tailor's tacks and second pin.

5 Small darts that may be visible from RS when pressed can be made even. Fold and baste the dart in usual way. Place a piece of straight seam tape or a piece of selvage from some lining fabric under the dart and stitch dart and tape together. Press dart to one side, tape to the other.

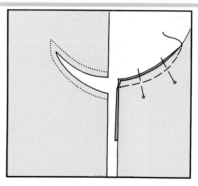

1 Curved dart This dart cannot be folded in the usual way. Mark seamlines of dart and cut away the centre, leaving 1.5 cm/⅝ in seam allowances. Place cut edges RS together and pin the dart, matching seamlines and lifting the fabric as you pin. Baste the seam. Remove pins.

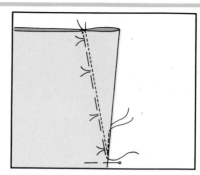

3 Press the stitching and press the dart to one side with the bulk pressed either downward or toward the centre of the garment. If the dart is very wide at the base or if it makes a noticeable ridge on the garment, press it so that the fabric lies evenly on each side of the stitching.

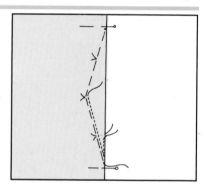

1 Double-ended dart Mark as for standard dart. Fold fabric RS together matching tacks. Insert a pin at each end of the dart beyond points and one at the centre. Baste, remove centre pin. Starting at centre, machine to one point reversing along fold. Turn the work around.

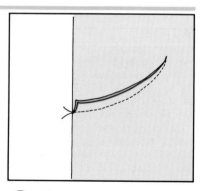

2 Place under machine and stitch slowly from base to point. Remove basting. Press stitching flat and then press both edges upward. Trim edges to 5 mm/¼ in and finish. Press dart again firmly.

TUCKS

Tucks, or parallel folds of fabric, can, if short, provide fullness. They can also be stitched over an entire area, as on a skirt or on the bodice of a dress, to give a purely decorative effect.

The style of garment and type and amount of fabric available govern the width of tucks. The spacing between each tuck depends on the effect desired in the finished garment.

If a complete section, such as a yoke or cuffs, is to be tucked and tucks are not allowed for in the pattern, make the tucks on a large piece of fabric and then cut out the appropriate pattern piece.

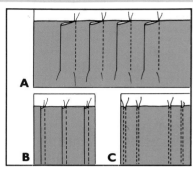

Short, or released, tucks (A) are useful for children's clothes and maternity wear. The amount of fullness required determines the size and number. Pin tucks (**B**) are very narrow tucks, ideal for lingerie or baby clothes in fine fabrics. Machine tucks (**C**) and pin tucks are purely decorative.

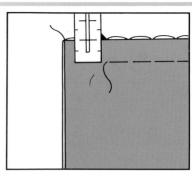

I **Wide tucks** To mark centre of first tuck, work a row of small basting stitches exactly on straight grain. Fold fabric WS together with basting on fold. Using an adjustable marker, measure required width of tuck. Mark stitching line and baste along it through both layers.

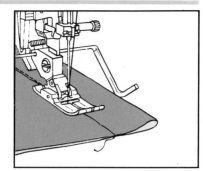

2 Attach machine quilting foot with adjustable bar. Adjust the end of the bar to the width of the fold and, using it as a guide, stitch the tuck. Alternatively, use the ordinary foot and hold the adjustable marker just in front of the foot to act as a stitching guide.

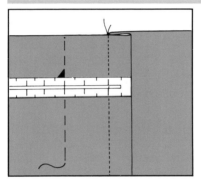

3 Remove basting. Press stitching flat and press tuck to one side. Note the tuck width and use the marker to mark a line indicating the centre of the next tuck, at the desired distance from the previous one. Fold fabric and baste and stitch second and subsequent tucks as for first tuck.

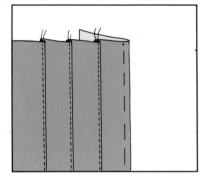

Pin tucks Mark centre of first tuck as for wide tucks. Fold fabric WS together and baste about 3 mm/$\frac{1}{8}$ in from fold. Press lightly. Stitch on fold with straight or zigzag machine stitch, running stitch, or hand or machine embroidery stitch. Remove basting and press. Continue in the same way.

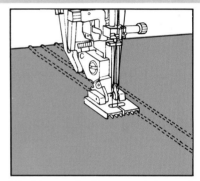

Machine tucks Use pin tuck foot and twin needle with two spools of thread. Work a row of basting on straight grain of fabric. Stitch tuck on RS with edge of foot on basting. Move fabric so that stitched tuck fits under a groove on foot and machine second and subsequent tucks. Remove basting.

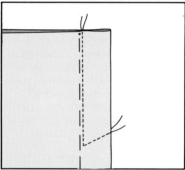

Released tucks Fold and baste as for wide tucks with RS together. Stitch from raw edge to release point (end of tuck). Turn fabric and stitch across to fold at an angle. Repeat for subsequent tucks. Remove basting. Press tucks to one side or evenly on each side of stitching.

GATHERS

Areas such as the shoulder, cuff, yoke or waist can have gathers set into them to introduce fullness. The amount of gathering and of extra fabric needed depends on the fabric.

Gathering threads can be inserted by hand or by machine, or fabric can be gathered automatically, in fixed amounts, with the gathering foot or ruffler.

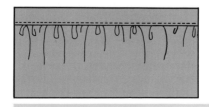

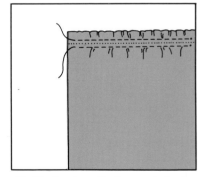

I **Gathering** To insert gathering threads by hand, take pieces of thread longer than the edge to be gathered. Knot one end. Work two parallel rows of running, one slightly below seamline and one above. Leave thread ends free. Do not make the rows too long: work in sections.

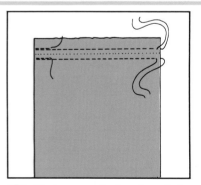

2 To insert gathering threads by machine, adjust machine to largest straight stitch. Reverse to anchor the thread and on RS machine two parallel rows on either side of seamline. Use a different coloured thread in the bobbin to distinguish it from that in the needle.

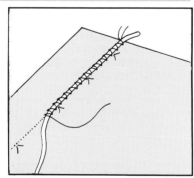

3 Alternatively, set machine to a medium to wide zigzag. Feed a thick thread, such as buttonhole or fine crochet cotton, under the foot and stitch over this thread, with fabric WS up. Some machines have a feed hole in the needle plate through which to pass the thicker gathering thread.

SHAPING

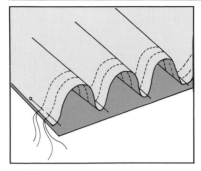

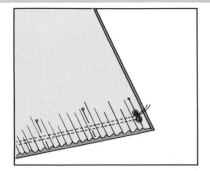

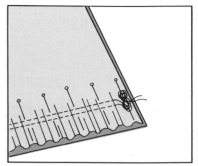

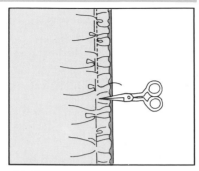

4 Mark centre of gathered edge and flat piece to be joined to it. If gathered section is long, divide both edges into four or more sections. Mark centre and ends of each section. With flat piece RS up, raw edge toward you, place gathered piece on top RS down. Match marks and pin.

5 Grasp the ends of gathering threads; if they have been inserted by machine, hold the bobbin threads. Do not pull them but gently ease fabric along them. When gathers lie flat on top of ungathered edge, insert a pin across loose threads at end and wind threads around pin.

6 To even out gathers, take hold of the fabric on either side of gathering and tug sharply. Hold the two layers together by inserting a pin in centre of gathering and one at opposite end from pin anchoring threads. Insert more pins until each section is evenly divided. Baste and remove pins.

7 With gathered side upward, place fabric under machine. Stitch slowly, exactly on seamline, adjusting gathers as they pass under the foot. Use points of small scissors to flatten or rearrange gathers and to prevent them being bunched. Remove basting and gathering threads.

SHIRRING AND GAUGING

Shirring is worked in parallel rows with shirring elastic, which gathers the fabric as it is sewn. Gauging gives the same outward effect, but as it is worked with normal thread it does not stretch. It is rather weak so the back must be covered.

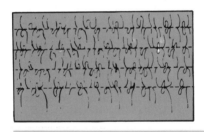

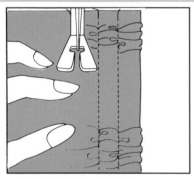

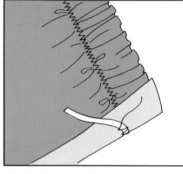

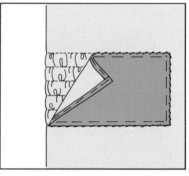

1 Shirring Mark area to be gathered. Using the bobbin winding mechanism, wind shirring elastic onto bobbin. Use polyester thread on top. Set machine to a large straight stitch and sew on RS. (The first row may not gather at all.) Use side of machine foot as a spacing guide.

2 Alternatively, set machine to a medium zigzag stitch. Thread end of shirring elastic up through hole in needle plate. Place the reel of elastic on the floor so elastic stretches slightly as it is machined down. The ends of elastic can be pulled up to tighten shirring.

Gauging Mark area to be gathered. Using normal thread, work parallel rows of gathering. Pull up bobbin threads evenly and sew them in on WS. Cut a piece of soft cotton to the size of gathered area and baste it to WS. Turn in raw edges and baste. Slip hem all around; remove basting.

WAFFLE

Waffle is suitable for yokes, sleeves and cushions. Use polyester thread for strength. The gathering is slight; use the gathering foot or insert rows of gathering threads by hand or machine. Work the waffling on a large piece of fabric and cut out the pattern piece afterward.

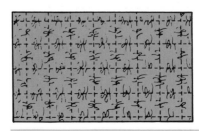

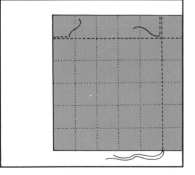

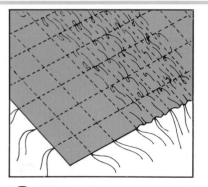

1 Waffle Mark area of fabric to be gathered on RS with horizontal and vertical rows of chalk dots. Insert gathers by hand or by machine, with large straight stitch, on RS along vertical rows and then horizontal. Reverse at the start of each row to anchor threads; leave long ends.

2 When all the rows are gathered, take hold of one set of threads (the bobbin ones if gathers were inserted by machine) and ease the fabric along them. Pull the threads up the desired amount and then pull the other set to balance.

Tips

1 Work parallel rows of tucks, gathers, shirring, gauging and waffling in the same direction on the fabric.

2 To judge how much material you will need for a gathering process, measure a small piece of fabric and try out the process. Re-measure the fabric to see how much fabric has been taken up.

3 When joining seams, stitch with the gathered piece uppermost so that you can keep a check on the gathering.

4 Hold a newly shirred area in the steam of boiling water for a few seconds to shrink the elastic and give it more grip.

ELASTIC

Elastic controls fullness at an edge or within a garment. Core elastic, baby and lingerie elastic and elastic webbing can all be threaded through a hem, channel or casing; elastic webbing can also be stitched directly to the fabric. A hem can be narrow at the edge of the garment or deep and stitched twice so that a frill is created below the elastic, or it can be double depth with two parallel rows of stitching which take two pieces of elastic. Measure elastic generously, adjust size after threading. It will pull up one and a half times its length if attached to fabric or up to three times if threaded.

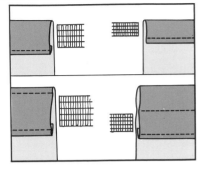

Casing width The width of the casing, hem or channel must be carefully calculated to ensure that elastic can move within it. Allow width of elastic plus 5 mm/$\frac{1}{4}$in ease plus twice thickness of elastic plus one seam allowance. If edge is to be stitched, add twice finished edge width.

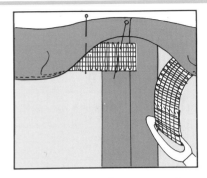

Threading elastic Use an elastic threader or, for long pieces, a rouleau tubing needle. Narrow elastic can be threaded through the eye and tied. Wide elastic and elastic webbing must be sewn firmly to the eye. Prevent elastic twisting by pinning across the hem while evening out the fullness.

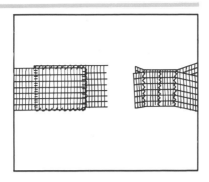

Joining ends Pin ends. For a flat finish in fine fabric overlap ends by 1 cm/$\frac{3}{8}$in; oversew overlapping edges and loop stitch over raw edges. Elastic webbing can be joined by stitching across with straight zigzag stitch. Make two or three rows 1 cm/$\frac{3}{8}$in apart enabling it to be loosened if necessary.

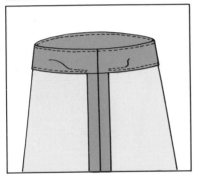

1 Slot for threading Baste hem or casing on WS garment. Stitch upper edge if required. Finish raw edge or press under. Stitch along lower edge, leaving a 1 cm/$\frac{3}{8}$in gap—more for wide elastic. Reverse stitching at each end. After inserting and joining elastic, hem or machine edge to close gap.

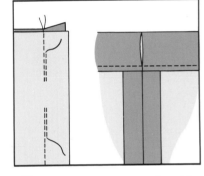

2 If the depth of hem and position of elastic can be established a neater slot can be made by leaving a gap in the seam. Stitch seam for 1.5 cm/$\frac{5}{8}$in at the edge, leave a suitable gap then stitch remainder. Press seam open. Fold edge to WS, press, baste and stitch.

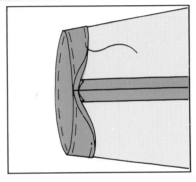

Integrated casing Allowance for casing must be added when cutting out garment. Fold hem to WS, baste the fold; press. Trim raw edge to depth to take elastic. Either zigzag or fold under; baste and stitch beside folded edge, or close to zigzag, leaving slot for elastic if not in seam.

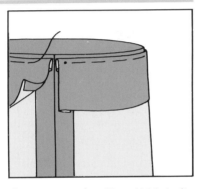

Separate casing Use self-fabric, lining or bias binding. Attach to RS garment, joining over a seam by turning ends in to meet. Trim edges, and roll casing to WS. Baste along edge and press. Finish lower edge; stitch upper edge if required. Stitch ends of facing, leaving a slot for elastic.

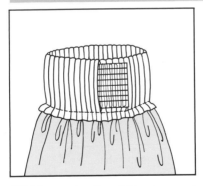

Ribbing casing Cut ribbing to correct length and width. With RS together join ends, leaving slot for threading. Zigzag raw edges. Stitch ribbing, stretched, to RS garment. Insert elastic. Alternatively, attach ribbing, insert elastic and *then* stitch along seam, stitching through ribbing and elastic.

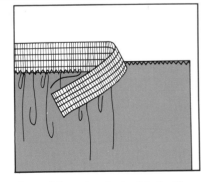

Attaching elastic to fabric Zigzag raw edge of garment or turn and stitch a narrow hem. Cut elastic to size, join ends, divide and mark elastic and garment edge into quarters. With fabric RS up zigzag along edge of elastic overlapping it onto the fabric. Stretch elastic, match up quarters.

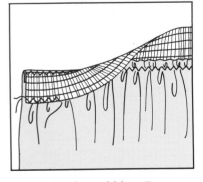

Wide elastic webbing For waist, ankles etc. Cut and join elastic, divide fabric edge and elastic into quarters. Overlap edge of elastic 1 cm/$\frac{5}{8}$in onto RS fabric. Zigzag along edge, stretch elastic and match quarters. Fold elastic to WS garment, zigzag along remaining edge keeping fabric flat.

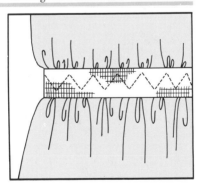

Attaching to fabric away from edge Cut and join elastic. Divide elastic and garment into quarters. Place elastic on WS fabric and attach down the middle with zigzag, elastic stitch or running zigzag. Stretch elastic, matching quarters. Wide elastic should be stitched along each edge.

SHAPING

FRILLS

Frills can be made in most fabrics, other than bulky ones. On fine fabrics make a double frill for extra body. Measure garment edge and decide on amount of fullness required: half as much again as the garment edge gives a slight gathering effect; twice as much provides a very gathered frill. The depth of the frill depends on its position—take care not to throw the design out of balance. Frills made from straight pieces of fabric are easier to handle.

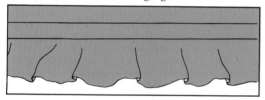

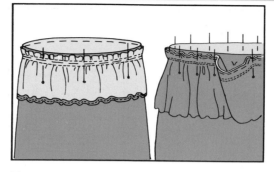

1 Frills For skirt or sleeve frills, join ends to form a circle. Hem outer edge. Insert two rows of gathers along other edge. Pin to garment, RS together. Pull up gathers to fit. Baste and machine frill to garment. For a double frill, cut out to twice finished depth; join ends. Fold RS together, press and baste raw edges together. Insert gathers through both layers and proceed as for single frill.

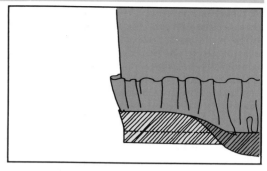

2 If the frill is to lie back on the garment, place hemmed frill RS up on RS of garment. Lay bias strip RS down on raw edge of frill. Baste and stitch through all layers. Remove basting. Fold strip over trimmed seam edges so that they are encased. On WS hem finished strip edge into machining.

RUFFLES

A decorative finish on necklines and cuffs, a ruffle is a piece of fabric cut in such a way that the outer edge is longer than the inner. This causes the ruffle to flute decoratively when attached. Make ruffles in fine fabrics so that they are not too bulky. As for frills, ruffles can be made single or double, and can lie back or extend from the edge of the garment.

Ruffles provide an opportunity for adding decorative stitches and edgings.

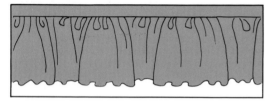

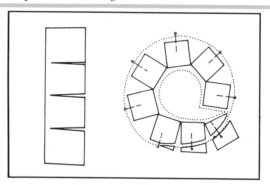

1 Ruffles Measure length of garment edge. Cut a piece of paper to that length by approximate width of ruffle. Fold the paper into equal squares. Open out and cut along each fold almost to edge of paper. Arrange on another piece of paper, spreading out the cut sections. Draw around the first piece of paper and cut along the drawn line; if the ruffle is to end in a point, trim off a corner.

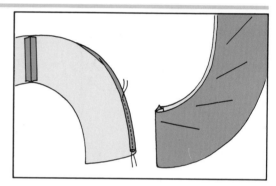

2 Use cut paper to cut out fabric for ruffle. For skirt or sleeve ruffle, join ends to form a circle. Turn up narrow rolled hem on outer edge of ruffle and machine or whipstitch along it. For double ruffle, cut two fabric pieces and baste along outer edge, RS together. Machine, press, remove basting and trim edges to 3 mm/⅛ in. Turn RS out, press outer edge and diagonally baste inner raw edges together.

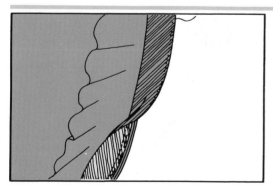

3 If the ruffle is to lie back on the garment, place hemmed ruffle RS up on RS of garment. Lay bias strip RS down on raw edge of ruffle. Baste and stitch through all layers. Remove basting. Fold strip over trimmed seam edges so they are encased. On WS hem finished strip edge into machining. Press bias strip and frill.

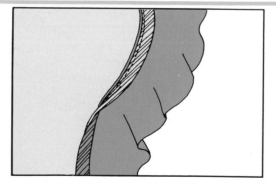

4 If the ruffle is to extend from the garment, attach it with a facing or a bias strip. Baste ruffle to garment, RS together. Baste bias strip or facing RS down on top of ruffle and machine through all layers. Remove basting. Turn bias strip or facing to WS; hem bias into machining and hold down facing in usual way.

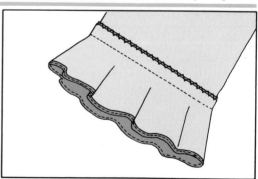

5 If the join will not show in wear, as at the end of a tight sleeve or the bottom of a skirt, attach the ruffle direct to the garment, RS together. Trim raw edges and finish together. Press finished edges toward garment.

FACINGS

A facing is a method of finishing an edge such as a neckline or armhole by applying a piece of fabric to one side of the edge and turning it completely to the other side. The facing is usually finished on the wrong side of the garment and is invisible.

For best results, cut facings from garment material if fabric is light- or medium-weight, but from lining material, nylon knit or thin cotton if garment fabric is bulky.

Facings are sometimes in one piece, but more often are in several pieces that are joined, for neatness, in places corresponding to the garment seams.

Before applying facing, stitch, finish and press as many garment seams as possible and mark seam allowances clearly on the garment edges. Interface areas that need support before facing. Always attach facing pieces to the garment before joining them.

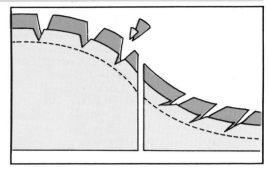

1 Layering and clipping Eliminate bulk in seams and help facings to lie flat by layering the edges and then clipping them. Trim interfacing, if used, very close to stitching; trim raw edge of facing to 3 mm/⅛ in. Trim garment edge to 5 mm/¼ in. Cut off corners diagonally close to stitching.

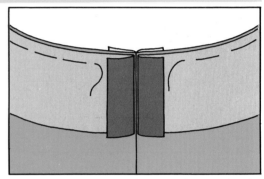

2 To ensure that facings will lie flat when finished, reduce bulk by clipping. Concave edges can have small V-shapes clipped out every 5 mm/¼ in if fabric is bulky. All curves should be clipped at an angle, almost to the stitching, every 5 mm/¼ in.

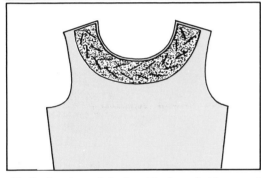

1 Basic shaped facing Used to finish curved edges such as necklines and armholes. If interfacing is needed, attach before facing. Cut out interfacing using facing pattern pieces. Trim 5 mm/¼ in from outer edge of each piece of interfacing to ensure that it will not extend beyond the finished edge of the facings. Diagonally baste interfacing to WS of garment.

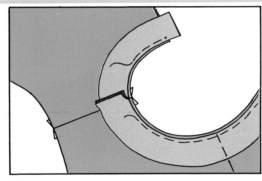

2 With RS together, place facing pieces in position on garment, matching shaped edges. Insert a few pins to hold. Baste along seamline finishing 2 cm/¾ in away from any joins that have to be made in the facing. On a neckline with a zipper at the centre back, baste to the end. (The seam allowance of 1.5 cm/⅝ in on the facing extends beyond the zipper.) Remove pins.

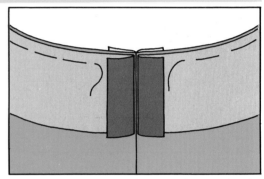

3 Make sure the facing is lying flat. Lightly press back all the unstitched facing ends so that the folds of each adjacent pair meet exactly over the garment seamline beneath them. These seam allowances may not be equal in depth if an alteration has been made or the facing has stretched.

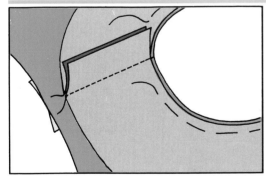

4 Lift pressed edges and place folds together. Insert one pin centrally across folds if fabric is slippery or springy. Baste along fold lines and remove pin. Keeping join away from garment, machine or backstitch along fold line. Remove basting. Trim seam allowances to 5 mm/¼ in and trim off corners at seam edge diagonally.

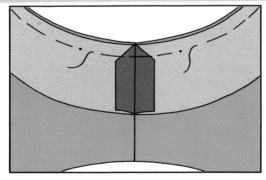

5 Press joins open and finish basting the facing to the garment by stitching across them.

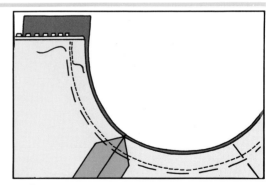

6 With garment WS up, machine slowly along marked seamline rather than on basting. On a neckline with a zipper, start just inside zipper, reverse for a few stitches, then sew forward. Stop frequently to turn work and produce a smooth curve. Lift work to make sure seams lie flat in the right direction and that facing joins are open and flat. Finish by reversing for a few stitches.

FACINGS

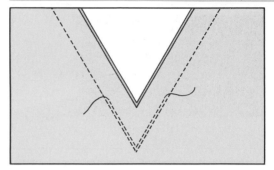

7 Work a second row of machining on top of first row around a sharp curve or at the point of a V-neck to prevent the fraying that will otherwise occur when this area is later clipped. Remove basting.

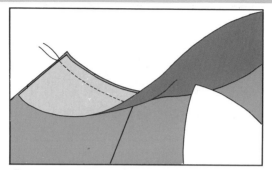

8 Place garment on sleeve board RS down. Press stitching flat, taking care not to distort the shaping of the edge. With RS up, slide iron under facing and run tip around join, lifting facing up vertically. Finish off by layering and clipping. For a V-neck, clip from point at outer edge almost down to point of machining.

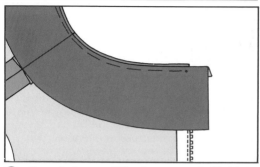

9 Turn facing to WS of garment; hold fabric across join and roll facing between thumb and finger to bring join to edge. Baste, rolling facing 2 mm/$\frac{1}{16}$ in to WS at each needle insertion so join does not show on RS. Baste about 2 mm/$\frac{1}{16}$ in from edge on fine fabrics, 4 mm/$\frac{1}{8}$ in on heavier ones. If basting is too close to edge it will not anchor facing, if too distant the join will roll back to RS.

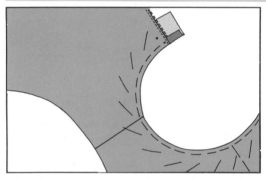

10 Press edge well on WS and RS. With RS of garment uppermost, hold faced edge over one hand to keep it in shape. Work a row of diagonal basting below edge to hold facing flat and in position.

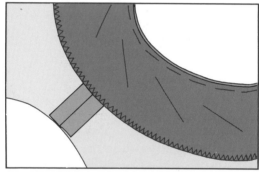

11 On WS trim any fraying sections from lower edge of facing and finish as for an open seam. A zigzag machine stitch tends to straighten a curved edge, so press with a damp cloth or steam iron after stitching to flatten any flutes. When pressing, keep facing edge away from garment to avoid making an imprint on garment.

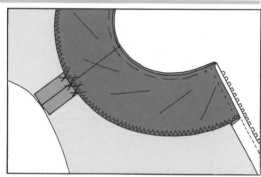

12 On WS attach facing to garment wherever facing edge crosses a seam. Use hemming stitches if facing edge has been turned under, or herringbone stitch if facing edge is flat. For knit fabric, lift facing edge and work a bar tack about 2 mm/$\frac{1}{16}$ in long between seam allowance and facing. Turn under facing end and prick stitch folded edge to zipper tape beside teeth. Remove basting.

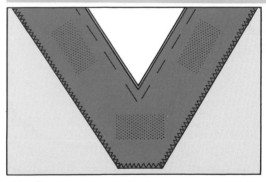

13 To anchor facing more securely—this is particularly important at armholes and V-necks—use fabric adhesive strip. Cut pieces 2 to 2.5 cm/$\frac{3}{4}$ to 1 in long. Place garment WS up on sleeve board. Slip pieces of adhesive web under facing every 2.5 to 4 cm/1 to 1$\frac{1}{2}$ in, or wherever edge is very shaped or fabric is springing up. Press well, using a damp cloth, to melt adhesive.

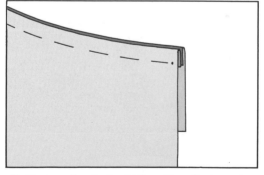

1 **Decorative facing** Follow (**1**) to (**8**) above, but place facing RS down on WS of garment. Hold garment WS up and turn facing over to RS. Roll edge between finger and thumb to reveal join and then roll it toward you until 2 mm/$\frac{1}{16}$ in of facing shows on WS of garment so that join is invisible on RS. Baste on WS with small stitches close to edge and press on WS and RS as for (**9**) and (**10**) above.

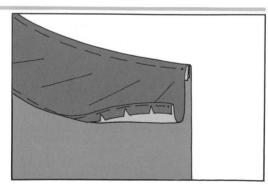

2 With garment and facing RS up, work diagonal basting beside top edge of facing. Mark hem allowance on lower edge with tailor's chalk or a row of basting. Turn in facing on marked line and baste it down beside fold. Trim raw edge to about 5 mm/$\frac{1}{4}$ in and clip any curves. Holding facing away from garment to avoid making an imprint, press hem allowance along basting line.

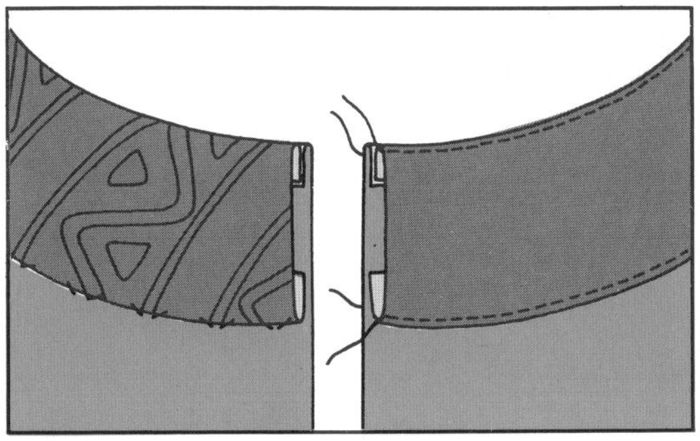

3 Baste facing flat to RS of garment. Finish by slip hemming, which may be preferable on patterned fabrics, or by machining with a straight or zigzag stitch along top and bottom edges. Alternatively, finish with a machine embroidery stitch along neck and facing edges. Remove all basting and press.

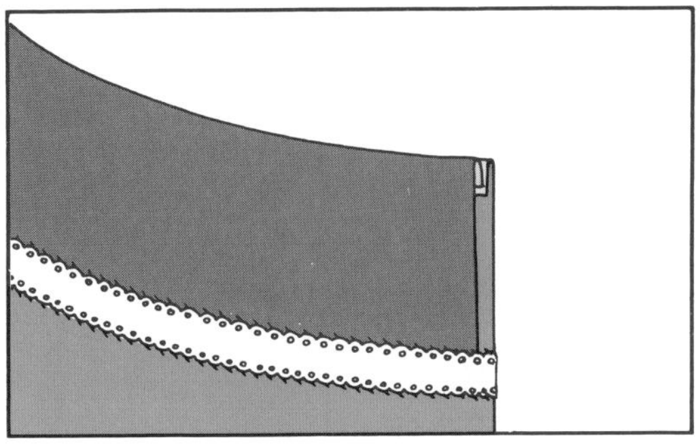

4 For extra decoration, mark or baste along hem allowance as in (**2**) and trim fabric exactly on this line. Baste facing flat to garment and cover raw edge with braid. Baste braid in place, turn in ends and hem them down. Attach braid along both edges by hemming or machine stitching. For a shaped facing, choose a braid that will ease around the curves. Remove all basting and press.

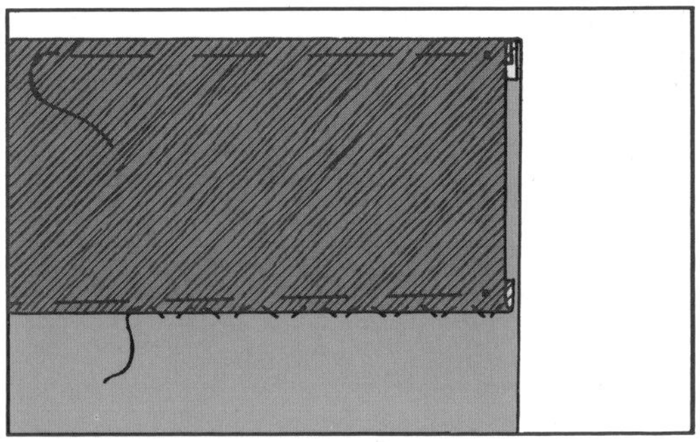

5 To apply decorative facing to a straight or nearly straight edge such as a hemline, cut strips of fabric on the bias or true cross and join to give required length. Baste to WS of garment with ends of strip joining over left side seam of skirt. Follow (**3**) to (**8**) of basic method. Roll facing over to RS as for standard decorative facing, baste and press. Hold down lower edge as in (**3**) or (**4**).

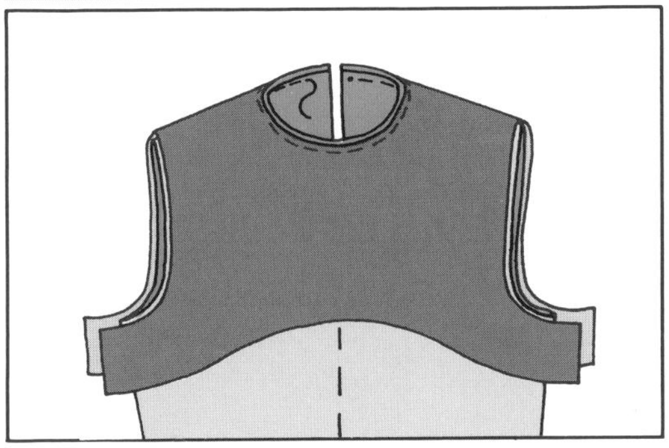

1 Combination facing If neck and armhole facings cut in usual way will overlap at the shoulder, one large facing can be cut to combine the two. Pin facing pattern pieces together to correct shape before cutting out; lower edge of facing must curve upward from armhole to avoid restricting the shaping in the bust or back. Follow (**1**) to (**9**) of basic method, but do not join underarm seams of facing.

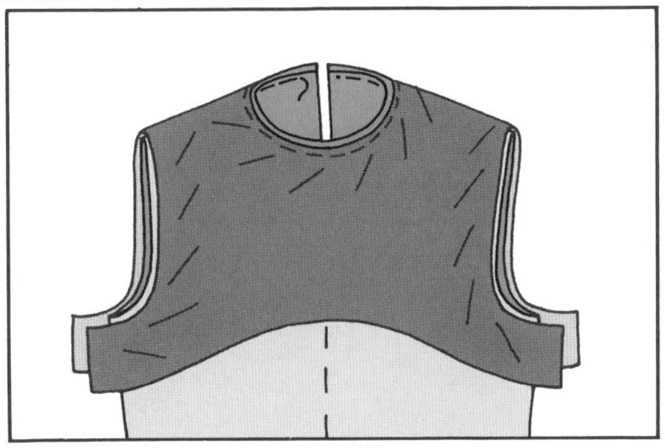

2 With WS of garment and RS of facing outermost, hold faced edge over one hand to keep it in shape. Work a row of diagonal basting around neck below edge to hold facing flat and in position against garment. Holding raw edges together, baste diagonally around armholes, but do not take basting too close to the edges.

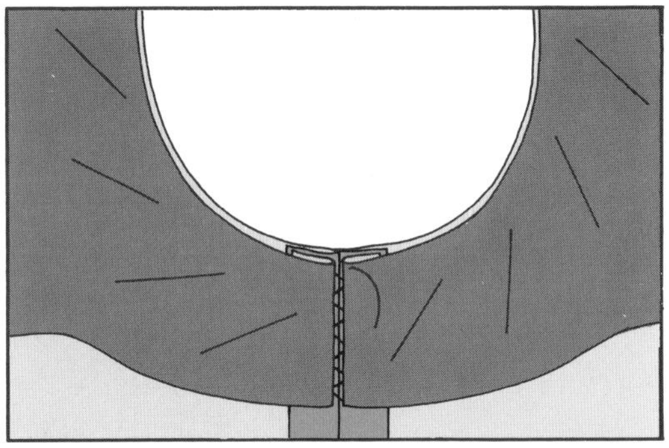

3 At underarm seam, turn in two facing edges to meet over seam. Slip stitch together.

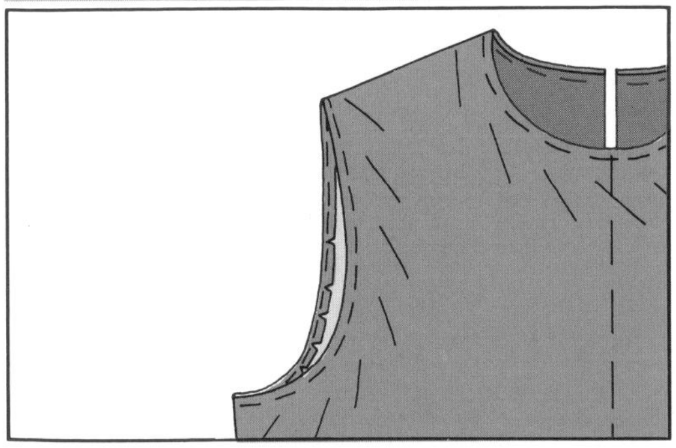

4 With garment RS out, turn in garment armhole edges along marked seamline. Baste along fold. Clip any curves using layering and clipping method. Press fold. If fabric is thick or springy, finish raw edges with herringbone stitch on WS.

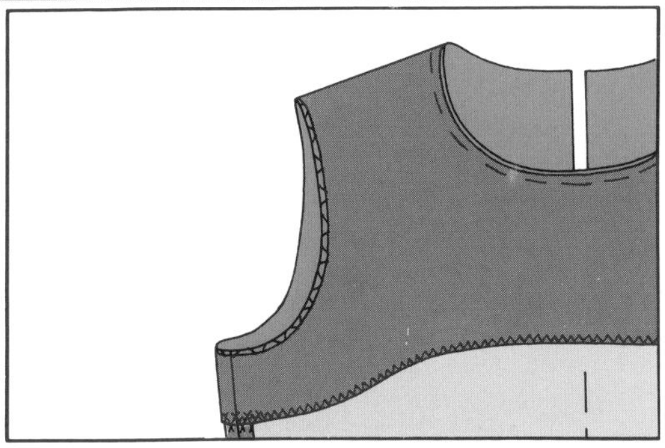

5 Trim 8 mm/$\frac{3}{8}$in from raw edge of facing at armhole edge. Turn in trimmed edge to WS of facing so fold is 2 mm/$\frac{1}{16}$ in from garment edge. Baste to garment and press. Finish by working hemming or fell stitch around armhole on WS. Finish lower edge of facing. Where facing crosses underarm seam hold down with herringbone stitch. Remove all basting and press again.

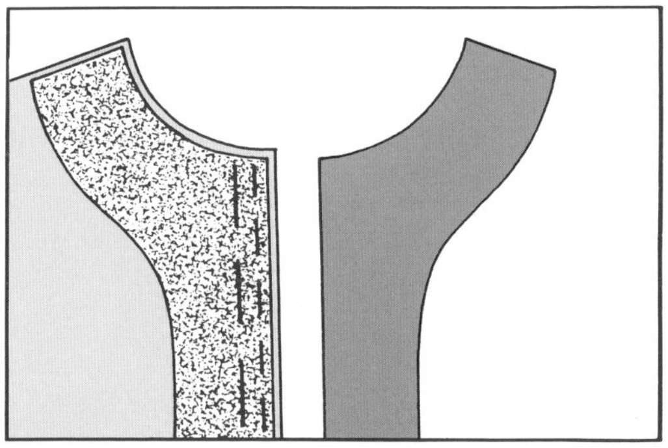

1 Neckline with front opening: facing separate Use this method if front edge is shaped or of contrasting fabric, or if loops or ties are used. Baste loops or ties in place. Folow (**2**) to (**7**) of basic method. When machining, start at bottom of centre front; continue around neck and down opposite centre front edge. Remove basting.

FACINGS

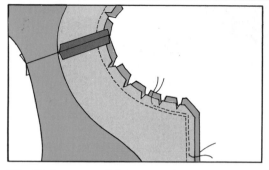

2 With garment RS down on sleeve board, press stitching flat. With RS up, slide iron under facing as far as possible and, lifting facing, run tip around join. Layer edges and clip neck edge. Do not clip front edge, unless it is curved (as for lapel), because this will weaken it and may lead to an uneven appearance. Trim top corners at neck edge diagonally.

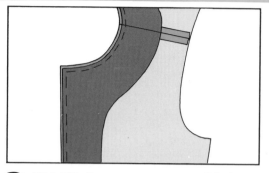

3 With WS of garment uppermost, roll facing to WS as for (9) of basic method so that join is 2 mm/$\frac{1}{16}$ in to WS. Baste close to edge. Work corner out by rolling it with fingers or pushing it out with a collar point turner. Press edge well on WS and RS.

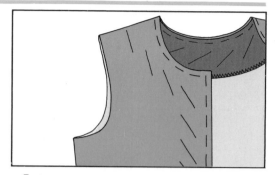

4 On RS of garment work a row of diagonal basting all around near edge. On WS finish lower edge of facing and attach facing to shoulder seams with herringbone or hemming stitch, or a bar tack, as for (11) and (12) of basic method. Remove basting, unless buttonholes are to be worked or completed.

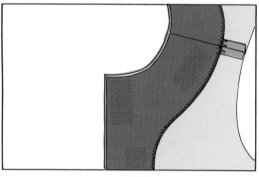

5 To prevent fraying, push a small piece of fabric adhesive into each corner of neckline front with a bodkin and press firmly. As for final stage of basic method, insert small pieces of adhesive strip between facing and garment at back of neck and in several places down front edges. Press well. If buttonholes are to be worked or completed, do not insert adhesive until this has been done.

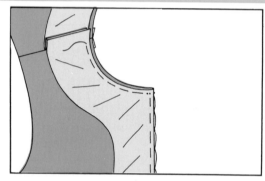

Neckline with front opening: facing attached To avoid bulky front-edge joins, cut front facings as garment extensions. Interface garment if desired. Mark centre front and seamlines. Work first stages of piped or bound buttonholes. Fold front facing to RS. Baste along fold and around neck and diagonally to within 2 cm/$\frac{3}{4}$ in of shoulder joins. Attach self-fabric back facing as for basic method (2).

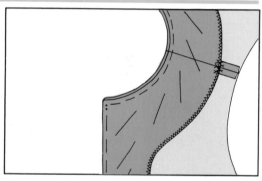

2 Join back neck facing at shoulders to front facing, following (3) to (9) of basic method. With garment RS up, machine all around neck, reversing a few stitches at both centre front edges. Finish facing as for last three stages of front neck opening with separate facing.

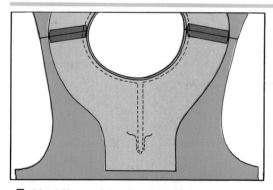

Neckline with slit opening Front facing extends 4 cm/1$\frac{1}{2}$ in below slit. Follow (1) and (2) of basic method, basting facings in position. On WS of garment, mark position and depth of slit at centre front. Follow (3) to (6) of basic method, leaving 3 mm/$\frac{1}{8}$ in between lines of stitching down sides of slit and stitching to a point at its base. Work a second row of stitching around point. Remove basting.

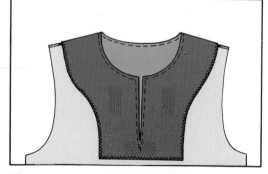

2 Cut slit carefully between stitching right up to machining at point. Layer all edges and clip neck edges. Turn facing to WS and proceed as for basic method (9) to (11), attaching lower edge of facing at shoulder seams. Remove diagonal basting and insert short pieces of fabric adhesive on each side of opening and at corners as for neck opening with separate facing. Remove basting and press.

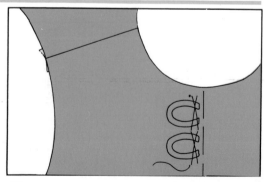

3 If ties or tubing loops are to be used to fasten slit, position them on RS at centre front edge so that they face away from the slit. Baste them down before applying facing. Place facing over ties or loops and complete opening as above. As the facing is rolled to WS the loops or ties will extend beyond the edge. For loops, attach buttons on other side of slit.

WAISTS

The position of the join between bodice and skirt varies with style and fashion from a high empire line to a low line on the hips. Whatever the style, the method of making a waist join is the same.

Fitting is particularly important in linking the bodice and skirt because the join must be in exactly the right place and neither too tight nor too loose. Patterns sometimes give instructions for joining the front of the bodice to the skirt front, the back of the bodice to the skirt back and then stitching the side seams from underarm to hem. This is a very unsatisfactory method, as the waist cannot be fitted properly.

Before making a waist join, make up the dress skirt except for the hem. Stitch the darts and seams in the bodice, but not the shoulder seams—the work is much easier to handle if these are left open. Leave openings of the correct length in both the skirt and the bodice for inserting the zipper or any other fastening.

Many people find a waistband restricting on skirts and trousers, and a more comfortable waist can be created by turning in the garment edge and adding tape, ribbon or, more usually, petersham. Petersham comes as a ribbon in different widths or as fabric. The fabric variety may be soft or boned, straight or curved. Curved petersham that fits slightly below the waist is often more comfortable than straight as it does not ride up during wear. Whichever petersham you choose should be washable and no wider than 4 cm/1½ in or it will curl up.

Stitch petersham in place after the waist edge has been turned in. Because the edge of petersham is stiff to sew, use a very small needle and polyester thread and hem into each bead at the petersham edge.

For the very best results do not use the waistband piece provided by the pattern. Instead, establish the waistband length by measuring your waist and allowing for seam allowances and any overlap. Calculate width according to personal taste, the garment style and the amount of fabric available. Do not cut out the waistband until you are ready to make it.

Tips

1 Always measure the band to fit your waist and make the garment fit the band.
2 Always baste on a band when fitting a garment, especially trousers, as it helps the hang. A length of petersham can be used.
3 Do not trim waist seam allowances too much as they act as support during wear. A guide is 5 mm/¼ in on bulky fabrics, 3 mm/⅛ in on medium or lightweight ones.
4 Never clip waist turnings or the waist will stretch during wear.

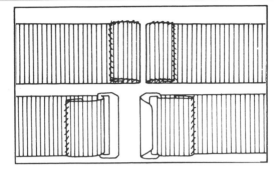

Petersham or petersham ribbon Turn in ends 1.5 cm/⅝ in and turn in raw edges; hem around. When fastened, petersham should fit waist loosely. Fasten with a hook and eye or hook and bar. A flat metal clip can also be attached to the petersham. Slip 1.5 cm/⅝ in of petersham through slots on clip, turn in raw edges and hem around. The hook should face toward the body during wear.

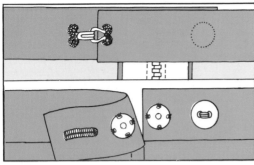

Overlap or underlap Attach a hook and eye supported with a snap. Place the well section of the snap on underlap and the other part directly above it on WS of end of overlap. Stitch eye to end of underlap on WS and hook to overlap. Hook should face toward the body during wear. Buttons and buttonholes can also be used, but back them up with a snap to prevent buttonholes losing their shape in wear.

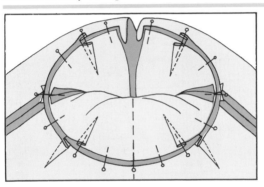

1 **Making a waist join** Arrange garment bodice RS up on a table. Place RS of skirt on bodice. Pin together at centre front and/or centre back, inserting pins vertically on WS of bodice. Match side seams, edges of opening and darts on skirt with those on bodice and pin; if darts will not match as a result of fitting adjustments, arrange them evenly. Match all other seamlines and pin.

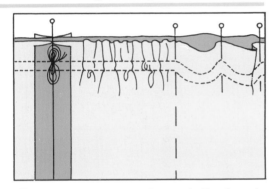

2 If any part of the skirt or bodice is to be gathered, insert two rows of gathering before pinning. Arrange bodice and skirt RS together as before and pin side seams, edges of opening and centre front and/or centre back, inserting pins vertically. Pull up gathering threads to fit and wind ends around pin. Insert extra pins around waist on joins, but use more, close together, if gathered.

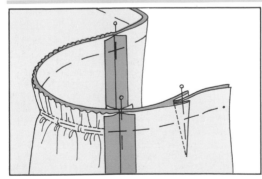

3 Baste all around waist with small stitches, working from the gathered side if appropriate, but from either side if both bodice and skirt are gathered. When basting across darts, make sure that they lie open or flat and face toward the centre. Remove all pins except those at seams and darts.

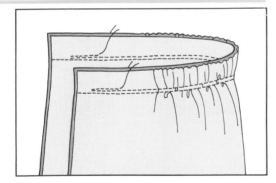

4 Machine waist join with gathers uppermost, making sure darts remain in position. Remove pins. For strength, work a second row of stitching 2 mm/¹⁄₁₆ in above the first, starting and finishing 2 cm/¾ in from opening. Reverse for a few stitches at each end. Remove basting and gathers. To prevent knit fabric from stretching, stitch seam binding into the join on bodice side, as for taped seam.

WAISTS

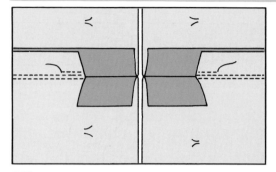

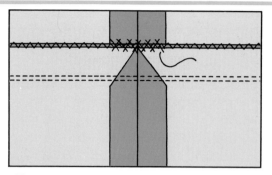

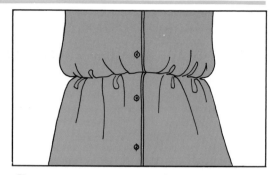

5 Trim raw edges to 1 cm/⅜ in. Clip into skirt seam allowance close to machining, 2 cm/¾ in from opening, and press seam open. This reduces bulk and makes the opening easier to finish.

6 Finish raw edges as appropriate to fabric. For fine fabrics, and garments that will be washed frequently, bind the edges, use a zigzag stitch, or work another row of machining and overcast. On WS press waist seam allowances up toward bodice. Press again on RS. At side seams hold waist join seam allowances in position with herringbone stitch.

Stays The appearance of a dress with a full skirt, or one made from fabric that is heavy or gives, is greatly improved by a stay inserted in the waist. A blouson dress needs a stay to lift the bodice so that the waist is in the correct position. If the dress is to be worn with a belt, a stay prevents the waist join from dropping and helps to ensure that the join remains invisible during wear.

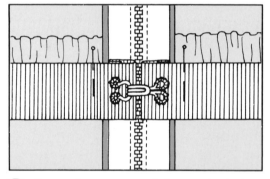

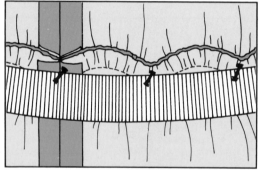

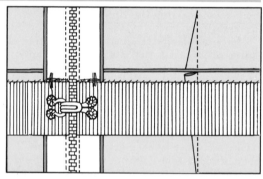

2 Do not insert stay until dress is finished or zipper has been put in. Cut curved or straight petersham (or, for fine fabrics, grosgrain ribbon), not wider than 2.5 cm/1 in, to waist size, plus 3 cm/1¼ in. Turn in ends and attach hook and eye. Press waist join up into bodice. With zipper closed, pin fastened petersham to waist join on either side of zipper, with top edge of petersham on waist join.

3 For curved petersham place concave edge on waist join so convex edge hangs below waistline. In loose-fitting or gathered blouson dresses the waist join is longer than the petersham. Insert more pins at intervals around waist join so garment waist is evenly positioned along petersham. Attach petersham with bar tacks at side seams, centre front or centre back and once between these points. Remove pins.

4 If the dress is close fitting, the petersham and waist join should be exactly the same length. After pinning at regular intervals, hold petersham firmly in place by hemming its top edge to seam allowances on waist join. On each side of zipper finish hemming at edge of tape and work a strong bar tack to anchor petersham to tape, 2 cm/¾ in from zipper teeth. Remove pins.

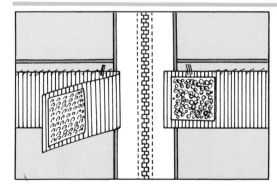

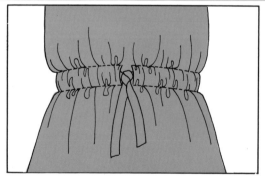

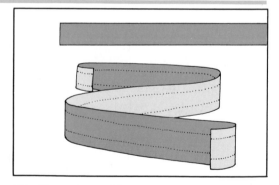

5 For easy fastening at centre back use two 2.5 cm/1 in pieces of Velcro rather than a hook and eye. Cut petersham 3 cm/1¼ in longer than required and turn in and finish end of underlap. Attach one piece of Velcro to underlap, the other to overlap. Hold overlap down with a bar tack 5 cm/2 in from edge of zipper tape. When fastening the dress, fasten the stay before the zipper.

Drawstring waistline A casing—a length of fabric through which a tie or elastic is threaded—applied to RS or WS of a garment can be used instead of a waist join. The tie can be rouleau tubing, a flat tie belt, cord, braided wool, crochet, macramé or elastic with fabric tie ends. On a lined garment, make the casing by working two rows of stitching through the fabric and lining at the required distance apart.

2 For casing width, measure width of tie insertion, allowing for its thickness, and then add 5 mm/¼ in for ease and 3 cm/1¼ in for seam allowances. For casing length, add 5 cm/2 in to garment waistline measurement. Cut a strip of fabric, preferably on the cross but on straight grain if there is insufficient material, joining if necessary. For a casing on WS purchased bias binding may be used.

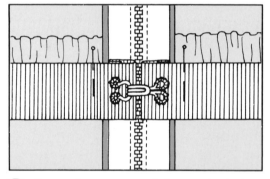

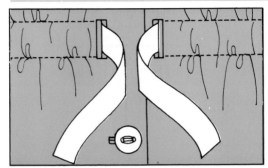

3 If drawstring is to emerge on RS of garment, work two large vertical buttonholes on the garment before attaching casing. Make them slightly narrower than width of casing and place 2.5 cm/1 in apart or, if the garment opening is fastened with buttons, far enough for opening to lie flat. The buttonholes may be worked by machine, but piped buttonholes give the best finish.

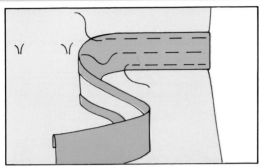

4 For a casing on WS of garment, mark waistline on WS with a row of basting or tailor's tacks. Centre casing, RS up, over marking and baste along centre. Turn in raw edge 1.5 cm/⅝ in on one side of casing and baste down. Using an adjustable marker, turn in 1.5 cm/⅝ in on other side and baste. Turn in ends to meet, or turn them in at edges of zipper tape or just behind worked buttonholes.

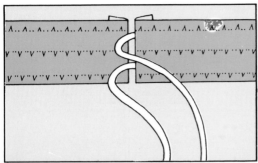

5 With casing uppermost, stitch along each edge of casing. A straight stitch may look crooked on RS of garment so use a small zigzag or blind hem stitch for a neater look, especially on plain fabrics. For an attractive effect, stitch again through the centre of the finished casing to allow space for two fine cord or tubing ties. Remove basting and insert ties.

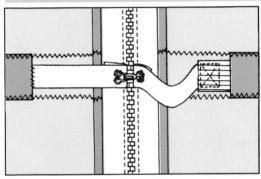

6 Attach casing for elastic before inserting zipper or finishing opening. Position casing, turn in edges and baste as in (**4**). Turn in ends 5 cm/2 in from opening and baste. Machine along both edges to opening. Remove basting. Insert zipper or finish opening. Cut elastic to fit waist and machine 5 cm/2 in of cotton tape to ends. Insert elastic and hem tape to casing. Turn in ends, hem and attach hook and eye.

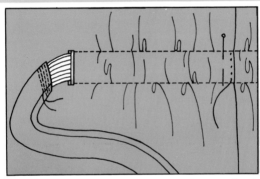

7 For elastic with fabric tie ends, cut elastic slightly shorter than waist and make a length of tubing. Turn tubing RS out, slot ends of elastic inside and machine across ends of rouleau several times to hold elastic. Slot elastic into casing, put on garment, arrange gathers and pin at side seams. Remove garment and prick stitch from RS through garment and elastic at side seams. Remove pins.

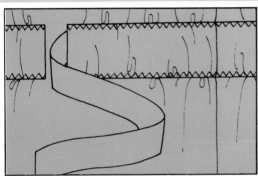

8 For a casing on RS of garment, a strip cut on the cross often improves the design, as with checked fabric. Any joins in casing should correspond with garment seams. Fold under seam allowances on casing sides and baste casing to waist join, with RS up. Turn in ends so they are 1 cm/⅜ in apart. Machine along both edges of casing in straight, zigzag or embroidery stitch. Remove basting. Insert tie.

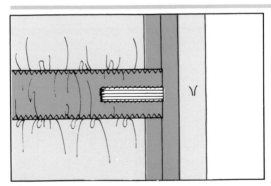

9 If casing is applied to only part of a garment, such as around the back of the waist, cut casing and baste in position as in (**4**) and turn in ends. Machine casing sides and remove basting. If elastic is to be threaded through casing, allow enough to turn back over casing; hem sides and loop stitch raw ends of elastic firmly in position.

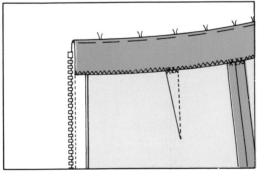

1 **Petersham waist finish** Insert zipper into garment. Turn top edge of garment to WS along marked waistline above zipper. Baste along fold. Press, taking care to avoid stretching. Finish raw edge with overcasting or zigzag. Where edge crosses a dart or a seam hold it in place with herringbone stitch. At the zipper hem ends down and across zipper tape and seam allowances.

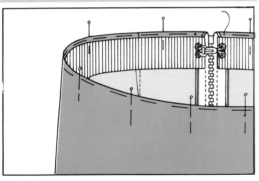

2 Cut petersham to the waist length plus 3 cm/1¼ in. Turn in 1.5 cm/⅝ in at ends and attach a hook and eye so petersham fits waist when fastened. Fasten zipper. With garment RS out, slip fastened petersham inside waist with hook and eye under zipper. With top edge of petersham 2 mm/1/16 in below waist edge, pin on each side of zipper. Pin all around from RS to ease any fullness.

WAISTS

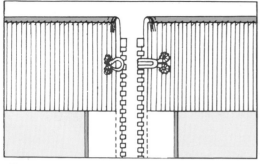

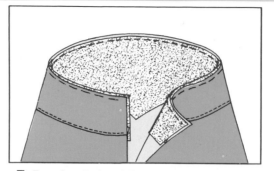

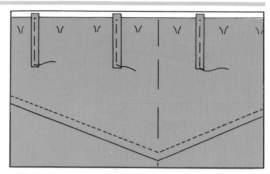

3 Baste petersham in position, remove pins and hem top edge to garment. Anchor ends of top edge of petersham on each side of zipper with a bar tack into zipper tape. Remove basting. Press.

| **Faced waistband** On casual clothes and those with yokes a soft waistline finish can be created with a facing. Baste interfacing to WS of waist area, over the yoke if there is one. Construct garment. Insert zipper.

2 If belt carriers are a feature of the style, make them up and baste in position on RS of garment up to raw edge of waist, basting along full length of each carrier to prevent ends from being caught in subsequent stitching. Alternatively, hold them in position with transparent adhesive tape. The minimum number of carriers should be one at each side seam, two at the back and two at the front.

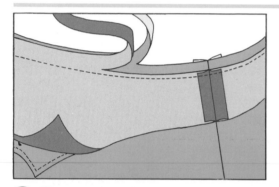

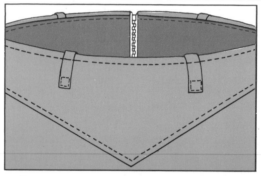

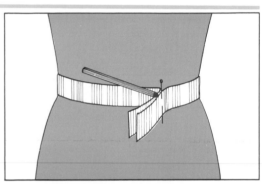

3 Place waist facing RS down on RS of garment. Baste and make joins as for other facings. Machine along seamline with garment uppermost. Layer as for facings, trimming seam allowances to no less than 3 mm/⅛ in on fine fabrics or 5 mm/¼ in on thicker ones. Do not clip. On soft or knit fabrics prevent stretching by inserting seam binding on WS garment into waist join, as for taped seam.

4 Roll facing to WS so join is 2 mm/1/16 in toward inside of waist edge. Baste close to join. Press. Belt carriers now extend from join. Bring them over to RS, turn ends under; baste down. Stitch carriers in a square, hemming around three sides and working prick or stab stitch across top of square. Remove basting. For decorative effect, machine around carriers or work topstitching around waist.

| **Straight waistband** Stiffen with petersham sew-in waistbanding or perforated iron-on banding. Measure it firmly around the waist, allowing at least 7.5 cm/3 in overlap—it can be reduced later. Mark the overlap with fabric pen.

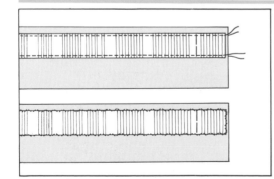

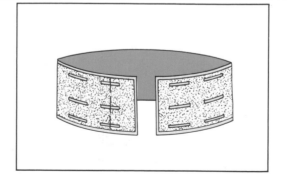

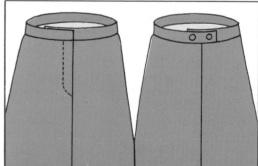

2 Cut a length of fabric on straight grain twice width of stiffening plus 3 mm/1½ in or, for perforated banding, same width. To attach petersham or sew-in banding place one edge along centre of fabric on WS. Stitch, using catch stitch all around or machining along each edge to end of fabric.

3 Perforated interfacing band is simply pressed to the WS of the fabric. Align central perforations on straight grain. Press with hot iron and damp cloth. With all types of stiffening the end can be level with the end of the waistband but with lightweight fabrics reduce bulk by trimming off 1.5 cm/⅝ in.

4 The longer end can overlap or underlap the shorter, depending on the style of the garment and the position of the fastening. Underlapping is preferable for side and back openings, because it is neater and less conspicuous, while an overlap looks more attractive for a front opening and creates a slimming effect if fastened with two buttons.

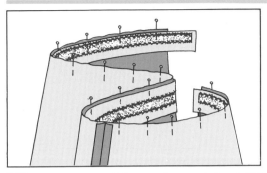

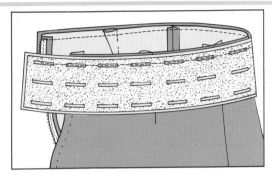

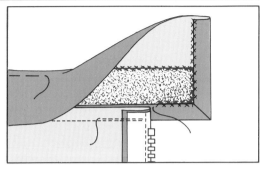

5 With garment RS out, place waistband RS down on RS of waist, matching raw edges and with interfacing at top. Pin band to garment at start of extension. Pin other end so end of stiffening aligns with zipper edge. Pin at intervals around waist. If there is much extra fabric in waist turn garment WS out and pin band at frequent intervals to RS, easing fullness. Baste. Remove pins.

6 With waistband uppermost, machine just above edge of stiffening or on perforations, finishing at edges of zipper and reversing for a few stitches at each end. Remove basting. Trim seam allowances to about 5 mm/¼ in—too much trimming may lead to stretching. Open out band away from garment and press waist join from RS so that seam allowances are pushed up into band.

7 Fold band along centre, along perforations or edge of stiffening to WS of garment; baste along fold, starting and finishing a little in from each end. Press. Turn in ends of band over stiffening, baste and press. On extension hold down seam allowances with herringbone stitch if fabric is springy, and remove basting.

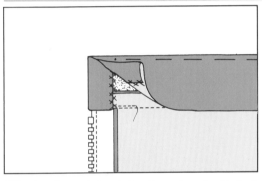

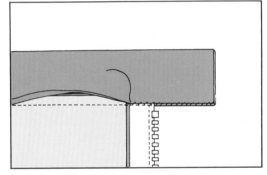

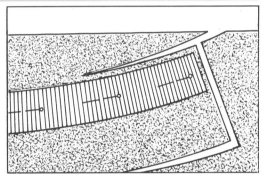

8 At other end of waistband turn in end to lie flush with zipper edge. Hold down seam allowance to stiffening with herringbone stitch if necessary and remove basting. Note that waistband can be attached to WS first and finished on RS with machine stitching.

9 Turn under raw edge of waistband and baste it down so that fold falls on line of machine stitching on WS of garment. Hem along band into machining. Remove basting. Slip stitch ends of band and lower edge of extension up to edge of zipper. Finish extension with hooks and eyes, buttons and buttonholes backed up with snaps, Velcro, or any other appropriate fastenings.

Curved waistband Curved petersham may be used to stiffen this band. If it is not the correct width, use it as a guide to the waist curve and stiffen band with heavy interfacing. Measure petersham to fit waist, allowing for extension as for straight waistband. Pin to interfacing. Cut around petersham not more than 5 mm/¼ in above concave edge and to desired width below convex edge.

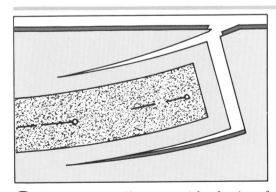

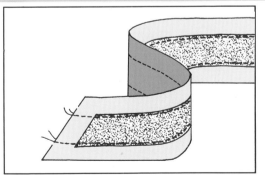

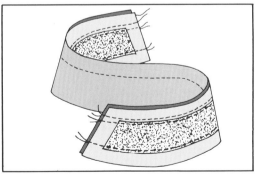

2 Lay out a piece of lining material and a piece of fabric RS together. The fabric can serve as lining with medium and lightweight fabrics, but bulky fabric waistbands are best lined with lightweight cotton or nylon knit or with lining material. Pin stiffening to the two fabric pieces and cut around, allowing 1.5 cm/⅝ in for seam allowances all around. Remove stiffening from fabric.

3 Place stiffening centrally on WS of fabric and baste down centre. Machine just inside both edges of stiffening, continuing stitching to ends of fabric, or work herringbone stitch over edges. Remove basting and press.

4 Place RS of band on RS of lining and baste the two raw edges together along the top, concave, edge just above edge of stiffening. Machine 3 mm/⅛ in from concave stiffening edge. This ensures that the lining does not show on the finished garment. Remove basting. Trim seam allowances as for faced waistband (**3**). Press.

WAISTS

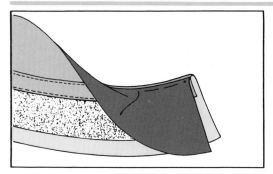

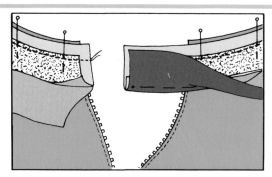

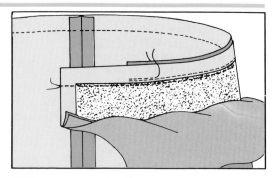

5 Roll lining over to WS of band so that join is slightly to WS and baste near edge. Press. Put waistband around waist and decide which end will be extension; the extension can overlap or underlap. Adjust length as for straight waistband (**3**) and mark extension with tailor's chalk.

6 Holding lining out of the way, place RS of band on RS of garment. The curved waistband will sit a little below the waist, so it must be fitted carefully and usually needs to be set below top edge of garment. Match extension chalk line to zipper edge and pin vertically. Match other end of stiffening to other zipper edge and pin. Insert pins all around waist and baste band into position. Remove pins.

7 Machine with band side uppermost, just above edge of stiffening, stopping at zipper edge and reversing for a few stitches at each end. Remove basting. Trim seam allowances to between 3 and 5 mm/$\frac{1}{8}$ and $\frac{1}{4}$ in. Open out band away from garment and press so that seam allowances face up into band.

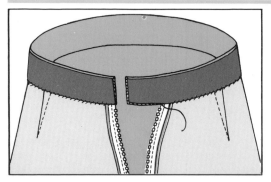

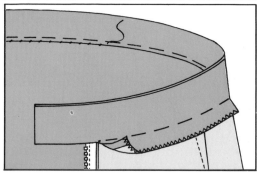

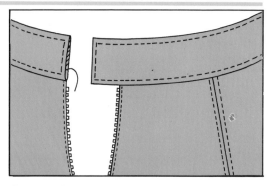

8 Turn in ends of band extension as for straight waistband (**7**). Turn up lower edge of lining along machining on WS and baste. Turn under lining edge on extension and short end of waistband and baste down. Press. Slip stitch ends of band and lining and lower edge of extension up to zipper. Hem lining into machining around waist. Remove all basting; press. Attach fastener to extension.

9 If using self-fabric lining on bulky fabric, attach waistband as in steps (**1**) to (**7**). Treat band and extension ends as in (**8**), but instead of turning in lower, raw, edge and hemming into machining, baste raw edge flat onto machining. Finish edge as appropriate to fabric and hold in place by working prick stitch through from RS at join of band and garment. Remove basting.

On casual clothes and those made from plain fabric such as denim, the waistband may be applied to WS of garment and then rolled over and finished by machining on RS so that the stitching matches any other topstitching on the garment. The stitching can also be worked in a contrasting colour thread.

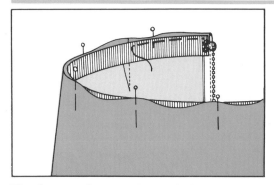

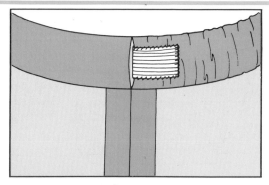

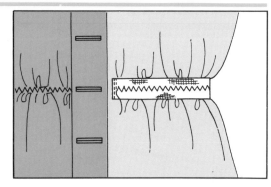

Elastic petersham may be attached to a waist edge for comfort. Stretch petersham slightly and measure to fit waist, plus 3 cm/1$\frac{1}{4}$ in for seam allowances. Turn in each end and attach hook and eye. Prepare waist edge of garment. Place fastened petersham inside waist. Pin vertically at intervals and then pin in between, stretching petersham to fit waist. Unfasten petersham, baste and hem to waist seam allowance.

Insert elastic rather than stiffening in garments for adults and children with variable waistlines. Cut waistband, allowing for joins to fall at side seams. Stitch joins, leaving section on inside of band open. Attach as appropriate to straight or curved waistband. Thread wide elastic in one opening and out the other. Turn ends over band toward back, oversew sides and loop stitch ends.

A loose-waisted dress can be drawn in with narrow elastic webbing sewn directly to garment or seam allowance. Measure elastic around waist, stretched. Divide elastic and dress waistline into quarters; mark with fabric pen. Anchor end of elastic beside opening with a few stitches then zigzag down centre, stretching elastic and matching quarters. If there is no opening, join ends of elastic first.

SLEEVE OPENINGS AND CUFFS

There are several methods for making an opening at the end of a long sleeve. You do not have to use the one in your pattern.

If the fabric frays, choose an opening such as the faced slit in which the cut edges are reinforced and the raw edges hidden. For bulky fabric select any flat opening, and for springy material avoid openings such as the bound type that involve layering several pieces of narrow fabric. Instead choose the faced slit or flat dart opening.

Before making an opening consider its finished look. This will depend on the style of the cuff and the length of the opening, but any opening must be long enough to prevent strain at the top.

If the sleeve is not altered to its correct length before the opening is made, any subsequent shortening will shorten the opening. Establish the sleeve length by measuring the seam of an existing garment.

Always cut and make the openings on both sleeves at the same time to ensure that they are correctly positioned. With the exception of the simple concealed opening, which falls at the underarm seam, the openings fall at the back of the sleeve, usually at the lowest part of the curve on the sleeve edge or in line with the little finger. Make the opening before joining the sleeve seam.

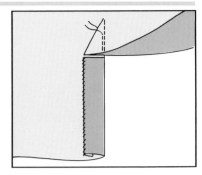

1 Flat dart opening This uncuffed sleeve is darted from the wrist. The lower part of the dart is left unstitched and split open to give a neat, flat opening. The bottom of the sleeve may have a narrow hem or be bound or faced, then fastened with loops and buttons, snaps or Velcro.

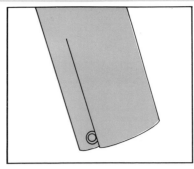

2 Stitch top 5 cm/2 in of dart, reversing for a few stitches at end, and press dart toward front of sleeve. Cutting on fold, split lower section of dart as far as the end of the dart stitching. Remove dart basting.

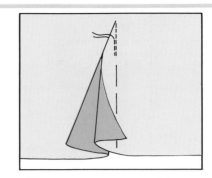

3 With dart still facing front of sleeve, lift back top edge and clip lower front edge horizontally in to end of stitching. Trim raw front edge vertically to 3 cm/1¼ in from marked line. Turn under raw edge and slip hem to sleeve to hold in position.

4 Similarly, clip back edge in to stitching and trim to 1.5 cm/⅝ in, finish and fold back. Overcast remaining raw edges of dart. Press.

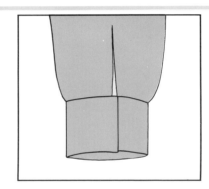

1 Simple concealed opening As it is flat it is suitable for any fabric and is the best choice of opening for adding an embroidered, beaded, quilted or other fancy cuff. As the opening falls at underarm seam on inside arm the cuff cannot have buttons. Fasten it with snaps or Velcro.

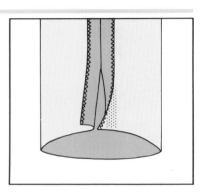

2 Fold sleeve RS together; baste and stitch underarm seam to within 7 cm/2¾ in of wrist, reversing at top of opening. Finish raw edges. Remove basting. Press seam open. The narrow seam allowances can be held down with fabric adhesive strips. Attach cuff.

103

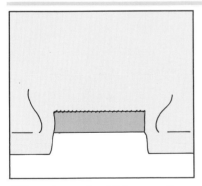

Clipped opening Make two clips at wrist edge of sleeve 1.5 cm/⅝ in deep and 2 cm/¾ in apart, at normal opening position. Press flap onto WS sleeve, overcast raw edge. Secure with a piece of adhesive web. Gathering threads if used must end level with the clip. Attach cuffs with ends level with clip.

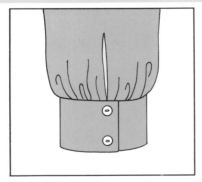

1 Faced slit opening A flat, neat, edge-to-edge opening. Quick to make and ideal for children's and casual clothes or on springy, fraying or bulky fabrics. For the latter, use lining or fine material for the facing. On adults' garments the opening should be about 7 cm/2¾ in long.

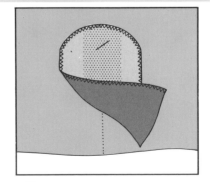

2 Cut a rectangle of fabric 9 by 5 cm/3½ by 2 in. Cut one end in a curve and finish sides and curved end. Press paper-backed adhesive web down centre of WS of facing. Peel off paper. Tack position of opening on RS of back of sleeve; baste facing, RS down, over it.

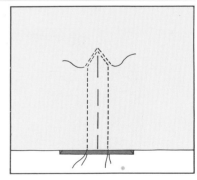

3 With sleeve side up, stitch 2 mm/ 1/16 in away from one side of the opening line almost to its top. Turn fabric; stitch diagonally to end of line. Turn; stitch away from line at same angle for same distance. Turn; stitch back to edge. Machine around point again. Remove basting.

SLEEVE OPENINGS AND CUFFS

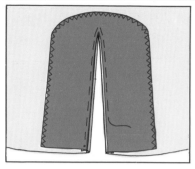

4 Cut carefully between the two lines of stitching right to point. Roll facing to WS of sleeve, so that join is slightly to WS. Baste around opening to hold join in position and press. Do not remove basting until cuff has been attached.

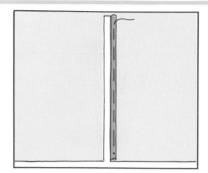

Shirt sleeve opening Suited to casual clothes, shirts and jackets. There are several ways of making this opening; the method described here is an easy one. The opening should be up to 15 cm/6 in long on a man's shirt to avoid strain and to allow the sleeve to be rolled up.

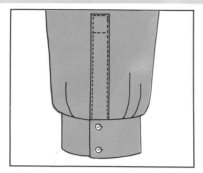

2 Measure and mark opening at back of sleeve on WS. Cut along mark. Make a narrow hem on back edge of opening, clip across at top of slit for 3 mm/⅛ in and roll hem that width to WS of sleeve. Baste hem, press and machine it, reversing a little at top of slit. Remove basting.

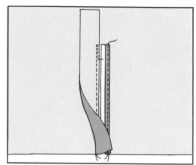

3 Cut fabric strip on straight grain 6 cm/2¼ in longer than opening and 4 cm/1½ in wide. Put one side RS down on WS of front edge of opening. Baste. Stitch, 2 mm/1/16 in from edges, from wrist to top of slit, reversing a little at top. Open out strip and press, RS up. Remove basting.

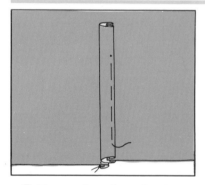

4 Turn under other side of strip 3 mm/⅛ in to WS. Press. Bring strip through to RS of sleeve. Baste down turned-under edge of strip so that it covers machine stitches. The strip now extends beyond slit on RS of sleeve. Press strip.

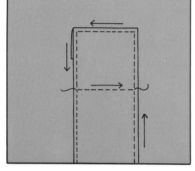

5 Turn under top of strip in a square or point. With sleeve RS up, baste and stitch up the turned-under edge, across top of opening and down the other side to slightly below start of slit—stitch across strip for strength at this level. Remove basting. Press. Attach cuff.

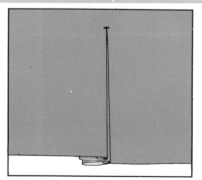

Bound opening Sometimes known as a continuous strip opening because it is made by attaching one piece of fabric. Its advantage is that it does not gape as the edges overlap. Use only on light- and medium-weight materials as it is often too bulky for heavy fabrics.

2 On RS at back of sleeve mark and cut slit for an opening about 7 cm/2¾ in long. Cut fabric strip on straight grain twice length of slit and 2.5 cm/1 in wide. Place one end, RS down, at bottom of RS of sleeve, and with edge of slit and one side of strip level. Baste 5 mm/¼ in from edge.

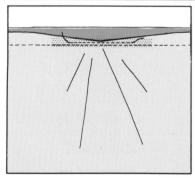

3 As you baste, open slit out straight; hem on slit edge becomes smaller at centre (top of slit). Machine on WS of sleeve, catching in the threads of material at centre. Remove basting. Stitch again for 2 cm/¾ in across centre and press adhesive web on top.

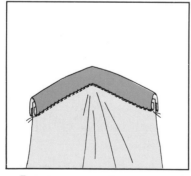

4 Fold over raw edge on other side of binding strip. Place fold on line of machining on WS of sleeve. Baste. Hem into machining or machine the binding down. Remove basting. For fine fabrics cut a bias or crosswise strip 1.5 cm/⅝ in wide; press and apply as for double binding.

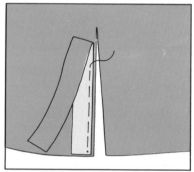

5 To finish opening, turn sleeve RS up and bring opening edges together. Press so binding on edge to front of sleeve is folded back onto WS of sleeve and so binding on back edge extends forward across the opening. Work a bar tack on RS of sleeve at top of opening.

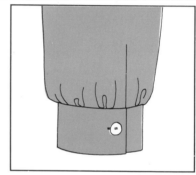

6 On WS of sleeve at top of strip adjust fold to lie flat and back-stitch through fold of strip from top of inside edge downward, at an angle, to outer edges. This keeps the binding in position during wear. Attach cuff.

CUFFS

A cuff can be a narrow band with a classic width of 3–5 cm/1–2 in, or it can be deep and shaped to fit the arm and not just the wrist. A cuff can be an added piece of fabric that draws the sleeve in at that point, or an extension of the sleeve that simply folds back. If the cuff is to fit the arm tightly there must be an opening in the sleeve and fastenings on the cuff. One button is sufficient for narrow cuffs; use two on cuffs 5 cm/2 in or more in depth and four on deeper cuffs. Establish sleeve length and adjust; make openings and stitch sleeve seam before attaching cuff.

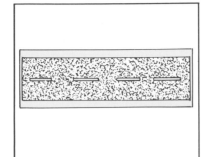

1 Iron-on interfacing Light-weight perforated banding makes cuffs 3 cm/1¼ in wide when finished. Test on fabric before use. Cut length of banding equal to cuff pattern; press to WS of fabric. Cut around outer edge adding 1.5 cm/⅝ in seam allowance to each long edge.

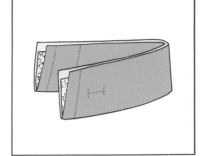

2 Using fabric pen, carbon paper or tailor's chalk, mark end seam allowances and overlap and, on RS, the buttonhole position. Attach cuff, stitching just beside edge of interfacing; cuff folds easily along the middle of the perforations. For heavy fabrics use two layers of interfacing.

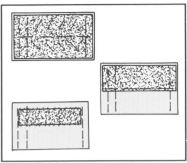

Sew-in interfacing On light-weight fabrics cut soft interfacing same size as cuff and baste to WS. On medium fabrics cut interfacing to extend 1 cm/⅜ in beyond centre of cuff. Cut heavy interfacing to centre line; omit seam allowances. Mark seams, overlap and centre line. Attach with catch stitch.

105

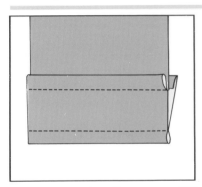

False turn-back cuff Fold sleeve WS together, and stitch two 5 mm/¼ in tucks. Make one tuck 4.5 cm/1¾ in from lower edge, i.e. hem of sleeve, the other 8 cm/3¼ in from edge. Fold sleeve hem to WS along lower tuck, fold under raw edge and hem to back of upper tuck.

Sleeve band Measure perforated interfacing around arm, adding ease. Press to WS fabric; cut out adding seam allowance all around. Fold band RS together, join ends, press open. Fold WS together along centre and baste. Attach band, folded to RS, gathering sleeve to fit. Stitch. Press.

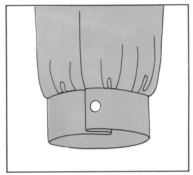

1 Easy wrap cuff Can be used on all light- and medium-weight fabrics. Excellent for fraying materials because no opening is necessary. Cuff wraps over from front to back of sleeve, in line with little finger. Interface whole cuff with light-weight interfacing.

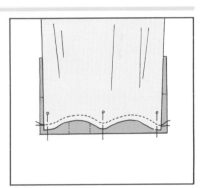

2 Mark hems and length and position of wrap-over on cuff. In lower edge of sleeve insert tucks or a row of gathering near seamline. Pin RS of one long cuff edge to lower edge of RS of sleeve, matching raw edges. Pull up gathering thread or adjust tuck width until sleeve fits cuff.

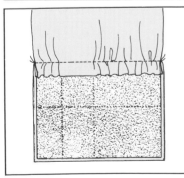

3 Arrange fullness so there is a flat section at cuff wrap-over. Baste sleeve to cuff. Remove pins and machine with gathers uppermost, taking usual seam allowances. Remove basting and gathers. Trim allowances. Open out cuff to extend beyond sleeve end; press seams toward cuff.

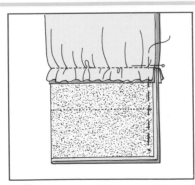

4 Fold sleeve RS together. Pin cuff at wrist to hold both sides of join level. Baste along cuff and underarm sleeve seam. Starting from bottom edge of cuff machine beside basting up to underarm, making sure that the seam allowances remain flat all the way up. Remove pin and basting.

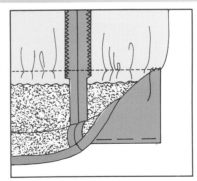

5 Press seam open and finish raw edges to just beyond cuff join. Trim away a little of seam allowances within cuff. Fold cuff along centre and baste close to fold. Turn under raw edge and baste to WS of sleeve so fold covers machining at join of cuff and sleeve. Press. Hem into machining.

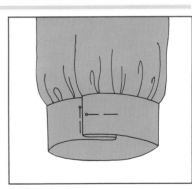

6 Remove basting. Slip sleeve onto arm and pin sleeve head to shoulder of the garment you are wearing. Fold over wrap in cuff, in line with little finger, toward back of sleeve. Pin. Mark end of wrap on under section of cuff with pins or chalk. Unpin cuff and take off sleeve.

SLEEVE OPENINGS AND CUFFS

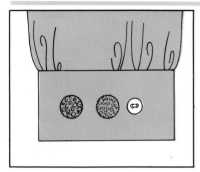

7 Open cuff out again and attach fastening—either snaps or Velcro—so that cuff fits when fastened. Remove any marker pins. For a decorative effect attach a button or buttons on outside of cuff overlap near folded edge.

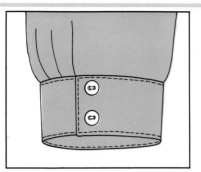

1 **Plain straight cuff** This classic shirt cuff can be made in almost any fabric and topstitched when complete. If there is insufficient material, make the cuff from two pieces of fabric joined lengthwise. This cuff can also be made very wide and then folded back and fastened with cuff links.

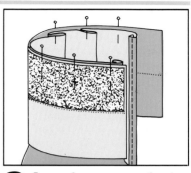

2 Interface WS of cuff to suit fabric. Mark seam allowances and fold lines. Except if attaching cuff to a shirt sleeve opening, mark length of underlap either from pattern or by trying on cuff around wrist—the underlap extension will be on the back of the sleeve.

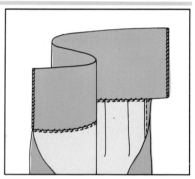

3 Insert pleats or a row of gathers in lower edge of sleeve. Pin RS of cuff to RS of lower sleeve edge, with back edge of sleeve opening on mark for start of underlap extension. Allow cuff to extend 1.5 cm/⅝ in beyond opening at front of sleeve. Draw up gathers or adjust pleats to fit cuff.

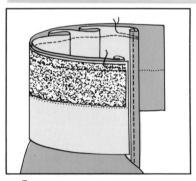

4 For a shirt sleeve opening, pin both cuff ends level with ends of opening. For all types of sleeve opening, baste and machine on WS of sleeve, making sure that pleats or gathers stay in place and taking usual seam allowance. Start and finish by reversing. Remove basting and gathers.

5 Trim interfacing close to machining, raw edge of cuff to 5 mm/¼ in and sleeve edge to slightly less. With cuff extending away from sleeve, press seam allowances into cuff. Fold in outer edge and ends of cuff along marked seamlines. Baste near edge. Trim raw edges to reduce bulk.

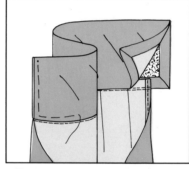

6 Fold cuff WS together along centre fold line so ends are level and basted outer edge of cuff lies on machining joining cuff to sleeve on WS. Baste ends and along edge over machining; baste diagonally along length of cuff.

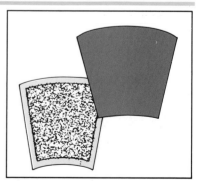

7 Press. Slip stitch ends and lower edges of extension. Hold down cuff edge to WS of sleeve by hemming into machining. Remove all basting and then press again.

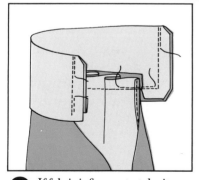

8 If fabric is fine or stretchy it may be better to fold cuff RS together after attaching interfaced side to sleeve and then to stitch across ends and extension. Trim seam allowances 5 mm/¼ in. Trim corners diagonally. Turn cuff RS out. Turn under free lower edge and hem into machining.

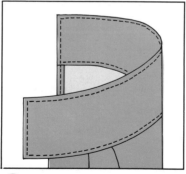

9 If cuff made by either method is to be topstitched, work this stitching around all four sides of completed cuff. Check for fit by trying cuff on as in (2). Attach fastenings as desired, but remember to choose ones that are easily manipulated.

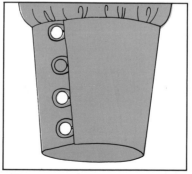

1 **Shaped cuff** If the cuff is deeper than about 6.5 cm/2½ in it must be shaped to fit the curve of the arm above the wrist. A shaped cuff is cut in two parts and has a seam along its lower edge. It looks very attractive decorated with topstitching and fastened with tubing loops and buttons.

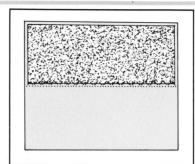

2 Cut two pieces (one may be in lining) for each cuff. Pin top piece around wrist, allowing for 5 mm to 2 cm/¼ to ¾ in extension. Mark where front end of cuff falls on back to give length of underlap, allowing usual seam allowances on both ends. Interface top piece. Mark seam allowances.

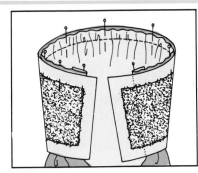

3 Insert a row of gathers in bottom of sleeve. Place interfaced cuff piece RS down on RS of sleeve with convex edge on bottom of sleeve. Insert pins from cuff side so cuff seam allowance extends beyond front edge of sleeve opening and underlap extension mark aligns with back edge.

4 Pull up gathers to fit cuff. Pin around cuff from gathered side. Baste sleeve to cuff. Remove pins.

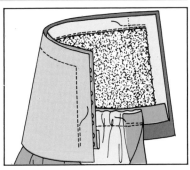

5 Machine, from gathered side, to edges of opening. reversing at each end. Trim seam allowances, open out cuff, press seam allowances into cuff. If tubing loops are being used, baste into position on front edge of RS of cuff so loops face away from raw edges. Machine across loop ends.

6 Place RS of second cuff (or lining) piece on RS of attached piece. Baste wrist edge and front edge. With interfaced piece uppermost, machine around wrist curve, turn corner and machine along front edge. Stop exactly where interfaced cuff joins sleeve. Reverse at each end.

7 Trim seam allowances to 5 mm/ $\frac{1}{4}$ in and trim interfacing very close to stitching. Trim corners diagonally. Turn cuff RS out. Roll edges until wrist join on cuff is slightly to WS. Baste wrist edge close to join. Press. Baste diagonally along centre of cuff and across ends.

8 Turn in raw edge along bottom of cuff onto machine stitching on WS joining interfaced cuff section to sleeve. Baste. Hem into machining.

9 At extension end remove basting. Turn in cuff edges to meet at end and along extension. Slip stitch together. Add any decoration such as topstitching. Remove all basting. Press.

10 For an easier method of attaching second cuff piece to first on fine fabrics, stitch, starting at front edge, around wrist curve and down back edge. Trim interfacing and seam allowances. Turn cuff RS out; finish as in (**7**) to (**9**), slip stitching lower edge of extension only.

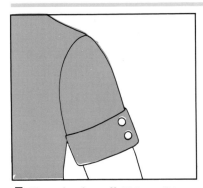

1 **Turn-back cuff** This cuff is a rolled back extension of the sleeve and is decorative rather than functional. It is interfaced with a strip of light perforated band interfacing and this establishes the depth of the cuff.

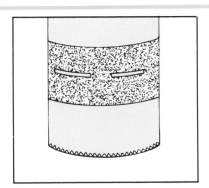

2 With sleeve WS out, press interfacing with perforations on the fold line marked at desired depth. Finish raw edge.

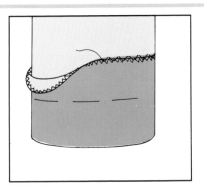

3 Turn up cuff to WS along perforations and baste. Insert a length of fabric adhesive web around sleeve under finished edge and press to attach adhesive or catch stitch finished hem edge to WS of sleeve.

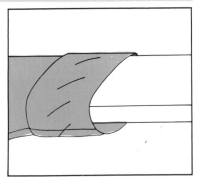

4 Turn sleeve RS out and roll cuff back over RS of sleeve. Diagonally baste cuff to sleeve. Arrange on sleeve board RS up and press lightly. Remove all basting. Press on WS to melt adhesive. Work topstitching if desired around top of cuff, stitching through turn-back only.

SLEEVE OPENINGS AND CUFFS

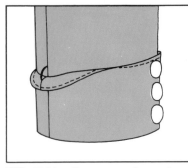

5 Hold cuff in position by working a bar tack at the sleeve seam, hidden between seam and cuff. Work another bar tack between seam and cuff on opposite side of sleeve or attach decorative buttons there through all layers of fabric.

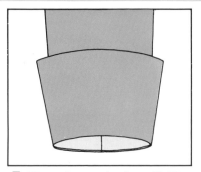

1 **Shaped turn-back cuff** This purely decorative cuff is wider at the top than at the wrist. If the fabric is bulky, the inside of the cuff should be made from lining. If there is a slit or a shaped part on the lower sleeve edge on the outside of the arm, the cuff pieces are also shaped.

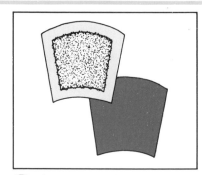

2 Cut out two cuff pieces in fabric and interface. Cut out two cuff pieces in lining material. Fold interfaced cuff piece with RS together and join side seam. Trim seam allowances to 5 mm/¼ in, but do not finish. Press seam open. Join seam in lining and trim. Turn cuff RS out.

3 Place RS of cuff to RS of lining, matching side seams, and baste together diagonally along seams. Baste cuff layers together diagonally all around. Baste wide, outer, edges of cuff together.

4 Machine outer edges beside basting. Remove all basting. Trim outer edges to 5 mm/¼ in and trim interfacing close to machining. Turn cuff RS out. Roll edge until join is slightly to inside of cuff. Baste around outer edge close to join. Press well. Baste diagonally around centre of cuff.

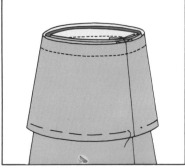

5 If cuff has a break in it, bar tack ends together on seamline. Then, with sleeve RS out, slip cuff, RS out, over sleeve end and match raw edges at wrist and side seam joins. Baste around cuff at wrist edge on marked seamline through all layers and machine. Remove wrist edge basting.

6 Move cuff down sleeve toward wrist so fold at wrist is slightly inside sleeve. Push raw edges at join up inside sleeve so they are hidden during wear. Clip seam allowances close to machining so they lie flat inside sleeve. Baste diagonally near lower cuff edge. Press cuff lightly.

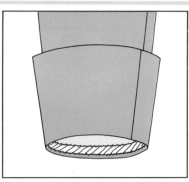

7 Turn sleeve WS out. Finish raw edges of medium or heavy fabric with herringbone stitch; finish those of fine fabric by covering with a bias strip and hemming along both edges. Turn sleeve to RS and remove basting. If sleeve is lined, bring lining over raw edges and fell stitch.

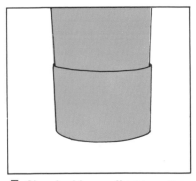

1 **Simple bias cuff** This cuff is made from bias material, often in a contrasting colour or pattern, joined to the end of the sleeve. The material can either be rolled back to form a cuff, or used as an extension to the sleeve end—a useful way of adding length.

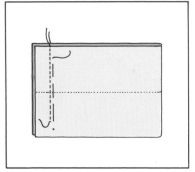

2 Cut bias strip twice desired depth of cuff (at least 5 cm/2 in), plus 4 cm/1½ in for seam allowances and an allowance for roll on a turn-back cuff. Press strip to stretch it. Mark turn-back line. Pin ends together to fit sleeve and, with RS together, baste and machine ends.

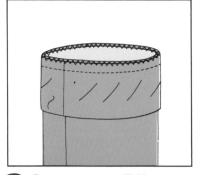

3 Press seam open. Fold strip in half lengthwise, WS together, and work diagonal basting all around. Slip cuff over RS of sleeve so cuff join falls at underarm seam. Baste and machine along seamline at bottom of sleeve. Remove basting. Trim raw edges to 5 mm/¼ in and finish together.

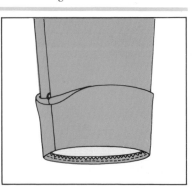

4 For turn-back cuff, pull cuff down until the join disappears inside the sleeve. Hold cuff in position and baste diagonally all around. Press. In lined sleeve cover the finished edges with lining. Remove basting. Work bar tack at side seam between cuff and sleeve.

SLEEVES

The style and line of sleeves, like other parts of a garment, are subject to the influences of fashion, but there are essentially only three types of sleeve—set-in, kimono and raglan.

The plain set-in sleeve is joined to the garment armhole with a seam that follows the underarm curve of the body exactly and then extends over the shoulder bone. The part of the seam on the shoulder may be high to give a cut-in look, or raised on a pad for a military style, or the sleeve head may be gathered into the armhole to create a high-standing sleeve; a set-in sleeve may be fitted, loose, gathered, straight or shaped. The section from shoulder to underarm always follows the same line on the body.

The kimono is the easiest sleeve to make. Simply an extension of the bodice, it is particularly suited to leisure clothes, but has the disadvantage of being bulky under the arm. This is because there is no shaped join at the shoulder and thus the sleeve must be loose fitting to allow for movement.

Commonly used on garments needing a fairly loose fit, the raglan sleeve is reasonably easy to construct. The seams joining sleeve to bodice run from neckline to underarm.

There are many possible variations on the three basic sleeves. For example, the sleeve may be set into a square armhole; the bodice yoke may be cut in one piece and the lower part of the sleeve gathered in; or a plain, short, set-in sleeve may have a gathered or circular lower section. The dropped shoulder line creates a shape similar to the kimono, but a separate sleeve section is joined to the bodice with a straight seam running across the arm (from the underarm) a little way below the shoulder bone. This style uses less fabric than the all-in-one kimono. Use appropriate seams, such as a lapped or open seam, to make all these types of sleeves.

Except for men's shirt sleeves, sleeves are generally attached to the garment after their seams have been joined and finished and their cuffs or sleeve ends finished.

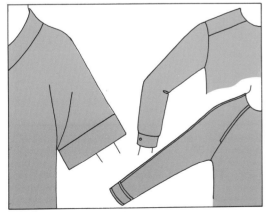

Kimono, set-in and raglan sleeves

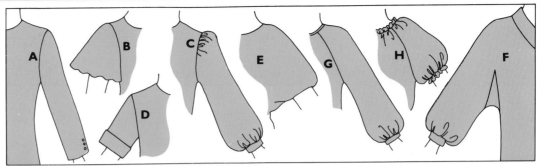

Variations on the basic styles The plain tailored sleeve (**A**) is usually straight, set into an armhole lowered sufficiently to allow room for other garments. A fluted set-in sleeve (**B**) is widened at the hem. The gathered sleeve (**C**) has additional height and width but it is set into the basic armhole. A shirt (**D**) usually has an extended shoulder so that the armhole seam runs across the top of the arm.

If kimono sleeve is short (**E**) and underarm seam long enough for arm to be raised, no gusset is needed. If shoulder seam is shaped to the body and sleeve is long or a tighter fit is required, an underarm gusset is needed (**F**). A looser fitting raglan sleeve (**G**) has a deeper armhole and fuller sleeve. Both sleeve and bodice neckline can have additional width that is gathered up (**H**).

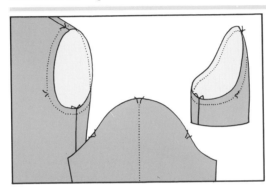

1 **Plain set-in sleeve** Mark armhole seamline on bodice and seamline at top of sleeve. It may also help to mark head point on sleeve, which is exactly in centre of fabric cross grain, and balance points/notches halfway down the armhole on sleeve and bodice. Remember that these are only guidelines and may be moved in fitting. Join and finish sleeve seam. Turn bodice and sleeve RS out.

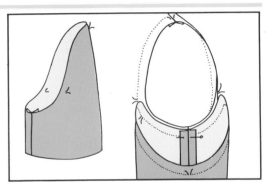

2 Check sleeves to establish right and left. On both sleeve and bodice the back of the armhole extends while the front is scooped. This shaping gives extra width across the back. Place RS of sleeve seam on RS of bodice seam, with raw edges at underarm matching, and pin across seams. Remember that seam positions may have been altered by fitting adjustments to sleeve or bodice.

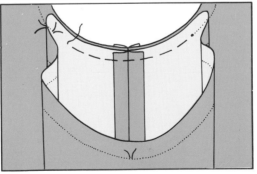

3 Hold RS of sleeve and bodice toward you. On underarm section only, and with raw edges together, match seamlines and pin on each side of first pin for about 10 cm/4 in (approximately the length of deeply curved section of sleeve). Do not worry if balance marks/notches on sleeve and bodice do not coincide. Baste underarm section. Fasten off basting. Remove all pins.

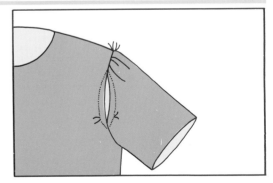

4 Put one hand inside shoulder at neck edge, bringing it out through the bodice armhole to grasp the sleeve head. Bring sleeve head up to end of shoulder seam and hold the two together.

SLEEVES

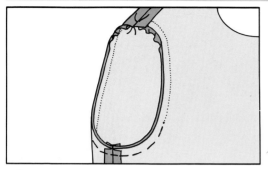

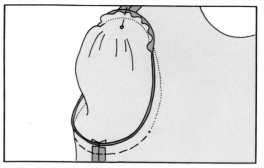

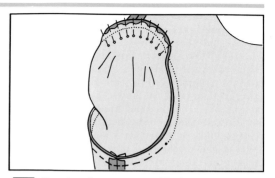

5 Pull bodice over sleeve so that bodice is WS out with sleeve hanging inside it and RS of sleeve and bodice are still together. In this position the sleeve head, which is larger than the armhole to allow for the shape of the shoulder, is wrinkled within the armhole because of the excess fullness.

6 To disperse fullness, keep hold of sleeve head and shoulder seam, and turn bodice and sleeve edges back over hand so that sleeve is on top, WS up. Pin sleeve head to bodice across marked seamline. There are now only two short stretches of sleeve head to attach to armhole and fullness has been largely eased away by holding sleeve and bodice correctly. Use this method for all types of fabric.

7 Keeping sleeve on top of bodice, insert pins at intervals across seamline, picking up fabric on seamline only. Continue around armhole to meet basting. Fullness in sleeve head flutes at sleeve edge but contracts to slight bumps of fabric where pins are inserted. Adjust pins until most ease lies over shoulder and there is very little fullness down the back of the armhole.

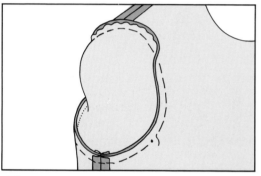

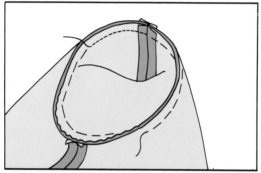

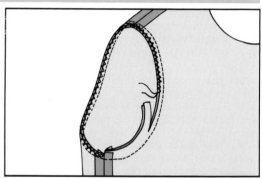

8 With sleeve still in same position, baste with small stitches across centre of pins, removing each pin as it is reached. Do not allow ease to form pleats. If this is a problem, take smaller stitches to divide up fullness. Try on garment, fit sleeve and adjust sleeve head basting if necessary.

9 Sew in sleeve, preferably by hand, starting from underarm seam and using a small half back-stitch. Remove basting. Sewing the sleeve in by hand enables you to hold the sleeve correctly, so that you can continue to control and take up the fullness in the sleeve head.

10 To machine sleeve in, stitch slowly from sleeve side, starting at underarm seam. Use points of small scissors to prevent pleats from forming, as for gathers. Remove basting. After stitching by hand or machine, trim seam allowances to no less than 1.5 cm/½ in and finish both edges together. Press seam into sleeve head for support. At underarm press stitching on WS and leave seam upright.

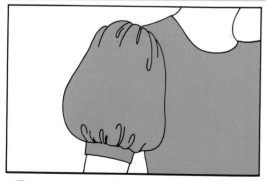

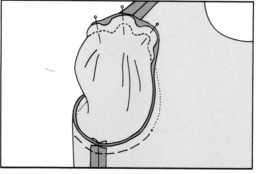

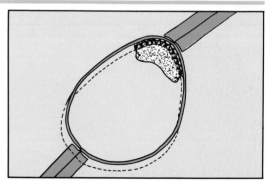

1 **Gathered head** The amount of fullness in the top of a gathered sleeve can be as little as 5 cm/2 in which will provide a very slight stand. Exaggerated styles may have as much as 15–20 cm/6–8 in to be gathered up. In crisp fabrics particularly this will produce a high vertical stand.

2 Mark balance points/notches as for set-in sleeve and insert one gathering thread in sleeve head between them. Proceed as for set-in sleeve (**1**) to (**5**). Pin between top of sleeve head and end of underarm basting. Pull up gathering thread until sleeve lies loosely on top of armhole. Arrange gathers. Pin frequently. Finish as for plain set-in sleeve (**8**) to (**10**).

Sleeve support to hold up gathers. Cut a piece of medium-weight iron-on interfacing 10 cm/4 in wide and 13 cm/5 in long. Fold along the middle, with the adhesive on the inside and press. Cover with fabric or lining if desired. Place inside top of sleeve equally either side of shoulder seam. Attach with zigzag, sewing through support and seam allowance of top of sleeve.

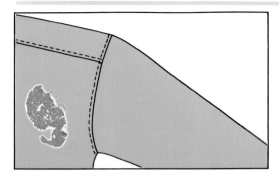

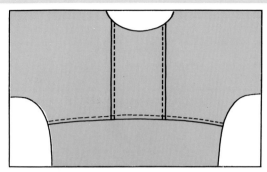

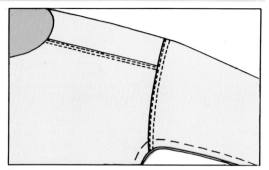

1 Shirt sleeve A man's tailored shirt sleeve usually has a loose, low armhole and a shoulder line that is almost dropped; the seam joining the sleeve to the bodice is only slightly shaped, especially if machine flat fell seams are used, which are difficult to make on a shaped armhole. Mark shoulder point on yoke with a tailor's tack.

2 With RS and raw edges together, place top of sleeve piece along open armhole edge on shirt, making sure that marked sleeve head aligns with shoulder point on yoke. Pin at sleeve head and at each end of seam. Baste, easing any fullness at top of sleeve evenly. Remove pins. Stitch together, using a machine flat fell, narrow finish or topstitched seam. Remove basting and press.

3 Fold shirt RS together so raw edges meet on sleeve underarm seam and on bodice side seam. Match ends of armhole seam at underarm and pin. Baste bodice side seam. Remove pin at underarm and baste down sleeve underarm seam. Join bodice and sleeve seams with a continuous machine flat fell seam from hem edge of bodice to sleeve wrist edge. Remove basting. Press on WS and RS. Attach cuff.

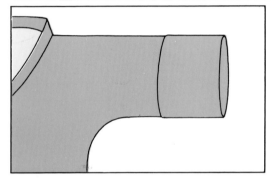

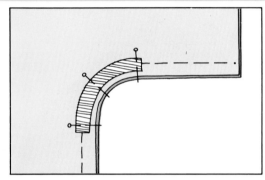

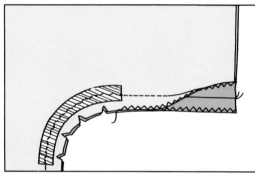

1 Kimono sleeve With this type of sleeve the shoulder seam is usually fairly straight or may even be eliminated by cutting out the pattern with the seam laid on a fold in the fabric so that the sleeve is all in one piece with the bodice. The more horizontal the shoulder seam or shoulder line the more room there is for movement (but this increases garment bulk).

2 With front and back garment pieces RS together, baste and machine shoulder seams, if any. Baste underarm seams. Cut a length of purchased bias binding (pressed out flat and folded in half for neatness) or stretch lace to match length of most curved section of seam. Pin and baste binding or lace around curved section, centring it over seamline.

3 Machine seam using a stitch suitable for the fabric, but along reinforced section change to a slight zigzag to retain necessary give. Remove basting. Along curve, clip seam allowances, but not reinforcement, halfway to machining. Press seam open. The curved section may spring up again, but do not try to press it too flat. Finish raw edges of seam.

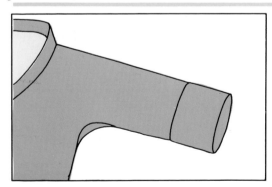

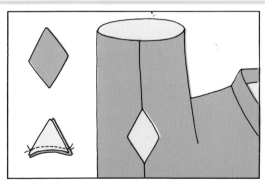

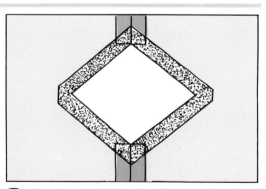

1 Kimono sleeve with gusset For a closer fitting sleeve, it is necessary to slope the shoulder more and sometimes, therefore, to narrow the sleeve at the wrist as well. The part of the seam around the underarm is then raised, which reduces the depth between shoulder and underarm. To prevent strain on seam when arm is raised, a gusset is inserted into the seam under the arm.

2 A gusset may be one diamond-shaped piece of fabric or two shaped triangles joined together. Sometimes the gusset forms part of a side panel on the main part of the garment. If a kimono style is found to be too tight, a gusset can be inserted. Mark a chalk line across the seam at the highest underarm point. Reinforce area by pressing a strip of light iron-on interfacing to WS.

3 Cut along chalk line 5 cm/2 in on each side of seam and open out slit to give four reinforced edges and a diamond-shaped hole. Measure the diamond and cut a piece of fabric to fit, allowing usual seam allowances on each edge. If cutting two triangles, add seam allowances for curved join in centre. Whichever gusset style you use, make sure that one side of it is on the straight grain.

SLEEVES

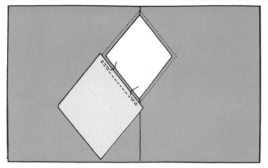

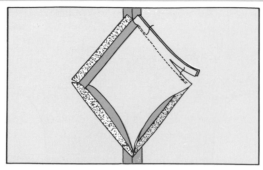

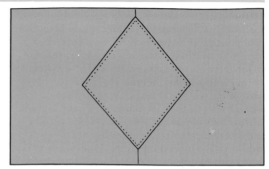

4 If gusset piece is provided, mark position of gusset opening and baste and machine underarm seam to start of each end of it. Reinforce raw edges of opening on WS with iron-on interfacing 3 cm/1¼ in wide and open into a diamond-shaped hole. Place gusset RS down on RS of garment. Baste and stitch along one edge, reversing at each end. Remove basting.

5 Trim seam allowances of stitched seam to 1 cm/ ⅜ in. Press seam open. Clip garment seam allowance at each end of machining right in to last machine stitch. Proceed as for an angled seam. Swing gusset around to work second side. Trim seam allowances and clip into corners as before. Turn work over to WS to complete third and fourth sides of gusset.

6 To further reinforce gusset seams and area, work a row of prick stitch from RS of gusset 3 mm/⅛ in inside join, stitching through all layers of fabric and around all four sides of gusset.

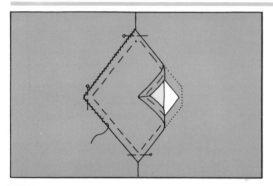

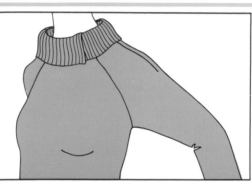

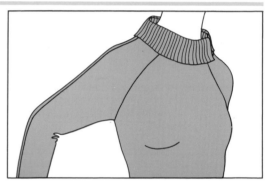

7 Alternatively, insert gusset by reinforcing WS of garment as in (2) to (4). Turn in gusset edges along seamlines, baste and press. Place gusset WS down on RS of garment to cover opening. Pin at corners. Baste around gusset so turned-in edges lie along seamline at opening. Hem or slip stitch all around. Work prick stitch from RS 3 mm/⅛ in inside join. Overcast seam allowances together.

| **Raglan sleeve** This sleeve is fairly easy to insert, but there are often fitting problems at the neckline. The excess width at the top of the sleeve is often drawn in with a dart. If the fullness at the point of the dart shows as a bulge on RS of garment, lengthen dart to help eliminate this. Top of sleeve and/ or neckline may be gathered into a band, yoke, or elastic.

2 A raglan sleeve that has a seam running all the way from neck to wrist generally fits much better than a darted sleeve, and adjustments can be made easily on this seam.

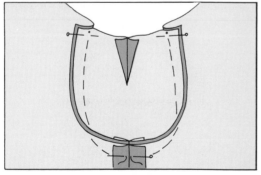

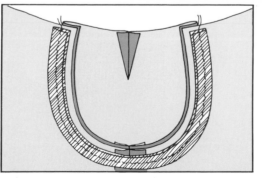

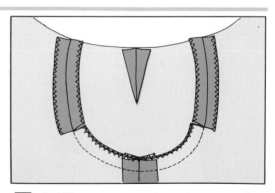

3 With sleeve folded RS together, baste and stitch underarm seam and dart or top seam. Remove basting. Press seam or seams. Cut dart and press open. Place sleeve underarm and bodice seams RS together with raw edges level and pin. Place edges together at neck and pin; remember that all edges are on bias and likely to stretch. Baste from neck to seam at underarm, holding armhole as for curved seam.

4 Remove pins. Machine around armhole from garment side; remove basting. If garment is of knitted fabric, reinforce seam with purchased bias binding, pressed out flat and then folded in half, or lining material cut on bias or true cross and folded in half. Baste binding down on garment side centred over seamline, and machine along on top of seamline, using a slight zigzag stitch. Remove basting.

5 On WS press upper sections of seam open from neck downward for the whole section that will be visible during wear. Press stitching of lower part of seam on WS so that seam allowances stand up together as for a plain set-in sleeve; finish these underarm edges together. Clip outer, garment, seam allowance down to just above machining and finish the opened parts of the seam separately.

YOKES

Attractive style details, yokes provide a good position for decorative stitching and also the opportunity to introduce fullness into the adjoining section, either as a fashion feature or for freedom of movement. Other reasons for making a yoke include the need to economize on fabric—the resulting smaller pattern pieces may fit more easily onto the fabric than one large skirt or bodice piece—and the desire to take out other seams—the saddle yoke, for example, is a one-piece yoke that joins the front and back sections and eliminates shoulder seams.

Yoke shapes

The shape varies according to the style of the garment and the position of the yoke. Stitch shaped yokes with lapped seams for ease of handling. Stitch angled yokes (**A**) with angled seams. A yoke seam on the chest line can run from armhole to neck edge (**B**) or centre front edge (**C**) but it will always be above the bust line. A yoke seam without fullness in the lower piece may be quite high as in a man's suit and will often be cut in one piece, called a saddle yoke (**D**). On a child's garment the yoke seam may be high but the fullness can be controlled almost to waist level with smocking (**E**). A raglan style garment can have a full, gathered body section joined to a round yoke (**F**).

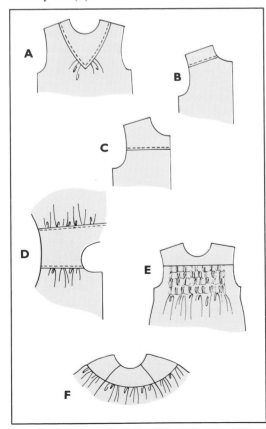

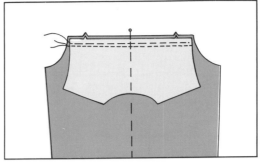

1 **Attaching plain yoke** Mark centre and balance marks/notches on yoke and adjoining garment section. Place pieces RS together; pin vertically at centre. Pin at balance marks/notches and at each end. Baste pieces together along seamline, easing garment onto yoke if there is slight shaping. Remove all except centre pin. Stitch from end to end. Remove basting and centre pin.

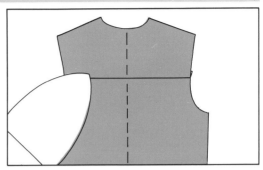

2 On WS of garment press the stitching flat and press seam allowances up toward yoke. If yoke is to be topstitched and is in medium or heavy fabric, press seam allowances open to lessen bulk. Turn yoke so that RS is uppermost and press.

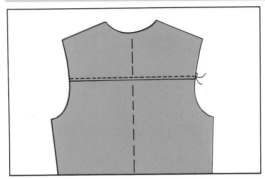

3 Topstitch, if desired, on RS of yoke, either very close to the yoke seam or a little way up from it, depending on the effect required. Press the stitching. If the seam allowances have been pressed open before topstitching, press lower seam allowance up toward yoke.

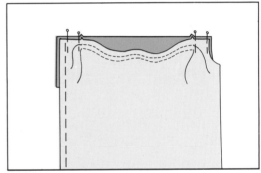

1 **Attaching gathered section to yoke** Insert two rows of gathering threads between balance marks/notches indicating extent of gathered area. If you are introducing this feature into a pattern, gather required length. Place gathered section on yoke, RS together. Match balance marks/notches and ends and pin vertically. If whole width of adjoining section is gathered, pin together at ends only.

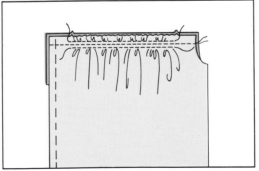

2 Gently pull up gathering threads until gathered section lies flat on yoke and anchor thread ends around a pin. Even out or bunch gathers in groups to achieve the desired effect and fit. Working from gathered side, baste along seamline. Remove pins. Machine beside basting with gathered piece uppermost. Stitch slowly, making sure gathers do not pleat or become uneven. Remove basting and gathers.

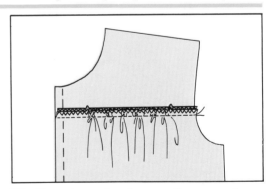

3 Trim the gathered seam allowance only to 5 mm/¼ in. Press the seam allowances up into the yoke, taking care not to flatten the gathering. Finish the seam allowance on the yoke piece. Zigzag or oversew the gathered edge, catching it down to the yoke seam allowance beneath.

YOKES

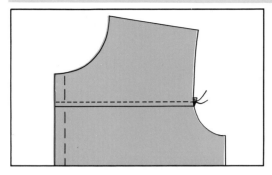

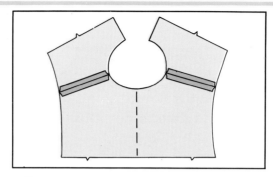

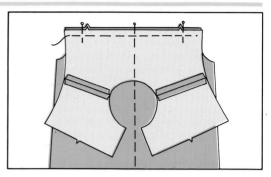

4 If you want to topstitch a yoke with a gathered adjoining section, there is no need to press seam allowances open as for a plain yoke, even on heavy fabric, as bulk is reduced when the gathered edge is trimmed in (**3**). Topstitch on RS of yoke as for a plain yoke, but work about 3 mm/⅛ in from the edge of the yoke. If the topstitching is right on the edge it will not hold up the seam allowances.

1 **Double or lined yoke** Cut out of garment fabric two sets of yoke pieces for front and back or cut out one set in fabric and one in thin cotton or lining material. Mark centres and balance marks/notches on yokes and garment. Join shoulder seams with RS together on both sets of yoke pieces. Press shoulder seams open and trim seam allowances to 5 mm/¼ in.

2 Place back yoke to lower back section of garment with RS and raw edges together. Match centres and balance marks/notches and pin, inserting pins vertically. Baste along seamline.

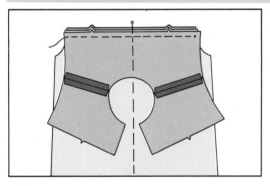

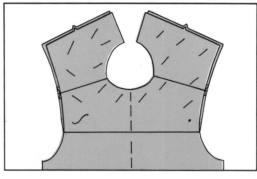

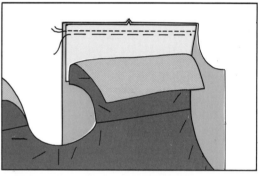

3 Take second, or lining, section for back yoke and place with RS of yoke to WS of garment so that yoke edge is level with basted edges of first yoke and garment section. Match centres and balance marks/notches and pin vertically. Baste along seamline through all layers. Leave centre pin in position; remove other pins. Garment edge is now sandwiched between the two yoke pieces.

4 With WS of first yoke piece uppermost, stitch beside basting through all three layers. Remove basting and centre pin. Trim seam allowances to 5 mm/¼ in. Smooth both yokes upward and garment section down. On WS press stitching flat and press seam allowances up toward yoke. Turn yoke to RS. Topstitch if desired. With layers flat and edges level baste around edges with diagonal stitches.

5 Fold back the under, or lining, yoke sections on the front yoke pieces. Place the front yokes onto the front garment sections with RS together. Pin and baste along seamline. Stitch beside basting through yoke and garment. Remove basting. On WS press seam up toward yoke and trim seam allowances to 5 mm/¼ in. If you want to add topstitching to the front yoke, work it at this stage.

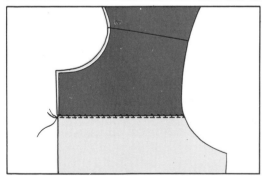

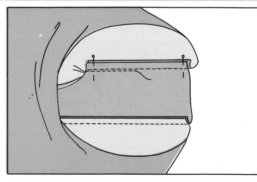

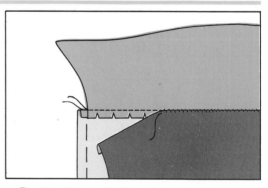

6 Bring under, or lining, yoke down onto seam. Turn under raw edge and baste. Press and finish by hemming into the seam stitching. Remove basting. This type of yoke is generally used on a shirt, so complete collar, sleeves and neck opening as usual, taking in both raw edges of yoke.

7 Alternatively, omit basting and bring yoke lining around WS out over the body of the garment and up again to the yoke itself. With RS lining to RS front yoke and edges carefully matched, pin ends. Arrange so that original line of stitching is uppermost and stitch again beside it on the yoke. As you work, take care not to catch in other parts with the yoke.

8 If a collar is added to a lined yoke, the lining can finish neck edge instead of a facing. Join outer yoke to garment. Baste and stitch collar to RS of neckline. Trim and clip seam allowances; press into yoke. Make up yoke lining and press. Place lining on yoke WS together. Baste on shoulders and diagonally on body of yoke. Trim lining edges. Turn in, baste and hem lining all around.

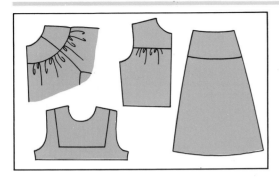

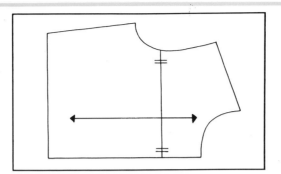

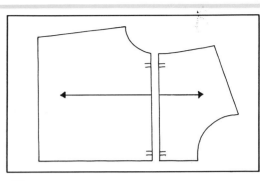

1 **Adapting a pattern to include a yoke** Draw a line on the existing pattern where you want the yoke seam to be. If it is to provide shaping it should fall *above* the bust, shoulder blades or hips. It can be any shape.

2 Draw two straight lines—balance marks/notches—across the yoke line. Write a note above and below the line that seam allowances must be added.

3 Cut the pattern on the yoke line and separate the pieces. If the yoke is purely decorative pin pattern pieces to fabric and cut out, adding seam allowances on yoke edges. Stitch together as for a plain yoke.

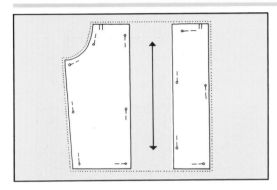

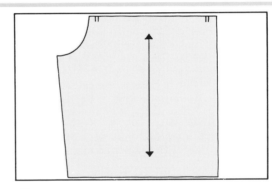

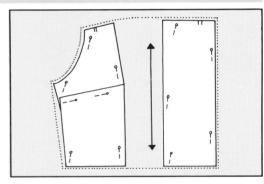

1 **Adapting a pattern to include gathers** To add gathers, tucks etc., cut the lower part of the pattern from hem to yoke line. With a fresh piece of paper beneath, spread out the pieces, allowing extra width between the edges and pin down. Allow 5–8 cm/2–3 in for bust fullness, less for shoulder blades, considerably more for a skirt.

2 Outline the pattern. Cut out, transferring the balance marks/notches. Place yoke and main pattern on fabric and cut out. Make up, matching balance marks/notches, as for gathered yoke.

Darts These will not be required if gathers are added, so remove them from the pattern before spreading the pieces. Fold the dart flat right across to the cut edge opposite. Flatten the paper and pin it to new paper.

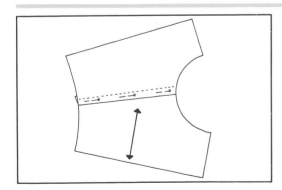

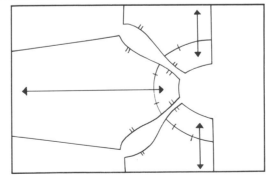

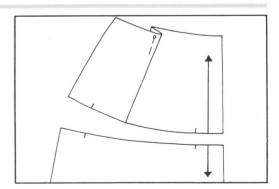

Saddle yoke To transform an ordinary yoke pattern into a saddle yoke pattern, overlap shoulder seam allowances of back and front yoke patterns and pin. Place pattern on double fabric with centre back to fold if opening is at front, with centre front to fold if opening is at back. Cut out and attach as for plain yoke.

Raglan yoke To create a yoke on a raglan style place back, sleeve and front pattern close together with raglan edges meeting. Draw yoke seamlines on each piece at required depth. Make balance marks/notches, cut off yokes. Cut and spread lower parts of back, sleeve and front and insert additional width for gathers. Outline new shapes and cut.

Skirt yoke When making a yoke on a skirt or trouser pattern, cut off the yoke section then remove the dart from waist to yoke edge. Flatten the paper and pin it to new paper. Gathers may be inserted in lower skirt piece by cutting pattern and spreading out. When yoke seam is made the yoke edge is more curved than the skirt edge and this gives the seam the correct line for the hips.

PLEATS

Pleats are folds of fabric treated in different ways to produce characteristic pleat types. Folds all pressed in one direction are knife pleats, while a single knife pleat that is left open below hip level on a skirt is called a kick pleat. Two knife pleats placed close together and pressed away from each other on the wrong side form an inverted pleat; if pressed toward each other they form a box pleat. Sunray pleats are accordion-like pleats graduating in width from almost nothing to about 2 cm/¾ in.

Pleats are most commonly used to create style and fullness in skirts, but can also be used as classic decoration on dresses, shirts and jackets and on pockets. Most skirt pleats are stitched down for part of their length and pressed flat. However, the pleat folds can be held in position at the waist but left unpressed below the waistband. Decorative pleats are usually pressed flat and then anchored at top and bottom so the pleat can open.

When choosing fabric for pleating remember that all thick, spongy or hairy fabrics are bulky when pleated. For such fabrics restrict pleats to one or two knife, inverted or box pleats. Nearly all closely woven fabrics of light and medium weight pleat well; light synthetic knits are the exception.

Sunray pleats should be permanently pleated professionally, but this is effective only on very fine or lightweight fabrics and is completely permanent only in synthetics. Always allow plenty of fabric. Shallow knife pleats can be done at home, but good results are difficult.

Success with pleats depends on accuracy, thorough pressing while the fabric is flat and before seams are joined, and a good fit. Choose a pattern for a pleated garment by its hip measurement and fit with pleats basted in place. Pleats do not provide body room: they should hang closed when the body is still.

PLEAT WIDTHS AND FOLD LINES

The width of a pleat—the width of the concealed fold of fabric on the wrong side of a garment—depends on the type of pleat, the number of pleats, the design of the fabric and the amount of fabric available. As a general guideline, knife pleats may be up to 7 cm/2¾ in wide if single, but if continuous or arranged in groups should be about 2 to 4 cm/¾ to 1½ in wide. A kick pleat should never be less than 3 cm/1¼ in wide. Inverted and box pleats should be at least 6 to 8 cm/2¼ to 3⅜ in wide if used in the back of a skirt, but narrower if in groups because the folds at the backs of adjacent pleats must not overlap. It is most important to mark the width of all types of pleats accurately.

On checked or striped fabric make sure the pattern matches at pleats by avoiding joins except at garment seams. Decide both the width and arrangement of pleats for the best effect on the fabric. Ideally, a pattern of checks should remain unaltered after pleating, but this is difficult to achieve and may involve alterations in pleat width. Striped fabric may be pleated so that part of the design is concealed in the pleat shaping to give a diagonal effect.

Most pleats are stitched down to a depth mark, or release point, whose position varies according to the style of the garment. If you make the pleats narrower than suggested on the pattern, lower the depth marks.

All pleats, apart from sunray, are marked out in the same way: an outer fold line, an inner fold line and a placement line onto which the outer fold line is brought. If more than one piece of fabric is used in a pleated section, place seams at the inner folds so the joins are invisible. The part under the fold between the inner fold and placement lines is the pleat backing. (For inverted and kick pleats a pleat backing cut in fabric of the same weight but of contrasting colour or pattern can produce a variety of attractive pleat effects.) How these lines are combined depends on the pleat type. To distinguish among them, mark fold lines with basting and placement lines with tailor's tacks.

Inverted and box pleats Both have two inner folds, **B**, and two outer folds, **A**; mark these and the centre line of the pleat backing, **C**, on which, for inverted pleats, the two outer folds will meet on RS, for box pleats the two inner on WS.

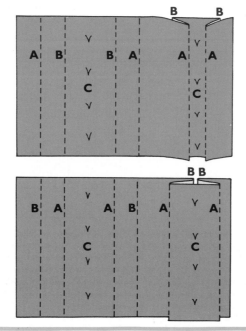

Knife and kick pleats Place outer fold, **A**, on placement line, **C**. Inner fold, **B**, falls between them.

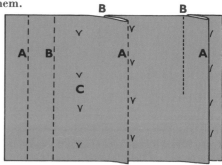

Separate backing If a separate backing, **D**, is used on inverted or kick pleats, seams should fall on inner fold lines, **B**. The advantage of a separate backing is that the pleat can be shaped so that it is wider at the hem than at the waist. Because the joins are not on the straight grain the skirt hangs well, and the waist shaping can be taken out of the pleat rather than with darts. If a separate backing is not used, only small adjustments can be made at the waist during fitting.

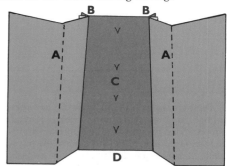

The part of the backing above the release point where a kick pleat opens may be cut from lining material if there is not enough fabric, as it will not show during wear. The two parts of the backing should be joined with an open seam. The backing of a kick pleat should always extend up to the waist or the pleat will drop, particularly if the backing hangs loose at the hem.

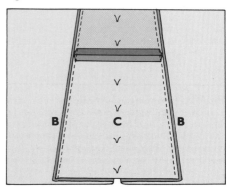

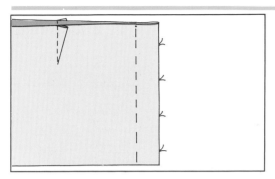

1 **Knife and kick pleats** Make all markings on garment pieces. Fold fabric RS together so that outer fold line of pleat meets placement line. Baste the two layers together from hem to waist along lines. For more than one pleat continue to fold and baste in same way. Baste any darts. Baste side seams. Try on. To fit skirt across hips and thighs adjust side seams, not pleat width.

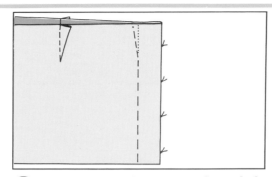

2 Adjustments at the waist can be made by altering the line of pleat basting (the pleat stitching line). To tighten waist, take in pleat stitching line a little at waist and then gradually run new line out to meet original line well above hip level. For grouped pleats, take in a little in this way equally on each pleat. For adjustment of continuous pleats see zipper insertion method, p. 118.

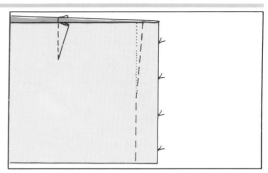

3 If the pleat stitching line is shaped and the skirt is too tight across the stomach, release basting down to hip and baste a new line up to the waist. Unless the skirt is much too small, never let out the pleat right to the hem because the narrowed pleat will not hang well. If pleats are grouped, alter each one a little and by an equal amount. For adjustment in continuous pleats see zipper insertion, p. 118.

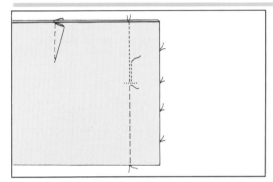

4 Decide pleat depth (distance from waist to which pleat will be stitched) during fitting, but do not use pleats to give figure room below waist: make skirt larger at sides instead. Mark depth with chalk at release point. Machine from mark up to waist along basted pleat line, reversing at start. Work large machine stitch from each release point down to hem. Remove basting. Repeat for all pleats.

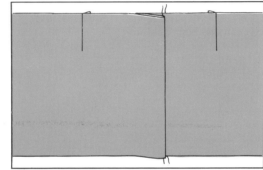

5 On WS press stitching flat and press fold (the pleat) to one side. Press again from RS. Repeat for all pleats. Pressing must be very thorough to guarantee a crisp pleat fold. Remove large machine stitches. For unpressed pleats complete stages (**1**) to (**4**), but stitch only within seam allowance at waist where waistband will be attached. Press stitching only.

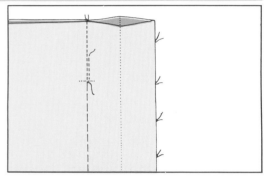

Inverted pleats Make all markings on garment pieces. Fold fabric RS together along centre line of pleat backing, matching inner fold lines and outer fold lines. Baste fabric together along outer fold lines. Repeat for any other pleats. Baste any darts and side seams. Fit, adjust, mark pleat depth and machine along basted line as for knife pleats (**2**) to (**4**). Remove all pleat basting.

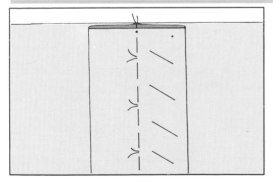

2 On WS press stitching flat. Open out the pleat and press centre line of pleat backing down onto stitched fold lines beneath. On RS smooth pleat seam flat with the fingers and press. Baste marked placement line to stitched folds. Repeat for any other pleats. Press lightly on RS. Baste diagonally along both folds of each pleat. Press all pleats thoroughly from both WS and RS. Remove basting.

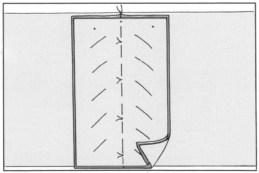

3 If separate pleat backing has been cut, baste and stitch along outer fold line on garment piece as in (**1**). Remove basting and press open on both WS and RS. Mark centre line on pleat backing. Place pleat backing RS down on WS of pleat with centre line of backing on pleat seam. Baste down. Lift raw edges of pleat and backing and hold together with diagonal basting. Repeat for all pleats.

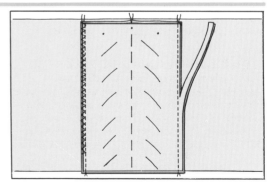

4 With tailor's chalk mark seamline down raw edges of pleat backing. Machine along seamline through backing and pleat edges only. Trim raw edges and finish. Complete finishing just above where the top of hem turn-up will come to as turning edges in hem area will be finished with the hem. Remove basting.

PLEATS

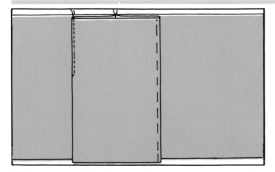

1 Box pleats Make all markings on garment piece. Fold WS of fabric together, match, baste and stitch fold lines as for inverted pleats. Press stitching on RS. Open each pleat out on RS and press so stitched folds are under centre of pleat. Baste pleat edges to garment from waist to hem. Press well. On RS stitch basted edges to garment from waist to release points. Remove basting.

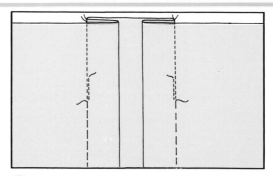

2 Alternatively, construct two separate knife pleats, but press folds toward each other on WS to form box pleat. Press well on RS and WS. Repeat for all pleats.

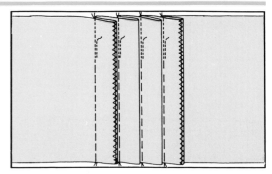

Joins For a better fit, the skirt may have a join or several joins in a group of pleats. Place joins at inner fold lines. Make up and press pleats in garment pieces according to type of pleat. Join raw edges on seamline and finish together. These seams are often shaped into the waist edge, as it prevents them overlapping. The distance from the waist at which the seams are shaped depends on the garment style.

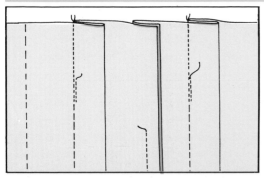

1 Inserting a zipper in continuous knife pleats Cut out skirt with wide seam allowances at zipper opening (at side seam) so seam position can be adjusted and to ensure even pleating at zipper. On skirt back leave two pleats unstitched for fitting adjustments. Stitch and press pleats on either side of zipper, except final pleat at zipper opening. Baste and stitch side seam up to zipper opening.

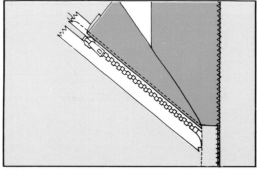

2 Remove side seam basting. Press side seam allowances to skirt front and finish together up to opening. Finish lower seam allowance up to waist. Clip across top allowance to seam stitching and turn back raw edge toward skirt back. Press along seamline. Baste along fold. With work still WS up, set in first side of zipper on turned-back edge and then remove the basting from this edge.

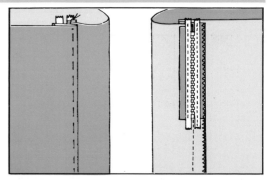

3 Baste and press fold of final pleat on RS of skirt and baste to other side of opening to cover zipper. On WS of garment baste second side of zipper tape to pleat edge along seam allowance. Do not take basting through to RS. Backstitch or machine zipper tape to pleat edge only. Remove basting and press. Fit skirt by adjusting and stitching the last few pleats at back of skirt on WS.

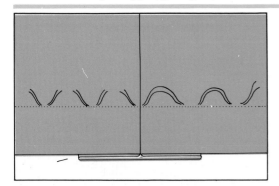

1 Hems Finish the seams and waist of garment. Try on and mark the hemline in the usual way with chalk and basting stitches. Mark hemline through to pleat backing using tailor's tacks with long loops. Part the three layers and clip the threads. Pull out the large stitching holding the pleat fold.

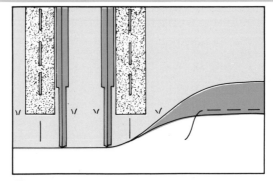

2 Open out the hemline, press open any seams in the pleat and trim to 5 mm/¼ in. On some fabrics cuff-weight interfacing band, pressed with perforations on the fold, will help keep pleats crisp and in place. Test on spare fabric first. Turn up hem, baste and press fold.

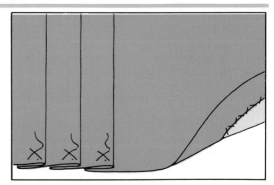

3 Trim raw edge of hem to a depth suitable for fabric, but keep hem as deep as possible—up to about 5 cm/2 in—to add weight and so help pleats to hang well. Finish raw edge. Baste to garment. Finish with catch stitch. On RS fold pleats back into position and work double diagonal basting to form a cross shape across each pleat and through all layers. Press well.

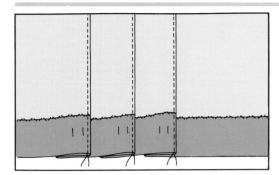

4 On WS edge stitch by machine along pleat fold only, from hem to as near waist as possible. If fabric is very bulky, backstitch through hem section by hand. Remove all basting.

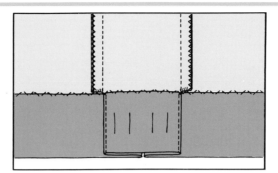

5 If pleat backing is separate, backs of pleats will have seams rather than folds. Clip seam edges at top of hem after hem has been completed to allow seam allowances to extend beyond hem edge. Overcast raw clipped edges. Pleats with a separate backing do not need edge stitching along their whole length, but the pleat fold at the hem must be edge stitched by machine or with backstitch.

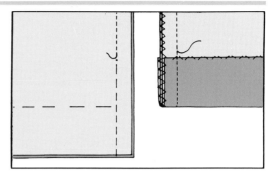

6 If a pleated skirt is cut in separate sections, the hem can be finished separately on each. Baste all seams and stitch to within about 13 cm/5 in of raw hem edge. Press seams to one side. Try on. Mark hemline as in (**1**). Remove basting. Turn up and stitch hem on each section. Baste seams again up to end of seam stitching and stitch very slowly. Remove basting. Finish seam allowances together.

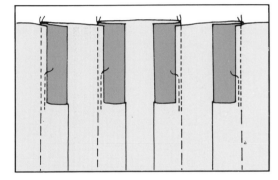

1 **Reinforcing pleat backs** Several pleats placed close together may produce excess bulk at the waist; if this happens or if pleats overlap, cut away top layer of fabric in pleat on WS from inner fold to within 1.5 cm/⅝ in of stitching and to 1.5 cm/⅝ in above pleat depth marks, leaving under-layer supporting pleat.

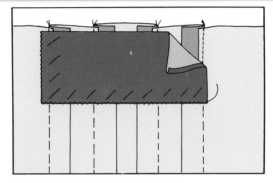

2 To reinforce, cut a piece of lining fabric to cover length of pleat section and depth from waist edge to pleat release point, plus seam allowances on all but waist edge. Baste diagonally in position to cover raw edges. Turn under lining edges and hem to pleats around three sides, leaving raw edge at the waist. Complete waist finish to include edge of lining.

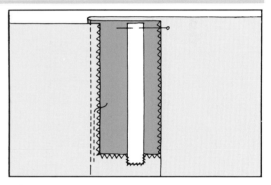

3 To reinforce single pleats or pleats in knits, cut away top layer of pleat as in (**1**). Finish raw edges where pleat was trimmed away. Cut a thin strip of seam binding or tape the length of stitched pleat depth. Turn under raw edge at base of tape and hem to back of pleat just below where top layer was trimmed away. Pin or baste other edge at the waistline and include it in waist finish.

PLEAT FINISHES

Pleats may be finished with decorative stitching or with arrowheads, which provide decoration and strength at points of strain.

Topstitching is added on the right side of the pleats after they have been stitched and pressed, but before the waist finish is completed. The pressed fold of the pleat can be edge stitched, but this stitching should never be used to keep the pleat in place or as a substitute for pressing. Its disadvantage is that it is worked after the hem has been completed and so the stitching may wobble as it has to be worked over uneven thicknesses of fabric.

Arrowheads should be worked in buttonhole thread or a thread to match that used for any other topstitching on garment. To preserve their raised appearance, press them right side down on a towel.

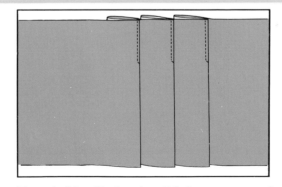

Topstitching Machine from RS. Start at waist and slope stitching in toward pleat release point for the last 5 mm to 1.25 cm/¼ to ½ in. Repeat for all pleats, making sure that stitching begins to slope at exactly the same level for each one. The size of the stitching and its distance from the pleat edge should match the position of any other topstitching on garment. If preferred, saddle stitch by hand.

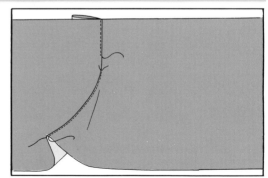

Edge stitching Undo about 2 cm/¾ in of pleat stitching on WS above release point. Edge stitch on RS along fold of pleat from release point to hem. Finish edge stitching at hem by sewing in thread ends on WS by hand. On WS backstitch long threads from pleat stitching down to release point one at a time.

PLEATS

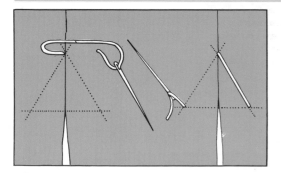

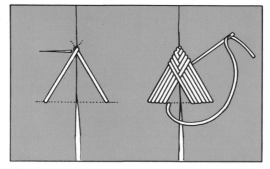

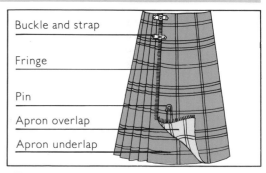

1 **Arrowhead** Using tailor's chalk, accurately mark out a triangle on RS of garment; make each side about 1 cm/⅜ in long and draw the base line so that the pleat release point lies just inside its centre. Bring needle up to RS from WS at top of triangle, slightly to the left of its point. Take needle down to bottom righthand corner of triangle and insert. Bring needle out at bottom lefthand corner.

2 Insert needle slightly to right of top point of triangle and bring up again at top left just below position of first thread. Continue until whole triangle is filled, keeping stitches very close together, so that threads within triangle touch, making sure that stitches are in a straight line along base of triangle and working gradually down its sides. Fasten off on WS with backstitches and cut off thread end.

1 **Making a kilt** A traditional kilt for an adult requires 3.75 m/4 yd of fabric 145 cm/54 in wide, but a kilt-style skirt can be made with 1.80 m/2 yd of fabric of the same width if the check is small.

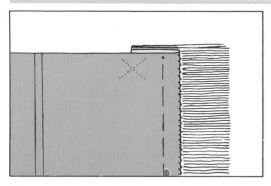

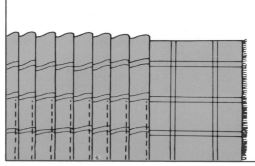

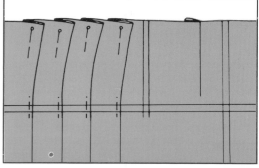

2 Cut off a strip 3 cm/1¼ in wide across the width, fold it lengthwise and press for fringe. Cut main fabric in half lengthwise and rejoin end to end with open seam. Keep checks matched and unbroken. Turn up hem. On outer overlap edge fold under 2 cm/¾ in. Press and place RS up over folded edge of fringe piece. Baste and stitch in place. Make fringe by fraying out raw edges.

3 Decide on the amount to be left flat and unpleated—the apron underlap and overlap—and mark off at each end. Turn under raw edge on unfringed edge and edge stitch. With RS up mark hip depth and pin pleats at this level adjusting until pleated section plus one apron section equals hip size plus 5 cm/2 in ease. Baste pleats from hip to hem.

4 Above hip level fold each pleat along same check but wrap further over to reduce waist edge. Pin all pleats and measure waist. Adjust until waist size is correct. On women's kilts small darts may be necessary as well. Baste pleats up to waist and press well on RS from hip to waist; or they can be topstitched by machine.

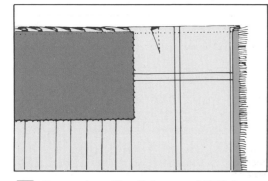

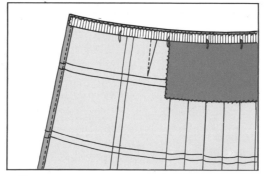

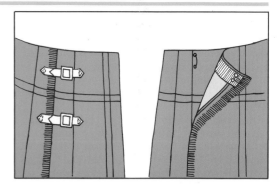

5 Baste a piece of firm lining material WS down to WS of pleated area to extend from hip line to waist and to edge of apron. Turn under and hem all edges except at waist. Put kilt on and mark overlap and position for fastenings. Women's kilts may wrap from right to left. Check waist size, make sure kilt hangs level, mark waistline with chalk.

6 Cut a length of curved petersham, baste to RS of waist with shorter curve on chalk line. Machine stitch or hem along edge. Turn in ends of petersham level with kilt and stitch. Remove all basting. Fold petersham to WS, press and work bar tacks at intervals to hold petersham to kilt.

7 Fasten traditionally with buckles, straps and eyelets (stitch straps with leather needle), or wrap apron over and fasten with large hooks and eyes, trouser hooks and eyes or Velcro placed on both parts of apron. For hooks or Velcro, add straps and buckles as decoration. On all kilts insert a large kilt pin through apron.

COLLARS

The collar is so often the focal point of a garment that it must be made and attached with care for a professional result. This is not always an easy task. Most difficulty with collars arises from the shape of the collar pieces. The neck edge of the collar—the edge that is attached to the neck edge of the garment—may be straight or curved in a slightly convex or concave shape. The concave edge—as on a flat collar, for example—is the easiest to attach because it is nearest in shape to the shape of the neck edge. The slightly convex edge often found on a tailored, classic collar with lapels (see p.158) or on a shirt collar is the most difficult to attach because, when placed against the neck edge of the garment, it curves away from it.

The variation in the shape of the neck edge of the collar also determines whether it lies flat or stands up against the neck. The less the neck edge of the collar follows the shape of the neck edge of the garment, the more the finished collar will stand up.

The outer edge of the collar is shaped in a variety of ways according to the style of the garment, and a paper pattern can easily be altered at this edge without affecting the fit of the collar. The neck edge of the garment may also vary in shape, but is usually slightly shorter than the collar neck edge. Position ease at the shoulder seam areas.

FITTING, ADJUSTING AND PRESSING

Always attach a collar at the latest possible stage in making a garment, after you have finished fitting and have made any necessary adjustments to the neckline. If the garment has a zipper at the neck, insert it before attaching the collar. If an alteration is made to the length of the neckline, alter the collar pattern accordingly. Lengthen a collar pattern by cutting it in two places on either side of the centre back or centre front line and inserting extra paper (1). Similarly, shorten it

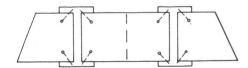

by taking out a small pleat on either side of the centre back or centre front line (2). When

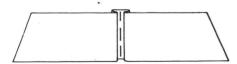

all adjustments have been made, cut out the collar in fabric.

If you are uncertain about the fit or shape

of the collar, or its effect on the finished garment, cut out a trial piece in spare fabric or interfacing and attach it at the fitting stage. If adjustments prove necessary, this piece can be altered and used as the collar pattern. Provided the length of the neck edge remains the same, any adjustments to collar shape or style can be made.

When attaching a collar always press the work well at every stage and never resort to topstitching instead of pressing to obtain a sharp outer edge. Press the neckline join as a curve over a pad, towel or sleeve board. If a dressmaker's dummy is available, put the garment on the dummy to press RS of neck join. If the collar has a roll line, keep the

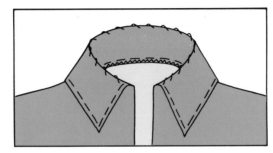

collar in its rolled shape after basting the roll (3). Use the dummy when pressing to establish the roll line that the collar will adopt during wear.

FACINGS

Although neck facing pieces are usually included in paper patterns, the facing generally makes the collar too bulky. To eliminate this unwanted bulk, omit facings wherever possible. This will give a professional finish.

If the collar stands up all around the neck, as in a stand or bias roll collar, or if the garment fastens up to the neck, as with a shirt, the neck join will not be visible and so no facing need be used. For a flat collar a simple alternative to a facing is to use a bias strip to conceal the neck join. However, if any part of the neck join is likely to be visible during wear, as in a classic collar with lapels, it must be faced to conceal the join.

A facing is also required on a shawl collar, which usually stands up at the back of the neck, and the neck join at the front of the garment must also be concealed. This is sometimes achieved with a separate facing, but it is generally better to cut the top-collar and facing in one piece in order to avoid a join.

Where a collar is to be placed at a faced opening, always attach the facing or fold back and finish a facing cut as part of the garment after the collar has been attached.

INTERFACING

All collars require some form of interfacing throughout the whole collar or in particular areas. If even more stiffness is needed in some parts of the collar, as at the points of a shirt collar, an extra layer of interfacing can be inserted.

The choice of interfacing depends on the style of the collar and the fabric. Select heavy, crisp, soft or thin interfacing accordingly. Always try out iron-on interfacing on a small piece of fabric first to ensure that it is not too crisp. Firm iron-on interfacing can be used, however, on stand-up collars, which do not fold over at the neck.

Always interface the section of the collar that is attached first to the neckline of the garment. For most collar styles this is the under-collar—the section that lies against the garment and does not show in wear. However, on stand-up collars it is the outer collar section that is interfaced, and often on men's shirts a better result is obtained by interfacing the outer collar.

Before attaching any type of collar, always make sure that the centre lines of both top- and under-collar pieces are marked with basting and that all seam allowances and any fold lines are appropriately marked. Also check that all markings on the neck edge of the garment have been made.

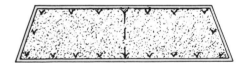

Cut lightweight or thin interfacing using collar pattern (4). If using iron-on interfacing, trim off 2 mm/$\frac{1}{16}$ in from all edges, to prevent interfacing sticking to ironing surface, and press on WS of under-collar. For sew-in interfacing, diagonally baste to WS of under-collar. The edges of both types of interfacing are later stitched into seams and light sew-in interfacing is trimmed close to the machining.

Cut heavyweight or thick interfacing to finished collar size using collar pattern. Either cut around collar pattern and then carefully cut off 1.5 cm/$\frac{5}{8}$ in all around interfacing, or trim seam allowances off pattern and then cut interfacing. According to type of interfacing, press or diagonally baste it in position on WS of under-collar. Cut off corners of interfacing at outer points of collar. Herringbone sew-in interfacing into place (5).

COLLARS

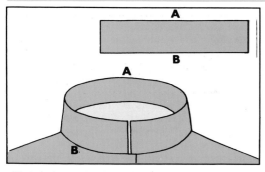

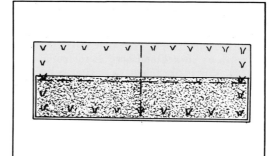

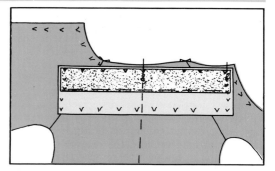

1 **Straight stand collar** stands away from the neck and is usually fairly narrow: outer edge (**A**) is the same length as neck edge (**B**). If the edges are together at the front of the garment the collar is Chinese in style; if they meet at the back it is Victorian. Cut a straight piece of fabric to twice the finished depth of the collar, plus two 1.5 cm/⅝ in seam allowances.

2 Mark seam allowances and centre front and centre back on garment. Attach suitable interfacing to WS of collar, to extend from one edge to 5 mm/¼ in past fold line. Mark all seam allowances on collar pieces and mark centre and fold lines.

3 Place RS of collar down on RS of garment, with interfaced section toward neck edge. Match centre line of collar with centre back (or front) line of garment. Insert a pin across seamline. Bring centre front (or back) markings at collar ends to meet centre front (or back) markings at opening on garment neckline. Pin across seamline at each end, picking up fabric on this line only.

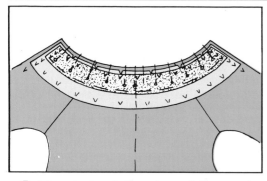

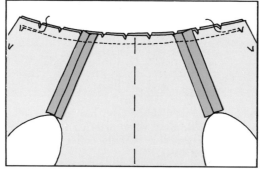

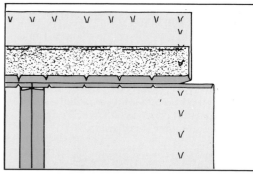

4 Clip neck edge of collar at intervals between pins to help collar lie flat against neckline. Lift neckline to keep it curved and pin collar to neckline. Use plenty of pins, inserting them across seamline and picking up fabric on this line only. Baste with small stitches on seamline. If any pleats or folds form, take smaller stitches. Remove pins.

5 Clip neck edge of collar and garment together, ending clips halfway between raw edges and basting line. Turn work over and machine close to basting. Stitch slowly and stop frequently to examine underside to make sure that pleats or folds are not being sewn in. Fasten off machining at each end exactly on centre front (or back) lines by reversing for a few stitches. Remove basting.

6 Arrange neckline on a sleeve board or pad with RS of garment uppermost and run tip of iron around neck join, between collar and bodice. On WS trim garment edge at neck join to 3 mm/⅛ in and collar edge to 5 mm/¼ in. If light sew-in interfacing has been used, trim close to machining to reduce bulk within seam allowance. On WS of garment press neck join open. Press again on RS.

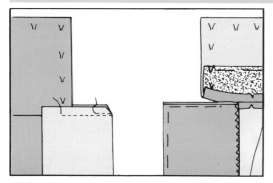

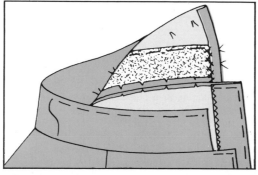

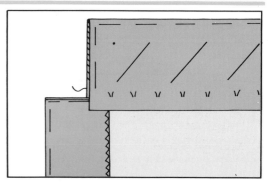

7 If facing is cut as part of garment, fold along marked line to RS; baste and machine top edge from collar seamline to folded edge. For a separate facing, attach it RS down on RS of garment. For both types trim seam allowances along top edge and outer corner; trim down the front on a separate facing. Turn through. Baste and press edges so that join is 2mm/1/16 in to WS. Finish outer edge.

8 With garment WS up, fold in collar ends along marked lines from neck join to 1 cm/⅜ in past centre fold line on collar. Baste folded ends. Press. Trim edges of turned-in ends to no less than 3 mm/⅛ in and, if fabric is springy, herringbone these edges to hold in place. Remove basting. Turn garment so that RS of collar is uppermost and fold collar along fold line. Baste along fold. Press.

9 On WS complete collar ends by trimming raw edges of inner (unfolded) sections to no less than 3 mm/⅛ in. Fold in ends of inner sections so that they lie 2 mm/1/16 in to WS of collar and are invisible from RS. Baste. Press and slip stitch ends. Work a row of diagonal basting along centre of collar through both layers to hold them together.

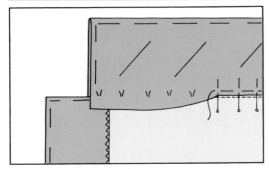

10 For lightweight fabric, press all neck join seam allowances toward collar. Turn under raw edge of collar and pin vertically to neck edge, starting at centre. Baste. Finish by hemming into machining of neck join. Oversew end of facing to collar edge at top corner. For other fabrics, complete neck edge as for shaped stand collar (**8**) by prick stitching from RS into neck join.

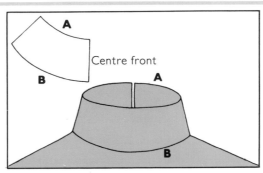

1 **Shaped stand collar** A slightly curved collar that fits well up against the neck and can be made to any reasonable depth. The garment usually fastens at the back with the collar standing above the zipper. Because of the shaping, two pieces of fabric are cut and then joined along their outer edges (**B**). The neck edge of the collar is the same length as that of the garment but the top, outer, edge (**A**) is shorter.

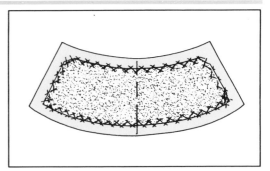

2 Mark seam allowances and centre front and centre back on garment. Insert zipper. Cut collar with straight grain running down centre front. If fabric is bulky, use lining material or cotton lawn for inner collar. Attach interfacing to outer collar as appropriate (see p. 121). Mark all seam allowances and centre front line on top and inner collar pieces.

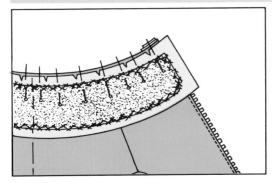

3 Place RS of outer collar on RS of garment neckline, matching centre front line on garment to centre line of collar. Pin across seamline. Clip collar at neckline edge to bring collar and garment together at centre back, matching seam allowances at centre back exactly. Pin at each end. Pin frequently across seamline, picking up fabric on this line only. Baste on seamline. Remove pins.

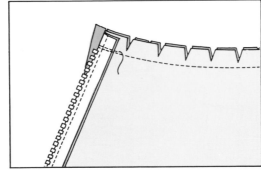

4 Clip collar and neckline edges together halfway into seam allowances to make sure that collar lies flat. With garment side uppermost, machine close to basting. Fasten off machining at each end exactly at centre back lines by reversing for a few stitches. Remove basting. Trim neck edge to 3 mm/⅛ in and collar edge to 5 mm/¼ in. Trim sew-in interfacing close to machining.

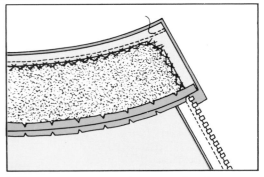

5 Press join open, making more clips if necessary so join lies flat. Press again on WS and RS. With RS of garment uppermost, place lining or inner collar against outer collar, RS together, matching centre front and seamlines. Baste along outer edge. Check depth of collar stand is equal all around—for accuracy use an adjustable marker. Machine from interfaced side beside basting. Remove basting.

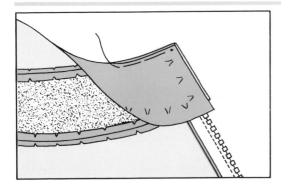

6 Layer collar seam allowances by trimming inner allowances to 3 mm/⅛ in and outer to 5 mm/¼ in and then trim interfacing close to machining if appropriate. Clip well. Roll inner collar to WS of garment, bringing join 2 mm/1/16 in over to WS. Baste along fold to hold join in place, leaving ends of collar free to be turned in. Press basted fold.

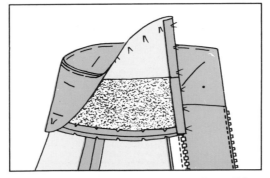

7 Baste diagonally along centre of collar on RS to hold lining flat. With WS of garment uppermost, turn in ends of collar along seamlines to 1 cm/⅜ in past join at top edge of collar and then slightly more so that inner collar edge lies 2 mm/1/16 in to WS of collar. Slip stitch ends as far as the marked seamline on neck edge.

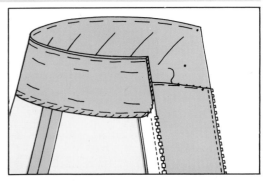

8 Trim raw edges of inner collar to 5 mm/¼ in and finish. Complete raw, clipped edge of garment only with overcasting. Baste edge of inner collar flat over neck join. Press. To prevent ends of inner collar from being visible beside zipper, either trim collar edge at an angle and finish or turn under and hem to zipper tape. Turn to RS and work prick stitch through into neck join. Remove all basting. Press.

COLLARS

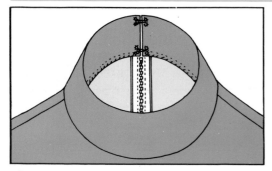

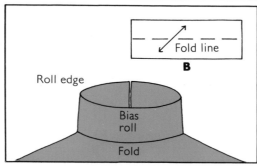

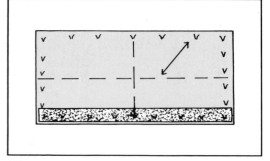

9 The ends of the finished collar can be fastened with hooks or Velcro. If using Velcro attach both pieces to inner collar on WS of garment, but arrange one piece so that it protrudes sufficiently to be fastened invisibly during wear, as for bias roll collar (**7**). Similarly, place hooks and eyes on WS, or work thread loops instead of eyes, just to inside of collar.

I **Bias roll collar** consists of a strip of fabric folded into a double roll. The finished collar can be of any reasonable depth, but if less than about 3 cm/1¼ in will not remain in rolled position during wear. Cut fabric on true cross to four times finished width of roll, plus two 1.5 cm/⅝ in seam allowances, and slightly longer than neck edge (**B**) of garment. There is usually a zipper at centre back.

2 Mark all seam allowances and centre back and centre front on garment. Insert zipper. Interface WS of collar along neck edge with a strip of iron-on interfacing of appropriate weight (see p. 121) and 2.5 cm/1 in wide (or proportionally wider for a deep collar). This interfacing is sufficient to support the collar. Mark all seam allowances, fold line and centre front line on collar piece.

124

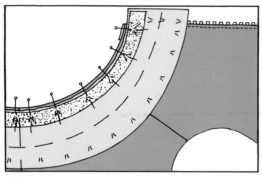

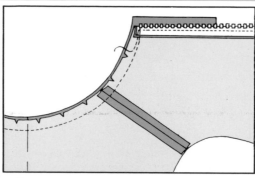

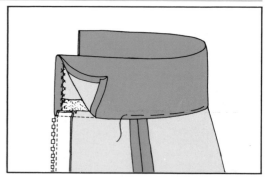

3 Place RS of collar on RS of garment neckline with interfaced section at neckline edge. Match centre front lines, and centre back lines on collar ends and garment, and pin across seamline. Pin at intervals around neck, picking up fabric on seamline only and easing in any fullness in collar to fall near shoulder seams. On firm fabrics it may be necessary to clip garment neckline to ensure collar lies flat.

4 Baste on seamline. Remove pins. Machine with garment side uppermost and fasten off machining by reversing for a few stitches, exactly at centre back lines above zipper. Remove basting. Clip seam allowances in garment neckline only. Press join open from WS and press again on RS.

5 Turn in, baste and press collar ends on marked lines. Trim raw edges of ends to 3 mm/⅛ in. On springy fabrics herringbone over raw edge of seam allowance on inner part of roll. On fine fabrics, press seam allowances at neck join into collar, bring raw edge down, turn under, baste and hem into machining. Slip stitch ends so that inner edge is 2 mm/1/16 in to WS of garment. Remove all basting.

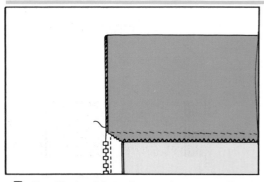

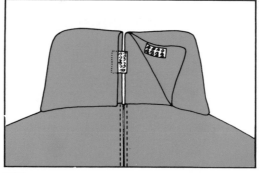

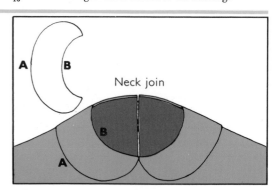

6 For all other fabrics, keep neck join open. Finish raw edges of collar and baste flat over neck join. Beside zipper, trim collar edge at an angle and finish or turn under and hem. On RS of garment, prick stitch into join between collar and garment as for shaped stand collar (**8**). Slip stitch collar ends as in (**5**) so that the join is 2 mm/1/16 in to WS of garment. Remove all basting.

7 Place fold edge of collar on pressing surface. Hold one end of collar and stretch edge with iron. This ensures that collar falls over and covers neck join. Roll collar to RS of garment, allowing it to find its own roll line. Fasten collar with small hooks and eyes placed under outer part of roll or with a small piece of Velcro hemmed in a similar position, but with one part extending slightly.

I **Flat collar** Neck edge is curved in a similar shape to garment neck. If both edges are exactly the same shape the collar lies completely flat with no stand. However, few flat collars are cut without a stand. The collar is usually in two parts, with outer edges (**A**) curved to form a Peter Pan style. It can also be in one piece and the outer edge any shape. A very long outer edge will produce a fluted collar.

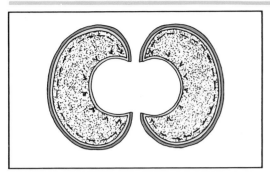

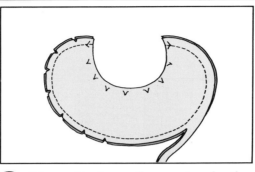

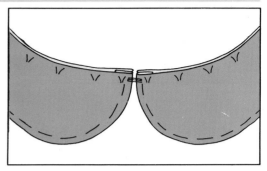

2 Mark seam allowances and centre front and centre back on garment. Cut out collar pieces. Interface whole of two under-collar pieces on WS as appropriate (see p. 121). Mark seam allowances on collar pieces. Place under-collar pieces against top-collar pieces, RS together. Baste and machine around all except neckline edges, working from interfaced side. Remove basting.

3 Trim machined seam allowances to no less than 3 mm/⅛ in. Trim interfacing close to machining if appropriate. Clip curved sections of machined outer edges of collar pieces every 5 mm/¼ in.

4 Turn collar pieces RS out. Roll edges so that join is 2 mm/1/16 in to underside of each collar piece. Baste rolled edges. Press well. Place two collar pieces together at centre front and work a bar tack to hold them together, exactly on seamline of neck edge.

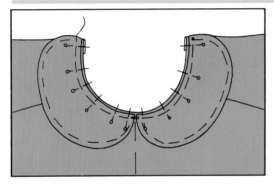

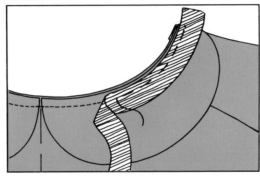

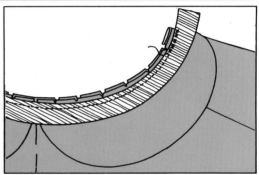

5 Place under-collar down on RS of garment. Match centre front of garment and collar and pin across seamline. Pin ends of collar to match centre back lines. Insert more pins at intervals, picking up fabric on seamline only. Clip garment neckline if necessary so collar lies flat. Baste. Remove pins. With collar side up, machine on fitting line, reversing at collar ends. Remove basting.

6 Unless garment is to be faced as in (**10**) or lined as in (**11**), cut a bias strip of fabric or purchased bias binding 2.5 cm/1 in wide to length of neckline, plus 1.5 cm/⅝ in at either end. On RS of garment centre strip RS down over machine stitches so an equal amount extends at each end. Taking a 5 mm/¼ in seam allowance on strip, baste along neck seamline on top of machining, attaching collar.

7 With garment WS up, machine just inside first row of stitching exactly from centre back edge to centre back edge, starting and finishing by reversing for a few stitches. Remove basting. Trim edge of bias strip to 2 mm/1/16 in, garment neckline edge to 5 mm/¼ in and collar edges to 3 mm/⅛ in. Trim interfacing close to machining if appropriate. Clip garment and collar edges at 5 mm/¼ in intervals.

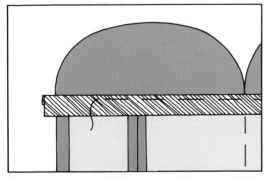

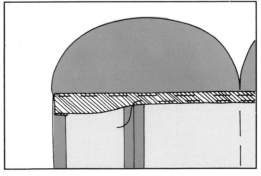

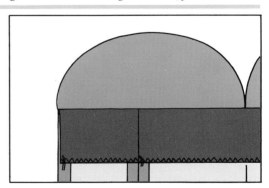

8 With garment RS up, run tip of iron around join under collar, and then place collar alone, RS up, on pressing surface and run tip of iron along join under edge of bias strip. With WS of garment uppermost, hold collar upright, smooth down bias strip over neck join to WS and baste just below join through seam allowances and garment. Press on WS.

9 Turn under both ends of bias strip so that they lie 2 mm/1/16 in from centre back edge. Baste. Trim 5 mm/¼ in off remaining raw edge of bias strip, turn under and baste to garment. Press. Slip stitch ends of bias strip and slip hem turned-in edge to garment. Remove basting.

10 A flat collar may be finished with a facing, but it can cause problems in laundering. Treat as a normal facing after attaching collar. Place RS down on RS of garment over collar, machine from garment side with garment WS up, trim and clip. Roll facing to WS, finish lower edge and anchor with bar tacks at shoulder seams and centre back.

125

COLLARS

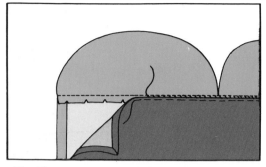

1 If garment is to be lined, machine collar to neckline, clip and layer seam allowances, trimming garment edge to 5 mm/¼ in and collar edge to 3 mm/⅛ in. Press seam allowances toward bodice. Insert lining and complete neck join by turning in edge of lining, basting it down and hemming into machine stitches at neck join. Remove basting.

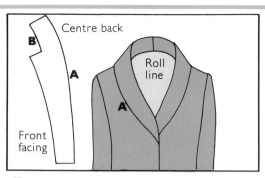

Shawl collar runs in two sections from centre front opening or seam to centre back. Garment neck is usually V-shaped and the collar has a stand at back of neck. Under-parts are usually cut in one with front bodice, but may be cut separately and joined to bodice before shoulder seams are joined and collar attached. Outer edge (**A**) may be curved, pointed or scalloped.

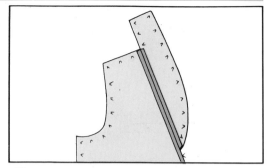

2 Mark all seams and centre front and centre back on garment. If separate pieces are to be attached to bodice for under-collar sections mark all seams. Place front bodice and under-collar pieces RS together from shoulders down centre front bodice edges, leaving back neck section of collar extending. Baste and machine along seamlines and press seam open. Make all markings on top-collar.

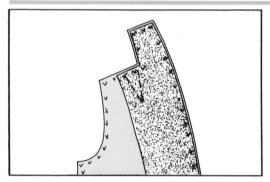

3 Attach soft iron-on or sew-in interfacing to WS of under-collar area of garment, extending it down centre front of garment if there is a front opening or fastening. If under-collar is cut in one piece with front bodice, make all markings on top-collar pieces and under-collar sections. On some patterns a dart is taken out of each side of collar neckline to improve its shape. Mark darts.

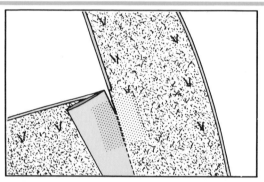

4 On WS of each under-collar, baste darts. Machine from seamline (not raw edges) to points. Remove basting. Trim away interfacing within dart to reduce bulk. Press darts toward armholes. If necessary, attach small pieces of paper-backed adhesive to WS of fabric at raw neck edges below base of dart to prevent fraying; clip fabric from neck edge to beginning of dart stitching.

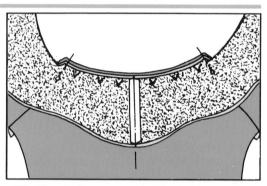

5 Place bodice pieces together at shoulders. Baste and machine shoulder seams. Press seams open and finish. Bring back neck edges of under-collar sections around to match back neck of garment. Pin to garment across seamlines at back neck and between shoulder seams. Baste and stitch centre back ends of under-collar RS together. Remove basting. Press seam open; trim to 5 mm/¼ in.

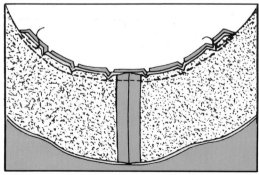

6 Trim interfacing close to stitching. To attach under-collar between shoulder seams along back of neck, baste, remove pins and machine with collar side up. Start and finish machining exactly at ends of shoulder seam stitching. Remove basting. Clip and layer seam allowances, trimming garment edge to 5 mm/¼ in, collar edge to 3 mm/⅛ in. Trim interfacing close to machining. Press seam open.

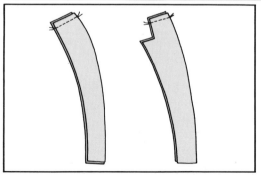

7 If top-collar is wide at shoulders, make darts in top-collar pieces as in (**4**). Stitch pieces together at centre back, RS together. Trim join to 3 mm/⅛ in and press open. Top-collar is not same shape as under-collar as front facing is cut in one piece with it—it may extend over shoulder seams, above right. If garment is unlined, finish outer edges of facing and, on all but fine fabrics, top-collar.

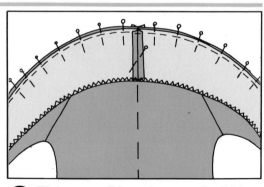

8 With garment RS up, place top-collar RS down on RS of under-collar. Match collar seams at centre back and pin, picking up fabric on seamline only. Match darts and pin. Pin around outer edge of collar and down centre front. Baste, remove pins and machine along seamline. Trim seam allowances on garment to 5 mm/¼ in and on top-collar to 3 mm/⅛ in. Trim interfacing. Clip.

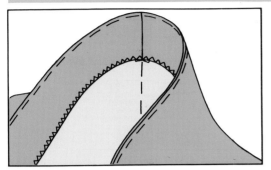

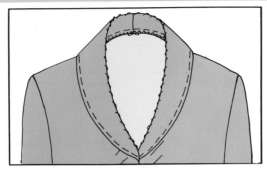

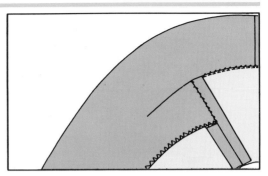

9 Press seam open up front edges and as far around outer edge of collar as possible. Turn top-collar to WS of garment. Roll edge and baste so join is 2 to 3 mm/$\frac{1}{16}$ to $\frac{1}{8}$ in to underside, depending on the fabric. Adjust position of top-collar and front facings so seamlines match on WS of garment.

10 Roll collar into position. Work diagonal basting over roll. Baste rest of front facings flat to WS of garment. Baste inside back neck between shoulder seams of top-collar flat to under-collar just above finished edge. Finish raw edges of collar and garment seam at back of neck; prick stitch into neck join between shoulder seams. Herringbone facing ends to seam allowances on WS.

11 On fine fabrics, press clipped seam allowances at neck join up into collar, turn under raw edge of top-collar and hem across back of neck between shoulder seams. If facing ends extend over shoulder seams, turn them under and hem to seam allowances. If desired, hold down rest of facing on fine and bulky fabrics with adhesive strip. Insert at intervals on WS of facing. Remove all basting.

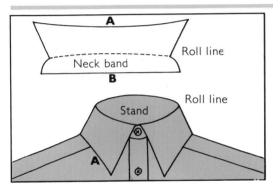

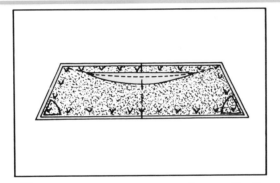

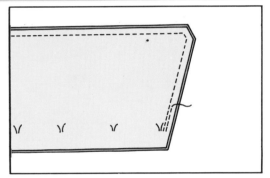

1 **Shirt collar** Made from two pieces of fabric joined at outer (**A**) edges so collar points can be shaped. Neck edge (**B**) is straight or slightly convex to give collar a stand at back of neck. Roll line is high at back but runs down to neck edge at centre front. A neck band can be cut as part of the collar or attached separately. Attach front facings and turn them to WS in the usual way before attaching collar.

2 Make all marks on garment. Cut out all collar pieces. Interface under- or top-collar as appropriate (see p. 121). Add additional triangles of stiffening of a crisper type to collar points if desired. With heavy interfacing cut away on roll line. If collar has a neck band, interface band twice. Mark seams, roll line and centre back line on collar pieces and seams and centre back line on band if separate.

3 For collar without band, place top- and under-collar pieces RS together, matching centre back lines. Baste and machine around all but neck edges, starting and finishing exactly on centre front seamlines and working one machine stitch across each point. Trim and layer seam allowances to no less than 3 mm/$\frac{1}{8}$ in. Trim interfacing close to machining. Trim corners and clip curves on outer edges.

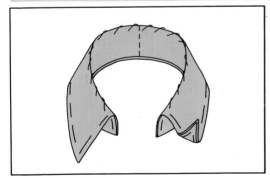

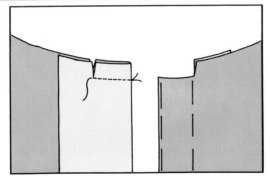

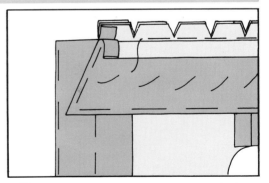

4 Place collar, still WS out, on pressing surface and run tip of iron inside it, along seamline. Turn collar RS out. Ease out points with a pin or collar point turner. Roll outer edges and baste so that join is 2 mm/$\frac{1}{16}$ in to underside of collar. Press. Fold collar into rolled position it will adopt in wear and baste diagonally across roll line.

5 Fold front facing to RS. Machine along top edge from fold to centre front mark. Clip seam allowances down to machining at centre front mark and trim off corner. Turn RS out. Baste facing down to WS.

6 Opening collar out slightly, place RS of top-collar on WS of garment neckline, matching centre back lines. Pin across seamline at centre back, picking up fabric on this line only. Pin centre front ends of top-collar to centre front lines of garment across seamline. Clip edges of top-collar and garment so that collar lies flat. Baste top-collar to garment along seamline at neck. Remove pins.

COLLARS

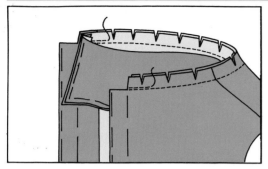

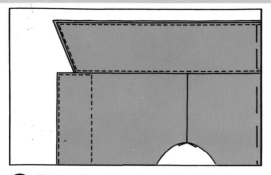

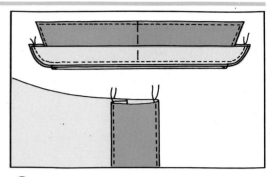

7 Machine from garment side with garment RS up, making sure that under-collar is not sewn in. Start and finish stitching exactly at collar ends and fasten off well here. Remove basting around neck edge. Trim seam allowance on top-collar to 3 mm/⅛ in and on neck edge to 5 mm/¼ in. Press seam allowances up into collar. Press neck join from WS of garment.

8 Trim under-collar edge to 5 mm/¼ in. Turn it under and baste in position so that it covers machine stitching. Machine on edge around neck with under-collar side up. Remove basting. Topstitch collar and front facing if desired from RS of collar and garment. Remove basting on facing.

9 If collar has a separate band, make up as in (**2**) to (**4**). Turn to RS and topstitch. Place two band pieces RS together and, matching centre back markings, insert neck edge of collar between two band pieces until raw edges of collar are level with shaped edges of band pieces. Stitch along marked seamline on band from end to end. Remove basting. Turn front garment facings to WS and machine.

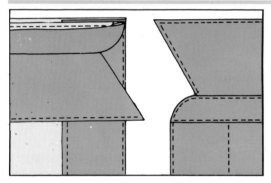

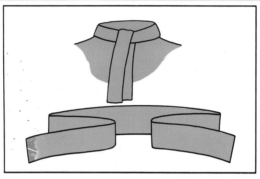

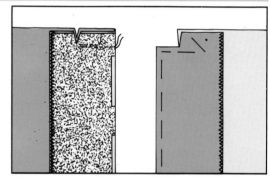

10 Trim one band seam allowance to 2 mm/ 1/16 in, one collar allowance to 4 mm/⅛ in, the second to 2 mm/1/16 in, and other band allowance to 4 mm/⅛ in. Clip allowances. Turn band RS out. Attach under-piece to neck as for under-collar in (**6**) to (**8**), but take ends to edges of centre front opening. On RS stitch along edge of top band piece on neck join; topstitch around rest of band.

1 **Stand collar with tie ends** Usually fairly wide and can be attached to a round or V-neck. There may be a buttoned front opening or the tie can be made of two pieces to provide for the tie at the front and a zippered or buttoned back opening. The tie can be cut on straight or cross grain, ends square or angled. Attach a narrow piece of interfacing to neck edge omitting tie ends.

2 For front opening fold garment RS together on fold line and stitch along neck edge from fold to centre front point. Fasten off stitching. Trim raw edges and corner. Clip up to end of stitching at centre front point. Turn corner of garment RS out, press, baste neck extensions together.

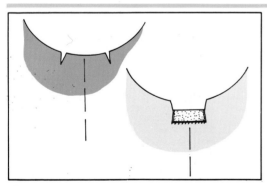

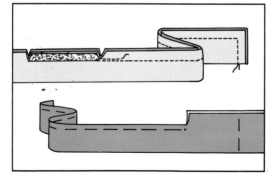

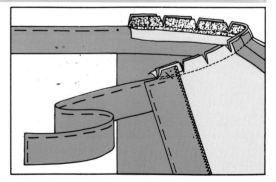

3 For a garment with centre back opening: complete the opening edges; at centre front make two clips 2 cm/¾ in apart, fold the flap that forms to WS and press; overcast edge and hold in place with a small piece of adhesive web.

4 Fold tie collar RS together and baste. Stitch along tie section and across each end. If tie is for a back opening garment stitch across both ends of each piece and along the tie edge as far as centre mark. Clip seam in as far as stitching at centre front point. Trim edges and corners. Turn tie RS out, roll edge, baste and press.

5 Clip garment neck edge at intervals. Matching centre back and centre front, place collar on RS garment with neck edges level. The strip of interfacing should be nearest to the garment. Pin and baste one edge of tie collar to neckline. Turn fabric garment side up and stitch from base of centre front clips across neck making sure free edge of tie does not become caught in stitching.

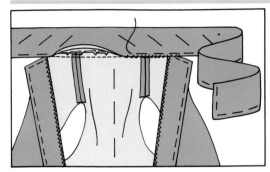

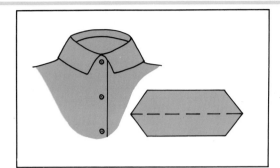

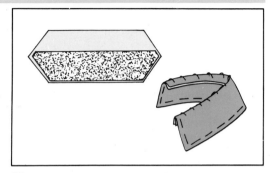

6 Trim neck seam allowances and clip every 5 mm/¼ in. Press seam into neck tie. Fold tie into position and baste along the middle. Trim remaining neck edge seam allowance, fold under raw edge and bring on to machine stitching. Baste in position. Hem along neck edge picking up the machine stitches. Work a bar tack on WS of neck at centre front point between collar and garment.

Convertible collar The classic pointed collar that can be made to fasten up to the neck or to be worn open so that the front facings form lapels. If the collar is fitted carefully in the closed position and the construction is accurate a small loop and button can be attached to the top corners so that it really can be converted from one style to the other.

2 Attach interfacing to one section to just beyond the centre line. Fold RS together, stitch across end, trim and turn RS out. Baste along outer edge, press, fold collar into wearing position and baste along roll line. Trim off the raw edge that extends so that they are level. The garment facing is often cut all in one with garment front edge; attach interfacing to WS.

129

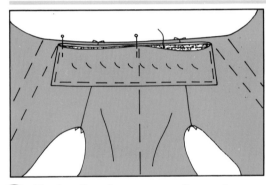

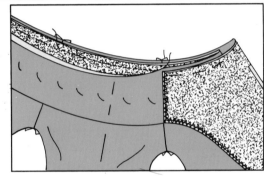

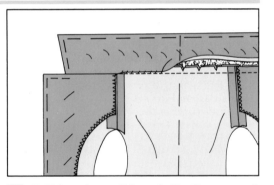

3 Match collar edges to centre front points on neckline; match centre back marks; pin collar to RS garment with interfaced edge to garment. Lift upper edge of collar and baste the edge underneath to the garment neck edge. Machine stitch with collar uppermost between the shoulder seams only, keeping upper edge clear of stitching.

4 Finish outer edge of facing along shoulder and along front edge to hem. Fold facing RS down on top of collar. Baste with neck edges level and with facing folded accurately along centre front line. Trim corners, snip neck edge.

5 Fold front facings RS out, hold collar to extend above neck edge and baste and press along front edges of garment. Baste along middle of facing up to shoulder. Clip and trim neckline seam allowance, press edges into collar, press neck join, collar and shoulders. Fold under remaining raw edge of collar onto machine stitching. Baste in position; hem into machining or machine close to fold.

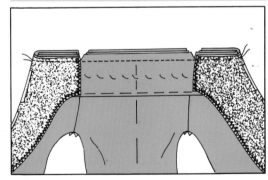

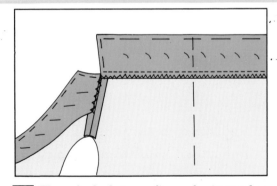

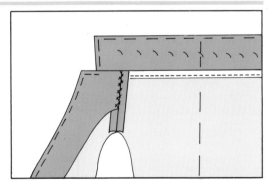

6 An alternative method for light fabrics is to baste through both neck edges of collar when attaching to garment, fold front facings over RS down on top, then machine stitch right across neck from centre front fold to the same point on the other end. Trim the raw edges and clip in as far as the stitching level with facing ends.

7 The neck edge between clips can be zigzagged or overlocked so that it lies flat inside back neck of garment when front facings are turned RS out and collar is pressed to extend beyond neckline.

8 Alternatively, fold a narrow strip of bias fabric and place it on the centre section of collar, overlapping facing edges by 1 cm/⅜ in. Stitch across neckline through bias, collar and garment. Turn facings RS out, press and baste with collar extending; hem or machine edge of bias to garment. Complete all versions by stitching shoulder edge of facing to seam allowance of shoulder seam.

POCKETS

Pockets may be decorative or functional or both. There are two basic types—patch pockets and bag pockets.

Always make pockets as early as possible in the construction of a garment and decide their position at the first fitting. The size of all visible pockets should be proportioned to both the garment and the wearer's figure. Most visible pockets create emphasis by breaking the line of a garment, so position them carefully.

Size and strength

A functional pocket must be placed so that the hand can be inserted easily and be big enough for you to feel into all parts without disturbing the opening. Unless pocket size is dictated by the style of the garment, as in a jacket, calculate the dimensions by measuring the size of your hand and adding 2 to 4 cm/$\frac{3}{4}$ to 1$\frac{1}{2}$ in all around for ease.

For all pockets the wrong side of the garment fabric should be reinforced. Pocket bags must also be strong. Calico and pocketing are toughest, but if strength is not essential use self-fabric or cotton, lining fabric or poplin.

Mitres

Corners can be folded in neatly to make right-angled corners but mitres are quick and easy to do, especially on crisp fabrics. Fold over two adjacent edges equal amounts and press. Open out. Fold corner over where creases meet, press. Open out. Refold with WS together and with edges level, then stitch along the crease. Trim, turn RS out and press.

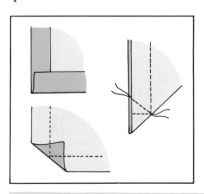

Pocket position Put on garment, make sure all fitting adjustments that might affect pockets are complete, e.g. shoulder and side seams. Using pattern piece or a piece of interfacing cut to shape, pin to the garment, adjusting position suitably. Mark garment at pocket corners, remove pattern.

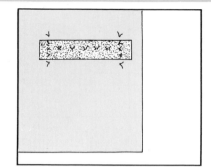

1 **To reinforce position** of a cut pocket opening on WS, or behind opening of a patch pocket on WS of garment, cut a piece of iron-on interfacing, of weight appropriate to fabric, 5 cm/2 in wide and 4 cm/1$\frac{1}{2}$ in longer than pocket opening. Centre over marked line on WS and press on.

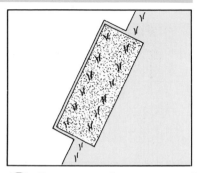

2 For a seam pocket in garment of medium- or heavy-weight fabric, press iron-on interfacing 3 cm/1$\frac{1}{4}$ in wide over both side seamlines on WS of garment. Interfacing should end 3 mm/$\frac{1}{8}$ in from raw edges. For lightweight fabric adhesive web is applied at a later stage (see seam pocket).

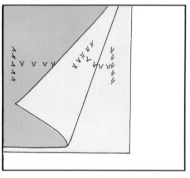

Marking Lay out piece of garment with position marked RS up. Draw chalk line for top of pocket and a line across at each end. To transfer marked position to corresponding garment piece, either put both together and tailor tack on chalk line or put them RS together and bang sharply.

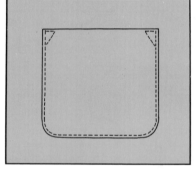

1 **Patch pocket** A piece of fabric applied to RS of garment. It may be shaped.

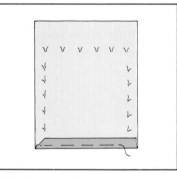

2 Mark pocket opening on garment. Cut pocket with side and bottom seam allowances of 1.5 cm/$\frac{5}{8}$ in, slightly more at top. Mark seam allowances. On WS of pocket turn up a single hem along base. Baste 3 mm/$\frac{1}{8}$ in from fold. Press. Trim corners diagonally.

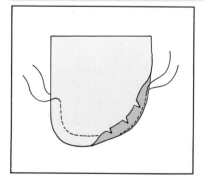

3 For accurate curved edges insert a gathering thread around the lower edge of the pocket on the stitching line. Pull it up slightly and ease the fabric along until the seam allowance begins to curl over. Clip the seam allowances around the curve so that they lie flat. Press the edge.

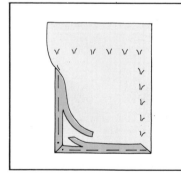

4 Fold side edges on marked lines to WS. Baste 3 mm/$\frac{1}{8}$ in from fold to top hem fold line. Press and trim bottom corners as in (**2**). Trim 3 to 5 mm/$\frac{1}{8}$ to $\frac{1}{4}$ in off turned-in edges; if desired, top-stitch them and remove basting. Press. Clip side seam allowances at top hem fold line.

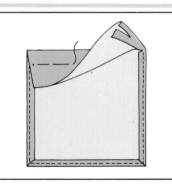

5 Turn in ends of top hem at an angle to WS and trim away extra fabric. Turn down hem along top edge; baste. Machine double hem with straight or zigzag stitch. Finish raw edge of single hem and hold down with catch stitch, machining or adhesive web. Remove basting.

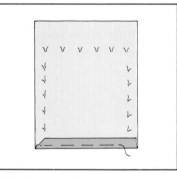

130

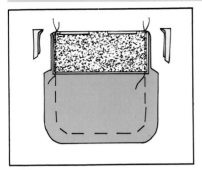

6 An alternative treatment for the top edge is to cut a piece of light perforated interfacing to fit, press to WS of top edge, zigzag the edge. Fold top of pocket to RS along perforations, stitch across the hem. Trim edges and corners. Turn RS out, fold in and press remaining edges.

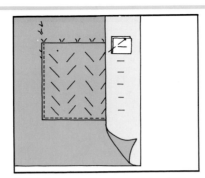

7 Place pocket in position RS up on RS of garment. If WS of garment has not been reinforced, pin pieces of cotton tape folded in half on WS of garment where top corners of pocket fall. Baste diagonally along top and sides of pocket, matching edges to tailor's tacks. Remove pins.

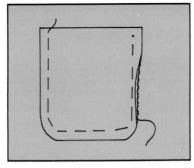

Attaching by hand A plain or top-stitched pocket can be sewn to the garment using small slip stitches placed just under the pocket edge. Alternatively with thick fabric turn garment WS up and backstitch through to pocket seam allowances, feeling the edge beneath as a guide.

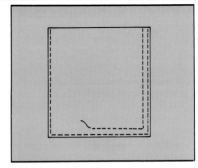

Attaching by machine Adjust machine to a stitch of suitable size or to match other topstitching on garment. At top right corner, lower foot so that it is completely on pocket, reverse stitching then stitch forward around pocket. If a second row is required use edge of machine foot to keep parallel.

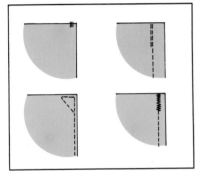

Reinforcing corners On RS make machine bar tack across corner; reverse machine stitching; stitch a triangle; or zigzag for 1 cm/$\frac{3}{8}$ in. To reinforce invisibly: on RS make hand bar tack under corners; on WS make hand bar tack from pocket to garment, or hem through garment and pocket corner.

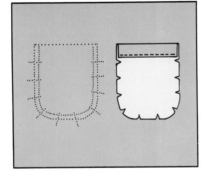

Attaching invisibly For curved pocket. Finish top edge, trim other edges to 5 mm/$\frac{1}{4}$ in. Using chalk or fabric pen, draw on garment outline of edge of pocket and another line 5 mm/$\frac{1}{4}$ in inside it. Mark points on outer line and clip raw edge of pocket to match.

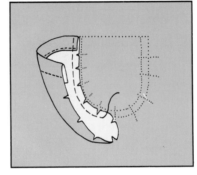

2 Place pocket RS down to RS garment, match pocket top *right* corner to top *left* garment corner and outer edge of pocket to *inner* line on garment. Reverse at top edge, stitch around pocket taking 5 mm/$\frac{1}{4}$ in seam, matching guide points accurately.

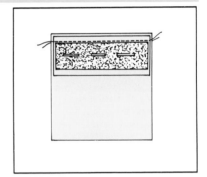

Facing on RS Press light perforated interfacing band to WS fabric, cut out allowing 1 cm/$\frac{3}{8}$ in seam allowance. Cut pocket 3.5 cm/1$\frac{3}{8}$ in shorter than pattern. Place RS facing to WS pocket and stitch taking 1 cm/$\frac{3}{8}$ in seam. Press seam toward band.

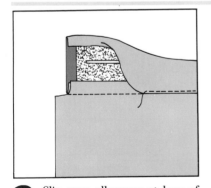

2 Clip seam allowance at base of facing to allow pocket to lie flat. Fold in ends of facing, fold facing along perforations and down onto RS pocket to cover machine stitching. Baste, stitch all around facing. Fold in remaining edges and attach to garment.

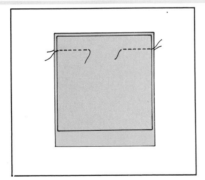

Lined patch pocket Interface upper edge of pocket with perforated banding. Cut lining 3.5 cm/1$\frac{3}{8}$ in shorter than pocket. With RS together stitch lining to upper edge of pocket for 4 cm/1$\frac{1}{2}$ in each end. Press seam open across pocket.

2 Fold pocket along perforations, align all outer edges of lining and pocket; baste. Stitch around outer edge of pocket. Trim seam and corners. Turn pocket RS out through gap in seam. Baste and press pocket. Slip stitch gap in seam. Attach pocket to garment.

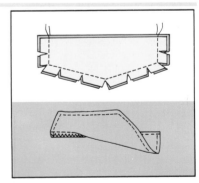

False flap Cut shape of flap in iron-on interfacing, press to fabric, cut out. Cut second piece the same. Place RS together, stitch outer edge, clip edges. Turn RS out, press, zigzag raw edges. Place RS down on garment, stitch beside zigzagged edge. Fold flap over, baste down, stitch below upper edge.

POCKETS

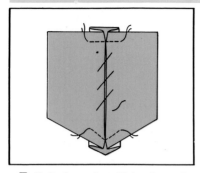

1 Safari pocket Make flap, edge stitch and zigzag raw edges. Baste a pleat in a piece of fabric, press, cut out pocket. Stitch across ends of pleat.

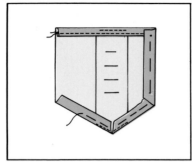

2 Turn narrow hem along top and stitch. Turn in remaining edges making pocket 2 mm/$\frac{1}{16}$ in narrower than flap; baste and press. Hold down edges with hemming web.

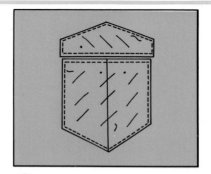

3 Place pocket on RS garment; baste. Place flap RS down with zigzagged edge against top hem of pocket. Baste. Stitch flap to garment 5 mm/$\frac{1}{4}$ in above edge. Stitch pocket to garment around outer edge. Fold flap over pocket, stitch again below upper edge.

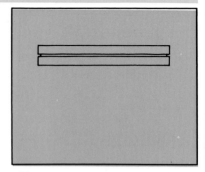

1 Piped pocket Narrow piping of even width finishes each side of the opening on RS of garment. If fabric is checked or striped, the piping may be cut on the bias for decorative effect. The pocket is formed by a bag placed on WS of garment.

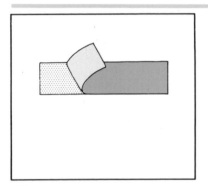

2 Mark pocket opening on garment. Cut two fabrics strips on straight grain (or bias for special effects) 3 cm/1$\frac{1}{4}$ in wide and at least 5 cm/2 in longer than pocket opening. Press on paper-backed adhesive web to cover whole of WS of each piece. Peel off paper backing.

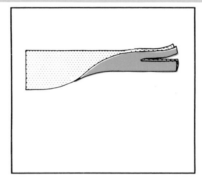

3 Fold each strip in half WS together and press. Trim to twice desired width of finished piping. Beginners should practise so that the strips are as narrow as possible.

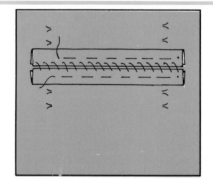

4 On WS of garment press down iron-on interfacing 5 cm/2 in wide and 4 cm/1$\frac{1}{2}$ in longer than opening. On RS centre strips against line of opening with raw edges touching. Baste in position and hold their raw edges together by oversewing across them.

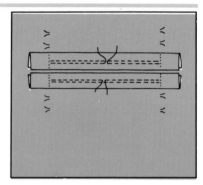

5 Using chalk, mark length of pocket opening accurately across strips. Machine along centre of each exactly between marks, starting and finishing at centre of each to give a double row of stitches. Cut off thread ends. Remove basting and the oversewing between strips.

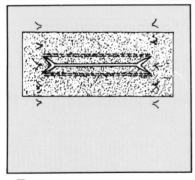

6 With garment WS up, cut between rows of machining to within 1 cm/$\frac{3}{8}$ in of ends and then cut out diagonally to ends of rows of stitching.

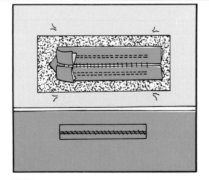

7 Push strips through to WS. Hold folds of strips together by oversewing on RS. Tuck triangles of fabric at each end of pocket opening back between garment and ends of strips. Press on WS and RS. From RS stab stitch across ends or machine stitch in seamline all around.

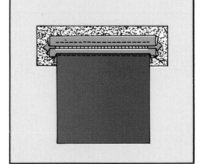

8 Cut two pieces of fabric (or one fabric and one lining) 3 cm/1$\frac{1}{4}$ in wider than length of piping and 15 cm/6 in deep—more for a man. Press under one edge of one piece, place it RS up on lower piping. Hem in position or machine using piping foot, holding garment well clear.

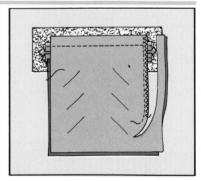

9 Place second piece of fabric RS down with upper edge level with upper piping. Backstitch to piping or machine using piping foot. Baste pocket pieces together. Chalk pocket outline, curving corners. Stitch on chalk line, trim and zigzag to finish.

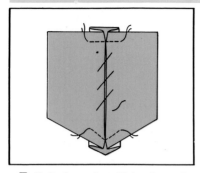

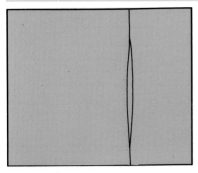

1 Seam pocket Formed from a bag, which is either cut out as part of the garment on garments in light-weight fabric, or attached to seam allowances of side or panel seams on those in heavy- or medium-weight fabric. A gap is left in the seam for inserting the hand.

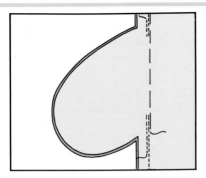

2 For pocket cut as extension of garment, make all markings and place garment pieces RS together. Baste whole of side seam. Machine seam, leaving gap for pocket opening between marks and reversing stitching at each end of opening. For separate bag pieces join to seam first.

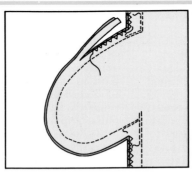

3 Finish stitched sections of seam. Baste bag pieces RS together. Machine around bag from top of opening, finishing about 5 mm/$\frac{1}{4}$ in below opening at bottom. Reverse stitching at each end. Trim edges of bag a little and finish together. Remove basting. Press pocket in correct direction.

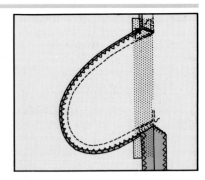

4 At each end of pocket clip diagonally into garment seam allowance (on side pocket faces away from). Loop stitch or overcast cut edges. On WS slip adhesive web 3 cm/ $1\frac{1}{4}$ in wide, and 1 cm/$\frac{3}{8}$ in longer at each end than opening, into fold between pocket and garment. Press.

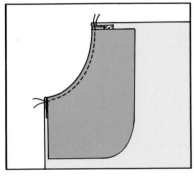

1 Pocket in shaped seam Cut out garment pieces, cut pocket bag with one edge shaped to correspond with seam edge. Attach interfacing to WS shaped edge of garment. Stitch pocket bag to garment with RS together and shaped edges level. Trim and clip, turn bag to WS. Press edge.

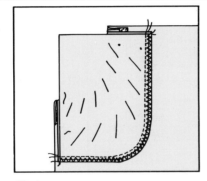

2 Place skirt section in position WS down on RS of under section, baste along shaped edge. Baste pocket pieces together around outer edge. Stitch and finish the edges. Continue making garment.

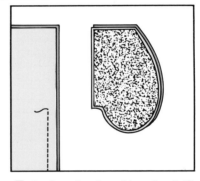

1 Pocket in the side of a full skirt, eliminating zipper. Stitch skirt seam leaving 18 cm/7 in open at waist. Cut two pocket bag pieces with one straight edge 19.5 cm/8 in long, the other edge curved, and waist edge straight and 8 cm/3$\frac{1}{4}$ in long. Press light interfacing to one piece.

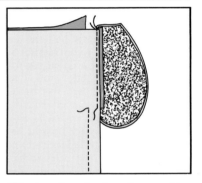

2 Attach pocket bag pieces to skirt seam edges, with RS together and stitching to the outside of the seamline. Press seam allowances toward pocket.

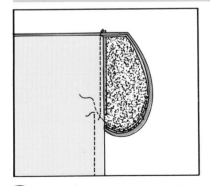

3 Mark a point on one pocket bag piece 15 cm/6 in below waist and stitch bag pieces together from there around to the top of the skirt seam.

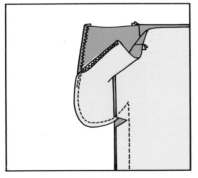

4 Finish raw edge of pocket between stitching and waist by turning a narrow hem or with zigzag stitch.

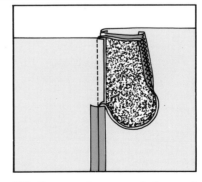

5 Press pocket toward front of skirt, clipping seam allowance at base of pocket to allow it to lie flat.

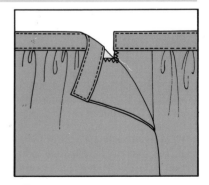

6 Insert gathers or pleats in skirt. Attach waistband keeping pocket facing front of skirt and making waistband long enough at the back to extend to the end of the top edge of the pocket bag.

BELTS

A belt should be planned as an integral part of an outfit rather than added as an afterthought. Its effect must be considered when fitting a garment; a belt should never be used to disguise or draw in poor fitting. It can, however, be a useful means of disguising or emphasizing a figure point. One that circles the waist completely emphasizes a neat waist, while a half belt at the back, or one around to the front panel lines of a garment, appears to break up a thicker one. Choose belt width, position and fabric according to figure type. A wide, tight, high belt, for example, suits a long-waisted figure, a narrow, low, loose one a short-waisted figure.

When selecting belt fabric remember that self-fabric provides least emphasis, and contrasting fabric the most. Belts may be made from one fabric or a combination of two. They may be left plain or decorated with stitching, motifs, leather thonging or braid; or they may be shirred, quilted or made from three lengths of tubing plaited/braided together. A self-fabric belt can be fastened with a matching or contrasting buckle. To reduce emphasis, however, use a concealed overlap at the left side seam.

All belts except very soft tie belts need either a backing or an internal stiffening (interfacing) to prevent them from creasing. Widths are limited for bought belt backing so choose the backing before the buckle. Other stiffenings which are easier to handle include heavy non-woven interfacing. These can be cut and used for very wide shaped belts. Buckram can also be cut, but is difficult to sew. Petersham, which may be straight or shaped, is easy to use and may be enclosed by the belt fabric or used to back it. The simplest way of interfacing a straight belt is to use iron-on perforated interfacing band.

Belt carriers

The position of belt carriers varies with the individual and the garment. If the waist is small and emphasized by a tight belt, both belt and carriers should be exactly on the waistline. A thicker waist usually needs carriers placed higher to accommodate a looser belt. A loose-fastening outer garment such as a coat needs carriers placed to allow for body movement.

Choose carriers according to the strength required and to the garment fabric and style. Straight fabric carriers, for example, are stronger than thread loops, but more noticeable and, unlike rouleau tubing carriers, cannot be inserted into garment seams.

Before attaching carriers, put on the garment, fasten the belt comfortably and use pins to mark edge of the belt at the side seams (or centre back). For each carrier move pins out to add a total of 5 mm/¼ in for ease.

Buckles

A conventional buckle has a central shaft over which the belt passes. If the belt has a metal prong fastener on this shaft, eyelets must be worked in the belt or the prong removed. With an unpronged buckle, the belt extension is fastened in place with hooks or Velcro, unless the belt is much wider than the buckle and so gripped automatically.

It is advisable to buy a buckle after buying the garment fabric. A large buckle will emphasize a trim waist, whereas a small matching buckle is preferable for a large waist. For a special buckle, however, such as an heirloom, it may be worth selecting garment fabric to enhance it or making a plain, classic belt that can be worn on several garments. A fabric-covered buckle can be purchased or made at home from a kit that includes a metal buckle which can be covered.

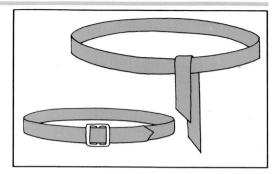

1 Calculating length Some types can be trimmed to size after being made. Calculate length as follows. Tie belt: Waist size plus double length of finished hanging ends, plus 25 cm/10 in allowance for single knot, 50 cm/20 in for a small bow, 130 cm/50 in for a large one. Buckle belt: Waist size plus 5 cm/2 in ease plus 2.5 cm/1 in for buckle and 20 cm/8 in overlap.

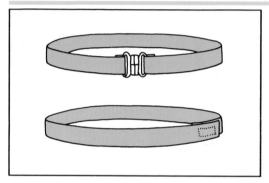

2 Clasp or rings: Waist size plus 4 cm/1½ in ease plus 10 cm/4 in overlap, to fasten with button. Velcro or hooks: Waist size plus 4 cm/1½ in ease plus 8 cm/3 in for overlap. For wide or shaped belts or cummerbunds add 8 cm/3 in ease to waist size plus sufficient overlap for the type of fastening chosen.

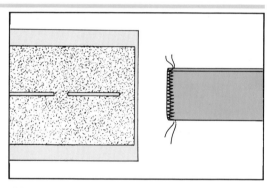

Simple belt for lightweight fabric Cut light perforated interfacing band to required length. Press to WS of fabric with perforations on straight grain. Cut out allowing 1 cm/⅜ in on each edge. Fold RS together along perforations; baste. Stitch beside edge of interfacing and across one end. Trim, turn RS out. Press. Finish end and pass around central bar of buckle; stitch to secure.

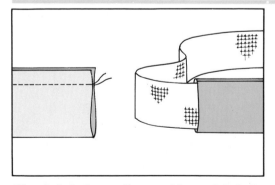

Simple belt for medium and heavy fabric Cut non-roll belt backing to required length. Cut fabric twice width plus 2 cm/⅜ in seam and 3 mm/⅛ in ease, fold RS together and stitch 1 cm/⅜ in from edge. Turn RS out and press. Insert belt backing, topstitch along each edge. Zigzag ends and attach clasp or, for buckle, stitch across one end before turning through.

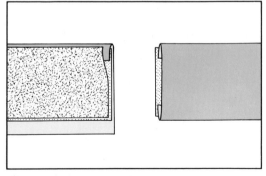

Simple belt without stitching This uses double layered iron-on belting, available in several widths. Cut belting to required length. Cut fabric same length but 2 cm/¾ in wider. Place belting adhesive side down to WS of fabric. Fold over edge of fabric along each side and tuck under the loose flap of the backing. Press carefully, first along edge, then over flap, then whole belt.

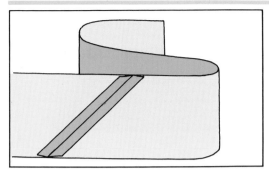

Joining fabric If belt cannot be cut from one strip of fabric, position joins at side seams or centre back of garment to make them less conspicuous. Cut diagonally across ends of strips and baste RS together, matching patterns. Machine. Remove basting and trim seam to 5 mm/¼ in. Press seam open. Because it is on the cross this seam will be less bulky than a straight join.

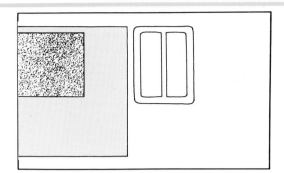

1 **Cutting interfacing** For a straight belt, purchase belt backing to fit the buckle, allowing 3 mm/⅛ in for thickness of fabric, or cut interfacing to finished width and length of belt. To find width, pin fabric to a small piece of interfacing and position buckle at one end. Draw a straight pencil line on interfacing to the correct length. Measure and pencil another parallel line the right width. Cut out.

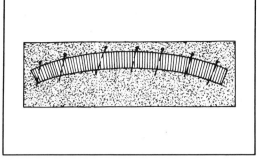

2 For narrow curved belt, cut curved petersham to width and length of finished belt. For wide belt, pin petersham the right length to interfacing. Pencil concave curve on interfacing. Mark ends. Remove petersham. With adjustable marker set to finished belt width, mark second curve at even distance from first. Cut out. For a pointed end, fold interfacing lengthwise; cut to a point.

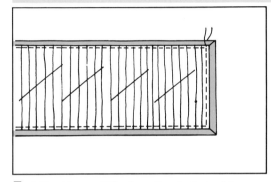

1 **Attaching stiffening** For belt backing or petersham, turn in all fabric edges so that fabric is 3 mm/⅛ in wider and longer than backing. Place fabric WS down on backing and baste diagonally down centre. With backing side up, machine at even distance from backing edges. Stitch petersham close to edge; stitch inside stiff double edge of belt backing. Remove basting.

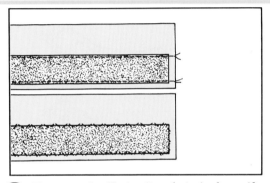

2 For internal stiffening (interfacing), place stiffening on WS of fabric as appropriate and baste. With stiffening side up, machine 2 mm/1/16 in from long edges and right out to raw fabric ends. Use a straight, blind hem or embroidery stitch. For a finish invisible on RS of belt, attach stiffening edges with herringbone or catch stitch, or with adhesive strips. Remove basting.

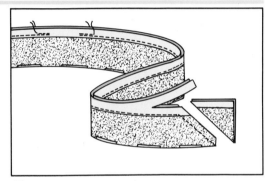

1 **Tie belt** Cut fabric to correct length on straight grain and twice finished width of belt, plus 1.5 cm/⅝ in seam allowances on all edges. Attach light perforated interfacing band to WS. Fold lengthwise, RS together; baste along edge and across ends. Machine, leaving gap of 10 cm/4 in centrally to turn belt through. Trim edges to 3 mm/⅛ in except at gap. Remove basting; press.

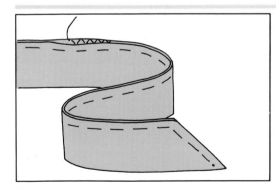

2 Turn belt RS out by pushing end of a knitting needle against stitched ends. Pull ends out through gap. Ease out corners. Roll edges so that join is on edge. Baste along stitched edges. At gap, turn in raw edges on seamline and baste. Press basted edges and then folded edge. Slip stitch gap. Remove basting. Press again. For looped belt attach fastenings at desired position.

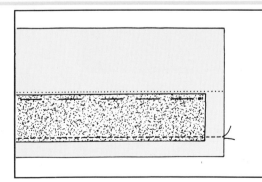

1 **Straight belt in double fabric** For all but very bulky fabrics, cut interfacing to correct dimensions and cut a length of fabric on straight grain to twice width of interfacing, plus 1.5 cm/⅝ in seam allowances on all edges. Mark centre of fabric on WS with chalk. Place interfacing against this line. Baste in position. Attach along edges to fabric ends by desired method. Remove basting.

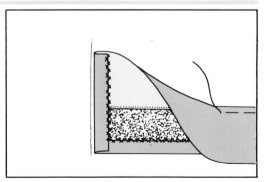

2 Turn in raw edges over interfacing along lower edge and across ends (interfaced half is RS or outside of belt). Baste in position. Press. Hold down with herringbone stitch. Remove basting. Fold fabric down over interfacing and baste in position along top fold. Press.

BELTS

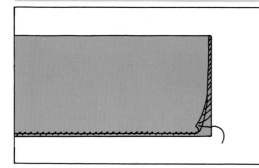

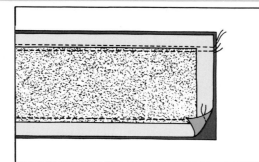

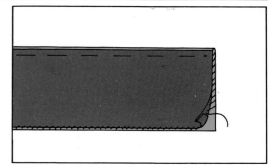

3 On WS (inside) of belt turn in lower edge of fabric that has been folded down over interfacing and baste along lower edge. Keep the edge 2 mm/$\frac{1}{16}$ in above lower belt edge so join does not show on RS. Slip stitch ends of belt and hem along lower edge. If interfacing was not machined into place, machine stitching may be worked all around belt at this stage. Remove basting and press.

4 For bulky fabric, cut fabric to width of interfacing, plus 1.5 cm/$\frac{5}{8}$ in for seam allowances on all edges. Cut another piece in lining fabric or nylon knit to same size. Centre interfacing on WS of fabric piece and attach as desired right to fabric ends; see p.135. Place lining and fabric strips RS together. Baste just above top edge of interfacing and machine. Remove basting and press.

5 Roll lining to WS of belt and baste along stitched top edge. Turn in fabric at each end of belt and then all edges of lining so that they lie 2 mm/$\frac{1}{16}$ in back from edge of belt and are invisible from RS. Baste and press. Slip stitch ends and hem along lower edge. Remove all basting. Press.

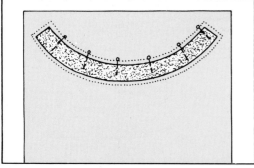

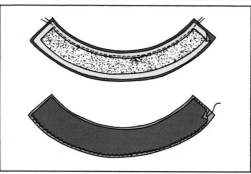

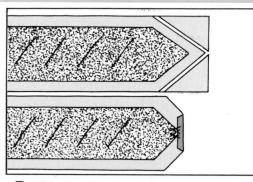

1 **Curved belt** Suitable for all but striped or checked fabrics. Place curved petersham or interfacing cut to correct dimensions on fabric and pin so curve is evenly placed across grain. Cut out around stiffening, allowing 1.5 cm/$\frac{5}{8}$ in for seam allowances on all edges. For patterned fabric, allow for a join at side seams. Cut out two pieces, or, for heavy fabric, cut out second piece in lining to reduce bulk.

2 Make any joins. Centre interfacing on WS of fabric and attach. Place two fabric strips or lining and fabric RS together, baste and machine along concave edge beside interfacing. Roll lining to WS; baste top edge. Turn in fabric edges all around and herringbone; then turn in lining edges and baste so folded edges are 2 mm/$\frac{1}{16}$ in in on WS of belt. Slip stitch ends; hem lower edge. Remove basting.

1 **Mitred end** If belt has a pointed end, reduce bulk by mitring. Cut interfacing to correct dimensions and cut one end of it to a point. Baste diagonally along centre to WS of belt fabric and attach. Cut end of fabric to shape, allowing 1.5 cm/$\frac{5}{8}$ in seam allowances. Fold fabric over point of interfacing and cut off so turning on point is 3 mm/$\frac{1}{8}$ in. Herringbone trimmed fabric edge to interfacing.

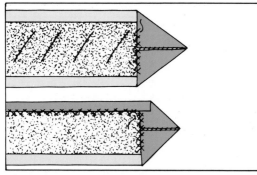

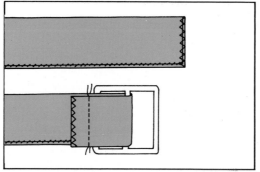

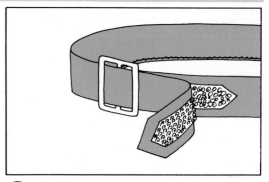

2 Fold in fabric along both angled edges of interfacing point. Press. Trim away excess fabric on overlapping folds and double layer at point. Slip stitch folded edges together to point. Herringbone down any raw edges that cross interfacing. Press well. Turn in raw edges along sides and herringbone to interfacing. To finish belt, cover with separate backing.

1 **Buckled belt** If making a belt to which a buckle is to be attached, do not turn in and slip stitch the buckle end of the belt. Instead, trim raw edges and finish by overcasting or with a zigzag stitch. For unpronged buckle, thread belt over shaft and fold back surplus to WS. Hold in place by machining across whole width. If belt is a little short, fold back a minimum of 1 cm/$\frac{3}{8}$ in and hem in place.

2 Hold belt extension down neatly to rest of belt with Velcro. This can be 13 mm/$\frac{1}{2}$ in wide and 8 cm/3 in long, or 3 cm/$1\frac{1}{4}$ in wide and 5 cm/2 in long, depending on width of belt. Fasten belt and mark position of extension end on main part of belt. Hem Velcro into position behind this mark and at extension end; it should be invisible on RS of belt. For pointed belt end trim Velcro to match.

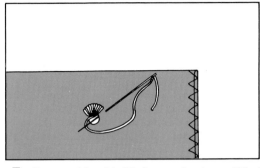

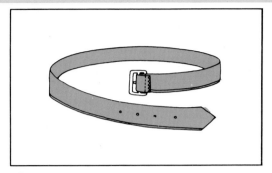

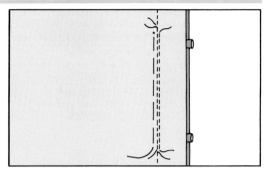

Pronged buckle Mark central point on RS of belt 3 cm/1¼ in from buckle end. On RS of belt make an eyelet here. For metal eyelet use an eyelet tool kit. For handworked type, make a hole with a punch tool, stiletto or awl and loop stitch around. If using a stiletto or awl, stitch quickly and reinsert during stitching to re-form hole. If tool will not pass through, use points of scissors.

2 Thread belt through buckle, insert prong through eyelet and fold back to WS of belt the 3 cm/1¼ in between eyelet and end of belt. Machine across whole width. Do up belt comfortably around waist. Mark position of prong in centre of belt extension. Work an eyelet at this point, another 4 cm/1½ in behind it (for a tighter fit) and two more at intervals of 4 cm/1½ in toward belt end.

Tubing carriers Measure between pins marking position of carriers. Cut tubing to this size, adding 1.5 cm/⅝ in for ease and 4 cm/1½ in for insertion at seams. On WS of garment measure equally from underarm to waist at side seams to re-mark positions. Remove pins, take out seam stitching between marks, insert ends of tubing and baste. Restitch seam. For strength, stitch again. Remove basting.

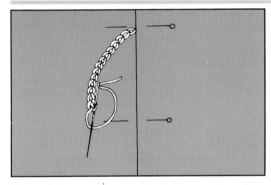

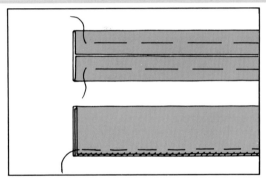

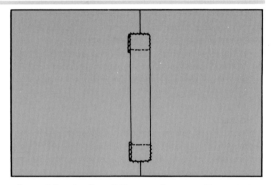

Thread loops Measure for loops as for tubing carriers; allow 5 mm/¼ in for ease, more for a thick belt. For a chain stitch loop, work stitches between pins, holding chains away from fabric; see also p. 24. For strength, make a loop-stitched bar (see pp. 66–7), working four or five strands between pins and backstitching through all layers at strand ends. Remove pins.

Straight carriers Cut a fabric strip on straight grain four times the finished carrier width, 2 to 4 cm/¾ to 1½ in wide and long enough to make all loops. Measure for loops as for tubing carriers but allow only 5 mm/¼ in for ease. Fold in sides of strip to meet in centre on WS. Baste. Fold again so folded edges meet. Baste, press and slip stitch folded edges of strip together or machine along both edges.

Attaching by hand Remove basting. Cut strip into lengths. Turn in ends to obtain required loop length (make seam allowances as small as possible). Baste loop to RS of garment in pinned positions. Remove pins. Hem around three outer edges of ends and backstitch across base of turned-in edge of strip, stitching through to garment. Remove basting.

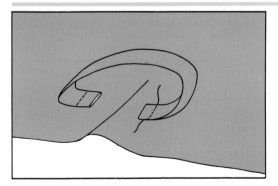

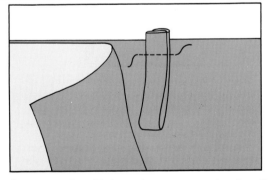

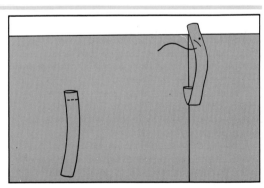

Attaching by machine Place carrier RS down on RS of garment below marked position. Stitch across carrier 5 mm/¼ in from end. Fold in other end 5 mm/¼ in and pin in position but pin through under layer only. Move carrier over so that you can get the machine foot inside to stitch across. Press carrier flat.

Loose carriers To insert in a seam or waist edge of skirt or trousers, fold carrier in half and press. Place raw ends on RS of garment with edges level. Stitch in place. Place facing or second piece of garment on top RS down and stitch seam.

Carriers on waistline Place carriers RS down on garment, depth of finished carrier plus two seam allowances below unfinished waist edges; stitch across ends of carriers. Press them up toward waist, loosen them a little and baste in place. Attach waistband facing, petersham etc., RS down on RS of skirt and finish on WS.

LINING

Lining consists of making up in lining fabric a replica of the garment and attaching it to the inside of the garment at various points or, as in a jacket, around all its edges.

The main advantages of a lining are that it conceals raw edges and, if stitched down around all its edges, controls fraying. However, lining increases the cost and may provide unwanted bulk and warmth.

Mounting

A good alternative to lining may be mounting, in which mounting—or backing—fabric is attached to each garment piece before the garment is made up. Mounting (sometimes called underlining) provides firmness, reduces clinging, creasing and stretching, can lessen the build-up of static electricity in synthetic fibres, and makes ironing easier because it reduces wrinkling during washing. All processes are easier to handle in double fabric and fraying tends to be reduced. Better machining results because stitching through four layers usually eliminates wrinkling. Pressing is also easier as there is no danger of raw edges making imprints on the right side of the garment. However, mounting increases cost, does not eliminate the need to finish raw edges and adds bulk.

Sometimes, as in winter coats and suits, both mounting and lining are advisable—the one improving the wearing qualities, the other making the garment easier to put on and take off. The two can be combined: in a dress the bodice may be mounted and the skirt lined.

Fabrics

Buy the garment fabric first and feel it in conjunction with several mounting fabrics before making a final choice. Most medium-weight woven fabrics, such as cotton, viscose/rayon and blends of these and other fibres, including acrylics, and also wool and tweed, should be mounted on lightweight cotton lawn, polyester and cotton or modal and cotton. Fine fabrics such as voile, chiffon and georgette can be mounted on another layer of the same or similar fabric. Only slippery, shiny fabrics should be mounted on slippery lining fabrics, while knitted fabrics must be mounted on nylon knit.

Lining fabric should never be thicker or heavier than the garment fabric. If it is to be seen, its colour should be a good match or contrast with that of the garment. If the garment is to be washed, choose a washable lining. Loose lining should be slippery but strong, which makes polyester, triacetate or cupro the best choices, although they may be noisy in wear. Nylon knit can also be used to line most fabrics, including wool, and is essential on jersey and other fabrics with give.

HOW TO MOUNT

Cut out the garment in top fabric. Place pattern pieces, with garment fabric still attached, on mounting fabric. Unless garment fabric is slippery or very fine there is no need to pin before cutting out as the weight of the pattern pieces is sufficient to steady them during cutting. Cut out mounting to exactly the same size as the pattern pieces (1), but omit collars, cuffs, belts, pockets and any other areas that are to be made double.

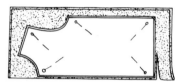

When the mounting is cut out, the darts, gathers, seam allowances and other points can be marked in two ways. For the first method mark garment pieces before removing pattern. Pin pattern pieces to cut mounting pieces and mark, using a tracing wheel and dressmaker's carbon paper. Remove pattern pieces. Place mounting fabric WS up on work surface and place each corresponding marked garment fabric piece WS down on top of mounting with all raw edges level. Work rows of diagonal basting to attach each piece of the garment to the mounting fabric, starting and finishing each row 2 cm/3/4 in from raw edges (2). Keep both layers flat and lift fabric onto needle by pushing it with forefinger of other hand. On larger pieces of fabric the basting stitches can be up to 5 cm/2 in long, but on small areas they should be no longer than 2.5 cm/1 in.

For the second, more accurate method of marking the mounting pieces, baste unmarked garment and mounting pieces together, pin pattern pieces back on and make all markings with tailor's tacks through both layers.

Attach any interfacing in appropriate way. Beginners should then make a practice seam to check they have chosen the correct mounting fabric. If the result is too bulky, the fabric is too bulky to be mounted or the mounting is too heavy. If a stiff mounting has been put under a soft fabric the feel of the fabric may have been spoilt. A slippery mounting will not adhere to and support cotton, wool or similar fabric. If the mounting

spoils the result on the seam, alter the mounting or do not use any at all.

Continue to make up the garment in the usual way, treating the two pieces of fabric as one. As there are two layers, it will probably be necessary to split darts and press them open. Trim all raw edges and finish, working over both fabric and mounting together. The garment hem can either be made in the normal way or, to reduce bulk, finish the raw edge rather than turning it under before sewing up the hem. The garment will hang better with a mounting. After completing the garment, remove all basting and press.

HOW TO CUT LININGS

Make up garment to a convenient stage and fit. If necessary, adjust pattern pieces to correspond to garment alterations. Lay pattern pieces out on double lining fabric where possible. If the lining fabric is narrow, it may be necessary to make seams in the lining; allow extra fabric for seam allowances.

When no separate pattern pieces are provided, use garment pattern pieces but make the following adjustments. Fold back facings and pin. If separate facing pieces are provided, pin into position on main pattern pieces, matching seamlines, before folding back. Fold up hemlines a further 1 cm/3/8 in. Chalk a line 3 mm/1/8 in outside seam edges of pattern pieces for ease (1). Cut on this line,

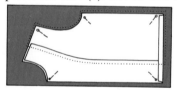

but, where facing is folded, cut approximately level with edge of facing, adding a seam allowance. If the lining is slightly too big it can be trimmed later.

If pattern pieces are provided for the lining, check them against garment pattern pieces to ensure that ease has been allowed. If not, cut 3 mm/1/8 in outside all edges of pattern.

If the lining is to be sewn in around all edges, add even more ease by placing centre back of pattern piece 1 cm/3/8 in away from fold of lining fabric to make a pleat. Cut out the lining and then baste this pleat along its entire length, stitching beside the edge of the pattern (2). Remove pattern and press pleat to one side. Make up and insert lining and, when garment is complete, remove basting.

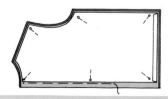

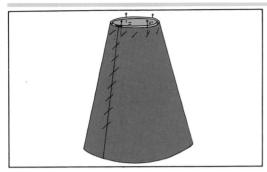

Lining a skirt Cut lining pieces, baste them together and fit. Make seams in lining. Complete skirt, including hem, except for waist finish. Place lining over skirt, WS together. Match and pin at seams, centre back and centre front. Diagonally baste lining to skirt all around waist, down seams to within 8 to 10 cm/3 to 4 in of hem and at centre front and centre back. Remove pins.

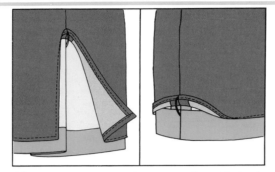

2 Complete waist, including raw edges of lining in finish. Turn up and finish lining hem to lie at least 2.5 cm/1 in above skirt hem. Hold lining in place with 1 cm/⅜ in bar tacks between garment hem and lining at each side seam, centre front and back. If skirt has a front or back pleat, leave a slit in lining to correspond with pleat. Turn in edges of slit and work a bar tack at top.

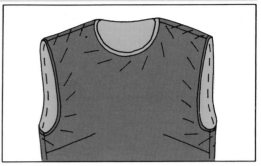

Lining a dress Cut lining pieces, baste them together and fit. Stitch seams in lining, but where they occur at garment openings, leave them unstitched for a corresponding length. Finish edges of armholes if sleeves are to be unlined. Pin lining to dress, WS together. Diagonally baste along shoulders, around neck and armholes. Remove pins. Turn in neck edge of lining and fell stitch.

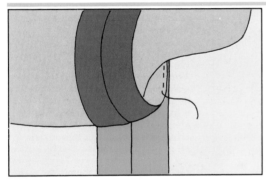

2 On RS of lining prick stitch shoulders by seam, working through lining and garment shoulder allowances only. Roll lining back and join lining side seam allowances to garment allowances from armholes to waist with flash basting or a large half backstitch. Turn up and finish lining hem and attach lining to garment hem with bar tacks as for skirt lining.

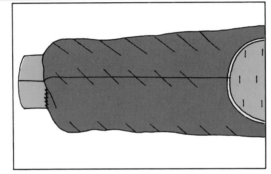

3 For lined sleeves, construct garment sleeves and complete hems. Make sleeve seams in lining. Slide linings over sleeve WS together. Align seams and baste diagonally from armhole to hem. With fabrics level, work several rows of diagonal basting around sleeve. Turn under wrist edge of lining 2 cm/¾ in from sleeve edge, draw it back a further 2 mm/1/16 in for ease, baste and fell stitch into position.

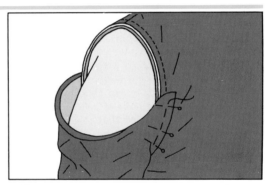

4 Set sleeves into garment in usual way, leaving lining edges free. Backstitch bodice lining allowances to garment allowances around each armhole. Turn under top edge of sleeve lining and pull up lining so the fold just covers the row of backstitching. Pin all around, pinning across fold and easing fabric between pins. Baste, remove pins and hem or fell stitch into place. Remove basting.

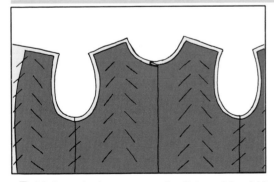

Lining a jacket or coat Cut lining with a fold at centre back. Stitch shaping and side seams in garment and lining and press. Place garment and lining WS together and baste lining into place all over garment with parallel rows of diagonal stitches starting at centre back and matching lining and garment at side seams. Make shoulder seams in garment and finish neckline.

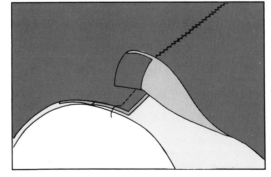

2 Lay back shoulder edges of lining flat over garment shoulder allowances and backstitch to allowances only. Turn under front shoulder edges of lining on seamline and fell stitch down. Set in lined sleeves as for a dress. Finish garment hemline. Turn under remaining raw edges of lining and baste into position, allowing 3 mm/⅛ in ease. Fell stitch lining in place.

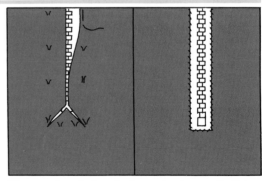

Zippers Just before the base of a zipper, clip lining out at an angle to lining seam allowances down sides of zipper tape. Turn under lining edges all the way down both sides of the zipper. Turn clipped point under so fold makes a straight line across base of zipper. Baste and hem lining into position. Remove basting.

FITTING AND ALTERING

Fitting depends not only on body shape but also on the style of the garment and the fabric. Good fitting produces a garment that is comfortable and looks pleasing.

Always spend as much time as necessary to achieve a good fit. Because fitting can be learned only by experience, and because new fitting problems arise from changes in the shape of the body with increasing years and from alterations in fabrics and styles, it is worth compiling a chart of possible faults to be identified.

When fitting, consider the way of life of the wearer and the occasions on which the garment will be worn, but always make sure that there is room for normal everyday movements. Knitted fabrics can help fitting problems as they allow for movement.

The main principles of fitting apply to all types of garments for people of all ages. They can also be used to improve the fit of bought clothes, provided that only minor changes of shape, such as lengthening or shortening a dart and taking in, are involved. Do not attempt, for example, to raise a neckline or to let a garment out, and avoid lifting at the shoulders if this makes the skirt too short. Collar alterations are generally unsuccessful.

Trousers are often the most difficult garments to fit, especially on women. It is often impossible to determine your shape until the trousers are cut out and basted, and by then it may be too late to correct faults. Choose women's trouser patterns by their hip size, men's and children's patterns by their waist size. Before cutting out trousers, measure the inside leg seam of existing trousers and add 8 cm/3 in for lifting (less for a child), plus a hem allowance.

Few garments can be made satisfactorily without at least three fittings, and if the garment is close fitting or complicated in style many more will be needed. Use your body measurements as a guide and use a dress model to help with fitting, shaping and positioning.

Fitting techniques

If you fit a garment on yourself, it will take longer than if you have someone to help, but it is perfectly possible to achieve a good fit by standing still in front of a mirror to identify faults. Restrict yourself, however, to styles and fabrics that will accommodate problems. When fitting any garment follow these guidelines:

1 Do not fit the garment too closely—remember that you are standing still.
2 Fit and correct only one area at a time, not the whole garment.
3 Attach interfacing before fitting to avoid stretching fabric edges during fitting.
4 Allow extra fabric in known problem areas and for the hem.
5 Until final fitting, fit the garment without a belt.
6 Do not fit a problem area too tightly. Make sure that the fabric does not cling to bulges and so emphasize them. It should brush gently against them.
7 Keep all seamlines even. Shoulder and side seams should not be visible from the front.
8 Choose a style with seams or darts over known problem areas.
9 Large areas of fabric are difficult to fit unless broken up by features such as gathers.
10 If your figure is lopsided in any part, do not make the same alteration on both sides.
11 Fit elbow darts with sleeves basted in position and arms slightly bent.
12 For large busts do not make bust darts too large.
13 Straining in any area indicates too little shaping.
14 Before fitting, baste centre front opening diagonally below and almost to waist and pin it securely above waist to neckline.
15 If both back and front of neckline are lowered, shoulder seams may need lifting to prevent garment slipping off shoulders.
16 Always check armhole fit before inserting sleeves, but remember that faults may not show until sleeves are basted in.
17 To fit a waisted dress, try on bodice only.
18 If natural waist is very low at back, do not fit too accurately.

How to fit

The following equipment is necessary for fitting: a full-length mirror; a back-view mirror or another mirror propped up on a chair for viewing the back; pins; tailor's chalk; a tape measure; hem marker or long ruler. Equally essential is plenty of time, and a bonus, if you are making a garment for yourself, is someone to help who knows your fitting problems.

Preparation

Tailor tack and interface the first part of the garment to be fitted, such as the bodice. Never prepare a whole garment before fitting. Mark centre back and centre front lines. Baste together the part to be fitted, but if fitting a bodice or dress with a back opening on yourself, baste up this opening but leave open left shoulder and side seam (or right if left-handed), which are easier to pin up for fitting than the back (1). For an overlapping opening, fold back the facing to the marking and baste. Stitch up any pleats. Wear correct undergarments and shoes and comb your hair into its usual style. If fitting a skirt or trousers, wear a close-fitting waist-length sweater, not a blouse. Never fit trousers with a dress or skirt bunched up.

Put on the garment and pin up any

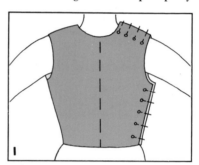

openings securely. It may help, at the first fitting, to put the garment on inside out so that alterations can be accurately marked, but try it on RS out for subsequent fittings.

Stand still and look front on in the mirror. Turn sideways, stand still again, and move the head only to view the side and some of the back. Turn and check the other side, then look in the back-view mirror. Consider each area in turn.

First check and adjust any darts or other shaping. Then proceed to the next area of fitting, usually the seams near the shaping that has already been corrected, then to seams such as waist joins that hold major sections of the garment together. When you are sure that these seams are correctly adjusted, check the shoulder seams, armholes, sleeves and, finally, the hem.

As few areas of a garment are completely isolated, when one fault is corrected another may be caused or cured elsewhere. Watch the overall effect of alterations and, throughout the fitting process, try to maintain the original balance of the garment design and remember that shortening an opening or raising a waistline may upset buttonhole spacing. Slip on part of a garment, such as a sleeve, yoke or trouser leg, or at least hold it up against

you, to check the general effect after basting the initial seams but before basting the main garment sections together.

What folds indicate

Loose vertical folds indicate that the garment is too wide. To correct, take in the side seams, but if the garment is much too wide it may be necessary to take in a pleat down the centre front or back of the appropriate pattern piece and then recut.

Tight vertical folds or wrinkles are a sign that the garment is too short between two points, for example between shoulders and waist or, in trousers, between waist and crotch. Correct by lengthening as necessary.

Loose horizontal folds indicate excess length in a particular area, for example between bust level and waist, back of waist and bottom, or front of waist and hips. Correct by shortening at the nearest seams.

On a pear-shaped figure a horizontal fold of surplus fabric may occur above the waist of a dress and on a top-heavy figure below the waist. If the dress has a waist join, it may help to alter this, but it may also be necessary to alter the centre front seam. This seam must be altered if the dress has no waist join. If no seam is included in the pattern, it is often possible to insert one by cutting out two separate pieces for the front, each with a seam allowance, rather than folding the fabric in two. Careful fitting of the centre front seam can also disguise a lopsided figure.

Tight horizontal folds or wrinkles indicate a tight garment and can be corrected by letting the garment out at the nearest seams.

Marking and checking alterations

The easiest way to mark alterations is with tailor's chalk but, if it is not suitable for the fabric, alternatives include a chalk pencil in pink, blue or white, or a fabric marking pen. Use the type of pen that automatically fades, not the kind that has to be washed out. Mark the end of a dart with a cross, mark basting lines with chalk lines and use chalk crosses to indicate where to start and finish any alteration. Use pins for taking out excess fabric.

After chalking these marks, take off the garment. If the garment has been fitted WS out, baste alterations and refit. If the garment has been fitted RS out, turn the fabric over where pins are inserted and insert pins between the original ones, picking up one layer of fabric only (2).

Turn back to the first side and slide the points of the first pins out of the double layer and reinsert through the

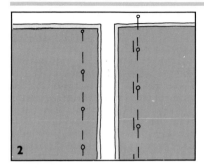

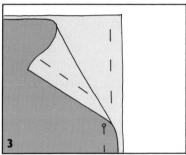

top layer only. Open out the fabric to reveal two adjusted lines (**3**).

If chalk shows up sufficiently, mark both sides of alteration and remove pins. If not, leave pins in.

Fold the garment in half, matching up the new lines, or place corresponding garment pieces together correctly and arrange them so they lie flat on the working surface. Mark new chalk or pinned line with tailor's tacks and clip tacks in the usual way. Baste the garment pieces together, then try the garment on. Finally, check the length of corresponding seams and darts to make sure that they are equal and mark dart lengths with chalk lines. Do not make any corrections to the length if your figure is lopsided.

Shaping

Darts, gathers and released tucks all contribute to shaping. A dart creates an area of fullness at its point and darts are placed to provide shaping for the bust, shoulder blades, elbows, abdomen and bottom. The dart should point toward the area being shaped, running right onto it for a close fit, or stopping short for a looser fit.

If the dart does not provide enough fullness, enlarge it or insert an extra one and make a compensatory adjustment in the nearest seam. If the dart creates surplus fullness, make it smaller or remove it altogether. If a dart is not in line with the bulge on the appropriate body area, move it to the correct position. For example, back darts in skirts and trousers usually fall midway between centre back and side seams, but if necessary, to improve fit, move them at the first fitting nearer to

the centre back, above the bottom.

If a dart is altered to adjust the amount of shaping, the width of its wider, base, end is automatically altered. This may affect other areas: for example, the size of the waistline may be reduced or expanded, or seam edges on the back and front of the garment may no longer be equal in length. The same applies if an extra dart is added. Correct discrepancies at the seams nearest the darts.

Gathers, like darts, provide shaping for bulges and the fullness they create should be sufficient to accommodate these. On small areas of gathering, such as on a yoke, the gathers should be above or below the bulge. Excess fullness in gathers can be removed in the nearest seam. A small amount of extra fullness can be obtained by letting out the nearest seam, but a correct fit is usually guaranteed by repositioning gathers.

For all shaping alterations your helper can clip any basting where faults occur and repin the shaping correctly. If fitting yourself, make a chalk mark or insert a pin to mark the position of a fault and estimate the size of the adjustment needed. Take off the garment. Mark and baste the alterations and try the garment on.

Seams

Functional and decorative seams also contribute to shaping. Check functional, fitting seams for position as well as fit. Make sure that shoulder seams run along the tops of the shoulders and slightly to the back and that side seams hang vertically. If side seams slope, either the front or back will have to be lifted or dropped to straighten them. If they wobble, the basting may be inaccurate, the garment may have been cut on the wrong grain or, more usually, is too tight. If the abdomen is very large or the back very narrow, an uneven alteration may be needed at the side seams. Trouser seams should hang straight and not twist. Yoke seams should run horizontally without dropping near the armholes. If the figure has one very exaggerated point, do not fit too closely over this area.

Side seams may be used to alter the width of a dress bodice that is too loose or too tight round the back, bust or diaphragm. The front of the pattern is usually slightly wider than the back, which may not always be correct for the figure, and side seams may have to be adjusted by unequal amounts from the front and back. Skirts and trousers can also be altered by taking in or letting out the side seams.

Like other seams, decorative seams may need moving or altering after fitting adjustments have been made.

IDENTIFYING THE PROBLEMS—SIDE VIEW

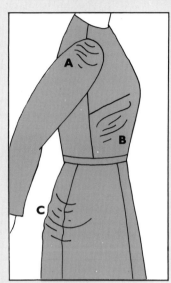

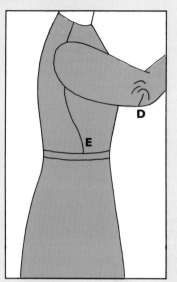

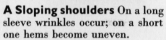

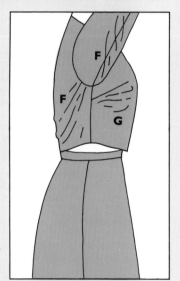

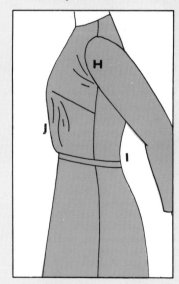

A Sloping shoulders On a long sleeve wrinkles occur; on a short one hems become uneven.

B Bust darts too low Garment loose over bust with unfilled fullness below.

C Too much shaping in shaped seam over bust, bottom or shoulder blades An

unfilled bulge of surplus fabric appears in the seam area.

D Elbow darts too high Unfilled pockets of surplus fabric appear at the end of the dart.

E Back or front shoulder needs lifting Side seams slope to front or back instead of hanging vertically.

F Armholes too low Entire garment is lifted when arms are raised.

G Bust darts too high Fabric strains across bust and may ride up.

H Armholes too tight Armholes may cut into the body at the

front, especially on a fleshy figure.

I Low natural waistline at back Waistline on waisted dress follows natural line, becoming uneven.

J Small bust If bust dart is too wide at the base, unfilled fabric results below bust.

FITTING AND ALTERING

IDENTIFYING THE PROBLEMS—BACK VIEW

A Sloping shoulders Folds of excess fabric appear just below shoulders, starting near neck and increasing toward armhole edges.

B Narrow back Centre back seam stands away from the body.

C Shoulder darts wrongly placed If back is flat, surplus fullness occurs at end of darts.

D Back bodice too loose Vertical folds form in armhole and underarm areas.

E Shoulder seams need to be lifted Horizontal folds of fabric form above waist or below bottom.

F Hollow back—skirt Folds form below back of waistband. In trousers waist appears too high at the back.

G Skirt or trouser side seams too loose Vertical folds of fabric form down centre; on a very straight-hipped figure folds form at sides.

H Flat bottom—skirts and trousers Unfilled fullness occurs at the points of back darts.

I Hollow back—dress In a one-piece dress fabric droops above the waist or below bottom. In a waisted dress folds form above waist or waist join dips at the back.

J Sleeves set in too far back Vertical wrinkles appear at back of upper part of sleeve.

K Trousers too loose Excess fabric may hang in folds below bottom.

L Elbow darts too low Garment wrinkles and strains on upper arms and across back.

M Neckline too tight or too high May cause horizontal wrinkling at back or front of neck.

N Overtight fit/uneven shoulder seams/poor assembly Centre back seam wobbles or sits at a bad angle.

O Bodice back too tight Horizontal folds form on bodice back and on upper part of sleeves.

P Side seams too tight—skirt or trousers Horizontal wrinkles appear in seam area.

Q Skirt or trouser darts too long or too narrow at base Garment strains over large bottom.

R Bodice darts too wide Garment feels tight round midriff and horizontal folds may result.

S Bodice darts too long Garment feels tight at base of armholes.

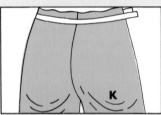

IDENTIFYING THE PROBLEMS—FRONT VIEW

A Tight fit over bust or below armholes Neckline gapes. This problem may also be caused by a narrow chest or prominent bust.

B Shoulder seams too long Garment is uncomfortable and on a sleeveless bodice armholes gape; on a sleeved bodice the sleeve heads drop.

C Small bust Sometimes bodice darts are unsuitable for the figure and empty pockets of fabric are produced above bodice dart point at bust.

D Hollow abdomen Unsightly fullness may appear at points of waist darts on trousers and skirts.

E Centre front opening too short Diagonal folds occur on each side of opening, running down to hem.

F Wrongly placed darts—skirt or trousers Pockets of fullness show below or on the abdomen.

G Sleeves set in too far forward When arms are at sides folds appear at front of upper sleeves.

H Bodice darts too short Too much fullness is produced below bust.

I Too much fabric in shaped area Gathers or released tucks create excess fullness or bulkiness or over-emphasize parts of the figure such as large bust, hips or thighs.

J Bodice darts too wide Garment too tight at waist.

K Skirt or trouser darts too wide Waist is too tight and garment may wrinkle on both sides of the darts.

L Centre front opening too long Diagonal folds run up skirt and out toward side seams.

M Bodice darts too long Bodice will be too tight across the bust and, if very tight, horizontal wrinkles will occur above and below the bust.

N Square shoulders Fabric drags from armhole level to outer ends of shoulder seams.

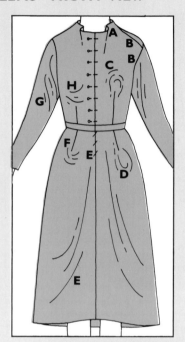

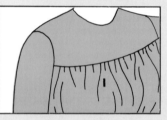

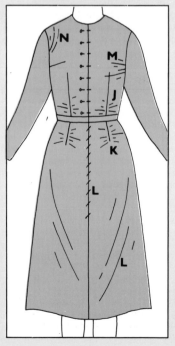

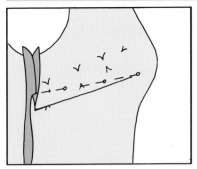

To lower bust darts clip basting of darts and side seams. Pick up fabric of each dart and adjust angle by pinning from base of original dart, a little below bust level, to bust point. Mark new dart, baste and fit.

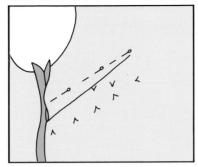

To raise bust darts clip basting of darts and side seams. Pick up fabric of each dart and, starting at base of original dart, repin dart at appropriate angle. Mark new dart, baste and fit.

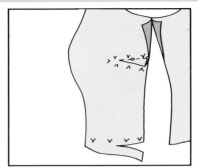

To take in surplus unfilled fabric in bust area, clip basting of darts and side seams. Repin darts, making them narrower and, depending on the figure, shorter. Cut away surplus fabric at waist so edge of front bodice aligns with bottom edge of back bodice. Mark corrections, baste and fit.

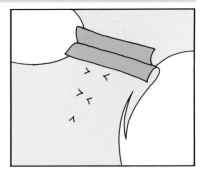

If shoulder blades are flat remove darts and trim away surplus fabric at armhole edge.

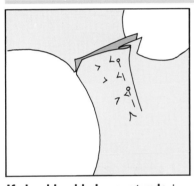

If shoulder blades protrude in a different place from where darts end, take out the dart and shoulder seam basting. Move darts to appropriate place, pin, mark and baste. Pin and baste shoulder seams along original seamlines and refit.

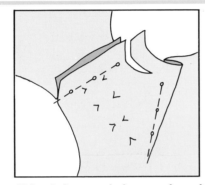

If back is rounded at neck and below take out the dart and shoulder seam basting. Move darts into neckline and repin shoulder seams, starting at outside sleeve edge. Mark and baste alterations. Trim excess fabric on back neckline to reshape. Refit.

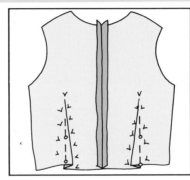

To reduce width of back bodice darts take out basting and repin darts, taking up less fabric at base of each one. Mark new darts, baste and refit.

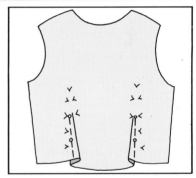

To shorten darts take out dart basting and repin to correct length. Darts should end at least 2.5 cm/1 in below armhole level, but they should be lower than this for a good fit if the figure has any surplus fat in the midriff area or above or below the bra fastening. Mark new darts, baste and refit.

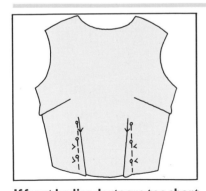

If front bodice darts are too short take out dart basting and repin, lengthening darts as much as necessary so they provide or add to bust shaping. Mark, baste and fit. If darts are too long or too wide, shorten them or reduce width at base as for back bodice darts.

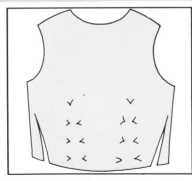

For a small bust remove darts and trim away fabric at side seams to bust level to compensate. However, if front bodice darts are the only means of bust shaping, they must be retained. Correct their length and position to give a smooth, comfortable fit. Pin, mark and baste darts and refit bodice.

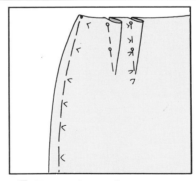

1 **For a large bottom** insert another dart on each side, balanced for a good fit. Pin new darts, mark and baste. Take out side seams to depth of dart, repin and baste, reducing width of seam allowances to keep waist size correct. Refit.

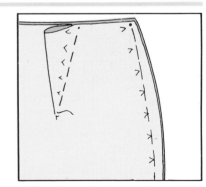

2 Alternatively, make existing darts wider at base, and shorten if necessary. (Darts should end at the start of the rise of the bottom.) Pin, mark and baste darts and adjust side seams as in preceding method. Refit.

FITTING AND ALTERING

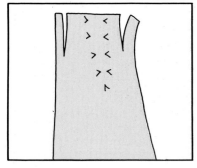

For a flat bottom make darts narrower at base as for back bodice darts. For a low bottom, lengthen darts as for front bodice darts. Alternatively, remove darts. Take out side seam basting and, on trousers, that of crotch seam to depth of darts; trim excess fabric, repin, mark and baste. Refit.

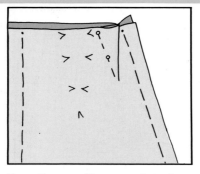

For a flatter effect move front darts in skirts and trousers at first fitting from their usual position midway between centre front and side seams nearer to side seams, make them shorter and slope them toward seams. Pin, mark and baste. Refit.

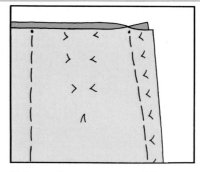

If front darts are too wide at the base, making the waist too tight, remove darts and take any extra fabric out of side seams by pinning and then basting; taper new line to meet original seamline below level of original darts. Refit.

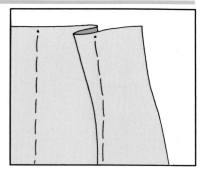

To remove excess fullness continue darts as panel seams from waist to hem. Pin, mark and baste seams and try on again to check alteration.

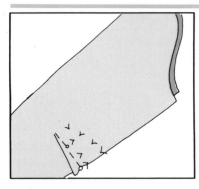

If elbow darts are too high—they should be just below the elbow—take out dart basting and move whole dart down to appropriate level. Pin new dart, mark and baste. If darts are too low, move whole dart up. Refit sleeve for both alterations.

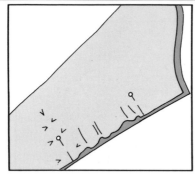

If darts are too long, making sleeves feel tight, shorten darts as for back bodice darts. If sleeves are still uncomfortable, remove darts altogether and ease back seam allowance of underarm sleeve seam onto front allowance when remaking sleeve seam, placing ease above elbow.

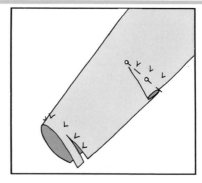

If arm is very slender reduce width of elbow dart at its base, as for back bodice darts, and trim off equivalent surplus fabric at sleeve wrist. Pin and mark dart, baste and refit.

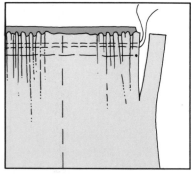

To reduce bulkiness of gathers undo basting and detach shaped section. Reduce gathering by flattening fabric along gathering thread and rearrange gathers in correct position. Baste altered section to remainder of garment and trim away excess fabric of gathered section at ends.

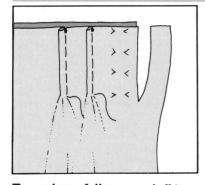

To reduce fullness or bulkiness created by tucks, reduce the number and/or depth of stitching. Remove excess fabric at side seams. Generally tucks over the bust should be fairly long, those from the waist down fairly short.

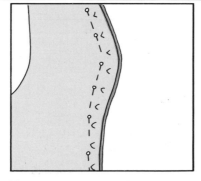

To remove excess shaping or to introduce more shaping, the curves or angles of shaped seam edges may be adjusted in the same way as darts. To remove any excess, take up surplus fabric on seams with pins and mark new lines. Baste and stitch new lines.

If the garment is too tight take out shaped seam at point of strain only and allow seams to open up as much as necessary. Pin in correct position, tapering alteration to meet original seamline. Mark and baste again. Stitch new lines to produce smooth seams without bulges.

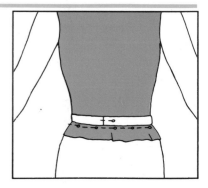

On bodice of a waisted dress side seams from underarm to waist should allow for movement but should not cause wrinkles. To fit, tie a tape around waist, over bodice, and mark waistline all around, level with bottom of tape, using pins or chalk. Check length of side seams.

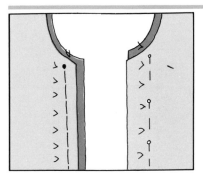

To widen bodice let out side seams, letting more out of back seam allowance than front for a broad-backed figure. To tighten, pin out surplus at side seams. Mark and baste all adjustments and refit the bodice.

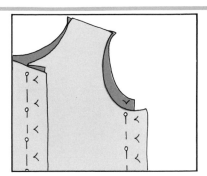

For a narrow-backed figure take more out of back seam allowance of side seam than front and, if necessary, a little out of centre back seam. Pin, mark and baste alterations and refit.

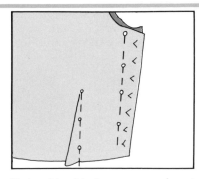

If shoulder blades are prominent adjust side seams and, if necessary, add a waist dart on either side of centre back. Pin alterations, mark and baste them and refit.

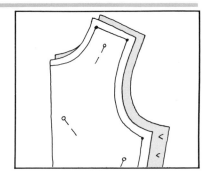

For a big reduction at side seams position pattern on fabric so pattern seamline aligns with new seamline. Pin pattern to fabric and recut armhole and, if necesary, shoulder. On outside leg seams of trousers run any large alterations down to hem to avoid wedge effect in finished seam.

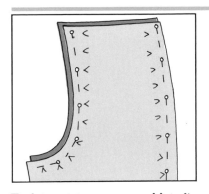

To let out trousers or skirt clip side seam basting in tight area and open up seams. Pin, mark and baste, as for shaped seams. Allow extra ease for a large bottom. For a large alteration let out centre back seam too and, if necessary, move waist darts. Reverse procedure for a loose garment.

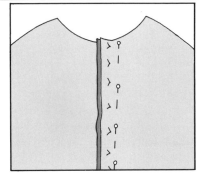

For a pear-shaped figure alter centre front seam to correct loose fit above waist on a non-waisted garment. On a waisted garment alter seam as well as waist join if necessary. Undo seam above waist and pin out surplus fabric, tapering to meet original seamline. Mark, baste and refit.

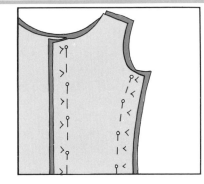

If the grain or pattern of the fabric will be altered detrimentally by taking in centre front seam, take in a little at centre front and remainder at side seams. Pin, mark and baste new seamlines and refit.

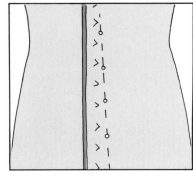

For a top-heavy figure correct loose fit below waist by taking out basting of centre front seam below waist. Take in appropriate amount from below waist area, tapering new seamline to meet original one above waist. Pin and mark new seamline, baste and refit.

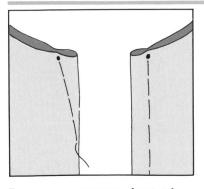

For a very narrow chest take a small amount from centre front to make a short dart at neck only. Alternatively, pin a tuck from neck edge all the way down centre front. Cut tuck open and treat as centre front seam. Mark and baste alterations. Refit.

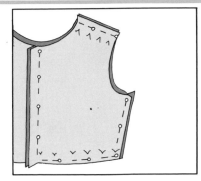

To lengthen centre front opening drop position of waist seam on bodice and skirt by same amount and/or raise shoulder seams by letting out seams until folds disappear. Take care not to unbalance the garment style. Pin and mark all altered seams, baste and refit.

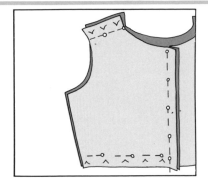

To shorten opening lift position of bodice and skirt waist seam by same amount and/or shoulder seams by taking in seams until folds disappear. Take care not to alter the balance of the garment style detrimentally. Pin and mark all altered seams, baste and try on again.

To tighten centre back seam, if zipper has been basted in, pin out surplus in a small fold on each side of zipper. Remove zipper. Mark and open out. Measure excess; incorporate it in seam allowances. Rebaste zipper; refit. If there is no zipper, pin out surplus as for centre front seam.

FITTING AND ALTERING

To correct a badly angled seam take out basting of side and shoulder seams and adjust seamlines, making sure shoulder seams are even in width. Pin, mark and baste. To loosen seam, release basting and let out seam where necessary as for side seam; pin, mark and baste again. Refit.

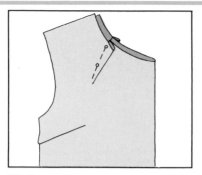

If chest is narrow and neckline gapes, pin out excess fabric in a tuck all down centre front (see p. 145). Alternatively, insert darts or small gathers in neck. Lifting the shoulders can help (see p. 147), but may not cure the fault. Pin, mark and baste all adjustments and refit.

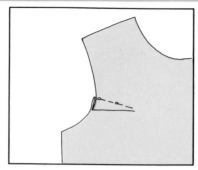

If gaping neckline is caused by a large bust, insert an extra dart in armhole. If armhole is then too tight, refit and release side seams (see p. 145). Pin, mark and baste all adjustments. Refit.

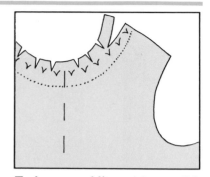

To lower neckline mark a possible new neckline with chalk on one half of WS of bodice, starting at original shoulder seam. Allow 2.5 cm/1 in for seam allowance and error. Clip raw edges of neck. Refit and, if correct, mark other half of neckline. Trim 1 cm/$\frac{3}{8}$ in at a time until neckline is correct.

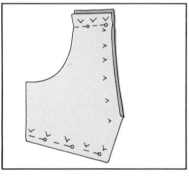

To raise neckline raise shoulders by necessary amount (see p. 147) and, in waisted garments, lower waistline accordingly. Pin, mark and baste adjustments and refit. When finishing neck edge take very small seam allowances.

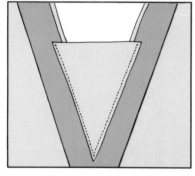

If neckline is too low on finished garment make an insert the desired shape and size from two pieces of matching or contrasting fabric. Stitch pieces WS together, leaving a gap, turn through to RS and slip stitch gap. Backstitch insert into position on front facings on WS of garment.

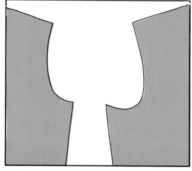

Armholes The back and front of an armhole should run in a fairly straight line from the shoulder. The back curves gently toward the underarm seam, the front scoops in a deeper curve and then turns up slightly toward the seam. This allows width at the back for arm movement.

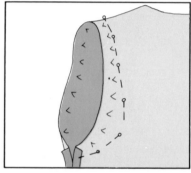

If armholes are too loose remove sleeves and undo side seams. Starting at underarm seam, pin and mark new, deeply curved seamline on front of bodice armhole to meet original seamline at top of armhole. Baste in sleeve and refit. Trim away fabric to follow curve, leaving seam allowance.

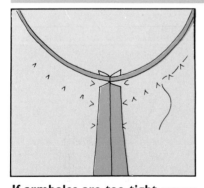

If armholes are too tight remove basting joining sleeve to armhole at underarm and release side seam in bodice and sleeve seam to allow more room. Pin, mark and baste altered seams and then refit.

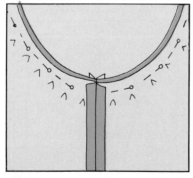

If armholes are too low correct by lifting shoulders (see p. 147), but check neck and darts afterward. Alternatively, take very small seam allowances in underarm sections when setting sleeves into armholes.

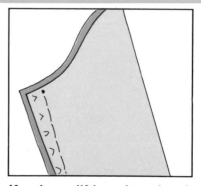

If a large lifting alteration is made the sleeves will be too big for the armholes. Adjust by taking them in at top of underarm seam. Pin and mark alteration, tapering it to meet original seamline. Baste and refit.

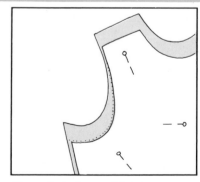

If armhole is too high (this generally occurs only if shoulders have been lifted) take out shoulder and side seam basting and lay fabric pieces flat WS up. Place paper pattern on fabric with pattern armhole at required depth below fabric armhole. Redraw armhole around pattern. Trim excess fabric.

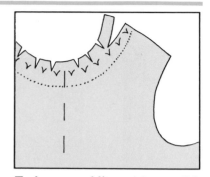

146

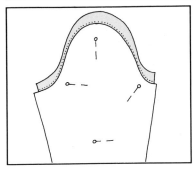

If sizeable scoops of fabric are removed from armholes, adjust sleeves accordingly. Position pattern on sleeves so pattern armhole is at required depth below fabric armhole. Using pattern as a guide, redraw sleeve armhole and head and cut along marked line.

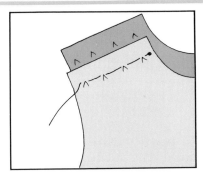

I **To lift shoulders** remove basting and lift back or front of shoulder seams until folds disappear. Pin, mark and baste alteration. On one-piece dresses lifting the shoulders is a useful alteration for a hollow back.

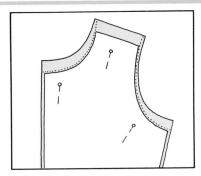

2 Take out bodice and shoulder seams and pin pattern on fabric so shoulder seam on pattern aligns with new seamline. Recut neck, armhole and shoulder length around pattern piece.

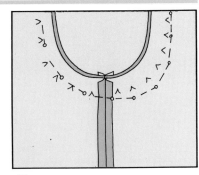

3 If necessary, before setting in sleeves, scoop out armhole a little on front or back of bodice, depending on which parts of shoulder seams were lifted. Taper alteration to meet original seamline. Pin, mark, baste and fit corrections.

If figure has sloping shoulders remove and repin shoulder seams to follow line of figure and to take out excess fabric. If figure is round-shouldered it may be necessary to take more out of the front of each seam than the back. Mark and baste alterations and refit.

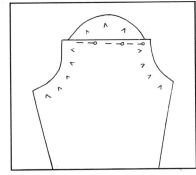

If garment has sleeves compensate for altered shoulder seams by pinning a small pleat in each sleeve pattern piece 2 cm/$\frac{3}{4}$ in below centre top of sleeve head; trim edge to follow curve. Recut sleeve accordingly.

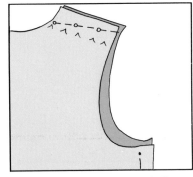

To fit square-shouldered figure clip basting at ends of each shoulder seam and open seam sufficiently for alteration to be made. Pin and mark seam, angling it from neckline up to outside edge. Baste. This alteration may be needed only at either front or back of each shoulder seam. Refit.

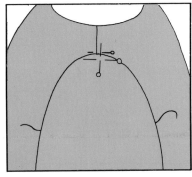

I **To shorten shoulder seams** so they may finish exactly on top of bone at top of arms, clip basting over each sleeve head and lift pinned fold of sleeve head seam allowance farther onto shoulder. Pin. Mark position reached by fold on shoulder seam with a pin.

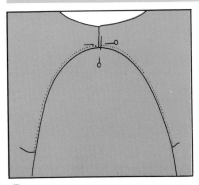

2 After removing garment, mark a new fitting line for each sleeve on bodice around edge of sleeve head. The new line should rejoin original marking above level where underarm curve begins. Baste and fit.

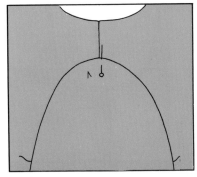

I **If sleeves are too far forward** take out basting at each sleeve head and pin fold of sleeve head seam allowance to garment at shoulder, placing sleeve head marking slightly to back of shoulder seam. If sleeves are too far back, place marking to front of shoulder seam.

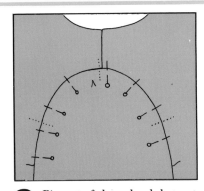

2 Pin rest of sleeve head, but not underarm, ensuring sleeve is hanging straight. (Elbow darts may cause lower parts of sleeves to hang at an angle.) Make three chalk marks across each sleeve head. Unpin and set sleeve in again, matching up marks. Fit.

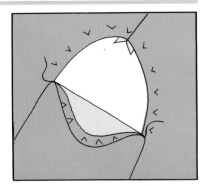

I **To correct wrinkles in sleeve head** first check whether they are caused by a sleeve that is too tight or a bodice that is too narrow at the back. If so, let out the appropriate seams. If not, take out basting in each sleeve head, fold raw edge under a little farther and pin in position.

FITTING AND ALTERING

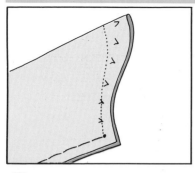

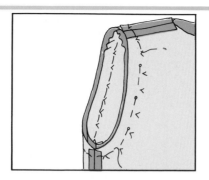

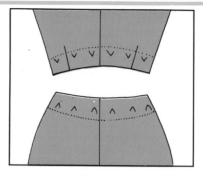

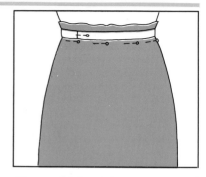

2 Unpin and mark new seamline on sleeve head. Remove sleeve from garment and set in again, following new line and making a smooth curve over sleeve head only. Fit.

Tightness blamed on sleeves is often due to a narrow garment back. In area of strain only, take out basting in back seams joining sleeves and garment. Pin new seamline, tapering it to meet original seamline and letting out appropriate amount, mark and baste again. Refit.

On a waisted dress correct fit for a hollow back by separating bodice and skirt and marking a curved waist seam allowance on back of skirt below original marking. Bodice may need similar alteration above marking. On a one-piece dress, lift shoulders (see p. 147).

On a skirt or trousers smooth fabric above waist, pin a tape around waist over fabric and, using chalk or pins, mark new back waistline level with bottom of tape. Finish waist following new line. Refit.

148

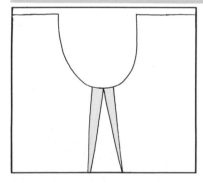

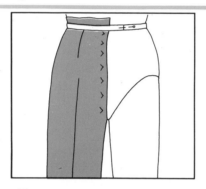

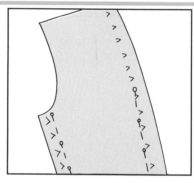

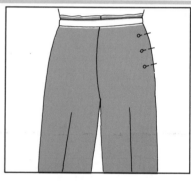

1 **Before cutting out trousers** place pattern pieces together at inside leg and check width of crotch. If pattern does not appear wide enough, extend back and front at top of inside leg 1 to 4 cm/⅜ to 1½ in when cutting out. For a large bottom extend back leg piece more than front.

2 Alternatively, if crotch is too wide at fitting, take in inside leg by required amount. When crotch width is correct, baste up one leg, press in crease and turn up and baste hem. Try trouser leg on, pin tape around waist and fit shaping of waist, hips and thighs as for a skirt.

3 If legs are too wide, take two-thirds of excess from outside seam, from just below thigh level to hem. On inside leg, take in other third, from crotch or thigh level to hem. Reverse procedure if leg is only slightly narrow. A big alteration must be done on the pattern.

4 If trouser leg is twisted, undo and rebaste vertically. After adjusting inside and outside leg seams baste crotch seam to join both legs and undo left side seam enough for trousers to be tried on. Pin tape around waist and pin up left seam. Mark and baste pinned seam and refit.

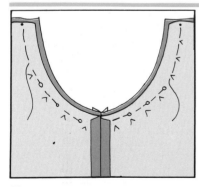

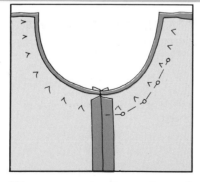

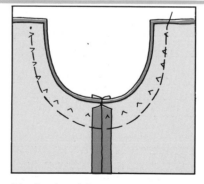

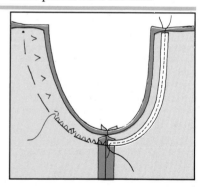

If trousers are too tight at crotch remove basting at base of front and back crotch seams. Repin seams, letting out front of crotch and a little at the back. Taper alteration to meet end of basting on either side. Mark new curves. Baste and try on again.

If trousers are too loose at crotch pin out surplus in back crotch and mark. Take off trousers and scoop out back of crotch seam on WS below original marking, tapering alteration to meet original seamline at inside leg. If trousers cut under crotch, scoop out seam a little at back and front. Refit.

Mark a level for waistline as for a skirt (see above) and lift trousers as much as necessary. If waistline is still too low, lower crotch curve the amount needed to lift the trousers. Pin, mark and baste alteration, tapering it to meet original seamline on front and back seam.

If waist is too big take excess out of centre back crotch seam from waist downward. This improves the appearance as it makes the centre back seam lie more on the cross. Zigzag for extra give. Reinforce front crotch seam by stitching tape into seam or insert zipper here.

REPAIRS

Repairing becomes necessary either because an area of fabric has given way as a result of constant wear or washing or because of accidents such as burns, tears or shrinking.

Wear in certain clothes, for example trousers and jackets, can often be foreseen and vulnerable areas such as knees and elbows can be reinforced with patches, either on the wrong side or, decoratively, on the right side. All repairs to worn areas are easier to manage before holes have formed in the fabric. Part of the good fabric must, however, be covered as well as the worn area; otherwise, the repair is stronger than the rest of the garment and creates more worn areas. It is not usually worth making a repair in one area if the fabric is weakening all over.

When repairing, use fabric that has already been washed and even worn. Old garments can often be cut up for this purpose. If a repair is needed at a point of strain, try to reinforce the whole area to stop the problem recurring. Use thread that is the same or finer than that used originally and take plenty of stitches. Generally, repairs intended to be unnoticed should be hand stitched rather than machined, but on furnishings machined repairs are stronger and look more professional.

The choice of repair depends on the degree and area of wear. Very small areas can be darned, but, except on knitwear, darning is not strong. Larger areas should be patched, or complete sections, such as trouser hems, may be removed and replaced with matching or contrasting fabric.

Repairs to burns and tears are more difficult to deal with. If they cannot be made invisible, make features of them by using contrasting fabric or adding items such as cuffs or pocket flaps in the same or contrasting fabric. If clothes and furnishings have shrunk, it is often better to lengthen them with contrasting fabric rather than to let down the hem, because hemline marks may show. Press all finished repairs to improve their appearance.

DARNING BY HAND

Select thread that matches perfectly the colour of the item to be darned. It should be slightly thinner than the original thread as the darn will be thicker than its surround. Darning wool is thinner than ordinary wool. On woven fabrics it may be possible to use yarn pulled from spare fabric or from the hem. This gives a perfect colour match although it makes a thicker darn. Use a long piece of thread and a long needle—a sharps or, for wool, a darning or tapestry needle. Spread the area to be darned over your fingers or over a darning mushroom. Darn on the right side.

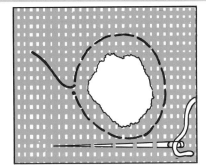

1 Darning fabric or knitting Work a circle or oval of running stitches around the worn area or hole to mark its extent and cut off thread. Beginning at left of worn area, just outside marking stitches, work running stitches in vertical line, weaving needle in and out of fabric.

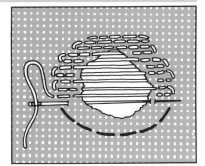

2 Leave a loop of thread at end of row, so darn is not too tight and continue weaving backward and forward across hole, keeping threads parallel. At beginning of rows insert needle over and under raw edge of hole alternately. Work each row to slightly beyond marked area.

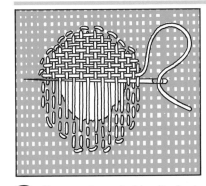

3 Turn work so stitching lies horizontally. Weave needle alternately over and under each of the previously laid threads, starting and finishing each row as in (**2**). Work over whole area. To finish, take thread to WS and run it in and out of fabric beside darn until secure.

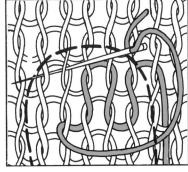

1 Swiss darning on knitting Use to repair a worn area before hole has formed. Mark extent of worn area as for standard darn. Start with two vertical running stitches on RS. Starting at top and working horizontally from right to left, pick up loops following formation of knitting.

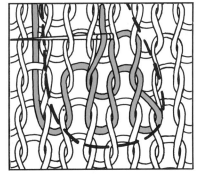

2 At end of first row turn work upside down so end of first row is on the right. Again following the knitting loops, work a second row to link with the first, as shown. Continue until whole area is reinforced. Finish off thread on WS with a row of running stitches beside darn.

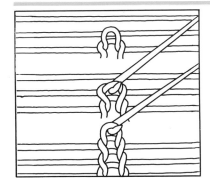

Ladders Use a fine crochet hook or a special latched hook. On RS catch loop at base of ladder and loop it over bar of yarn above it. Catch that bar, loop it over next bar, and so on. If ladder ends in a hole, anchor final loop firmly in darn. If not, pull final loop to WS and anchor with backstitches.

DARNING BY MACHINE

Machine darning is ideal for worn areas, but on holes the machining has to be worked so closely that it can produce a hard area. Use darning foot, below, and machine embroidery thread.

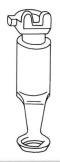

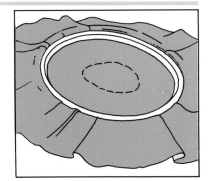

1 Lower feed teeth mechanism and set stitch length indicator to 0. Insert fabric RS up in an embroidery hoop so fabric lies flush on machine bed. Mark area to be darned with a circle or oval of running stitches in matching thread.

REPAIRS

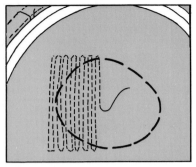

2 Place hoop under machine foot, lower needle into edge of worn area and lower foot. Hold outside of hoop with thumbs and little fingers. Machine to opposite edge, moving hoop to position each stitch. Work further parallel rows fairly close together.

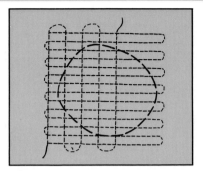

3 When area is covered, stop, with needle in fabric. Raise foot, turn hoop and lower foot again. Stitch back and forth across the first rows but allow more space between lines. If darning a hole, turn fabric again and work a third, vertical set of stitching over hole.

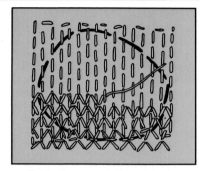

4 To darn wool by machine, use woollen thread and work first rows of stitching as for normal machine darning. Work second set of stitching in zigzag stitch and do not work a third set of stitching, even if darning a hole.

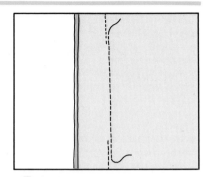

I **Split open seam** Cut off ends of thread if stitch has broken. Machine seam up, overlapping original stitching by at least 5 cm/2 in at each end. Fasten off firmly. On knit fabric restitch split area of seam using polyester thread and a small zigzag stitch.

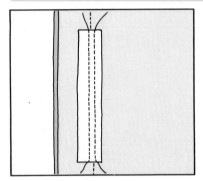

2 If fabric seems weak where seam has broken or if fabric has split, baste a strip of narrow tape or seam binding along seam, overlapping original stitching by 3 cm/1¼ in at each end. Stitch through tape and seam. Work two rows of stitching for strength.

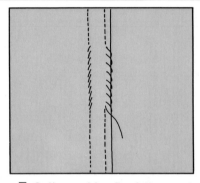

I **Split machine flat fell seam** A repair often needed on jeans. On old jeans the easiest method is to hem the seam edges closely by hand on both RS and WS. If thread from original stitching is hanging loose, thread it into a needle and backstitch to match original stitches.

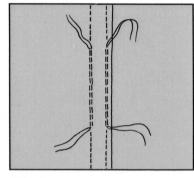

2 On new jeans or to repair a very visible split, thread machine with heavy topstitching thread in matching colour or with two reels of normal sewing thread and machine split section on RS with a large stitch. Take all thread ends through to WS and backstitch by hand.

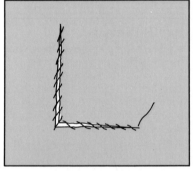

I **Right-angled tears** These occur when the fabric catches on something sharp and both warp and weft threads give way. If the fabric is not very worn, the edges can be drawn together by running stitch. Use matching thread and begin by loosely oversewing the two raw edges on RS.

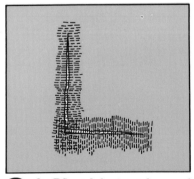

2 On RS work horizontal rows of close running stitch from top of tear down to angle and a little beyond. Vary length of rows to make darn less obvious. Fasten off thread on WS and begin again on RS at other end of tear. Work rows of running stitches a little beyond corner and fasten off.

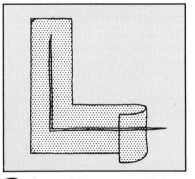

3 On an old garment, work large close zigzag stitch on RS to draw edges together. Alternatively, diagonally baste raw edges of tear together; press lightly. Remove basting and press to ensure edges meet. Cut an L-shaped piece of adhesive interfacing and iron onto WS.

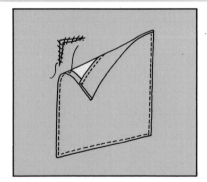

I **Patch pocket tears** Frequent use often results in a hole in the garment fabric at top corners. Undo stitching at these corners. Darn tear or, if it is small, oversew raw edges together. Cut a strip of seam binding, tape or firm interfacing 3 cm/1¼ in longer than width of pocket.

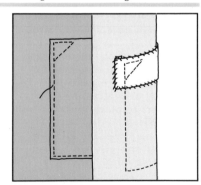

2 Place strip on WS of garment level with pocket top. Turn in ends and attach by hemming all around or, if using iron-on interfacing, press in position. Restitch pocket corners firmly by hand or machine, working through pocket, garment and tape reinforcement.

1 **Garment patch** Cut patch at least 3 cm/1¼ in larger than needed, matching grain of fabric and pattern, if any, with garment area. Trim patch to a square or an oval. Place RS up over RS of hole or worn area. Baste, turning in edges 5 mm/¼ in and clipping curves.

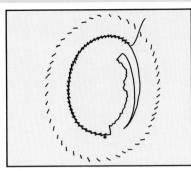

2 Press, and hem around with very small stitches. On WS trim away surplus fabric within patch to a width of 3 mm/⅛ in. Overcast raw edges to finish them.

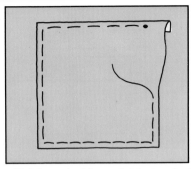

1 **Household patch** Ideal on bed linen, towels and other household items. Take fabric from another similar article or use new fabric that has been washed. Cut a rectangular patch 3 cm/1¼ in larger than worn area. Baste in position, turning in edges 3 mm/⅛ in. Press.

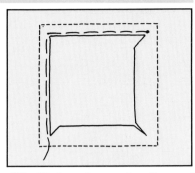

2 Machine close to edge all around patch, using straight or zigzag stitch. Remove basting. On WS trim surplus worn fabric within patch to 1.5 cm/⅝ in. Make 1.25 cm/½ in clips into corners. Turn in raw edges and baste. Press. Machine on fold. Remove basting and press.

Quick hard-wearing patch Apply purchased patches of adhesive-backed denim or motifs. Press patch RS up into position on RS of fabric and work loop stitch or machine zigzag around the edge. Trim away surplus fabric on WS and loop stitch, overcast or zigzag raw edges to finish.

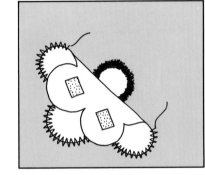

Burn holes Cover hole with a form of decoration suitable for garment, such as rows of braid or appliqué motifs. Attach appliqué with pieces of fabric adhesive, press in place and embroider by hand or machine around outer edge. Attach braid by hand or machine.

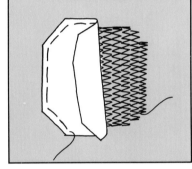

Reinforcing knees Apply decorative patches to RS of new clothes. If a hole has formed, patch on WS before patching RS. If area is worn, reinforce with rows of zigzag machining parallel with straight grain of fabric before adding decorative patch to RS.

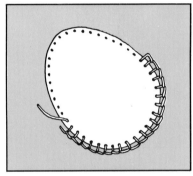

1 **Reinforcing with suede and leather** Pre-cut patches are available, often with holes around edge to aid sewing. Alternatively, cut oval patches and machine around edge without thread to make holes. Using buttonhole thread, loop stitch patch to sleeve through holes.

151

2 To reinforce frayed cuff edges, cut a strip of leather about 2 to 2.5 cm/¾ to 1 in wide for each cuff. Apply to RS first, starting level with sleeve seam and hemming along top edge. Trim ends of leather level and oversew together. Fold leather over to WS and hem in place.

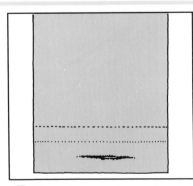

1 **Worn trouser hems** On trousers with turn-ups/cuffs, unstitch turn-ups/cuffs and press out all creases. Try trousers on and turn up to correct length. Trim surplus fabric and finish with conventional hem.

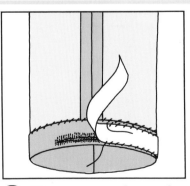

2 If trousers are worn because they are too long, undo hems and press flat. Draw together fraying edges with hand or machine darning. Turn up hem so trousers are shorter. Reinforce WS with trouser kick tape. Position tape 2 mm/1/16 in from bottom of trouser hem and hem all around.

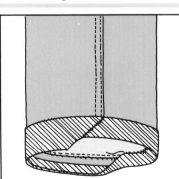

3 On casual trousers or jeans repair worn hems by binding bottom edge with purchased binding. Apply binding so it encases worn edge.

REPAIRS

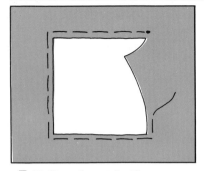

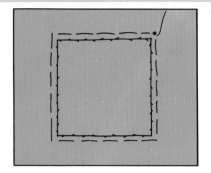

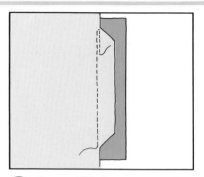

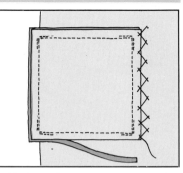

1 Tailored patch Use on garments such as suits and coats. Cutting exactly on straight grain, trim away worn area of fabric into a rectangular shape. On checked fabric cut exactly on line of check. Make clips of 1.25 cm/½ in into corners, turn edges under to WS, baste and press.

2 Cut a piece of fabric 3 cm/1¼ in larger all around than hole, matching grain and pattern to garment area. Place patch RS up behind hole and baste in position. Using basting thread, slip stitch on RS between patch and folded garment edge. Remove basting.

3 Turn to WS. Open out raw edges of garment and patch where slip stitching appears. Join edges by hand or machine on slip stitching, sewing each edge separately and reversing at end of each edge.

4 On WS trim edges to 5 mm/¼ in and then trim underneath edge a little more. Press flat and press seam allowances outward from patch. Herringbone on WS to hold down raw edges.

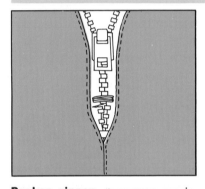

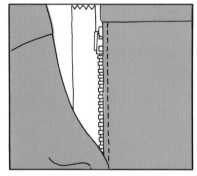

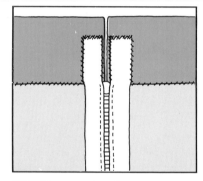

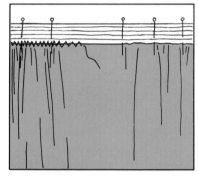

Broken zipper—temporary repair. If zipper teeth part, take slider to base. On side that has come away from slider clip into tape below last visible tooth. Lift that tooth and slot it firmly into top of slider. Move slider up to close teeth. At top of remaining gap work a strong bar tack into tape across teeth.

1 Zipper replacement Remove broken zipper, noting how it was inserted. Press opening edges, keeping them folded under. Baste in new zipper and machine or prick stitch on original stitching lines. Work any extra rows of stitching needed to hold layers together. Remove basting.

2 If tape ends of original zipper were included in waistband, cut off old zipper at base of band. When inserting new zipper, lay it in position with tape ends on back of band and hem ends into position all around.

Elastic edging Remove worn elastic and attach open-weave or ribbed elastic with a plain edge, cut to required length. Join ends with zigzag stitch. Stretch elastic and pin bottom edge at intervals to RS of garment. Zigzag over bottom edge of elastic, keeping it stretched as you stitch.

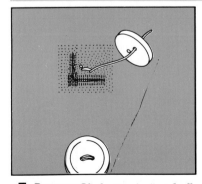

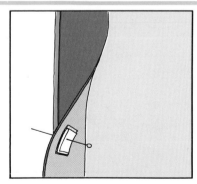

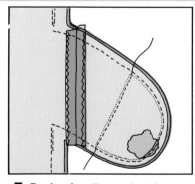

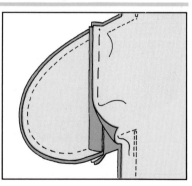

1 Buttons If a button is ripped off, the fabric may also tear. Remove button and all adhering thread. On a lined garment, slip a piece of iron-on interfacing through tear, bring edges of tear together and press interfacing in place. Repair tear by right-angled tear method. Replace button.

2 If garment is unlined, lift or undo outer edge of facing and pin a piece of interfacing and a square of folded tape or seam binding on WS of facing at button position. Settle button on RS, remove pin and sew on button through interfacing, tape and facing.

1 Pocket bag To mend a hole in the bottom, buy a pack of replacement bag sections. With garment WS out, slip new bag piece WS out into pocket. If new piece is adhesive, press it into place; if not, turn under top edges and machine or hem to pocket. Trim away worn part.

2 To replace bag: with garment WS out, undo stitching and remove worn bag. With new bag WS out, turn top edges back to WS. Place pocket edging over turned-back edges and baste together. Turn pocket RS out and hem bag to edging on basted join. Remove basting.

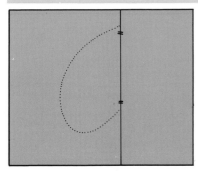

Worn seam pocket Support sagging pocket bag by pressing on medium-weight iron-on interfacing cut to shape. On RS press to make small pleat to cover ends of seam. Work a bar tack through all layers over the pleat at each end of pocket opening but 5 mm/¼ in further in.

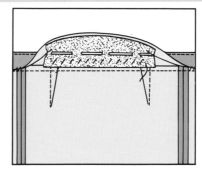

Frayed buttonholes Remove remains of stitching. Apply fray-check liquid to edges. Lift edge of facing; place two pieces of soft iron-on interfacing RS together between layers of garment. Or, insert through buttonhole. Draw together buttonhole edges on both sides. Restitch.

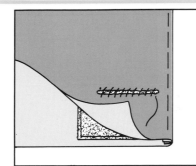

Reinforcing waistband Undo the section of stitching but leave band attached. Press waistband flat as far as possible. Insert a piece of iron-on interfacing band and *baste* along one edge. Fold waistband back into position and replace all stitching. Press to attach new interfacing.

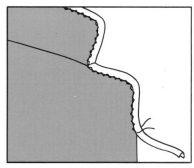

Worn coat edges Slip folded braid over the edges, up to the neckline and around collar. Attach with wide zigzag stitch in thread to match braid. Secure braid with basting tape before stitching if coat edge is bulky. Treat sleeves in the same way whether worn or not.

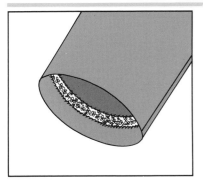

Worn cuff lining Place decorative braid over lining edge right around sleeve. Hem along each edge.

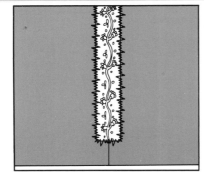

Pulled seam Soft fabrics, knits and twill weaves may show signs of strain up to 5 mm/¼ in from the seam itself. Apply flat braid, ribbon or bias binding to cover and reinforce the area. Attach with decorative machine stitching.

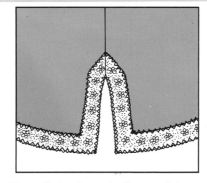

Torn lining hem Apply stretch lace to RS with one edge of lace level with hem edge. If hem was torn through being too tight, make a slit by undoing 15–20 cm/6–8 in of a seam. Turn a narrow hem on each edge and apply lace. Attach lace with small zigzag stitch along each edge.

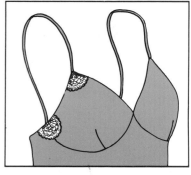

Underwear repair Points of strain or wear or small areas spoilt by too hot an iron can be covered with lace motifs. Attach with machine satin stitch or hand loop stitch. Motifs near a garment edge should be trimmed to shape after stitching. Apply more motifs if necessary to achieve a pleasing design.

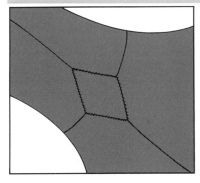

Worn underarm lining Where a coat or jacket lining has split or worn, cover the area with a large square patch of similar fabric. Hem in place all around.

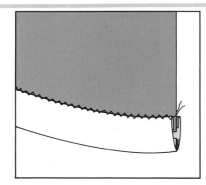

Worn, torn or dirty evening dress hem Cut contrasting fabric wide enough to cover torn hem, shaping it to match. Turn in upper edge, stitch to RS garment. Trim away torn fabric. Cut pieces of lining, join to edge of contrasting fabric, turn to inside and hem in place.

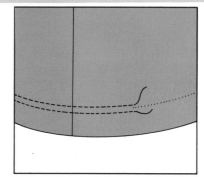

Let-down hem Despite careful stitch removal and pressing the old hemline may show. Turn up and finish at the new level, adding a false hem if necessary. On RS work a row of twin-needle stitching in matching or contrasting thread exactly over the old hem mark.

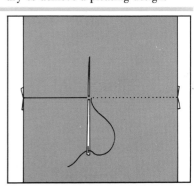

Rantering A technique for concealing a seamline on wool and soft fabrics after a repair has been made by applying a patch. Press the seam open. From RS draw together the fibres with hand stitches, passing the needle back and forth.

3

TRADITIONAL TAILORING

Step-by-step instructions for making jackets, coats and trousers: the special stitches used in tailoring; the various types of interfacing; details such as pockets, vents, collars and cuffs; techniques to ensure a professional-quality garment that will last

COATS AND JACKETS

Suits and coats for men and coats and jackets for women are timeless classics that are never out of fashion. They are subjected to a lot of wear and are expected to last, keeping their shape, for a long time. The coat (or jacket) will vary in outline according to fashion: length will change even in men's overcoats; style of sleeve may alter; fastening will be double- or single-breasted, or, for women, wrap-over; lapels may be long or short, wide or narrow, but the basic construction techniques that form the craft of tailoring remain the same.

Tailored clothes are measured, cut, assembled and fitted like other clothes but after that much of the sewing is traditionally done by hand so that the shape can be set as the stitches are put in. The skill of the tailor lies in carefully building up a garment that will not lose its shape, that is structured to give a pleasing outline and disguise figure faults, yet is comfortable to wear.

It is essential to have considerable experience of dressmaking and a fair degree of skill before embarking on tailoring but no additional equipment is required. The stitches and seams used in dressmaking are employed, with the addition of padding and serging. Additional time and patience are required, especially when pressing, but the results more than compensate for the painstaking construction.

Use best quality fabric whatever the weight, type or fibre, remembering that woollen cloth is easiest to handle, with worsted, and wool with some polyester, almost as easy. If possible try to start by making a coat for someone who is a standard size and shape so that you can concentrate on the techniques. Use a commercial paper pattern, adapting it if necessary in order to follow the instructions on the following pages. Use a dress form or dummy if you have one—for establishing roll lines, as a base for some basting, for deciding on pocket positions, and to support the shape that you are so carefully putting in.

Findings

The term is used to describe the materials needed for the multi-layered underpinning that supports the garment. They include soft canvas, hair canvas/haircloth, collar canvas, domette, melton, silesia/pocketing, linen, stay tape. You will also need foam shoulder pads, wadding/batting to add to them and padding or lambswool for sleeve head rolls.

Notions

In addition to sewing thread, zippers and waistbanding you will need trouser clasps, coat buttons, cuff buttons, backing buttons (large holes), gimp and buttonhole twist.

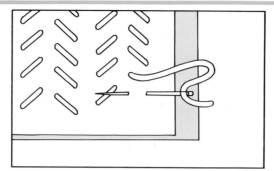

Padding or pad stitch Used to attach interfacing to collars and lapels. A flat stitch penetrating both layers, worked in rows. The visible stitch should be 5 mm/¼ in wide and deep, picking up a very small amount on the needle. Insert needle horizontally, each stitch falling between two on previous row. Work left to right, up and down. Fasten off with backstitch; start next stitch with knot.

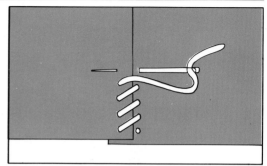

Serging A strong flat stitch used in tailoring for anchoring raw edges. It has limited use in other types of sewing; under-fabric must be thick, stitch will not restrain fabrics that fray badly. Insert needle horizontally beside raw edge and bring it up to 3 mm/⅛ in into the upper edge, more on thick tweed and coating. Do not pull thread tight.

Assembling a coat, jacket or blazer Before starting on sewing techniques baste a layer of interfacing in place, baste coat pieces together and check the fit, particularly length if it is a short jacket, and pocket positions. Take the pieces apart and construct the pockets (see p. 161–2), then follow the sequence of construction described on the following pages.

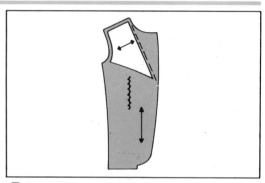

I **Interfacing** Exclude all seam allowances. Cut canvas for coat front following armhole, shoulder, neckline, front edge and two thirds of hem; curve remaining edge. With soft fabric or woman's coat cut canvas to fit entire front. Mark lapel roll line. Insert darts. Cut haircloth for chest area on bias grain following roll line and two-thirds of armhole; trim 2 cm/¾ in in from edge.

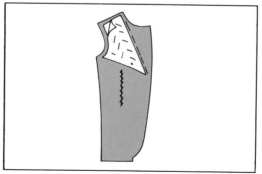

2 Place haircloth on top of canvas. Cut domette to go on top following roll line, shoulder, armhole and 5 cm/2 in of seam but trim 1 cm/⅜ in all around. On women's coats haircloth can be replaced by soft canvas; domette can be omitted from thin fabrics. Baste together permanently over chest area; keep flat. Press on both sides with hot iron and damp cloth, shape to a curve while warm.

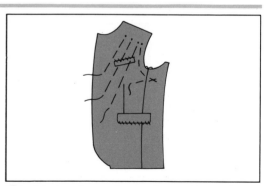

3 Stitch and press darts and seams in coat fronts. Arrange interfacing assembly, domette side down, and coat front on top WS down; align roll lines. Baste between shoulder and hem, further toward front edge and along roll line. Baste around armhole and across to dart. Smooth out the cloth as you stitch; backstitch where pockets occur. On WS cut canvas to fit under pocket.

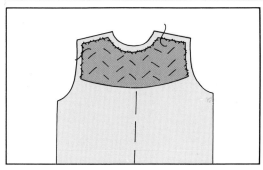

4 On women's coats and loosely woven fabric add support by attaching soft canvas to back shoulder area to halfway down armhole. Curve lower edge, exclude seam allowances, insert darts and baste to WS. Work catch stitch along shoulders, neck and armholes. Leave all temporary basting in place until final pressing of garment.

5 Make a bridle of stay tape, basting it tautly along roll line from just inside front edge to within 4 cm/1½ in of neck and leaving an extra 10 cm/4 in unattached to be stitched to the collar later. Hem along each edge of stay tape. Remove basting.

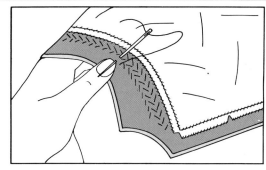

6 Pad the lapel, folding it along the roll line and holding it so that it curves over your hand and curls into rolled position as you stitch. Begin at the roll line with a row of stitches on the tape then stitch up and down in rows to within 1 cm/⅜ in of edge of canvas, covering the lapel with padding stitches and using sewing thread. Press well on a ham or pad to preserve curl.

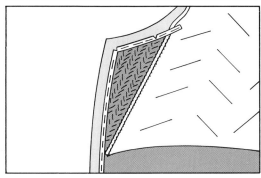

7 Trim outer edge of canvas so that it follows the seamline along front edge and around lapel corner as far as gorge line, i.e. point where collar will join neckline. Baste stay tape with one edge on seamline, pulling it taut around gorge line and clipping the edge. Pull taut to lapel corner and clip; baste tape flat as far as buttons. Pull taut between buttons and around hem.

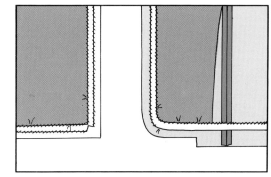

8 Hem along both edges of tape. If fabric is loosely woven continue tape along hemline, except in full length coat where linen would be used. If bottom corners are square, clip tape to turn corner. On women's coats in light fabrics catch stitch over edge of canvas instead of using tape. Press coat fronts on WS and RS, preserving lapel curl.

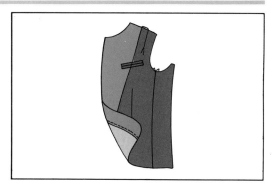

Facing Baste and stitch front dart and shoulder tuck in coat front linings. Place facing RS down to RS lining, match seam edges from shoulder to hem, ease lining over chest. Stitch, press seam toward lining. Make jetted pocket (see p. 162) at chest line. Place facing assembly RS down on coat front, match front edges, stitch and baste on seamline.

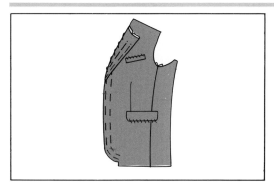

2 With thin fabrics stitching can go around lapel corner to end of gorge line. Trim and layer seam allowances, press stitching flat, turn facing RS out over coat. Seamline must be out of sight, so roll edge to inside from hem to base of lapel and to outside for length of lapel and baste. Hold lapel in rolled position while stitching. Baste again 2.5 cm/1 in inside and also over lapel roll. Press edges.

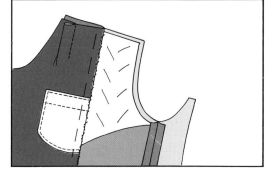

3 Smooth facing flat on inside, baste from neck to hem beside lining seam. Fold lining back and catch stitch seam allowance to interfacing, also stitching one layer of pocket bag to interfacing. Replace lining and baste to coat, easing slightly. On a woman's coat without inside pockets attach facing to coat without joining to lining, turn to WS, baste, press and catch stitch raw edge to interfacing.

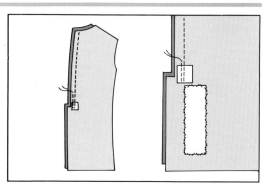

Vent Reinforce bottom of centre back seam at top of vent by basting a small square of linen on the seamline. Stitch and press seam. Reinforce vertical edges of vent; catch stitch a strip of linen to upper edge, placing edge of linen on fold line. Hem a piece of stay tape to seamline of under edge. With RS up fold vent edges over reinforcements, baste and press. Herringbone edges to coat.

COATS AND JACKETS

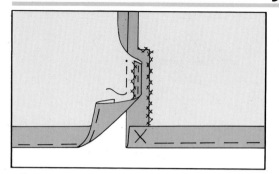

2 With RS up baste vent closed far enough to ensure hemline can be marked level on each edge. With WS up fold up hem on outer part of vent, keeping inner piece out of the way. Ease back so that it will not show. Baste hem for 10 cm/4 in. Fold and baste hem on other side of vent.

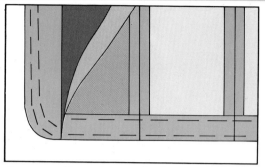

Seams and hem Join coat back to coat front, press seams. Open out WS up. On women's jackets and full-length coats catch stitch a bias strip of linen 2–4 cm/ $\frac{3}{4}$–$1\frac{1}{2}$ in wide, with one edge on hemline. Fold up and baste hem. Trim hem evenly, baste and secure to garment or linen.

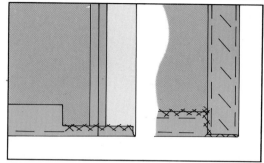

Square corner Open out facing, press seam open. Fold up hem and baste, measuring both sides evenly from neckline. From facing seam to edge, fold up at an angle. Press. Trim to 1 cm/$\frac{3}{8}$ in within the facing. Herringbone over raw edges. Fold facing into position, baste down to corner and along hem with RS up, curling corner under. Press. Slip stitch bottom edge; herringbone or serge across hem.

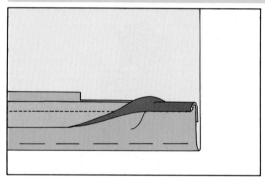

Bound hem Unlined jackets and full-length coats should have a neatly bound hem. Also use on sleeve hems, facing edges and seams of unlined jackets. Stitch bias strips of lining fabric to RS marked hemline of coat. Trim raw edge to 5 mm/$\frac{1}{4}$ in or less. Press bias so that it extends beyond hem RS up. Roll bias over edge and prick stitch from RS in seamline. Baste hem to coat and catch stitch.

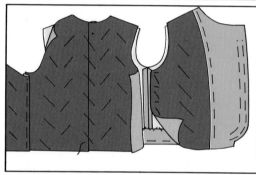

Lining Stitch and press lining seams, basting a pleat at centre back for ease. Place lining WS down on WS coat. Align centre back, shoulders and hem and baste in rows starting at centre; do not pull lining taut. Smooth front lining into place, flash baste edge to coat seam allowance. Bring edge of back lining over front, fold under and baste. At vent turn in edges and baste.

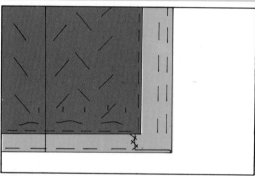

2 On women's coats or jackets bring front edges of lining over facing edge, fold under, ease back 3 mm/$\frac{1}{8}$ in and baste. On all garments baste through coat and lining from RS, 5 cm/2 in above hem. Turn coat WS up, trim lining, fold edge under 1 cm/$\frac{3}{8}$ in from hem, ease back 3 mm/$\frac{1}{8}$ in and baste. Hems on women's full-length coats may have lining hem stitched separately.

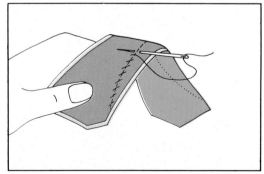

Collar Prepare neck edge by joining shoulder seams, holding lining and interfacing clear. Cut out bias under-collar in melton or fabric, join centre back seam and trim. Cut bias collar canvas excluding seam allowances and baste to WS collar. Mark roll line. Backstitch along roll line with canvas uppermost, pulling thread taut. Pad stitch along roll line over the backstitching.

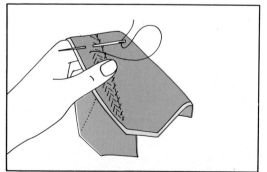

2 Pad the collar stand first, holding the edge and putting three or four rows between the roll line and the neck edge. Stitch to within 5 mm/$\frac{1}{4}$ in of the edge of the canvas. Turn collar around and pad stitch the remainder, the fall. The collar will curl into the correct shape.

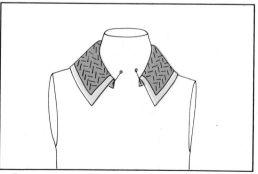

3 Press up to the roll line on RS and WS then press outer edge up to roll line, stretching it to shape it and lengthen the edge across the back of the neck. Turn collar and stretch centre section of neck edge in the same way. Finally, fold collar on fold line and press fold. These last stages can be done on a dress form giving you a chance to make sure both sides are equal.

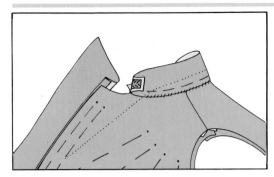

4 Replace pattern, re-mark stitching line and trim canvas and melton to the line. To attach collar, overlap neck edge of under collar on RS coat neck, using a dress form if you have one. Match centre backs, match collar roll line with lapel roll line, baste and hem or serge firmly over the edge of the collar.

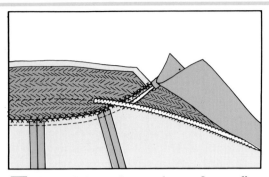

5 On inside herringbone neck seam flat to collar. Lay end of bridle across seam and onto collar along roll line. Baste and hem each side of tape. Press, preserving collar shape.

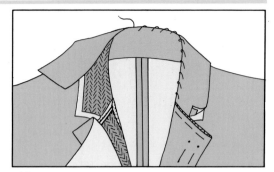

6 With under-collar and lapels folded into position, place top-collar piece WS down on under-collar. Align centre backs and baste around roll line with big stitches. Bring front facing into position and baste lapel step if not stitched. Trim and fold in top-collar seam allowance along gorge line and baste through to under-collar. Trim, fold in and baste facing edge to meet it.

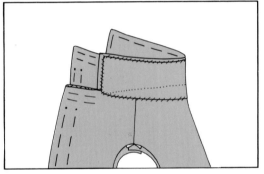

7 Press basted seams, join invisibly with draw stitch. Trim edge of top-collar so that only 6 mm/$\frac{1}{4}$ in extends beyond under-collar. With RS top-collar toward you fold edge on seamline, tucking it between the edges of the melton and the canvas and baste. Press. On under-side hem melton to edge of top collar.

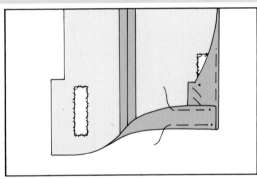

Sleeves Stitch and press underarm seam. On WS baste a strip of linen 3 cm/1$\frac{1}{4}$ in wide against each vent extension with one edge on seamline. Catch stitch all around. Add bias strip of linen to hemline if soft fabric. Fold each vent edge to WS and baste, turn up sleeve hem, baste and catch stitch. Press.

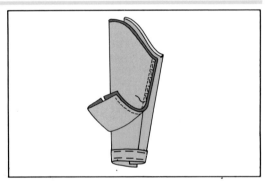

2 Stitch and press upper sleeve seam as far as top of vent. Baste vent in closed position. Prick stitch on RS across top of vent. Turn sleeve inside out. Stitch lining seams allowing ease. With lining WS out place on sleeve matching underarm seams. Flash baste or backstitch centre section of lining seam allowance to sleeve seam allowance.

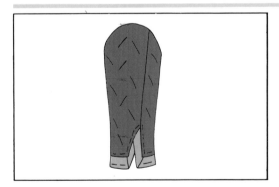

3 Turn lining over sleeve by putting one hand inside, grasping both edges and pulling through. With sleeve WS out baste lining to sleeve allowing ease, basting vertically and then 5 cm/2 in above hem. Trim sleeve lining, fold under raw edge 1.5 cm/$\frac{5}{8}$ in from hem, ease back and baste. Turn in and baste edges around vent.

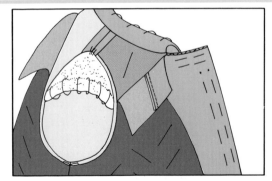

4 Smooth interfacing over shoulder seam toward back. Backstitch to shoulder seam allowance. Insert sleeves in armholes. Put shoulder pads in position with edge extending into top of sleeve 5–10 mm/$\frac{1}{4}$–$\frac{1}{2}$ in, and thickest part of pad to back of shoulder seam. Oversew loosely to attach to armhole seam allowance holding shoulder in shape. Oversew the other corner to the interfacing.

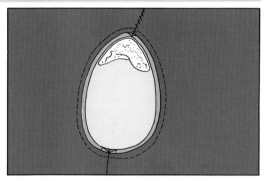

5 Attach sleeve head roll by placing it evenly over sleeve head, backstitch it to seam allowance. Smooth front lining seam allowances around armhole. Pull out edge of sleeve head lining, turn edge under and baste over armhole edges, distributing ease in the same way as the sleeve.

159

COATS AND JACKETS

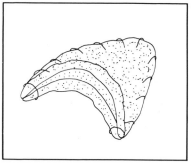

Shoulder pads Use shaped foam pads and cover each side with a piece of wadding/batting. This softens the outline, eliminates the noise foam makes and corrects faults. Experiment, using it under pad to fill hollows and on top to level up uneven or sloping shoulders. Baste through all layers.

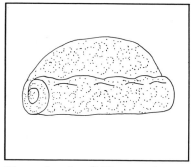

Sleeve head roll These can be purchased but to make your own use a bias piece of wadding/batting, domette or lambswool 6 cm/2½ in wide, 25 cm/10 in long, less for women, and tapered at the ends. Fold in one edge 3 cm/1¼ in and stitch. Attach single edge to armhole seam allowance over sleeve head.

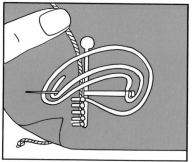

1 **Tailor's buttonholes** Fell stitch lining edges. Attach hanging loop. Mark buttonholes. Punch or clip a hole at round end, cut slit. Thread needle with gimp, knot, sew between layers, bringing needle out beside slit. Using buttonhole twist, stitch over gimp toward round end.

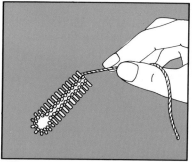

2 Pull gimp taut, curl it around the hole and make five stitches over it around the hole, pulling knots to the surface. Stitch the second side; stitch a straight bar at the other end. On WS cut gimp and oversew over the ends. Close buttonholes with oversewing. Press coat. Sew on buttons.

SPEED TAILORING

This is a modern method of structuring a coat or jacket using non-woven iron-on interfacing in place of traditional canvasses. The technique of heat-fusing stiffening to fabric is basic to the clothing industry and now that a variety of similar fusible sewing aids is available to the home dressmaker some of the techniques can be copied.

Speed tailoring is quick because it reduces the amount of hand sewing necessary, but just as much skill in cutting and pressing and accuracy in stitching are required as in traditional tailoring. As speed is the keynote choose a simple style, perhaps a pattern you have used before. The garment can be lined or, for speed, unlined. Use a fabric that is easy to sew such as wool or wool and polyester, in tweed, plain weave, birdseye or pinstripe. Avoid pile fabrics, checks and fabrics that need matching. With very heavy fabric use two layers or a heavier weight of interfacing. Press all interfacings in position steadily and firmly, using a steam iron and a damp cloth to achieve a lasting bond. Exclude seam allowances on medium and heavy interfacings to reduce bulk in seams and edges. The speed tailoring technique can be applied to several stages of coat construction.

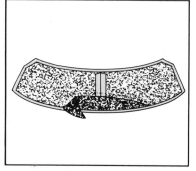

Under-collar Cut medium interfacing on the bias and press to WS of each half of collar. Stitch centre back seam and press open. Mark roll line. Cut a second piece of interfacing the size and shape of collar *stand* only. Trim 5 mm/¼ in from roll line edge and press on top of first layer.

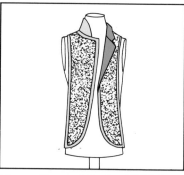

Top-collar and facing If fabric requires extra stability attach soft or ultra-soft interfacing to WS top collar and front facings. Join top collar to facings along gorge line RS together. Press open seams. This eliminates hand drawn gorge seams which are difficult to do with interfacing attached.

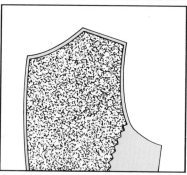

Coat front Using medium interfacing cut shape of front to midway down armhole, using pinking shears on outer edge to prevent a ridge on the fabric. Press to WS coat fronts. Alternatively press soft interfacing to WS entire coat front. If required press light or medium interfacing to back shoulder area.

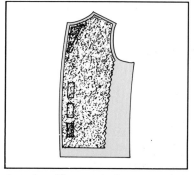

Lapel and buttonholes Cut medium interfacing for lapel excluding seam allowance and trimming 5 mm/¼ in from roll line. Cut rectangles at least 2 cm/¾ in wider than buttonholes and 5 cm/2 in long. Press all in place.

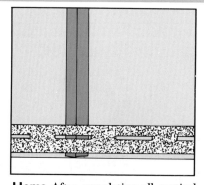

Hems After completing all vertical seams and also darts, arrange coat WS up to reinforce hemline. Trim one side of light perforated band to half width to avoid a ridge on the finished garment. Press in position with perforations along hemline and narrow side of band on garment.

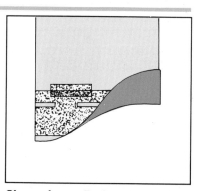

Sleeve hems Perforated band with one edge trimmed can also be used on sleeve hems and vent edges. On lightweight fabrics all hems should be stitched but others may be held in place with pieces of hemming web; test first to make sure it does not stiffen the hem too much.

POCKETS FOR COATS AND JACKETS

Patch pockets can be used, but it is more usual to make pockets that involve cutting the garment as described here.

Make all pockets after attaching interfacing but before main seams are sewn.

Size guide (excluding seam allowances):

Women Main body pockets 12 cm/4¾ in wide; bag 15 × 14 cm/ 6 × 5½ in.

Men Main body pockets 17 cm/ 6¾ in wide; bag 20 × 18 cm/ 8 × 7 in; welts 3–4 cm/1–1½ in deep; flaps 4–7 cm/1½–2¾ in deep; jettings—as narrow as fabric will allow; breast pockets 11 cm/4¼ in wide; breast welt 2.5 cm/1 in deep; bag 14 × 13 cm/5½ × 5 in.

1 **Welt pocket** Formed by attaching a folded piece of fabric, or welt, to lower edge of pocket opening on RS of garment. The welt is then turned upward so its folded edge forms top of opening. The welt may be cut on the cross for decorative effect. A pocket bag is attached on WS of garment.

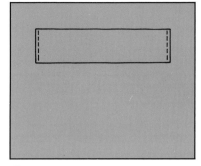

2 Mark opening on garment. Cut out welt piece, allowing 1.5 cm/ ⅝ in seam allowances. Mark seams and fold line. Interface top half of welt to fold line, but within seam allowances at sides. Turn in sides so welt length equals that of opening, folding in sides on lower half at a slight angle.

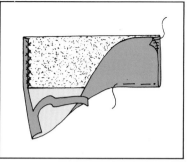

3 Trim 3 mm/⅛ in from the turned-in edges. Press and hold in place with herringbone stitch. Fold welt WS together at centre fold line. Baste fold. Baste folded ends together (angled fold falls on WS of finished welt). Baste raw edges of welt together. Press well. Slip stitch ends.

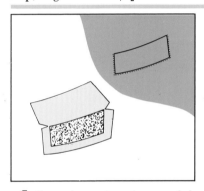

4 To make a shaped or angled welt, or one for a breast pocket (slightly curved to run at an angle between armhole and coat front), cut interfacing to size and shape of finished welt. Mark fold line along top edge and use as pattern to cut fabric, adding seam allowance on outer edge.

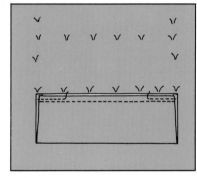

5 Trim seam allowance on raw edges of welt to 6 mm/¼ in. On RS of garment mark a line to depth of welt below pocket opening. Place welt RS down on garment below this line, with raw edges touching it. Baste and machine 6 mm/¼ in from edge. Remove all basting and press well.

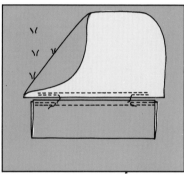

6 Cut two bag pieces. On RS of garment place one bag piece above marked opening, RS down, with lower edge touching raw edges of welt. Baste and machine 6 mm/¼ in from edge, but make stitching on bag piece 2 mm/1/16 in shorter at each end than stitching on welt.

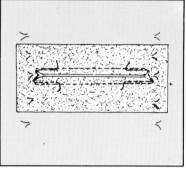

7 Remove basting. On WS of garment cut carefully between rows of stitching. Then, 1.5 cm/⅝ in from ends of shorter row of stitching, cut out to ends of rows of machining.

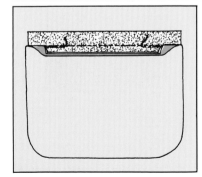

8 Push bag piece through to WS and allow to hang down inside. Lift bag piece and attach second piece to welt stitching by folding under edge and hemming in place.

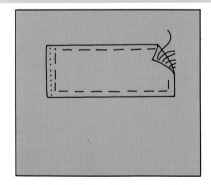

9 On RS fold welt up. Baste flat to garment. Press well. Slip stitch each end of welt to garment. Then prick stitch ends from RS, stitching no more than 4 mm/⅛ in from edges. Remove basting. Press.

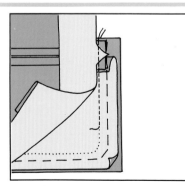

10 Baste bag pieces together. Leaving about 1.25 cm/½ in seam allowance, mark final shape with chalk, rounding corners. Machine on chalkline, stitching close to original machining at pocket ends. Stitch again 5 mm/¼ in outside first row. Remove basting. Press.

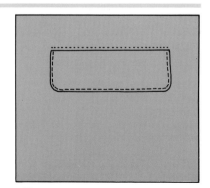

1 **Flap pocket** This has a shaped flap attached on RS to upper edge of opening. The lower edge of it is finished with a jetting, or binding, which is concealed by the flap during wear. The pocket has a bag attached on WS of garment.

POCKETS FOR COATS AND JACKETS

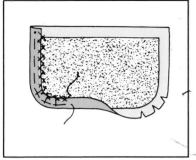

2 Mark opening on garment. Cut flap and lining, allowing 1.5 cm/ $\frac{5}{8}$ in seam allowances. Mark seams. Interface as appropriate. Clip curves. Turn in all but top edge to WS along marked lines. Baste. Check flap length equals length of opening. Trim allowances and herringbone edge.

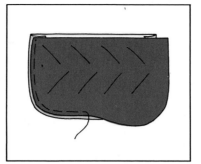

3 Turn in lining on all but top edge. Baste folded edges to lie 1 mm/ $\frac{1}{16}$ in from edges of flap, press and fell stitch. Remove basting except along top. Trim top of flap and lining to leave 6 mm/ $\frac{1}{4}$ in seam allowance. Cut fabric strip 2.5 cm/1 in wide and 5 cm/ 2 in longer than flap.

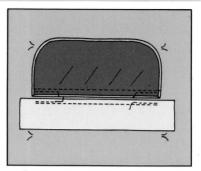

4 Baste flap RS down above opening on RS with raw edges on marked line. Place strip below flap and baste to garment with raw edge touching flap edge. Stitch flap 6 mm/ $\frac{1}{4}$ in from edge and strip 3 mm/ $\frac{1}{8}$ in from edge: finish strip stitching 3 mm/ $\frac{1}{8}$ in from ends of flap stitching.

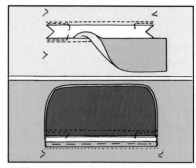

5 Push strip (jetting) through slit to WS. Fold it over the seam allowances and roll it tightly. Baste jetting down and on RS prick stitch in join between jetting and garment. Press. Push triangles of fabric at ends of pocket slit through to WS and stab stitch across pocket ends.

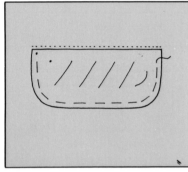

6 On RS of garment pull flap over pocket opening. Baste to garment, using straight stitches around edge and diagonal ones across centre. Prick stitch or machine 3 mm/ $\frac{1}{8}$ in above join between flap and garment, stitching through garment and allowances. Remove basting. Press.

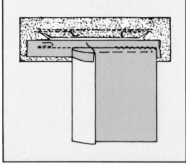

7 For each pocket cut two rectangles to size, press under top edge of one piece on seam allowance and place RS up on WS of garment with fold against machining on lower jetting. Baste in position and hem into machining. Remove basting.

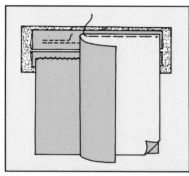

8 Place second bag piece RS down on top of first, with lower edges level and top edge level with raw edges of fabric of upper part of flap. Baste and machine to raw edges, taking a 6 mm/ $\frac{1}{4}$ in seam allowance. Remove basting. Mark, stitch and trim bag.

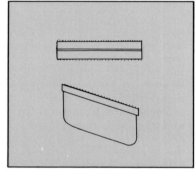

Jetted pocket Similar to a piped pocket or buttonhole, both edges are finished with a piece of fabric that forms a narrow edge or jetting. A piece of fabric is placed behind the opening. The bag is attached on WS of garment. A variation has a flap inserted between the jettings.

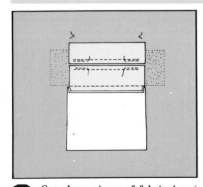

2 Cut three pieces of fabric 4 cm/ $1\frac{1}{2}$ in wide and 2 cm/ $\frac{3}{4}$ in longer than pocket width. Baste one piece RS down on RS garment above pocket marking with one edge on mark. Cut pocket bag pieces. Join one to second jetting RS together. Baste RS down on garment. Stitch in place.

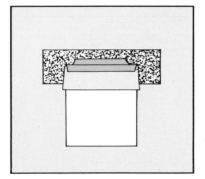

3 On WS cut between rows of stitching along centre of pocket then cut diagonally toward ends of stitching. Press seams open. Push jettings and bag through slit. Roll edges evenly, baste and press. Push end triangles to WS. On RS oversew jettings together. Press.

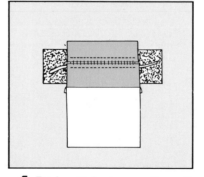

4 Prick stitch in seamline all around pocket on RS. On WS work a bar tack at each end of pocket opening. On men's jackets or on soft loose fabrics, a strip of light interfacing or linen can be placed under lower jetting after pushing it through but before prick stitching.

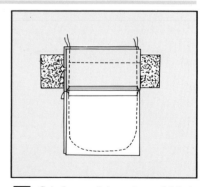

5 Stitch remaining piece of fabric to second piece of bag RS together. Press seam open. Place RS down on WS garment with raw edge level with upper edge jetting. Baste. Stitch through fabric and jetting. Stitch bag pieces together sewing through ends of jettings.

TROUSERS

MEN'S TROUSERS

The style and outline may vary with changes in fashion: trouser legs may be straight, flared or drainpipe with plain or cuffed hems; the waist may be fitted at the front with darts or with shallow or deep pleats; there will be darts in the back unless, as with jeans, a yoke provides the shaping. The waistband usually sits on the hip bone because men do not have an indented waist, but it may be lower and tight-fitting or higher and loose, to be supported by braces/suspenders. Whatever the styling the construction techniques remain unchanged in classic tailoring.

Check the measurements of the paper pattern and adjust it to fit including width of leg at hem level (check against an existing pair of trousers). Baste together each leg and fit separately before doing any stitching. After fitting and re-basting leg seams if necessary, press in creases in each leg separately (see p. 41).

Trousers can be made for women on the same principle, although a softer waistband should be used. Also, pockets with a shaped, faced edge might be preferred to men's side seam pockets.

Plain open seams are used unless a welt seam is preferred on the outside leg. If welt seams are used the waistband and pocket edges are stitched to match.

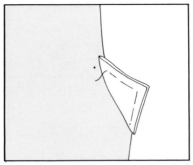

Reinforcements Attach crotch stays to front trouser legs to prevent stretching. Cut two 13 cm/5 in squares of pocketing, fold RS out to form triangle; press. Baste each on WS of leg, with fold level with zipper base point on crotch seam and level with a point 10 cm/4 in along inside leg seam.

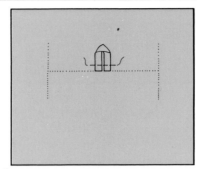

1 Back pockets On RS of back trouser legs chalk a horizontal line 9 cm/3½ in below waist edge. Starting 5 cm/2 in from side seam mark pocket 10 cm/4 in wide. If pocket is to be fastened, stitch piece of tubing 1 cm/⅜ in wide and 3 cm/1¼ in long, folded into a loop, above marking.

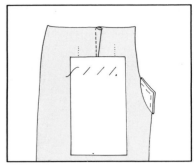

2 Cut a piece of pocketing 15 cm/6 in wide and 43 cm/17 in long or less if preferred. Place WS down on WS trouser with one edge 2.5 cm/1 in above pocket position and extending equally each end of the line.

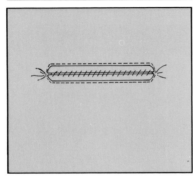

3 Cut two pieces of fabric 13 cm/5¼ in long and 4 cm/1½ in wide. Make jetted pocket with 3 mm/⅛ in jettings. On RS pinch ends together, baste all around; press. Stitch around in a rectangle. Fold trouser leg away, stitch beside lower edge of lower jetting to attach it to pocket bag.

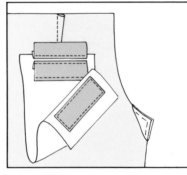

4 Fold pocket bag over RS together until raw edge extends 2 cm/¾ in above waist edge. Mark position of pocket opening on upper layer of bag. Unfold bag. Cut a piece of fabric 6 cm/2¼ in wide and 13 cm/5¼ in long. Centre it RS up over chalk mark on bag. Stitch all around.

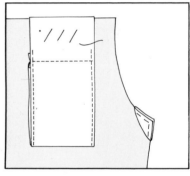

5 Fold pocket bag back into position, baste and stitch through free edge of upper piping and pocket bag. Baste pocket bag to WS trouser above stitching. Stitch along both sides of bag, stitching close to pocket ends.

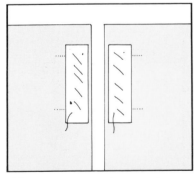

1 Side seam pockets Mark pocket position from 5 cm/2 in below waist edge to extend for 20 cm/8 in on side edge of both front and both back trouser legs. Reinforce fronts by basting a strip of linen 23 cm/9 in long and 3–4 cm/1¼–1½ in wide on WS with one edge level with trouser edge.

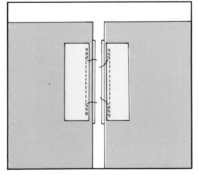

2 Cut two pieces of fabric for each pocket 5 cm/2 in wide and 23 cm/9 in long. Baste one to each seam edge on RS over marked pocket position, with raw edges level. Stitch on seamline to attach strip to trouser leg. Stitching lines must be exactly equal in length, i.e. 20 cm/8 in.

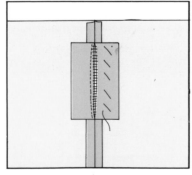

3 Place front and back trouser leg RS together; pin across seam at pocket. Stitch seams holding edge strips clear and ending at ends of pocket. Press all seams open. Roll pocket strips to WS, baste, press, prick stitch along front 5 mm/¼ in from edge. Baste pocket edges together.

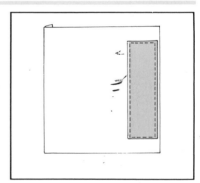

4 Clip seams at ends of pocket. Press. Cut a piece of pocketing for each bag 40 cm/16 in wide and 35–40 cm/14–16 in deep or as preferred. Fold one side 1 cm/⅜ in to WS and press. On the opposite edge attach a strip of fabric 8 cm/3 in wide with edges level.

TROUSERS

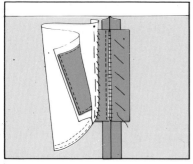

5 Place pocket bag in position with fold beside prick stitch line. Baste and hem to pocket strip. Fold bag RS together; bring fabric edge to meet edge of pocket strip on back trouser. Pin layers together. Draw a curve from base of pocket stitching to fold at lower edge. Trim, stitch twice.

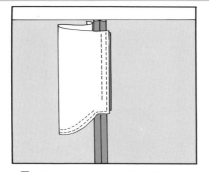

6 Place remaining edge of pocket bag level with outer edge of pocket piece. Baste flat. Stitch bag to fabric beneath with backstitch. Stitch again, by machine, close to raw edges. Hem or backstitch across bottom of bag to attach it to the seam. On RS work bar tacks at ends of pocket.

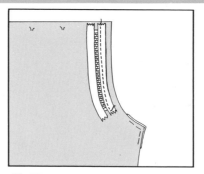

I **Zipper** (right side) Curved trouser zippers are usually 25 cm/10 in long, extending into curve of crotch seam. A straight zipper may have to be shorter. Place zipper face down on RS trouser leg with slider just below seamline and teeth to inside of it. Baste; stitch beside teeth.

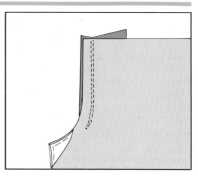

2 Cut a piece of fabric for fly extension 6 cm/2⅜ in wide and 5 cm/2 in longer than zipper. Place fabric RS down over zipper, baste with edges level, turn trouser leg over and stitch again on top of first row.

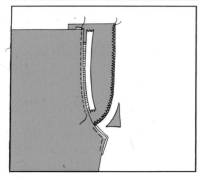

3 Roll fly extension and zipper to extend, folding seam allowances onto WS. Baste beside zipper teeth, press. With trouser RS up stitch beside teeth. On fly extension trim outer edge curving it below zipper, zigzag raw edge beside teeth. Baste and stitch front waist pleats or tucks.

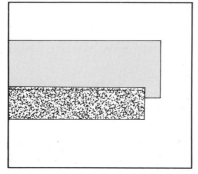

I **Waistband** (right side) Cut piece of fabric 6 cm/2¼ in wide or 3 cm/1¼ in wider than selected stiffening and length of trouser waist plus fly extension. Cut interfacing 4.5 cm/1¾ in wide, and attach to WS fabric, overlapping edge by 1.5 cm/⅝ in. Stitch along edge of interfacing.

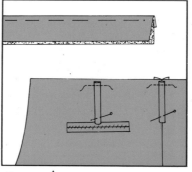

2 Fold fabric over interfacing, baste along upper edge. Press. Make belt loops and stitch on RS of each trouser leg at waist edge. Pin other loops appropriately. Make each loop 9 cm/3½ in long and stitch to seam allowance.

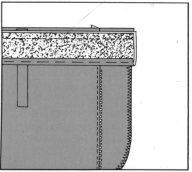

3 With zipper open and tops of pockets pinned out of the way place waistband RS down to RS trouser leg and baste with edges level; include fly extension. Stitch seam, press open. Topstitch waistband if required.

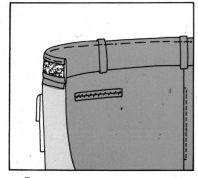

4 Stitch belt loops again 1 cm/⅜ in below waistband seam. Fold loops up and pin to waistband. Fold over ends of loops level with waistband, trim surplus and stitch end of loops to waistband. Press waistband.

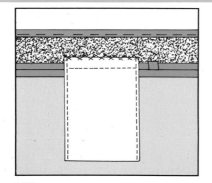

5 On WS trouser unpin pocket tops and fold up over WS waistband. Baste pocket to trouser waist seam allowance using strong basting. Trim surplus pocket bag 1 cm/⅜ in above and catch edge to waistband interfacing with herringbone stitch.

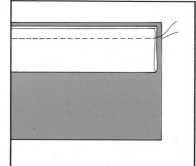

6 To face back of waistband cut a piece of pocketing 6 cm/2¼ in wide and same length as waistband. Cut a piece for trouser curtain 8 cm/3 in wide, fold in half lengthwise and press. Place on RS facing with upper raw edges level and stitch together 1.5 cm/⅝ in from edge.

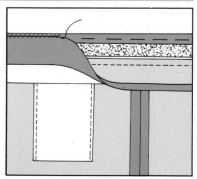

7 Place facing WS up on WS trouser, raw edge level with seam allowances edge of waist seam. Lift seam allowance, backstitch facing and curtain edges to it. At centre back leave facing unstitched for 8 cm/3 in. Turn in final facing edge level with edge of waistband and fell.

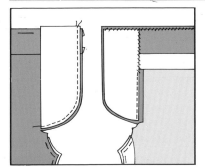

8 Cut pocketing to depth and width of fly extension plus waistband. With RS together stitch along outer edge and around below base of zipper. Trim edge; turn RS out; press. Fold in raw edges and hem to waistband. Below waistband, backstitch edge to seam beneath.

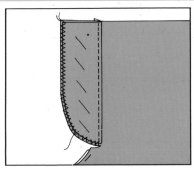

Left fly Cut pieces of fabric and pocketing same size as fly extension on right leg. Baste together RS out. Baste to RS left trouser front with long edge matching fly edge of trouser. Stitch. Trim edges and press so that fly piece extends. Prick stitch or machine beside seam. Finish raw edges.

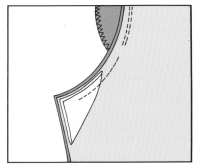

2 Join legs. Place right and left front crotch seam edges RS together, matching crotch points and waist edges. Baste and stitch from base of zipper to within 4 cm/1½ in of crotch point. It is easiest to stitch by hand using double thread and backstitch. Press seam open. Do not clip.

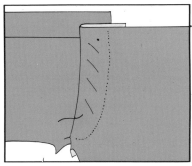

3 Fold fly piece on left side to WS, baste with seam on edge. Press. Fasten zipper. Lap left fly edge over fly extension and pin in position, adjusting until zipper is correctly aligned on left fly piece. Pin or baste. Mark position of centre of zipper tape. Also mark waist seam allowance.

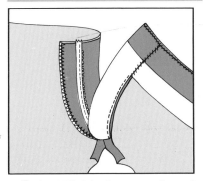

4 On WS lift fly pieces free of trouser and baste zipper tape to it, keeping it in the position established when basting from RS. Open zipper. Machine or backstitch through tape and fly piece.

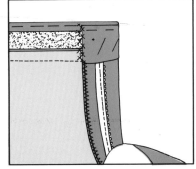

5 Remove basting and spread out waist of left trouser leg with fly piece extending. Stitch loops, waistband and pocket edges as for right leg. Fold back fly piece and end of waistband to WS and baste. Slip stitch along edge of waistband, herringbone over edge across it.

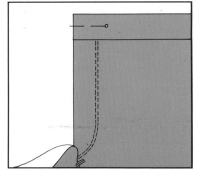

6 Close zipper; pin band. Check stitching line; open zipper then machine or prick stitch from base of band finishing with a bar tack over crotch seam. On WS hem zipper tape to fly piece, also backstitch any parts of tape not held by original stitching; this usually happens around the curve.

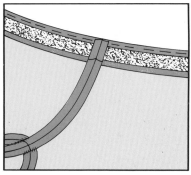

7 Stitch and press inside leg seams. Baste crotch seam from base of zipper and through ends of waistband. Machine stitch or hand backstitch with double thread. Press open. Where crotch seam crosses inside leg seams serge the seam allowances to hold them flat. Do not clip crotch seam.

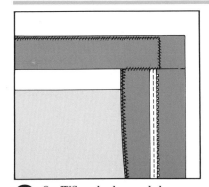

8 On WS make bar tack between fly extension and crotch seam at base of zipper. Complete the trouser waist by attaching facing and curtain as for right trouser leg. At centre back overlap ends, fold in upper raw edge. Fold in all remaining raw edges and hem.

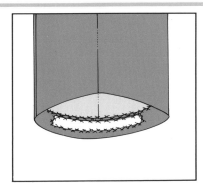

Hem Mark length, checking that inside leg seams are equal. Baste and press hems, trim to 3–4 cm/1–1½ in. Overcast fraying fabrics. Complete with herringbone stitch, use serging stitch where hem crosses seams. Stitch kick tape or seam tape along back of trouser to take shoe wear.

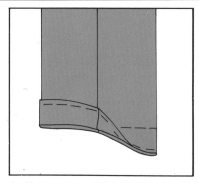

Cuff or turn up The trousers should be cut 9 cm/3½ in longer. Mark hemline then chalk another line 9 cm/3½ in below. Turn hem on this line, baste and press. Trim hem depth to 4 cm/1½ in and stitch. Fold cuff to RS along chalk line, baste the fold, press. Attach kick tape.

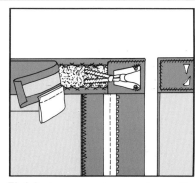

Finish trousers by pressing well. Make buttonhole, attach button or use a trouser clasp. Sew to WS waistband before facing is attached. Use tape tied through holes of hook and stitch firmly. Attach bar by pushing points through waistband and press flat.

4

SEWING FOR THE HOME

A thoroughly practical introduction to home furnishings: all the sewing techniques related to the making of cushions and pillows, slipcovers, curtains, blinds and shades, table linen and bed linen; and ideas for coordinating your décor

CUSHIONS AND PILLOWS

A few cushions or pillows can quickly transform the plainest chair or sofa, garden bench or hammock, and help to make a setting, whether indoor or outdoor, attractive and welcoming. Not only do they add comfort but they can also be used as decorative accents in a colour scheme, tying together colours and textures.

If your furnishings are fairly restrained, make a feature of the cushions. Design your own shapes and styles, making a paper pattern to cut around if the shape is irregular. (It is also advisable to make a pattern for cutting out circular cushions.)

Most fabrics can be used for cushion covers, including leather, suede, handicraft felt, vinyl-backed fabrics and fake fur. Bear in mind whether the fabric can be washed or has to be dry cleaned and try to avoid those that shed pile or fluff. Covers with zippers can be easily removed for washing and cleaning. Alternatively, stitch the opening by hand so that it may be opened easily.

Choosing a filling

There are many suitable fillings for cushions. The most luxurious are feather and down; among the cheaper range, foam chips, foam slabs, polyester fibrefill and kapok are the most widely used; and the most convenient are ready-made cushion pads or pillow forms.

Foam chips and polyester fibrefill can be bought loose or in bags. They must be enclosed in a fairly thick inner cover and packed tightly or the cushion will flatten and become lumpy. Wear an apron when filling a cushion, as the chips are full of static electricity and cling to clothes and skin.

Slabs of latex or polyurethane foam for box cushions are available cut to size, or they can be cut to shape at home. (Dip the knife in water occasionally as you cut to help it slide through the foam.) Latex foam tends to be heavier and bouncier than polyurethane, but the latter is made in various densities. Ask advice when buying foam since different types of cushions require different densities.

Kapok, a vegetable fibre, is used mostly for lightweight cushions. Buy it by weight, packing the covers well or they may flatten.

Inner cover

It is important to have a strong inner cover to facilitate cleaning and to keep the filling in place (this is particularly important if the cover is made from a knitted or stretchy fabric that may lose its shape). Calico is the most widely used material, particularly for foam slabs, which eventually tend to crumble. Make inner covers in the same way as the outer ones, using open seams but omitting a zipper or piping. For speed, turn in and machine zigzag the opening.

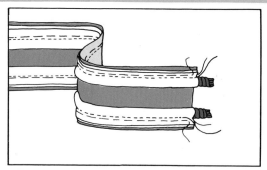

1 **Piping** Prepare and apply piping as for piped seams (see p. 47), using a piping or zipper foot and stitching as close as possible to cord. For a box-edge cover, attach piping to RS of gusset strip along top of bottom edge, or both, as desired. Proceed as for a box-edge cover, using piped seams when attaching gusset and piping to cover.

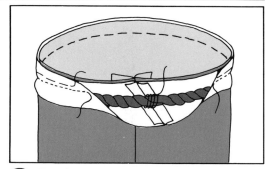

2 For a bolster, stitch side seam of cover to make a tube. On RS, pin and baste piping, the length of the circumference, around each end of tube, starting at seamline and placing raw edges together. Leave a short piece extending at both ends and join piping at seamline as for piped seam. Finish bolster as for round box-edge cover.

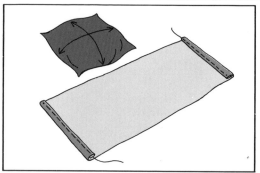

1 **Quick cover** Transform an old squashy cushion with this flapped cover. Cut a strip of material 2.5 cm/1 in wider and two-and-a-half times the length of the cushion. Turn both short edges under 1 cm/3/8 in, baste and press. Turn both edges under another 1.25 cm/1/2 in to make double hems, baste, press and slip hem or machine on WS.

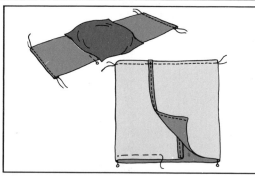

2 Centre cushion on RS of fabric, marking fabric at each end of cushion with a pin. Remove cushion and fold over both hemmed ends on the pins so that they overlap. Remove pins. Making sure raw edges are level, baste and stitch both side seams through all layers, leaving 1.25 cm/1/2 in seam allowances at each side. Turn cover RS out and insert cushion through overlapped opening.

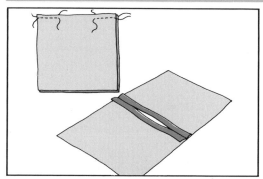

1 **Square cover with zipper** Cut two pieces of fabric to fit cushion, plus 1.25 cm/1/2 in seam allowance on all sides. Choose a zipper about 7.5 cm/3 in shorter than side of cushion and centre it along one edge of one piece of fabric, marking ends with chalk or pins. Remove zipper, place fabric RS together and baste and stitch from ends of zipper opening to edge of fabric. Press seam open.

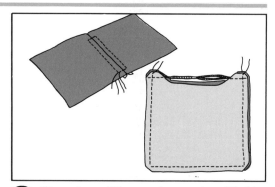

2 Place zipper RS up under opening. Working from RS baste and stitch zipper in place, stitching across both ends. Remove basting and press; open zipper enough to allow you to turn the cover through when stitched. Refold cover with RS together and baste and stitch remaining three side seams. Trim excess fabric diagonally at corners and turn cover through opening to RS. Insert cushion.

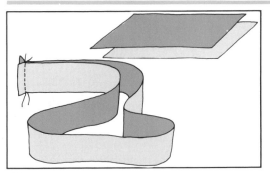

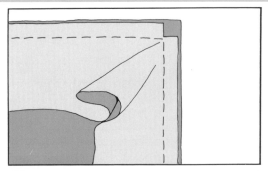

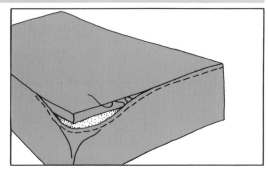

1 **Square box-edge cover** Cut two squares of fabric 1.25 cm/½ in larger all around than top of cushion, and cut a side gusset the thickness of the cushion, plus 2.5 cm/1 in, by twice the combined length and width of the cushion, plus 2.5 cm/1 in. (Join pieces of fabric if you do not have a large enough single piece.) Join ends of gusset RS together, leaving 1.25 cm/½ in seam allowances. Press seam open.

2 With RS facing and raw edges together, pin and baste one edge of gusset to all sides of one square. Ease corners by clipping into gusset seam allowance. Stitch with gusset uppermost, leaving 1.25 cm/½ in seam allowances and pivoting stitching at corners. Press seam down toward gusset.

3 Attach other edge of gusset in same way to three sides of second square, leaving fourth side and about 7.5 cm/3 in of the two adjoining seams unstitched. Turn in seam allowance of unstitched gusset, baste and press. Turn fabric RS out and insert cushion. Smooth down seam allowance of unstitched section of square over edge of cushion and slip stitch it to basted turning of gusset.

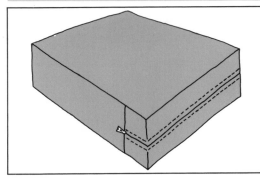

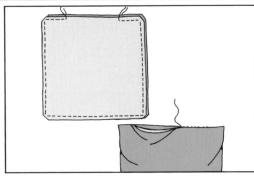

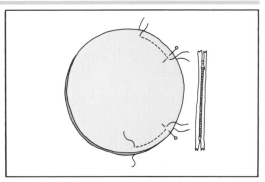

4 For a square box-edge cover with a zipper, choose a zipper that matches the colour of the fabric and measures about 15 cm/6 in longer than one side of the cushion. (It is easier to insert the cushion if the zipper extends along the whole of one side and a few inches along the adjoining sides.) Cut gusset, insert zipper and make up cover as for round box-edge cover with zipper.

Simple cover Cut two pieces of fabric the same size as the cushion, plus 1.25 cm/½ in seam allowance all around. With RS together, baste and stitch around three sides and a little way along each end of fourth. Press stitching and trim corners diagonally. Turn cover RS out. Press under 1.25 cm/½ in seam allowances on unstitched edges, insert cushion and slip stitch edges together.

Round cover with zipper Cut two circles the diameter of the cushion, plus 1.25 cm/½ in seam allowance. With direction of fabric grain matching, place circles RS together and position zipper on edge, easing it around curve. The zipper should measure approximately one-third of circumference. Mark ends of zipper and baste and stitch 5 cm/2 in from each end. Press seam open.

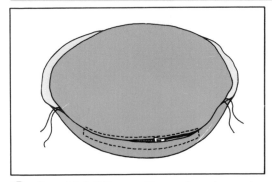

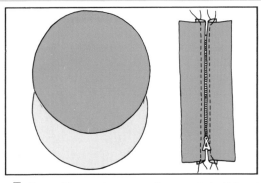

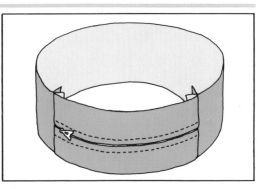

2 Turn fabric RS out and insert zipper in opening by an uneven hems method, sewing across both ends. Turn fabric back again to WS, leaving zipper partly open, and baste and stitch seam around the rest of the cover. Turn cover through opening to RS and insert cushion through opening.

Round box-edge cover Cut two circles 2.5 cm/ 1 in larger in diameter than cushion. For a cover without a zipper, cut a gusset and make up the cover as for square box, making sure that the fabric does not stretch as you slip stitch the opening. For a cover with a zipper, cut two gusset strips 2.5 cm/1 in longer than zipper and half the cushion thickness plus 2.5 cm/1 in. Attach strips to zipper.

2 Cut another strip 2.5 cm/1 in wider than cushion thickness and long enough to complete the gusset, adding an extra 2.5 cm/1 in to the length for seam allowances. Join ends of strip to ends of zipper section, RS together, taking 1.25 cm/½ in seam allowances. Press seams open.

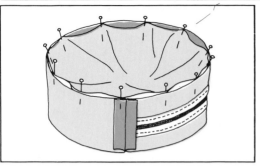

3 With RS together, pin one circle to one edge of gusset, matching raw edges. Baste and stitch in place, open zipper enough to put your hand through. Attach second circle to other side of gusset, matching direction of fabric grain on both circles. Press seam toward gusset. Turn cover RS out through zipper and insert cushion.

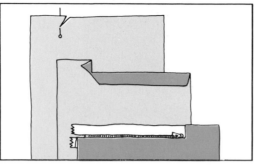

Bolster cover with zipper Cut a rectangle the length of the bolster by the circumference, plus 1.25 cm/½ in seam allowance all around. Cut out two circles 2.5 cm/1 in larger in diameter than bolster. Place zipper along a short edge of rectangle; mark end with a pin. Clip diagonally into seam allowance to pin and fold under along zipper section. With RS up, place zipper so teeth centre under folded edge.

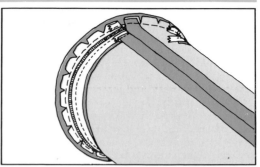

2 Baste zipper tape to folded edge and stitch, continuing across top of zipper. Fold rectangle in half lengthwise RS together, and join to make a tube, taking 1.25 cm/½ in seam allowances. Press seam open. With RS together, pin circle to edge of rectangle, treating exposed zipper tape as fabric edge. Baste and stitch. Attach other circle of fabric to other end of rectangle; finish as for round box-edge cover.

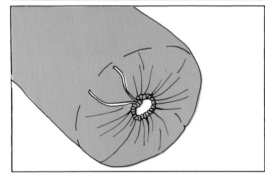

Bolster cover with gathered ends Cut a rectangle the length plus the diameter of the bolster, by the circumference plus 2.5 cm/1 in. Fold in half lengthwise, RS together, and join. Press seam open, turn in and stitch 1.25 cm/½ in at ends of fabric. Turn cover RS out and insert bolster. With a bodkin run tape through each hemmed end, draw up tape ends, tie and tuck in. Cover gap with a patch.

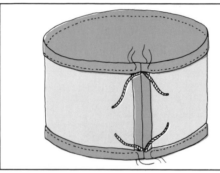

Powder puff cushion Cut a rectangular strip the length of the circumference of the cushion, plus 2.5 cm/1 in, by the width from the centre of the top side to the centre of the bottom. Join short sides RS together. Press seam open. Turn in top and bottom edges 2.5 cm/1 in and stitch. Thread tape, about 10 cm/4 in longer than circumference, through each hem, leaving ends free.

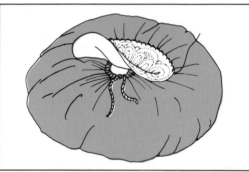

2 Turn cover RS out and insert cushion. Draw up tapes as far as possible and knot securely. Cover small central hole on each side with a circle of fabric, oversewing it in place.

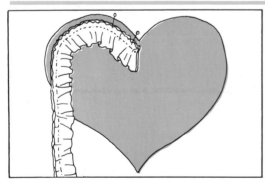

Fancy cushion with frill Cut two pieces of fabric to shape of cushion, plus 1.25 cm/½ in seam allowance all around. For the frill, cut a strip twice the intended finished width, plus 1.25 cm/½ in, and at least one and a half times the cushion's circumference. Fold strip in half lengthwise, RS together, stitch across ends, and turn strip RS out. Gather on seamline. Pin one end of frill to cushion.

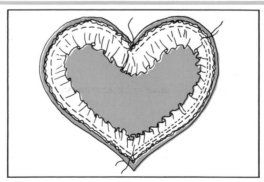

2 Draw up gathers evenly. Pin and baste frill to one of fabric pieces, RS and raw edges together, adjusting the gathering if necessary so that it is full at each corner. Stitch together for approximately one-third of cushion's circumference.

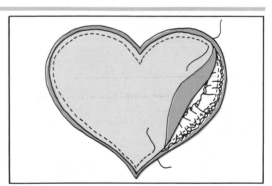

3 Place other cushion shape RS down on top, pin, baste and join remaining two-thirds of circumference where frill is not stitched to first cushion shape, stitching through all three layers. Turn to RS and press under 1.25 cm/½ in seam allowances on unstitched edges, insert cushion and slip stitch edges together.

SLIPCOVERS

A set of well-fitting slipcovers, or loose covers, can give furniture a new lease of life. Chairs of different shapes and styles can be covered in matching or complementing fabrics to form a coordinated group, or a single chair can be covered in a different fabric from the main suite to add variety and interest.

Choose a sturdy, firmly woven fabric to ensure the cover wears well and retains its shape. A medium weight is best as heavy fabrics can be difficult to handle on intricate sections. Make sure the fabric is shrink-resistant if it is to be washed, or shrink it before making up. Also check that it is colourfast.

Linen union—a tough blend of linen and cotton fibres—is traditionally used for slipcovers and lasts well. Chintz is also popular, but is not quite as hard-wearing. Firmly woven synthetic fabrics can be used. Avoid silky fabrics, which show marks easily, and also stretch fabrics, which sag. Most furnishing fabrics are 122 cm/48 in wide.

If there are old slipcovers on the furniture that fit well, use them as a pattern, but do not remove any fixed upholstery fabric as this helps keep padding in shape. Try out and adjust each section as you work to ensure a good fit. Open and piped are the most suitable seams, and corded piping can be made in contrasting or matching fabric. For the latter allow an extra 50 cm/20 in of fabric on an average chair; scraps can also be used.

The basic methods may be adapted for different chair shapes. To avoid wasting fabric, make patterns as instructed for armchair covers for any awkward shapes. For all covers use the sewing machine as much as possible, as machine stitching is more durable.

Equipment

Suitable fasteners are Velcro, extra long zippers with metal or nylon teeth and snap fastener tape. Use T-pins to hold fabric to chair while fitting.

Two types of slipcover pins are available to keep the cover in place: twist-in pins and double-pronged pins.

Use screw-in snaps to attach cover to a wooden base. Insert screw half into base and sew other half to fabric.

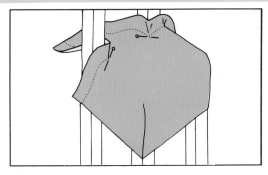

1 Padded dining chair seat Make pattern and cut fabric as for simple stool cover (**1**). Stitch front corners. Place cover RS out on chair and pull back section out between uprights. Starting at front edge, smooth cover over seat. Mark position of uprights on fabric with pins across inside angles.

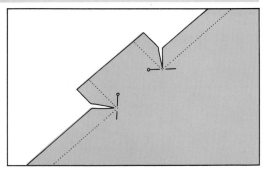

2 Remove fabric from chair and clip it diagonally from edge of angle to pins.

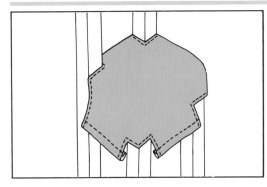

3 Replace cover on chair and pin side hems so they lie neatly on each side of inside angle of upright. Remove cover and trim away excess fabric at side hems. Stitch double hems if there is sufficient fabric; if not, stitch single hems and finish edges. Finish lower edge of cover and insert cord and secure as for simple stool cover (**4**).

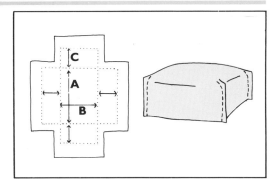

1 Simple stool cover Measure length **A**, width **B** and depth **C** of stool seat. Make a cross-shaped paper pattern, adding 1.25 cm/½ in seam allowances in angles of cross and 5 cm/2 in to each arm of cross to turn under base. Cut out fabric. Baste and stitch corner seams RS together, tapering slightly at top of cover to give a rounded edge to seat. Press seams open.

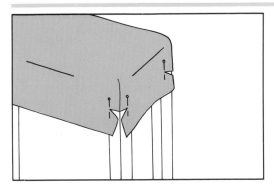

2 Place cover RS up on stool. At each corner insert two pins to mark position of stool leg either side of seam. Remove stitches from base of seam to just below seat level and clip diagonally to pins.

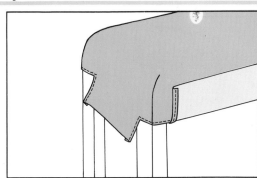

3 Turn under and pin centre section between pins level with base of stool seat to give a neat straight edge across each side of leg. Remove cover and baste and machine central single hem. Trim and turn in a narrow single hem down both sides; baste and machine.

SLIPCOVERS

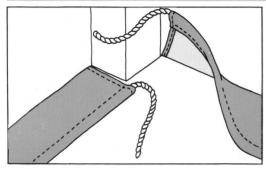

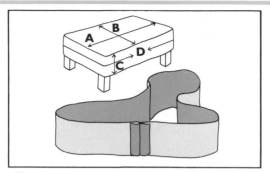

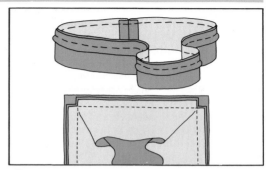

4 Stitch each corner in the same way. Turn up a 4 cm/1½ in double hem along base of each side of seat. Baste and stitch. Place cover on stool RS up. Take a length of cord and thread it through the hem at the base of each side in turn, taking it to inside of legs at corners. Pull ends of string firmly so that cover fits stool tightly, knot them together and tuck ends under hem.

Piped-edge stool cover For top piece, measure length **A** and width **B** of stool top. Add 2.5 cm/1 in seam allowance to each measurement and cut out fabric. Measure depth of seat **C** and add 10 cm/4 in, measure girth of seat **D** and add 2.5 cm/ 1 in seam allowance and cut gusset to these measurements. Place ends RS together and baste and stitch 1.25 cm/½ in seam.

2 Make a piece of corded piping the length of the gusset. Baste piping to top edge of RS of gusset and pin seat section RS down over gusset. Baste and stitch as for piped seam, clipping into seam allowance of gusset and piping at corners and pivoting stitching.

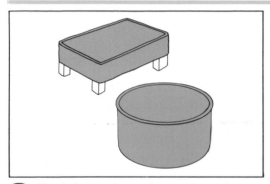

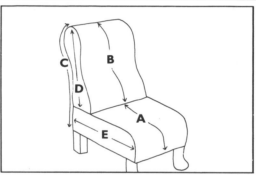

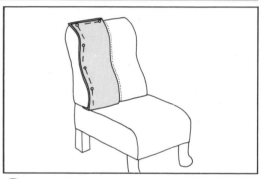

3 Finish lower edge as for simple stool cover, dealing with legs in same way. If suitable use elastic in the hem instead of cord or string. Adapt this cover to fit any shape of stool, but, if the top is not square or rectangular, make an accurate paper pattern for it, adding seam allowances as for standard piped-edge stool cover.

Armless chair There is no need to make a pattern. Estimate fabric needed from three main sections: seat **A**, inside back **B** and outside back **C**. Side gussets **D** and **E** can often be cut from scraps; otherwise allow extra fabric. Measure **A**, **B** and **C** at longest and widest points and add 1.25 cm/½ in seam allowances all around. Add 10 cm/4 in to length of seat and inside back for tucking in.

2 Cut out three main pieces. If chair seat and back are shaped, trim fabric pieces to fit exactly. Draw a chalk line down centre of inside back of chair. Fold fabric down centre and place on chair with fold on chalk line. Pin to side and top of chair and tuck extra 10 cm/4 in down back of seat. Trim to fit, allowing exactly 1.25 cm/½ in for seams at top and sides. Leave fabric pinned to chair.

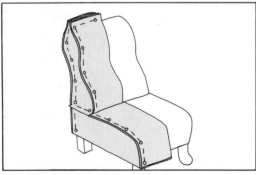

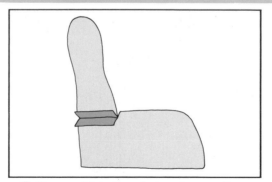

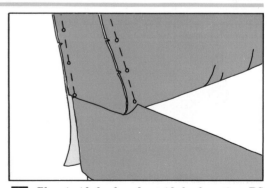

3 Fold other main sections and pin to chair as in (**2**). Tuck extra 10 cm/4 in on seat section down back of seat. Measure longest and widest points of **D** and **E**, adding 2.5 cm/1 in seam allowances to length and width. With fabric on straight grain cut one strip for **D** and one strip for **E**. Pin both gussets to main fabric sections and trim to fit, allowing 1.25 cm/ ½ in for seams.

4 Remove fabric from chair and unpin. Reverse gussets left to right and use as patterns to cut another set. Place one set RS together, the base of gusset **D** to top gusset **E**, so that back gusset aligns with back of seat gusset. Baste and stitch 1.25 cm/½ in seam. Clip seat gusset beside end of stitching and press seam open. Join other set. If required make piping to fit all around gussets.

5 Place inside back and outside back sections RS together, baste and stitch seam at top of back. Press. Place RS out on chair, tucking extra on inside back down back of seat. Pin back side gussets RS out to main pieces, fitting fabric as close to chair as possible. Trim again if necessary; seam allowances should be exactly 1.25 cm/½ in; notch them at intervals to help rematch them exactly.

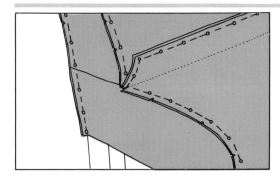

6 Fit seat gussets to seat cover in same way. Clip tuck-in allowances of **A** and **B** where they meet—level with join of back and seat gussets. Pin around edge of tuck-in allowance. Remove fabric from chair and unpin gussets from main sections. If using piping, pin and baste it to outside back, inside back and to seat edges of gussets on RS.

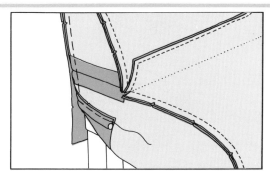

7 Pin main sections to gussets RS together, matching notches, but leave one outside back seam open for fasteners to about three-quarters of way up chair or to its widest part. Arrange clipped allowances of inside back and seat so they fall exactly at corner where gussets join and tuck-in fabric extends. Join gussets to main sections. Baste and stitch seam for tuck-in. Finish and press seams.

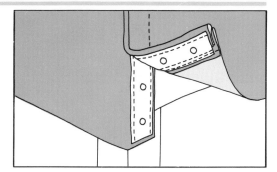

8 Insert zipper, head downward, in unstitched outside back seam, treating piped edge as fabric edge. Or place one half of Velcro or snap fastener tape on RS within seam allowance without piping. Stitch down both edges. Attach second half to RS of opposite seam allowance so it overlaps first half when seam allowance is folded to WS on seamline and piping extends from edge. Topstitch this section.

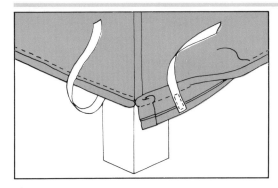

9 Baste and stitch piping to RS of edge on seamline, turning ends under toward cover so they meet. Press seam so piping extends down from lower edge and press seam allowances up toward cover. At edge of leg on each side stitch a length of tape to WS to tie around back of legs and keep cover in place. Topstitch all around edge just above piping through tapes and seam allowances.

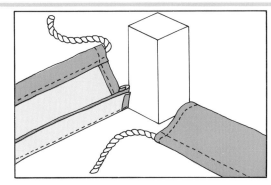

10 Alternatively, attach a false hem with the piping. Cut four fabric strips about 10 cm/ 4 in deep by length of each side of chair plus 2.5 cm/1 in for seam allowances. Stitch narrow double hem at each end of strips and baste and stitch a double hem on bottom of strips. Baste piping and then strips to edge of cover, RS together, and machine. Finish as for simple stool cover.

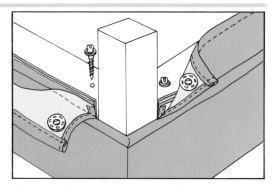

11 On chairs with wooden frames covers can be held in place with special screw-in snaps. Attach a false hem as in (**10**) and turn to underside of chair. Attach well half of snap to underside of fabric hem. Screw snap half into timber beneath. Fasten snap to well to hold fabric down. Use several snaps on each side of chair depending on size.

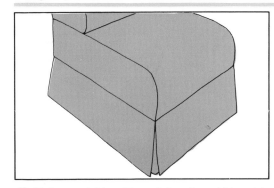

1 **Valances/skirts** For a plain valance/skirt with pleats at the corners, measure from lower edge of cover to within 1.25 cm/½ in of floor and add 4 cm/ 1½ in for a bottom hem and a 1.25 cm/½ in seam allowance. Measure length of each side of chair, adding 7.5 cm/3 in hem allowance to each side. Cut four strips of fabric to these measurements.

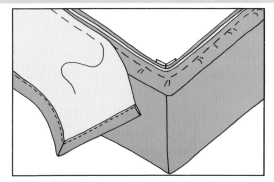

2 Turn in double hems on lower and side edges of all four strips. Remove cover from chair. Make a length of piping to extend around lower edge of cover. Starting at fastened edge, baste piping to lower edge of cover as in armless chair (**9**). Place raw edge of each strip RS down over piping. Make sure hemmed side edges meet at corners. Baste and stitch through all layers.

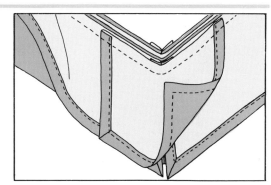

3 Cut four square pieces of fabric the same depth as the valance/skirt, plus double hem allowances on three sides. Turn up and stitch hems. Trim about 1.25 cm/½ in from top of each square so it will not hang below edges. Centre a pleat backing over the three unfastened corners, placing each square RS down on WS of valance/skirt. Baste along seamline and stitch through all thicknesses.

SLIPCOVERS

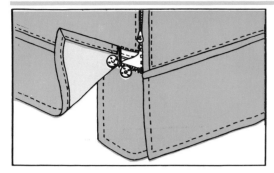

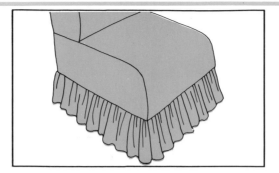

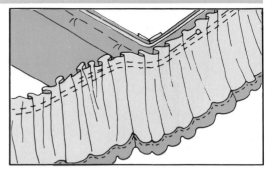

4 At fastened corner stitch half of pleat to one side of cover so that other half extends beyond fastened edge. Finish top edge and stitch one section of a snap to top of extending half. On valance/skirt press seam allowance upward and topstitch above piping if desired. Mark position of second section of snap on seam allowance and attach snap.

Gathered valance/skirt Use only on soft fabrics that drape well. Calculate depth as for plain valance/skirt and measure length, allowing one and a half times the measurement around base of cover for fullness. Cut the valance/skirt strip, joining pieces if necessary, and stitch a double hem on lower and side edges. Make a length of piping to extend around base of cover.

2 Work two rows of gathering stitches around top of strip. Draw up threads until valance/skirt fits base of cover exactly and distribute gathers evenly. Remove cover from chair. Baste piping strip to RS of lower edge of cover along seamline. Starting at fastened corner, pin valance/skirt RS down on cover, matching raw edges. Baste and stitch through all layers.

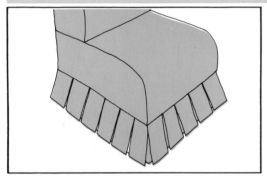

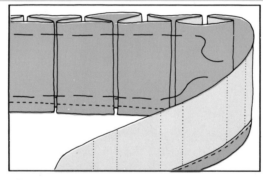

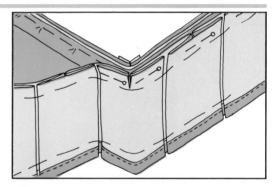

Pleated valance/skirt Box pleats are generally used, with the same width for front and concealed back folds. Calculate depth as for plain valance/skirt. For the length, measure around base of cover and treble the measurement. Add an extra 2.5 cm/1 in for hemming ends. Cut a strip of fabric to these measurements, joining pieces if necessary.

2 Turn in and stitch double hem on lower edge and side ends. Work out size and number of pleats to fit side of chair so that corners of chair come between pleats. Mark pleats and press in place, basting along top and bottom edges as you press. Make a length of piping to extend around lower edge of cover. Remove cover from chair.

3 Baste piping to RS of lower edge of cover along seamline. Starting at fastened corner, place valance/skirt RS down over piping and edge of cover, matching raw edges. Pin in place, positioning so that corner seams of cover come between pleats on RS. Clip at corners. Baste and stitch seam. Press seam allowances upward. Topstitch on RS of cover above piping if desired.

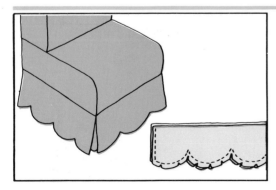

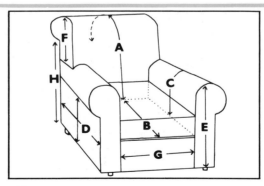

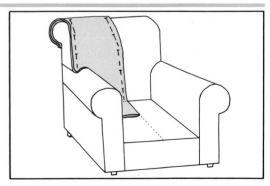

Shaped valance/skirt Measure as for plain valance/skirt; add 1.25 cm/½ in seam allowances all around. Cut two strips for each side. Make a paper pattern of the shaped bottom edge and mark shape on WS of one section on each side. Place sections RS together; stitch along shaping line and each end. Clip curves. Trim seam allowances to 6 mm/¼ in and press. Turn RS out. Attach as for plain valance/skirt.

Armchair Make a fabric pattern, according to the following instructions, for each area of the chair marked on the diagram. Use old sheets or curtains or cheap cotton, as a paper pattern would not stand up to fitting and pinning. Although final seams are only 1.25 cm/½ in, add seam allowances of 2.5 cm/1 in all around so there is room for adjustment if the pattern is not correct.

2 Remove seat cushion. Chalk a line down centre of back **A** and seat **B**. Measure length and width of **A** and cut pattern about 7.5 cm/3 in wider than **A** and at least 20 cm/8 in longer. Fold in half and place on chair, leaving about 2.5 cm/1 in extra at top and rest of extra length at bottom. Pin fabric to chair and trim to 2.5 cm/1 in at top of back and down side to seat, following shape of arm.

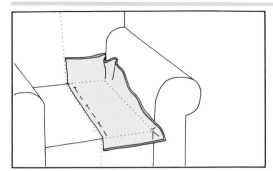

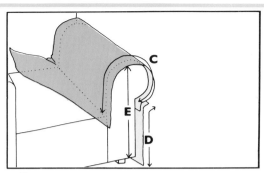

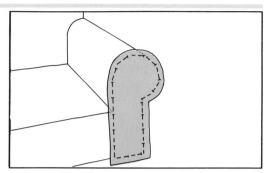

3 Measure seat **B** and cut pattern at least 20 cm/8 in longer and 25 cm/10 in wider. Fold in half and position on chair with fold on chalk line and all extra length except about 2.5 cm/1 in at back of seat. Pin to chair. If necessary trim seam allowance to 2.5 cm/1 in along front edge and at front of sides so pattern piece **B** extends gradually to full width at back edge. (The extra fabric is tucked in later.)

4 The chair arm is in three sections: inside arm and over curve **C**, outside arm beneath curve **D**, and shaped front gusset **E**. Measure length and width of **D** and cut pattern 2.5 cm/1 in larger all around. Measure **C** and cut pattern, adding 12.5 cm/5 in to length of back edge and 10 cm/4 in extra to width for tucking in, tapering to 2.5 cm/1 in extra elsewhere.

5 For arm gusset **E** pin pattern fabric to chair and mark gusset shape with chalk. Cut out pattern, adding 2.5 cm/1 in all around. Cut back gusset pattern **F** in same way. Mark the two gussets to differentiate between them.

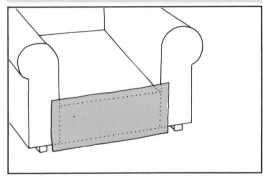

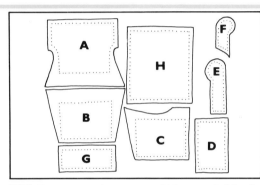

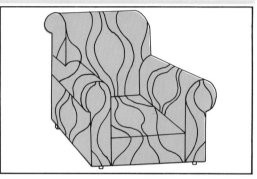

6 Measure depth of front seat area **G** and length of **G** across to inside edge of gusset **E**. Cut pattern 2.5 cm/1 in larger all around. For outside back **H**, pin pattern fabric to chair, mark shape with chalk and cut out pattern 2.5 cm/1 in larger all around. Sections **G**, **D**, **E** and **H** should fall to the same distance from the floor. Decide on the type of valance/skirt, if desired, and measure as for armless chair.

7 To estimate the amount of fabric needed for the eight pattern pieces, lay them out on the floor within the width of the fabric to be used and measure the length needed. Remember that sections **C**, **D**, **E** and **F** must be cut twice. Add extra for the valance/skirt and for matching patterns if the fabric is patterned.

8 With patterned fabric, position motifs carefully on the chair. Centre a large motif on inside back, seat and outside back and, if possible, on the inside and outside of each arm. Centre a motif, not necessarily the main one, on the arm and back gussets. Avoid placing patterned fabric so there is half a motif on one half of a section and nothing on the other half.

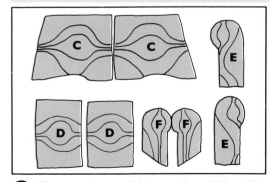

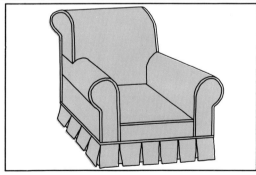

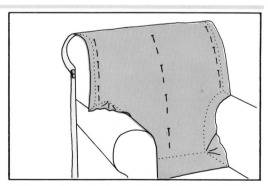

9 To ensure that any fabric motifs are fully visible and can be well positioned, place all pattern pieces on single fabric and on the straight grain. Place gussets **E** and **F** so warp runs vertically top to bottom. Cut out all pieces; reverse **C**, **D**, **E** and **F** to cut a second piece for each. Mark seamlines and centres on all sections.

10 For piping, measure the length of the seams that emphasize the shape of the chair and give definition to its edges—top of seat front, arm front gussets down to valance/skirt, between base of cover and valance/skirt and from top of arm around back gusset and down to valance/skirt at back. Make separate lengths of piping for each seam.

11 Place back section **A** and outside back **H** RS together and baste and stitch 2.5 cm/1 in open seam along top edges. Trim seam allowances to 1.25 cm/½ in and finish this seam and all subsequent seams. Press seam open. Place back sections on chair RS out and pin in place down sides and centre, making sure top back seam is straight and any fabric motif is centred.

SLIPCOVERS

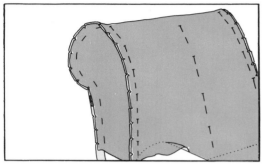

12 Position gussets **F** on chair RS out. Pin to edges of main back sections **A** and **H**, fitting fabric as close to chair as possible. Adjust until fabric fits chair tightly and then carefully trim seam allowances to exactly 1.25 cm/½ in beyond pins. Notch seam allowances at intervals to help match seams at next stage. Unpin and remove fabric from chair.

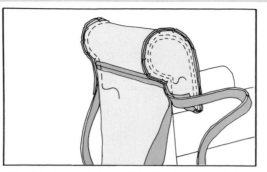

13 Baste piping to RS of back gussets **F** along seamlines, clipping around curves. At back edge, leave piping long enough to reach to top of valance/skirt. Do not pipe lower edge of gussets. With RS together, pin and baste gussets **F** to **A** and **H**, placing main sections over piping and matching notches. Stitch as for a piped seam; press seam allowances toward gusset.

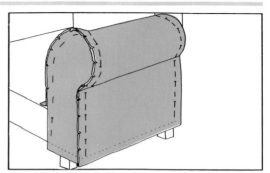

14 Join sections **C** and **D**, RS together, with a 2.5 cm/1 in open seam. Trim seam allowances to 1.25 cm/½ in. Place joined sections RS out on chair and pin in place, checking that seam is straight and that it falls just below the curved part of the outer arm. Fit front arm gussets **E** in same way as back gussets (**12**), trimming and notching seam allowances. Remove all pins and take fabric off chair.

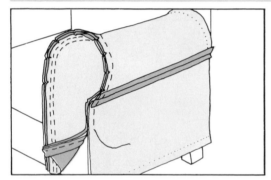

15 Baste piping to RS of front arm gussets **E** along seamlines, clipping piping around curves to fit. Do not pipe lower edges. With RS together, pin and baste gussets **E** to joined arm sections **C** and **D**, placing arm sections over piping and matching notches. Stitch as for a piped seam and press seam allowances toward gusset.

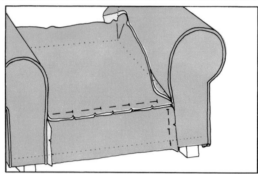

16 Place seat cover **B** and arm covers RS up in position. Pin front strip **G** to seat cover **B**, matching centres, and pin **G** to gusset **E**. Adjust pins for a good fit, trim and notch seams as in (**12**). Unpin and take **B** and **G** off chair, leaving arm sections in place. Baste piping to RS of top edge of seat front **G** on seamline. Place **B** RS down on **G**, matching notches, and stitch as for a piped seam. Press.

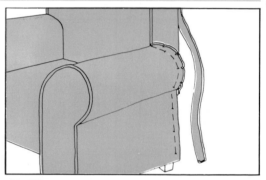

17 Place joined back sections on chair RS up. Pin seams between arm sections **C** and **D** and back sections **F** and **H** on each side, starting at inner edge of back gusset **F**. Adjust pins so fabric fits well, trim and notch seam allowances as in (**12**). Unpin and remove fabric from chair. On one side of chair only baste seam RS together, sandwiching piping extending from **F** in seam. Stitch and press.

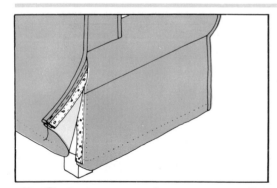

18 At the opposite side join arm section **C** to back gusset **F** only. To complete seam between **D** and **H**, baste end of piping to edge of **H**. Choose a zipper to extend three-quarters of the height of the chair or to the widest part. Insert zipper, Velcro or snap tape as for armless chair (**8**). Baste and stitch sides of seat front **G** to front of arm gusset **E**, RS together, as for piped seam.

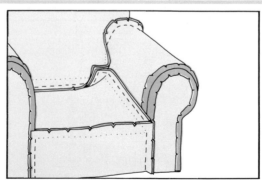

19 With RS together, baste and stitch seam on each side between **A** and back edge of **C**. No fitting is necessary as seams are later tucked in around seat. With RS together, join sides and back of seat **B** to seat edge of arms **C** and of inside back **A**. Trim edges if necessary to help them fit together, but make sure there is still sufficient surplus for tucking down back and sides of seat.

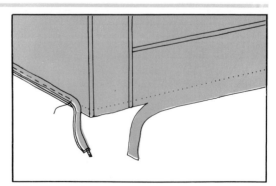

20 Place cover on chair. Smooth it into position, pulling it down and tucking it in around seat. Close fastener. Trim lower unfinished edge level all around. Baste piping to RS of lower edge. To finish with a valance/skirt, check required depth and attach to edge of cover. Alternatively, finish base as for armless chair. Cover loose cushions as for box cushion (see p. 169).

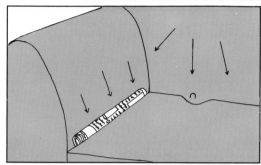

21 For a good finish, pull cover into place firmly and anchor it by inserting slipcover pins through fabric into padding down sides and back of seat. Alternatively, push rolled-up newspaper down into tuck-in around seat to wedge cover down. Disguise any lumpy areas in the chair padding by arranging a layer of upholstery wadding on the chair before putting on the cover.

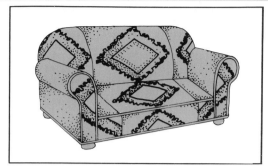

Sofa Adapt basic armchair instructions by adding an extra central panel of fabric to the inside back, outside back, seat and front of seat. Place any fabric design centrally on these panels. If the sofa is wide enough, use the whole width of fabric for the central panels and match the side panels to them. Allow extra fabric on each panel for seams. Join panels and proceed as for armchair.

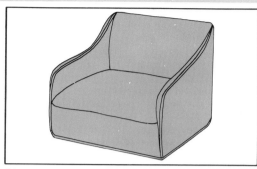

Narrow-armed chair No back opening is needed for a fastening and an arm gusset is unnecessary. Join outer arm to outer back and then join inner arm to inside back, allowing enough extra between them for tucking in. Join inner and outer sections with or without piping around top of arms and back. Add front and seat pieces, allowing tuck-in at sides and back of seat.

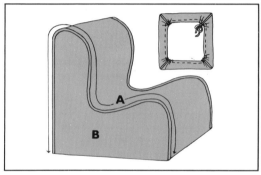

Foam unit seating This type of furniture is easy to cover as there are only three sections: one long centre piece **A** extending down the back and front and two side gussets **B**. Cut out the sections, allowing about 15 cm/6 in extra fabric on all lower edges. Join with piped or open seams. Double hem lower edges and thread with elastic or cord to hold them under base of chair.

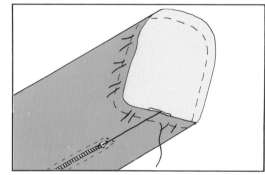

Foam-filled furniture For a softer look omit piping and gather fabric into shape. Measure each cushion and cut fabric, adding 7.5 cm/3 in at each end. Cut out two gussets for each cushion, 5 cm/2 in smaller in diameter than ends of cushion. Stitch base seam, inserting in the centre a zipper long enough to enable the cushion to be removed easily. Run a row of gathers around each end of cover.

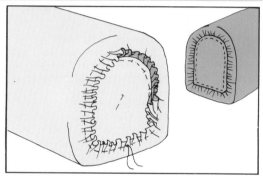

2 Place cover WS up on cushion. Pull up gathers. Place each gusset RS down on gathered end and pin to cushion in centre. Tuck gusset into gathered end and, pulling out edge of gusset as you work, pin gusset to gathered edge RS together. Remove cover. Baste and stitch gussets to cover and press seams toward gussets. Topstitch close to edges of gussets to hold gathers.

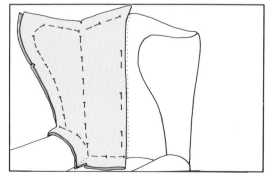

Wing chair Cut inside back pattern in one piece. Chalk a line down centre of chair, fold pattern and place it on line, with tuck-in allowance at bottom and about 2.5 cm/1 in extra at top as for armchair (**2**). Pin pattern fabric together around edges. To fit pattern, pin it very closely to chair down inside angle of wing and chair back. If insufficient fabric is allowed, the cover will be too tight.

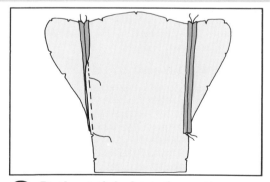

2 Divide outside back into three sections: centre back and two wings. Cut and fit all three. Stitch one wing to centre back and baste the other in place. Fit and pin outside back to inside back, trim and notch seam allowances, then unpin. Starting at the top, stitch 10 cm/4 in of the second wing seam on outside back. Choose a zipper long enough to extend from end of stitching to bottom of outside back.

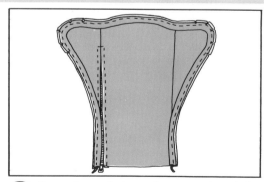

3 Insert base of zipper into seam just below stitching. On centre back edge stitch zipper down entire length. On other edge stitch down to bottom of wing. Baste piping around top and sides of outside back, treating unstitched side of zipper as outer edge of outside back. Join inside and outside back along top and down sides as for piped seam, matching notches. Proceed as for armchair.

CURTAINS

Professional-looking curtains are well within the scope of even a complete novice. The two basic requirements are a sewing machine and the ability to stitch in a straight line.

Start by choosing a fabric to go with your colour scheme and décor and decide on the style of curtain heading before buying the fabric, as the heading governs the amount you need. Remember to add extra for matching patterns and for shrinkage. Never skimp on the amount of fabric allowed for fullness. Styles such as pencil pleats will not hang well if the full amount of fabric is not used and the appearance of the curtains will be spoiled.

Most curtain fabric is 120 cm/48 in wide, although wider fabrics are also available; curtain lining is a little narrower so that it does not have to be trimmed before being sewn.

Modern lightfast chemical dyes have minimized the problem of fading, but some fabrics such as printed cottons still have a tendency to fade, so avoid using them in a very sunny room. As strong sunlight also weakens fabric fibres, line the curtains to prolong their life in addition to preventing fading.

As well as thinking about colour, pattern and texture, bear in mind, when choosing the fabric, that curtains give privacy, help to reduce noise and add to the warmth and comfort of the room. If you have draughty windows, it is well worth spending extra money on specially treated lining fabrics that provide insulation.

Remember, too, that curtains are not only for windows. Sheers and semi-sheers, hung from ceiling tracks, can make attractive room dividers, while a simple curtain in front of low shelving makes an instant cupboard and can hide a multitude of odds and ends.

MEASURING CURTAINS
If possible, install tracks and rods before measuring for curtains. They are fitted in different positions depending on the window shape and the style of the curtains.

Inside the window recess
Spring wires, rods and tracks for net and sheer curtains are generally fitted inside the window recess, **A**, and should be close to the top. Multiply measurement **A** two and a half or three times (depending on the desired style of the curtain heading) for the fullness of the curtains. Take measurement **B** for the length and add about 20 cm/8 in for hems.

If a straight track is fitted on a dormer window, the curtains may cover too much of the window and block out the light when they are drawn back. To prevent this, if the recess walls on either side of the window are deep

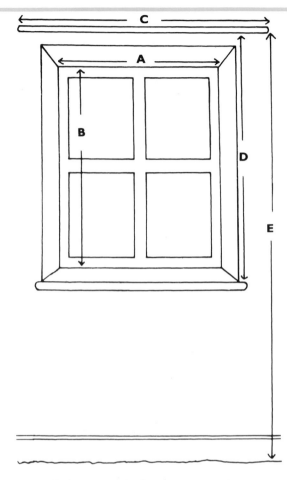

enough, buy a track about 15 cm/6 in longer than the width of the window and at each end carefully bend 7.5 cm/3 in to fit around the recess. The curtains can then hang against the side walls.

Measure for half-length café curtains fitted inside the recess in the same way. Their length depends on the height of the rod from the window sill; extra fabric may be needed for a fancy heading or if the curtains extend outside the recess.

Outside the window recess
Where possible, a wall-mounted track or rod should extend a little to either side of the window to allow for maximum daylight when the curtains are open. The amount of the extension depends on the overall proportions of the window and the thickness of the fabric when bunched together.

For sill-length curtains take measurement **C** and multiply according to the type of curtain heading to be used. Take measurement **D** for length and add about 20 cm/8 in for hems. Sill-length curtains should hang clear of the sill by about 2.5 cm/1 in to prevent wear along the bottom. Or if draughts are a problem, let the curtains hang slightly below the sill.

For floor-length curtains take measurement **C**, and multiply for fullness, and measurement **E**, adding on 20 cm/8 in for hems. Floor-length curtains should clear the floor by about 2.5 cm/1 in.

For floor-to-ceiling curtains, the track can be fixed to the top of the wall or to the ceiling. Neat, unobtrusive ceiling tracks are obtainable, but be sure to fix them securely—a batten screwed into the ceiling joists gives good support. Measure the length of the track, **C**, and multiply for fullness: measure from track to floor and add about 20 cm/8 in for hems. With ceiling tracks use a tape with pockets at the top; special hooks may also be needed, depending on the style of heading and weight of the fabric.

Headings
Curtain headings can be straight or gathered or have pencil or pinch pleats. For a straight heading no extra fullness is needed; make it with cotton heading tape. Special tape is available for all three shaped styles.

Gathered headings are the simplest and usually the most economical on fabric. Allow at least one and a half times the track length for fullness.

Pleated headings are particularly suitable for floor-length nets and sheers. Pencil pleats normally need about two and a half to three times the track length for the best result. Wide pleating tape is available with pockets nearer to one edge than the other. If you want a firm stand-up heading to cover a plain track (the pockets are nearer the bottom edge), add the depth of the tape to the length of the fabric required.

The various tapes for single, double or triple pinch pleats differ in fabric requirements. As estimating the amount required can be complicated, take the track measurements with you when buying the tape and fabric and ask the shop assistant for advice on the amount needed for fullness. When estimating the length of the fabric, decide whether you want the hook pockets at the top or bottom of the tape, as for pencil pleats.

If draw cords are to be used, the curtains must fit the width of the track exactly.

Joining widths and placing patterns
Join pieces of fabric selvage to selvage, to obtain required width. The cut edge should be to the outside of the window. Join plain, colour-woven fabrics with a narrow open seam, clipping selvages to allow fabric to drop evenly. If selvage is wide and a different colour, trim off and join widths with French seams. Match patterns carefully at seams; they must also match up where curtain edges meet when closed.

CURTAIN FITTINGS

Metal track with wall bracket and gliders; mainly for heavy curtains. Can be fitted with draw cords and a 7.5 cm/3 in overlap extension track, below, at the centre of the window. An alternative form of extension, for use with two separate rails, each longer than half the width of the window, consists of two plastic end stops for the track and a central metal bracket. The bracket has two grooves into which the tracks are slotted; it can be fixed to the top or side of the window recess.

White plastic track with gliders; unobtrusive and ideal for curtains without pelmets/valances. Obtainable in different clip-on or stick-on finishes such as teak, silver, gold and other colours.

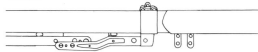

Slimline track in plastic or metal with ceiling fitting; for curtains fixed to the ceiling or to inside top of the window recess. Ideal for lightweight nets and sheers.

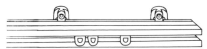

Traditional wooden café curtain pole with wooden rings and wall-mounted brackets. Available in different wood finishes and colours.

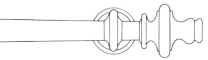

Traditional brass rail with brass rings and wall-mounted brackets. Made in many designs and diameters for all weights of curtain.

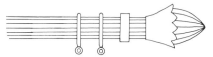

Imitation brass pole with a concealed track; the gliders look like rings from the front. Can be fitted with draw córds.

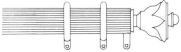

Plastic-coated spring wire attached by hooks and eyelets within the window recess. Generally used for sheers, nets and other lightweight curtains.

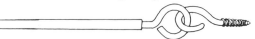

Brackets for fixing slimline wooden or brass rails to the inside of a window recess. Can be face-fitting (fixed to the wall behind the curtain), (**1**) and (**2**), or end-fitting (fixed to the wall on the side of the window), (**3**). Various sizes take different diameter rails. Generally used with lightweight or café curtains.

Rings For narrow rods or spring wires use small nylon or plastic rings (**1**), which are non-corrosive and washable. The ring is sewn onto the curtain. Alternatively, slot a split brass ring (**2**) through pocket tape or through the fabric instead of hooks. For wooden poles use a heavy wooden ring (**3**). A curtain hook is passed through the small eyelet at the ring base. Hollow brass rings (**4**) for brass rails are made in a range of sizes and fixed to the curtain in the same way as wooden rings. Hang shower curtains with metal pin rings (**5**) inserted through sail eyelets (**6**) at top of curtain. Eyelets are sold with instructions and a tool for inserting them.

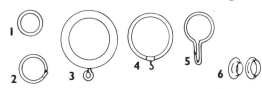

Weighted tape, below left, consists of small pieces of lead encased in a fabric tube. Insert in bottom curtain hem for a better hang. **Curtain weights**, below right, are small button-like pieces of lead. Attach at intervals to bottom of shirred sheers.

Equipment for headings

Special tapes and hooks are available for making different styles of curtain heading and for hanging the curtains. Headings can also be shaped by hand using standard heading tape.

Cotton heading tape; white and coloured available.

Gathering tape for a gathered heading; available in cotton, nylon or polyester, in white, cream or a variety of colours.

Pencil pleat tape for a pencil pleat heading; available in cotton/nylon or nylon/polyester. Sheer pleating tape is also available for sheers and nets.

Pinch pleat tape for single, double and triple pleats, in cotton/nylon or polyester/nylon. Pleats are made at set intervals by gathering up the cords.

Metal pronged hook for use with pinch pleat tape without cords for triple pleats at variable intervals.

Cotton lining tape

Standard hooks for use with gathering and pleat tapes. Left, clear plastic, white plastic; right, brass, steel.

Pin hook for gathered and pleated headings made with standard heading tape; the point pierces fabric.

Plastic cord pull keeps the end of the cord out of the way behind the curtain and prevents tangling. It is hung by a hook from one of the tape pockets at outside edge of curtains.

Cording set with draw cords for straight runs of curtain (and some shallow bay windows) saves wear and tear and soiling of the curtains. Available in a range of sizes and styles to fit different tracks. The draw cord is joined to the two gliders at inside edges of curtain and draws the curtain open or closed.

Pelmet/valance bracket and rail for simple gathered pelmets or valances. Can be fitted to most windows over the curtain track.

Right-angled brackets, below left, or **"glass" plates made of brass**, below right, can be used to fix the sides of a box pelmet/valance frame to the wall. The plates screw into the sides of the frame.

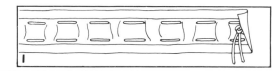

MAKING CURTAIN HEADINGS

There are three ways to shape a curtain heading using tape specially prepared for each method.

Gathered heading

Cut a piece of standard gathering tape about 7.5 cm/3 in longer than the top edge of the curtain, draw out 4 cm/1½ in of the cords at one end of the tape and knot them together. Trim off surplus tape and fold end over knotted cords on WS (**1**).

CURTAINS

Turn down and baste a single hem at curtain top. Place tape RS up with folded end on one side of curtain and over raw edge of hem (**2**).

Baste in place, leaving about 4 cm/1½ in extra tape at the other end. Take out cords from extra tape back to curtain edge; trim end of tape and fold under, leaving ends of cord free. Sew the tape to the curtain, stitching close to top and bottom edges and avoiding cords (**3**).

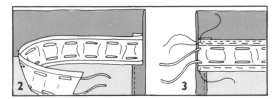

Fasten off thread securely and press curtains well. Draw up cords until the curtain measures half the track width and knot free ends of cord together. Repeat for second curtain, leaving loose cords at opposite side of curtain. The cords on both curtains should be at the outside of the window. Place hooks in tape at intervals of about 7.5 cm/3 in (**4**).

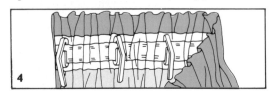

Pencil pleats

Turn down top hem 2 cm/¾ in. Draw out 4 cm/1½ in of cord at both ends of tape; knot cords at one end only. At this end, trim off surplus tape and turn under as for gathered heading. Place tape close to top of hem (**5**) and attach as for gathered heading.

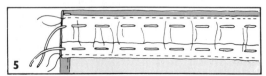

If you want to hang the curtains from a decorative rail without obscuring it, apply tape with pockets toward the top. Use the other way up for a firm stand-up heading to cover a plain track. Draw up pleats evenly and insert hooks every 5 to 7.5 cm/2 to 3 in (**6**), depending on the weight of the fabric.

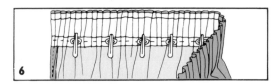

Pinch pleats

Attach tape to curtains as for pencil pleats (**7**).

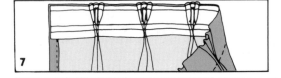

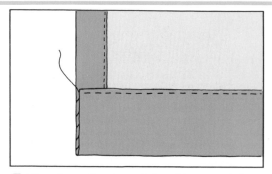

1 **Simple unlined curtains** Measure window according to style of curtains required and cut fabric. Turn in 1.25 cm/½ in double hem down each side of curtain, clipping any selvages, and baste. Machine hem or hand sew satins and velvets. At bottom edge press up a 1.25 cm/½ in fold and turn up again to form a double hem. Stitch hem and slip stitch folded edges at hem corners.

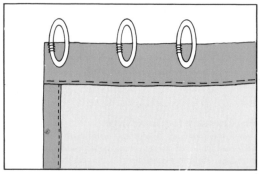

3 Stitch hem by hand or machine, depending on fabric. If the heading is not to be gathered (leave fabrics such as brocades and heavily patterned sheers ungathered to show off their design), sew hooks or rings to top edge of curtain.

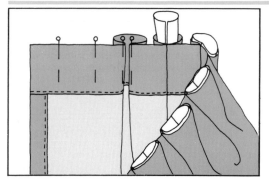

5 Simple pleats can be made without pleating tape. Decide on width of pleats and spaces between them. Measure and mark pleats on WS along top hem. Bring marks together and on RS baste and stitch down them at right angles to top of curtain for 5 to 7.5 cm/2 to 3 in. Insert cartridge paper tubes into each pleat to hold the shape. Insert pin hooks in back of alternate pleats.

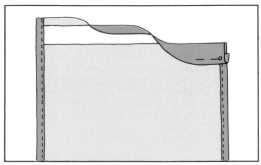

2 For a crisper look, stiffen top of curtains with iron-on interfacing. Cut interfacing 1.25 cm/½ in narrower than intended depth of top hem and iron it to WS of fabric 1.25 cm/½ in from raw edge. Do not overlap ends on side hems. Turn the 1.25 cm/½ in over it, pin and baste hem. (If using gathering tape for heading—see p. 179—cut interfacing to same depth as top hem and place it along fabric edge.)

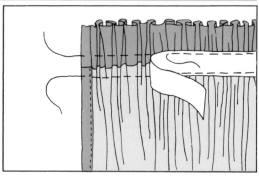

4 To make a gathered heading without gathering tape, work a row of gathering about 2.5 cm/1 in above turned-down edge, and another row 2.5 cm/1 in below. Draw up threads until curtain is the right width and distribute gathers evenly. Pin, baste and machine ordinary 2.5 cm/1 in tape along rows of gathering over edges of top hem. Remove gathering threads; insert pin hooks or split rings in tape.

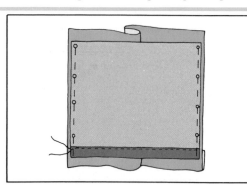

1 **Simple lined curtains** Cut out curtains. Cut lining 15 cm/6 in shorter than curtain and about 12.5 cm/5 in narrower. Turn up double hem of 7.5 cm/3 in at bottom of curtain and 5 cm/2 in at bottom of lining and machine with a long loose stitch. With RS together, pin lining 5 cm/2 in from top edge of curtain so bottom of lining hem overlaps top of curtain hem by about 2.5 cm/1 in.

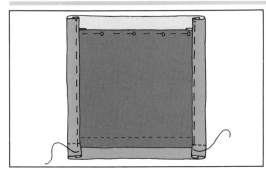

2 Baste and stitch side edges of curtain and lining together, leaving 1.25 cm/½ in seam allowances. Clip selvages and press seams open. Turn curtain RS out and lay it RS down. Fold in equal seam allowances on both sides so lining is centred on back of curtain. Baste, making sure neither fabric nor lining is creased or puckered. Pin and baste top edge of lining to curtain.

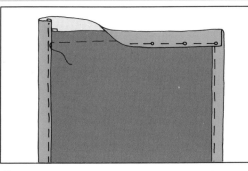

3 Press side edges. Turn down a single hem at top of curtain over lining edge, pin and baste. Attach curtain tape (see p. 179). Alternatively, turn down double hem, stitch and hand pleat as desired. Remove all basting. Interfacing is not usually necessary. For a very stiff hem for hand pleating, attach interfacing to top hem allowance before turning down hem as for unlined curtains (**2**).

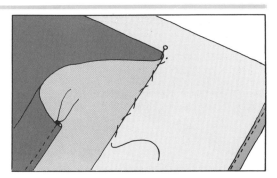

Extra wide curtains Linings may need anchoring. Make up curtain and linings separately, with side and lower hems as for unlined curtains. Place curtain RS down with lining centred, RS up, 5 cm/2 in from top. Pin lining to curtain down centre, turn back one side and catch with large, loose slip hemming. Repeat at intervals between centre and edges. Slip hem side hems together and finish as for lined curtains (**3**).

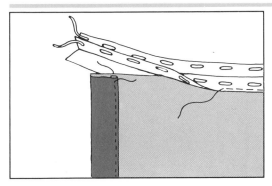

1 **Detachable linings** are made with lining tape and can be used with most heading tapes with pockets. Linings need not be as full as curtains, e.g. on triple-pleated curtains. Cut out lining fabric as for unlined curtains and double hem along sides and bottom so lining is 2.5 to 5 cm/1 to 2 in shorter than curtain. Slip top edge between bottom edges of tape. Baste and machine along bottom of tape.

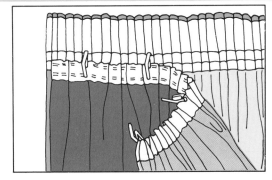

2 Knot cords of tape at one end and draw up at the other as for curtain tapes. Distribute gathers evenly. Join lining to curtains by curtain hooks, pushing hooks through slots in top of lining tape, up into pockets of main curtain tape and through into rings or gliders on track.

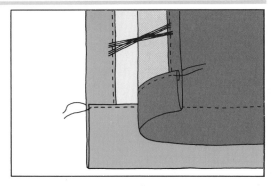

3 To keep linings neatly in place at sides of curtains, work long catch stitches between lining and curtain at intervals down sides. This allows some give and stops the edges puckering. Alternatively, slip stitch edges of lining and curtain loosely together, or sew on snap fasteners at intervals on side hems, stitching to seam allowances only so they cannot be seen from RS.

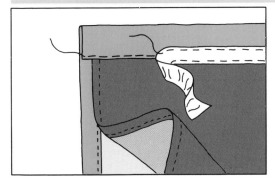

Stretch or loosely woven fabrics Cut curtain and lining as for lined curtains. Make up separately, with side hems as for unlined curtains. Stitch double hem along bottom of lining. Baste lower, double hem of curtain. Join curtain and lining together and finish heading. Hang curtain for a few days to drop. Adjust lower curtain hem if necessary and machine. Slip hem lining to curtain down side hems.

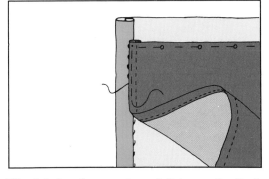

Pile fabrics Cut curtain and lining as for lined curtains, but make them up separately, with side and lower hems as for unlined curtains. Stitch curtain hems by hand to avoid marking the pile. With WS together, centre lining on curtain and pin top of lining 5 cm/2 in from top edge of curtain. Baste and slip hem lining to curtain down side hems. Finish heading by machine.

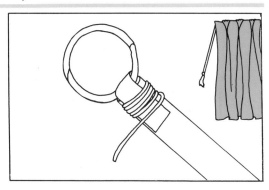

Draw rods Easy-to-reach draw rods save handling curtains. To make rod, hold a split curtain ring against end of a length of thin dowelling with a piece of tape and bind tape ends tightly with string. Attach rod to curtain by passing ring through end pocket of heading tape at inside edge. Bind rod with bias or ribbon to match curtain, or decorate with braid and trim bottom with a tassel.

CURTAINS

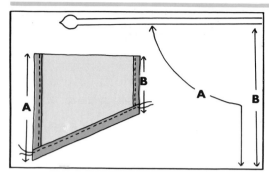

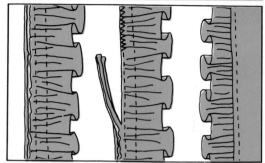

Draped curtains If curtains are to be permanently drawn back, make inside edge **A** longer than outside edge **B** so hemline appears straight. Take measurement **A** from where open curtain will fall on rail and loop tape measure loosely up to side and then down to hem length. Take measurement **B** from rail to hem length. Cut curtain twice desired width to allow for fullness and construct with sloping hem.

1 **Frilled edge for drawn-back curtains** Measure longer side of curtain. Cut strip of fabric one and a half times this length and double the width of the finished frill, plus two 1.25 cm/$\frac{1}{2}$ in seam allowances. Fold frill in half lengthwise RS together, stitch across ends and turn RS out. Keeping raw edges level, work two rows of gathering close to seamline. Draw up gathering threads until frill fits curtain.

2 Distribute gathers evenly and, with RS together, pin and baste raw edges of strip to edge of curtain. Stitch along seamline. Stitch again, halfway between raw edge and seam; then trim away fabric close to second line of stitching. Zigzag all raw edges together with closely set stitches; press seam toward curtain so frill extends out from curtain and on RS topstitch along middle of seam allowance.

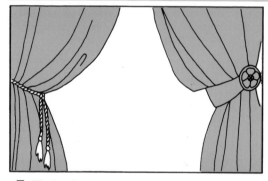

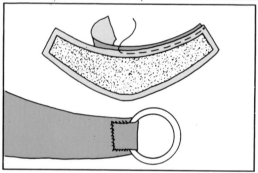

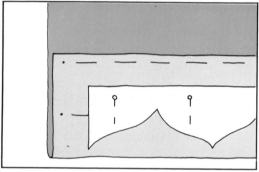

1 **Tie backs** Curtains can be drawn back and fixed to hooks or brackets on the wall with matching fabric tie backs, chains or a tasselled cord. Some brackets have chains to go around the curtain, others stand out from the wall so the curtains fit behind. For a simple tie back, fix a hook in the wall behind the curtain, thread a cord over it and tie the cord around the front of the curtain.

2 For a matching tie back, cut two curved strips of fabric long enough to go loosely around curtain. To WS of one, attach iron-on interfacing 1.25 cm/$\frac{1}{2}$ in smaller all around than fabric. With RS together, join long curved edges of fabric strips with a 1.25 cm/$\frac{1}{2}$ in seam. Press RS out. Slip a curtain ring over each end, turn back 1.25 cm/$\frac{1}{2}$ in and hem. Hang rings on wall hooks behind or at side of curtain.

1 **Shaped hems** Prepare hem before stitching the lining to the curtain. From a piece of folded paper cut a repeat pattern for the hem. Cut curtain to required size, allowing pattern depth plus 5 cm/2 in for bottom hem. Turn lower hem allowance up on RS of fabric and hold with several lines of basting. Place pattern 1.25 cm/$\frac{1}{2}$ in from fold on hem and 5 cm/2 in from one end. Pin in place.

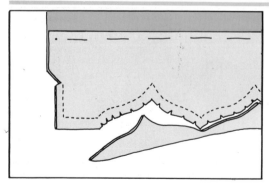

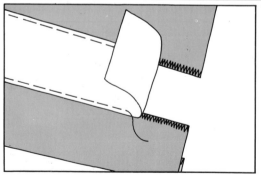

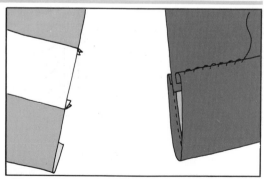

2 Chalk around shaped edges of pattern. Remove pattern. Baste and stitch along shape. Also stitch a 1.25 cm/$\frac{1}{2}$ in vertical seam at each end of curtain the depth of the pattern. Clip into side seam allowance at top of stitching. Trim seams to 5 mm/$\frac{1}{4}$ in, clip curves and turn RS out. Finish hem and proceed as for simple lined curtains, cutting lining to finish 2.5 cm/1 in above top of decoration.

1 **Lengthening curtains** Insert a lengthening band rather than letting curtains down, since the old hemline generally shows. If curtains are only slightly short, insert wide braid. Free bottom of lining from curtain; measure from bottom of curtain the depth at which you want to insert braid, cut along line and zigzag raw edges. Overlap braid on edges and stitch in place. Let down lining.

2 If curtains are very short, insert a band of contrasting fabric. Cut a strip the width needed, plus 2.5 cm/1 in for seam allowances. Cut curtain bottom as before and join raw edges of strip and curtain, RS together. Press seams toward strip. Let down lining and join lining fabric twice the extra width needed to the bottom, RS together. Press. Turn up new fabric and hem to seamline.

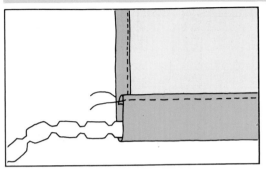

Weighted hems All curtains, except very heavy ones, and nets and sheers in particular, hang better if the bottom hem is weighted down with weighted tapes. The tapes consist of small pieces of lead enclosed in a fabric tube, which is passed through the bottom hem when the curtain is finished. Available in different grades, the tapes are very flexible and can be used even on full, gathered curtains.

NETS AND SHEERS

There are many suitable natural and synthetic fabrics, the choice ranging from fine, almost transparent nets and sheers to heavy textured, patterned and coloured weaves. Many nets and sheers, especially cotton ones, shrink, so buy extra material if necessary. If the fabric is not too bulky, wash it before cutting out. Otherwise, baste generous hems in place until after the first wash. Then adjust and sew permanently.

Nets and sheers are hung from tracks or poles if they are to be opened, spring wires if they are to stay closed. They are made in the same way as simple unlined curtains with a few minor differences. For example, if you are using several drops of fabric for one window, leave them separate. Lost in the folds, the selvages are less conspicuous than seams and the curtains are easier to wash.

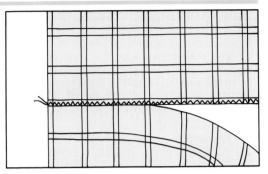

Cutting nets/sheers level Carefully follow the line of the weave to ensure the cut edge is level. Prevent excess fraying on cotton and some synthetic fabrics by zigzagging along cutting line first, and then cut fabric outside the stitched line. With a large-holed pattern cut along the solid part of the design, to give a definite edge to turn in and hem.

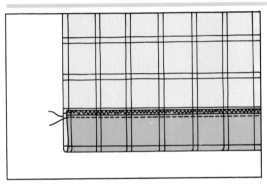

Stitching the hem Sometimes only a single turning is needed, especially if you have stitched before cutting. Fold fabric along centre of a pattern repeat or between patterns, whether the hem is to be single or double. This makes the hem neater and less noticeable as the holes in the pattern on the turnings fall exactly over those on RS. Use a long stitch and a loose tension and keep fabric taut.

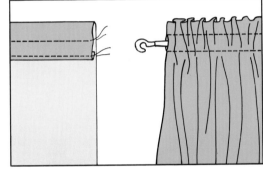

Self-heading can be used with a spring wire on narrow windows or dowelling or a slim brass rod on wider ones. Allow about 5 cm/2 in top hem for a spring wire, a little more for a rod. Turn down 1.25 cm/½ in and turn down fabric again to make a 4 cm/1½ in hem. Stitch close to hem edge and then about 2 cm/¾ in from it. Insert wire or rod in lower channel of hem to leave top edge as a frill.

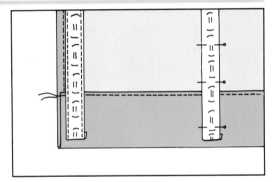

Shirred curtains Cut and join fabric so it is one and a quarter times track width, plus hem allowances, and about two and a half times desired length. Hem curtain, with self-heading at top. On WS stitch lightweight gathering tape vertically every 15 cm/6 in, finishing 1.25 cm/½ in from bottom. Knot cords and turn under tape at lower end as for gathered heading. Leave cords free at top.

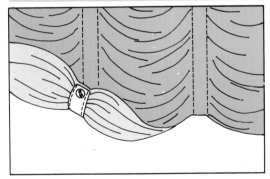

2 Draw up cords so curtain fits length of window and distribute gathers evenly down each tape. Hide ends of cords in cord pulls or by winding them around small pieces of cardboard and pinning these on WS of top hem. For a better hang on very lightweight fabrics, sew curtain weights to lower end of each piece of tape before hanging the curtains.

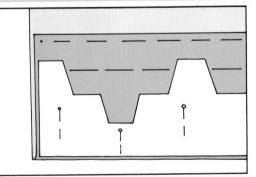

Fancy hems can be made with doubled fabric. Hem bottom is straight, but top edge is stitched to form a pattern. Work out a fairly simple pattern on paper. Turn up a single hem slightly deeper than the pattern shape and hold in place with several lines of basting. Pin pattern to fabric and mark shaped edge on fabric with tailor's chalk, pencil or basting. Remove pattern.

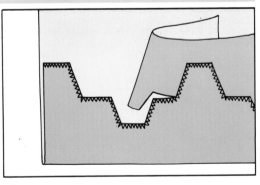

2 Set the machine to a medium-width, fairly close zigzag with a loose tension and stitch carefully along marked lines. Keep fabric taut while you stitch and do not allow it to pucker within the zigzag. A coloured thread adds to the decorative effect. Carefully trim away surplus hem allowance above stitching with small sharp scissors.

CURTAINS

CAFE CURTAINS

The perfect screen, café curtains hang across the lower half of a window from a rod or pole, to which they are attached by rings or fabric loops. The spacing of the loops and rings, and the width and depth of the loops depend on the thickness of the rod, the size of the window and the finished effect desired.

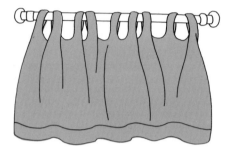

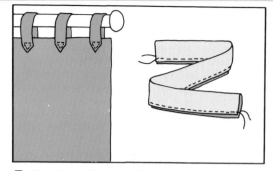

1 **Simple unlined café curtains** Hem a rectangle of fabric the required size. To make the loops, cut a long strip of fabric twice the finished width desired, plus two 1.25 cm/½ in seam allowances. Fold in half lengthwise and stitch with RS together.

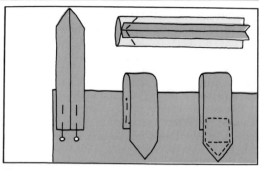

2 Cut strip into lengths, twice as long as finished loop. Press seam open down centre of each length and stitch a right-angled point at one end, trimming excess fabric. Turn RS out. Pin and baste unstitched end of one loop to RS of curtain top, so about two-thirds extends at top, and turn down shaped end over this to cover raw edge. Pin and baste; stitch to curtain through all thicknesses as shown.

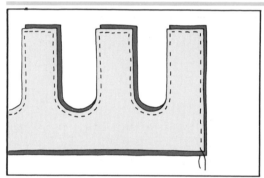

1 **Scalloped-top café curtains** Decide on number and width of tabs and width of curved spaces between them. To length of curtain add depth of scallop, plus 1.25 cm/½ in seam allowance. For fabric tabs extending from curtain, allow enough to go up over rod and down to 2.5 cm/1 in below base of scallop. From folded paper cut a pattern of about four tabs in a row.

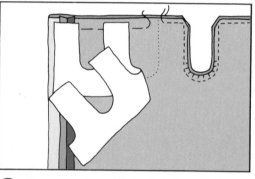

2 Cut out curtain and lining. Stitch double hem on bottom of curtain and lining and, RS together, join sides as for lined curtains. Baste layers together along top. Pin pattern along top of lining, starting with a tab at one side, and mark outline with chalk or pencil. Baste and stitch through both layers along marked line. Trim seam to 5 mm/¼ in; clip around curves and trim corners. Turn RS out; press.

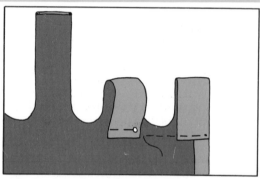

3 If curtains are to be hung with rings, stitch one at each corner of each tab; if with fabric tabs, fold tops of tabs over to WS, pin in place 2.5 cm/1 in below base of scallops, and baste across back of curtains. Stitch in place, either by hand to lining only, or through all thicknesses by machine, in a straight line of stitching across whole width of curtain. Press curtain and thread rod through loops or rings.

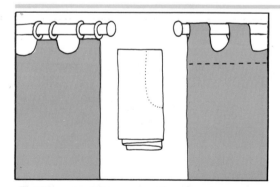

1 **Pleated café curtains** For shaped top band, cut fabric the length of the finished width of the curtain, plus 2.5 cm/1 in for seam allowances, by the depth required for the band, plus seam allowances of 2.5 cm/1 in. Line band as for lined curtains. Make pattern for band and cut band to shape as for scalloped-top café curtains.

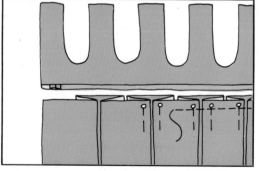

2 To work out curtain fabric, decide on width of pleat and double. Multiply doubled pleat measurement by number of tabs in top band, excluding two end ones, and add to window measurement. Cut fabric to these dimensions. Mark pleats, arranging them so they fall from centre lower edge of tabs. Pin and baste in place 1.25 cm/½ in from top. Work second row of basting 2.5 cm/1 in below.

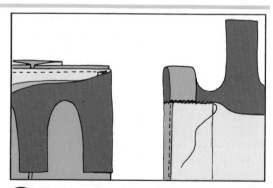

3 Turn in and stitch double hems down each side of curtain and at bottom edge. With RS together, leaving band lining free, join lower edge of band to top edge of curtain. Turn in seam allowance along lower edge of band lining and baste along machining to WS of curtain. If fabric loops are allowed for, baste lining and loops in place at the same time. Stitch by hand or by machine.

SHOWER CURTAINS

The ideal fabric for waterproof shower curtains is vinyl-backed material, but it requires extra care in making up as pins, needles and basting leave marks. To avoid the marks showing, pin the fabric within the seam allowance or hold it together with paper clips.

The plastic coating of the fabric tends to cling to the smooth underside of the machine foot when the fabric is stitched on the right side so, if you intend to sew a lot with vinyl, invest in a special foot with a small roller set into it. Otherwise, place tissue paper over the stitching line and tear it away after sewing. Sew plastic that has no woven backing with a large stitch to prevent tearing along the seamlines. Clean out the bobbin area of the machine thoroughly after sewing vinyl or plastic; bits of fabric tend to lodge in the works and can cause the bobbin to jam.

1 **Lined shower curtains** For a curtain that is waterproof on the inside and attractive outside, use towelling, lined with vinyl-coated fabric, or plastic shower curtaining. Construct as for simple lined curtains with towelling as main fabric and allowing for 10 cm/4 in to hang down inside bath edge. To save on fabric, do not gather curtains but use sail eyelets inserted through top hem and pin rings.

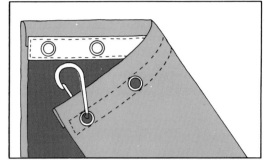

2 Sail eyelets are sold with an instruction leaflet and tool for inserting them. To make a sail eyelet heading, turn down a 5 cm/2 in single hem over lining edge and baste. Baste wide standard tape over hem edge to cover it and stitch close to tape edges and across ends. Insert eyelets along centre of tape about 7.5 to 10 cm/3 to 4 in apart. Insert pin rings.

PELMETS/VALANCES

Pelmets/valances are not used as often as they used to be. Some windows, however, need pelmets/valances to set them off to best advantage. In high-ceilinged rooms particularly, they help to give the impression of height and width to a window. Illustrated, right, are six of the most popular styles.

The size and shape of a pelmet/valance depend on the style of the window, but leave enough space between the pelmet/valance and the curtain track behind to give access to the track and to allow the curtains to run freely.

For lightweight gathered pelmets/valances there are special extension supports to carry a standard type of track several inches in front of the curtains. The heavier, shaped, box type needs a wooden frame, which should extend at least 30 cm/12 in on either side of the window.

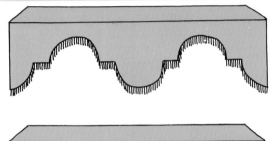

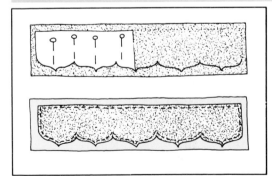

1 **Box pelmet/valance to match curtains** Add length of front and sides of pelmet/valance together and make a paper pattern to required style. Cut shape for entire pelmet/valance around pattern from buckram interfacing. Cut two strips of curtain fabric the length and width of interfacing, plus 1.25 cm/½ in all around. Centre interfacing on WS of one strip and baste and machine to fabric.

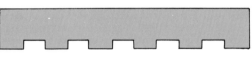
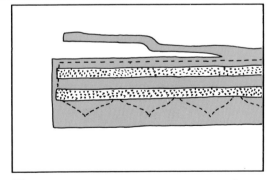

2 Cut two strips of Velcro the length of interfacing and glue hooked sections along top and bottom of front and side sections of box frame (before fixing box to wall if possible). Turn buckram-backed strip RS up and position the two loop sections of Velcro on fabric to correspond with those on frame. Machine in place down both edges of each strip. Trim top edge of fabric level with top of buckram.

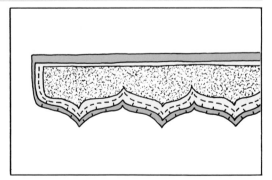

3 Place strip, RS down, on a second, matching fabric strip and baste and stitch at ends and along bottom edge, following decorative shape of buckram. Trim fabric 5 mm/¼ in from stitching; clip curves and turn RS out.

CURTAINS

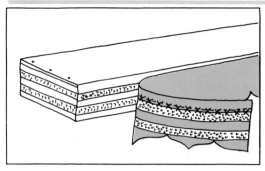

4 Turn down top hem of second strip over first strip and buckram and cross stitch to Velcro. If decorating with braid, sew it to side without Velcro. Fasten fabric to frame by pressing the sections of Velcro together.

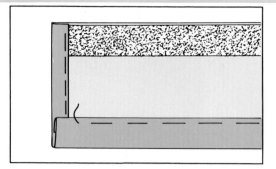

Frilled pelmet/valance Cut a strip of fabric about three times the length of the pelmet/valance by the depth required, plus 7.5 cm/3 in for both top and bottom hems. Stitch double hems along bottom and sides. Cut a strip of 7.5 cm/3 in iron-on interfacing as long as the fabric and iron to WS of top edge. Turn down top hem 7.5 cm/3 in and baste.

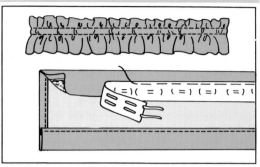

2 Stitch gathering tape over raw edge, draw up cords, and hang from track as for gathered curtains.

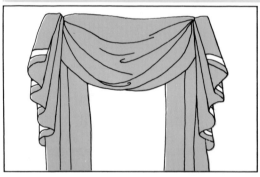

Draped pelmet/valance A luxurious heading for long formal windows. This simple style has only three shaped pieces of fabric, used double so that each piece is self-lined. Braid or trimming can be added to side drapes.

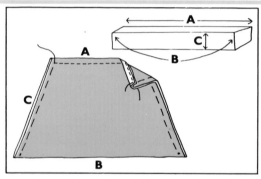

2 To make centre loop, measure length of front of pelmet/valance, **A**, then drape tape measure loosely across front to estimate length of drape's lower edge, **B**. Multiply depth, **C**, by four to allow for folds and cut a piece of double fabric based on these dimensions, with folded edge at bottom. Baste side edges WS together. Turn down and stitch a narrow single hem along top edge.

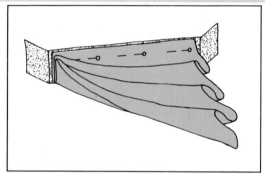

3 Cut a strip of buckram the length and depth of pelmet/valance front and sides. Cut and attach bands of Velcro to frame and back of buckram as for box pelmet/valance (**2**). Taking pleats of equal depth on each side, fold fabric up to front section of buckram. Pin folds in place and stitch by hand through all layers along top edge of buckram. Stitches at side edges will be hidden behind drapes.

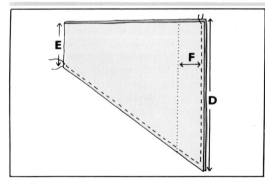

4 Decide on number and width of folds at side and add length of pelmet/valance side, **F**. Decide length of longest edge, **D** (roughly half length of curtain), and shortest edge, **E**, and add 5 cm/2 in to both for hems. Fold fabric in half and cut shape based on these dimensions. Mark extent of **F**. With RS together, join lower edge and long edge, **D**, with a 2.5 cm/1 in seam. Turn RS out and press.

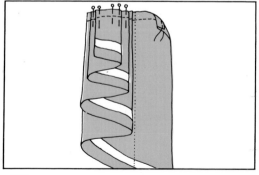

5 If using braid or trim, sew approximately 4 cm/1½ in away from lower edge. Turn down 2.5 cm/1 in to WS along top edge and machine. With RS (trimmed side) facing you, arrange and pin fabric in slightly decreasing folds so top fold is narrowest. Keep top edge level and leave enough of it unpleated at the widest end to pin along side of frame. When effect is right, mark folds and open out fabric.

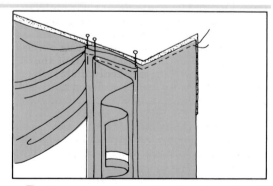

6 Pin and stitch top of unpleated section, RS up, to one buckram side extension. On one side of centre section, pin and stitch widest fold through all thicknesses and, if possible, buckram to cover ends of centre drape. Work stitches so they are covered by next fold. Continue like this until narrowest fold and slip stitch this fold down each side about 2.5 cm/1 in. Attach to frame along Velcro strips.

BLINDS AND SHADES

An economical and easy way of covering small windows, blinds or shades are traditionally made from Holland, a coarse linen fabric, but canvas, cotton, linen union and many of the medium-weight synthetics as well as vinyl-coated cottons can be used.

Those with a spring roller are the most popular type. They are available in kit form, with instructions and all the necessary fittings and screws. Roller blinds/shades are a practical choice for kitchens and bathrooms, but can also be used to provide privacy when used together with full, frilled, permanently drawn back curtains. The bottom edge can be shaped and trimmed with braid, fringes, tassels or lace and the cord can be finished with one of many decorative ends.

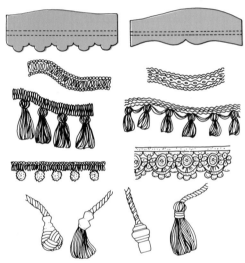

Roman or pleated blinds/shades fold into soft accordion pleats as they are drawn up and hang straight when down. They do not need stiffening and can be made with heavier and more textured fabrics than can the roller type. Pleated blinds are elegant but not fussy, and are particularly suited to dining rooms, sitting rooms and bedrooms.

Straighten the fabric before cutting out as it must be cut on the straight grain or the blind/shade will hang crookedly. Fabric for roller blinds/shades can be stiffened to give a smooth crisp finish. Apply spray-on stiffener before cutting out as it may shrink the fabric a little. Press the fabric well first, spray and allow to dry flat. As stiffener prevents fraying, no side hems are needed. However, if stiffener is not used, make the side hems narrow and not too bulky. A single hem, zigzagged, gives a much neater finish than a double hem.

MEASURING
Only two measurements are needed, the width, **A**, and length, **B**. Blinds/shades may be fitted inside or outside the window recess.

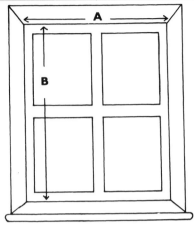

For inside, measure the exact size of the recess, making sure that width is the same at top and bottom. If there is no recess or you want to cover the window completely, the fabric should not extend too far beyond the edge of the window and should not drop below the sill.

Roller blinds/shades
Buy a kit to measurement **A** or longer. Remove the metal cap from the end opposite the spring and cut off surplus on wooden part of roller. When the cap is replaced the complete roller should be about 2.5 cm/1 in shorter than the width of the recess (the pins, fitted into the brackets, make up the rest). Trim batten to fit.

Cut fabric measuring **B**, plus about 30 cm/12 in, by **A**, if fabric needs side hems. Cut fabric 2.5 cm/1 in narrower than **A** if stiffened or vinyl-coated because the sides will not need finishing.

Pleated blinds/shades
Cut two pieces of dowelling the length of **A**. Cut fabric measuring **A**, plus 2.5 cm/1 in, by **B**, plus 30 cm/12 in, joining fabric lengths if necessary.

MOUNTING
Blinds/shades are generally mounted so they hang close to the window (**X**). If preferred, they can hang the other way (**Y**). There will be a gap between the blind and the window, but only the face of the fabric will be visible from the room.

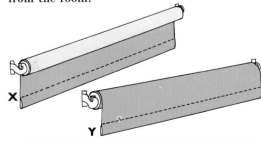

Joining widths
Avoid joins as seams tend to interfere with the free running of the roller. Choose instead an extra wide fabric or make two blinds/shades. If you have to join widths, make a central panel with an extension on either side, not a central seam. Keep seams flat and straight; trim and finish seam allowances.

FITTINGS
For the roller type kits are available containing instructions and the following fittings: a spring-loaded roller with a flat pin at the spring end and a round pin at the other; top-fitting or face-fitting brackets; stretcher batten for base; nylon or cotton pull cord with two end fittings. The kit may also contain tacks and glue for fixing the fabric to the roller and screws for the brackets.

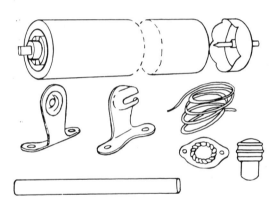

For the pleated type you need two lengths of dowelling, or one length for the bottom and a slim brass rod for the top; face-fitting brackets; a cord, heavier than that for a roller blind and without end fittings; a cleat to hold the cord ends when the blind is pulled up; and screw-in eyelets or metal pulleys with a plastic roller disc. The cleat is attached to the side of the window recess just above the cord end; pulleys or eyelets carry the cord and are fixed to the top and side of the window recess. The pulleys facilitate raising and lowering heavy pleated blinds/shades.

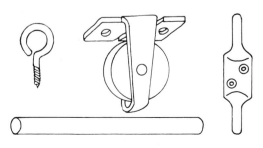

BLINDS AND SHADES

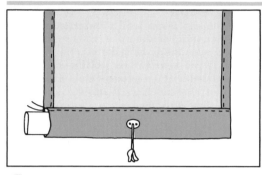

1 Roller blind/shade Cut roller and batten to size and fix brackets to recess wall. Straighten fabric grain and stiffen if desired. Cut out fabric and, if not stiffened, stitch 1.25 cm/$\frac{1}{2}$ in side hems. Turn up and stitch double lower hem to take batten. Insert batten. On WS attach cord to batten centre with fitting provided.

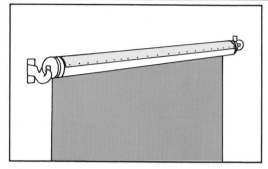

2 Turn top of fabric over roller, glue and tack down. Place roller on brackets and work to adjust spring tension.

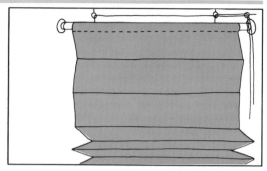

1 Pleated or Roman blind/shade Cut two pieces of dowelling the width of the blind/shade or, for the top, choose a slim brass rod the required size. Fix brackets at either side of window recess. Cut a rectangle of fabric on straight grain to fit window measurements **A**, plus 2.5 cm/1 in for side hems, by **B**, plus 30 cm/12 in for top and bottom hems.

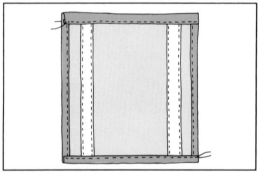

2 Turn in double hems down the sides and stitch. Press under 1.25 cm/$\frac{1}{2}$ in along top and bottom edges and then turn in hems wide enough to take dowelling, or, at top, brass rod. On WS, about 10 cm/4 in from each side, stitch two lengths of narrow tape vertically between top and bottom hems, sewing down both edges of tape.

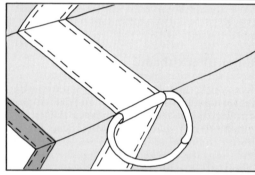

3 Work out width of pleats (10 cm/4 in is average width), mark pleats, fold fabric at marks and press pleats, one by one. Mark both pieces of tape at back edge of each pleat and push a small split brass curtain ring between tape and fabric at each mark, inserting last two rings at top edge of bottom hem. Fit dowelling into top and bottom hems. Slip stitch bottom hem ends together.

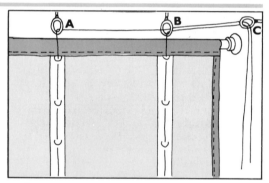

4 Fix eyelets or pulleys, **A** and **B**, to top of window recess in line with rings, and another, **C**, at top of one side of recess. Hang blind/shade. Thread cord through **C** and **B**, down through rings on one tape and up through those on the other. Take cord through **A**, back through **B** and **C**. Cut ends level and pull to raise blind/shade. Attach cleat to side of recess near bottom of cord and wrap cord ends around it.

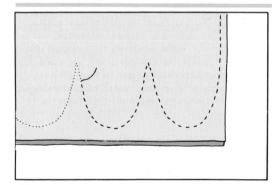

1 Shaped decorative hem Cut two straight bands of fabric the length of the finished width, plus 2.5 cm/1 in, by the depth of the shaped motif, plus batten width and 2.5 cm/1 in. Trace decorative shape on WS of one band, leaving 1.25 cm/$\frac{1}{2}$ in seam allowances and, with RS together, sew both bands along tracing line and at both ends. Trim seams, clip curves and turn band RS out.

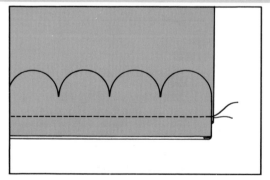

2 Invert band over RS of blind/shade base, with batten allowance extending over raw edge at bottom, and stitch to bottom seamline of blind/shade.

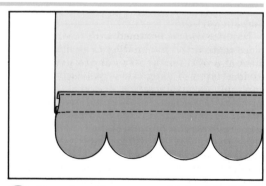

3 Press shaped hem to extend below blind/shade and press turnings up to WS. Turn under raw edges on batten allowance and stitch to WS of blind/shade.

TABLE LINEN

Create the perfect setting for every meal by making your own table linen. For a sophisticated dinner party make matching place mats and napkins and set them on a polished wood table. For afternoon tea try a pretty flowered cloth to complement your tea service, with a set of napkins in the predominant colour. Or, for brightening up breakfast on a dull morning, try a gingham or colourful non-iron seersucker cloth with matching or contrasting egg cosies and tea cosy. Breakfast tray cloths can be made to match with bedroom décor.

Fabric designers often use a selected range of colours in a variety of prints. These can be used to create an interesting and coordinated table setting, with tablecloths, place mats, napkins, padded mats and bread holders in different patterns and toning colours. It is also possible to buy the same design on different types of fabric—polyester and cotton mixtures for tablecloths, vinyl-coated for children's place mats and quilted for tea and coffee pot covers.

Choose washable fabric for all tablecloths and napkins. Linen is the traditional choice for table linen that is likely to be in regular use. It is, however, fairly expensive and cotton or a cotton and synthetic mixture is equally suitable. Braid, appliqué and other forms of decoration should also be washable, colourfast and shrink resistant.

Napkins can be in the same fabric as the tablecloth or can contrast in colour or design. Place mats for daily use should be made from a heavy washable fabric, or one that can be wiped clean. If you want to make matching mats in the napkin fabric, make them double or line them with a thicker material for extra protection.

For square or rectangular napkins, follow the method for a rectangular cloth; for place mats follow the appropriate method for the shape required.

Napkins can be trimmed with lace, and place mats with bias binding or braid. Table linen also offers an opportunity to practise various types of patchwork, quilting, appliqué, embroidery and decorative machine stitching. Make a patchwork tea cosy, for example, before embarking on a more ambitious patchwork project.

If your table is fairly large and you want to avoid joining pieces of fabric to obtain the required width for a cloth, it is worth looking for extra wide fabric such as polyester and cotton sheeting, which is now available in many colours and designs.

Table linen can also be used to conceal or disguise. Hide an old or damaged table under a floor-length cloth; cover improvised board and trestle tables for a buffet lunch or supper with attractive long cloths.

MEASURING

For all shapes of tablecloth measure the area of the table top plus depth of side overhang.

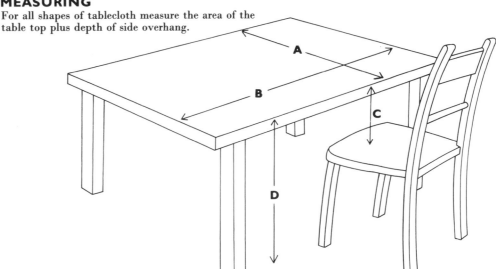

For a square or round table there is only one top measurement, **A**; for an oval or rectangular table, measure the width, **A**, and the length, **B**. For all shapes of cloth add twice the overhang, **C**, plus two double hem allowances, to the top measurement. The standard double hem allowance is 2.5 cm/1 in, but it can be wider if desired. The depth of the overhang depends on personal preference, but generally a cloth ends just above the dining-chair seat; a long cloth on a side table can come to within a short distance of the floor, **D**.

Joining fabric

Preferably try to find a fabric that is as close as possible to the width required for the cloth. However, if it is necessary to join fabric to make up the width needed, buy a piece of fabric twice the estimated length of the finished tablecloth; remember to allow extra for hems and for matching up the pattern when joining the pieces. Fold the fabric in half crosswise and cut on the fold. One piece forms the centre top panel. From the second piece cut two pieces of equal size to make up the width (**1**), leaving a centre scrap, and join

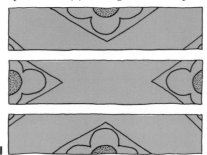

1

one to each side of the main part of the cloth, selvage to selvage and with any pattern motifs matching (**2**). The joins should, ideally, be placed in the overhang as seams across the table top are ugly and can unbalance crockery. Open seams are adequate for a cloth on a side table, but for cloths such as dining cloths that will be in more frequent use, stitch a flat fell seam or, if you do not want the stitching to show on the right side, a

French seam. (The centre scrap, if wide enough, can be used to make matching table napkins.)

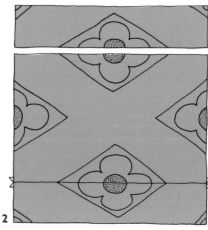

2

Place mats

For everyday use place mats are generally made from heavier fabric than that used for tablecloths.

Estimate the size required for mats by setting a place on the table. Measure the area it takes up, allowing enough for a surround. To this add 2 cm/¾ in extra all around for double hems. Make up, following appropriate tablecloth method. Alternatively, on a woven fabric, fray the edges and zigzag all around to hold them.

TABLE LINEN

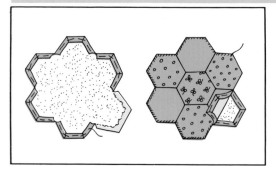

Reversible patchwork mat Make 14 7.5 cm/3 in patchwork hexagons backed with iron-on interfacing. Join patches in two sets of seven. Baste a piece of thin padding to WS of one piece; trim padding to within seam allowance. Fold in, baste and press raw edge all around both pieces; place WS together and oversew all around outer edge.

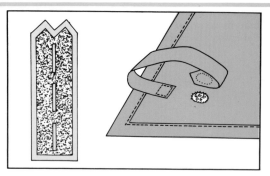

Napkin holder Attach a tab to the left edge of a breakfast tray cloth to hold a matching napkin. Cut light perforated interfacing band 12 cm/4¾ in long, press to WS fabric and cut out, adding seam allowances. Fold RS together, stitch around edge of interfacing, trim, turn RS out and press. Place on RS of tray cloth 3 cm/1¼ in from edge. Attach by stitching in a small square. Sew on Velcro circles to fasten.

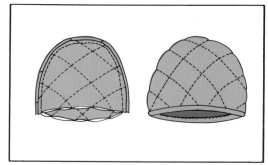

Tea cosy Measure circumference and height of pot, adding 7.5 cm/3 in ease. Make a loose cover by joining two semicircles of quilted fabric to fit over handle and spout of pot. Insert an extra layer of padding. Make lining to fit. Bind around lower edge to finish.

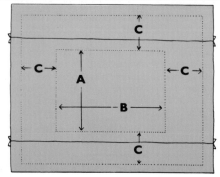

Fitted tea or coffee pot cover Cut four flat-topped triangles of quilted fabric; bind three sides. Join two pieces WS together leaving gap for spout. Join the other two, leaving lower part unstitched for handle. Stitch remaining two seams. On WS gather top, pull up and fasten off firmly. Make a 10 cm/4 in tab of fabric and stitch to base of opening on RS. Stitch Velcro circles in position to fasten tab.

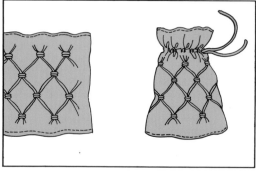

Egg cosy For a decorative smocked effect cut checked fabric 30 cm/12 in by 12 cm/4¾ in; hem both long edges. Smock from RS; start 4 cm/1½ in below top edge, pulling together alternate corners of check with double stitches. Use embroidery thread and stitch back and forth, passing needle through tubes of fabric. Fold fabric RS together; join ends and gather top of cosy.

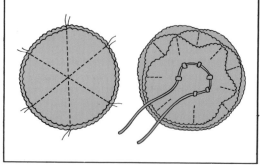

Bread holder Hem, bind or decorate edges of three 30 cm/12 in diameter circles of fabric. Join two circles with three lines of stitching to divide into six segments. On RS top (third) circle attach six ribbon loops 5 cm/2 in from edge. Join top and middle circles with six short rows of stitching midway between rows beneath. Thread ribbon through loops and pull up to form pockets.

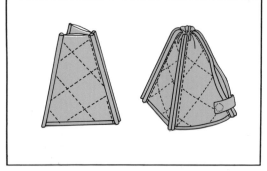

1 Rectangular cloth and napkins For square or rectangular napkins cut fabric to desired size, plus hem allowances of approximately 2 cm/¾ in all around. For a cloth, measure **A** and **B**. To both measurements add twice the overhang, **C** or **D**, and two hem allowances. For both cloth and napkins, mark top and centre of hem allowance with tailor's chalk on WS.

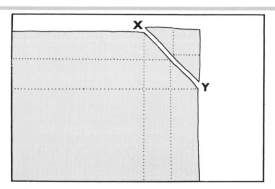

2 Turn in a double hem all around to give a finished hem of about 1.25 cm/½ in for a cloth, slightly less for a napkin. Press fold lines. Open out folds and cut off a triangle of fabric diagonally across each corner from **X** to **Y**.

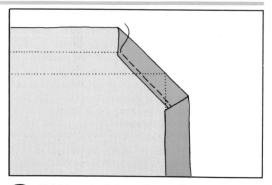

3 Fold in a single hem diagonally across corners. Press the folds and baste them down across corners. Taking each corner in turn, fold in first fold of hem on one side of the fabric.

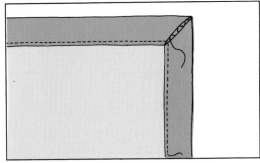

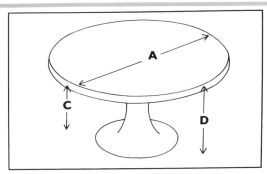

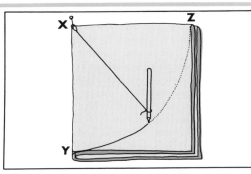

4 Turn in first fold on the other side and then second fold on each side. Pin and baste folds in place. Machine close to inner folded edge all around, pivoting stitching at corners. For neatness, slip stitch folds together at corners on wide hems. Remove basting and press cloth well.

I **Round cloth** Double the length of the overhang, **C** or **D**. Add to it the diameter of the table top, **A**, plus two 1.25 cm/½ in single hem allowances. Cut a square of material based on this dimension, joining widths of fabric if necessary.

2 Fold square into quarters. At **X**, pin a piece of string and tie a pencil to it at the distance of **Y** from **X**. Using the pencil and string as a compass, draw a curve between the two diagonally opposite corners **Y** and **Z**. Be careful not to wrinkle the fabric as you draw and keep the string taut. Cut through all four layers of fabric along the pencil line and open the fabric out.

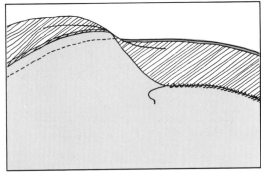

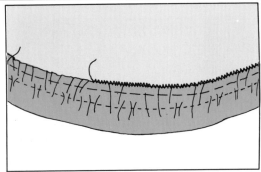

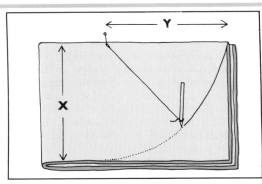

3 The easiest method of hemming a round cloth is to attach a length of single or double bias binding. With RS together, stitch binding around edge of cloth, roll binding and seam to WS and stitch in place by hand or machine.

4 Alternatively, work a row of gathering around cloth about 6 mm/¼ in from edge. Turn up a single hem and press, drawing up gathering thread to ease in fullness around edge. Baste hem in place and machine satin stitch around raw edge to finish and hold hem. Remove basting and press.

Oval cloth Measure and cut fabric as for rectangular cloth and fold into quarters as for round one. Measure width, **X**, of folded fabric and on one long edge mark this distance from corner of raw edge, **Y**. At marked distance pin a piece of string. Measure length of **X** along string and tie on a pencil at this point. Draw a curve between corner and lower raw edges. Proceed as for round cloth.

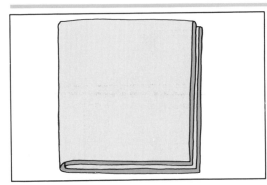

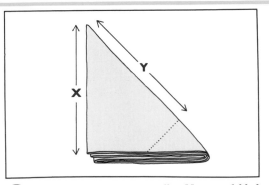

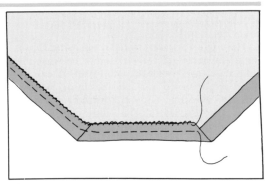

I **Octagonal cloth** An attractive shape for a round table and easier to hem than a round cloth. To the diameter of the table top, **A**, add two side overhangs, **C** or **D**, and two double hem allowances. Cut a square of fabric based on this dimension. Fabric must be exactly square to make an even-sided octagon. Make sure sides of square are exactly in line with fabric grain. Fold square into quarters.

2 Fold cloth again diagonally. Measure folded edge **X** and, measuring from the top corner, on folded edge **Y** mark the length of **X** with a pin. At right angles to folded edge **Y** cut off the corner below the pin, taking care to cut in a straight line. (This gives a cloth with eight equal sides.)

3 Unfold fabric and trim edges to neaten. Turn up narrow single hem all around, overlapping corners and pressing them in place. Turn up a second, wider hem in the same way. Pin, baste and stitch in place by hand or machine. For a decorative finish stitch a tasselled braid to the hem.

BED LINEN

By making your own bed linen you will not only save money, but you also have the greatest possible flexibility in the choice of colour, design and fabric, enabling you to coordinate your bedlinen with the colour scheme and décor of your room.

As bed shapes and sizes vary considerably, check the dimensions of your bed before buying the material. Sheeting is usually sold in widths of 175 cm/70 in and 230 cm/90 in for standard single and double beds. Extra wide fabric for king-size beds is not as easily available, but it is well worth searching for as it avoids uncomfortable joins. As a general rule, a plain sheet should be long enough and wide enough to cover the mattress and also to tuck in all around.

Pure cotton and linen fabrics are ideal for making luxurious, long-wearing sheets and pillowcases. Comfortable and absorbent, cotton and linen will be expensive purchases initially, but the sheeting should last a very long time. The only real drawback to using natural fibres is that they wrinkle badly and will need to be ironed after washing. Easy-care polyester and cotton mixtures are the most practical form of sheeting and are available in a wide range of colours and patterns. These mixtures are particularly useful for fitted bottom sheets, which can be difficult to iron. They are also ideal for valances or dust ruffles, which cover the base of the bed, and for quilt covers. Quilt covers can also be made to match printed cotton curtains, providing the curtain fabric is smooth, washable and colourfast. It is now possible to coordinate the fabrics you select for your bed linen with wallpaper, accessories and even carpeting, creating quite a dramatic effect.

Whatever the style of valance or dust ruffle, it will stay in place more securely and with the minimum of pins if joined to a piece of fabric, ideally an old sheet, large enough to cover the bed base.

The main considerations in choosing fabric for pillowcases are that it should be washable, colourfast and preferably non-iron. It can be plain or patterned and can match or contrast with the sheeting. Give a plain fabric added interest by decorating the pillowcase with embroidery or appliqué or stitching lace to the edges.

Of all items of bed linen, bedspreads can be the least utilitarian and most eye-catching. Although heavier materials hang better than lighter weight ones, almost any material can be used. Accentuate the lines of a tailored cover with piping or braid. Highlight a plain fabric with appliqué motifs or embroidery in contrasting colours. Or try luxury quilted or lacy fabrics, or ornate jacquard weaves, for a simple yet stunning effect.

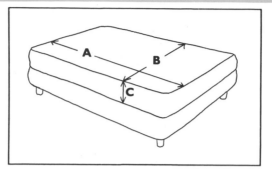

Sheets Take the following measurements: **A** length of mattress top; **B** width of mattress top; **C** depth of mattress. In addition to these measurements allow 25 cm/10 in for hems and tuck-in on a single bed, 30 cm/12 in for a double bed.

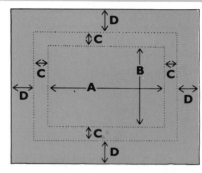

Plain sheet For the width of sheeting required, add **B** to twice **C**, plus two tuck-in and hem allowances, **D**. For the length, add **A** to twice **C**, plus two tuck-in and hem allowances, **D**.

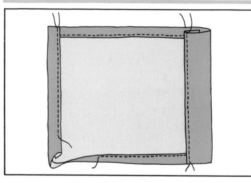

2 If sheeting is correct width for the bed, leave selvages or stitch a single hem down each side. If fabric is too wide, trim to size and stitch a double hem down each side. Stitch a double hem 7.5 cm/3 in wide at top of sheet and another at the bottom 2.5 cm/1 in wide. On the top hem a zigzag or machine embroidery stitch may be used. Slip stitch folded edges together at ends of double hems.

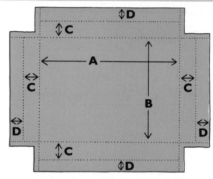

Fitted bottom sheet This is shaped and elasticated at all corners to fit around the mattress. For the width of sheeting required, add **B** to twice **C**, plus two tuck-in and hem allowances, **D**. For the length, add **A** to twice **C**, plus two hem and tuck-in allowances, **D**. Trim fabric to size if necessary and cut into corners as shown, leaving 1.25 cm/½ in hem allowance on each edge of corners.

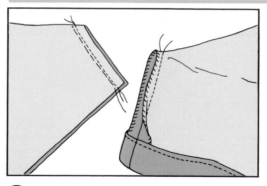

2 Join edges at each corner, RS together, with an open seam, taking 1.25 cm/½ in seam allowances. Alternatively, for extra strength, join edges with French seams. Turn in and stitch a 2.5 cm/1 in double hem around all edges of fabric.

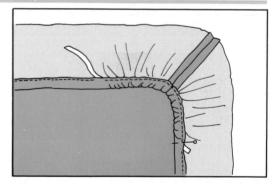

3 Undo a small section of hem, wide enough to take a bodkin, on both sides of each corner, approximately 25 cm/10 in from corner seam. Cut four 20 cm/8 in lengths of strong elastic and with a bodkin thread each through hem section at corners, holding free end in place with a pin. Stitch both ends of elastic firmly in place. Remove pins. Sew in thread ends.

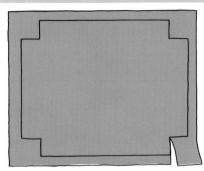

To convert a flat sheet into a fitted one, take measurements for a fitted sheet as in previous method and compare with those of flat sheet. If existing sheet is too small, undo one or more of the hems, as necessary; if it is too large, trim it to required size. Mark out shape with chalk or pins, cut out and proceed as for fitted sheet.

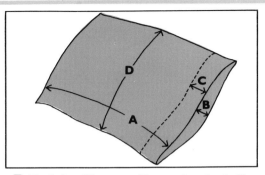

| **Tuck-in pillowcase** Measure length of pillow **A**, double it and add 20 cm/8 in for tuck-in **B** and 7.5 cm/3 in for top hem **C**. Measure width of pillow **D** and add 2.5 cm/1 in for seam allowances. To both length and width measurements add another 2.5 cm/1 in to ensure that the pillow can be removed easily from the cover. Cut fabric to size.

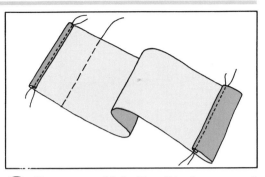

2 Baste across fabric 20 cm/8 in from one end. Turn down and stitch a narrow double hem across this end. At the other end, which will be the top hem, turn in 1.25 cm/½ in and press; turn in a further 6 cm/2¼ in and stitch in place. If you wish to decorate the top hem, do so now before joining side seams.

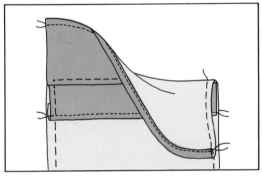

3 Working on a flat surface, RS together, fold top hem up to basted line and baste fabric together down both sides. Fold other end of fabric along basting line to cover top hem and baste it down through all layers. Stitch down entire length of each side, leaving 1.25 cm/½ in seam allowances. Turn cover RS out and press well.

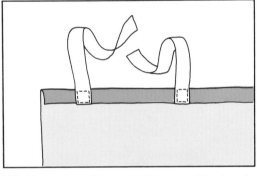

| **Economy pillowcase** Measure pillow length, double it and add 15 cm/6 in. Measure width and add 5 cm/2 in. Cut fabric to these dimensions. Turn in 1.25 cm/½ in single hem on short edges and press. Cut four 24 cm/9 in lengths of 1.25 cm/½ in tape and position two tapes on each side, with one end of tape on turning edge. Sew tape to turnings in a square.

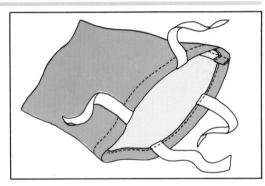

2 Turn in both edges another 6 cm/2¼ in and press, flipping tapes back over fold of hem. Hem turnings by hand or machine, stitching through tapes. Fold fabric in half crosswise, WS together, and join two long sides with French seams.

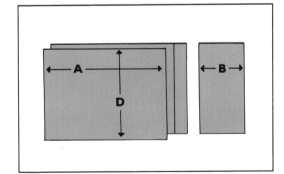

| **Frilled pillowcase** Cut out fabric in three sections: top, bottom and tuck-in. Top section measures pillow length (**A**) plus 6.5 cm/2½ in for ease and seam allowance, by width (**D**) plus 6.5 cm/2½ in. Bottom section measures (**A**) plus 6.5 cm/2½ in plus 7.5 cm/3 in for top hem, by (**D**) plus 6.5 cm/2½ in. Tuck-in measures (**D**) plus 6.5 cm/2½ in by 20 cm/8 in. Length of frill is three times **A** plus three times **D**.

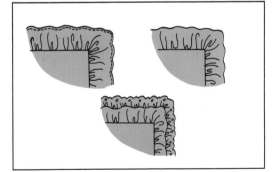

2 The frill can be made from purchased trimming or from fabric to match or contrast with pillowcase. It can be single with a narrow hemmed edge or double with a fold along the edge. To cut frill from fabric decide on desired depth and add 3 cm/1¼ in seam allowances; for a double frill cut twice desired depth plus 3 cm/1¼ in. An alternative is a layered frill: trimming on top of a fabric frill.

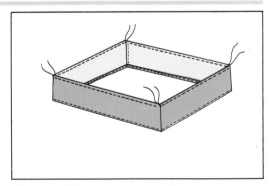

3 Join frill along short edges. Hem along one edge of single frill; fold double frill WS together and press. Fold into four and press creases to mark quarters. Mark centre of each side of top pillowcase section by creasing with the iron. Run gathering threads along raw edges of frill, one to each quarter.

BED LINEN

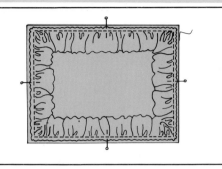

4 Place frill on top section RS together, match the quarter marks and pin with raw edges level. Pull up each gathering thread until frill fits perimeter of pillowcase. Arrange gathers evenly, with more fullness at corners so that frill will lie flat when it extends beyond the edge. Pin all around, baste and stitch. Remove pins, basting and gathering threads.

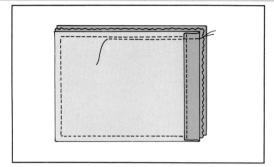

5 On top section turn in a 5 cm/2 in hem and stitch along one short edge. Place on bottom section RS together, pin and baste with edges level. Turn pillowcase over and stitch around three sides, excluding hemmed side, following previous line of stitching.

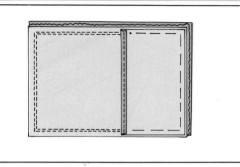

6 Turn in and stitch a narrow hem along one long edge of tuck-in. Place tuck-in RS down on WS of bottom of pillowcase, matching side edges and matching raw edge to deep hem on bottom section. Pin and baste across end and down sides to edge of tuck-in. Stitch in place following previous stitching and taking care not to catch in the hem of the bottom section. Turn pillowcase RS out.

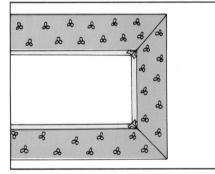

Wide borders Contrasting fabric, eyelet lace etc., can be added to pillowcases and one end of sheets. Cut two strips of fabric to desired depth for each edge of pillow, mitre the corners by making joins at 45° angles, trimming surplus off after stitching. Join borders together around outer edge, turn RS out. Make pillowcase following method for frilled pillowcase.

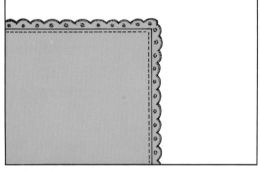

Satin stitch edges Cut fabric in three sections; stitch a hem on tuck-in. Stitch tuck-in to top section WS together and work satin stitch scallops. Place bottom section against top section WS together. Stitch and scallop around remaining three sides, enclosing all edges. Trim close to satin stitch. Add eyelets for decoration.

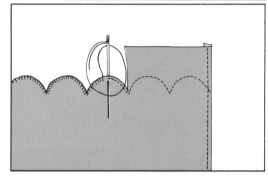

Scallops To add hand-stitched scallops to ends of sheets, hem along three sides, divide end of sheet into equal sections according to size of scallop required. Use the edge of a plate to outline scallops on the straight grain. Mark with basting or fabric pen, stitch along outline with running stitch or machining then trim close to stitching and loopstitch or buttonhole stitch over the edge.

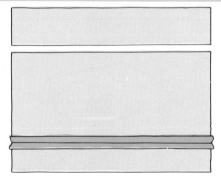

1 **Continental quilt cover** Cut two pieces of sheeting the length of the quilt by its width, adding 2.5 cm/1 in to both measurements. If joins are necessary, place them centrally or on either side of central panel, matching patterns and placing selvage to selvage. Join widths with open seams and press seams open.

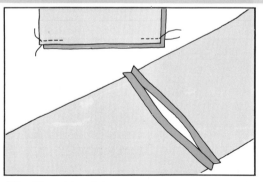

2 Place fabric RS together and, leaving a central opening approximately 45 cm/18 in shorter than the length of the edge, stitch along bottom edge from each end, taking 1.25 cm/½ in seam allowance. If the cover is to be fastened with a zipper, press under seam allowance on opening and, with fabric up, insert zipper. Stitch remaining three seams, RS together; turn cover to RS through opening.

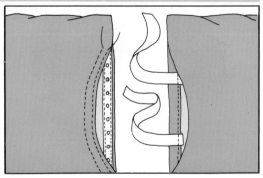

3 For a cover fastened with snap fastener tape or pieces of tape, leave opening and stitch remaining three seams. Turn cover to RS and press under seam allowance on opening. Apply fastener tape to each seam allowance so the fittings coincide. Stitch along both edges of tape. Alternatively, stitch pieces of tape every 10 cm/4 in under finished allowances as you hem them down.

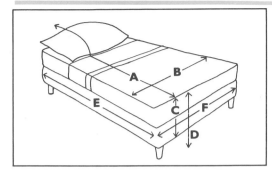

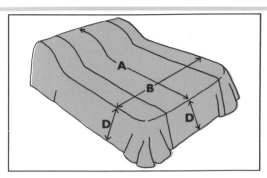

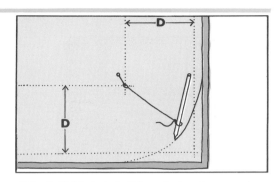

Bedcovers Make up the bed. Measure **A** length of mattress top, including extra for pillow; **B** width of mattress top; **C** depth from mattress top to bottom of bed base; **D** depth to within 2.5 cm/1 in of floor; **E** length of bed base; **F** width of base. Take 1.25 cm/½ in for seam allowances, 2.5 cm/1 in for single hem allowance, 4 cm/1½ in for a double hem.

⏐ **Simple throw-over cover** The easiest and quickest bedcover to make. For the length of fabric required, take **A** plus **D**, and add two double hem allowances, or more if the fabric is very heavy. For the width, add **B** to twice **D**, plus two double hem allowances. If necessary, join widths of fabric as for quilt covers, using one whole width for centre panel and joining two side panels.

2 Fold fabric in half lengthwise. At one end, on either side of corner, measure **D** plus hem allowance from raw edges and mark with chalk lines. At intersection of the two lines (top corner of the mattress) anchor a pin attached to a length of twine. Tie a pencil or chalk to twine and, with twine taut, draw an arc from edge to edge. Cut through both layers along curve. Double hem all fabric edges.

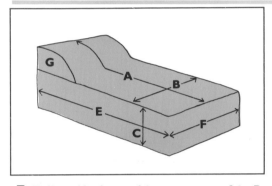

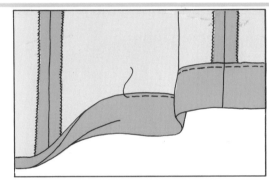

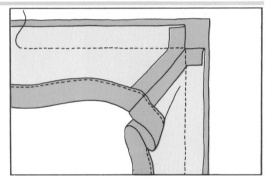

⏐ **Tailored bedspread** Cut main section **A** by **B**, plus seam allowance on three sides and double hem allowance at top edge. Cut two gussets **G** as for bedspread with gathered skirt (**2**) and (**3**), and two side sections **C** by **E**, adding one seam and double hem allowance to each dimension. Cut the foot section measuring **F**, plus two seam allowances, by **C**, plus one seam and double hem allowance.

2 If necessary, join widths for main panel as for simple throw-over cover and decorate with piping or braid if desired. Join pillow gussets to main panel as for bedspread with gathered skirt (**3**). With RS facing, join foot and side sections with open seams and press seams open. Turn up and stitch double hem on lower edge of this strip.

3 With RS facing, join strip to top panel and gussets with an open seam. Before stitching the corners, undo seams of strip the depth of the seam allowance so fabric lies flat. Pivot stitching around corners. Press seam toward panel. At top end of cover, turn in and stitch double hem along unstitched skirt edges, gussets and main panel as for bedspread with gathered skirt(**6**).

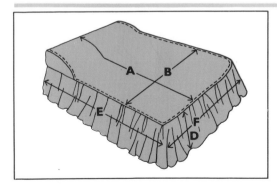

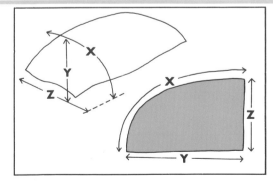

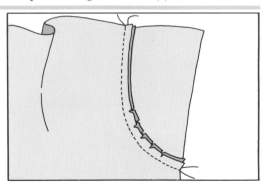

⏐ **Bedspread with gathered skirt** For top panel, cut a rectangle **A** by **B**, adding two seam allowances to both measurements. For skirt length, add twice **E** to **F**, plus half their combined length for fullness; for skirt depth, take **D**, plus one double hem and one seam allowance. Different fabrics can be used for skirt and top panel, but choose one that drapes well for the skirt.

2 With pillow in position, measure length from head of bed over pillow to mattress at bottom edge of pillow **X**. Measure under pillow from head of bed to same point on mattress **Y** and measure thickness of pillow **Z**. Add seam allowances to **Y** and **X** and a double hem allowance to **Z**. Make a paper gusset with two straight sides the dimensions of **Y** and **Z** and a curved side the length of **X**.

3 With fabric RS together, cut two gussets from pattern. If cutting them on single fabric, reverse pattern for the second. With RS together, join curved side of gusset to edge of top end of main panel with an open seam, keeping edges level and easing fullness around curve. Clip seam allowances around curve and press seam toward gusset.

BED LINEN

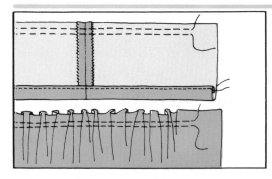

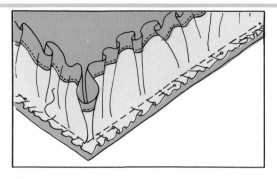

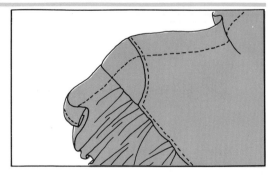

4 Cut sufficient lengths of fabric to make a strip for the skirt, adding seam allowances for joining strips. Join lengths with open seams and press seams open. Turn up and stitch a double hem along bottom edge of skirt. Leaving double hem allowance at both ends of skirt, work two rows of gathering stitches along top. Draw up threads until skirt fits sides and foot of main panel.

5 Measure and mark centres of gathered edge and foot of main panel. With RS facing, pin centres together and, working outward to corners and then along sides of main panel to head end, pin rest of skirt to panel, distributing gathers evenly, and baste. Join with an open seam, pivoting stitching at corners, and press seam allowances toward panel.

6 On RS topstitch near seam join to secure seam, sewing through seam allowances underneath. Press stitching. At top end of cover, turn in and stitch double hem along unstitched skirt edges, gussets and main panel.

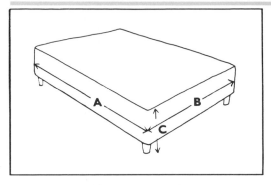

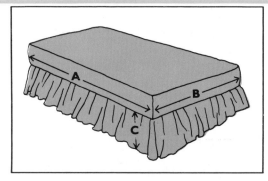

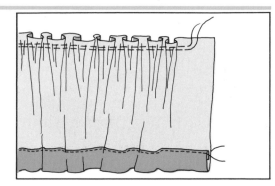

Valances/dust covers Measure **A** length of bed base; **B** width of base; **C** depth from top of base to within about 2.5 cm/1 in of floor. Take 1.25 cm/$\frac{1}{2}$ in for seam allowances, 2.5 cm/1 in for single hem, 4 cm/1$\frac{1}{2}$ in for a double hem. Cut a fabric cover for bed base, with seam allowances on three sides and double hem allowance at side against wall.

1 **Simple gathered valance/dust cover** For the length, add twice **A** to **B**, plus two double hem allowances and half as much again for fullness. For the width, add one seam and one double hem allowance to **C**. Cut out fabric, joining pieces with open seams to make the required length. Press seams open.

2 Turn up and stitch double hem along lower edge and work two rows of gathering stitches along top, leaving double hem allowance ungathered at both ends. Draw up thread until valance/dust cover fits around sides and foot of base cover. Measure and mark centres of gathered edge and foot of cover.

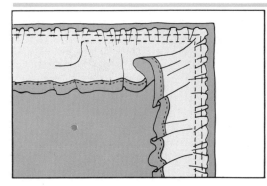

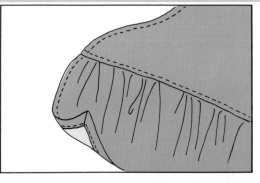

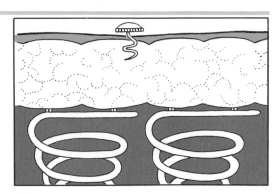

3 With RS facing, pin centres together and, working outward to corners and then along sides, pin rest of strip to cover, distributing gathers evenly, and baste. Join with an open seam, pivoting stitching at corners, and press seam toward cover.

4 On RS topstitch near seam join to secure seam, sewing through seam allowances underneath. Press stitching. Turn in and stitch double hem along unstitched edges and top end of base cover.

5 Place valance/dust cover on bed base. To anchor it securely to a sprung-edge divan base, insert slipcover pins at intervals along top edge of base, twisting them down into padding of base. To anchor on a firm-edge divan base, insert a tack at each corner through the fabric into the wooden corner block of the divan and insert slipcover pins at intervals along top edges of base into padding.

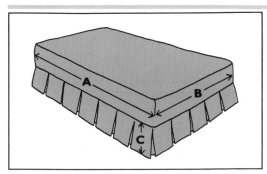

1 Pleated valance/dust cover Choose heavy fabric to match bed cover. Pleats are distributed so bottom corners of bed come between pleats. (Adjust pleat size toward top end of bed if necessary.) For the width, take **C**, plus one seam and one double hem allowance; for the length, add twice **A** to **B**. To this add the extra length needed for type of pleat used, plus two double hem allowances.

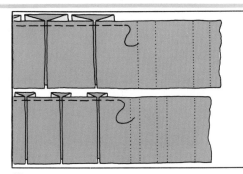

2 For deep box pleats (same width for front and concealed back folds), treble the length of valance/dust cover. For shallow pleats (back fold half the width of front), double the length. Ideally, front folds of shallow pleats are 10 to 15 cm/ 4 to 6 in wide. Cut out fabric, joining lengths if necessary. Hem; mark pleats and press in place, basting along both top and bottom edges of pleats as you press.

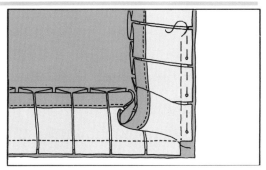

3 Find centre of pleated strip and on each side measure outward half **B**. Pin the pleats at these points to bottom corners of base cover, RS together and taking usual seam allowances on sides of cover. Fit and pin rest of pleats along foot. Join with an open seam, clipping seam allowance of strip at corners. Pin pleats along sides of cover, baste and join. Finish and attach as for gathered valance/dust cover.

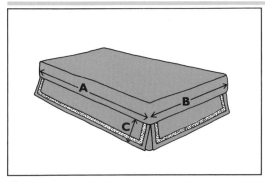

1 Plain valance/dust cover Decorate with braid or team with a tailored divan cover. Measure length of side **A** and deduct 1.25 cm/½ in; measure depth **C**. Cut two sections to these measurements, adding a seam allowance for top edge and double hems on other sides. Measure length of foot **B** and deduct 2.5 cm/1 in; measure depth **C**. Cut one section with seam and hem allowances as for sides.

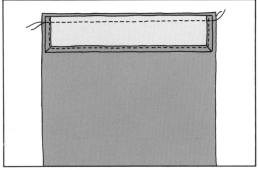

2 Turn in and stitch double hem along side and lower edges of skirt sections, mitring corners. If using braid, attach it to sides and lower edge of skirt, mitring corners. With RS facing, centre foot section of skirt on foot of base cover so that ends of foot section are 1.25 cm/½ in from edges of cover; baste and stitch in place, continuing the stitching to edges of cover.

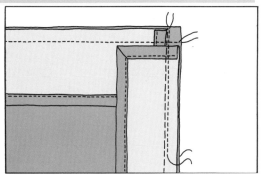

3 With RS facing, pin one of side sections of skirt to base cover, so bottom end is 1.25 cm/½ in from bottom edge of cover. Baste and join with an open seam, taking care not to catch foot section of skirt in seam and stitching to bottom edge of cover. Join other side section to cover in the same way. Turn in and stitch narrow double hem along top edge of base cover.

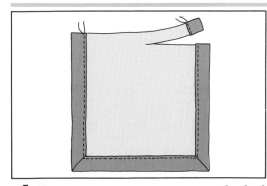

4 Measure two square corner gussets to depth of **C**, add double hem allowance on three sides and cut gussets out. Turn in and stitch hems, mitring corners. Trim off about 1.25 cm/½ in from top edge of each square so that the gussets will not hang below skirt sections.

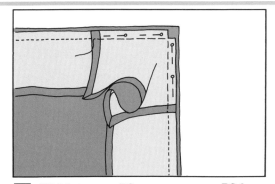

5 With base cover RS up, centre gussets RS down over bottom corners. Clip seam allowance in centre of top edge of gussets and, working out from centre, pin gussets to foot and sides of skirt and cover and baste. Join with open seams, pivoting stitching at corners so it forms a right angle and aligning it with previous rows of machining. Trim off bottom corners of base cover diagonally.

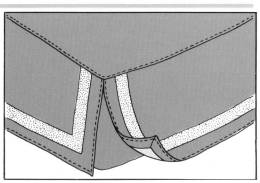

6 Press seams toward cover and topstitch as for gathered valance/dust cover. Position on bed base, pull firmly into place at corners and edges and attach to base with slipcover pins as for gathered valance/dust cover. Crease centre of gusset vertically between thumb and finger to help it to hang well.

5

DECORATIVE SEWING

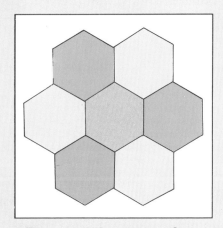

An introduction to three popular needlecrafts and some of their variations: patchwork – crazy, honeycomb, diamond and log cabin; quilting – padded, tied, stuffed and corded; appliqué – hemmed, machined, persé, découpé, inlay, lacework and reverse appliqué

PATCHWORK

The ideal craft for anybody who enjoys sewing, patchwork is the formation of a new piece of fabric by joining small scraps of fabric in different colours and designs.

Patchwork is an ancient craft. Some years ago pieces of patchwork were found in a walled-up chapel in India which date back to the 6th and 9th centuries. In general, however, there are few extant examples of patchwork which date back to before the 19th century.

Europeans who left their countries to settle in America from the 17th century onward probably took patchwork quilts with them across the Atlantic. Patchwork remained well loved in the United States and quilting parties became an important feature of domestic life.

Patchwork patterns were often peculiar to certain regions and many have fascinating names, such as "Bear's paw", "Rocky road to California" and "Duck's foot in the mud", reflecting local events and the environment. The same pattern may have different names according to where it is made. Many patterns popular in North America are identical to traditional patchwork designs in the North of England, which illustrates the continuity of the craft.

The appearance of patchwork depends on the shapes being meticulously stitched together so that they link perfectly to form the pattern. There are two basic methods of making patchwork by hand. In the first, prepared patches, with seam allowances turned over the backing papers, are stitched together one by one. In the second method, overlapping patches are laid out on another piece of fabric, the foundation fabric, and stitched down. Patchwork can also be done with a sewing machine.

The equipment needed for patchwork is readily available: a pair of sharp scissors for cutting fabric accurately; a sharp craft knife or scalpel for cutting backing papers or templates; white basting thread; fine sewing thread—use cotton on cotton fabrics, all-purpose or synthetic thread on synthetic fabrics and silk on silk; needles, sharps or betweens, sizes 8 or 9 depending on the fabric; fine pins; a thimble; a soft pencil for marking shapes on the fabric; and templates for cutting out shapes. It is often helpful to have an old cork mat or cork tile on hand when planning a design, so that when you have arranged the patches satisfactorily you can pin them down in position until needed.

For some patchwork designs firm paper is required for cutting the backing shapes for patches. Papers hold the patches firmly in shape until they are stitched together and are usually removed when the patchwork is complete. Alternatively, if an article needs extra body, cut backing shapes in iron-on interfacing and attach to the wrong side of the patches. These can be left in place when the patchwork is finished.

It is important to choose suitable fabrics for patchwork as its durability depends on the material used. Do not combine fabrics of different weights and thicknesses as the stronger fabrics tend to pull and strain the lighter ones. If mixing different fabrics, make sure they have the same washing and wearing qualities. Old and new fabrics can be used together, but check the old fabric is still strong by tugging it firmly in both directions, and wash new fabric before using it in case of any shrinkage or colour loss.

Cotton and cotton mixtures are the best fabrics for a beginner as they combine well. Velvets and silks are more difficult to work with than other fabrics and should be used only when you are more experienced. They look splendid, however, on mounted patchwork such as crazy work, where they can be used together as the foundation fabric helps bear the strain of wear and tear.

Patchwork can be used to make a wide variety of items. Although the term is often thought of as referring only to quilts, many other items, such as tablecloths, garments, bags and other accessories, can look very attractive in patchwork.

Successful patchwork depends not only on good technique but on a well-balanced design and a pleasing colour scheme. Many different shapes can be used, such as triangles, hexagons, diamonds, circles and squares. Experiment with new shapes to create unusual patterns. By the clever combination of different shapes and imaginative use of fabric patterns and colour, you will be able to create an infinite range of aesthetic and individual designs.

FINISHING AND LINING
Perfect a beautiful piece of work and make it strong and long-lasting by finishing it well and lining it. Choose a weight of lining which is suitable both for the patchwork fabric and for the item: cotton poplin, linen and calico can be used to line quilts and coverlets, for example.

To line a patchwork garment, lay patchwork on lining fabric and pin from centre, smoothing out lining to avoid creases. Cut out lining, allowing for seam allowances, and construct garment in usual way. If you have a pattern for the garment, use this to cut out the lining.

TEMPLATES
Templates are shapes used as patterns for cutting out patchwork pieces and backing papers. They are available in plastic and metal in different sizes and shapes such as hexagons, diamonds, squares and

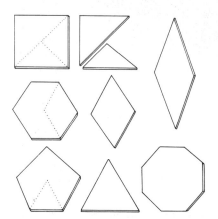

triangles. Cardboard templates can be made at home and, although not so long-lasting as

plastic or metal, enable interesting new shapes to be made. It is essential for templates to be accurately shaped so that patchwork pieces fit together exactly.

Templates for hand quilting are often sold in pairs: one solid shape the exact size of the finished patch, used for cutting the backing papers, and one larger window template, for cutting fabric patches with seam allowances. The window template is 5 mm/$\frac{1}{4}$ in larger all round than the solid template and is shaped like a frame—the turning allowance is a solid border around a space the size of a finished patch. When the template is placed on the fabric any motif is visible as it will appear on the patch.

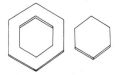

If you have only a solid template the size of the finished patch, make a window template to use with it for cutting materials. Place the solid template on a piece of cardboard and draw around the outline. Draw a second outline 5 mm/$\frac{1}{4}$ in away; cut around both outlines to form the window template.

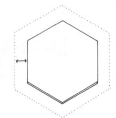

INSTANT PATCHWORK
Squares and triangles of various sizes are printed onto one side of soft non-woven material. Seam allowances are indicated by a dotted line. Bought by the panel, this type of patchwork is quick to do because it eliminates the normal cutting and backing necessary for conventional patchwork. The iron-on backing prevents fraying. Seams can be made by hand or machine.

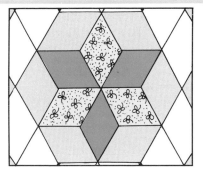
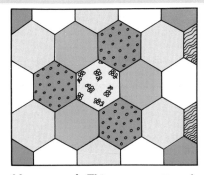
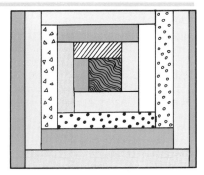

Basic designs

Crazy Patches of any size, shape and colour are stitched to foundation fabric.

Honeycomb This rosette pattern is based on the hexagonal patch—a popular shape as its blunt angles make it easy to combine with other shapes. Seven hexagons are joined together to make a rosette.

Diamond A star pattern, each star being made with six diamonds. Diamonds also combine well with other shapes.

Log cabin This pattern is made in separate squares which are then sewn together. Each square consists of strips of fabric stitched around a central square on foundation fabric.

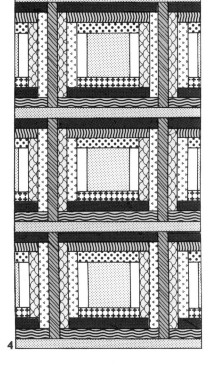

SPECIAL EFFECTS

1 "Starburst", also referred to as "Star of Bethlehem", is made with the long diamond, which is narrower than the lozenge diamond. Eight long diamonds are needed to make a star. More diamonds are arranged in circles around the central star. The circles radiate from light to dark tones.

2 The lozenge diamond based on the hexagon is used in this pattern known as "Baby blocks". Light and dark diamonds are arranged to give a three-dimensional cube-like effect.

3 Triangles in light and dark fabrics are juxtaposed to create attractive zigzag patterns.

4 In this variation of log cabin, blocks are arranged in a pattern known as "Courthouse steps". Light and dark strips are placed at opposite ends of each square so, when the pattern is complete, the light strips stand out to create a pattern of their own.

5 This wave-like pattern is created by hexagons arranged in undulating lines. Light and dark tones are placed to accentuate the pattern.

PATCHWORK

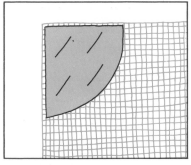

1 Crazy No templates or papers are required. Use fine cotton or muslin as foundation fabric and cut out whole shape, allowing 4 cm/1½ in extra on each edge. At one corner of foundation fabric diagonally baste a right-angled patch into place, matching raw edges.

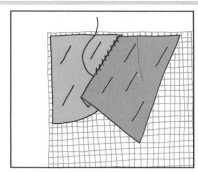

2 Place a second patch so it overlaps or underlaps first patch. Diagonally baste in position. Turn under and hem or work running stitch on any raw edges not to be covered by other patches, to anchor them to foundation fabric, or machine in place. Finish thread securely.

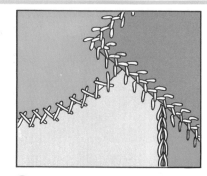

3 Continue until foundation fabric is covered. Traditionally, crazy work is finished by embroidery such as herringbone, feather and chain stitches in matching or contrasting thread around each shape. Embroidery may also be worked by machine. Press work on WS.

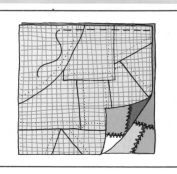

4 If making a large item such as a quilt, it may be easier to cut the foundation fabric into smaller squares. Stitch patches to squares. When squares are complete, place them RS together and stitch by hand or machine. Make sure colours and patterns are well distributed.

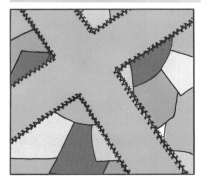

5 Alternatively, blocks of patchwork may be appliquéed separately to a large piece of background fabric. Arrange patches at regular intervals so that background fabric forms a border around them. Fold under edges of background fabric and hem invisibly.

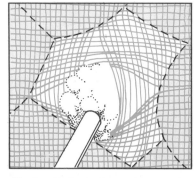

6 Small finished articles can be padded from the back with synthetic padding or cotton wool. When cutting out fabric add about 5 cm/2 in to desired finished size. Using a wooden skewer, push threads of foundation fabric apart in centre of shape and push in padding.

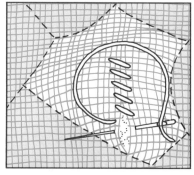

7 Work stuffing into corners of shape until it is well padded. Push parted threads of foundation fabric together again with wooden skewer. Alternatively, cut a small hole in back of shape to insert stuffing. Oversew hole neatly when shape is padded.

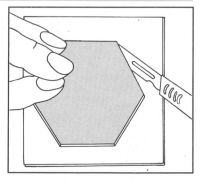

Honeycomb Prepare backing papers using a solid template. Place template over one or two pieces of paper on a board. With a sharp knife cut firmly around hexagon. Do not cut more than two papers together or the shapes will be inaccurate.

2 Cut material patches using a window template. Place template on fabric with one side of hexagon on straight grain of fabric and make sure any fabric design is well positioned. Draw around outer edge of template with a pencil and cut out patch on this line with scissors.

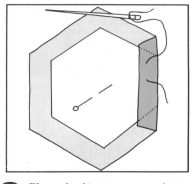

3 Place a backing paper exactly in centre of fabric hexagon on WS and pin. Fold seam allowance of one side over paper, but do not fold paper. Crease fold and, beginning near centre of seam allowance, take a long basting stitch through fabric and paper, leaving end of thread loose.

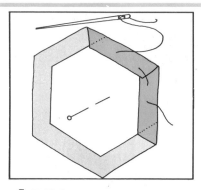

4 Fold down next seam allowance in same way, overlapping corners. Make a basting stitch across corner with first seam allowance and bring needle up again near next corner. Continue folding and basting down seam allowances in this way until sixth side is reached.

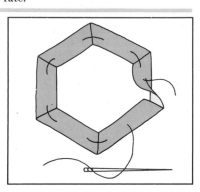

5 On sixth side, fold fabric and crease as before. Lift corner of first seam allowance and tuck corner of sixth seam allowance underneath. Secure with last basting stitch. Cut off thread leaving loose ends. Remove pin. Press patch lightly on WS. Prepare required number of patches.

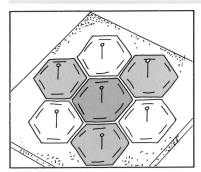

1 Joining A good start for many articles is a rosette of honeycomb patches. Take seven patches that complement each other in colour and pattern. Arrange on a cork tile until satisfied with the design and then pin down to cork.

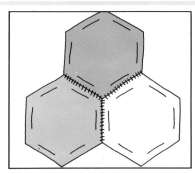

2 Place centre patch and one other RS together with corners matching exactly. Oversew patches along one side, taking small stitches—16 to 18 to the inch. Take needle through edge of fabric only as the paper must be easy to remove. Start and finish stitching very securely.

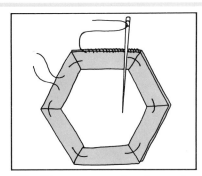

3 Matching RS and corners as above, join third patch to first two patches. Take care to stitch whole length of seam and secure corners. Oversewing appears as straight stitches on RS. Continue until all patches are attached around central patch.

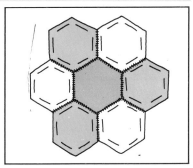

4 When the rosette is formed, remove basting and paper from central patch. As the basting is not held by knots or backstitches it is quickly removed. Leave other papers in position until the patches are surrounded on all sides. Press seams lightly on WS.

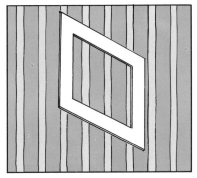

1 Diamond The lozenge diamond is based on the hexagon and measures the same across its width as along each side. Cut backing papers as for hexagon using a diamond template. Cut fabric patches, placing template so that two opposite sides are parallel with straight grain of fabric.

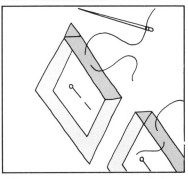

2 Centre paper on WS of patch and pin. Fold top right fabric seam allowance over edge of paper, taking care not to roll paper. Hold with a long basting stitch, leaving a loose end, and bring needle out near top of diamond.

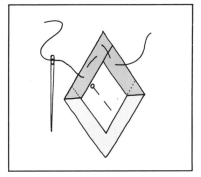

3 Fold over projecting end of fabric at top of diamond so that fold lies parallel with left side of diamond. Fold over the top triangular point of diamond and crease firmly.

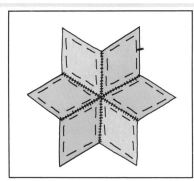

4 Fold over seam allowance on top left of diamond, tucking folded point underneath. Secure with a basting stitch. Take another basting stitch and bring needle up near next angle. Fold allowances one under the other here as for honeycomb and baste to secure.

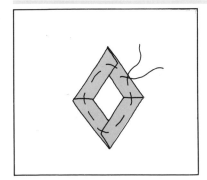

5 Fold bottom point of diamond in the same way as top and fold seam allowances one under the other as for honeycomb at fourth and last angle. Baste to secure and leave end of thread loose. Press each patch lightly on WS.

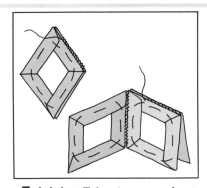

1 Joining Take six prepared patches and arrange design on cork as for honeycomb. Place two patches RS together, matching angles. Oversew from **A** to **B**. Open out and join third patch to central patch in same way. Make sure points meet exactly at centre.

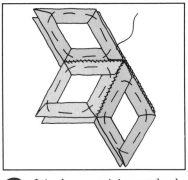

2 Join three remaining patches by same method. Place the two sets of patches RS together with points matching. Oversew along central join, checking that all six points meet neatly at centre of star.

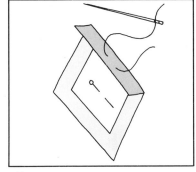

3 Press star open. Do not remove papers and basting until diamonds are stitched on all sides. This method applies also to triangles.

PATCHWORK

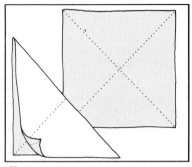 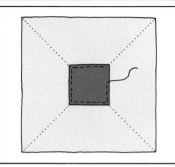 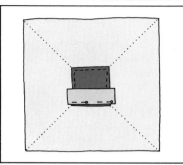 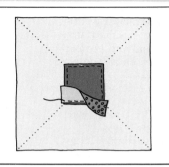

1 **Log cabin** Make a template for foundation squares in firm cotton about 30 to 40 cm/12 to 15 in square for a large item such as a quilt or 15 cm/6 in square for a cushion. Allow 1.25 cm/½ in all around for joining finished squares. Fold and press diagonally to find exact centre.

2 Cut small squares in patchwork fabric about 4 cm/1½ in square. Matching centres pin a small square RS up on foundation square. Stitch around small square 5 mm/¼ in inside raw edges by hand, with running stitch, or by machine. Raw edges will be covered by patchwork strips.

3 Cut strips of fabric on straight grain no less than 2.5 cm/1 in wide. For contrast, use light fabrics on two sides of square, dark on two sides. Cut a dark strip 2.5 cm/1 in longer than central square. Pin RS down on square, matching raw edges, with 1.25 cm/½ in protruding at sides.

4 Making 5 mm/¼ in seam allowances, backstitch strip down, working through strip, central patch and foundation fabric. Roll strip toward you over stitching; do not pull it too tight. Press lightly and pin down to foundation fabric. Strips may also be attached by machine.

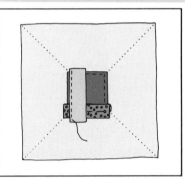 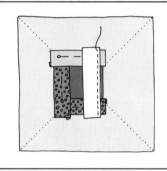 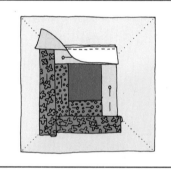 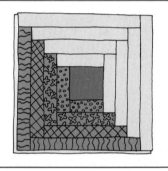

5 Cut a second strip in dark fabric long enough to extend over side edge of central square and end of first strip. Place RS down over side of square, matching raw edges and overlapping first strip. Pin, stitch and finish second strip as in (**4**).

6 Cut a third strip in light fabric, long enough to cover top edge of central square and end of second strip. Attach to top edge as in (**4**). Cut a fourth strip in light fabric long enough to overlap both first and third strips. Pin to remaining free side of square, stitch and finish as first strip.

7 Cut and attach second row of strips to overlap in same way as first row. Place light and dark fabric at the same sides each time. Place each strip RS down, matching raw edges with strip beneath. Remove pins from first row. Stitch strips as before, roll back, press and pin down.

8 Continue until foundation square is covered. Fold final strips so that raw edges lie on edges of foundation square. To join squares, place them RS together and backstitch or machine, making sure corners of squares correspond exactly and are securely stitched.

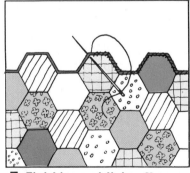 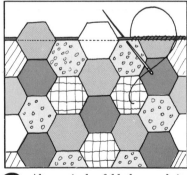 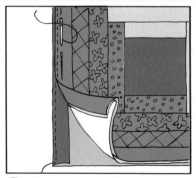 

1 **Finishing and lining** Choose a weight of lining which is suitable both for the patchwork fabric and for the finished item. On some patchwork designs, such as honeycomb, simply turn in the edges and hem them to the lining to give an attractive shaped edge.

2 Alternatively, fold the patch in half to give a straight edge and hem to lining.

3 Quilts may also be finished by turning in the patchwork and lining so that the folded edges match exactly. Work a row of neat running stitches 5 mm/¼ in from folded edge.

4 Alternatively, attach a binding strip to finish patchwork and lining edges. Covered piping cord can also be used and gives a strong finish.

QUILTING

Quilting is a satisfying combination of utilitarian purpose and decorative result. Its insulating and protective qualities have long been appreciated. Quilting is today enjoying a revival as a relatively cheap yet effective way of providing strong, warm clothes and bedclothes.

All quilting, whatever its ultimate function, is based on the same sandwich principle—two pieces of material enveloping one layer of wadding/batting. (The only exception is flat quilting.) The incidental patterns that emerged when the layers were stitched together were later elaborated until the pattern dominated.

There are several forms of quilting. Padded, commonly called English or American quilting, is the most straightforward and functional. It has a worldwide following but has always been considered a peasant tradition. The upper classes practised the more elaborate techniques of stuffed and corded quilting. Corded, or Italian, quilting developed later than stuffed, or trapunto, work and became extremely popular for bedcovers and hangings in the 17th century. Apart from providing extra weight to give a better hang, the stuffing for both varieties is purely decorative. Tied quilting can be even more ornamental, with the addition of non-structural buttons and bows. In contrast, flat quilting incorporates no stuffing at all; instead two pieces of fabric are held together by an all-over pattern of stitches.

For all forms of quilting choose closely woven, smooth materials, preferably natural fabrics such as cotton, linen or silk. Synthetics are usually too springy to give the soft, undulating surface characteristic of good hand work. Synthetic wadding/batting, however, is a vast improvement on traditional materials, as it is lighter and easier to wash and less quilting is required to hold it in place.

When quilting small articles by hand, a lap frame or quilting hoop should be used. For quilting large articles, a special frame is a good investment. Extra large articles can be made up in sections and then sewn together; this is known as the "quilt-as-you-go" method.

BASIC QUILTING

The following processes are common to padded, stuffed, corded and flat quilting.

Marking the design

On RS of top fabric mark design with a pencil, embroidery transfer or dressmaker's carbon. Or, after the layers have been basted together (see below),

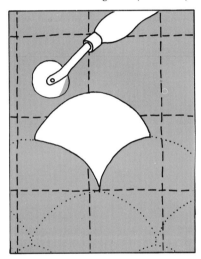

mark design on top fabric around a metal, plastic or cardboard template with a tracing wheel or by indenting a line on the fabric with a blunt needle—if using this method it is best to mark small areas at a time. The design for stuffed quilting must be composed of small enclosed shapes; for corded it must be linear. For quilting by machine, with the quilting foot and gauge, mark only one line in each direction for repeating patterns such as diamonds and squares.

Basting

Iron top fabric and backing. Spread backing flat on a table or on the floor. Smooth filling over it (for padded and tied quilting) and then top fabric, RS up. Baste small pieces in a vertical and horizontal grid and large ones radially from the centre, smoothing out all creases.

If, however, you wish to combine stuffed quilting with padded in order to emphasize or highlight a part, or parts, of the design, work all of the stitching for the stuffed area and insert the stuffing before basting the filling and

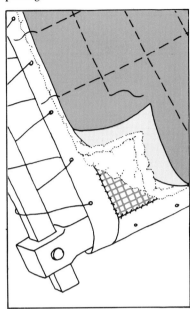

backing into position for the padded quilting.

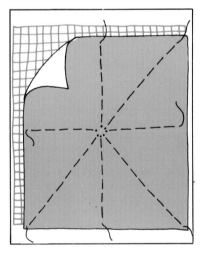

Stitching

Work stitching along design lines. The most common stitch for hand quilting is running stitch, although any line stitch is suitable. To stitch padded quilting start with a knot hidden between layers. Using a thimble on the middle finger of the stitching hand,

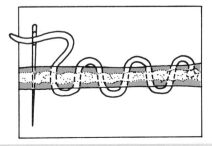

make a series of small, even running stitches, placing the index finger of the other hand beneath the area to be quilted to ensure that the needle penetrates all layers of material. Work with a rhythmic motion, making three to five stitches at a time.

Quilting by machine

For corded or stuffed quilting, use a normal foot as only two layers of fabric are being stitched. For padded quilting, attach a quilting foot and gauge, or bar. The foot has a short front and moves over thick layers of material easily. Adjust gauge so it is required distance from foot. Use it as a stitching guide, to maintain even spacing between rows of stitching or adjust it for each row as required. Set machine to medium-length stitch for all fabrics except vinyl, which needs a long stitch to stop the fabric tearing and being spoiled.

Choose thread to match top fabric—silk on silk, synthetic on synthetic—and a needle suitable for both the top fabric and the filling.

Stitch alternate lines in opposite directions to counteract any tendency for top fabric to slip.

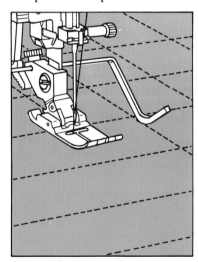

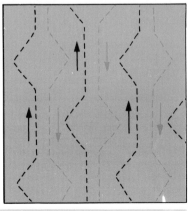

QUILTING

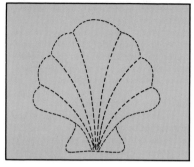 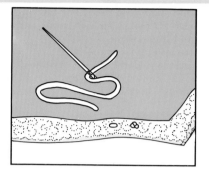 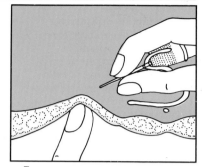 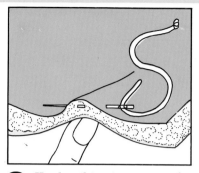

1 **Padded quilting** has a top fabric and a backing, which can be of similar material to the top fabric or of muslin. Between these is a filling, which can vary from a layer of re-processed wool to several layers of padding. Prepare and mark as for basic quilting.

2 Hand quilting is necessary for intricate designs. Thread a quilting needle with quilting thread; knot the end. Insert needle through top fabric and filling only.

3 Pull thread until knot pops through top fabric and is buried in the filling.

4 With end of needle pressing against thimble on middle finger of sewing hand, work each running stitch through all three layers, making contact with finger of other hand (below quilt) with each stitch.

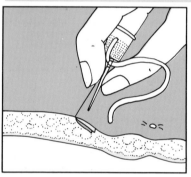 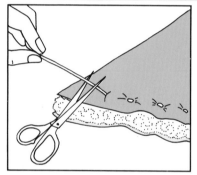 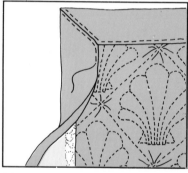 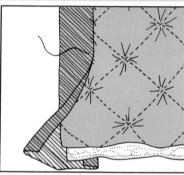

5 When crossing a seam, work stab stitches across bulky area to keep stitching neat and even.

6 To end a row of quilting, work two to three backstitches over the last stitch, then run needle and thread about 4 cm/1½ in away from backstitches. Pull taut and clip off excess thread.

7 After design has been quilted there are several ways of finishing the edges. If the backing is of a good material, cut it slightly larger than the top fabric and bring it over to RS of finished quilting to form a neat border. Turn in edges, mitre and stitch corners and all around border.

8 Padded quilting can also be finished with binding. Use strips of suitable fabric in a matching or contrasting colour and apply to all edges as for single or double binding.

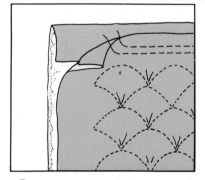  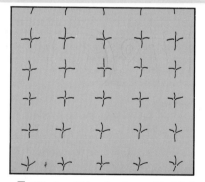 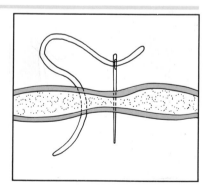

9 For a traditional finish, end quilting pattern slightly away from edge (distance depends on scale of work) and fold in edges of top fabric and backing. Work one or two rows of stitching close to edge.

10 Alternatively, work buttonhole or machine satin stitch along edge of quilting pattern. Trim away surplus fabric and filling.

1 **Tied quilting** is a form of padded quilting. The layers of fabric are held together at intervals by a knot rather than stitching. A bow or bead can be attached for decoration. Use a strong thread such as linen thread, buttonhole twist, pearl cotton or embroidery floss.

2 Prepare work in a frame as for basic quilting (there is no need to mark a design). Thread needle with a fairly short length of thread and bring through to RS, leaving about 5 cm/2 in on WS.

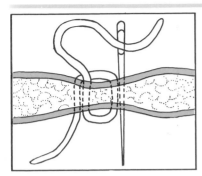

3 Work two small backstitches over each other and take needle through to WS.

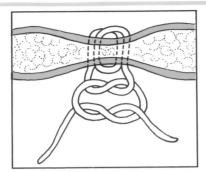

4 On WS tie both ends of thread together to form two or three firm knots and, on RS, a small hollow. Trim off ends close to last knot. Repeat knots at intervals (these do not have to be regular) to create desired pattern.

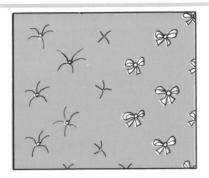

5 For a decorative effect, attach a bead or button on RS when working second small backstitch, or start on RS and take needle through to WS and back to RS, leaving ends of thread long enough to tie into a bow on RS. Use ribbon for more conspicuous bows.

Stuffed quilting is essentially decorative as only parts of the design are stuffed—with teased wool or small pieces of wadding/batting. The article must be lined, with lining fabric. The backing fabric should be loosely woven muslin.

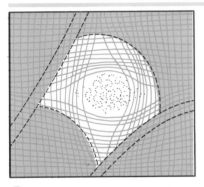

2 Prepare as for basic quilting. Stitch around shapes by hand or with a fairly short machine stitch. For small shapes, part warp and weft threads of backing sufficiently to insert desired amount of filling. Stroke threads of backing fabric into place with a needle.

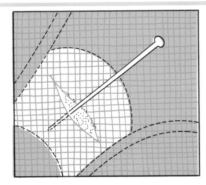

3 For larger shapes, make a slit in backing taking care not to cut through the top fabric, and push filling into every point or corner of the design with a knitting needle.

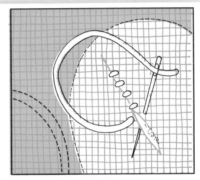

4 Oversew slit to keep filling in place.

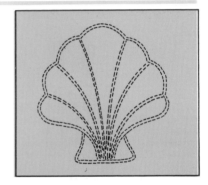

Corded quilting is linear, with padding inserted between parallel rows of stitching. Use cotton cord or thick wool for padding. The quilting can be worked on single fabric or on fabric backed with muslin. If it is worked on backed fabric, line the quilting with lining fabric.

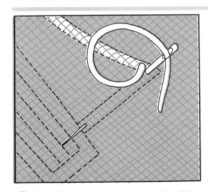

Corded quilting on double fabric Prepare and stitch as for basic quilting. Secure thread ends and remove basting. With backing uppermost, insert tapestry or rug needle, threaded with cotton cord or wool, through muslin and push between parallel stitching lines.

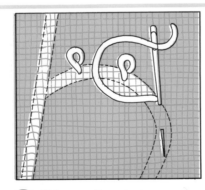

2 Bring needle out at corners or curves and insert at same place, leaving a small loop of cord or wool projecting. This prevents puckering and allows for shrinkage. Where lines intersect, cut filling to leave short end and start a new length.

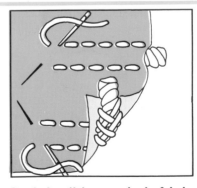

Corded quilting on single fabric Choose firm cotton cord the desired width for the filling. Hold it under fabric and backstitch alternately above and below the cord to secure it to the fabric. Cut off surplus cord at end of channels.

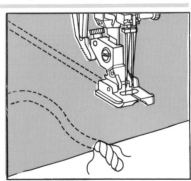

Corded quilting can be worked on the machine with the twin needle and cording foot, through which the cord is threaded. Narrow lines of corded quilting can also be simulated—no filling is inserted—by using the twin needle and a tight bottom tension.

QUILTING

SPECIAL EFFECTS

Create a wide range of original and attractive effects by combining different forms of quilting such as corded and stuffed, or by working them in special ways, as for shadow or contour methods. Quilting is also very effective when used with appliqué or patchwork.

Contour quilting

A quick and easy method of padded, flat, stuffed or corded quilting, this involves stitching around the design motifs in a patterned fabric, and around the contours within them if desired. This method does away with the need to make and mark on designs, but choose a fabric with a simple pattern or the quilting effect will not show. Baste layers of fabric together and stitch as for basic quilting. Stuffed motifs look most effective worked in this way, either on their own or in conjunction with padded quilting.

Stuffed motifs on a corded ground

This is traditionally worked on white fabric so that the stuffed motifs stand out against the solidly corded background. It provides a similar weight to padded quilting. Prepare work as for basic quilting and complete all stitching before inserting filling as for corded and stuffed quilting.

Shadow quilting

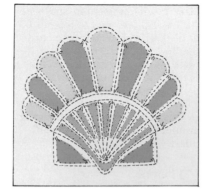

In contrast to most other forms of quilting, shadow quilting uses colour as an intrinsic part of the design. It can be padded, corded or stuffed. The effect is achieved by quilting through two layers of transparent fabric such as organdy, and inserting a strongly coloured filling. No separate backing is used. Insert felt shapes between the layers as filling for padded quilting, baste them in place and work quilting stitches around them. Use knitting wool in one or more thicknesses for corded quilting and tease it out for stuffed quilting.

Appliqué quilting

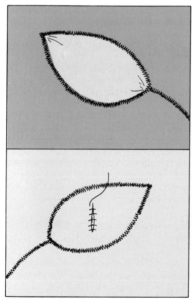

Appliqué combines easily with all forms of quilting. For stuffed quilting baste and machine satin stitch motifs to RS of fabric. Slit fabric carefully behind motif, making slit as small as possible; do not cut right to edges of motif. Insert padding and oversew slit. No backing is needed as the main fabric acts as a backing.

Apply braids or ribbons to RS of top fabric and machine along both edges to form channels for corded quilting. Or, for padded quilting, work an automatic stitch down centre of braid and a quilting stitch around it.

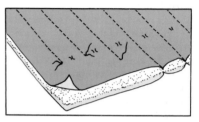

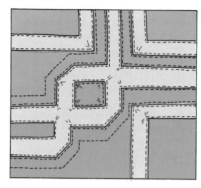

For motifs on padded quilting, baste motifs to RS of top fabric before basting fabric to backing and filling. Proceed as for ordinary padded quilting, stitching around the motifs with satin stitch through all layers of fabric.

Quilted patchwork

Also known as Swiss or raised patchwork, this is an effective way to give patchwork extra warmth and bulk. Put any two matching patchwork shapes, e.g. hexagons or diamonds, RS together and sew around all but one side. Turn through to RS, stuff and slip stitch remaining side. Join prepared patches by oversewing.

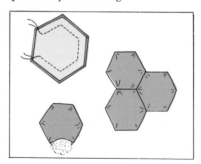

MAKING UP A QUILTED GARMENT

Making up a garment from ready-made quilted fabric poses problems because of the bulk of the fabric. Choose a pattern without pleats, gathers or fullness and, if possible, a style with loose sleeves such as the kimono. Alternatively, design quilting to fit the pattern pieces. Bear the following rules in mind, particularly if you are using a conventional dress pattern:

Ready-made quilted fabric

1 Do not cut out pattern pieces with fabric double or folded, as the bulk of the fabric causes distortion.
2 When the pattern pieces are cut out and the seamlines are marked, take out quilting stitches from the seam allowance, remembering to finish off all ends securely.

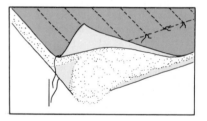

3 Remove padding up to seamline to eliminate bulk in the seams. Do the same for any other areas that are likely to be bulky, such as darts, openings and facings.

4 Never turn up a double hem on quilted fabric. Either remove padding up to hemline, as above, and turn up a single hem, or bind edge of fabric and make a single turning.
5 Set the sleeve head into the armhole before stitching the sleeve underarm seam and the garment side seam, so that any surplus fabric can be accommodated in these seams rather than being eased into the armhole and so creating unwanted bulk.

Designing for pattern

1 The entire garment need not be quilted. A quilted hem may be incorporated for weight or quilted sleeves for warmth. Quilt details such as collars and cuffs to make them more hard-wearing as well as more decorative. The quilting can be padded, corded, stuffed, flat or any combination.
2 Place pattern pieces on fabric and work tailor's tacks at a slight distance beyond pattern edges to allow for shrinkage during quilting. Mark seamlines and remove pattern.
3 Mark quilting design on RS of fabric, keeping within seamlines. Back fabric appropriately for the kind of quilting and stitch by hand or machine.
4 When the quilting is complete, cut out garment pieces, using tailor's tacks as a guide, and make up the garment.

APPLIQUÉ

Appliqué has a long and ancient history and was probably first used by the Persians in the 9th century BC. The term is derived from the French *appliquer*, to put on, and it denotes the attachment of one piece of fabric to another, traditionally by hand with fine hemming stitches. Motifs can be attached effectively by imaginative use of other hand stitches or by machine with both straight and zigzag stitches.

Throughout its history appliqué has offered a wide scope for individual expression. Wall hangings and tents made by the Egyptians in the 8th century BC showed a subtlety of design far removed from the bold and colourful use of appliqué for both the tunics and banners of the knights of the Crusades. On medieval church banners and vestments appliqué achieved a new dimension of beauty and delicacy, whereas the early American settlers, with their quilts embellished with appliqué motifs, introduced a more personal, homely effect.

Appliqué motifs should ideally be strongly defined and the designs simple. Buildings can be broken down into a series of rectangles and trees shown as silhouettes. Basic shapes can be grouped to suggest leaves on a branch or petals on a flower. Add detail with embroidery.

The choice of fabric is an important feature of the design. Virtually any type of fabric can be used, the only consideration being the use to which the article will be put—on a child's garment, for example, do not apply fabrics that are not easily washable. If you are starting from scratch rather than applying a motif to an existing garment, choose a background fabric that will complement the design without dominating it and group a selection of fabrics of different textures and colours on the background before choosing the final pieces.

The method of applying the fabrics depends on those used. Felt and leather do not fray and, therefore, do not need seam allowances, whereas fine fabrics need the edges turned under, or need backing with iron-on interfacing. Wherever possible, except for appliqué pictures, cut motifs to follow the same grain line as the background fabric. Material cut on the bias has a tendency to pull and pucker when attached.

Press all fabric motifs before applying. After the appliqué is completed, press very gently, but as little as possible, on the wrong side to avoid flattening the work.

No special equipment is needed—only a sharp cutting knife, scissors, needles and matching or contrasting thread, depending on the type of appliqué and the effect desired. Mercerized cotton or polyester thread is ideal for all types of appliqué. For planning the design you will need a soft pencil and drawing or tracing paper or stiff cardboard for the templates for each motif. If necessary, pin the templates in place on the background fabric to arrange the design satisfactorily.

Appliqué has a wide range of uses, from decorating clothing, home furnishings and banners to making pictures and wall hangings. With the correct amount of care and preparation any of the basic types of appliqué on the following pages—hemmed, machined, persé, découpé, inlay, lace or reverse—will be a satisfying reflection of your imagination.

QUICK APPLIQUÉ

The types of appliqué described on the following pages are mainly finely sewn and fairly time consuming. However, the basic principle of applying pieces of fabric to a background can also be used for bold, quick appliqué that is particularly suitable for children's toys, clothes, wall hangings, headboards and curtains.

Press paper-backed adhesive web to the WS of pieces of felt, cotton or other fabric. If stiffening is required attach iron-on interfacing first and adhesive web on top. Cut out motifs—letters, numbers, fruit, houses, cars etc. Peel off paper backing, place motifs in position and press with warm iron and damp cloth until motifs are firmly bonded to the backing. Turn to WS and press again. Add extra features to motifs with felt tip pens, fabric paint or bold machine embroidery. If the article is likely to be washed a great deal, zigzag around the outer edge of each motif.

STITCHES

A variety of ordinary sewing stitches can be used to attach motifs: hemming—ideal for catching down the turned-in edge of closely woven fabrics; slip hemming, if decorative stitching is to be added; running stitch; loop stitch—excellent for wools and felts and very effective if worked in contrasting thread; buttonhole—ideal, closely worked, for covering the raw edge of fine fabric to give a decorative but firm edge; fishbone, particularly suitable for inlay appliqué where two edges are butted together; three-sided punch stitch (see below), which gives an openwork effect to the edge of the motif and is ideal for lingerie; and both straight and zigzag machine stitches. Many interesting effects can be obtained by the careful use of various automatic machine embroidery patterns.

For decorative surface stitching the following stitches can be worked: stem, which gives a continuous line—the thickness can be varied by using different types of thread; chain; running stitch; couching—a thread is laid on the edge of a motif and held down with loop, herringbone or cross stitch worked in a matching or contrasting thread; French knots; and, for a heavier effect, spider's web, or wheel, and star stitches—star is the first, spoked stage of the wheel. Machine embroidery can also be worked.

Three-sided punch stitch

Use fine thread—mercerized or polyester 50 is ideal—and a tapestry needle 18 or 14. Thread needle and tie end of thread around eye to prevent it slipping. Work right to left along edge of motif. At each stage work two stitches.

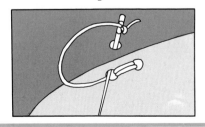

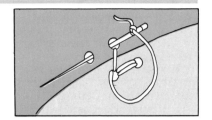

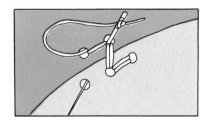

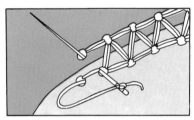

APPLIQUÉ PICTURES

Appliqué pictures give plenty of scope for the imagination, both in the composition and in the choice and mixture of fabrics.

The background fabric should not detract from the picture; a dull surface with a pleasing but not dominant texture is ideal. The straight grain should run the length of the picture. Allow enough fabric to be turned over the backing.

Design ideas can be taken from a wide variety of sources including children's books, posters and greetings cards. Trace the design on tracing paper for each shape and enlarge or reduce if required. Cut shapes out, allowing for hems where necessary (this depends on the type of appliqué to be worked), and pin shapes to chosen fabrics, to RS or WS as appropriate. Attach by hand or machine, by any of the above methods.

Hand embroider extra detail on attached motifs if desired. A variety of beads, buttons, sequins and other trimmings can also be sewn on.

To back picture, cut a piece of cardboard or wood to size of picture. Stretch picture, RS up, over board and turn edges of background fabric over board. Mitre corners and glue edges to board. Glue a piece of strong paper or fabric to back of board to cover it. Alternatively, use a fabric backing such as calico. Turn in raw edges of background fabric, mitre corners and hem edges down to backing.

APPLIQUÉ

1 Hemmed appliqué is particularly suitable for a design based on colour and shape alone. The motifs are attached by hand, by hemming; the stitches should be almost invisible on RS. The material for the motifs should be lightweight and closely woven; fine cotton is ideal.

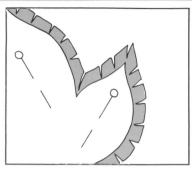

2 Cut a paper template for each motif. Pin template to fabric and cut around it with sharp scissors, adding 5 mm/¼ in for hems all around. On curves clip into design line so that the hems can be tucked in smoothly and stitched easily.

3 Place the motif, RS up, on RS of background fabric. Baste diagonally down centre, then work out to edges to avoid puckering. Using a fine needle and thread to match motif, hem around shape, tucking in hem allowances. Mitre points or fold them in, keeping outline sharp.

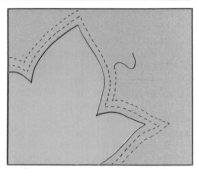

4 The finished design should have a soft, raised appearance. Emphasize individual shapes by working running stitch (any number of rows) around them on the background fabric, using thread that contrasts with the motif. Do not press too heavily.

1 Machined appliqué is hard-wearing and therefore suitable for household articles and children's wear. It is particularly important that the fabric for the motifs should be similar in fibre content and weight to the background fabric, especially if the article is to be washed.

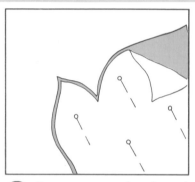

2 Cut a paper template for each motif. Pin template to fabric and cut around it; no hem allowances are needed.

3 If fabric for motif is very fine or frays badly, back it with iron-on interfacing. Place the motifs, RS up, on RS of background fabric, overlapping if necessary for the design. Baste diagonally in place. Work a row of straight machining around each motif, as close as possible to edge.

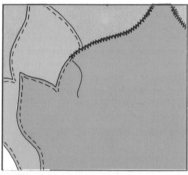

4 Use satin stitch foot and machine embroidery thread to match or contrast with background fabric or motif. Set for satin stitch—for most motifs to half the full zigzag. Using straight machining as guide, work satin stitch over raw edges and machining. Add details by hand or machine.

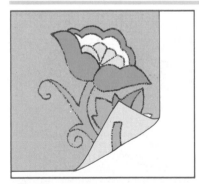

1 Découpé is a simple form of inlay and can be worked by machine. The main, or surface, fabric is cut away to reveal applied motifs of contrasting colour underneath. Designs should be simple, bold and planned to ensure that the surface fabric holds them together adequately.

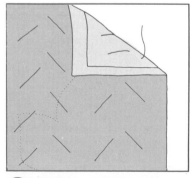

2 With tailor's chalk, mark design on RS of surface fabric. Cut a piece of contrasting coloured fabric slightly larger than required (it can be a rectangle and does not have to be cut to the shape of the motif). Baste diagonally, as for hemmed appliqué, with RS to WS of surface fabric.

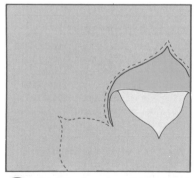

3 On RS of surface fabric, work straight machine stitching along chalk line. Cut away surface fabric just inside stitching.

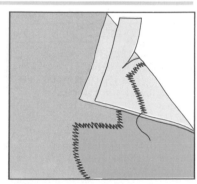

4 Cover cut edge with machine satin stitch worked as for machined appliqué. On WS cut away surplus contrasting fabric, leaving a small margin outside satin stitching.

1 **Reverse appliqué** produces a padded, multicoloured effect and is ideal for table mats, yokes or cushions. The design is created by cutting through layers of fabric to reveal the different colours beneath. The number of layers of fabric depends on how many colours are required.

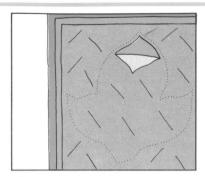

2 Practise on three layers of fine cotton first. Diagonally baste layers together, RS up. On top layer mark design with tailor's chalk. Cut away all areas of design where top fabric is not required about 5 mm/¼ in within chalk line; cut slightly nearer to chalk line on a corner or tight curve.

3 Clip around curves as for hemmed appliqué. Turn cut edges of first layer under to WS and hem down, working small neat stitches. Mark design on second layer of fabric, undoing basting if necessary. Cut away second layer where not required for design; turn under and hem edges.

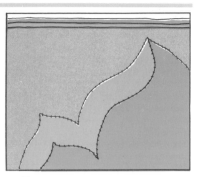

4 Proceed as for practice piece, using as many layers of fabric as required. If desired, in some areas of the design cut middle layers back to design line on top layer so that top layer can be hemmed to any layer beneath those that have been cut back.

1 **Inlay appliqué** is used for banner and church work, box lids and stools. The motif is inserted into an area of identical shape cut out of the background fabric. Choose fabrics that contrast in colour with that of the background and that do not fray; suede and leather are ideal.

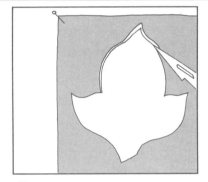

2 Pin main fabric RS up to a board. Cut template of stiff cardboard and place on fabric. Hold it down with one hand and, with a sharp knife, cut around template and through fabric to make appropriate shaped hole. Cut motif from contrasting coloured fabric in same way.

3 Working on a flat surface or in a circular embroidery frame, diagonally baste a backing fabric such as calico with RS to WS of main fabric. Diagonally baste motif RS up to RS of backing fabric over cut-out shape, matching raw edges with raw edges of main fabric.

4 Using a fine needle and a thread that blends with the colour of both the main fabric and the motif, work fishbone stitch through motif and main fabric only. Remove calico or, for a stiffer effect, leave it in place.

1 **Lacework appliqué**, with its lacy openwork effect, is most suitable for lingerie and gives semitransparent fabrics a delicate, luxurious appearance. Choose designs with a simple outline and avoid very sharp curves as the fabric tends to fray when stitched.

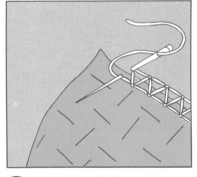

2 Cut out motif. Diagonally baste motif to RS of garment. With fine thread, work three-sided punch stitch. Pull each stitch to achieve lacy effect. This can be done by machine set for zigzag at half full width of swing and stitch length 1½ with hem-stitching needle.

1 **Appliqué persé** motifs are cut from patterned fabrics, traditionally chintz, which is ideal for its bold patterns and close weave. Avoid fabric with intricate patterns and try to create something original rather than copy the fabric motifs. As chintz is liable to shrink, wash before using.

2 Cut out motif using small sharp scissors. Place motif, RS up, on RS of background fabric and baste in place. Work straight machining and satin stitch as for machined appliqué; use a thread to match background fabric for working satin stitch. Motif can be padded from the back.

INDEX

INDEX

hips
   fitting and altering garment 142
   measuring 76
Holland 34, 187
honeycomb patchwork 201, 202–3
honeycomb stitch (machine) 17
hoods
   fasteners for 70, 71
hook fasteners 64
Hooke, Robert 28
hooks and eyes 69–70
houndstooth 34
Howe, Elias 8
Hunt, Walter 8

I

Indian silk 34–5
inlay appliqué 211
insertion seam 47, 48
instant patchwork 200
interfacing 84–7
   for belts 135
   for collars 121, 122
   inserting with diagonal basting 23
   in tailoring 156–7
   see also iron-on interfacing; sew-in-
     interfacing
inverted pleats 116–17
invisible stitches see catch stitch;
   draw stitch; felling; prick stitch;
   slip hemming; slip stitch
iron-on interfacing 85
   for appliqué 209
   for cuffs 105
   for speed tailoring 160
ironing see pressing
irons 38
Italian quilting 205

J

jackets
   fasteners for 70
   lining 139
   tailored 156–62
   see also pleats; repairs
jeans
   open seams 42
   zipper stitching strengthened 59
   see also repairs
jeans buttons 70
jersey 33, 35
   hems on 53
jetted pockets
   tailored 162

K

kapok 168
kick pleats 116–17
kilts 120
kimono sleeves 81, 109, 111–12
knife pleats 116–17

knitted fabrics 29, 35
   cutting 54
knots, for hand sewing 22

L

lace 35
   seams in 46
lacework appliqué 211
lambswool for tailoring 156
lamé 35
lapels
   edges joined by draw stitch 25
   in speed tailoring 160
lapped seam 47, 48
lawn 35
leather 168, 209
   reinforcing with 151
   sewing and equipment 72
legs and thighs
   adjusting pattern for 81
linen 28, 35, 156, 189, 192, 205
linen union 171, 187
lingerie
   blind hemming 53
   insertions seams 47
   see also nightwear
linings 138–9
   for curtains 178, 180–1
   fabrics for 138
   felling for joining to garments 25
   holding with diagonal basting 23
   joined to seam by flash basting 24
   for patch pockets 131
   for patchwork 200, 204
   repairing 153
   in yokes 114
   see also mounting and individual
     articles
log cabin patchwork 201, 204
loop stitch 26
   for appliqué 209
loops and ties 66–7

M

machine flat fell seam 42, 44
machine sewing 13–15
   appliqué 209, 210
   buttonholes 64
   buttons 68
   direction of stitching 14–15
   fastening off 15
   how to start 13
   patchwork 200
   quilting 205
   repairs 149–50
   tension 13–14
   tucks 89
   zippers 59
   see also appliqué; quilting; sewing
     machines; stitches, machine
Madras 35
matelassé 35
maternity clothes
   fasteners for 71

measurements
   for curtains 178
   for pattern choosing 76–7
measuring equipment
   for hand sewing 20–1
melton 156
mercerized fabrics 30
mitring 130
   on belt ends 136
modacrylic 29, 35
modal 35
mohair 28, 35
moiré fabrics 30, 35
moleskin 35
monograms 18
mothproof fabrics 30
mounting (underlining) 138
mousseline 35
mungo 35
mushroom fastener 71
muslin 35

N

nap 31
napkin holders 190
napkins 189, 190–1
narrow finish seam 42, 45
natural fibres 28
neckline
   fitting and altering 142, 146
   fitting facing to 95–6
   gaping, adjustment for 81
"needle down" button 10
needle holder, with tightening screw
   10
needle plate 10
needle thread tension control 10
needle threader 10, 20–1
needlecord 35
needles
   for patchwork 200
   for suede, leather and fur 72
needles (hand sewing) 20–1, 31
needles (machine) 9
   faults 19
   positioning 14
nightwear
   French seams on 42
   hems 50
   see also lingerie
ninon 35
non-iron fabrics 30
notions 20–1
   for tailoring 156
nylon 28, 35, 36
nylon tricot binding 20, 49

O

ombré 35
open seams 42, 43
   binding 56
   finishing 43
   topstitched 47, 48
organdy 35

organza 35
overcasting 26, 47
overlock or serging machine 11
overlock foot 12
overlock stitch (machine) 17
oversewing 26

P

padding or pad stitch 156
pads, hams and rolls 38
Panama 35
panné 35
patch pockets 130–1
   repairing 150
   tailored 161
patching (repairs) 149, 151
patchwork 200–4
   history of 200
   finishing 200, 204
   quilted 208
   special effects in 201
pattern markings 76
patterned fabrics
   matching design 42, 178
   placing pattern for 83
   seams in 46, altered 145
   zipper insertion 62
patterns 76–83
   adapting to include a yoke 115
   altering and adjusting 78–81
   cutting out 83
   designing quilted 208
   in patchwork 200
   placing 82–3
   for slipcovers 175
   for tailored garments 156
Payen, A. 28
Pe-Ce fibres 28
pelmets/valances 185–6
pencil pleats
   in curtains 178, 180
percale 35
petersham 35, 97, 102
   for belts 135
petersham waist finish 99–100
pillow forms 168
pillowcases 192, 193
pillows and pillow covers 168–70
pin tuck foot 12
pin tucks 89
   see also tucks
pinch pleats
   in curtains 178, 180
pins 20–1
   for slipcovers 171
piping and piped seams
   made from bias strips 57
   on pockets 132
   on seams 47
   on soft furnishings 168, 171
place mats 189–90
pleats 116–20
   in curtains 180, 184
   finishes on 119–20
   placing joins in 118
   pressing 40
   reinforcing backs of 119

INDEX